PELOUBET'S NOTES
1973-1974

PELOUBET'S NOTES
1973-1974

*Based on the International Bible
Lessons for Christian Living
Uniform Series*

by

RALPH EARLE

100th ANNUAL VOLUME

Founded by Francis N. Peloubet

BAKER BOOK HOUSE ● GRAND RAPIDS, MICHIGAN

ISBN: 0-8010-3304-7

Copyright © 1973 by

Baker Book House Company

Lessons based on International Sunday School Lessons; the International Bible Lessons for Christian Teaching, copyright by the Committee on the Uniform Series

PREFACE

This is a particularly significant year in the life of *Peloubet's Notes*, for this volume marks the one hundredth annual publication of this indispensable guide for thousands of teachers and students using the International Sunday School Lessons. Baker Book House is grateful to have been the publisher for the past five years.

Dr. Ralph Earle, Professor of New Testament at Nazarene Theological Seminary, Kansas City, Missouri, serves as editor of this centennial volume. His ability as a Bible expositor is well known by those who used the 1972-73 volume. The detailed outlines he includes with each lesson contribute to the logical presentation of the subject. Following his predecessors, Dr. Earle quotes extensively from a wide field of commentators and presents a variety of theological thought on the passages treated. His contemporary applications and discussion questions are particularly helpful in applying the Scripture passages to the everyday life of the Bible student. Stress is laid upon the need for a thorough knowledge of the Word in order to live a victorious Christian life.

Baker Book House sends out this centennial volume with the prayer that it may help to usher in the time when "the earth shall be full of the knowledge of the Lord, as the waters cover the sea" (Isaiah 11:9).

CONTENTS

FIRST QUARTER

The Gospel According to Paul

Unit I: Ministry of Reconciliation

Unit II: The Message of Reconciliation

Unit III: The Life of Reconciliation

SECOND QUARTER

The Gospel of John

Unit I: The Son of God Came to Us

Unit II: The Son of God Active Among Us

Unit III: The Son of God Victorious for Us

THIRD QUARTER

Acts: How the Church Grew

FOURTH QUARTER

Letters to Young Churches

September 2, 1973

PAUL SPEAKS TO THE CHURCH

DEVOTIONAL READING	I Corinthians 3:1-9

Topic: *Paul Speaks to a Divided Church*

Background Scripture: I Corinthians 1:1-15; 3:1-9; 5:1-2; II Corinthians 1:23—2:11; 12:19-21

ADULTS

Scripture Lesson: I Corinthians 1:10-15; II Corinthians 12:19-21

Memory Verse: *There is one body and one Spirit, just as you were called to the one hope that belongs to your call.* Ephesians 4:4

Topic: *The Fractured Church*

Background Scripture: I Corinthians 1:1-15; 3:1-9; 5:1-2; II Corinthians 1:23—2:11; 12:19-21

YOUTH

Scripture Lesson: I Corinthians 1:10-15; II Corinthians 12:19-21

Memory Verse: *Is Christ divided? Was Paul crucified for you? Or were you baptized in the name of Paul?* I Corinthians 1:3

Topic: *Paul Persecutes the Church*

Background Scripture: Acts 6:1-3, 5, 8-14; 7:54—8:4; 9:1-2

CHILDREN

Scripture Lesson: Acts 7:54—8:4

Memory Verse: *Bless those who persecute you; bless and do not curse them.* Romans 12:14

DAILY BIBLE READINGS

Mon., Aug. 27: Fellow Workmen for God, I Corinthians 3:1-9.
Tues., Aug. 28: The Mind of Christ Jesus, Philippians 2:1-11.
Wed., Aug. 29: Stand Firm in Your Faith, II Corinthians 1:23—2:11.
Thurs., Aug. 30: Servants of Christ, I Corinthians 4:1-7.
Fri., Aug. 31: Our Unity in Christ, Ephesians 4:1-13.
Sat., Sept. 1: Christ's Prayer for His Church, John 17:20-26.
Sun., Sept. 2: United in the Same Mind, I Corinthians 1:10-17.

LESSON AIM

To show the danger of division in the church, and the divine remedy for it.

1

Time: I Corinthians was written about A.D. 54 or 55; II Corinthians in A.D. 55.

Place: I Corinthians was written at Ephesus; II Corinthians in Macedonia, probably at Philippi. Corinth was located in Greece.

Paul Speaks to a Divided Church

I. Greeting and Thanksgiving: I Corinthians 1:1-9

II. The Problem of Divisions: Corinthians 1:10-15
   A. A Plea for Unity: v. 10
   B. The Report of Dissension: v. 11
   C. The Four Cliques: v. 12
   D. The Seriousness of Division: vv. 13-15

III. Carnal Christians: I Corinthians 3:1-9

IV. A Case of Immorality: I Corinthians 5:1-2

V. The Grace of Forgiveness: II Corinthians 1:23—2:11

VI. Paul's Compassionate Concern: II Corinthians 12:19-21
   A. All for the Sake of the Church: v. 19
   B. The Threat of Further Contentions: vv. 20-21

Today we begin a series of thirteen lessons on "The Gospel According to Paul." It is really the gospel of Jesus Christ as proclaimed by Paul. The material for this quarter is drawn from Romans and I and II Corinthians.

The first unit of four lessons introduces us to the Corinthian church and Paul's relationship to it. We see something of the problems that plagued this church and what solutions the apostle proposed. Here we are dealing with "The Ministry of Reconciliation."

The second unit (lessons 5-9) points up "The Message of Reconciliation." Here the material is drawn from the first eight chapters of Romans, where Paul gives the heart of his gospel of salvation from sin.

The third unit (lessons 10-13) discusses "The Life of Reconciliation," noting the application of the gospel to our daily lives. For this we turn to the rich devotional material found in Romans 12, 13, and 14, plus some passages in the Corinthian Letters. The quarter's study ends with Paul's personal testimony of faith and hope.

These lessons will help us to face our problems today, both in the church and in our private lives. The gospel of Jesus Christ is as applicable to modern living as it was to the days of Paul.

Social and moral conditions in the first century were strikingly similar to what they are in the twentieth. There was a permissive society then as there is now. Corinth was a notoriously wicked city, and the church there was affected by its pagan surroundings.

It was also a fractured church, split into cliques. Grown people were showing childish attitudes. And yet it was a community of Christians, with a spiritual ministry.

Sometimes we get discouraged and are tempted to be disgusted with the faults we see in the church. But we must always remember that the church is composed of human beings like ourselves, with all the frailties and weaknesses that are common to humanity. We must, therefore, be patient and charitable.

What are some things that divide a church today? Is the so-called generation gap a divisive factor? If so, are we contributing to that division, or are we helping to heal it? In other words, do all of us have a ministry of reconciliation?

CONCEPTS FOR CHILDREN

1. Paul persecuted the Christians because he thought they were disobeying God and he didn't want them to lead other people to do the same.
2. It sometimes happens today, also, that people do wrong to their neighbors because they are misguided. They may sincerely think that they are doing right.
3. As the early Christians remained true to Jesus even though they suffered persecution, so we must be willing to take ridicule and taunting if it comes to us because of our stand for Christ.

THE LESSON COMMENTARY

I. GREETING AND THANKSGIVING:
I Corinthians 1:1-9

The first word of each of Paul's thirteen Epistles is his name. This is in keeping with the custom of that day. Actually, this is a much more sensible practice than our modern habit of putting the writer's name only at the end. The first thing a person wants to know when he opens a letter is: "Who wrote it?"

In writing to the recalcitrant church members at Corinth, Paul emphasizes the fact that he was "called to be an apostle of Jesus Christ through the will of God." He had to assert his apostolic authority in dealing with these unruly people.

He calls them "sanctified in Christ Jesus," though in 3:1 he addresses them as "carnal." It is obvious that "sanctified" here has its minimum meaning of "set apart to God." As

such they were "called to be saints" (literally, "holy ones").

The apostle finishes his salutation with a twofold greeting—"Grace . . . and peace." These are the two special blessings that only God can bestow.

As in all of Paul's Epistles except Galatians, the greeting (vv. 1-3) is followed by a thanksgiving (vv. 4-9). The apostle thanks God for the grace that has been given to the Corinthian Christians, and that they have been enriched "in all utterance, and in all knowledge," so that they "come behind in no gift" (vv. 4-7). These were gifted people and as such they should have made an ideal church. Unfortunately, such was not the case.

II. THE PROBLEM OF DIVISIONS:
I Corinthians 1:10-15

A. A Plea for Unity: v. 10

Though these Corinthian believers were far from what they should have

been, the apostle calls them "brethren." He says, "I beseech you." The
verb also means "exhort." He didn't
command them, but pleads with them.

He asks them to do three things.
First, he urges them to "speak the
same thing." This does not necessarily
mean to say the same words but to
agree on meaning the same thing. God
is interested in unity, not uniformity.

In the second place he pleads that
there will be no divisions among them.
The Greek word is *schisma*, "schism."
They were in danger of having a
church "split," and Paul was seeking
to avoid it.

Above all, the apostle wanted them
to "be perfectly joined together in the
same mind and in the same judgment."
The word for "joined" was used for
mending torn nets (Matthew 4:21) and
setting broken bones. So it was a fitting term here to express the idea of
"patching up" the strained relations
that threatened to tear the church
apart. The greatest need in the Corinthian church at the moment was for
Christian unity. The people needed to
have "the same mind"—the mind of
Christ.

B. The Report of Dissension: v. 11

Some members of "the house of
Chloe" had told Paul that there were
"contentions" at Corinth. The word
literally means "strife" or "wran-
gling." The Christians at Corinth were
quarreling with each other. Things
were so bad that people were hearing
about it.

We do not know anything further
about Chloe—the name means "tender
foliage." If she had been a member of
the church at Corinth, it would seem
unwise for Paul to mention her by
name. It is thought that she may have
been a slave-owner living at Ephesus,
where Paul wrote this Epistle. Some
slaves ("house") of hers had visited
Corinth, perhaps on business for her,
and had learned of conditions in the
church there.

C. The Four Cliques: v. 12

The first was composed of those
who said, "I belong to Paul." They
looked back to him as the founder of
the church. He was their highest authority. There was nothing wrong in
their being loyal to him. The real
trouble was they had a divisive spirit.
They were following a human leader,
rather than giving their full loyalty to
the real Head of the church.

Today there are people who never
get weaned away from their first pastor, or the one under whom they were
converted. They keep on talking about
him and telling how wonderful he was.
They never really accept a new pastor,
and so they make his work more difficult.

The second party consisted of
those who claimed, "I belong to Apollos." They liked eloquent preaching.
They were sermon-tasters. Paul had a
keen mind and enforced the truth with
firm logic. But he was not an orator.
Some in the church were so cruel as to
say that his speech was "contempt-
ible" (II Corinthians 10:10). That is,
he did not conform to the rules of
rhetoric.

Apollos was a different type. In
Acts 18:24 he is described as a Jew
who was "born at Alexandria, an eloquent man, and mighty in the scriptures." Robertson and Plummer say of
Apollos: "His brilliancy and Alexan-
drian modes of thought and expression
readily lent themselves to any tendency to form a party, who would
exalt these gifts at the expense of
Paul's studied plainness" (*First Corinthians*, p. 11).

There are still people who would
rather have their ears tickled with ora-
tory than their souls stirred with
straightforward truth. There is such a
thing as worshiping words instead of
searching out true meanings.

A third group was composed of
those who said, "I belong to Cephas."
This is the Aramaic word for "stone."
We know the man better as "Peter"
(Greek *petros*, "stone"). But Paul
regularly refers to him as Cephas (ex-

cept Galatians 2:7-8). He had been the chief spokesman for the twelve apostles, even during Jesus' ministry. On the day of Pentecost he preached a powerful sermon, and three thousand were saved. Unquestionably, Peter was honored at first in the early church as the main leader.

As the church spread to distant points, it was finally recognized that Peter was the leading apostle to the Jews and Paul the special apostle to the Gentiles (Galatians 2:7-8). So it may be assumed that those who claimed Peter as their leader were the Jewish Christians at Corinth, if not actually a Judaizing party. They probably emphasized the central authority of the Jerusalem church and tended to think of Christianity as a sect of Judaism.

In addition to the followers of Paul, Apollos, and Peter, there were those who said, "I belong to Christ." On the surface this sounds like a noble declaration. They were not following human leaders; they belonged only to Christ!

But Paul refers to them as comprising one of the divisive cliques. A study of the entire Epistle gives us the impression that the members of this party may possibly have been more obnoxious than the others. Perhaps they were the supersaints, who put themselves on pedestals as being better than all the rest of the Christians. "To say, with special emphasis, 'I am of Christ,' is virtually to say that Christ is mine and not yours'" (Robertson and Plummer, p. 13).

There is nothing worse than spiritual pride. Were these the ones who gloried in displaying the gifts of the Spirit in a divisive way, creating the problem that Paul has to deal with at length in chapters 12—14 of this Epistle? Perhaps so.

D. The Seriousness of Division: vv. 13-15

The church at Corinth was being divided by these four parties that had emerged. The apostle challenges his readers with the question: "Is Christ divided?" If He is one, the church must be a unity in Him.

The Greek could just as well be translated, "Christ is divided!" Some have preferred this interpretation as more striking. Since the church is the body of Christ, to divide the church is to divide Him. But the other two parts of this verse are clearly questions, and so probably this should be taken as such.

The second question Paul asks is this: "Was Paul crucified for you?" All three parts of this verse are rhetorical questions with the obvious answer, "No!" If Paul was not crucified for them, they had no right to say, "I belong to Paul."

The apostle asks a third question: "Were ye baptized in the name of Paul?" No, it had been in the name of Jesus (Acts 8:16). The Corinthians were wrong in elevating Paul as some of them had been doing.

In fact, the apostle had been especially careful to avoid any impression that he wanted to gather followers about himself. He declares, "I thank God that I baptized none of you but Crispus and Gaius, lest any should say that I had baptized in mine own name" (vv. 14-15). Crispus was the chief ruler of the synagogue at Corinth (Acts 18:8); so it was natural that Paul would accord him this special recognition. Gaius was Paul's host at Corinth when he wrote to Rome (Romans 16:23). He had filled a large place in the Corinthian church.

Apparently as an afterthought, Paul does remember that he had baptized "the household of Stephanas," who was probably one of his earliest converts at Corinth (v. 16). He cannot recall having baptized anyone else there.

III. CARNAL CHRISTIANS: I Corinthians 3:1-9

In spite of the claimed superspirituality of many Corinthian Christians, Paul writes: "And I, brethren, could not speak unto you as unto spiritual, but as unto carnal, even as unto babes in Christ" (v. 1). Why does he declare that they are still carnal? "For whereas there is among you envying, and strife, and divisions, are ye not carnal, and walk as men?" (v. 3). The divisions in the church were inescapable evidence that they were carnal. W. D. Davies says: "Disunity among Christians is a sign of the absence of the Spirit" (*Invitation to the New Testament*, p. 362).

The apostle finally mentions the specific situation that we have studied in chapter one. He asks: "For while one saith, I am of Paul; and another, I am of Apollos; are ye not carnal?" v. 4). He goes on to say: "Who then is Paul, and who is Apollos, but ministers by whom ye believed, even as the Lord gave to every man?" (v. 5). The word translated "ministers" simply means "servants." Servants are not supposed to be substituted for leaders.

What were the respective roles of Paul and Apollos? The apostle states it in familiar terms of the farm: "I have planted, Apollos watered; but God gave the increase. So then neither is he that planteth any thing, neither he that watereth; but God that giveth the increase" (vv. 6-7). Paul's logic is simple but devastating.

There was one thing more that the apostle wanted to say emphatically. The cliques at Corinth gave the impression that Paul and Apollos were rivals, each wanting separate followings. But

the apostle asserts categorically, "Now he that planteth and he that watereth are one" (v. 8). Any supposed division between Paul and Apollos existed only in the minds of the carnal church members at Corinth. It had no basis in fact.

IV. A CASE OF IMMORALITY:
I Corinthians 5:1-2

The pride and self-satisfied complacency of the Corinthian Christians was pathetic. They boasted of their superior spirituality, but were morally deficient. They were tolerating, right in the membership of the church, a case of immorality which was particularly offensive to the pagans. It was a matter of incest, a man living in sin with his own stepmother. Instead of mourning over this, the "Christians" were puffed up with pride. Paul said, "Put him out of the church."

V. THE GRACE OF FORGIVENESS:
II Corinthians 1:23—2:11

Apparently some of the members at Corinth had wondered why Paul had not paid them a visit. He had sent Timothy and Titus on separate missions, but why had he not come himself?

Paul tells them plainly why it was: "Moreover I call God for a record upon my soul, that to spare you I came not as yet unto Corinth" (1:23). He was determined not to come to them in a sorrowful spirit (2:1), holding court and pronouncing judgment on the offender. So he had stayed away. Instead of going to them, he had written them a letter (v. 3).

This letter is often referred to as the "Tearful Letter." Paul tells them: "For out of much affliction and anguish of heart I wrote unto you with many tears; not that ye should be grieved, but that ye might know the love which I have more abundantly unto you" (v. 4).

Where is this letter? There are two possible answers. Some scholars think that the so-called Severe Letter has

---

DISCUSSION QUESTIONS

1. How can we have a ministry of reconciliation?
2. What kind of Christian unity should we seek?
3. What people or groups should be united?
4. How far should we seek organic union?
5. What is more important than that?
6. What should be our attitude as regards unity in the local church?

been lost; it was never a part of our Bible. Others feel that our I Corinthians fits the description given here. Either one of these theories seems acceptable to us.

Paul says that the man he condemned in his earlier letter has now been sufficiently punished and should be forgiven (vv. 6-7). He writes: "Wherefore I beseech you that ye would confirm your love toward him" (v. 8).

Who is this man that he refers to? The most natural suggestion would be that it is the one who was condemned for his immorality in I Corinthians 5:1-2. He had evidently now repented and should be forgiven.

VI. PAUL'S COMPASSIONATE CONCERN:
II Corinthians 12:19-21

A. All for the Sake of the Church: v. 19

In verse 14 the apostle writes: "Behold, the third time I am ready to come to you; and I will not be burdensome to you: for I seek not yours, but you." He goes on to say: "And I will very gladly spend and be spent for you; though the more abundantly I love you, the less I be loved" (v. 15). He had not asked them to help him out financially at all, nor had Titus done so (vv. 16-18).

Is he trying to excuse himself to them? No! Paul's great, unselfish spirit is shown in his assertion: "But we do all things, dearly beloved, for your edifying" (v. 19). Though the apostle had been slandered and insulted by some of the leaders at Corinth, he still loved the Christians there. Everything he did was for the sake of the church. He was the model pastor!

B. The Threat of Further Contentions: vv. 20-21

Paul feared that if he came to Corinth at this time, he would be disappointed in the church members there and they would not understand him. The result would be "strife, jealousy, angry tempers, disputes, slanders, gossip, arrogance, disturbances" (v. 20, NASB). These Paul did not want. So he was staying away.

The apostle's heart was so burdened for conditions at Corinth that he evidently feared he would speak too strongly on the matter. Apparently cases of "uncleanness and fornication and lasciviousness" had multiplied, and Paul knew he would be broken and filled with tears with what he found. As a true pastor, he cared!

CONTEMPORARY APPLICATION

Today there is much division in Christendom. Our consciences sometimes bother us when we sing: "We are not divided, all one body we." The sad fact, of course, is that this is not true, unless we are talking about the mystical body of Christ.

True Christians ought to be more and more united in a spirit of loving fellowship. Thank God, this is taking place at many points. We need to pray with our Lord: "That they all may be one" (John 17:21).

GOD'S WISDOM FOR MAN'S FOLLY

DEVOTIONAL READING	I Corinthians 3:10-23

ADULTS

Topic: *God's Wisdom for Man's Folly*

Background Scripture: I Corinthians 1:18—3:23

Scripture Lesson: I Corinthians 1:18-24; 2:9-13

Memory Verse: *The word of the cross is folly to those who are perishing, but to us who are being saved it is the power of God.* I Corinthians 1:18

YOUTH

Topic: *Who Is Wise?*

Background Scripture: I Corinthians 1:18—3:23

Scripture Lesson: I Corinthians 1:18-25; 2:9-13

Memory Verse: *The word of the cross is folly to those who are perishing, but to us who are being saved it is the power of God.* I Corinthians 1:18.

CHILDREN

Topic: *Paul Meets the Lord*

Background Scripture: Acts 9:3-30

Scripture Lesson: Acts 9:3-6, 20-22

Memory Verse*: You will be a witness for him to all men of what you have seen and heard.* Acts 22:15

DAILY BIBLE READINGS

Mon., Sept. 3: The Wisdom of God, I Corinthians 2:1-8.
Tues., Sept. 4: No Other Foundation, I Corinthians 3:10-17.
Wed., Sept. 5: We Preach Christ Crucified, I Corinthians 1:18-25.
Thurs., Sept. 6: Not Lacking in Any Spiritual Gift, I Corinthians 1:1-9.
Fri., Sept. 7: Fools for Christ's Sake, I Corinthians 4:8-13.
Sat., Sept. 8: The Rich Fool, Luke 12:13-21.
Sun., Sept. 9: Spiritually Discerned, I Corinthians 1:26-31; 2:14-16.

LESSON AIM

To show the difference between man's wisdom and God's wisdom.

LESSON SETTING

Time: About A.D. 54 or 55

Place: Ephesus

God's Wisdom for Man's Folly

SUGGESTED INTRODUCTION FOR ADULTS

The ancient Greeks worshiped wisdom. Modern Americans worship science. Both attitudes are wrong. All the true wisdom that the Greek philosophers had they received from Christ, "in whom are hid all the treasures of wisdom and knowledge" (Colossians 2:3). And all the knowledge that scientists have accumulated through experimentation is simply a discovery of the divine laws written into the universe by its Creator. Man should glory in God, not boast in himself.

The ancient philosophers sought to explore the ultimate meanings of life. Many of them concluded that the primal force in the universe was fire. What they failed to see and acknowledge was that it was God.

Human wisdom led to human folly. If history proves anything, it is that man alone cannot find his way. He wanders about, lost in the mazes and morasses of his own foolish thinking. Only God can show us the right path.

SUGGESTED INTRODUCTION FOR YOUTH

There are only two kinds of people in the world, those who are wise and those who are otherwise. But who is wise?

When we say, "Oh, he's a wise guy," we are not handing out a compliment. We are cataloguing the fellow as one who thinks he is wise, when he is really a "nut."

Young people today are allergic to sham. That is something to be thankful for, not something to be decried as dangerous. Some of us older people need to give more careful attention to downright, upright, absolute honesty. When a teacher tries to cover up his ignorance by looking and sounding wise, students turn him off. And rightly so.

But wisdom is more than intellectual knowledge. True wisdom comes only from God. That is what our lesson today seeks to teach us.

CONCEPTS FOR
CHILDREN

1. Paul's conversion resulted from a personal meeting with God.
2. It is necessary for each person to meet God personally in order to be saved. (We are not saved just because our parents are Christians, or because we go to Sunday school and church.)
3. Because of his past, Paul wasn't trusted by his fellow Christians at first. This may happen to others who have just been saved after living a godless life.
4. Those who had been Paul's friends when he persecuted the Christians became his enemies after he became a Christian. This often happens to new Christians.

THE LESSON COMMENTARY

I. THE WISDOM OF THE WISE: I Corinthians 1:18-20

A. Rejection of the Cross: v. 18

Paul speaks of "the preaching of the cross." The Greek says, "the word of the cross" (cf. RSV), that is, the message of salvation through the death of Christ at Calvary. To those who are perishing through unbelief, this message is "foolishness." But to us who are being saved it is "the power of God."

This is the paradox of the gospel. It would seem to man's unaided wisdom that the cross revealed the weakness of God: He let His Son die there at the hands of cruel men. But actually, it was the divine plan for man's redemption. And so the Crucifixion becomes the greatest display of divine power in history. For it was there and then that God dealt a deathblow to sin and shook Satan's kingdom from center to circumference. Calvary was Love's finest hour.

All this is foolishness to the unsaved, simply because they do not understand the meaning of the cross. To them the Crucifixion was a personal tragedy in the life of a mistaken prophet who died a martyr's death. But we realize that the crucifixion of Christ has cosmic significance. We who are saved by the blood of Calvary know that the cross is the power of God for our salvation.

B. Doomed to Destruction: vv. 19-20

In verse 19 Paul quotes from Isaiah 29:14 to support his argument. Through His ancient prophet God had said that He would destroy the wisdom of the wise. Worldly wisdom is wisdom "under the sun," to use one of the key phrases of Ecclesiastes. It is wisdom with a low ceiling, earthbound. Only as the divine dimension is added can one find the true wisdom that is eternal. Wisdom related only to this world will perish with the world.

Then Paul asks, "Where is the wise? where is the scribe? where is the disputer of this world?" The first question is quoted from Isaiah 19:12, though in that place "wise" is plural ("wise men"). The whole of Isaiah 19 is addressed to Egypt, the country that was especially noted for its wise sayings. Some of this wisdom literature has been discovered by archaeologists. But God asks, "Where are thy wise men?" They have all perished, and their wisdom with them.

The second question—"Where is the scribe?"—is a quotation from Isaiah 33:18. The context there is that of Assyrian scribes taking inventory of the spoils they had captured in Judah. On the tablet of Shalmanezer in the Assyrian Gallery of the British Museum there is a description that corroborates what we read in Isaiah.

In Paul's day "the wise" would refer mainly to the Greeks (cf. v. 22), for Athens was the great center of wisdom at that time, and had been for some centuries. But its wise philosophers, like those of ancient Egypt, have long since disappeared. The apostle appropriately asks, "Where is the wise?"

Also in Paul's day "the scribe" would most naturally refer to the Jew. The term is found frequently in the Gospels (62 times) and Acts (4 times), but elsewhere in the New Testament only here. While it is used for the "townclerk" in Acts 19:35, in every other instance it refers to the Jewish scribes, or teachers of the law, and should probably be taken that way here.

The Greek word for "disputer" is found only here in the New Testament. The term could probably apply equally well to Jews and Greeks, for both were fond of endless arguments and debates. The Jewish rabbis haggled over fine points in the letter of the Law. And the Greek philosophers debated day after day in the Agora at Athens.

It is startling to read that God has "made foolish the wisdom of this world." But history furnishes numerous examples of this. Man's plans for world peace, for instance, have all failed. What modern man needs most is humility, a willingness to say, "We don't know how to do it," and a repentant turning to God for guidance. But pride is man's besetting sin. It caused the fall of Satan, and it is the main cause of people's downfall today.

II. THE WISDOM OF GOD:
I Corinthians 1:21-25

A. Christ Crucified: vv. 21-23

God, in His wisdom, ordained that men by their own wisdom should not know Him. This statement must be read in the light of the Fall of man (Genesis 3). Since man deliberately rebelled against God's will, sinful man cannot find out God. We only know Him by divine revelation. And the su-

preme revelation of God was made at the cross.

So Paul goes on to say that "it pleased God by the foolishness of preaching to save them that believe." Too often people take this as meaning that preaching seems a foolish way to try to save men. But the Greek word translated "preaching" is *kerygma*, which does not refer to preaching as a *method*, but rather to the *message* proclaimed. It is the message of salvation through the crucified, risen Christ that seems foolish to unregenerate mankind.

There was one outstanding difference between Jews and Greeks. Paul puts it this way: "The Jews require a sign, and the Greeks seek after wisdom" (v. 22). The truth of the second statement is well known. The first statement is documented in the Gospels. Four times we are told that the scribes and Pharisees asked Jesus for a sign (Matthew 12:38; 16:1; Mark 8:11; Luke 11:16). They wanted a spectacular "sign from heaven" (so Mark and Luke) something that would prove His messiahship. But Jesus chided His generation for seeking a sign and declared that the only sign it would be given was that of the prophet Jonah (Matthew 12:39; 16:4; Luke 11:29; cf. Mark 8:12).

What is God's answer? Paul says: "But we preach Christ crucified, unto the Jews a stumbling block, and unto the Greeks foolishness" (v. 23). The oldest Greek manuscripts have "Gentiles" instead of "Greeks," but the two terms seem to be used somewhat interchangeably in the New Testament.

The Greek word for "stumblingblock" is *scandalon*, from which we get "scandal." This is the origin of the phrase, "the scandal of the Cross." The Jews expected a Messiah who would come as a mighty conqueror and with great signs, dispersing their Gentile overlords and establishing a glorious kingdom like that of David and Solomon. Instead Jesus went around humbly teaching the common people and healing the sick. Finally He was arrested, condemned, and exe-

cuted by the ignominious method of
crucifixion. Surely this could not be
the Messiah! The Jews stumbled over
the cross, and it is still a scandal to
them. Since Jesus did not fulfil their
Messianic expectations, they rejected
Him.

B. Christ the Power of God: v. 24

To both Jews and Greeks the death
of Christ seemed to be a proof of His
weakness. But Paul asserts that to
those who believe, whether Jew or
Greek, Christ is "the power of God,
and the wisdom of God." Christ is
God's power for the salvation of weak
sinners, and He is the wisdom of God
for human ignorance. That is why Paul
teaches so strongly in his Epistles that
Christ is all we need. In Him we find
the answer to our two greatest needs,
strength and wisdom.

C. Divine "Foolishness" vs. Human Wisdom: v. 25

The "foolishness of God"—what a
strange phrase! Of course Paul means
what *men* consider foolish. He declares
that "the foolishness of God is wiser
than men; and the weakness of God is
stronger than men." Lias comments:
"What was folly in the eyes of the
Greek, or weakness in the eyes of the
Jew, was yet far wiser and stronger
than their highest conceptions. The
revelation of God in the man Christ
Jesus—the foolishness of God, the Infinite allying itself to the finite—was the
perfection of the Divine Wisdom; the
crucifixion of sin in the Death of
Christ—the weakness of God, God suffering, dying—was the highest manifestation of Divine power, in that it destroyed what nothing else could destroy" (*I Corinthians*, pp. 39-40). Robertson and Plummer sum it up briefly:
"God's wisdom, at its lowest, is wiser
than men, and God's power, at its
weakest, is stronger than men" (*I Corinthians*, p. 23). The distance between
God and man is infinite, but bridged in
Christ.

III. CHRIST, THE WISDOM OF GOD: I Corinthians 1:26-31

Paul reminds the members of the
church at Corinth that not many of
them were "wise men after the flesh"
—that is renowned for human wisdom
—or "mighty" (influential), or
"noble"—the Greek means "well-
born." The fact that he says "not
many" rather than "none" shows that
there were some Corinthian Christians
from backgrounds of education, culture, and status. But, as in the case of
Jesus' followers, most of them were
poor people with no prominent standing. The names of Paul's converts suggest that many were slaves or freedmen.

The apostle goes on to say that
"God hath chosen the foolish things of
the world to confound the wise; and
God hath chosen the weak things of
the world to confound the things
which are mighty; and base things of
the world, and things which are despised hath God chosen, yea, the
things which are not, to bring to
nought things that are." The purpose
of all this is "that no flesh should
glory in his presence." The expression
"things which are not" is explained by
Lias as meaning "'things which by
comparison are non-existent'—things
which by the side of other things of
higher importance in our human eyes
appear to us as nothing" (*I Corinthians*, p. 40). Findlay comments: "The
classes to which Christianity appealed
were *non-entities* for philosophers and
statesmen, cyphers in their reckoning"
(*Expositor's Greek Testament*, II,
772).

Verse 30 contains one of Paul's
comprehensive characterizations of
Christ. He writes: "But of him [God]
are ye in Christ Jesus, who of God is
made unto us wisdom, and righteousness, and sanctification, and redemption." The Greek suggests that the last
three terms are explanatory of the previous one. Robertson and Plummer
comment: "The terms, linked into one
group by the conjunctions, are in ap-
position to *sophia* (wisdom) and de-

fine it ... the four terms are not co-ordinate" (*I Corinthians*, p. 27). Findlay agrees. The meaning then is that Christ became God's wisdom to us, shown in our salvation, which has three aspects or phases—"righteousness" (justification, initial salvation), "sanctification" (the cleansing, empowering work of the Holy Spirit in our hearts), and "redemption" (final salvation in the redemption, or glorification, of our bodies, Romans 8:23).

IV. THE WISDOM OF MEN vs. THE POWER OF GOD:
I Corinthians 2:1-8

Paul had made an appropriate speech before the august Court of the Areopagus (Acts 17:22-31). Doubtless disappointed with the meager results, he went to Corinth "determined not to know anything among you, save Jesus Christ and him crucified" (v. 2). He goes on to say: "And my speech and my preaching was not with enticing words of man's wisdom, but in demonstration of the Spirit and of power: that your faith should not stand in the wisdom of men, but in the power of God" (vv. 4-5). Anything that stands on the wisdom of men will ultimately fall. Men's ideas have changed again and again across the centuries. But the power of God gives solid support to our faith.

The apostle adds that among the "perfect" (or mature) Christians he speaks wisdom—not the wisdom of this world, but "the wisdom of God in a mystery" (vv. 7-8). This mystery is the divine plan for the salvation of both Jews and Gentiles through Jesus Christ and His death on the cross.

V. THE WISDOM OF GOD REVEALED:
I Corinthians 2:9-13

A. Revelation by the Spirit: vv. 9-10

In verse 9 we find a rather loose quotation from Isaiah 64:4. Some people are disturbed by this lack of preciseness. But Lias wisely warns us: "It is unreasonable to require greater literary accuracy in the citation of words in the N.T. from the O.T. than is customary in a modern preacher, who is frequently content with giving the general drift of the passage he quotes. Such a practice was even more likely to exist in days when the cumbrous nature of books prevented them from being so readily at hand as at present" (*I Corinthians*, p. 45). It must be remembered that at that time all copies of the Scriptures were copied by hand. Not only was there no division into chapters and verses; neither was there any separation between sentences or words. Checking a passage in the Old Testament would be a tedious task indeed.

We often hear verse 9 quoted by itself as indicating that we cannot know in this life what God has prepared for those who love Him. Obviously, this is a careless distortion of Scripture. For the next verse declares: "But God hath revealed them unto us by his Spirit." We cannot know them by human wisdom. But the divine revelation in the Bible does give us some knowledge of the future. It should also be noted that these things God has prepared include the spiritual blessings which we receive as His children in this life. The Holy Spirit searches out these things and reveals them to us.

DISCUSSION QUESTIONS

1. Why is the wisdom of this world not in tune with the wisdom of God?
2. How may we receive God's wisdom?
3. What is the basic difference between the wisdom of men and the wisdom of God?
4. Why does the wisdom of God appear foolish to men?
5. Why does the preaching of the cross offend people?
6. How may young converts mature spiritually?

B. The Holy Spirit as Teacher: vv. 11-13

The apostle draws an analogy between man's knowledge of himself and his knowledge of God. Robertson and Plummer write: "Even a human being has within him secrets of his own, which no human being whatever can penetrate, but only his own spirit. How much more is this true of God" (First Corinthians, p. 44). A man can only know the thoughts of his heart by his "spirit," his inner consciousness. Likewise, man can only know the thoughts of God as the Holy Spirit reveals them to him.

Fortunately, we have not received the spirit of the world, but the Spirit of God (v. 12). Findlay puts it well: "'The spirit of the world' breathes in men who are a part of the world; 'the Spirit that is from God' visits us from another sphere, bringing knowledge of things removed from natural apprehension" (Expositor's Greek Testament, II, 782).

So the Holy Spirit teaches us and enables us, in turn, to share the things of God with others. Without the Holy Spirit, no amount of intellectual brilliance nor advanced education can help a man to understand even the elementary truths of God's kingdom. This fact is illustrated every day. One often wonders how men of great learning, even noted theologians, can miss the simple truths of the gospel.

The last part of verse 13—"comparing spiritual things with spiritual"—has caused a great deal of discussion. The problem rises partly out of the fact that the second adjective "spiritual" may be either masculine or neuter. (The forms are the same in the dative case.)

Many interpretations have been given, but Lias gives the four basic ones: "(1) explaining spiritual things to spiritual men (so Wycliffe), (2) explaining spiritual things by spiritual, (3) explaining spiritual things in spiritual ways (so Luther), and (4) comparing spiritual things with spiritual (so Vulgate and A.V.)" (I Corinthians, p. 46).

The first of these seems to be preferable (cf. RSV, Phillips, NEB). However, the New American Standard Bible reads: "combining spiritual thoughts with spiritual words," adopting the neuter, as did its predecessor (ASV). Findlay (Expositor's Greek Testament, II, 783) opts for this also. The lack of the definite article with the second "spiritual" is perhaps the main argument for this. We cannot be sure which of these meanings was in the mind of Paul.

The closing verses of this chapter highlight the fact that "the natural man" cannot understand spiritual truths. Only the Holy Spirit can enable us to comprehend the things of God.

CONTEMPORARY APPLICATION

Paul's statement that "the Jews require a sign" has been vividly illustrated in modern times. The superintendent of the Hebrew Mission in one of our large cities told of a Jewish young lady who was seeking salvation. Her trouble was that she could not seem to believe that Jesus was the Messiah.

One day she was riding in the back seat of the superintendent's car. The sky was clear and the sun was shining brightly. Suddenly a ball of fire struck the road in front of the car, causing the driver to jam on the brakes.

To the surprise of the superintendent and his wife, the young lady immediately exclaimed: "Thank you, God. Now I know that Jesus of Nazareth is your Messiah." She then explained that on that very morning she had prayed: "O God, if Jesus is the Messiah, give me a sign today, so that I will know it." God accommodated Himself to her needs, and she was satisfied.

UNITY AT THE LORD'S TABLE

DEVOTIONAL READING	John 6:35-48

ADULTS

Topic: *Unity at the Lord's Table*

Background Scripture: I Corinthians 11:17-34

Scripture Lesson: I Corinthians 11:17-26

Memory Verse: *For as often as you eat this bread and drink the cup, you proclaim the Lord's death until he comes.* I Corinthians 11:26

YOUTH

Topic: *One at the Lord's Table*

Background Scripture: I Corinthians 11:17-34

Scripture Lesson: I Corinthians 11:17-26

Memory Verse: *For as often as you eat this bread and drink the cup, you proclaim the Lord's death until he comes.* I Corinthians 11:26

CHILDREN

Topic: *Problems at Antioch*

Background Scripture: Acts 13:14-52

Scripture Lesson: Acts 13:44-50

Memory Verse: *I will give you as a light to the nations, that my salvation may reach to the end of the earth.* Isaiah 49:6

DAILY BIBLE READINGS

Mon., Sept. 10: The Lord's Supper—According to Matthew, Matthew 26:17-29.
Tues., Sept. 11: The Lord's Supper—According to Mark, Mark 14:17-31.
Wed., Sept. 12: The Lord's Supper—According to Luke, Luke 22:14-27.
Thurs., Sept. 13: The Bread of Life, John 6:48-58.
Fri., Sept. 14: The Lord's Supper—According to Paul, I Corinthians 11:23-32.
Sat., Sept. 15: The Broken Body and the Shed Blood, John 19:28-37.
Sun., Sept. 16: Known in the Breaking of Bread, Luke 24:28-35.

LESSON AIM

To show the proper attitude one should have at the Communion table.

LESSON SETTING

Time: About A.D. 54 or 55

Place: Ephesus

Unity at the Lord's Table

I. Schisms at the Lord's Supper: I Corinthians 11:17-19
   A. Censure, Not praise: v. 17
   B. Report of Schisms: v. 18
   C. Cliques in the Church: v. 19

II. Selfishness at the Lord's Supper: I Corinthians 11:20-22
   A. Insincerity at the Sacrament: v. 20
   B. Drunk at the Lord's Table: v. 21
   C. Desecrating God's House: v. 22

LESSON OUTLINE

III. Sacrament of the Lord's Supper: I Corinthians 11:23-26
   A. A Revelation from the Lord: v. 23
   B. The Broken Bread: v. 24
   C. The Cup: v. 25
   D. A Memorial and Anticipation: v. 26

IV. Seriousness of the Lord's Supper: I Corinthians 11:27-34

   A. Self-examination Necessary: v. 27-30
   B. Self-judgment Needed: vv. 31-34

SUGGESTED INTRODUCTION FOR ADULTS

Paul had his problems with the church at Corinth. He had heard about three of them. First he had been told that there were divisions in the church (I Corinthians 1:11). He devotes the first four chapters of his First Epistle to the Corinthians to this very serious matter. Then he noted that it was "reported commonly" that there was a bad case of immorality in the church membership: a man was living with his stepmother. He discusses this problem in the fifth chapter. In chapter 6 he deals with the third problem, lawsuits between Christians.

Chapter 7 begins by saying: "Now concerning the things whereof ye wrote unto me." Paul proceeds to deal with some half dozen problems the Corinthians had written him about. The first was that of marriage (chap. 7). The second concerned things offered to idols (chaps. 8-10). The third had to do with church worship (chap. 11). The fourth, discussed at considerable length, dealt with spiritual gifts (chaps. 12-14). This is followed by a long chapter on the Resurrection (chap. 15) and a brief discussion of the collection for the saints that was to be taken at Corinth (chap. 16). It is with the third of these problems that we are concerned today—conduct in church worship, and particularly at the Lord's Supper.

SUGGESTED INTRODUCTION FOR YOUTH

Youth Classes. The Communion service should always be a sacred time. It is no place for levity or thoughtlessness, but a time for extreme reverence. And yet it should be an occasion of real joy in the sense of fellowship with the risen Lord.

Young people should not hesitate to partake of Communion if they are conscious that their sins have been forgiven and that they belong to Christ. Even if this is not true, anyone who comes with a truly repentant heart, confessing his sins, is welcome at the table.

CONCEPTS FOR CHILDREN

1. When Paul preached, some accepted his message and believed in Christ, while others did not.
2. The same thing happens today every time the Word of God is preached.
3. We should be sure that we are among those who accept and believe the gospel, for it is by doing so that we show that we are God's children.

THE LESSON COMMENTARY

I. SCHISMS AT THE LORD'S SUPPER:
I Corinthians 11:17-19

A. Censure, Not Praise: v. 17

As noted in the introduction, the eleventh chapter deals with Christian conduct at church worship, and especially at the Communion service. The last item comes in the second half of the chapter, in our lesson for today.

The opening words of this chapter —"Be ye followers [Greek, "imitators"] of me, even as I also am of Christ"—form a fitting capstone to the previous chapter, and should be put with it. (There are no chapter divisions in the early manuscripts of the New Testament.) Only Paul would dare to utter such words. But he walked so close to the Lord that he could invite others to stay right behind him, imitating his spirit.

Then the apostle commends the Christians at Corinth for keeping the traditions that he had handed down to them (v. 2). These included the instructions that men should pray in public with their heads uncovered (vv. 4, 7). It is interesting to note that Jews follow the reverse practice. As a young man we visited the oldest Jewish synagogue in America, on Truro Street in Newport, Rhode Island. On entering,

we men removed our hats. Immediately the elderly men who were saying their prayers protested. A young man who could speak English asked us to put our hats on again in reverence to God. Today at the famous Wailing Wall (now called the Western Wall) in Jerusalem all the men wear either a hat or a skull cap.

This is the opposite of our American way of showing respect or reverence. But the great medieval Jewish philosopher Maimonides wrote: "Let not the wise men, nor the scholars of the wise men pray, unless they be covered" *(Cambridge Greek Testament)*. Among the ancient Germans and Romans it was the custom for men to pray with covered heads.

The Greek practice was different. Among the Greeks, slaves had their heads covered; the uncovered head was a sign of freedom. This may have influenced the Gentile Christians to adopt the custom of having men pray with heads uncovered. At any rate, over the centuries the church has followed Paul's instructions here.

Regarding the women, the apostle ordered that they should always have their heads covered, or veiled, when praying (vv. 5-6). This was a symbol of their subordination to men. Until very recently the Roman Catholic Church has held rigidly to this practice. No woman was supposed to enter a place of worship without at least a kerchief on her head.

In Protestant churches the customs have changed. One can remember when most women wore hats to church, at least on Sunday morning. This is no longer the case. In most places only a few elderly women—or ultra-modern girls!—wear hats.

Are we disobeying a divine command? The reasonable answer seems to be "No." Paul was dealing with a Greek custom at Corinth. For a woman to appear in public with her head uncovered would advertise the fact that she was a person of bad character. Paul did not want Christian women to be so imbued with their freedom in Christ that they flouted the accepted standards of their culture. The same should be true of us today.

Now to come specifically to grips with the lesson for today. Paul says that in the instructions he is about to give he cannot commend the conduct of his readers, "for it seems that your church meetings do you more harm than good!" (Phillips). What good is the church when conditions reach that stage?

B. Report of Schisms: v. 18

The apostle has heard that in their services there were "divisions." The Greek word is *schisma*, from which we get "schism." There were church "splits" at Corinth, because of the selfish attitude of too many members. When each one is for himself, the church is divided. When every one is for the Lord, the church is united. It is as simple as that.

How sad that Paul would have to say about the report of divisions, "And I partly believe it." The Corinthian Christians were a quarrelsome crowd, as Paul had discovered when he was with them. It must be noted here that people's backgrounds have a way of carrying over into their Christian life. Some allowance has to be made for this. Corinth was noted for its contentiousness, and this local fault

showed up in the church. "All things become new," but it often takes time for this to take place fully.

C. Cliques in the Church: v. 19

The apostle says that there must also be "heresies" among them. The Greek word is *haereseis*, from which we get "heresies." But the main meaning of this word as used in Paul's day was "factions." Later in church history the factions in the church represented wrong doctrines, and so *haereseis* came to be used in its modern sense of "heresies." But here it clearly means "factions." The only place in the New Testament where it means "heresies" is II Peter 2:1. In the other three places where it is so translated in the King James Version (Acts 24:14; I Corinthians 11:19; Galatians 5:20) it should be rendered "factions." In the other five occurrences of this word in the New Testament (all in Acts) it is correctly translated in King James Version as "sect." We read about the sect of the Sadducees (5:17), the sect of the Pharisees (15:5; 26:5), "the sect of the Nazarenes" (24:5), and "this sect"—Christianity (28:22). Factions were inevitable ("must be") in a city like Corinth.

But what does the rest of verse 19 mean? Robertson and Plummer make this suggestion: "Either by coming to the front in the interests of unity, or by keeping aloof from all divisions, the more stable characters will become manifest." They add: "To have religious zeal, without becoming a religious partisan, is a great proof of true devotion" (*I Corinthians*, p. 240). Our first loyalty must be to Christ, not to human leaders.

II. SELFISHNESS AT THE LORD'S SUPPER: I Corinthians 11:20-22

A. Sincerity at the Sacrament: v. 20

The apostle declares that when the Corinthian Christians came together "this is not to eat the Lord's supper." That is, they did not have the right motive in coming to the Communion table. They came for food rather than fellowship. Perhaps the correct meaning is: "You do not eat the *Lord's supper*" (Phillips, from *International Critical Commentary*). They ate supper, but it was not truly the Lord's meal of spiritual communion.

The Gospels portray Jesus as instituting the Lord's Supper at the close of the Last Supper, the night before His crucifixion. So the early believers ate a Love Feast (Agape) and then celebrated Communion. Later the Eucharist was put first, with the Agape following it. Probably the expression here, "the Lord's Supper," takes in both. Today it is used synonymously with Communion and Eucharist. But here a full meal is implied.

B. Drunk at the Lord's Table: v. 21

When the Christians at Corinth met together for their fellowship meal, "everyone seizes first his own supper" (Weymouth). The result is that "one goes hungry while another gets drunk" (Moffatt).

Getting drunk at the Lord's Supper! Such a thing is hard to imagine. It is only in the light of the very low moral conditions at Corinth that one can envision church members acting that way. Some versions try to weaken the wording here. But the Greek verb means "to be drunk." We would agree with Lias when he writes: "We have no right, with some commentators, to soften down the force of this word, as though no such abominations were possible at Corinth. The permeation of the Christian community by the Spirit of Christ . . . was a more gradual process than is generally supposed" (*I Corinthians*, p. 130).

C. Desecrating God's House: v. 22

Paul speaks sharply and sternly to these selfish, self-indulgent people. "Don't you have houses in which to

eat and drink?" he asks. "Why do you despise the church of God and humiliate the poorer members who have nothing?"

Now we see the practical effect of the schisms (v. 18) and factions (v. 19) in the church at Corinth. When the people came together for the Love Feast, they separated into cliques. Those who were cultured, educated people of means ate together, with an abundant supply of rich food and beverages. The poorer people ate by themselves. Some of them had little or no food. In fact, the implication of the two longest questions in this verse is that some of these poor people had no homes of their own—"Have ye not houses to eat and to drink in? . . . and shame them that have not?"

Almost in despair the apostle writes: "What shall I say to you? shall I praise you in this? I praise you not." Their contempt for the church of God and their callous lack of compassion for the poor were utterly unchristian. What *could* he say to them?

III. SACRAMENT OF THE LORD'S SUPPER: I Corinthians 11:23-26

A. A Revelation from the Lord: v. 23

Paul claimed to have received directly from the Lord his instructions about the Lord's Supper. He does not say, "from the disciples of the Lord," but "from the Lord." Doubtless Peter and John had told him in detail what took place in the upper room when Christ instituted the Lord's Supper. But Paul seems to assert here that this historical knowledge of the event had been validated to him by a direct revelation as to its meaning and significance for the church.

"The Lord Jesus the same night in which he was betrayed took bread." From the Gospel accounts we learn that this was at the close of the Passover meal, which we now call the Last Supper.

B. The Broken Bread: v. 24

"When he had given thanks" is all one word in the Greek—*eucharistesas.* From this we get the term Eucharist, which is one name for the Lord's Supper. It literally means "thanksgiving." At every Communion service we should give thanks to God for the sacrifice of His Son at Calvary. We should also give thanks to Christ for His presence with us at the table, which makes the Sacrament a real Communion. And we should be thankful for the fellowship of the saints that we experience with special meaning when we gather for the Lord's Supper. Thanksgiving should be an integral and important part of every Communion service. In the midst of the sacredness and solemnity of the occasion, our hearts should well up with "the joy of His salvation."

The broken bread symbolizes the Body of Christ, given for us on the cross to make an atonement for our sins. "This is my body" is taken by most Protestants to mean "this represents my body." (The following word "broken" is not in the oldest manuscripts and should be omitted.)

C. The Cup: v. 25

At the close of the Supper, Jesus also shared the cup with His disciples. As He did so He said: "This cup is [represents] the new testament in my blood: this do ye, as oft as ye drink it, in remembrance of me." The word translated "testament" is better translated "covenant." It was common in those days to make what was called a "blood covenant." A contract was drawn up between two men. Then each pricked his own arm and signed his name with his blood. A covenant so made was considered especially binding. And that is the kind of a covenant of salvation that Christ has made with us; it is signed with His own blood.

Some churches hold that the bread of the Communion service is actually Christ's body and the wine is actually His blood. It seems to us that Jesus Himself gave the answer to this idea during His earthly ministry. He had mentioned His body as being the living bread that gives eternal life (John 6:51). In consternation the Jews said, "How can this man give us his flesh to eat?" (v. 52). Then Jesus became more explicit: "Except ye eat the flesh of the Son of man and drink his blood, ye have no life in you. Whosoever eateth my flesh, and drinketh my blood, hath eternal life" (vv. 53-54).

When the disciples began to murmur about this "hard saying" (v. 60), Jesus set the whole matter in its proper light. He said: "It is the spirit that quickeneth; the flesh profiteth nothing: the words that I speak unto you, they are spirit, and they are life" (v. 63). We are to feed on Christ *spiritually.* We do this by "eating" His Word, which gives spiritual life.

D. A Memorial and Anticipation: v. 26

This verse indicates the three tenses of the Communion service. It looks back to the *past:* "Ye do show the Lord's death." It has the *present* of spiritual fellowship with Christ: "as often as ye eat [are eating] this bread, and drink this cup." It looks forward to the *future:* "till he come."

Too often it is only the first of these three that is emphasized. The whole service revolves around a meditation on the meaning of the Crucifixion. Our minds are turned back to Calvary and stay there. But there ought to be a rejoicing in the fact that the risen Christ, our living Lord, is present with us at the table. That makes it a real Communion. In the fellowship of His presence we receive purity and power for living as we should in this sinful world. As His love bathes our souls, we are made more like Him and so enabled anew to live a more Christlike life.

But that is not all. There is the forward look—"till he come." Seldom do we ever hear anything about the Second Coming in a Communion message. But Paul indicates that this is an integral part of it. Whenever we gather for the Lord's Supper we should not only memorialize the Lord's death at Calvary but anticipate His coming in glory at the end of this age.

The early church did this. Here is the picture we find of a Communion service in the beginning years of the second century. The worshipers met long before sunrise in some private home, in order to avoid detection. In fact, they had to finish their meeting and disperse to their homes while it was still dark if they wanted to be safe.

Communion was celebrated every Sunday, for they knew that each Lord's Day might be their last one on earth. At the close of the Communion the whole congregation repeated in unison the Aramaic phrase found at the end of I Corinthians, *Maran atha* — "Our Lord, come!" This should be the note on which our Communion services end today. In fact, it would be entirely appropriate to sing a Second Coming song for the close of that service.

IV. SERIOUSNESS OF THE LORD'S SUPPER:
I Corinthians 11:27-34

A. Self-examination Necessary: vv. 27-30

The last verses of this eleventh chapter are a part of the lesson, though not so indicated, and comprise an important phase of Paul's instructions concerning the Lord's Supper. So we shall take a brief look at them.

The apostle warns that whoever eats the Communion bread and drinks the "cup of the Lord, unworthily, shall be guilty of the body and blood of the Lord." This is a serious sin.

How, then, are we to approach the Lord's table? The answer is given clearly in verse 28: "But let a man examine himself, and so let him eat of that bread, and drink of that cup." One of the greatest values of taking Communion lies in our examining our hearts to make sure that we are worthy to partake. Frequent Communion services would be spiritually helpful if sufficient emphasis were put on the importance of self-examination.

Paul even asserts that many people are "weak and sickly" and many have died ("sleep") because they partook of the sacred elements unworthily. The word "damnation" (v. 29) is simply "judgment" in the Greek. The context suggests that the reference is to sickness and divine judgment rather than to eternal "damnation."

B. Self-judgment Needed: vv. 31-34

The way to escape God's judgment is to judge ourselves (v. 31). When He judges us, He chastens us so that we will not be "condemned with the world" (v. 32). This shows clearly that "damnation" in verse 29 is an incorrect translation.

The apostle finishes his discussion where he began it. When the Christians gather for the Love Feast, they should wait for each other. If hungry, they should eat at home (vv. 33-34; cf. vv. 20-22).

DISCUSSION QUESTIONS

1. To what extent are Christians affected by their culture?
2. How did the atmosphere at the Last Supper (Luke 22:14-24) resemble the situation in Corinth?
3. What is the meaning of Communion? of Eucharist?
4. How should we approach the Lord's Supper?
5. Who should partake?
6. What value does the Communion have for us?

CONTEMPORARY APPLICATION

Some years ago we were holding a week-long revival effort in an overseas church where the culture was rather caste ridden. On one side of the center aisle sat the professional people—school teachers and the like. On the other side sat the working class, including clerks in stores. At the close of each service the people on each side shook hands among themselves, but there was no fellowship across the aisle. And yet most of these good people professed to have perfect love!

Needless to say, this situation burdened our hearts. The Lord graciously answered prayer. On the closing Sunday we had the privilege of seeing people from all over that congregation kneeling together at the altar, their hearts melted in love for each other. That is true revival.

September 23, 1973

THE MINISTRY OF RECONCILIATION

DEVOTIONAL READING

II Corinthians 5:11-15

ADULTS

Topic: *Ministers of Reconciliation*

Background Scripture: II Corinthians 5:11—6:10

Scripture Lesson: II Corinthians 5:16—6:2

Memory Verse: *God was in Christ reconciling the world to himself, not counting their trespasses against them, and entrusting to us the message of reconciliation.* II Corinthians 5:19

YOUTH

Topic: *Agents of Reconciliation*

Background Scripture: II Corinthians 5:11—6:10

Scripture Lesson: II Corinthians 5:16—6:2

Memory Verse: *God was in Christ reconciling the world to himself, not counting their trespasses against them, and entrusting to us the message of reconciliation.* II Corinthians 5:19

CHILDREN

Topic: *Paul in Corinth*

Background Scripture: Acts 18:1-17

Scripture Lesson: Acts 18:5-11

Memory Verse: *Be not afraid of them, for I am with you to deliver you, says the Lord.* Jeremiah 1:8

DAILY BIBLE READINGS

Mon., Sept. 17: The God of All Comfort, II Corinthians 1:3-11.

Tues., Sept. 18: Letters from Christ, II Corinthians 3:1-11

Wed., Sept. 19: Treasure in Earthen Vessels, II Corinthians 4:1-12.

Thurs., Sept. 20: A House—Eternal in the Heavens, II Corinthians 4:16—5:10.

Fri., Sept. 21: Ambassadors for Christ, II Corinthians 5:16-21.

Sat., Sept. 22: Now Is the Acceptable Time, II Corinthians 6:1-10.

Sun., Sept. 23: The Grace of God in Macedonia, II Corinthians 8:1-12.

LESSON AIM

To learn how we may be agents of reconciliation between God and man, and between man and man.

23

Time: About A.D. 55

Place: Somewhere in Macedonia, probably at Philippi

The Ministry of Reconciliation

I. Reconciliation Provided: II Corinthians 5:11-15

II. Reconciliation Effective: II Corinthians 5:16-17
   A. Knowing Christ Spiritually: v. 16
   B. A New Creation in Christ: v. 17

III. Reconciliation Explained: II Corinthians 5:18-19
   A. Reconciled in Christ: v. 18
   B. Reconciling the World: v. 19

IV. Reconciliation Applied: II Corinthians 5:20-21
   A. Ambassadors for Christ: v. 20
   B. Christ the Sin-offering: v. 21

V. Reconciliation Urged: II Corinthians 6:1-2
   A. The Earnest Plea: v. 1
   B. The Accepted Time: v. 2

LESSON OUTLINE *(margin label)*

SUGGESTED INTRODUCTION FOR ADULTS *(margin label)*

Today we conclude our study of the Corinthian church and Paul's relationship to it. Our lesson is taken from II Corinthians. This Epistle has three main divisions. First, Paul defends his ministry (chaps. 1-7). Then he discusses the collection for the saints (chaps. 8-9), which he had already introduced briefly in the last chapter of I Corinthians. In the third division (chaps. 10-13) the apostle defends his own character against the malicious slanders of some of the church members at Corinth.

Our present lesson is taken from the first division. It will be remembered that the overall topic of this quarter's lessons is "The Gospel According to Paul." In our study today we find the very marrow of this gospel: God's ministry of reconciliation in Christ. This, in turn, should produce in us a ministry of reconciliation toward the world.

Every true Christian should be involved in this ministry. If we are helping to stir up strife in politics, in racial relations, in social situations, in religious groups, then we are acting in a non-Christian way. Are we true ministers of reconciliation in the outreach of our lives?

SUGGESTED INTRODUCTION FOR YOUTH *(margin label)*

Youth Classes. The decade of the sixties was marked by violent conflict. Riots and demonstrations broke out on college campuses and in the asphalt jungles of our cities. The causes were racial, political, economic, social, and ultimately spiritual.

What are the seventies going to be like? That depends on what attitude you and I take. If we are agents of strife, the conflicts will continue. But if we are truly Christian, we will seek to be agents of reconciliation. Instead of hate, there will be love. Instead of violence, there will be understanding. The decision lies with us.

CONCEPTS FOR CHILDREN

1. Paul worked hard in Corinth. He worked unselfishly to bring the good news to those who did not know.
2. He preached wherever he could find people who would listen.
3. We also should present Christ to everyone who is willing to listen.

THE LESSON COMMENTARY

I. RECONCILIATION PROVIDED: II Corinthians 5:11-15

"Knowing therefore" (v. 11). The word "therefore" links this verse with the previous one. In verse 10 Paul declares that "we [believers] must all appear before the judgment seat of Christ; that every one may receive the things done in his body, according to that he hath done, whether it be good or bad." He goes on to say: "Knowing therefore the terror of the Lord, we persuade men."

Instead of "terror" the Greek simply has "fear" (*phobos*). Philip Hughes comments: "By 'the fear of the Lord,' then, the apostle does not mean that terror . . . which the ungodly will experience when they stand before God's judgment throne (cf. Rev. 6:15ff.), but that reverential awe which the Christian should feel towards the Master whom he loves and serves and at whose hand he will receive 'the things done in the body.' " (*II Corinthians*, p. 186).

In the light of the rest of verse 11, as well as verse 12, it seems that "we persuade men" does not refer to pleading with sinners to be saved (as in v. 20), but rather to Paul's effort to persuade "certain members of the Corinthian church of the integrity of his personal character (see 1:12 ff., 4:1 ff., 7:22 ff.) and of the authenticity of his status as their apostle (see 3:1 ff, 10:1 ff.)" (Hughes).

But in verse 14 Paul moves right into the subject of our lesson. He makes the magnificent statement: "The love of Christ constraineth us." The phrase "of Christ" can be taken in three ways: (1), subjective genitive: "Christ's love for me constrains me to crucial commitment"; (2) objective genitive: "My love for Christ constrains me to complete consecration"; (3) possessive genitive: "Christ's love in me constrains me to compassionate concern" for others. All these ideas are implied in this great declaration.

Paul then makes an important point: If Christ died for all, then all men were dead in sin (v. 14). The atonement of Christ was made for "all." All men need it and can have it by accepting Christ's death for them. The purpose of that death was that people should not "live unto themselves, but unto him which died for them, and rose again" (v. 15).

II. RECONCILIATION EFFECTIVE: II Corinthians 5:16-17

A. Knowing Christ Spiritually: v. 16

"Wherefore henceforth know we no man after the flesh." The "henceforth" means after his conversion. What is the meaning of the phrase "after the flesh"? Apparently it indicates, "according to the standards of the world." As Hughes says, "Typically worldly distinctions, such as those of race, social status, wealth, and title, should no longer govern the Christian's estimate of his fellow-men (cf. Gal. 3:28)" (*II Corinthians*, p. 197).

Paul continues: "Yea, though we have known Christ after the flesh, yet now henceforth know we him no more." Some have taken the expression "after the flesh" to mean that Paul had been acquainted with Jesus during our Lord's earthly ministry. But we have already noted that the phrase means "according to worldly standards." Before his conversion Paul had judged Christ by human standards and had rejected Him as an impostor. But on the Damascus Road he had discovered who Jesus really was—Son of God and Savior.

The last clause presents a good opportunity for sounding a warning against a purely literalistic interpretation of a Scripture passage, without taking the context into account. Taken by itself, this clause asserts that Paul no longer knew Christ. Obviously, this is not true. The context clearly indicates that he means "know Christ in this way," that is, "according to the flesh."

B. A New Creation in Christ: v. 17

The apostle declares that if any man is "in Christ" he is "a new creature," or "a new creation." Each born-again Christian, is, in a sense, a fresh creation from God's hand. And so, "old things are passed away; behold, all things are become new."

The first of these two clauses is illustrated in the case of every newly regenerated person. The old sinful habits and actions are gone. The old life of selfish indulgence is past. Now he belongs to Christ and wants to please Him. It is a real miracle that takes place in the new birth, a marvelous transformation that affects the whole person.

But this is only the negative side. The positive side is even more wonderful. Hughes remarks that "the exclamation 'behold!' sounds an unmistakable note of spontaneous jubilation" (*II Corinthians*, p. 203).

"Are passed away" is in the aorist tense, pointing back to a definite moment, the time of the new birth. On the other hand, "are become" is in the perfect tense, which signifies a continuing state. The old life is wiped out in the crisis of conversion; the new life comes to stay. What a glorious exchange!

It is obvious that the last clause of this verse needs to be interpreted intelligently. In the new birth we receive a new heart, a new nature, a new life in Christ. But we still live in the same old, sinful world. We still have the same physical body, subject to the same temptations. As long as we live in this world we will be surrounded by old things.

The description of the Corinthian Christians sounds a warning to us. Paul said they were "babes in Christ," but still "carnal" (I Corinthians 3:1-3). Our hearts are changed in a moment. But it takes time to make our whole personalities new—our thoughts, words, attitudes, temperaments, and dispositions. A failure to realize this will result in stunted growth spiritually. After we have received the grace of God we need to "grow in grace."

It should be noted that it is only "in Christ" that we are new creatures—never in ourselves! It has often been stated that the whole of Paul's theology can be summed up in the one phrase "in Christ." This is very true. Everything we receive from God is "in Christ." Apart from Him we have nothing and are nothing. This is really the central emphasis in Paul's Epistles.

III. RECONCILIATION EXPLAINED: II Corinthians 5:18-19

A. Reconciled in Christ: v. 18

Paul reminds us that "all this is God's doing" (Phillips); that is, "From first to last this has been the work of God" (NEB). In other words, all the work of redemption comes from God, initiated by His love. Men like to take the credit for all the great works they have accomplished in the world through scientific progress. But the greatest accomplishment of all is the transformation of human hearts and lives by the grace of God.

When people boast of the massive monuments of man's genius and prowess, they seem to forget that only the mind of man could have planned and executed it all. So man himself is the supreme creation, not his works. That is why the salvation of man is the greatest work in the universe. Man is worth more than all the material universe.

The title of our lesson is "The Ministry of Reconciliation." We have been leading up to this and have noted the provision for it in the death of Christ and the effectiveness of it in the new creation. Now in verse 18 we come to the term itself. We are told that God has "reconciled us to himself by Jesus Christ, and hath given to us the ministry of reconciliation." It was Jesus Himself who began the ministry of reconciliation, and He wants us to carry it on in our day.

Reconciliation is a very popular term in religious circles today. But unfortunately it is usually given a merely social significance, with no spiritual meaning. We are told repeatedly that we should be concerned for the reconciliation of blacks and whites, of employers and employees, of Communists and Christians, and of all the separated classes and groups of modern society. This is to be done by social and political action. It is a beautiful dream. But without a Biblical foundation it will utterly fail.

What is needed is the divine perspective, which gives the proper priorities. These are stated very clearly in this verse. The first thing is that God has reconciled us to Himself by Jesus Christ. The second thing is that God has committed to us the ministry of reconciliation. The tendency today is to leave God out of the picture entirely. We begin with men's opinions in the fields of psychology and sociology. Then we go on to "social action,"

which is the battle cry of most of Christendom.

What we refuse to see is that many of these man-made ideas are non-Christian and some of them are actually anti-Christian. Ignoring God, we start with the human and end with the human—in failure! We will never succeed in any ministry of reconciliation unless we begin with God. And until we are reconciled to God we cannot hope to be reconciled to each other. This is the fallacy of most of the talk today about reconciliation. It is an expression of man's pride in his own ability to work out his problems without divine help.

The verb here translated "reconcile" means "to change," and "hence, of persons, *to change* from enmity to friendship, *to reconcile*" (Abbott-Smith, *Lexicon*, p. 236). But that change must be effected in the hearts of men, and that can be done only by the regenerating power of the Holy Spirit on the basis of Christ's death for us at Calvary. This is the order of priority that is spelled out precisely in this Scripture. As long as men ignore this Biblical basis for reconciliation they will continue to fumble and fail. The pages of history are covered with the records of such failures.

B. Reconciling the World: v. 19

What is the message of reconciliation? It is that "God was in Christ, reconciling the world unto himself." This is the very heart of Paul's gospel. It could not be put more succinctly or forcefully than it is in this brief statement. Here we have the gospel in a nutshell.

"God was in Christ." That is what made Christ's death on the cross efficacious for us. It was not just a human sacrifice. That could never have atoned for the sins of all mankind. It was a divine sacrifice. It was not merely the human Jesus who died at Calvary. It was the divine-human God-man. This is what is meant when it says, "God was in Christ."

Notice that God takes the initiative. Religion has often been defined as man's search for God. False religion is this, and it always fails. True religion is God's search for man. It began back in the Garden of Eden, when God called to Adam, "Where art thou?" (Genesis 3:9). It came to its finest focus on the cross, where Christ died to reconcile us to God. It continues in the work of the Holy Spirit who urges us to repent of our sins and accept this divinely provided reconciliation.

The word "atonement" occurs many times in the Old Testament but only once in the New Testament (KJV). In Romans 5:11 we learn that through our Lord Jesus Christ "we have now received the atonement." But the Greek word there for "atonement" is the one that is here translated "reconciliation." *Atonement* literally means "at-one-ment." That is exactly what it is: we are made at one with God. Only when this has happened can we be made at one with our fellowmen.

There is just one barrier that separates us from God, and that is sin. What can be done about this? The answer is given here—"not imputing their sins unto them." Our sins were laid on Jesus, imputed to Him. Because of this we can go free and not have to suffer the penalty for our sins. The barrier is broken down, and in Christ we are united to God in love.

DISCUSSION QUESTIONS

1. What was the heart of Paul's theology?
2. What is meant by "reconciliation"?
3. What was God's work of reconciliation?
4. What kind of a ministry of reconciliation should we have?
5. How is this related to world peace?
6. What is the role of the church as such?

That is real reconciliation, which only the divine-human Christ could bring about.

After we have been reconciled to God, He commits to us "the word [that is, the message] of reconciliation." Sometimes we forget this. We rejoice in the fact that we have been forgiven through Christ's atoning death, but we fail to carry this message of reconciliation to others. We thus reveal our lack of gratitude to God. We can repay Him by telling others that He can save them, too.

It should be obvious from verses 18 and 19 that the current use of *reconciliation* in a merely sociological and political sense is not Biblical. The whole emphasis of this passage is on men being reconciled to God. This is our "ministry of reconciliation" and the "word of reconciliation" that we are to proclaim. When men are truly reconciled to God they will be reconciled to their fellowmen; for no genuine Christian can harbor hate in his heart toward any man.

IV. RECONCILIATION APPLIED: II Corinthians 5:20-21

A. Ambassadors for Christ: v. 20

It is a real honor to be selected as an ambassador from one's country to the capital of another nation. How much greater honor is it to be chosen as an ambassador of the King of kings! And yet that honor is offered to every Christian. We are to be Christ's ambassadors. In His "stead" we are to sound the divine appeal: "Be ye reconciled to God."

An ambassador does not represent himself; he represents another. He does not speak in his own name, but in the name of the ruler he represents. He does not have his own authority, but carries the authority of his government.

So it is with us. It is in Christ's name and by His divine authority that we plead with men to be reconciled to God. We do not air our own opinions, but proclaim His message. And we should always conduct ourselves as those who are conscious that they are ambassadors of the King of kings—not with a stuffed shirt attitude but with Spirit-imbued humility. It is a great honor, and at the same time a great responsibility, to be an ambassador of the Lord of heaven.

B. Christ the Sin-offering: v. 21

This verse states unequivocally the fact of the vicarious atonement made by Christ at Calvary. It is a mighty affirmation of the gospel: "For he hath made him to be sin for us, who knew no sin; that we might be made the righteousness of God in him."

Now it is obvious that the holy Christ did not actually become sinful. That would be morally impossible. We are specifically told that He was sinless—"who knew no sin." What, then, is meant by the statement that He was made sin for us? Hughes expresses it this way: "That is to say that God the Father made His innocent incarnate Son the object of His wrath and judgment for our sakes, with the result that in Christ on the cross the sin of the world is judged and taken away" (*II Corinthians*, p. 213).

As a result of this, we are "made the righteousness of God in him." In Christ, and only in Him, do we have God's righteousness. When we are in Christ and Christ is in us, then God sees His own righteousness as having become our righteousness. Apart from this our own righteousness is like filthy rags. Only as we receive God's righteousness in Christ can we be acceptable to God.

V. RECONCILIATION URGED: II Corinthians 6:1-2

A. The Earnest Plea: v. 1

As workers together with God (cf. 5:20), says Paul, we "beseech you also that ye receive not the grace of God in vain." This grace is received in vain when we do not accept it fully and act upon it. We must, by faith and obedience, permit that grace to continue to work in our hearts.

B. The Accepted Time: v. 2

"Succoured" is the translation of a vivid Greek verb that means, "I have come at your cry for help." When we call on God, He always comes to our aid. The reason we so often fail is that we forget or neglect to call on the divine resources that are always available to us.

The statement "now is the day of salvation" is very important. In Hebrews 3:7-8 we find a quotation from Psalm 95:7: "Today if ye will hear his voice, harden not your hearts." God has only one day of salvation—today. Actually, there is no tomorrow with God. He deals with us always in terms of "today." This is a solemn admonition to respond to God's call to salvation when it comes to us.

CONTEMPORARY APPLICATION

David Livingstone was born and brought up in a two-story stone house in Blantyre, Scotland. In this building are twenty-four rooms, each ten by fourteen feet. In each of these small rooms lived a family—twenty-four in all!

This building has now been turned into a museum, what John R. Mott called the finest Christian shrine anywhere. One can see the room where David Livingstone lived with his parents and four brothers and sisters.

As one comes down the last corridor he reads at the end this legend: "I will hold nothing I have or possess of any value except in relation to the kingdom of God." No one has ever expressed a more noble philosophy of stewardship than did this pioneer missionary to Africa's jungles.

The last room is especially impressive. Behind a small wooden altar is a plaque on the floor, a replica of the one over David Livingstone's body in Westminster Abbey. On the wall there is a cross. On one side are inscribed the words: "The love of Christ con- straineth us—St. Paul." The other side reads: "The love of Christ compels me—David Livingstone." His life was one long commentary on II Corinthians 5:14.

GOOD NEWS FOR SINNERS

DEVOTIONAL READING	Romans 1:1-12

ADULTS

Topic: *Good News for Sinners*

Background Scripture: Romans 1:1—2:16

Scripture Lesson: Romans 1:16-25

Memory Verse: *I am not ashamed of the gospel: it is the power of God for salvation to every one who has faith.* Romans 1:16

YOUTH

Topic: *Needed—Good News*

Background Scripture: Romans 1:1—2:16

Scripture Lesson: Romans 1:16-25

Memory Verse: *I am not ashamed of the gospel: it is the power of God for salvation to every one who has faith* Romans 1:16

CHILDREN

Topic: *Stand Up for the Right*

Background Scripture: Acts 19:23—20:1

Scripture Lesson: Acts 19:24-27, 35-41

Memory Verse: *You shall worship the Lord your God and him only shall you serve.* Matthew 4:10

DAILY BIBLE READINGS

Mon., Sept. 24: Not Ashamed of the Gospel, Romans 1:1-6, 16-17.
Tues., Sept. 25: Under Obligations to the Greeks, Romans 1:8-15.
Wed., Sept. 26: God Shows No Partiality, Romans 2:1-11.
Thurs., Sept. 27: God Judges Men, Romans 2:12-24.
Fri., Sept. 28: Entrusted with the Oracles of God, Romans 3:1-8.
Sat., Sept. 29: What We Have Seen and Heard, Acts 4:13-22.
Sun., Sept. 30: Made a Minister, Ephesians 3:7-13.

LESSON AIM

To show what God's good news for sinners is—that they may be forgiven and accepted as God's children.

LESSON SETTING

Time: The Epistle to the Romans was written about A.D. 56.

Place: It was apparently written from Corinth, on Paul's brief (3 month) visit there near the end of his third journey.

Good News for Sinners

Good News for Sinners

LESSON OUTLINE

I. Greetings and Thanksgiving: Romans 1:1-15

II. The Righteousness of God: Romans 1:16-17
   A. What the Gospel Is: v. 16
   B. Justification by Faith: v. 17

III. The Wrath of God: Romans 1:18-20
   A. Against All Unrighteousness: v. 18
   B. The Revelation of God in Nature: vv. 19-20

IV. The Rejection of God: Romans 1:21-25
   A. Intellectual Pride: v. 21
   B. Idolatry: vv. 22-25

V. The Rejection by God: Romans 1:26-32

VI. The Judgment of God: Romans 2:1-16

SUGGESTED INTRODUCTION FOR ADULTS

We have had four lessons on "The Ministry of Reconciliation." Today we begin a unit of five lessons on "The Message of Reconciliation," looking at the central content of the gospel as preached by the apostle Paul. The material for these lessons comes from the first eight chapters of Romans.

The Epistle to the Romans divides itself naturally into three parts. The first (chaps. 1–8) is theological. The second (chaps. 9–11) is eschatological, dealing with the problem of Israel in God's plans for the future. The third division (chaps. 12–16) is practical, making the application to Christian living.

The first division, again, has three main parts. After the introduction to the book (1:1-17) we have the doctrine of sin (1:18–3:20), the doctrine of justification (3:21–5:21), and the doctrine of sanctification (chaps. 6–8). These are in logical order. The main theme of Romans is "the redemption that is in Christ Jesus" (3:24). So we have first the doctrine of sin, showing the need for redemption. Then we have redemption shown in two stages: first in justification, dealing with the problem of *sins*, and second in sanctification, dealing with the problem of *sin*. Romans is the most systematic of Paul's Epistles.

SUGGESTED INTRODUCTION FOR YOUTH

Our generation is very problem-conscious. Young people have their hang-ups: drugs, sex, pollution, and parents! But the greatest problem of all, for everybody, is the problem of sin. It is universal—all races, social classes, and ages. Nobody is immune. All have sinned.

There is only one solution for the problem of sin and that is the gospel of Jesus Christ. Christ, the sinless One, died for our sins. Through His blood shed at Calvary we can be forgiven for our sins and have our hearts cleansed from all sin. That is the message of salvation presented by Paul in his Epistle to the Romans.

CONCEPTS FOR CHILDREN

1. It was because Demetrius was afraid he would lose money if many people became Christians that he urged the men who made and sold the statues of Artemis to cause a demonstration against Paul's friends. Money is the reason for many demonstrations today, as well.
2. Sometimes we will find that we must change our plans if we are to be used in the way that is best for the glory of God and the good of our fellowmen.
3. Boys and girls may sometimes have to pay a price (give up something they have wanted) for standing up for what they believe is right.

THE LESSON COMMENTARY

I. GREETINGS AND THANKS-GIVING:
Romans 1:1-15

We find here the longest salutation in any of Paul's thirteen Epistles. Usually it covers only one or two verses. But here it runs through six verses. The greeting is in verse 7.

The reason for the lengthy salutation is that Paul was writing to a church that he had never visited. Furthermore, it was at the capital city of the great Roman Empire. He wanted to lay a solid foundation for the gospel message he was going to present.

Usually Paul begins by calling himself an apostle. But here he first says, "a servant of Jesus Christ," and then "an apostle" (v. 1). This shows the humility of Paul as he addresses the Christians at Rome.

What is the foundation of the gospel? It is Jesus Christ, who is both human—"made of the seed of David according to the flesh" (v. 3)—and divine—"declared to be the Son of God" (v. 4). It is the God-man, Christ Jesus, who alone is able to save us from our sins.

The thanksgiving (vv. 8-12) regularly follows the greeting in Paul's Epistles (except in Galatians). Here the apostle thanks God "for you all, that your faith is spoken of throughout the whole world" (v. 8). The church at Rome was already an outstanding one. Paul was praying for the Christians there (v. 9) and expresses a strong desire to see them (vv. 10-12).

He goes on to tell them that he had often wanted to visit them but until then had been hindered (KJV, "let," v. 13). Because he had received the gospel as a free gift, he declared: "I am debtor, both to the Greeks, and to the barbarians; both to the wise, and to the unwise. So, as much as in me is, I am ready to preach the gospel to you that are at Rome also" (vv. 14—15).

II. THE RIGHTEOUSNESS OF GOD: Romans 1:16-17

A. What the Gospel Is: v. 16

Paul says that he is not ashamed of the gospel. Why? Because it is "the power of God unto salvation to every one that believeth." The power of God was shown in creating our vast astronomical universe. It is manifested every day in thousands of ways in nature. The electricity that lights our cities and runs our factories is but one form of it.

But the greatest manifestation of God's power is in the gospel. When we think of the sum total of human sin, only the gospel can cope with it. Man can manipulate physical forces. He can pass criminal codes. But he cannot cure the disease of sin in men's hearts. Only the power of God can handle this, the biggest problem in the universe.

This power is released only in the lives of those who believe. It is available to all. But it becomes effective through faith. It is faith that throws the switch and releases the power of the gospel to surge through our hearts, making them new and clean.

It might be said that verse 16 sounds the keynote of the Epistle to the Romans. The word *gospel* literally means "good news." It is good news for sinners that Christ has died for them on the cross so that their sins can be forgiven.

B. Justification by Faith: v. 17

The Greek says that "a righteousness" of God has been revealed. This can be taken in either of two ways: either as God's righteousness, one of His attributes that has made salvation possible, or a righteousness which God has provided for those who believe. Very wisely Sanday and Headlam suggest that it need not be a case of either/or. It can be both/and. The two views "are not mutually exclusive but rather inclusive." They go on to say: "The righteousness of which the Apostle is speaking not only proceeds from God but is the righteousness of God Himself: it is this, however, not as inherent in the Divine Essence but as going forth and embracing the personalities of men. It is righteousness active and energizing; the righteousness of the Divine Will as it were projected and enclosing and gathering into itself human wills" (*Romans*, p. 25). It is actually God's righteousness which is made available to men.

In support of his statement Paul quotes from Habakkuk 2:4: "The just shall live by faith." The background there was the threat of Babylonian invasion. So the passage in Habakkuk

might be paraphrased: "The righteous man shall save his life by his faith, or loyalty to Jehovah, while his proud oppressors perish" (Sanday and Headlam, p. 22). As quoted in Romans the statement becomes a bit clearer if we word it: "The righteous man by his faith shall live"; that is, he will live as a result of his faith.

With Paul faith is one of the prime elements in the gospel. We are not saved by our own efforts, but by faith in Jesus Christ.

III. THE WRATH OF GOD: Romans 1:18-20

A. Against All Unrighteousness: v. 18

Not only is God's righteousness revealed in answer to faith; His wrath is revealed "against all ungodliness and unrighteousness of men." If we were to distinguish between these two terms we would say that "ungodliness" has to do particularly with inner attitudes and "unrighteousness" with outer actions. Men are unrighteous in their lives because they are ungodly in their hearts.

These men are described as those "who hold the truth in unrighteousness." But the Greek verb probably means "hold down." So a better translation is "who by their wickedness suppress the truth" (RSV; cf. NEB: "are stifling the truth"). The truth of God's Word is covered over by men's sin, so that it becomes hidden to most people. That truth is revealed in the lives of the righteous.

B. The Revelation of God in Nature: vv. 19-20

The apostle asserts that what may be known of God—or "is known of God"—is "manifest in them," that is, in their hearts and consciences; "for God hath shewed ["manifested"] it unto them." Every man intuitively has a consciousness of God.

Some scholars prefer to translate "in them" as "to them." Perhaps "in them" means primarily "in their thoughts," as they contemplate nature around them.

In verse 20 this thought is carried a step further. God's "invisible" attributes "are clearly seen" in creation. His "eternal power and Godhead" (deity) are revealed in nature about us, so that all men are "without excuse" for rejecting Him. John Murray writes: "This is but another way of saying that God has left the imprints of his glory upon his handiwork and this glory is manifest to all" (*Romans*, I, 40).

Missionaries tell of an elderly man they once found in Japan. As soon as he heard the gospel for the first time he said, "That's the God I have been worshiping." In his contemplation of the stars at night he had come to the conclusion that there must be a great Creator-God who had made all this. As best he knew, he began to worship this God, without knowing His name. Except for the antagonism of sin in the human heart, cases like this would probably be far more common. But sin causes men to rebel against what they do know of God.

It is especially God's "eternal power" that is revealed in nature, and so His deity. His omnipotence and His omniscience come through rather clearly. But His love and holiness are not so evident. These are revealed particularly in the Bible and in human history.

IV. THE REJECTION OF GOD: Romans 1:21-25

A. Intellectual Pride: v. 21

Most books written in this century on the origin of religion describe it as beginning with primitive animism, and then proceeding through crude polytheism to henotheism (one god for each nation) and finally to ethical monotheism (only one God exists, and He is holy). It is claimed that this last stage was not reached until the eighth century B.C., when the great Hebrew prophets expressed it.

The picture given by Paul is quite different. In Romans 1:21-32 we have the divine revelation of the true "descent of man." It was literally a *descent* from the high plane of knowing God down to the lowest depths of idolatry and immorality. History supports this view of what actually happened.

So we start at the top: "when they knew God." The first step downward was *ingratitude:* "they glorified him not as God, neither were thankful." Denney comments: "Nature shows us that God is to be glorified and thanked, *i.e.*, nature reveals Him to be great and good" (*Expositor's Greek Testament*, II, 592).

The second step was *intellectual pride:* "they became vain in their imaginations." The last word in Greek gives us our word "dialoguing." Here it probably refers to "perverse, self-willed, reasonings or speculations" (Sanday and Headlam, p. 44).

Intellectual pride brought mental and moral *darkness:* "their foolish heart was darkened." When men close the doors of their hearts to the sunlight of God's love and truth, they are left in darkness, both intellectually and spiritually.

B. Idolatry: vv. 22-25

The next step down was *folly.* They professed to be wise, but showed themselves to be fools. And this folly led to *idolatry.*

Within this idolatry there were again steps downward. First they made images of men, then of birds, then of beasts, and finally of "creeping things." Snake worship, still practiced today, is the cellar of idolatry. Men did not begin with idolatry and evolve to a higher spiritual worship; they began with a knowledge of God and descended to the depths of ridiculous idolatry. It was a sad change—from "the glory of the uncorruptible God" to images of animals and snakes.

Because they rejected Him and turned away from Him, "God gave them up" (v. 24), or "handed them over" to go the way they wanted to go. The worst thing that can happen to any man is to be abandoned by God. But people bring this on themselves. We first forsake God and then He forsakes us. Man has nobody to blame but himself.

This same verb "gave them up" is repeated in verses 26 and 28. ("Gave them over" in verse 28 is exactly the same Greek word as "gave them up" in verses 24 and 26.) It describes a divine judgment of the most serious kind. When God gives us up, we are lost!

Men do not rise any higher than what they worship. They become like their gods. When they worship the images of animals, it is only to be expected that they will live like animals. And so idolatry almost inevitably leads to immorality. Since this is their choice, God lets them have their own way.

So here we read that God gave them up "to uncleanness through the lusts of their own hearts, to dishonour their own bodies between themselves." As someone has said, "To lose God is to lose everything." When men refuse to worship God, they can go in any direction. Some go into the depths of immoral depravity. Their religion is to make a god of their own bodies and live only for sensual pleasure.

The word translated "changed" in verse 25 is a different verb, a compound of that used in verse 23. This one means "exchanged." The correct translation is: "Who exchanged the

truth about God for a lie." When they did so they made a bad bargain! People who reject the truth are left only with a lie. This is the penalty that people pay for turning away from the light of truth; they walk in the darkness of self-deception. The most serious sin that man can commit is deliberate rejection of the truth.

A familiar characteristic of Paul in his Epistles is that he easily breaks forth in spontaneous praise. The very mention here of "the Creator" causes him to add a doxology: "who is blessed for ever. Amen."

Again the close comparison between idolatry and immorality is emphasized. The one follows the other in verses 23 and 24 and in verses 25 and 26. The use of "lie" to designate idolatry is found elsewhere. The truth is God—Jesus said, "I am the truth"—and the lie is any false god.

V. THE REJECTION BY GOD: Romans 1:26-32

When men reject God, He rejects them. So once more we read that "God gave them up" (v. 26). Before, it was to "uncleanness" (v. 24). Here it is to "vile affections." This stronger expression is used to point out the vileness of homosexuality, which is spelled out very precisely in verses 26 and 27. This has become one of the outstanding sins of our generation. A few years ago there were comparatively few homosexuals in Europe and the United States. Now there are multiplied thousands of them and they are widely approved in our permissive society. Several church denominations have put themselves on record that homosexual relations between consenting adults should not be considered a crime. There are "Christian" congregations of homosexuals, which have united into a denomination. They call themselves "the gay people." But there will be nothing gay about their eternal doom. Since they rejected the light of God's truth, they will be abandoned by Him to outer darkness.

DISCUSSION QUESTIONS

1. How is the gospel the power of God?
2. What is God's good news for the sinner?
3. What part does faith play in our salvation?
4. What is God's attitude toward sin? toward the sinner?
5. Why does idolatry lead to moral breakdown?
6. What hope do you see for America today?

The chapter closes with a black picture of the sins of those who forsake God. The list contained in verses 28-31 seems hauntingly familiar in our day. This is what happens to those who stubbornly reject God's way and take their own way.

VI. THE JUDGMENT OF GOD: Romans 2:1-16

The main theme of the second chapter is judgment, and the key phrase is "the judgment of God." Three things are said about it: (1) it is "according to truth, v. 2; (2) it is according to one's deeds, v. 6; (3) it is "according to my gospel," v. 16

The first chapter describes and condemns the twin sins of the Gentiles—idolatry and immorality. The second chapter condemns the twin sins of the Jews—insincerity and inconsistency.

Paul begins by saying: "Therefore thou art inexcusable, O man, whosoever thou art that judgest: for wherein thou judgest another, thou condemnest thyself." Clearly he is addressing the Jew, (cf. v. 17), who is judging the Gentiles. Yet in his heart, the one judging is doing the same thing, even though outwardly he may avoid the gross sins of the heathen. But God's judgment will be "according to truth," in the light of divine knowledge about the real condition of the heart. One will not escape just because his outward life is ordered with care. Because God's judgment is based on truth it will be "righteous judgment" (v. 5).

We will be judged not only according to truth but according to our deeds. It is not enough to claim that we are sincere; our conduct must be above reproach. If we do wrong, we shall be punished. God knows all about our deeds, including our motives for doing them. And "there is no respect of persons with God" (v. 11). Here is one judge who will never be guilty of partiality. Each man will get justice.

The question is sometimes raised, on the basis of careless statements made, as to how a just God can punish people for not believing in Jesus when they have never heard His name. The answer, of course, is that He will not punish them for this. The basis for judging such people is clearly stated in verses 12-16. Paul writes: "For as many as have sinned without law shall also perish without law: and as many as have sinned in the law shall be judged by the law" (v. 12). That is, Gentiles would not be judged by the law of Moses, but Jews would be. To place it in the modern setting we could simply substitute "the Bible" or "the gospel" for "the law." Those who have had the Bible available to them—people in so-called Christian lands—will be judged by the Bible, but those who have not known the Bible will be judged apart from it.

What will be the basis of judgment for such? It is spelled out in verses 14 and 15. God has written a measure of His law on every human heart, in what we call *conscience*. It is described here as: "their thoughts the mean while accusing or else excusing one another" (v. 15). The Greek says, "or *even* excusing." The implication is that most of the time their consciences will be accusing them of doing wrong. Perhaps once in a while conscience would approve, excusing them for what they do.

The lesson closes with the solemn warning that there will be a day when God will "judge the secrets of men according to my gospel" (v. 16). Our hearts must be pure and our thoughts acceptable in His sight.

CONTEMPORARY APPLICATION

Some years ago Bishop Robinson wrote a book entitled *Honest to God*.

In it he dismissed the idea that there is any God "out there" and contended that this idea is the figment of man's imagination.

After bowing God out of His universe, Robinson wrote a chapter in his book, and titled it "The New Morality." In it he advocated permissiveness. As we read the first part of the book, we said: "With God gone, morals will go." And that is exactly what has happened in our generation. Modern man has forsaken God, and God has given him up to wild licentiousness as exhibited in pornography and filthy movies.

LAW AND GOSPEL

DEVOTIONAL READING	Galatians 2:11-21

ADULTS

Topic: *Law and Gospel*

Background Scripture: Romans 2:17—3:31

Scripture Lesson: Romans 3:19-28

Memory Verse: *We hold that a man is justified by faith apart from works of law.* Romans 3:28

YOUTH

Topic: *Rules or Relationships?*

Background Scripture: Romans 2:17—3:31

Scripture Lesson: Romans 3:19-26

Memory Verse: *We hold that a man is justified by faith apart from works of law.* Romans 3:28

CHILDREN

Topic: *Paul Goes to Jerusalem*

Background Scripture: Acts 21:17-36

Scripture Lesson: Acts 21:17-19, 27-28, 30-36

Memory Verse: *Praise the Lord, all nations! Extol him, all peoples!* Psalm 117:1

DAILY BIBLE READINGS

Mon., Oct. 1: Fulfilling the Law, Matthew 5:17-26.
Tues., Oct. 2: Justified Through Faith in Jesus Christ, Galatians 2:11-21.
Wed., Oct. 3: What Was Promised by Faith, Galatians 3:11-22.
Thurs., Oct. 4: No Confidence in the Flesh, Philippians 3:3-16.
Fri., Oct. 5: The Righteousness of God, Romans 3:21-31.
Sat., Oct. 6: A Shadow of Good Things, Hebrews 10:1-10.
Sun., Oct. 7: Abolishing the Law of Commandments, Ephesians 2:11-21.

LESSON AIM

To show the true relationship between law and gospel.

LESSON SETTING

Time: About A.D. 56

Place: Corinth

39

Law and Gospel

I.   False Security in the Law: Romans 2:17-29

II. The Advantage of Being a Jew: Romans 3:1-8

III. The Universality of Sin: Romans 3:9-18

IV. No Justification by the Law: Romans 3:19-20
     A. All the World Guilty Before God: v. 19
     B. The Law Gives Knowledge of Sin: v. 20

V.   Justification by Faith: Romans 3:21-28
     A. A Righteousness Apart from Law: vv. 21-23
     B. The Redemption That Is in Christ Jesus: v. 24
     C. A Propitiatiory Sacrifice: v. 25
     D. Justice in Justification of the Sinner: v. 26
     E. No Place for Boasting: v. 27
     F. Final Conclusion: v. 28

VI. The Relation of Faith and Law: Romans 3:29-31

One of the main problems that Paul had to face was the Jewish attitude toward the relation between law and gospel. The non-Christian Jews, of course, insisted that the Law given at Sinai was final. It was obviously of divine authority and must be obeyed—all of it. But even the Christian Jews, at least some of them, asserted that the Gentile converts must be circumcised and commanded to keep the law of Moses (Acts 15:5). This caused much debate in the church.

Paul wrote the Epistle to the Galatians specifically for the purpose of counteracting the work of the Judaizers. He declared emphatically that no one can be saved through the works of the law; it is only through faith in Jesus Christ. And so the lines of battle were clearly drawn.

When Paul wrote to the Romans he was still very much concerned about this problem. So he takes even more space and time than in the Epistle to the Galatians to point out the sharp contrast between law and gospel. Salvation through the law is bad news: when can you be sure you have fulfilled its requirements? Salvation through faith in Jesus Christ is good news: you can know right now!

Is Christianity mainly a matter of rules, or of relationships? The former is the law, the latter is the gospel.

The answer of the New Testament is that it is primarily a matter of relationships—our relationship to God and to our fellowmen. If these relationships are ones of pure, holy love, we are Christians. If they are not, no measure of keeping rules and regulations will save us.

Yet life can never be entirely free from rules. Paul himself lays down many regulations for Christian conduct, as did Jesus. But salvation is through faith in Christ, who in His life fulfilled the law and in His death satisfied its righteous demands for us sinners.

CONCEPTS FOR
CHILDREN

1. Paul was willing to face any danger or hardship for the sake of Christ and the salvation of souls.
2. We should be willing to follow Christ (live a Christian life) no matter what it may cost us in the way of friends, money, or prestige.
3. Even though those we help do not show appreciation, we should continue to help them for Christ's sake.

THE LESSON COMMENTARY

I. FALSE SECURITY IN THE LAW: Romans 2:17-29

It is obvious that in chapter 2 Paul is primarily addressing Jews. He says to his reader: "Behold, thou art called a Jew, and restest in the law, and makest thy boast of God . . . being instructed out of the law" (vv. 17-18). Because he had been circumcised and had kept the law of Moses, the Jew felt secure in his acceptance by God. This is all he had to do. He boasted of his relationship to God.

From his high vantage point the Jew looked down on the poor Gentiles who did not have the law. He was confident that he was "a guide of the blind, a light of them which are in darkness, an instructor of the foolish, a teacher of babes" (vv. 19-20). Some have treated the language here as sarcastic, holding the Gentiles up to ridicule. But it need not necessarily be taken that way. God had designed that the Jews, to whom He had given the revelation of His truth, should teach it to the Gentiles.

The trouble was that the Jews were not always obeying their own teaching and preaching. Paul challenges them to teach themselves (v. 21). They preached that men should not steal, but they were guilty of stealing. Probably they did not commit outright theft, but by crooked business transactions they were actually robbing others. Hosea makes reference to this: "He is a merchant, the balances of

deceit are in his hand" (12:7). Amos spells it out in more detail: "Hear this, O ye that swallow up the needy, even to make the poor of the land to fail, saying, When will the new moon be gone, that we may set forth wheat, making the ephah small, and the shekel great, and falsifying the balances by deceit? That we may buy the poor for silver, and the needy for a pair of shoes; yea, and sell the refuse of the wheat" (8:4-6). Skimping the measure, charging high prices, cheating on the weighing, selling poor quality grains—all these were forms of stealing.

There is evidence that some Jewish teachers were guilty of adultery and sacrilege (v. 22). The latter may have been a matter of accepting objects stolen from pagan temples. By breaking the law they were dishonoring God (v. 23). Because of this, God's name was blasphemed among the Gentiles (v. 24).

Paul goes on to say that circumcision means nothing apart from keeping the law (v. 25). When the Gentiles "keep the righteousness of the law" they are treated by God as His covenant people, as though they had been circumcised (v. 26). Thus these godly Gentiles condemn the Jews who transgress the law (v. 27). A real Jew is not one who is such outwardly, nor is true circumcision simply the cutting of flesh. The real Jew is one inwardly, and true circumcision is the circumcision of the heart, in cutting off sin (vv. 28-29; cf. Colossians 2:11).

II. THE ADVANTAGE OF BEING A JEW:
Romans 3:1-8

In the light of what Paul has just said, someone might ask: "What advantage then hath the Jew? or what profit is there of circumcision?" (v. 1). The apostle gives an immediate answer: "Much every way: chiefly, because that unto them were committed the oracles of God" (v. 2). The main advantage the Jews had was in their possession of the sacred Scriptures (our Old Testament). This was an incomparable privilege, but one that carried heavy responsibilities.

Again Paul asks: "For what if some did not believe"—in Jesus as the Messiah? If they had read their Scriptures properly, they would have accepted Him. But does their unbelief invalidate or annul the faithfulness of God? The answer is No! God will be justified and emerge victorious (vv. 3-4).

All this raises another question: "If our unrighteousness commend [better, "establishes"] the righteousness of God, what shall we say?" (v. 5). Is God not unjust to inflict His wrath on the sinner?

Paul's reaction is emphatic: "God forbid: for then how shall God judge the world?" (v. 6). The fact that God overrules man's sin to His own glory does not make Him unjust in punishing the sinner. It is a false logic which would draw this conclusion.

But again he comes at the problem: "For if the truth of God hath more abounded through my lie unto his glory; why yet am I also judged as a sinner?" (v. 7). The answer is the same as above. Some were even slanderously reporting that Paul said: "Let us do evil, that good may come" (v. 8). The apostle has only one thing to say about such malicious liars: "whose judgment [not "damnation" (KJV)] is just." Anyone who would accuse Paul of advocating sin must have been morally bankrupt. The apostle's entire teaching in his Epistles is in favor of holy living, and utterly opposed to sinful living.

III. THE UNIVERSALITY OF SIN:
Romans 3:9-18

Paul calls attention to the fact that he has already "proved" [better, "charged"] both Jews and Gentiles, that they are all under sin" (v. 9). In support of this he proceeds to quote a rather lengthy string of isolated passages from the Old Testament. Verses 10-12 are taken from Psalm 14:1-3. The first part of verse 13 is from Psalm 5:9 and the last part from Psalm 140:3. Verse 14 is quoted from Psalm 10:7, verses 15-17 from Isaiah 59:7-8, and verse 18 from Psalm 36:1.

The last part of verse 12—"there is none that doeth good, no, not one"—has often been quoted as proof that no one can live without sin in this world; everybody sins. This use of the passage obviously does violence to the context. Would we want to apply verses 13-15 to all Christians? To ask the question is to answer it. What we obviously have here is a description of unregenerate people, not believers. Apart from the grace of God, men are like this in their hearts, even though all these things may not show up in their outward lives.

Looked at in this light, we recognize that we find here an awful revelation of human depravity. The sinful nature is like this. It contains the seeds of unrighteousness, rebellion, evil, deceit, lying, cursing, bitterness, murder, hatred, irreverence toward God. Only as we realize the deep-seated depravity of the human heart can we understand all the violence and wickedness we see in the world around us.

The late Dr. George Craft Cell of Boston University said one day in class: "Thirty years ago when I started teaching, I didn't believe in original sin. But thirty years of studying history have compelled me to believe in it. There is no other explanation for the diabolical acts of men." Another day he made a similar statement about belief in a personal devil.

IV. NO JUSTIFICATION BY THE LAW: Romans 3:19-20

A. All the World Guilty Before God: v. 19

What is the connection of this verse with what precedes? First, it should be recognized that "the law" means the entire Old Testament. The expression was often used in that sense. So the reference in "what things soever the law saith" is to the passages just quoted in verses 10-18. Probably the Jews would have said that these horrible descriptions didn't apply to them, but to the Gentiles. But Paul reminds them that what is written in the Old Testament was primarily for those "who are under the law." They could not shove these Scriptures aside and apply them only to the Gentiles. At least potentially, all this corruption lay in their hearts and might explode in their lives. They needed to be on their guard.

The result of all this is "that every mouth may be stopped, and all the world may become guilty before God." This takes in both Jews and Gentiles, and it includes all classes and levels of people today. The Greek word translated "guilty" literally means "subject to the judgment of God." It is a technical, judicial term, found only here in the New Testament.

B. The Law Gives Knowledge of Sin: v. 20

Paul declares that by doing the deeds of the law "no flesh"—"no man"—will be justified in God's sight. Godet writes that by "deeds of the law" are meant: "works such as man can do when he has no other help than the law—that is to say, in fact, in his own strength. The law is perfect in itself. But it does not provide fallen man with the means of meeting its demands" (*Romans*, p. 143).

What, then, is the function of the law? The last clause of this verse states, "for by the law is the knowledge of sin." People may not be conscious of the fact that something they are doing is wrong. But when they read God's Word they discover that it is. And so they have a sense of guilt. But the law in itself cannot remove that guilt. It takes the gospel to do that.

Paul expresses this same thought in 7:7: "I had not known sin, but by the law." The law was intended for the enlightenment and guidance of men, not their salvation.

V. JUSTIFICATION BY FAITH: Romans 3:21-28

A. A Righteousness Apart from Law: vv. 21-23

Apart from the law there has been manifested "a righteousness of God" (so the Greek). It is the same expression we have already seen in 1:17, where we noted that it could mean both God's righteousness and specifically that righteousness made available to us. It does not come to us through the law but, as the next verse says, through faith.

When Paul says that this righteousness is "witnessed by the law and the prophets" (the Old Testament), he is emphasizing, as always, the close connection between the Old and New Testaments. The latter does not contradict the former; it complements it. As Augustine wrote: "The New is in the Old concealed; The Old is in the New revealed."

This righteousness by faith rather than by human effort is implicit in the older revelation. For instance, Abraham and David were justified by faith (4:1-8). The New Testament simply makes this fact explicit.

This "righteousness of God," or justification by God, is "by faith of [rather, "in"] Jesus Christ unto all

... them that believe" (v. 22). What Paul is saying emphatically is that justification comes only through faith in Jesus Christ; there is no other way to find acceptance with God.

What is faith? Many years ago D. L. Moody, the great evangelist, gave an excellent definition. He said that saving faith is: (1) assent, (2) consent, and (3) laying hold. It is not just the acceptance of a creed; it is a personal commitment to Christ. Then one can "lay hold" of salvation in the final step of faith.

Too many people stop with a mere assent of their minds to the doctrines of Christianity. But our wills must be involved in moral commitment. In fact, Christ must have our whole personality—intellect, emotions and will.

This wonderful salvation comes to all who believe; "for there is no difference" between Jews and Gentiles. All alike are justified by faith. Since it is by faith, and not by works of the law, all are on an equal footing.

This fact that there is no difference between Jews and Gentiles is again emphasized in verse 23: "For all have sinned, and come short of the glory of God." The comma after "sinned" should not be ignored. "Sinned" is in the aorist tense of past action. "Come short" is in the present tense of continuing condition. "All have sinned"— every man's conscience documents that truth. But the sad fact is that we all, apart from divine grace in forgiveness, do now fall short of God's glory—what He planned we should be.

We have already noted that the first chapter of Romans describes the sins of the Gentiles, and the second chapter the sins of the Jews. The third chapter climaxes this by asserting the sinfulness of the whole world. Paul says "that ... all the world may become guilty before God" (v. 19). and that "all have sinned" (v. 23). The whole human race is under the curse of sin. The only salvation for any man lies in coming to the Savior.

B. The Redemption That Is in Christ Jesus: v. 24

All have sinned. But all may be "justified freely by his grace through the redemption that is in Christ Jesus." We have already noted that the last part of this might be taken as the theme of the Epistle to the Romans. It all deals with redemption through Christ.

The Greek word for "redemption" is an interesting one. It is compounded of the word for "ransom," and so originally meant the buying back of a slave, making him free by payment of a ranson. This was its meaning at the time Paul wrote. The next verse indicates the price that Christ paid to free us from the slavery of sin.

C. A Propitiatory Sacrifice: v. 25

Paul declares that God has "set forth" (literally, "put forward") Christ as a "propitiation through faith in his blood." The original word for "propitiation" is used in the Greek translation of the Old Testament for the "mercy-seat." Here the blood of the sin offering was sprinkled annually on the Day of Atonement to make reconciliation for the sins of all the Israelites. Christ is our sin offering, making atonement for all our sins. Only His blood can cover sin. The Epistle to the Hebrews suggests that Christ is the Tabernacle (the place of meeting between God and man), the altar, the sacrifice on the altar, and the mercy-seat where the atoning blood is sprin-

---

DISCUSSION QUESTIONS

1. What was the function of the law?
2. How can God justify the sinner?
3. What is the basic difference between law and gospel?
4. How has Christ freed us from the law?
5. What part does the law play in the Christian's life?
6. How can we know that we are saved?

kled. It takes all these types to bring out the fullness of Christ's ministry. Here the word translated "propitiation" could be translated as "propitiatory sacrifice."

Because of the coming death of Christ on the cross, God could be righteous in the "remission," or "passing over," of the sins of Old Testament times. Those who exercised faith and obedience were justified on the basis of the future sacrifice that would be made on their behalf.

D. Justice in Justification of the Sinner: v. 26

One of the great problems that Paul faces in this Epistle is: How can God "be just and the justifier of him which believeth in Jesus?" The answer to that question is Calvary. James Denney expresses it very well: "God's righteousness, therefore, is demonstrated at the Cross, because there, in Christ's death, it is made once for all apparent that He does not palter with sin: the doom of sin falls by His appointment on the Redeemer. And it is possible, at the same time, to accept as righteous those who by faith unite themselves to Christ upon the Cross, and identify themselves with Him in His death: for in doing so they submit in Him to the Divine sentence upon sin, and at bottom become right with God" (*Expositor's Greek Testament*, II, 613).

But we must not forget that it is only those who believe in Jesus that are justified. It is all by faith in His blood.

E. No Place for Boasting: v. 27

In the light of this, "Where is boasting?" The answer is obvious: "It is excluded." If we were justified by keeping the law, we might feel that we could boast of our achievement. But since Christ has done it all for us, there is no room whatever to boast. It is all His work, and we simply accept it by faith.

F. Final Conclusion: v. 28

On the basis of his presentation thus far in our lesson, Paul writes: "Therefore we conclude that a man is justified by faith without the deeds of the law." Justification by faith is one of the main emphases of both Romans and Galatians.

This doctrine is so deeply implanted in our thinking that it is difficult for us to realize how revolutionary it was in Paul's day. He was cutting across the current thinking of Judaism. No wonder there was opposition! This glorious truth of the New Testament was somewhat lost sight of during the Middle Ages. Then Luther rediscovered it, and it became the cornerstone of the Reformation. But many church members today still do not fully understand and appropriate it. Yet here is our only hope of forgiveness now and heaven hereafter.

VI. THE RELATION OF FAITH AND LAW: Romans 3:29-31

Again Paul asserts that there is only one means of justification for both Jews and Gentiles, and that is "by" or "through" faith. Probably both prepositions mean the same here.

The apostle asks his last question in this chapter: "Do we then make void the law through faith?" In answer he uses his favorite form of protest, "God forbid." Then He asserts: "Yea, we establish the law," or, put it on a secure footing by showing its real meaning. He thus agrees with Jesus' statement that He did not come to destroy the law but to fulfill it (Matthew 5:17).

CONTEMPORARY APPLICATION

The ancient Jews thought they were acceptable to God because they had been circumcised, they attended the required feasts, and they kept the law of Moses. Today in America there are millions of church members who believe they are Christians because they have been baptized, they attend Communion, and they live a decent life outwardly.

Both assumptions are wrong. We are not saved on the basis of anything we do outwardly. God looks at the heart. If in sincere faith we have repented of our sins and accept the sacrifice of Christ on the cross, we are saved. There is no other way.

RECONCILIATION THROUGH CHRIST

DEVOTIONAL READING	Romans 5:15-21

ADULTS

Topic: *Reconciliation Through Christ*

Background Scripture: Romans 5

Scripture Lesson: Romans 5:1-11

Memory Selection: *God shows his love for us in that while we were yet sinners Christ died for us.* Romans 5:8

YOUTH

Topic: *Good News for Modern Teens*

Background Scripture: Romans 5

Scripture Lesson: Romans 5:1-11

Memory Selection; *God shows his love for us in that while we were yet sinners Christ died for us.* Romans 5:8

CHILDREN

Topic: *Plot Against Paul*

Background Scripture: Acts 23:12-35

Scripture Lesson: Acts 23:12-16, 23-24

Memory Verse: *A worthless man plots evil, and his speech is like a scorching fire.* Proverbs 16:27

DAILY BIBLE READINGS

Mon., Oct. 8: Peace with God, Romans 5:1-11.
Tues., Oct. 9: Eternal Life Through Jesus Christ, Romans 5:12-21.
Wed., Oct. 10: The Faith of Abraham, Romans 4:1-12.
Thurs., Oct. 11: Jesus, the Expiation for Our Sins, I John 2:1-11.
Fri., Oct. 12: God Sent His Son, I John 4:7-12.
Sat., Oct. 13: The Suffering Christ Was Necessary, Luke 24:13-26.
Sun., Oct. 14: The Christ Must Die, John 12:20-33.

LESSON AIM

To discover how we may be reconciled to God, and to rejoice in the fact of reconciliation through Christ.

LESSON SETTING

Time: About A.D. 56

Place: Corinth

Reconciliation Through Christ

LESSON OUTLINE

I. The Results of Justification: Romans 5:1-2
   A. Peace with God: v. 1
   B. Access into This Grace: v. 2

II. The Fruits of Justification: Romans 5:3-5
    A. Rejoicing and Endurance: v. 3
    B. Character and Hope: v. 4
    C. The Love of God in Our Hearts: v. 5

III. The Price of Justification: Romans 5:6-8
     A. Christ Died for the Ungodly: v. 6
     B. Christ Died for Sinners: vv. 7-8

IV. The Life of Justification: Romans 5:9-11
    A. Saved from Wrath: v. 9
    B. Saved by His Life: v. 10
    C. Saved by the Atonement: v. 11

V. The Scope of Justification: Romans 5:12-21

SUGGESTED
INTRODUCTION
FOR ADULTS

Paul writes in I Timothy 2:5: "There is one God and one mediator between God and men, the man Christ Jesus." Christ is the only means of reconciliation between God and man.

If a bridge is going to span a river or gorge it must be firmly planted on both sides. Jesus Christ is the only one who meets these conditions, because He is the only God-man. Christ has closed the gap between deity and humanity. He has crossed the grand canyon that yawned so deep and wide between heaven and earth. He has bridged the chasm that separated man from God. With one foot planted in eternity, He planted another in time. He who was the eternal Son of God became the Son of man. And across this bridge—Jesus Christ—you and I can march into the very throne room in heaven, knowing that we are "accepted in the Beloved."

That is the gospel of reconciliation through Christ. No man needs to remain alienated from God, separated by his sins from fellowship with the Eternal. The barrier has been broken down. A bridge has been built. The way is prepared, waiting for all of us to take. And the welcome mat is out for all who will come.

SUGGESTED
INTRODUCTION
FOR YOUTH

There's good news for modern teens. Believe it or not, that's true!

Too many young people today feel alienated—from their parents, their teachers, their elders, and, worst of all, from God. In frustration they turn to demonstrations, to drugs, to anything that will relieve the boredom of life.

But there is good news for all such. Put in three words, it is "reconciliation through Christ." He, the eternal Son of God, came to earth for the express purpose of reconciling man to his Creator. He brings harmony within, and peace, and love. Reconciled to God, living a new life in

Christ, we find that we can now be reconciled to our fellow human beings.

CONCEPTS FOR CHILDREN

1. Paul's life was threatened, even though he was innocent.
2. We may sometimes have to suffer when it is not our own fault.
3. We should be ready to help those who are in danger.

THE LESSON COMMENTARY

I. THE RESULTS OF JUSTIFICATION:
Romans 5:1-2

A. Peace with God: v. 1

Having been justified by faith, "we have peace with God through our Lord Jesus Christ." But some of the very earliest Greek manuscripts have the subjunctive form of the verb: "let us have peace."

In ancient days there were no printing presses running off thousands of identical copies of the same book. All copies were made by hand. The nearest thing to a publishing house would be a room full of scribes—anywhere up to forty—each one taking down from dictation the text that was being read aloud slowly by the man who had the master copy. It is obvious that errors of the ear would inevitably occur, and we find such errors in the early manuscripts. They can easily be spotted, since they consist of words that sound alike.

In this case, there is only the difference of one letter between the indicative form ("we have") and the subjunctive form ("let us have"). Both were probably pronounced exactly alike. As a result, some scribes wrote the indicative and some the subjunctive.

In the case of the majority of variant readings in the Greek manuscripts of the New Testament we can be reasonably certain as to which is the correct reading, that is, the original one. But we cannot be sure here.

In such cases the only thing we can do is to recognize both readings. This combination is beautifully expressed in Phillips' translation: "let us grasp the fact that we *have* peace." That is the best way to take it.

"Peace with God"—what a wonderful concept! No more war, enmity, or alienation. Peace is one of the most precious treasures of life. We should be devoutly thankful that we have peace with God through our Lord Jesus Christ, and we should do nothing to disturb that peace by failing to live in Christ.

B. Access into This Grace: v. 2

Through Jesus Christ we have access, or "the introduction," into "this grace wherein we stand." God wants us to be established in Christ.

But it is not a matter of gritting our teeth and holding on. Instead, we "rejoice in hope of the glory of God," or in the hope of attaining to God's glorious ideal for us. This may have some application to this life, but probably refers primarily to the glories of the heavenly world into which we shall be brought in the future. It is only through Christ that we can share in the glory of God. How grateful to Him we ought to be!

II. THE FRUITS OF JUSTIFICATION:
Romans 5:3-5

A. Rejoicing and Endurance: v. 3

The words translated "rejoice" (v. 2) and "glory" (v. 3) are exactly the same in the Greek text and should be translated the same way in English. We not only rejoice at the thought of the future glory, that is ours in Christ, but we rejoice in our tribulations down here.

The word *tribulation* is an interesting term. The Greek word comes from the verb meaning "to press." It was used of pressing the juice out of grapes. This suggests the pressures of life, as when we say that we are in "a bind" or in "a squeeze." Sometimes we feel as though these pressures would squeeze the very life out of us. Our English word *tribulation* comes from the Latin *tribulum*, the flail used for thrashing out grain in ancient times. Such flails are still used in Taiwan. As a boy on the farm I used a long stick as a flail when beating the bean vines to pound dry beans out of their pods. So we have here the figure of the pounding that comes in daily life.

Putting these two ideas together, we get the picture of life pressing and pounding us, sometimes almost unendurably. This is what tribulation means. It is the squeezing and beating of daily circumstances that seem at times to nearly crush us to death.

How can we rejoice in tribulations? Because we know that tribulation works "patience." But the Greek term means "steadfast endurance." Denney notes that the Greek word "has more of the sense of bravery and effort than the English 'patience': it is not so passive" (*Expositor's Greek Testament*, II, 624). Patience never got a person to heaven; that takes endurance.

B. Character and Hope: v. 4

This steadfast endurance produces "experience." The Greek word is *dokime*, which means: "the result of trial, *approval, approvedness, proof*" (Abbott-Smith, *Lexicon*, p. 120). Denney writes: "Endurance produces approvedness—its result is a spiritual state which has shown itself proof under trial. . . . Perhaps the best English equivalent of *dokime* would be *charac-*

ter" (*Expositor's Greek Testament*, II, 624). Weymouth translates it "ripeness of character." This can come only through the steadfast endurance that results from the right reaction to tribulation in our daily lives.

All of this, in turn, produces "hope." When we find that God is faithful and takes us safely through the trials of this life, our hope for the future is strengthened. He who has helped us hitherto will help us hereafter. It also brightens our hope for a glorious future in heaven.

C. The Love of God in Our Hearts: v. 5

This hope, which has not been extinguished under trial, but rather confirmed, does not "disappoint us" (RSV), or make us ashamed. It will prove to be true. How do we know? "Because the love of God is shed abroad [literally, "has been poured out"] in our hearts by the Holy Ghost which is given unto us." God is love and the Holy Spirit is God. So when our hearts are filled with the Spirit, He floods them with divine love. This love gives us the assurance that we belong to God and will someday live with Him in heaven. It should also flow out through our lives to others.

III. THE PRICE OF JUSTIFICATION: Romans 5:6-8

Christ Died for the Ungodly: v. 6

One way of describing our condition before we were saved is that we were "without strength," or, as the Greek simply says, "weak." That is, we were too weak to do what we knew we ought to do. Many sinners want to do right. They want to quit their bad habits and live a good life. They know that they would be much better off if they did. But they do not find the strength to carry out their good resolutions.

So, "in due time Christ died for the ungodly." The last word literally means "irreverent." It refers to those who treat all of life as secular; nothing is sacred. They live their worldly lives as though God did not exist. And yet Christ died for them, to save them! This reveals the marvelous forgiving love of God. In His Son He has provided a free and full salvation for those who do not deserve it.

B. Christ Died for Sinners: v. 7-8

Few men would be willing to die for a righteous man, though some might do so. But God "commendeth ["shows" or "proves"] his love toward us, in that, while we were yet sinners, Christ died for us." The essence of sin is disobedience. Yet when men were disobeying God, Christ was willing to die for them.

We should not fail to observe the reiterated emphasis on the death of Christ as the basis for our salvation. This note is sounded in verses 6, 8, 10. It was the price of our justification.

Some people think they can be saved by simply following in the footsteps of Jesus, trying to live a good life like His. But we cannot take one step with Him until we have first found Him at the cross. There, in answer to repentance and faith, we can find forgiveness for the sins of the past and begin to follow Him. Deciding to turn over a new leaf and live a good life from now on does not take care of our past sins.

IV. THE LIFE OF JUSTIFICATION: Romans 5:9-11

A. Saved from Wrath: v. 9

We are "justified by his blood." This is the same as saying "by His death." Christ had to die in our place before God could justify us. Somebody had to pay the penalty of our sins.

Because of Christ's death we are "saved from wrath through him." Jesus took on Himself God's holy wrath against sin, and so turned it aside from us. How grateful we ought to be to Him!

B. Saved by His Life: v. 10

In verse 6 Paul says that Christ died for us when we were *weak*, helpless to save ourselves. In verse 8 he says that Christ died for us when we were *sinners*, which is all the more remarkable. But here he says that this happened when we were *enemies*. This is far more amazing. When we hated God, He loved us and gave His Son to die for us.

The word *enemies* underscores the fact that the essence of sin is rebellion against God. Sinners are not only weak, they are wicked. As rebels, they need to be "reconciled to God," and this can be done only through the death of His Son. This is the main emphasis in our lesson.

But Paul goes one step further. He says that, "being reconciled, we shall be saved by his life." This points up the important fact that Christ's death for us would have done no good had it not been preceded by a perfect life. He had to be the spotless Lamb of God. Peter declares that we were redeemed "with the precious blood of Christ, as a lamb without belmish and without spot" (I Peter 1:19). The law of Moses required that the sacrificial lamb must be unblemished in any way. Christ's sacrifice atones for our sins because His life was blameless, His character without any blemish. He was the only available perfect sacrifice.

This is the objective side of "by his life." But the phrase could also be translated "in His life," which is the subjective side. Phillips puts it this way in his translation: "If, while we were his enemies, Christ reconciled us to God by *dying for us*, surely now that we are reconciled we may be perfectly certain of our salvation through his *living in us*."

Salvation is more than reconciliation to God on the basis of Jesus' death at Calvary. It is also a new life in us, *His* life in us. We are fully saved, in subjective experience, only as we live in Him and He in us. The transformation of our characters takes place through His indwelling presence. We are truly Christians only because Christ lives His life in us.

Without doubt the primary emphasis here is on the objective side of the atonement. But probably the subjective aspect should also be given its place.

C. Saved by the Atonement: v. 11

The word translated "joy" here is the same verb that is translated "rejoice" in verse 2 and "glory" in verse 3. The love for variety in the King James Version is sometimes a bit confusing!

Paul says that we rejoice "in God through our Lord Jesus Christ, by whom we have now received the atonement." This is the only place where the great word *atonement* occurs in the King James Version of the New Testament. But the same Greek word is translated "reconciliation" in II Corinthians 5:18, 19 and "reconciling" in Romans 11:15.

As we noted in a previous lesson, the word *atonement* is literally "at-one-ment." It means that we have been made "at one" with God. Probably "reconciliation" is a better translation now, since this is a current term. The verb "reconciled" (same root in Greek) we have already found twice in this chapter, in verse 10.

There is no greater need in the world today than for reconciliation. It is sorely needed between husbands and

wives, between parents and children, between employers and employees, between whites and blacks—and on and on the list goes. But the reconciliation that is most needed is between God and man, and that reconciliation is found only in Christ. If all men were reconciled to God, the intrahuman relationships could be worked out.

On the meaning of the Greek word for "reconciliation," Denney writes that it is "not a change in our disposition toward God, but a change in His attitude toward us. We do not *give* it (by laying aside enmity, distrust, or fear); we *receive* it, by believing in Christ Jesus, whom God has set forth as a propitiation through faith in His blood. We take it as God's unspeakable gift" (*Expositor's Greek Testament*, II, 626).

V. THE SCOPE OF JUSTIFICATION:
Romans 5:12-21

The remainder of the chapter is taken up with a contrast between Adam and Christ. The main point is that as sin and death reached the entire human race through Adam, so righteousness and life are available to all men through Jesus Christ. The scope of justification is thus seen to be universal in its provision.

The foundation fact is this: by one man, Adam, "sin entered into the world, and death by sin; and so death passed upon all men, for that all have sinned" (v. 12). Since Adam was the federal head of the human race, his sin has affected all mankind.

The fact that sin causes death goes back to the second chapter of Genesis. God commanded Adam not to eat from the tree of knowledge of good and evil, and then warned him: "for in the day that thou eatest thereof thou shalt surely die" (2:17). Adam disobeyed. Spiritual death ensued at once, and physical death came in due time. Since all men have sinned, all likewise die. The universality of death, which is an observable fact, is based on the universality of sin.

DISCUSSION QUESTIONS

1. What is the relation of faith and peace?
2. How can we rejoice in tribulations?
3. How can our hearts be filled with divine love?
4. In what way are men enemies of God?
5. What is the meaning of atonement?
6. How are we saved by Christ's life?

Death exercised its dominion over men from Adam to Moses, even though men did not sin "after the similitude of Adam's transgression." That is, during that period there were no explicit commands from God which people might disobey. But because all men sinned in disobeying their conscience, all died. After Moses received the law at Sinai the Israelites were judged on the basis of their obedience of that law. Again disobedience brought death.

The main point that Paul makes is that the universality of grace in Jesus Christ exceeds the power of sin. He says: "For if through the offence of one many be dead, much more the grace of God, and the gift by grace, which is by one man, Jesus Christ, hath abounded unto many" (v. 15).

Again he writes: "For if by one man's offence death reigned by one [Adam]; much more they which receive abundance of grace and of the gift of righteousness shall reign in life by one, Jesus Christ" (v. 17). Adam brought death; Christ brings life. But God's grace is far greater than man's sin.

Then Paul relates this specifically to our topic, justification. He says: "Therefore as by the offence of one judgment came upon all men to condemnation; even so by the righteousness of one the free gift came upon all men unto justification of life; for as by one man's obedience many were made sinners, so by the obedience of one shall many be made righteous" (vv. 18-19). Adam's sin had cosmic significance. But so did Christ's death on the cross. Provisionally and potentially that death reaches as far as sin has gone.

CONTEMPORARY APPLICATION

A. B. Simpson tells of an evangelist who was praying with a lady seeking salvation. Finally a verse of Scripture sparked her faith, and she found peace. The evangelist wrote the verse on a piece of paper and gave it to her. She went home rejoicing in her new-found faith.

The next morning the emotion had subsided. She said to her little boy, "I thought I was saved last night. But I don't feel like it this morning."

Without a word the young lad went into her bedroom. Opening her purse, he extracted the piece of paper. Running back to her, he exclaimed joyfully: "Why, it's all right, mama. It says the same thing it said last night."

Faith is not based on feelings but on the unchanging Word of God. "Being justified . . . let us have peace."

FREE BUT STILL BOUND

DEVOTIONAL READING	Romans 6:5-14

ADULTS

Topic: *Freedom and Its Temptations*

Background Scripture: Romans 6:1—7:25

Scripture Lesson: Romans 6:15-23

Memory Verse: *If we live by the Spirit, let us also walk by the Spirit.* Galatians 5:25

YOUTH

Topic: *Whose Slave Are You?*

Background Scripture: Romans 6:1—7:25

Scripture Lesson: Romans 6:15-23

Memory Verse: *If we live by the Spirit, let us also walk by the Spirit.* Galatians 5:25

CHILDREN

Topic: *Storm and Shipwreck*

Background Scripture: Acts 27:1—28:16

Scripture Lesson: Acts 27:39-44

Memory Verse: *Let them thank the Lord for his steadfast love, for his wonderful works to the sons of men!* Psalm 107:31

DAILY BIBLE READINGS

Mon., Oct. 15: Dead to Sin—Alive to God, Romans 6:1-11.
Tues., Oct. 16: Slaves of Righteousness, Romans 6:12-19.
Wed., Oct. 17: The New Life of the Spirit, Romans 6:20—7:6.
Thurs., Oct. 18: Doing the Good, Romans 7:7-12.
Fri., Oct. 19: Thanks Be to God, Romans 7:13-25.
Sat., Oct. 20: The Son Makes You Free, John 8:31-38.
Sun., Oct. 21: Christ Has Set Us Free, Galatians 5:1-14.

LESSON AIM

To discover God's plan for dealing with man's inward nature of sin.

LESSON SETTING

Time: About A.D. 56

Place: Corinth

LESSON OUTLINE

Free but Still Bound

I. Union with Christ: Romans 6:1-14
   A. In His Death: vv. 1-7
   B. In His Resurrection: vv. 8-14

54

II. Freedom from Sin: Romans 6:15-23
   A. Under Grace, Not Law: v. 15
   B. Slavery Is Inevitable: v. 16
   C. Slaves of Sin: v. 17
   D. Slaves of Righteousness: v. 18
   E. Slavery and Freedom: vv. 19-22
   F. Wages of Sin—Gift of God: v. 23

III. Married to Christ: Romans 7:1-6

IV. The Law and Sin: Romans 7:7-13

V. The Law of Sin: Romans 7:14-25
   A. Sin That Dwelleth in Me: vv. 14-20
   B. The Law of Sin: vv. 21-25

SUGGESTED INTRODUCTION FOR ADULTS

The sixth and seventh chapters of Romans, which comprise the lesson for today, deal realistically with the problem of man's inner nature of sin. Salvation is more than forgiveness for the sins of our past life. It is more than being justified before God by faith. If it does not do something about the continuing presence of sin in the believer's heart, it is obviously not an adequate salvation. Sin is more than an act or attitude; it is an attribute of fallen human nature.

The Graeco-Roman world of Paul's day was defective in its understanding of sin. The Greeks put more emphasis on aesthetics than on ethics. Many of Paul's contemporaries tended to ignore or explain away the idea of sin.

The same kind of sophisticated intellectualism dominates society today. To talk about sin is to be hopelessly old-fashioned, to be a "square." There is no such thing as "sin" today. We have behavior patterns, but no problem of sin.

But whatever we call it, sin is very much with us. Paul gives us help in seeing what God wants to do about it.

SUGGESTED INTRODUCTION FOR YOUTH

Whose slave are you? There is no such thing as absolute freedom. Every man is the slave of someone. The question is: of whom?

In these chapters Paul discloses and describes his past slavery to sin. But over and over again in his Epistles he refers to himself as "the slave of Jesus Christ." Romans itself begins with this: "Paul, a slave of Jesus Christ." The word translated "servant" is literally "slave." Paul had simply exchanged one slavery for another. But what a glorious exchange! He had once been a miserable slave to sin; he was now the love slave of Christ.

CONCEPTS FOR CHILDREN

1. Life isn't always smooth sailing; sometimes storms come.
2. Christ will be with us in our difficulties just as he was with Paul.

3. Just knowing that Christ is with us brings courage and confidence.
4. We should be concerned for others in distress, as Paul was, and do all we can to help them.

THE LESSON COMMENTARY

I. UNION WITH CHRIST: Romans 6:1-14

A. In His Death: vv. 1-7

Frequently in Paul's Epistles we meet up with questions of his opponents. They are especially prominent in I Corinthians, and a number appear in Romans. We find two in this chapter (vv. 1, 15).

The apostle has just been emphasizing the triumph of grace over sin. He declared: "Where sin abounded, grace did much more abound" (5:20). Immediately the objection is raised: "What shall we say then? Shall we continue in sin, that grace may abound?" (6:1). The more there is of human need, the greater is the display of divine grace!

Against this specious kind of reasoning Paul responds typically with an emphatic denial: "God forbid." The Greek literally says, "May it not be!" Perhaps the best translation is, "By no means!" or "Not at all!" This is a favorite expression of the apostle. Sanday and Headlam describe it as "a formula of negation, repelling with horror something previously suggested" (Romans, p. 71). Burton writes: "Fourteen of the fifteen New Testament instances are in Paul's writings, and in twelve of these it expresses the apostle's abhorrence of an inference which he fears may be (falsely) drawn from his argument" (Moods and Tenses, p. 79). The expression occurs ten times in Romans, where theological debate is prominent. Outside Paul's Epistles it is found only in Luke 20:16.

Paul had no sympathy for the idea that a Christian must keep on sinning. The whole thrust of this chapter is an emphatic rejection of that heresy. He immediately asks, "How shall we, that

are dead to sin, live any longer therein?" The Christian is supposed to be dead to sin, not alive to it.

This is shown in the symbolism of baptism. The apostle says that those who have been baptized into Jesus Christ have been baptized into His death (v. 3). Going under the water is a symbol of our being dead and buried with Him. Coming up out of the water symbolizes our rising with Him in a new resurrection life of victory. We are to "walk in newness of life" (v. 4). Paul goes on to say: "For if we have been planted together in the likeness of his death, we shall be also in the likeness of his resurrection" (v. 5).

Then comes the sixth verse, with its tremendous message: "Knowing this, that our old man is crucified with him, that the body of sin might be destroyed, that henceforth we should not serve sin."

What is "the old man"? Sanday and Headlam say that it means "our old self" (Romans, p. 158). Godet, the great French commentator, writes: "The expression, our old man, denotes human nature such as it has been made by the sin of him in whom originally it was wholly concentrated, fallen Adam reappearing in every human ego that comes into the world under the sway of the preponderance of self-love, which was determined by the primitive transgression. This corrupted nature bears the name of old only from the viewpoint of the believer who already possesses a renewed nature" (Romans, p. 244).

What is "the body of sin"? This has commonly been thought to refer to our physical bodies. Since sin is inherent in the human body, so it is argued, we cannot be rid of sin until "the hour and article of death." But this point of view is Gnostic, not New

Testament. Sin does not reside in matter, but in the will. Godet points out the conclusive truth that the Incarnation proves that the human body is not inherently sinful. Jesus had a true body of flesh, but it was not a body of sin. "The body of sin," then, is the sin principle in men's hearts.

Some have thought to reduce the force of "destroy." It is true that sometimes the verb used here means "annul" or "render inoperative." The context here, however, suggests the stronger meaning. Godet comments: "But the translation *destroyed* probably renders the thought best" (p. 245).

B. In His Resurrection: vv. 8-14

Paul had just made the point: "For he that is dead is freed from sin" (v. 7). Probably the reference is to those who have died physically. But "if we be dead with Christ" (v. 8) means dead to sin and the old self. That is the ground of our faith "that we shall also live with him." It is obvious that we cannot rise from the dead until we have first died. So we cannot experience the resurrection life of victory in Jesus until we have been crucified with Him. The simple truth is that every resurrection must be preceded by a crucifixion. We have to die to live. This is one of the great paradoxes of Christianity.

How do we experience this death to sin and new life in Christ? Paul has the answer: "Likewise reckon ye also yourselves to be dead indeed unto sin, but alive unto God through Jesus Christ our Lord" (v. 11). The word *reckon* here does not have the colloquial sense of "guess" or "think." The Greek word was a technical commercial term in the first century, meaning to "account" or "put to the account of." This is not a matter of wishful thinking or of "hope so" salvation. Rather, it is put down on the books, signed and sealed that it is so! True faith brings certainty, not uncertainty.

But we are to account ourselves not only as dead to sin, "but alive unto God through Jesus Christ our Lord"—better, "in Christ Jesus." If we would remain dead to sin, we must be increasingly and continually alive to God. We do not conquer sin by concentrating on it. We do it by turning to Christ and letting Him give us the victory. He alone can conquer sin and Satan.

Our "members"—the parts of our physical body—are to be yielded "as instruments of righteousness unto God" (v. 13). God wants all of us—body, soul, and spirit.

II. FREEDOM FROM SIN: Romans 6:15-23

A. Under Grace, Not Law: v. 15

Paul has just asserted: "Sin shall not have dominion over you: for ye are not under the law, but under grace" (v. 14). As in the first verse of this chapter, an objector immediately asks: "What then? shall we sin, because we are not under the law, but under grace?" And once again the apostle emphatically says, "God forbid."

The attitude expressed in this verse is what is called antinomianism ("against law"). Throughout the history of the church, from the first century to the twentieth, there have been those who have taught that if we are under grace we are not subject to law. But there is no liberty without law. Though freed from the Mosaic law, we are subject to the law of Christ.

There is no more room for sinning under grace than under law. The seriousness of sin is shown at Calvary. When Christ took upon Himself our sins, the Father forsook Him—or at least so it seemed in Christ's own consciousness. God cannot condone sin. This is just as true now as it was in the Mosaic dispensation. Grace does not give license to sin.

B. Slavery Is Inevitable: v. 16

We are all slaves to someone or something. We cannot choose whether we will be slaves or not; we can only choose whose slaves we will be. We can be the slaves of sin and end up with death—spiritual death forever—or we can be obedient slaves of God and inherit righteousness as our eternal reward.

C. Slaves of Sin: v. 17

Throughout this whole section the term translated "servants" should be translated "slaves." Paul reminds his readers that they were the slaves of sin. But all that was changed when they "obeyed from the heart" the form of teaching "which was delivered to" them—or, "to which you were committed."

D. Slaves of Righteousness: v. 18

When they believed and obeyed the gospel, they were freed from the slavery of sin and "became the slaves of righteousness." What a glorious exchange!

There is no neutral ground. We cannot choose to be unattached. Unless and until we give ourselves in loving obedience to Christ to be His slaves, we remain the slaves of sin. There are no alternatives, no other options open to us.

You say: "I'll be my own boss; I'll not be subject to any authority outside myself." That may sound good, but it is only an illusion. When we choose self as our only master, it is not long until we discover that the old self is our sinful nature. So we are right back where we were—the slaves of sin.

Jesus Christ has paid the ransom price to free us from slavery to sin. Because He has purchased us with His own blood, we belong to Him by right of purchase. To refuse to be His is to rob Him of what belongs to Him.

But when we give ourselves in gratitude to Him we are His slaves, His own rightful property. He is our Lord, telling us what to do. Our only responsibility is loving obedience.

E. Slavery and Freedom: vv. 19-22

Paul gets down to grassroots and speaks in human terms about these great truths. As sinners we yielded the various parts of our body as slaves "to uncleanness and to iniquity unto iniquity"; or, "slaves to impurity and to lawlessness, resulting in further lawlessness" (NASB). This was the pattern of our living. But now we are to yield the parts of our bodies as slaves "to righteousness unto holiness." Probably "righteousness" refers more to the outward life and "holiness" to the inward character.

What is meant by "the infirmity of your flesh," which limited what Paul could say to his readers? Sanday and Headlam write that *sarx* (flesh) equals "human nature in its weakness, primarily physical and moral, but secondarily intellectual. It is intellectual weakness in so far as this is determined by the limitations of character" (*Romans*, p. 169).

When we were the slaves of sin, we were free from the control of righteousness (v. 20). But what was the "fruit," the consequences, of that condition? The only reward it gave was eternal death (v. 21). But now that we have been freed from slavery to sin and have become God's love slaves, we have the results in "holiness, and the end everlasting life" (v. 22).

We are free to choose our master, but we are not free to choose the consequences of that decision. If we choose sin, the inevitable and inescapable result is eternal death. If we choose righteousness, the reward will be everlasting life. We should weigh the consequences when we make the decision.

F. Wages of Sin—Gift of God: v. 23

This verse sums up all the preceding discussion: "For the wages of sin is death; but the gift of God is eternal life through Jesus Christ our Lord." The Greek says, "*in* Christ Jesus our

Lord." It is only in Him that we have life. He said, "I am the life." When we have Him, we have life. The adjective here is qualitative as well as quantitative. It is not only life that lasts forever; it is eternity in the heart. It is a quality of life that cannot die.

Life is a Person. That is, of course, an unfathomable mystery. But it is also a glorious fact. The highest form of life we know on earth is human personality. When we receive the divine Person, Christ, into our hearts, we have the highest form of life. Because it cannot be described, it is simply called eternal life. John puts it beautifully: "For the life was manifested, and we have seen it, and bear witness, and shew unto you that eternal life, which was with the Father, and was manifested unto us" (I John 1:2). In the previous verse he identifies "that eternal life" as "the Word of life"— Jesus Christ, the Son of God. When we have Him, we have eternal life. It is as simple as that; and at the same time, as profound as that. The message of the New Testament is that when we have Him, we have all.

III. MARRIED TO CHRIST:
Romans 7:1-6

Paul begins by saying that the law "has dominion over"—literally, "is lord of"—a man as long as he lives. Then he illustrates. A married woman is bound by law to her husband as long as he lives; when he dies, she is free. This legal fact is spelled out more fully in verse 3.

Then Paul makes the application to his readers. He writes: "Wherefore, my brethren, ye also are become dead to the law by the body of Christ; that ye should be married to another, even to him who is raised from the dead, that we should bring forth fruit unto God" (v. 4). In the death of Christ on the cross, the reign of the law of Moses came to an end. That was because Jesus identified Himself with it and fulfilled it completely. So His death meant that all people, and particularly the Jews, were free from the law so

that they could be united to Christ, the One who was raised from the dead. The outcome would be "that we should bring forth fruit unto God."

In a very real sense, salvation comes only through union with Christ. As we have already noted, we cannot have eternal life without receiving Him. In fact, He is our eternal life. There is no other way for us. We cannot have *it* unless we have *Him.* But when we have Him, we have it, and in it all that is really worthwhile.

IV. THE LAW AND SIN:
Romans 7:7-13

In verse 6 the apostle says: "But now we are delivered from the law, that being dead wherein we were held; that we should serve in newness of spirit, and not in the oldness of the letter." The last phrase simply means legalism. The previous one means true, vital religion.

Now Paul asks a third question (cf. 6:1, 15): "What shall we say then? Is the law sin?" (v. 7) And once more he protests, "God forbid."

What was the real function of the law? It was to give people a keen consciousness of sin. The apostle puts it this way: "Nay, I had not known sin, but by the law: for I had not known lust, except the law had said, Thou shalt not covet." That is, the law gave

---

DISCUSSION QUESTIONS

1. What does it mean to die with Christ?
2. How can we keep alive to God?
3. How should the Christian use his body?
4. What place should sin have in the Christian's life?
5. What was the purpose of the law?
6. Was Paul himself living under the conditions he describes in the seventh chapter of Romans, or under those he describes in the eighth chapter?

the awareness of sin. When the law said to Paul, "Thou shalt not covet," he sensed an inner rebellion, a covetous desire to have what was forbidden. As a result he became conscious of the virulence of sin; it filled his heart with evil desire. It seemed that the coming of the law to Paul when he was a young man had sparked the activity of sin in him. This he expresses vividly in verse 9: "For I was alive without the law once: but when the commandment came, sin revived, and I died." The law was not sin (cf. v. 7), but it did become the occasion for sin becoming more vigorous and aggressive. This is, at least in part, because sin is essentially a spirit of rebellion. That spirit asserts itself whenever it hears the words, "Thou shalt not." So the commandment, which was intended to result in life actually resulted in spiritual death for Paul.

Far from being sin, "the law is holy, and the commandment holy, and just, and good." But it would seem that Paul has been saying that the law had been the cause of his spiritual death. Had that which was holy in itself brought death to him? Again he cries out, "God forbid!" (v. 13). It wasn't the law that did this, it was sin. The law only exposed the exceeding sinfulness of sin.

V. THE LAW OF SIN:
Romans 7:14-25

A. Sin That Dwelleth in Me: vv. 14-20

In this paragraph the personal pronoun *I* becomes even more emphatic and frequent than in the previous section. Most scholars agree that verses 7-25 are autobiographical. But to what time in Paul's life do they refer, preconversion or postconversion? The early church fathers held to the former view, as do many today. In the Reformation period there was a tendency to adopt the latter.

Perhaps the both/and theory might help us a little. All would probably agree that the language here does not describe a *normal* Christian life. On the other hand, too many Christians find this the *average*. And even born-again believers discover that they still have "the sin that dwelleth in me" (vv. 17, 20).

B. The Law of Sin: vv. 21-25

Here the sin nature is labeled "the law of sin" (vv. 23, 25). What is the remedy? It is found in the fullness of the Spirit, described in chapter 8.

CONTEMPORARY APPLICATION

Though we are not under law, but under grace, we are still under law to Christ. And His law, "the royal law," is the law of love. This should control all our actions and attitudes, all our words and thoughts.

We are freed from the slavery of sin to become the love slaves of Christ. As such we must be in complete obedience to His will. We cannot do or say things we know would displease Him.

VICTORY IN SUFFERING

DEVOTIONAL READING	Romans 8:18-25

ADULTS

Topic: *Confidence of Victory in Suffering*

Background Scripture: Romans 8

Scripture Lesson: Romans 8:31-39

Memory Verse: *He who did not spare his own Son but gave him up for us all, will he not also give us all things with him?* Romans 8:32

YOUTH

Topic: *A Life Guarantee*

Background Scripture: Romans 8

Scripture Lesson: Romans 8:31b-39

Memory Verse: *He who did not spare his own Son but gave him up for us all, will he not also give us all things with him?* Romans 8:32

CHILDREN

Topic: *Paul in Rome*

Background Scripture: Acts 28:17-31

Scripture Lesson: Acts 28:17-22, 30-31

Memory Verse: *May God be gracious to us and bless us and make his face to shine upon us, that thy way may be known upon earth, thy saving power among all nations.* Psalm 67:1-2

DAILY BIBLE READINGS

Mon., Oct. 22: Walking by the Spirit, Romans 8:1-11.
Tues., Oct. 23: Saved by Hope, Romans 8:12-21.
Wed., Oct. 24: God Works for Good, Romans 8:22-32.
Thurs., Oct. 25: The Love of God, Romans 8:33-39.
Fri., Oct. 26: Overcoming the World, I John 5:1-12.
Sat., Oct. 27: Who Through Faith Conquered, Hebrews 11:32—12:2.
Sun., Oct. 28: I Have Overcome the World, John 16:25-33.

LESSON AIM

To see why the Christian can be victorious through times of suffering.

LESSON SETTING

Time: About A.D. 56

Place: Corinth

Victory in Suffering

LESSON OUTLINE

SUGGESTED INTRODUCTION FOR ADULTS

The contrast between Romans 7 and Romans 8 is startling indeed. In the former we find defeat and discouragement. The man who is giving us his spiritual autobiography under the law cries out: "O wretched man that I am! who shall deliver me from the body of this death?" (7:24). This is the dismal tone of chapter 7.

The writer gives us the answer in verse 25: "I thank God through Jesus Christ our Lord." But then he goes on to say: "So then with the mind I myself serve the law of God; but with the flesh the law of sin." It has been claimed that this is Paul's final statement as to his spiritual condition at the time he wrote to the Romans. If so, what kind of a gospel did he have to offer to them? This is no good news!

What are we going to do then with this last part of verse 25? The answer seems to be that it is to be taken as "a terse compressed summary of the previous paragraph, vv. 7-24, describing in two strokes the state of things prior to the intervention of Christ" (Sanday and Headlam, *Romans*, p. 184). In other words, Paul sums up in order to conclude.

The Holy Spirit does not appear anywhere in the seventh chapter. But in the eighth chapter He is mentioned some twenty times. The life of victory is life in the Spirit.

SUGGESTED INTRODUCTION FOR YOUTH

Life in Christ is not always easy. But neither is life outside of Christ. Suffering is the common fate of all humanity—saints and sinners alike. The difference is that God has promised to be with His children in their hardships and difficulties. Instead of frustration, the Christian has the joy and peace of the divine presence. So we have victory in suffering.

CONCEPTS FOR CHILDREN

1. In spite of hardship and danger, Paul reached Rome safely.
2. We do not always reach our goals by the way we have planned.
3. God is always faithful; He fulfills all of His promises.
4. Though a prisoner, Paul continued to witness.

THE LESSON COMMENTARY

I. NEW LIFE IN THE SPIRIT: Romans 8:1-13

When we enter the eighth chapter of Romans we find ourselves in a new world. "In contrast with the thirty occurrences of "I" in ch. vii are the twenty references to the Holy Spirit in ch. viii" (W. H. Griffith Thomas, *Romans*, p. 201). In chapter 7 we see man's failure in himself; in chapter 8 we discover man's victory in the Spirit.

Someone has said that this chapter begins with no condemnation and ends with no separation, while in between there is no defeat. It has always been a favorite with those who love the Lord. W. R. Newell writes: "There is scarcely a passage in the New Testament that is more delightful reading to the spiritual Christian than the eighth of Romans . . . . There is an atmosphere of blessing all through it. Of course there is, for the blessed Holy Spirit breathes throughout it—the indwelling Deliverer, Quickener, Guide, Assurer, Helper, Intercessor."

Verse 2 expresses the theme of the chapter: "For the law of the Spirit of life in Christ Jesus hath made me free from the law of sin and death." The term *law* seems to refer to an inward "principle" at work in us. "The law of sin and death" is the same as "the law of sin" in chapter 7 (vv. 23, 25). It is the sinful nature within, variously designated "inbred sin," "inherited depravity," "the carnal nature," or "original sin."

The only deliverance from this is found in a new law, introduced in chapter 8. It is called "the law of the Spirit of life in Christ Jesus." The law of sin brings death. The law of the Spirit brings life. But it is always life "in Christ Jesus." For it is only as we are in Him that we can have life in the Spirit.

In verse 3 it would appear that "law" refers to the Mosaic law, under which the Israelites lived until the coming of Christ. The trouble with that law was that it was "weak through the flesh." It told man what to do but did not give him the power to do it. Hence it failed.

What was God's remedy? He sent His own Son "in the likeness of sinful flesh, and for sin," and so "condemned sin in the flesh." Here "flesh" seems to refer to the physical nature.

The purpose of all this was that the righteousness of the law might be fulfilled in those "who walk not after the flesh, but after the Spirit" (v. 4). The part quoted here occurs at the end of the first verse in the King James Version. But the oldest Greek manuscripts have it only at the end of verse 4. The righteousness of the Mosaic law was fulfilled and is now fulfilled in those who follow the Spirit, not the flesh.

What is meant here by "flesh"? John Murray writes: "'The flesh' is human nature as corrupted, directed, and controlled by sin" (*Romans*, I, 284-85). The term is often used by Paul to refer to the physical body. But here it means the moral nature.

The apostle picks up the two phrases of verse 4 and makes a further statement about them in verse 5: "For they that are after the flesh do mind the things of the flesh; but they that are after the Spirit the things of the Spirit." Commenting on this, Griffith Thomas says: "The 'flesh' when used, as here, with a moral meaning, is always

to be understood as referring to the
old, unrenewed, sinful nature . . . . It
implies the entire unrenewed life apart
from God; and it should be carefully
observed that this does not necessarily
mean a gross, vicious life, for the flesh
as unrenewed may be educated, refined, and cultured. Indeed there is
even a religion of the flesh that consists in outward ceremonial observances, asceticism, and self-denial,
which, however, does not touch the
springs of the heart and provide acceptable worship" (*Romans*, pp.
208-209).

Paul goes on to say: "For to be
carnally minded is death; but to be
spiritually minded is life and peace"
(v. 6). The whole phrase "to be carnally minded" is literally "the mind
[or perhaps better, "the mind-set"]
of the flesh." The Greek word occurs
only in this chapter (vv. 6, 7, 27). It
indicates the "way of thinking." Griffith Thomas observes: "It always
means the entire bent of thought, feeling, motive, and will" (p. 212). John
Murray writes: "To 'mind the things
of the flesh' (vs. 5) is to have the
things of the flesh as the absorbing
objects of thought, interest, affection,
and purpose. And 'the mind of the
flesh' (vs. 6) is the dispositional complex, including not simply the activities of reason but also those of feeling
and will, patterned after and controlled by the flesh" (*Romans*, p.
285).

What is the outcome of living this
kind of a life? Griffith Thomas writes:
"The outcome of 'minding the flesh' is
death, which is to be regarded as separation from God" (*Romans*, p. 212).
This is because "the carnal mind
["the mind of the flesh"] is enmity
against God" (v. 7). Unless surrendered to God to be slain, it will separate us forever from Him. For those
who are "in the flesh [in the control
of the sinful nature] cannot please
God" (v. 8). If we let the Holy Spirit
have control of our hearts we are not
"in the flesh [but] in the Spirit" (v.
9).

II. NEW SENSE OF DIVINE FATH-
ERHOOD:
Romans 8:14-16

We have devoted considerable
space to the opening verses of this
great eighth chapter of Romans, because they are foundational. Now we
must pass rapidly over the intervening
section and come to that part of the
lesson found in the last part of the
chapter.

Who are sons of God? Those who
are "led by the Spirit of God" (v. 14).
This is a very challenging statement.
Are we led by the Holy Spirit day by
day?

It is the Holy Spirit who gives us
the sense of divine sonship, so that our
hearts cry out, "Abba, Father" (v. 15).
Abba is the Aramaic word for "father." It is here coupled with the Greek
term for "father" to suggest a warm
feeling of sonship, of belonging to a
loving Father in heaven, who has made
us His children. So we have the inner
witness of the Spirit that we are children of God (v. 16).

III. NEW SHARING OF DIVINE SUF-
FERING:
Romans 8:17-18

We cannot understand what Paul
says about victory in suffering in the
last paragraph of this chapter without
noting what he writes here about the
place of suffering in the divine plan for
our lives. He says that if we are God's
children we are His heirs and "joint-
heirs with Christ." But this is only if
we suffer with Him, "that we may be
also glorified together" (v. 17). This is
a fact from which we naturally shrink.
Some would-be Christians are completely turned off by it. But there is
no way of escaping it. The simple
truth is: no suffering, no glory!

But the apostle assures us that "it
will be worth it all," to adopt the
words of a familiar song. He declares:
"For I reckon that the sufferings of
this present time are not worthy to be
compared with the glory which shall
be revealed in us" (v. 18). The coming

glory we shall share with Christ will far outweigh our sufferings with Him here.

What we need to realize is that in the Christian life suffering is not for the purpose of punishment, but rather to develop Christlike character. If we are going to follow Christ we must follow Him in His sufferings before we can follow Him in His glory.

IV. NEW HOPE OF COMING RE-DEMPTION:
Romans 8:19-25

This is a unique passage in the New Testament. It pictures all creation as under the curse because of man's sin (vv. 20, 22). This is in keeping with what we read in Genesis 3:17-19. But, amazingly, we are told here that all creation waits eagerly "for the manifestation of the sons of God" (v. 19), when it will "be delivered from the bondage of corruption into the glorious liberty of the children of God" (v. 21). Sin has affected the whole universe, and all creation will share in man's redemption through Christ.

Then Paul makes the application to us: "we ourselves groan within ourselves, waiting for the adoption, the redemption of our body" (v. 23). Our souls are redeemed when we receive new life in Christ—"have the firstfruits of the Spirit." But the redemption of our bodies awaits the resurrection. Then the whole man—body, soul, and spirit—will be fully and finally redeemed. This is what is often referred to as our glorification, when we shall be clothed forever in our glorified bodies, which Paul describes as "a spiritual body" (I Corinthians 5:44).

V. NEW POWER IN PRAYER:
Romans 8:26-27

This is one of the most important passages on prayer in the New Testament. Without the help of the Holy Spirit we cannot pray effectively. He knows the mind of God and can help us to pray according to His will. God, who searches the hearts, understands and answers the prayers that are prayed in the Spirit, even though we ourselves may not fully comprehend them. How wonderful to have the Holy Spirit interceding for us!

VI. NEW ASSURANCE IN TRIBULA-TION:
Romans 8:28-30

Probably no single verse of Scripture has been of greater comfort and encouragement to Christians across the centuries than Romans 8:28. In the best Greek text it literally reads: "And we know that God causes all things to work together for good to those who love God, to those who are called according to His purpose" (NASB). Often in life it seems that everything is working against us. But behind the scenes is God, weaving the pattern and causing *everything* to work together for our ultimate good.

The assurance of this truth can hold us steady in the most excruciating trials of life. If we believe that our heavenly Father is all-powerful, all-knowing, and all-loving, we can trust ourselves fully to His care!

VII. NEW ASSURANCE OF COM-PLETE VICTORY:
Romans 8:31-39

Of this section of the chapter Griffith Thomas writes: "Now comes the Apostle's paean of triumph, as he closes this magnificent view of the life of the people of God. After emphasizing God's side of the Christian redemption he describes the resulting feeling of absolute confidence, and shows how that confidence rises into positive assurance" (*Romans*, p. 229).

Gairdner puts it this way: "The impassioned but subdued tones of verses 18-30, which succeeded the calm logic of verses 1-17, now pass into a sort of lyric outburst, which quickens and swells to its magnificent climax" (*Helps to the Study of the Epistle to the Romans*, p. 77).

Anyone who reads through this chapter at one sitting will feel a quickening of his pulse as he nears the end. The tempo picks up and lifts up.

This closing paragraph of the great eighth chapter of Romans forms a fitting climax to the doctrinal section of this Epistle. The first half of it consists of a series of rhetorical questions, eloquent and challenging. The last half is a ringing affirmation of Paul's faith in God's faithfulness.

A. The Divine Guarantee: vv. 31-32

He begins by asking: "If God be for us, who can be against us?" The answer is obvious: No one can successfully oppose us if God is on our side— or, as Abraham Lincoln put it, if we are on God's side.

Then comes the unanswerable guarantee of divine provision for our every need: "He that spared not his own Son, but delivered him up for us all, how shall he not with him also freely give us all things?" The logic is inescapable. If God did not withhold His most precious possession, His own beloved Son, but freely gave Him up to die for us, we know that with Christ He will "also freely give us all things."

In verse 32 there seems to be an allusion, probably intended, to Abraham's offering of his son Isaac. In the Greek translation of the Old Testament (the Septuagint) the same Greek word is used for "withheld" in Genesis 22:16 as we find here for "spared."

The word translated "freely give" is *charisetai*, from *charis*, "grace." So it means "graciously give." Whatever God gives is given not grudgingly but graciously.

The last words of the verse, "all things," call for comment. Alexander Maclaren writes: "Everything is given us when Christ is given to us, because Christ is the Heir of all things, and we possess all things in Him; as some poor village maiden married to a prince in disguise, who, on the morrow of her wedding finds that she is lady of broad lands, and mistress of a kingdom" (*Expositions of Holy Scripture*, "Romans," p. 197).

B. Freedom from Condemnation: vv. 33-34

Once more the apostle asks a question: "Who shall lay anything to the charge of God's elect?" The answer is given: "It is God that justifieth." The Greek could just as well be translated as a question: "Shall God who justifies?" The obvious answer is "No!"

Marcus Rainsford many years ago wrote a striking book on the eighth chapter of Romans. On this verse he said: "There is no ground for condemnation since Christ has suffered the penalty; there is no law to condemn us since we are not under law but under grace; there is no tribunal for judgment since ours is a Throne of Grace, not a judgment; and, above all, there is no Judge to sentence since God Himself, the only Judge, is our Justifier."

Again Paul asks: "Who is he that condemneth?" And again the reply could be put in the form of a question: "Shall Christ?" Certainly not He who died for us!

C. No Separation: vv. 35-36

Another question is asked: "Who shall separate us from the love of Christ?" Then the apostle names a number of possibilities: tribulation,

---

DISCUSSION QUESTIONS

1. Why do we need the Holy Spirit?
2. What is the main secret of Christian victory?
3. Why do Christians have to suffer?
4. What are some of the values of suffering?
5. What difference does Christ make in our suffering?
6. What should be our attitude toward suffering?

distress, persecution, famine, nakedness, peril, sword. To make it more emphatic, he quotes Psalm 44:22: "For thy sake we are killed all the day long; we are accounted as sheep for the slaughter." Will any or all of this separate us from the love of God?

D. More Than Conquerors: vv. 37-39

To the above question Paul has an emphatic "Nay!" He goes on to say: "In all these things we are more than conquerors through him that loved us." The phrase "we are more than conquerors" is a translation of only one Greek word. Paul took the preposition *hyper* (equivalent to the Latin "super") and put it with the word *nike*, "victory," to form a verb which means "we are super-victors." But how? Only "through him that loved us."

Then he asserts: "For I am persuaded that neither death, nor life, nor angels, nor principalities, nor powers, nor things present..." "Stop!" says someone; "I think I can take care of today, but how about that unknown tomorrow?" Paul continues: "Nor things to come, nor height, nor depth [nothing above or below us] nor any other creature [nothing in all God's vast creation] shall be able to separate us from the love of God." But where is that love shown? It is "in Christ Jesus our Lord."

The doctrinal section of this Epistle opens with a dirty, ugly picture of man's sin, in the last part of the first chapter. The second and third chapters declare that all have sinned. Then comes the good news of justification by faith, in 3:31—5:21. This is followed by Paul's treatment of sanctification, which culminates in his description of the spirit-filled life in chapter eight. And this last paragraph is the rapturous climax of it all.

CONTEMPORARY APPLICATION

Older readers will remember the electric trolley cars that used to run in all our cities. The source of power was in a live wire that ran overhead. Contact with this was made by the "trolley pole" on the roof of the car. Sometimes when going around a curve, this pole would be jolted off the wire. That meant that the car came to a stop. The conductor or motorman had to get off, walk back, and adjust the pole back to the wire. Then we were on our way again.

It is like that in the Christian life. The Holy Spirit is the power. But we must keep constant contact with Him if we are to live victoriously.

LIFE IN THE CHRISTIAN COMMUNITY

DEVOTIONAL READING	I Thessalonians 5:12-22

ADULTS

Topic: *Life in the Christian Community*

Background Scripture: Romans 12:1-13; I Corinthians 12:1—13:13

Scripture Lesson: Romans 12:1-8; I Corinthians 12:12-13

Memory Verse: *Do not be conformed to this world but be transformed by the renewal of your mind, that you may prove what is the will of God, what is good and acceptable and perfect.* Romans 12:2

YOUTH

Topic: *You Are the Church*

Background Scripture: Romans 12:1-13; I Corinthians 12:1—13:13

Scripture Lesson: Romans 12:1-8; I Corinthians 12:12-13

Memory Verse: *Do not be conformed to this world but be transformed by the renewal of your mind, that you may prove what is the will of God, what is good and acceptable and perfect.* Romans 12:2

CHILDREN

Topic: *Paul Writes About a Treasure*

Background Scripture: II Corinthians 4:7-12

Scripture Lesson: II Corinthians 4:7-12

Memory Verse: *We have this treasure in earthen vessels, to show that the . . . power belongs to God and not to us.* II Corinthians 4:7

DAILY BIBLE READINGS

Mon., Oct. 29: Be Transformed, Romans 12:1-13.
Tues., Oct. 30: Varieties of Gifts, I Corinthians 12:1-11.
Wed., Oct. 31: The Unity of the Body, I Corinthians 12:12-26.
Thurs., Nov. 1: Spiritual Gifts, I Corinthians 12:27—13:3.
Fri., Nov. 2: The Greatest of These Is Love, I Corinthians 13:4-13.
Sat., Nov. 3: Living as Children of God, I Thessalonians 5:12-25.
Sun., Nov. 4: Put on the New Nature, Ephesians 4:25-31.

LESSON AIM

To discover what the church really is and what Christ meant it to be.

68

LESSON SETTING

Time: About A.D. 55 or 56

Place: Romans was written at Corinth, I Corinthians at
Ephesus.

Life in the Christian Community

I. Christian Character: Romans 12:1-5
   A. Consecration: v. 1
   B. Transformation: v. 2
   C. Humility: v. 3
   D. Unity: vv. 4-5

LESSON OUTLINE

II. Christian Service: Romans 12:6-8
   A. Gifts and Graces: v. 6a
   B. Different Gifts: 6b-8

III. Christian Fellowship: Romans 12:9-13
   A. Brotherly Love: vv. 9-10
   B. Caring for others: vv. 11-13

IV. Christian Unity: I Corinthians 12:12-13
   A. Many Members: v. 12
   B. One Body: v. 13

SUGGESTED
INTRODUCTION
FOR ADULTS

"We are not divided, all one body we." So we sing.
But every well-informed person knows it is not so. We are
very much divided! Instead of being one body, we are
about 250 denominational bodies in the United States
alone. The words of the song seem to have a hollow ring, a
sting of rebuke.

That is the picture of the outward church. It is split up
into hundreds of factions that too often have refused to
have any fellowship with each other. Closed communion
has been the rule in many denominations. At the famous
meeting of the World Council of Churches in New Delhi,
India, some years ago, the best they could finally manage
was to have four separate communion services. And all
this in the name of church unity! It was a caricature.

Are we to say, then, that the words of the old song are
pure lie? No, thank God there is a sense in which they are
profoundly true. The church of Jesus Christ, composed of
born-again believers, is undivided. It is one body. But no
church rolls on earth reveal its membership. The record is
kept in heaven. The names of the members of the true
church are written in the Lamb's Book of Life (Revelation
21:27).

SUGGESTED
INTRODUCTION
FOR YOUTH

You are the church! This is a great privilege and at the
same time a great responsibility.

One concern that many observers feel about the modern "Jesus Movement" among young people is that it has
sometimes had a strong antichurch emphasis. The "Jesus

People" are found on the streets witnessing. They are meeting in homes for Bible study.

All this is wonderful, and we thank God for it. But you need the church, and the church needs you! In our lesson today we shall see the value of Christian fellowship as it is to be found in the meeting of believers to work and worship together.

CONCEPTS FOR CHILDREN

1. Our memory verse speaks of "earthen vessels." This is another way of saying "earthenware," which is the material of which some of the bowls and containers in our mothers' kitchens are made. When our text says that we are made like earthen vessels it means that we are weak when it comes to obeying God's will.
2. Even though we are Christians, we still are not perfect, and we must fight against the sin in our lives all the time.
3. But God loves us so much that even when we sin against Him, He lives in our hearts. It is much like putting something very precious, like gold or diamonds, in a poor, cracked flower pot; except that with God's love in our hearts, it makes us better people, while putting something precious in a flower pot doesn't make the flower pot better.
4. We should always show love to others so they will feel God's love flowing out of our hearts and want to know God themselves.

THE LESSON COMMENTARY

I. Christian Character: Romans 12:1-5

A. Consecration: v. 1

Paul makes his plea for Christian consecration on the basis of "the mercies of God." Those mercies have been shown to us in our conviction for our sins, in the repentance that the Spirit works in our hearts, and climactically in the forgiveness of all the sins of the past.

The apostle writes: "I beseech you *therefore.*" This points back to what precedes. In its largest context this includes the first eleven chapters of the Epistle. It takes in God's mercies in justification (chaps. 3—5) and sanctification (chaps. 6—8). These all come to us in Christ. It is only in and through Him that God's mercies in salvation are experienced by men.

But the mercies must also include

the immediately preceding chapters (9—11), which tell of God's dealings with Israel. In spite of centuries of unbelief and disobedience, the promise is: "And so all Israel shall be saved" (11:26)—as a nation.

It is particularly Christ's sacrifice for us that moves us to give ourselves to Him. Alexander Maclaren says: "If we will open our hearts to the sacrifice of Christ, we shall be able to offer ourselves as thank offerings" (*Expositions of Holy Scripture,* "Romans," p. 229).

Paul says, "I beseech you." Martin Luther comments: "He does not say: 'I command!' for he is preaching to those who are already Christians."

For what does the apostle plead? "That ye present your bodies"— literally, "to present your bodies." The infinitive is in the aorist tense, which suggests a crucial commitment to Christ, a real crisis in Christian experience. R. C. H. Lenski says that the verb form used here means "present completely." And the term *body* stands for the whole person. What Paul is saying is this: "I plead with you as Christians, who have experienced God's mercies, to present your entire selves to God, right here and now, once and for all." Of course, this will be followed by daily commitment to Christ and His will.

We are to present ourselves to God as "a living sacrifice." The original expression means "a living slaughter sacrifice" (Lenski, *Interpretation of Romans*, p. 747). This reminds us of the truth emphasized so clearly in the sixth and eighth chapters of this Epistle: We have to die to live. We are crucified with Christ (Romans 6:6; Galatians 2:20), so that we may live in Him, our Risen Lord, the resurrection life of victory.

But God does not want a dead sacrifice. He is not looking for martyrs, but for living witnesses. In some ways it is easier to die for Christ than to live fully for Him day by day. This takes real consecration. The sacrifice of our lives must be "holy" and as such it will be "acceptable" to Him.

Anyone who has used different versions of the New Testament will have noticed a considerable variation in the translation of the last two words. The King James Version has "reasonable service." The American Standard Version (1901) has "spiritual service." The Revised Standard Version reads, "spiritual worship." The New American Standard Bible combines these two: "spiritual service of worship."

Which of these is correct? The answer is: "All of them!" The noun may be translated either "worship" or "service." This is reflected today in the fact that we call our Sunday session at church either "morning worship" or the "morning service." Worship is a form of service and service is a form of worship. The two should never be divorced.

Also the adjective *logicen* (cf.

"logical") can mean either "rational" or "spiritual." The context suggests that the latter is meant here.

B. Transformation: v. 2

The apostle goes on to warn his readers against being "conformed to this world." Phillips has expressed this idea vividly and beautifully in his translation: "Don't let the world around you squeeze you into its own mold, but let God remold your minds from within." This points up the fact that Paul is not talking about conformity in dress or other external matters. He is dealing with a far more important thing: We are not to be conformed to the world in our thinking. It is in our thought life, particularly, that we are to be different from the world.

The verb *transformed* is in the present tense of continuous action. The first verse deals with the crisis experience of complete consecration of ourselves to God. The second verse deals with the long process of daily transformation into the image of Christ. This should go on all our lives.

"Transformed" is a translation of the Greek verb from which we get the scientific term "metamorphosis." Paul is here calling for a spiritual metamorphosis. It is the same verb which is rendered "transfigured" in connection with Jesus' Transfiguration on the mount (Matthew 17:2; Mark 9:2). It occurs only one other place in the New Testament, II Corinthians 3:18, where it is translated "changed." These passages, taken together, suggest that as Christians we are to live "the transfigured life."

According to Romans 12:2, how does this spiritual transfiguration take place? It is "by the renewing of your mind." What we think molds our whole personality. In fact, our thoughts write their stories on our faces. Charles Reznikoff put it well: "The fingers of your thoughts are molding your face ceaselessly." If we think joyous, loving thoughts, our faces will have a happy, kind look on them that will help to attract people to our Christ. It is a great tragedy that so many Christians have a solemn, if not sour, look on their faces most of the time. Someone has well said: "Religion that makes people look sick will not cure the ills of the world."

It is only as we think God's thoughts, by prayerful meditation on His Word, that we can know "what is that good, and acceptable, and perfect, will of God." This is the goal of Christian living.

C. Humility: v. 3

This is a primary virtue in Christian character. Jesus emphasized it more than any other. Paul followed his Master in this. In Philippians 2:3 he writes: "Let nothing be done through strife or vainglory; but in lowliness of mind let each esteem other better than themselves." Then he goes on to say: "Let this mind be in you, which was also in Christ Jesus" (v. 5). And what was that mind? It was the mind of humility (vv. 6-8).

So here the apostle writes: "For I say . . . to every man that is among you, not to think of himself more highly than he ought to think." What is humility? This passage indicates its true nature. It is not self-deprecation. It is not striking a pious pose, overwhelmed with our humility! It is not taking a Mr. Milquetoast attitude toward life. No, it is something far different from all of these. Humility is simply honest self-appraisal! It is refusing to think of ourselves more highly than we ought to think. Spiritually, it is recognition of the fact that we are nothing, and can do nothing of eternal value, apart from Christ. That truth alone should keep us truly humble. Instead of thinking proudly, we shall "think soberly"—literally, "have a sound mind." The proud person is out of his mind.

D. Unity: vv. 4-5

The church is the body of Christ (Ephesians 1:22-23). So it is symbolized by the human body. Paul reminds his readers that the physical body has many "members," with differing functions. Yet it is all one body. So it is with the church. Though it includes many people, yet we "are one body in Christ, and all members one of another." This being true, we ought to live in perfect unity as fellow Christians. When we fail to do so, we sin against Christ, our Head.

II. Christian Service: Romans 12:6-8

A. Gifts and Graces: v. 6a

Not all Christians have the same gifts, nor the same graces. God distributes these gifts according to His will. We should be thankful for the gift that He gives to us, and not covet someone else's gift.

B. Different Gifts: 6b-8

Here Paul mentions seven gifts that God gives to different individuals in the church: prophecy, ministry, teaching, exhorting, giving, ruling, showing mercy. In the New Testament, *prophesying* means "preaching." The term *ministry* is literally "service," "serving others" (Phillips). Teaching is an important ministry in the church, and should not be taken lightly. If called to that, whether in Sunday school, college, or seminary, we are to give it all we have. The word translated "exhortation" can be translated "encouragement." The exhorter seeks to encourage people to greater faith and obedience. The one who is able to give substantial funds to the church should do it with "simplicity"—better, "liberality." The one who "rules," or "presides," should do it with "diligence"—with earnestness or eagerness. The one who does merciful deeds to others should do it with "cheerfulness"—the Greek word used here gives us our word "hilarity." We should be joyous in our service to others.

It is the obligation of each Christian to ascertain what gift or gifts God has given to him and then to exercise them in the most effective way for the good of the church. This subject is dealt with at greater length in chapters 12—14 of I Corinthians. The implication is that each member of the body of Christ has some gift, and so a particular function and responsibility. When everyone finds his appointed place and fills it well, the work of the church moves on efficiently and effectively. When even one fails to do his duty, the whole body suffers.

III. Christian Fellowship:
    Romans 12:9-13

A. Brotherly Love: vv. 9-10

Love is the heart of Christianity. An unloving Christian is really not a Christian. But Paul warns his readers: "Let love be without dissimulation." The Greek says it is to be "unhypocritical." Hypocritical love is only a caricature. Only sincere love is true love.

The apostle goes on to say: "Abhor that which is evil; cleave to that which is good." We cannot hold on to the good unless we let go of the bad. We cannot love good unless we hate evil. God loves righteousness, but he hates sin. A holy God cannot do otherwise, and neither can His holy people.

Again we say, Christianity is a religion of love. Paul writes: "Be kindly affectioned one to another with brotherly love; in honour preferring one another." There is a beautiful relationship of holy love between fellow Christians that is unmatched anywhere else in the world. And all true love is unselfish love. So we sincerely seek the best good of others, rather than spending all our energies to promote our own interests. This is the real test of love. This shows whether it is "unhypocritical."

B. Caring for Others: vv. 11-13

In these three verses the apostle sums up some remaining Christian duties in short, punchy clauses. We are not to be "slothful in business." The word translated "business" actually means "zeal" or "earnestness." This should always be strong. "Fervent in spirit" is beautifully translated as "Be aglow with the Spirit" (RSV). In all these things we are to be "serving the Lord." "Rejoicing in hope" and "patient in tribulation" go very naturally together; it is our hope that gives us "patience," or better, "endurance." But all of this requires us to "steadfastly maintain the habit of prayer" (Phillips). Then Paul adds two other items that were especially important in the culture of that day, though still significant: "Distributing to the necessity of saints; given to hospitality."

Since Christian love is unselfish love, it involves caring for others who need our help. This is one of the evidences of genuine Christianity.

IV. Christian Unity:
    I Corinthians 12:12-13

A. Many Members: v. 12

In the twelfth chapter of Romans, as we have already noted, Paul spoke of several gifts that God bestows on the members of His church. In this chapter we have another list.

We are told first that "there are diversities of gifts, but the same Spirit" (v. 4). If these gifts are administered in the Spirit, obviously there will be no clash or conflict. It is only when people are out of the Spirit that trouble ensues.

DISCUSSION QUESTIONS

1. What is the church?
2. Who are its members?
3. What difference should there be between the church and the world?
4. What are some of the functions of the church?
5. How are we as individuals related to them?
6. What should bind us together as one body?

Paul goes on to say that "there are differences of administrations [or, "ministries"] but the same Lord. And there are diversities of operations, but it is the same God which worketh all in all" (vv. 5-6). Then he lists: "word of wisdom . . . word of knowledge . . . faith . . . gifts of healing . . . working of miracles . . . prophecy . . . discerning of spirits . . . kinds of tongues . . . interpretation of tongues" (vv. 8-10). All these are given by the sovereign will of the Holy Spirit, "dividing to every man severally as he will" (v. 11). It is not our place to choose a gift or seek for a particular one. It is the Holy Spirit who dispenses them in accordance with the divine purpose.

Then Paul writes: "For as the body is one, and hath many members, and all the members of that one body, being many, are one body: so also is Christ." Unity in diversity and diversity in unity—this is the divinely planned pattern of the Christian community.

The apostle takes time to spell out distinctly the resemblance of the church to the physical body. The latter has "many members" as any good book on anatomy will make clear. By casual observation we are all conscious of the considerable number of which we are aware by our senses. Yet the entire complex is all one body. Then Paul makes the application: "so also is Christ." He is the head of a body which has many members, each with an assigned function.

B. One Body: v. 13

Both the diversity and the unity of the body were strongly stressed in verse 12. Here it is particularly the unity: "For by one Spirit we are all baptized into one body, whether we be Jews or Gentiles, whether we be bond or free; and have been all made to drink into one Spirit." In the church of Jesus Christ there is no distinction of race, color, culture, or economic status. When and where these distinctions are made, the church has ceased to be truly Christian.

Paul points up the absurdity of envy or ill-will between members of the church by illustrating this in the case of the physical body. Suppose the foot should say, "Because I am not the hand, I am not of the body; is it therefore not of the body?" (v. 15). Similarly, if the ear should say, "I am not the eye," does that make it any less a part of the body? The body could not function if it were all eye, ear, or nose. All the organs, with all their diversified functions, are needed if the body is going to live normally.

Again the apostle asserts: "But now are they many members, yet but one body" (v. 20). So the eye has no right to say to the hand or to the foot, "I don't need you."

The climax of the apostle's comparison comes in the statement that when one member suffers, all the rest of the body suffers with it. So we should have real compassion for each other and seek to avoid hurting each other.

CONTEMPORARY APPLICATION

We are the church wherever we are! Too many people think of the church as confined to a single building and meeting at a certain hour on Sunday morning. But we are just as much the church when at work as when at worship. The church exists on Monday as truly as it does on Sunday—or does the "church" disappear for the week?

The truth of the matter is that we cannot escape being the church all the time and everywhere. We not only represent the church in the sanctuary on Sunday, but much more significantly at the office or shop or school on Monday. What image of the church do people derive from our daily lives?

LIVING VICTORIOUSLY IN SOCIETY

DEVOTIONAL READING	Romans 13:8-14

ADULTS	Topic: *Living Victoriously in Society* Background Scripture: Romans 12:14—13:14 Scripture Lesson: Romans 12:14—13:1 Memory Verse: *Love does no wrong to a neighbor; therefore love is the fulfilling of the law.* Romans 13:10
YOUTH	Topic: *What Can I Do in Secular Society?* Background Scripture: Romans 12:14—13:14 Scripture Lesson: Romans 12:14—13:1 Memory Verse: *Love does no wrong to a neighbor; therefore love is the fulfilling of the law.* Romans 13:10
CHILDREN	Topic: *Bringing People Together* Background Scripture: II Corinthians 5:16—6:10 Scripture Lesson: II Corinthians 5:17-20 Memory Verse: *All this is from God, who through Christ reconciled us to himself and gave us the ministry of reconciliation.* II Corinthians 5:18
DAILY BIBLE READINGS	Mon., Nov. 5: Overcome Evil with Good, Romans 12:14-21. Tues., Nov. 6: The Christians in the State, Romans 13:1-7. Wed., Nov. 7: Put on the Armor of Light, Romans 13:8-14. Thurs., Nov. 8: Walk by the Spirit, Galatians 5:15—6:10. Fri., Nov. 9: Walk in Love, Ephesians 5:1-4. Sat., Nov. 10: Be Subject to One Another, Ephesians 5:21-33. Sun., Nov. 11: Blessed Are the Peace Makers, Matthew 5:3-11.
LESSON AIM	To see how a Christian should live in a secular society.
LESSON SETTING	Time: About A.D. 56 Place: The Epistle to the Romans was evidently written at Corinth, near the end of Paul's third missionary journey.

Living Victoriously in Society

LESSON OUTLINE

I. **Living in Love:** Romans 12:14-17
   A. Blessing for Cursing: v. 14
   B. Compassionate Sympathy: v. 15
   C. Humility and Unity: v. 16
   D. Kindness and Honesty: v. 17

II. **Living in Peace:** Romans 12:18-21
   A. With All Men: v. 18
   B. No retaliation: v. 19
   C. Returning Good for Evil: v. 20
   D. Overcoming Evil with Good: v. 21

III. **Living in Obedience:** Romans 13:1-14
   A. Obey Authority: v. 1
   B. Be in Subjection: vv. 2-5
   C. Pay Your Taxes: vv. 6-7
   D. Love Your Neighbor: vv. 8-10
   E. Walk Honestly: vv. 11-14

SUGGESTED INTRODUCTION FOR ADULTS

Can one live victoriously in modern society? This is a very pertinent question. How are we answering it?

In last week's lesson (Romans 12:1-13) we studied Paul's admonitions to Christians about their relation to the church, to their fellow believers. But in today's lesson (Romans 12:14—13:14) he deals with the Christian in relation to a non-Christian society in which he lives.

Admittedly, the apostle's instructions about how to treat our brothers and sisters in the Lord call for complete consecration on our part and the Holy Spirit's presence filling our hearts with divine love. The standards are high, and without the constant supply of supernatural grace we could not possibly meet them.

But the same is true of our relation to those outside the Christian community. The fact is that most Christians spend more time with non-Christians than with fellow Christians. This is due to the demands of work or school. During the week we have to rub shoulders day after day with those who do not care about spiritual things. What is to be our attitude toward them? If we are to have a redemptive witness to them we must treat them with fairness and Christian kindness.

SUGGESTED INTRODUCTION FOR YOUTH

What can I do in a secular society? That is a crucial question for every young Christian. Can he be spiritual in an unspiritual environment?

Probably there never was a time in recent history when it was more difficult for young people to live clean, Christian lives than right now. There are many more avenues of temptation confronting the present generation than any previous generation. Between pot and pornography, the youth of our day are bombarded on every side. Can they take it? Can you take it?

The simple answer is that in your own strength you cannot. But you can be more than conqueror through Christ (Romans 8:37). With Him you can win.

CONCEPTS FOR CHILDREN

1. To be reconciled means to become friends again after we have had a disagreement with someone. We can become God's friends by believing that Jesus died for our sins so that God now accepts us as His children for Jesus' sake.
2. As God forgives us when we pray, we should forgive those who tell us they are sorry they have offended us.
3. When everyone lives a forgiving life, everyone is happier and it is easier to work with each other.

THE LESSON COMMENTARY

I. Living in Love:
   Romans 12:14-17

A. Blessing for Cursing: v. 14

There is perhaps no greater test of our Christian experience than our reaction to those who curse us. Do we return "tit for tat"? Do we give our enemy "just what he deserved"? Or do we return love for hate, kindness for cruelty, graciousness for persecution? This is the way to prove that we have God's grace in our hearts and that our religion works.

All of us have to suffer persecution in some way. In the first generation of the church it was largely from the synagogue. In the latter part of the first century and during the second century it was increasingly from the Roman rulers. With us today it is mainly social pressure. People may treat us with contempt if we do not conform to their worldly patterns. They may actually berate us or apply economic pressures on us. There are many forms that persecution can take besides physical harm. Sometimes these more refined types are harder to take in love.

B. Compassionate Sympathy: v. 15

There is no way that we can get close to people and help them more than by showing real sympathy, enter-ing into their heartaches and sharing their sorrows with them. This is a redemptive ministry in which all Christians can participate, for there is no more effective witness we can give than a loving concern for those who are in need. People's hearts are wide open at such times, and we can walk right in with Christ to minister to them.

But it is also important that we rejoice with those who are rejoicing. To congratulate people on their successes or share their joy in the coming of a baby to the home may open the way for leading them to the Lord. At such times our witness can be far more effective.

C. Humility and Unity: v. 16

Paul writes: "Be of the same mind one toward another." Lenski says that this means "having in mind for another the same thing that under like circumstances one has in mind for oneself." He continues: "I am to want you to have what, if I were in your position, I should want myself to have" (*Interpretation of Romans*, p. 775).

The middle sentence of this verse has caused much discussion. The King James Version reads: "Mind not high things, but condescend to men of low estate." But the American Standard Version (1901) has: "Set not your mind on high things, but condescend to things that are lowly." Which is the correct meaning?

The answer this time is that we cannot be sure. The word translated "lowly" is an adjective in the Greek that can be either masculine or neuter. Since the same form is used for both (in the dative case), we cannot say dogmatically which is intended.

Sanday and Headlam comment: "The neuter seems best to suit the contrast with *ta hypsela* ("high things") and the meaning of the verb" (*Romans*, p. 364). On the other hand, James Denney writes: "Elsewhere in the New Testament (seven times) *tapeinos* (lowly) is only found in the masculine, and so some would render it here: condescend to *men* of low estate; let yourself be carried along in the line of *their* interests, not counting such people beneath you." He notes that some prefer to take the adjective as neuter, and then concludes: "The first of the two alternatives impresses me as much more in harmony with the nature of the words used than the other" (*Expositor's Greek Testament*, II, 693).

Since it is impossible to be certain which of the two translations is correct, some modern versions put one in the text and the other in the margin. The best way for us as readers of the Bible is to apply both interpretations to ourselves. The first is well expressed by Phillips: "Don't become snobbish but take a real interest in ordinary people." We should always be willing to "associate with the lowly" (RSV), as Jesus did constantly.

But there is also an important message in the other interpretation. One way of putting it is this: "Accept humble tasks" (Goodspeed). It can equally well be rendered: "Accommodate yourselves to humble ways" (Weymouth). Similarly, the Berkeley Version says: "Adjust yourselves to humble situations." It has even been translated: "Be content (or, satisfied) with lowly things."

It is obvious that all these ideas are very relevant to Christian living. We are to be content with the simpler things of life and not crave what is expensive. But also we are to associate with humble people and do it without any attitude of condescension. True humility is one of the surest evidences of Christian character. And so the apostle warns: "Be not wise in your own conceits."

D. Kindness and Honesty: v. 17

The Christian is not to pay back "evil for evil." As Denney says, "Nothing can justify revenge." When we seek to give "tit for tat" we are not acting like Christians. This is true, no matter who wrongs us. This important admonition has its application in the home, at church, and among our friends, as well as in our relation to the outside world.

But along with this kindness must go honesty or goodness. Literally the second sentence of this verse reads: "Providing good things in the sight of all men." Phillips renders it: "See that your public behavior is above criticism."

This factor in Christian living cannot be emphasized too much. When we stoop from what is "excellent" (Lenski) or "noble" (RSV) to low practices or attitudes, we deny our Lord.

II. LIVING IN PEACE: Romans 12:18-21

A. With All Men: v. 18

This verse has often been misinterpreted. It tells us: "If it be possible, as much as lieth in you, live peaceably with all men." We hear someone say, "Yes, but it doesn't lie within me to live in peace with So-and-So!"

But that is no alibi, no way of escape. For what the verse really means is: "If possible, *so far as it depends upon you* . . . ." That is, the occasion of the quarrel is not ever to come from our side. Denney comments: "Over others' conduct we have no control; but the initiative in disturbing the peace is never to lie with the Christian" (*Expositor's Greek Testament*, II, 694).

Alexander Maclaren expounds it thus: "These words are, I think, unduly limited when they are supposed to imply that there are circumstances in which a Christian has a right to be at strife. As if they meant: Be peaceable as far as you can; but if it be impossible, then quarrel. The real meaning goes far deeper than that. . . . We cannot determine whether our relations with men will be peaceful or no; we are only answerable for our part, and for that we are answerable. . . . Your part is to be at peace; it is not your part up to a certain point and no further, but always, and in all circumstances, it is your part. It may not be possible to be at peace with all men; there may be some who *will* quarrel with you. You are not to blame for that, but their part and yours are separate, and your part is the same whatever they do. . . . Don't you quarrel with them even if they will quarrel with you" (*Expositions of Holy Scripture*, "Romans," pp. 298-99).

In other words, there is no place for quarreling in the Christian life. For, as the old adage says, "It takes two to make a quarrel."

B. No Retaliation: v. 19

We are not to avenge ourselves, "but rather give place unto wrath." Probably the true meaning is: "Leave it to the wrath of God" (RSV), or "Leave a place for divine retribution" (NEB). Sanday and Headlam explain it: "Give room or place to the wrath of God." That is, "Let God's wrath punish" (*Romans*, p. 364). Similarly, Denney comments: "The wrath spoken of, as the following words show, is that of God; to give place to God's wrath means to leave room for it, not to take God's proper work out of His hands" (*Expositor's Greek Testament*, p. 694).

This principle of no retaliation was emphasized strongly by Jesus in the Sermon on the Mount. The Christian is not to practice the old rule, "An eye for an eye, and a tooth for a tooth," but to forgive, and show love to all, even his enemies. In line with verse 14 above, Jesus said: "Bless them that curse you, do good to them that hate you, and pray for them which despitefully use you, and persecute you" (Matthew 5:44).

C. Returning Good for Evil: v. 20

Jesus said, "Love your enemies." Paul, in spelling this out a bit more, writes: "Therefore if thine enemy hunger, feed him; if he thirst, give him drink: for in so doing thou shalt heap coals of fire on his head." This is quoted from Proverbs 25:21-22.

What is the purpose of "heaping coals of fire" on the head of an enemy or one who has wronged us? Some have suggested—certainly facetiously—that they would gladly do a kind deed to an enemy if it would burn his head! But that is the kind of legalism that has no love in it and so is not Christian. Others have thought that we are to be consoled by the assurance that the enemy will be punished for his evil deed. But this is not Christian, either.

Sanday and Headlam point to the proper interpretation: "Coals of fire must, therefore, mean, as most commentators since Augustine have said, 'the burning pangs of shame,' which a man will feel when good is returned for evil, and which may produce remorse and penitence and contrition" (*Romans*, p. 365).

D. Overcoming Evil with Good: v. 21

"Be not overcome of evil, but overcome evil with good." The primary application of this is noted by Sanday and Headlam: "Do not allow yourself to be overcome by the evil done to you and be led on to revenge and injury, but conquer your enemies' evil spirit by your own good disposition." But then they add: "A remark which applies to the passage just concluded and shows St. Paul's object, but is also of more general application" (*Romans*, p. 365).

It is this more general application that we should like to note. Actually, this verse contains one of the greatest secrets of success in Christian living. It is especially important for young people, but equally applicable to all ages.

The best way to overcome temptation is not to struggle with it. Whatever gets our attention gets us. When we concentrate on anything, it becomes more powerful in its influences on us.

The simple truth is this: The harder we try to push a thought out of our minds the more persistent it becomes. But the solution is simple; and best of all, it works. Replace that bad thought with a good thought! We can only think of one thing at a time, unless we are mental jugglers. If we fill our minds with good thoughts, there will be no room for the bad ones.

For teen-agers and many young adults the evil thoughts will often be related to physical desire. To concentrate on these thoughts, even in a desperate effort to resist them, may only result in the increasing of physical desire, so that one's plight worsens.

What is the answer, then? Not to try to forget or banish these thoughts. Rather, just turn away from them and begin immediately to think of some good, pleasant experience. The more exciting and enjoyable it is, the more effective it will be in gaining full possession of our minds and crowding out the bad thoughts. We should recall

as vividly as possible this pleasurable experience, until it grips and holds us safe in its grasp. Later we may wonder where those evil thoughts went.

For older people it may not be unclean thoughts but unkind thoughts—which are actually unclean in God's sight. As soon as our minds begin to dwell on critical thoughts about someone else, we should immediately shift to something else. One way to do this is to recall some pleasant association with this person in the past that will help to mitigate the present criticism. Perhaps the best way to dispel unkind thoughts about another is to begin to pray for that person. It is hard to feel unkind toward someone when you are praying for him. And when we are on our knees in the presence of the Lord, some supposedly big faults in others begin to look rather picayunish.

So the best way to overcome evil thinking is not to fight it but to forget it. And the fastest and most effective way to do this is to replace it with good, positive thinking.

The applications of this verse reach into every area of life. Are we accused unjustly? The best way to silence slander is to live a good life that is obviously above reproach. And it is not only in the realm of thinking, but also in that of action that we can overcome evil with good. If we find ourselves tempted to do something wrong or even unwise or wasteful, the best solution is to keep busy doing what is good. If our lives are filled every day with worthwhile, productive activity, there will be little opportunity for wasting time or using it wrongfully.

The old saying is still true: "The devil finds work for idle hands to do." Those who are constantly busy doing good have little temptation to do wrong.

DISCUSSION QUESTIONS

1. How does our relationship to God affect our relationship to man?
2. How are we to measure what is good in modern society?
3. Why should we not avenge ourselves?
4. How can we influence society to be more Christian?

III. LIVING IN OBEDIENCE: Romans 13:1-14

A. Obey Authority: v. 1

There are two outstanding passages in the New Testament on the relation of the Christian to his government. One is found here in Romans 13:1-7. The other is in I Peter 2:13-17. Both Paul and Peter simply spell out more specifically the principles that Jesus laid down in this matter.

The first verse gives the general command: "Let every soul be subject unto the higher powers." The Christian is not to resist governmental authority, but submit to it. This is because "there is no power but of God: the powers that be are ordained of God." This does not mean that every government official is God's choice for that position. That would certainly not be true. But it does mean that the fact of government is ordered by God. Without governmental authority there would be chaos. No one would be safe anywhere. Violence and crime would control our cities. We must have government in any orderly society.

B. Be in Subjection: vv. 2-5

Since government is divinely ordained, whoever resists its authority is resisting God. The result will be condemnation (v. 2).

As a regular thing, "rulers are not a terror to good works, but to the evil." There have been exceptions, of course, as in the case of the Roman emperors who persecuted the Christians.

Some people feel that they cannot submit to the government because it is the instrument of evil. But what about the first generation of Christians to whom Paul and Peter wrote? Surely the Roman administration was at least as godless as the government under which we live. Yet those early believers were commanded to submit to Roman rule.

Of course it is recognized that God is the supreme authority for every Christian. When the government issues orders contrary to Christian conscience, the individual must refuse to obey. But this seldom happens.

C. Pay Our Taxes: vv. 6-7

This principle is laid down clearly here. But Jesus had already enunciated this divine prescription (Luke 20:25). We are obligated to pay taxes to support the government that serves and protects us.

D. Love Your Neighbor: vv. 8-10

Jesus called this the "second commandment" (Matthew 22:39). It summed up the second tablet of the Decalogue, which spelled out man's duties to his fellowmen. When we love our neighbor as ourselves we fulfill the law (v. 10).

E. Walk Honestly: vv. 11-14

Putting the prophetic telescope to his eyes, Paul declared that the night of man's sin would soon end; the day of God's righteousness would dawn. Meanwhile we should walk honestly with each other.

CONTEMPORARY APPLICATION

To live victoriously in our contemporary society we must maintain right relationships to both our fellow Christians and the outside world. In all cases these relations must be governed by holy, unselfish love. There is a sense in which we have an obligation to all men, as our world shrinks in size. That responsibility is to apply the principles of Christ to every area of our lives. Thus we can live victoriously and redemptively.

November 18, 1973

THE STRONG AND THE WEAK

| DEVOTIONAL READING | Romans 14:13-23 |

ADULTS

Topic: *The Strong and the Weak*

Background Scripture: Romans 14; I Corinthians 8:1-11:1

Scripture Lesson: Romans 14:1-4; I Corinthians 8:7-13

Memory Verse: *We who are strong ought to bear with the failings of the weak, and not to please ourselves.* Romans 15:1

YOUTH

Topic: *Don't Trip Your Brother*

Background Scripture: Romans 14; I Corinthians 8:1—11:1

Scripture Lesson: Romans 14:1-4; I Corinthians 8:7-13

Memory Verse: *We who are strong ought to bear with the failings of the weak, and not to please ourselves.* Romans 15:1

CHILDREN

Topic: *Love Within the Church*

Background Scripture: Romans 12:3-13; I Corinthians 13:1-13

Scripture Lesson: Romans 12:9-10; I Corinthians 13:4-7, 13.

Memory Verse: *Faith, hope, love abide, these three; but the greatest of these is love.* I Corinthians 13:13

DAILY BIBLE READINGS

Mon., Nov. 12: We Live to the Lord, Romans 14:1-9.
Tues., Nov. 13: Helping Our Brothers, Romans 14:10-23.
Wed., Nov. 14: Bear with the Failings of Others, Romans 15:1-13.
Thurs., Nov. 15: Supporting the Weaker Brother, I Corinthians 8:1-13.
Fri., Nov. 16: Plowing in Hope, I Corinthians 9:1-11.
Sat., Nov. 17: Winning Men for Christ, I Corinthians 9:15-23.
Sun., Nov. 18: God Is Faithful, I Corinthians 10:1-13.

LESSON AIM

To help us see what our attitude should be toward our weak brother.

LESSON SETTING

Time: About A.D. 55 or 56

Place: Romans was written in Corinth; I Corinthians in Ephesus.

82

The Strong and the Weak

LESSON OUTLINE

SUGGESTED INTRODUCTION FOR ADULTS

It is easy for those who are strong to feel condescending, if not actually contemptuous, toward those who are weak. But this is not a Christian attitude. Instead of contempt, we should always feel compassion toward others, and especially toward those who need help.

This operates in every area of life. People who are physically strong look down on those who have weak bodies. It is true that some people "enjoy ill health," partly because it gets them extra attention and relieves them of the responsibility of working. Some of these have changed dramatically to good health when they took a job or assumed a challenging task. But we must not forget that many people enter life with congenital defects or weaknesses. Such persons deserve compassion, not contempt.

Again, a person who is mentally acute is apt to be impatient with those who seem slow and dull. What we always need to remember is that the masses of people around us may well have been deprived of our advantages in heredity and environment.

But our lesson deals particularly with the attitude of those who are strong spiritually toward those who are weak spiritually. Here, as in all other areas of life, the rule is that thoughtful, unselfish love should govern all our attitudes and actions.

SUGGESTED INTRODUCTION FOR YOUTH

Don't trip your brother! This is the main thrust of today's lesson.

Suppose you have a buddy in school. He comes from a strict home or church; so he has strict standards. There are some things he believes a Christian shouldn't do, while you think they are all right. What are you going to do about it?

There are several paths you could take. You might make fun of his conscientious scruples. Of course, that would be utterly cruel and unchristian. Or you might say nothing, but do as you please, flaunting your liberty in his face. This might cause him to join you, violate his own conscience, and so stumble spiritually. The proper path, of course, is to avoid putting a stumbling block in his way.

CONCEPTS FOR CHILDREN

1. Paul's great poem on love (I Corinthians 13) was written to a church whose members were not showing love to each other.
2. Love alone can bring people who are fighting each other to become friendly again. This is true for children and children as well as for children and parents.
3. If we truly love one another we will be willing to treat others as we want them to treat us.

THE LESSON COMMENTARY

I. THOSE WHO ARE WEAK IN FAITH: Romans 14:1-4

A. Accepted, Not Criticized: v. 1

We think of weak Christians as those who are easily tempted to do wrong and who are unstable in their experience. But the term *weak* as used here means "overscrupulous." Sanday and Headlam write: "'Weakness in faith' means an inadequate grasp of the great principle of salvation by faith in Christ; the consequence of which will be an anxious desire to make this salvation more certain by the scrupulous fulfilment of formal rules" (*Romans*, p. 384). In other words, these weak Christians are the same as what we today call "legalists," those who make a fetish of adherence to external rules and regulations.

In a similar vein Denney comments: "The weak man is one who does not fully appreciate what his Christianity means; in particular, he does not see that the soul which has committed itself to Christ for salvation is emancipated from all law but that which is involved in its responsibility to Him. Hence his conscience is fettered by scruples in regard to customs dating from pre-Christian days" (*Expositor's Greek Testament*, II, 700). Denney thinks that the "weak" may

have been primarily Jewish converts, while the "strong" were Gentile Christians. This may well be the case, at least in part.

Legalists usually think that they are the strongest Christians. But Paul here exposes the fallacy of this. When we give primary emphasis to externals it shows that actually we are unspiritual.

Paul instructs the church at Rome to "receive" the weak believers into its fellowship. Why? Because Christ has received us, unworthy as we all are. The apostle expresses it this way: "Wherefore receive ye one another, as Christ also received us to the glory of God" (15:7). The church should have room for many different types of personalities in its membership. While discretion must be observed in taking in new members, equal care should be taken not to exclude those who love the Lord and sincerely want to do His will. We should be willing to "receive" such with a warm welcome and make them feel wanted in our fellowship. An "offish" spirit is unchristlike.

What is meant by "not to doubtful disputations"? Denney defines it: "Not with a view to deciding (or passing sentence on) his doubts." He adds: "The strong, who welcome him to the fellowship of the Church, are to do so unreservedly, not with the purpose of judging and ruling his mind by their own" (*Expositor's Greek Testament*, II, 701). Similarly Sanday and Headlam say: " ... but not to pass judgments on their thoughts. Receive them as members of the Christian community, but do not let them find that they have been merely received into a society in which their somewhat too scrupulous thoughts are perpetually being condemned" (*Romans*, pp. 384-85).

Godet gives a different slant to this phrase. He says it means: " ... but do not get by this very reception into debates ... which would terminate in the end only in vain reasonings" (*Romans*, p. 454). This is nearer to what seems implied in the King James Version.

Luther makes the admonition go both ways: "That is, no one should judge the opinion or conviction of the other" (*Commentary on Romans*, p. 180). The strong should not judge the weak, nor the weak judge the strong. Each should respect the opinion of the other. This is in keeping with verse 13: "Let us not therefore judge one another any more." Paul in his Epistles gives strong emphasis to the necessity of Christian unity. This demands that we do not criticize or judge each other.

B. Vegetarians vs. Meat-eaters: vv. 2-3

The question of vegetarianism is still with us. There are many Christians who feel that one is better off both physically and spiritually if he avoids eating meat. Some groups teach this strongly.

An illustration might be pertinent at this point. Some years ago an athlete who was winning honors in running felt called to the ministry and went to seminary. But he continued to exercise under the supervision of his coach.

One weekend he went out to preach. On Monday he ran his daily mile as usual, timing himself as always. When he reported his time to the coach, the latter exploded. It was the worst the young fellow had done in years. The coach demanded to know what he had been doing that weekend.

Here was the explanation: "I stayed in the home of some people who had religious scruples against eating meat. So I ate only vegetables Saturday and Sunday."

The coach's orders were crisp: "Get yourself a good steak dinner tonight and eat another steak for lunch tomorrow. Then run the mile and report to me." The result: right back in prime shape again and on target. Those misguided vegetarians made their innocent victim not only weak spiritually, according to Paul's definition here, but also weak physically!

So the apostle writes: "For one [the "strong"] believeth that he may eat all things: another, who is weak, eateth herbs." Vegetables are an important part of a healthful diet; but a properly balanced diet requires more proteins, such as are found in meat or fish.

Those who believe that eating meat is not pleasing to God have not read their Bibles carefully. After the Flood God said to Noah and his sons: "Every moving thing that liveth shall be meat for you; even as the green herb have I given you all things" (Genesis 9:3). The only stricture was against eating blood (v. 4).

Furthermore, Paul condemns as heretics those who command people to "abstain from meats, which God hath created to be received with thanksgiving of them which believe and know the truth." He continues: "For every creature of God is good, and nothing to be refused, if it be received with thanksgiving: for it is sanctified by the word of God and prayer" (I Timothy 4:3-5). People have a right—and an obligation—to eat what is scientifically good for them, but they have no Scriptural foundation for making a religious scruple of it.

How are vegetarians and meat-eaters to treat each other? Paul writes: "Let not him that eateth despise him that eateth not; and let him which eateth not judge him that eateth: for God hath received him" (v. 3). If the Lord receives people, we should receive them too. That is what Paul says in the opening verses of this chapter, although many churches have not obeyed this admonition.

C. Not to Be Judged: v. 4

Jesus said, "Judge not, that ye be not judged" (Matthew 7:1). Paul echoes this principle. Particularly here, the "strong" are not to judge the "weak." God is the Master of both; He alone has the right—and the ability—to judge. The "weak" person we might be tempted to knock down, God is able to make stand.

II. THE NATURE OF THIS WEAKNESS:
Romans 14:5-9

The "weak" person is the one who "esteemeth one day above another." The "strong" person is the one who "esteemeth every day alike" (v. 5). The reference is probably to the fasts and feast days of Judaism. The believer is freed from the obligation to observe these. He is a free man in Christ. But, says Paul, "Let every man be fully persuaded in his own mind." That is, we must do what we believe to be right.

In verse 6 the apostle declares that the one who observes the prescribed fasts and feasts does it "to the Lord," and the same is true of the one who ignores these. The meat-eater eats "to the Lord, for he giveth God thanks." Likewise the vegetarian who abstains does it "to the Lord," and also "giveth God thanks." Both should be respected.

A great principle is expressed in verse 7: "For none of us liveth to himself, and no man dieth to himself." There is a real sense in which this is a universal principle of life. We are all related to other human beings, so that none of us can live in complete isolation. But the next verse seems to sug-

gest that here Paul is thinking primarily of believers, who are vitally related to Christ.

III. HOW THE STRONG SHOULD TREAT THE WEAK:
Romans 14:10-19

Paul warns his readers that they must not judge their Christian brothers, "for we shall all stand before the judgment seat of Christ." He is the Judge; all men are under His judgment. When we judge our fellow Christians, we arrogate to ourselves the prerogatives of deity. This we dare not do! We must leave the judgment to Him. He knows all the facts—the motives as well as the deeds and words—so that He alone is capable of judging fairly. We do not know the motives of people and so should refrain from passing judgment on them.

Instead of judging others we should be concerned not to "put a stumblingblock or an occasion to fall" in any brother's way. This is one of the most serious sins we can commit. For this affects not only our own salvation but that of someone else.

Paul then comes back to the problem of eating meat. He declares: "I know, and am persuaded by the Lord Jesus, that there is nothing unclean of itself: but to him that esteemeth any thing to be unclean, to him it is unclean" (v. 14). This shows that the "weak" were primarily Jewish Christians, who were making a distinction between clean and unclean foods. In Christ all such distinctions have been done away, abolished at the cross.

But we still have to be careful not to offend other Christians and cause them to stumble. So Paul again sounds a warning: "But if thy brother be grieved with thy meat, now walkest thou not charitably. Destroy not him with thy meat, for whom Christ died" (v. 15). We are not to parade our liberty in the Lord in such a way as to harm a fellow Christian in his spiritual life. To do so is to sin against him.

It is a good thing to be free in Christ; in fact, it is the best thing that can happen to us. But the apostle admonishes us: "Let not then your good be evil spoken of" (v. 16). If our liberty in Christ brings reproach to His name, we should restrain ourselves for the sake of others.

Verse 18 points up vividly the difference between the old religion of Judaism and the new religion of Christianity. Paul writes: "For the kingdom of God is not meat and drink; but righteousness, and peace, and joy in the Holy Ghost." True religion is not a matter of externals, such as eating and drinking. It is entirely an internal, spiritual thing. It is "righteousness"—a right relation to God and to all our fellowmen. It is "peace," which can only come from righteousness. And we must never forget that it is also "joy." A joyless religion is only a caricature of Christianity. If we do not manifest joy in our lives we are denying Christ. Real joy is always the fruit of righteousness and peace. This verse gives us a striking description of the nature of true religion.

The closing verses of this chapter sum up what Paul has been emphasizing throughout. He writes: "Let us therefore follow after the things which make for peace, and things wherewith one may edify another" (v. 19). Literally the Greek says: "Let us then keep on pursuing the things of peace and the things of mutual upbuilding."

And so our conduct should always be governed by consideration for others. We should not be the occasion for a Christian brother violating his conscience. The conclusion of the whole matter is found in the first verse of chapter 15: "We then that are strong [free in Christ] ought to bear the infirmities of the weak, and not to please ourselves." That is the Christian attitude.

IV. A WEAK CONSCIENCE:
I Corinthians 8:7-8

The First Epistle to the Corinthians deals with a number of problems that had arisen in the church at Corinth. In the first six chapters Paul discusses three of these, about which he had heard: divisions, immorality, and lawsuits. Then in chapter 7 he says: "Now concerning the things whereof ye wrote unto me." The first question he dealt with was marriage (chap. 7). In chapters 8—10 he discusses whether Christians should eat meat that had been offered to idols and then put on sale in the public market. He affirms that "an idol is nothing in the world, and that there is none other God but one" (v. 4).

But he goes on to say: "Howbeit there is not in every man that knowledge; for some with conscience of the idol unto this hour eat it as a thing offered unto an idol; and their conscience being weak is defiled" (v. 7). The person with a "weak" (overscrupulous) conscience thinks that the meat has been contaminated religiously by having been offered to an idol. For him to eat it, then, would be to violate his conscience.

All this points up an important fact about the nature of the human conscience. Our consciences do not tell us what is right or wrong. They simply tell us not to do what we believe to be wrong. As has often been said, conscience is the monitor of the soul. But it has to be educated as to what is really wrong. The person with a "weak" conscience thinks some things are wrong that in God's sight have no moral or spiritual significance.

DISCUSSION QUESTIONS

1. What responsibilities do the "strong" have toward the "weak"?
2. How is true strength demonstrated?
3. What are some areas in which there may be a difference of individual consciences?
4. What is the importance of time in the education of conscience?
5. How is love related to knowledge?
6. How did Christ show us the way in this?

A "strong" conscience is an enlightened conscience that only condemns us when we do something that is really wrong. Eating meat or refraining from eating it makes no difference whatever spiritually, as Paul affirms in verse 8.

V. THE CHRISTIAN ATTITUDE TOWARD THE WEAK: I Corinthians 8:9-13

A. Thoughtfulness and Forbearance: vv. 9-11

Again Paul sounds a warning: "But take heed lest by any means this liberty of yours become a stumbling block to them that are weak." Just because we have a strong conscience that does not get bogged down in the minutiae of legalism, it does not mean that we are free to cause our weaker brother to stumble and fall. The fact that Paul reiterates this warning in both Romans and in I Corinthians shows how important he felt it to be. Our liberty must always be limited by the rights of others.

The apostle then pictures a specific scene to make his point clear. Suppose a brother with a weak conscience sees you, who have a strong conscience enlightened by "knowledge," eating in an idol temple. He may "be emboldened to eat those things which are offered to idols" (v. 10). Paul asks:

"And through thy knowledge shall the weak brother perish, for whom Christ died?" (v. 11). We must live redemptive lives. And this means not only that we try to lead sinners to Christ but that we do nothing to cause those that are in Christ to fall away from Him.

B. Christian Charity: vv. 12-13

Once more the apostle points out the seriousness of using our Christian "liberty" in such a way that it causes someone to be led astray. He says: "But when ye sin so against the brethren, and wound their weak conscience, ye sin against Christ." And that is the last thing that any sincere believer would want to do. Paul is pleading with us to weigh carefully the consequences of our actions. What may be, in itself, perfectly all right for us to do would be actually sinful if it causes some brother in Christ to stumble and fall.

There is no greater statement of large-hearted, unselfish charity than that expressed in the last verse of this chapter. Paul declares: "Wherefore, if meat make my brother to offend, I will eat no flesh while the world standeth, lest I make my brother to offend." That is total consecration. It is putting kingdom interests ahead of all personal desires. This is being a real Christian.

CONTEMPORARY APPLICATION

The Church of Jesus Christ consists of all those who by faith have accepted him as Savior and Lord. Within this fellowship there are people with many different temperaments and differing ideas. But we must learn to live together if we are to be truly Christian.

This takes kindness and forbearance, understanding and sympathy, love and compassion. It means that we think of others as well as ourselves, that we seek their best good. It means putting Christ first, others second, and ourselves last. We show our real strength by our care for others.

November 25, 1973

ALWAYS OF GOOD COURAGE

DEVOTIONAL READING	II Corinthians 4:1-15

ADULTS	Topic: *Always of Good Courage*
	Background Scripture: II Corinthians 4:1—5:10
	Scripture Lesson: II Corinthians 4:16—5:5
	Memory Verse: *We know that if the earthly tent we live in is destroyed, we have a building from God, a house not made with hands, eternal in the heavens.* II Corinthians 5:1

YOUTH	Topic: *Don't Lose Heart*
	Background Scripture: II Corinthians 4:1—5:10
	Scripture Lesson: II Corinthians 4:16—5:5
	Memory Verse: *We know that if the earthly tent we live in is destroyed, we have a building from God, a house not made with hands, eternal in the heavens.* II Corinthians 5:1

CHILDREN	Topic: *Love for Neighbors*
	Background Scripture: Romans 12:14—13:10
	Scripture Lesson: Romans 13:1-8
	Memory Verse: *He who loves his neighbor has fulfilled the law.* Romans 13:8

DAILY BIBLE READINGS	Mon., Nov. 19: Rooms in the Father's House, John 14:1-8.
	Tues., Nov. 20: The Good News You Received, I Corinthians 15:1-11.
	Wed., Nov. 21: If Christ Be Not Risen, I Corinthians 15:12-19.
	Thurs., Nov. 22: Christ the First Fruits, I Corinthians 15:20-28.
	Fri., Nov. 23: How Are the Dead Raised? I Corinthians 15:35-41.
	Sat., Nov. 24: It Is Raised in Glory, I Corinthians 15:42-50.
	Sun., Nov. 25: The Mortal Puts on Immortality, I Corinthians 15:51-58.

LESSON AIM	To show how we can always be of good courage because of what Christ has done for us and is now doing in us.

LESSON SETTING

Time: II Corinthians was written about A.D. 55.

Place: II Corinthians was written somewhere in Macedonia, probably at Philippi.

Always of Good Courage

   I. We Faint Not: II Corinthians 4:1-6

  II. This Treasure in Earthen Vessels:
       II Corinthians 4:7-11

 III. All Things for Your Sakes: II Corinthians 4:12-15

LESSON OUTLINE

 IV. The Temporal vs. the Eternal:
       II Corinthians 4:16-18
       A. The Outward Man vs. the Inward Man: v. 16
       B. Momentary Affliction vs. Eternal Glory: v. 17
       C. The Seen vs. the Unseen: v. 18

  V. The Earthly vs. the Heavenly: II Corinthians 5:1-5
       A. Our Earthly Tabernacle: v. 1
       B. Clothed with Immortality: vv. 2-4
       C. The Earnest of the Spirit: v. 5

 VI. Walking by Faith, Not by Sight:
       II Corinthians 5:6-10

SUGGESTED
INTRODUCTION
FOR ADULTS

The fourth chapter of II Corinthians is one of the most striking passages in Paul's Epistles. And it becomes even more striking when we read Phillips' translation of it.

During the Second World War, J. B. Phillips was in charge of a large group of young people in southeast London. As the German blitzes intensified, the people were spending long nights in bomb shelters. They needed the comfort of God's Word.

Phillips was reading the Bible to his parishioners to give them assurance of God's care. But he found that the King James Version, with its old-fashioned English, did not communicate adequately. So he began making a fresh translation from the original Greek of the New Testament and reading parts of it to his people each week. He began with Paul's Epistles. The Bible came alive for his listeners.

We would suggest that you begin the class session this week by reading, or having some capable person read, Phillips' translation of II Corinthians 4:1-15, the assigned devotional reading for this lesson. If it was already read in the opening exercises in the King James Version, this will do no harm. The vigor and freshness of Phillips' rendering will shine out all the more clearly.

SUGGESTED
INTRODUCTION
FOR YOUTH

Don't lose heart! That is the message of today's lesson. And it is a word that young people today need to hear. Many are becoming discouraged, disheartened, and disillusioned. They need to know that in Christ there is victory and worthwhileness in life.

If you haven't tried using one of the recent translations of the New Testament, we would suggest you do so. Good News for Modern Man and The Living Bible are both very readable. They are free paraphrases, however, and are not so reliable as The New American Standard Bible, which adheres very closely to the original. These recent versions of the Bible will help this lesson come alive with fresh meaning.

CONCEPTS FOR CHILDREN

1. "They will know we are Christians by our love." This is the ideal we must strive for. How much influence we have in the world will depend directly on how well we attain this ideal.
2. The basic way to fulfill God's law is to love our neighbor.
3. Love goes beyond the law: the law says we may not harm; love says we must help.

THE LESSON COMMENTARY

I. WE FAINT NOT:
II Corinthians 4:1-6

On his second missionary journey Paul had spent a year and a half at Corinth, longer than at any other place so far, founding a strong church there (Acts 18:11). Corinth was a great commercial metropolis, with sailors and travelers from all over the Roman Empire walking its streets. Today one can walk on the very pavement on which Paul walked in the first century. The outstanding feature pointed out to modern visitors is the large number of taverns that lined its main streets. The impressive ruins of ancient Corinth are mute testimony to a depraved citizenry.

The apostle realized the importance of establishing a strong center of evangelism there, so that its influence would reach far and wide. But unfortunately the Corinthian temperament was proud, quarrelsome, and pseudo-intellectual. These characteristics showed up in the members of the growing congregation, as we learn from I Corinthians. The church at Corinth gave Paul more heartache and heartbreak than any other.

In his First Epistle to the Corin-

thians the apostle scored them sternly for their divisions, immorality, and lawsuits among church members. He hoped this would bring about a reform. But instead there was considerable negative reaction.

Paul had written the first letter from Ephesus, where he spent three years on his third missionary journey. From there he sent Timothy across the Aegean Sea to check up on things in the church at Corinth. Timothy had a gentle disposition, and the belligerent opponents of Paul in the Corinthian church defied his efforts to improve the situation. Evidently the apostle himself made a quick trip to Corinth but was rebuffed and humiliated. Finally, in desperation, he sent Titus, who had a stronger personality than Timothy.

Titus was apparently gone for a long time, leaving Paul with increasing concern as to what was happening at Corinth. The apostle describes his experience this way: "We would not, brethren, have you ignorant of our trouble which came to us in Asia, that we were pressed out of measure, above strength, insomuch that we despaired even of life" (II Corinthians 1:8). The burden of the situation in the Corinthian church had so depressed Paul that he almost died under the pressure of it.

Unable to wait any longer for Titus, Paul started out for Corinth, going by land. He describes what took place on the way: "Furthermore, when I came to Troas to preach Christ's gospel, and a door was opened unto me of the Lord, I had no rest in my spirit, because I found not Titus my brother: but taking my leave of them, I went from thence into Macedonia" (2:12-13). Though faced with a good opportunity for preaching at Troas, Paul was so restless that he could not settle down. He must find out what was taking place at Corinth. So he crossed over to Philippi in Macedonia, on the continent of Europe.

And there it happened. But we let Paul tell the story in his own words: "When we were come into Macedonia, our flesh had no rest, but we were troubled on every side; without were fightings, within were fears. Nevertheless God, that comforteth those that are cast down, comforted us by the coming of Titus" (7:5-6). That is, when the apostle first arrived at Philippi and didn't find Titus returning from Corinth, his fears about the situation there simply increased. He was burdened so much that his body had no rest or relaxation. Paul was human and very intense by temperament. He was deeply hurt by the vicious attacks made on him personally by some of the members at Corinth. He was concerned about the whole future of the church there.

Then the Lord came to his rescue. One day Titus arrived with good news from Corinth. The apostle was greatly comforted and relieved by this. Apparently he wrote II Corinthians at Philippi and sent Titus back to Corinth with it, to prepare the way for his own three months' visit there (Acts 20:1-2).

All this background is needed if we are going to understand the fourth and fifth chapters of II Corinthians, our lesson for today. In the furnace of deep affliction and discouragement the apostle had learned how to have good courage in facing difficult circumstances, how to trust God more fully.

The first thing he says is, "We faint not." It seems that he had almost fainted at Ephesus, Troas, and Philippi. But in spite of it all, or because of it all, he could now say, "Nothing can daunt us" (Phillips). The simplest translation is, "We do not lose heart" (RSV).

The first half of the second verse is rendered strikingly by Phillips: "We use no hocus-pocus, no clever tricks, no dishonest manipulation of the word of God." What Paul declared he did—and what all of us must do—is to let the Word of God speak to us as it will. We must not try to twist it around to suit our wishes. We have no right to make it say something we want it to say. All heresies are guilty of manipulating the Scriptures to support their theories. This we, as honest Christians, cannot do. We must not allow "the god of this world" (v. 4) to blind our minds, perverting our understanding.

As a true preacher of the gospel, Paul could write: "For we preach not ourselves, but Christ Jesus the Lord; and ourselves your servants for Jesus' sake" (v. 5). Those who seek to advance themselves for their own glory are not true servants of either God or their fellowmen.

Verse 6 is a beautiful description of what salvation does for us in this life. God, who first said "Light be! [and "Light was" (Genesis 1:3)] has shined in our hearts, to give the light of the knowledge of the glory of God in the face of Jesus Christ." It is in Jesus that we see God, and seeing Him are saved. Why do people want to live in darkness when they can dwell in the glorious light of God's presence within their hearts?

II. THIS TREASURE IN EARTHEN VESSELS:

II Corinthians 4:7-11

A Christian is a person in whom Christ lives and who lives in Christ.

But we have to realize the stark truth that we have "this treasure [Christ] in earthen vessels," or as Phillips says "in a common earthenware jar." That's what our bodies are, made from dust (Genesis 2:7). Even our human personality is very earthy. In a sense we are a combination of dust and deity. And sometimes we seem awfully dusty!

Since we are, so to speak, but earthenware jars in which Christ dwells, we should be very conscious "that the excellency of the power [is] of God, and not of us." We have nothing of which to boast.

Then Paul describes his own experience, which is paralleled in a measure in every Christian's life. He writes: "We are troubled on every side, yet not distressed; we are perplexed, but not in despair" (v. 8). Again Phillips puts it beautifully: "We are handicapped on all sides, but we are never frustrated; we are puzzled, but never in despair." This infers that when we are frustrated we are not trusting fully in God. We are denying Romans 8:28. Admittedly, we may be sorely tempted to have a feeling of frustration. But faith quickly rejects it.

Paul goes on to say: "Persecuted, but not forsaken; cast down, but not destroyed" (v. 9). Phillips has a characteristically striking translation of the last half of this verse: "We may be knocked down but we are never knocked out!" That expresses the truth graphically. Many a time life seems to knock the Christian to the floor. But to the man of real faith in Christ, life's blows never become knock-out blows.

In verse 10 the apostle sounds again the note that one must die in order to live: "Always bearing about in the body the dying of the Lord Jesus, that the life also of Jesus might be made manifest in our body." If we want to experience the life of victory in Christ, we must first die with Him on the cross (Galatians 2:20). There is no resurrection without a prior crucifixion. To put it most briefly, we cannot fully live *in* Christ until we have died *with* Christ.

Paul is also thinking of the constant threat of physical death that he faced as a Christian (v. 11). This made the life of Jesus even more manifest in his "mortal flesh."

III. ALL THINGS FOR YOUR SAKES:
II Corinthians 4:12-15

"So then death worketh in us, but life in you." What does the apostle mean? Apparently that his dying to his own will and accepting God's will had resulted in their being saved, and so having life in Christ. Spirit-empowered evangelism, whether "mass" or "personal," can only be carried on effectively by those who have died with Christ.

Because these Corinthians had found new spiritual life in Christ, Paul is assured that God who "raised up the Lord Jesus shall raise up us also by [rather, "with"] Jesus, and shall present us with you" (v. 14). As the apostle has already argued in I Corinthians 15, the resurrection of Jesus is the guarantee of our own resurrection.

Paul could say to these Corinthians that in his ministry "all things are for your sakes" (v. 15). The great apostle did not live for himself, but for others.

IV. THE TEMPORAL vs. THE ETERNAL:
II Corinthians 4:16-18

A. The Outward Man vs. the Inward Man: v. 16

The apostle repeats the statement he had made in the first verse of this chapter: "We faint not." In spite of persecution and threat of martyrdom for the faith, in spite of constant trouble and perplexity, in spite of all the hardships of his ministry, he had not lost heart. He was "always of good courage."

He recognized that his "outward man," his physical body, was decaying. There is a sense in which it can be said that in our bodies death sets in the moment life begins. As one gets older he becomes more conscious of this process of decay. A certain measure of it is probably inevitable in old age.

But there is a counter truth: "The inward man is renewed day by day." The life of Christ within us is not dying or decaying. With the passing of the years it becomes more vibrant, more alive.

B. Momentary Affliction vs. Eternal Glory: v. 17

For Paul to speak of his hardships and sufferings (see 11:24-28) as "light affliction" manifested true faith. But it also showed real insight into the proper standard of values. A casual onlooker might say that the apostle's life was filled with trouble and at least threatening tragedy. How could Paul call it "light affliction"? First, because it "is but for a moment." True, it had gone on for many long years. But—and this is the point—in the light of an endless eternity of bliss and blessing, these agonizing experiences were actually "but for a moment." The longest life on earth is only a fleeting, flitting moment in comparison with eternity.

In the second place, the apostle could speak of all his excruciating suffering as "light affliction" because it "worketh for us a far more exceeding and eternal weight of glory." The last expression, "weight of glory" may reflect the fact that in the Hebrew Old Testament the same verb means "to be heavy" (Job 6:3) and "to be glorious" (Job 14:21). In heaven we shall be literally loaded down with glory.

When we realistically face this fact we can endure whatever sufferings and hardships we may have to endure down here. It will all be abundantly compensated for in the next life. If we really believe this, we will not complain about our present experiences. We can accept anything that is God's will for us with the assurance that ultimately all will be well.

C. The Seen vs. the Unseen: v. 18

How do our afflictions help us to become more spiritual? It happens while we "look not at the things which are seen, but at the things which are not seen." As long as our whole attention is taken up with material things, we will be materialists. If we want to be spiritual, our major attention must be given to the unseen, spiritual values. What we see with our physical eyes is all temporal; it is only the unseen that is eternal.

The last part of this verse would seem to imply that matter is not eternal, that it will sometime be completely destroyed. It is only the spiritual that will last forever.

V. THE EARTHLY vs. THE HEAVENLY:
II Corinthians 5:1-5

A. Our Earthly Tabernacle: v. 1

The body in which we live down here is only a "tent"; that is what the word for "tabernacle" means. It is only pitched for a short time, and we "camp" in it for a few years at most. But we have "a building of God, an house not made with hands, eternal in the heavens."

We spend the major part of our money feeding, clothing, and housing this physical body. Probably most of this is necessary. But we are neglecting our souls, which will last forever? The great temptation in this temporal life

---

DISCUSSION QUESTIONS

1. What did Paul teach about the next life?
2. What does he say about our resurection body (I Corinthians 15:44)?
3. What is the importance of hope in the Christian life?
4. What gives us courage to face life?
5. How can we show that we believe in the reality of heaven?
6. What is the value of suffering?

is to let the material dominate us. We must refuse to let this happen, resolutely resisting all secularizing of the spiritual.

B. Clothed with Immortality: vv. 2-4

In the midst of all the aches and pains of these physical bodies, or even in their limitations of strength and endurance, we often wish we could exchange them for our glorified bodies. We are "burdened" (v. 4) with these bodies of flesh. We long for the day when mortality will be "swallowed up" by immortal life. That is the final goal of our salvation. Elsewhere Paul expresses it this way: "We ourselves groan within ourselves, waiting for the adoption . . . the redemption of our bodies" (Romans 8:23).

We do not know much about heaven. We don't need to! All we need to know is the way of salvation, so that we can be saved ourselves and also be used by the Lord in saving others. We know that heaven will be far beyond our fondest dreams, and that is enough.

C. The Earnest of the Spirit: v. 5

The one who has worked in our lives to bring all this about is God, who has given us "the earnest of the Spirit." This expression is also found in 1:22. In Ephesians 1:14 we read that the Holy Spirit is "the earnest of our inheritance until the redemption of the purchased possession." The Greek word for "earnest" (*arrabon*,

only in these three passages) means "a down payment or first installment." The Holy Spirit in our hearts is the down payment of our heavenly inheritance. What will heaven be like? It will be like those moments when the Holy Spirit makes the presence of Jesus most real to our hearts. For in heaven we shall live forever in His presence.

VI. WALKING BY FAITH, NOT BY SIGHT: II Corinthians 5:6-10

There is a sense in which as long as we are in these physical bodies we are "absent from the Lord" (v. 6). How do we know that the One we have never seen with our physical eyes really exists? Because "we walk by faith, not by sight" (v. 7).

Paul says that he would prefer to be absent from the body and present with the Lord (v. 8). In Philippians 1:23 he says that this would be "far better." But he immediately adds: "Nevertheless to abide in the flesh is more needful for you" (1:24). Apparently he felt the same way at this time. But at any rate, he writes to the Corinthians, "we labour, that, whether present or absent, we may be accepted of him" (v. 9). The all-important thing is to be in the center of God's will and so live that we please Him.

The fact we must never forget is that "we must all appear before the judgment seat of Christ" (v. 10). It is there that we shall all be judged on the basis of how we have lived in this life. Since that is true, we should constantly seek to do God's will.

CONTEMPORARY APPLICATION

If we are governed by what we see and hear with our physical senses, we cannot avoid being discouraged and disheartened. The only way that we can "always be of good courage" is to keep tuned to the spiritual and to look

through the eyes of our heart. As has often been said, "The outlook is bad, but the uplook is glorious." It is glorious as long as we keep our eyes on Jesus, who always leads us on to victory if we follow Him.

WHY THE GOSPEL OF JOHN?

DEVOTIONAL READING	John 1:29-34

ADULTS

Topic: *Why the Gospel of John?*

Background Scripture: John 1:6-13; 17; 20:30-31; 21:24-25

Scripture Lesson: John 20:30-31; 1:6-13; 17:1-3

Memory Verse: *These are written that you may believe that Jesus is the Christ, the Son of God, and that believing you may have life in his name.* John 20:31

YOUTH

Topic: *Why the Gospel of John?*

Background Scripture: John 1:6-13; 17; 20:30-31; 21:24-25

Scripture Lesson: John 20:30-31; 1:6-13; 17:1-3

Memory Verse: *These are written that you may believe that Jesus is the Christ, the Son of God, and that believing you may have life in his name.* John 20:31

CHILDREN

Topic: *Why Jesus Came*

Background Scripture: John 17

Scripture Lesson: John 17:3-10, 26

Memory Verse: *I made known to them thy name, and I will make it known, that the love with which thou hast loved me may be in them.* John 17:26

DAILY BIBLE READINGS

Mon., Nov. 26: A Witness to Jesus, John 1:6-11.
Tues., Nov. 27: "This Is the Testimony," John 1:19-23.
Wed., Nov. 28: To Make His Name Known, John 1:29-34.
Thurs., Nov. 29: To Bring Abundant Life, John 10:7-18.
Fri., Nov. 30: To Bring Peace, John 16:28-33.
Sat., Dec. 1: "That the World May Believe," John 17:17-21.
Sun., Dec. 2: "That You May Have Life," John 20:26-31.

LESSON AIM

To discover why the Gospel of John was written and what its purpose is.

LESSON SETTING

Time: The Gospel of John was probably written about A.D. 95, during the reign of the Roman Emperor Domitian.

96

Place: According to early church tradition, this Gospel was written at Ephesus, in the Roman province of Asia in Asia Minor, which is now Turkey.

Why the Gospel of John?

I. The Purpose of the Gospel: John 20:30-31
   A. The Profusion of Signs: v. 30
   B. The Purpose in Writing: v. 31

II. The True Light: John 1:6-13
    A. The Witness of That Light: vv. 6-8
    B. A Light to Every Man: v. 9
    C. The Light Rejected: vv. 10-11
    D. The Light Accepted: vv. 12-13

III. Christ's High-Priestly Prayer: John 17
     A. For Himself: vv. 1-5
        1. The Giver of Eternal Life: vv. 1-3
        2. The Restoration to Glory: vv. 4-5
     B. For His Disciples: vv. 6-19
     C. For His Church: vv. 20-26

This quarter is devoted to a study of the Gospel of John. The thirteen lessons seek to show who Jesus was, why He came to earth, and what He can be to us today.

There are three units. The first, entitled "The Son of God Came to Us," comprises lessons 1—4. It presents the purpose of John's Gospel and introduces major themes which are found throughout the book. The second, "The Son of God Active Among Us," discusses six topics in chapters 3—6. It includes examples of both the works and the teachings of Jesus. The third unit, "The Son of God Victorious for Us," covers the trial, death, and resurrection of Jesus. Out of seeming defeat came the greatest triumph of history. The main thrust of the Book, belief in Jesus Christ, is emphasized again in the last lesson.

The early church fathers tell us that the apostle John lived in Ephesus during the latter part of the first century, surviving until the time of Trajan (A.D. 98). It is thought that he wrote his Gospel near the end of this time, around A.D. 95.

The Gospel of Mark presents a moving picture of the public ministry of Jesus, changing rapidly from one scene to another. Matthew and Luke give us series of colored slides, thrown on the screen for us to look at more closely. But in John's Gospel we find a studied portrait of Christ, its lines drawn with loving care. After some sixty-five years of contemplation (A.D. 30-95), John the Apostle sat down to describe not only the Jesus he had walked and talked with for three years, but also the Christ He had come to know more and more intimately through the abiding Holy Spirit.

SUGGESTED INTRODUCTION FOR YOUTH

Why do we have four Gospels, or lives of Christ, in the New Testament? The answer is that no one human individual could possibly portray the many aspects of Jesus' character and ministry. Even a building has to be photographed on all four sides if one is to get an adequate knowledge of what it really looks like. How much more is this true when we are seeking to understand who and what Jesus is! The four Gospels present four pictures of Christ, the Son of God who became the Son of Man.

CONCEPTS FOR CHILDREN

1. Jesus is God brought near to us.
2. Jesus came to earth to help us know God.
3. Jesus is God's gift of love to the world.
4. God wants us to accept that gift into our hearts.

THE LESSON COMMENTARY

I. THE PURPOSE OF THE GOSPEL:
John 20:30-31

A. The Profusion of Signs: v. 30

The Synoptic Gospels refer to the miracles of Jesus as "powers," because they demonstrated the divine power of the Master, and "wonders," because they describe the effect of the miracles on the people who witnessed them. But John prefers another word, which literally means "signs"—though often translated "miracles" in the King James Version. John used this term because for him the miracles of Jesus "sign-ified" some spiritual truth, and also because they were signs or evidences of Jesus' deity.

John declared that Jesus did "many other signs" in the presence of His disciples, "which are not written in this book." Actually, John records only seven miracles of Christ, in contrast to several times that number in the other Gospels. And each of those seven miracles illustrated some spiritual truth. Here is a list of these "signs," with the lesson each teaches:

1. Turning the Water into Wine (chap. 2). The joy of the Gospel is better than the drabness of legalism.
2. Healing the Nobleman's Son (chap. 4). Jesus' divine power is not lim-

ited by space, time, or any other circumstance.
3. Healing of the Impotent Man at the Pool of Bethesda (chap. 5). Sin is a disease that paralyzes men's souls, but Christ can heal them.
4. Feeding the Five Thousand (chap. 6). Jesus is the Bread of Life.
5. Walking on the Water (chap. 6). With our hand in His, we can walk safely over life's troubled sea.
6. Healing the Man Born Blind (chap. 9). Sin blinds men's eyes to spiritual truth but Christ can open their eyes to see Him as Son of God and Savior.
7. Raising Lazarus from the Dead (chap. 11). Sin is death, but Jesus is "the resurrection and the life," now and forever, for those who believe on Him.

Besides the "many other signs," recorded and unrecorded, John tells us: "And there are also many other things which Jesus did, the which, if they should be written every one, I suppose that even the world itself could not contain the books that should be written" (21:25). This is an obvious hyperbole. But it is a striking truth, even though exaggerated for effect. Jesus lived a very busy life. In some three years of public ministry He accomplished more than any other man has in a long lifetime. Though He died in

His early thirties, His life was complete.

B. The Purpose in Writing: v. 31

Some people hang the house key at the back door. This is what John has done. The key to understanding his Gospel is found in this verse, which closes the main body of the Gospel. (Chapter 21 is in the nature of an Epilogue.)

The purpose of writing the Gospel is spelled out very clearly. John wrote "that ye might believe that Jesus is the Christ, the Son of God; and that believing ye might have life through his name." It will be seen that the purpose was twofold: first, to induce belief in the deity of Jesus, and second, to produce life as a result.

The main thrust of this Gospel is to demonstrate the deity of Jesus so that people will believe in Him. This again is twofold. They must believe that Jesus is "the Christ"; that is, the Messiah of the Jews, predicted in the Old Testament and awaited for so many centuries. But in the second place they must accept Him as "the Son of God," the only One who can save us from our sins. The deity of Jesus is the foundation doctrine of Christianity. If Jesus is not God as well as man, He cannot be our Savior.

But the Bible is never interested in theology for theology's sake. The purpose of belief is in order that we might have life.

A word needs to be said about the term *believe*. It is the key word of John's Gospel, occurring ninety-eight times. So it is important that we understand what it means.

D. L. Moody defined saving faith as (1) assent, (2) consent, and (3) laying hold. It is more than *assent* of the mind; it is the *consent* of the will. Too many people claim to be Christians on the basis of the fact that they give mental assent to the truths of Scripture. With their heads they believe that Jesus is the Son of God and that He died for their sins. But there is no moral consent to follow Christ in conformity to His will. Real faith is a commitment.

To believe is to obey. This is one of the most important facts to be faced in the Christian life. Faith and obedience cannot be divorced in experience. Unless we obey, we do not really believe. It is obedient faith that brings us into vital relationship with Jesus Christ as Savior and Lord.

The term *life* also calls for a word of comment. In John's Gospel *life* regularly means "eternal life." This is the fruit of genuine faith, as defined above.

II. THE TRUE LIGHT: John 1:6-13

A. The Witness of That Light: vv. 6-8

One of the several internal hints that John the Apostle, the son of Zebedee, is the writer of the Fourth Gospel is the fact that this important disciple of Jesus is never mentioned by name in this Gospel. In the Synoptics he is one of the inner circle of three—Peter, James, and John. He also plays a significant role in the early chapters of Acts. But in the Fourth Gospel he is anonymous. The only plausible explanation for this is that he was the writer of that Gospel.

Coupled with that is the fact that John the Baptist, so-called again and again in the other three Gospels, is always referred to in John's Gospel as simply "John"—because he is the only John named in this Book. So we read in verse 6: "There was a man sent from God, whose name was John" (cf. Matthew 3:1; Mark 1:4). This John "came for a witness, to bear witness of the Light that all men through him might believe" (v. 7). Always the purpose in John's Gospel is to induce belief in Jesus.

The author is careful to tell us that John the Baptist "was not that Light, but was sent to bear witness of that Light." This explicit denial may suggest that some of John's disciples were claiming that he was the Messiah. In Acts 19:3 we read about some of John's followers who had not heard about Pentecost. These were in Ephesus, the very city where John the Apostle was now writing his Gospel. Furthermore, in the second century we read of a John the Baptist sect. So the apostle, writing near the end of the first century, may have been sounding a note of warning against this heresy.

The use here of the word *Light* prepares us for the great declaration of Jesus in John 8:12: "I am the Light of the world." He is the only one who can dispel our spiritual darkness.

B. A Light to Every Man: v. 9

Jesus is described as "the true Light." The word *true* here means "real" or "genuine." Someone has suggested that here it means "divine" in contrast to human and earthly lights, some of which lead men astray.

There is no way of being sure whether "that cometh [literally "coming"] into the world" modifies "Light" or "man." Either way makes good sense. Throughout all human history Christ has lighted every man coming into the world, at least in a measure through conscience. But when He came into the world, in the Incarnation, He became even more fully "the true Light." He Himself declared: "As long as I am in the world, I am the light of the world" (9:5).

C. The Light Rejected: vv. 10-11

"He was in the world" may well refer to the presence of Christ as the eternal Logos before His incarnation. In a very true sense, He has always been "in the world" as the Creator and Sustainer of all life. But though the world was made by Him, yet "the world knew him not." People were ignorant of their Creator; they did not recognize Him.

"He came unto his own, and his own received him not" (v. 11). This translation in the King James Version is inadequate. For it gives the impression that "his own" in both clauses refers to the same thing, which is not the case. In the Greek original, "his own" in the first clause is neuter gender, while in the second clause it is masculine. The literal translation would be: "He came to His own things and His own people did not receive Him." Perhaps the best translation is: "He came to His own home, and His own family did not receive Him." His home was Palestine, the land promised to Abraham. His family was Israel; they should have welcomed Him as the promised Messiah. Instead the Jews rejected Him. He fulfilled the prophecies of their ancient Scriptures (our Old Testament), but still they refused to accept Him. This was the greatest tragedy in their long history.

It is far more unreasonable for people to reject Jesus today, after nineteen hundred years of Christian history. Christ has made good His claim to be the Son of God and the Savior of all who believe. His holy footprints are clearly seen in the sands of time. In country after country He has proved to be the true Light, dispelling the darkness and illuminating men's minds and hearts.

D. The Light Accepted: vv. 12-13

Though the Jewish leaders of that day rejected Jesus, yet many of the common people believed on Him. And so we are told that "as many as received him [tax collecters, sinners, Samaritans, prostitutes, the poor, as well as some from the higher and respected classes] to them gave He power to become the sons of God, even to them that believe on his name." The Greek word for "power" is not *dynamis* (Acts 1:8), from which comes "dynamite, dynamo, dynamic," but *exousia*, which means "right," "privilege," or "authority." All those who accept Jesus as Savior are accepted by God as His children. It is as simple as that!

"Received him" is further defined as "believe on his name." Faith is reception. As we have already indicated, believing must be a matter of the heart as well as of the head. To believe on His name is to accept Him for what His name declares Him to be—Messiah, Savior, Lord. It is not just believing that He is the Savior of the world, but accepting Him as our personal Savior. It is not just believing that He is Lord over the universe, but accepting Him as Lord of all in our lives. Those who thus believe in Jesus become God's children.

John makes much of the New Birth, which is described more fully in chapter 3. But here he says that those who believe in Jesus are "born, not of blood, nor of the will of the flesh, nor of the will of man, but of God" (v. 13). This means: not of physical life, nor of natural instinct, nor of human will. The Jews trusted in their physical birth as descendants of Abraham to make them children of God. One of the distinctive emphases of John's Gospel is that a person enters the family of God only through a spiritual birth.

Jesus spelled this out more explicitly in His conversation with Nicodemus. To that famous teacher of religion the Master said, "Except a man be born again, he cannot see the kingdom of God" (3:3). In answer to Nicodemus's incredulous query, Christ explained: "Except a man be born of water and of the Spirit, he cannot enter into the kingdom of God" (3:5). That is, the New Birth includes cleansing and spiritual renewal. Then Jesus asserted, "Ye must be born again" (3:7). Why? Because "that which is born of the flesh is flesh; and that which is born of the Spirit is spirit." There is only one way to enter this physical world and that is by a physical birth. Just as truly, there is only one way to enter the spiritual realm and that is by a spiritual birth. The logic of this is so clear and incontrovertible that it is difficult to understand why so few people recognize the absolute necessity for the New Birth. To all today Jesus still says, "You must be born again."

III. CHRIST'S HIGH-PRIESTLY PRAYER:
John 17

A. For Himself: vv. 1-5

1. The Giver of Eternal Life: vv. 1-3

The Gospel of John divides itself quite naturally into two parts. Chapters 1—12 tell of Jesus' ministry to the world; chapters 13—21, of His ministry to His own. All four Gospels emphasize the fact that toward the close of His life on earth the Master concentrated on preparing His disciples to carry on after He went back to heaven.

So chapter 13 describes the Last Supper in the upper room at Jerusalem. Chapters 14—16 give the Last Discourse of Jesus. This is followed by Christ's high-priestly prayer in chapter 17.

He began by saying, "Father, the hour is come." At the wedding feast in Cana of Galilee He had said to His mother, "Mine hour is not yet come" (2:4). Again we are told that the Jewish leaders tried to arrest Jesus, "but no man laid hands on him, because his hour was not yet come" (7:30). This statement is repeated in 8:20: "No man laid hands on him; for his hour was not yet come." It is obvious that "his hour" was the time when He was to culminate His earthly ministry with His sacrificial death on the cross.

And so we find a startling change at 12:23, where Jesus declares: "The hour is come, that the Son of man should be glorified." He had just offered Himself to the Jewish people as their Messiah, in His so-called Triumphal Entry into Jerusalem (12:12-16). That this was intended as a Messianic act is shown by the quotation from Zechariah 9:9 in verse 15: "Fear not, daughter of Zion: behold, thy King cometh sitting on an ass's colt." But the religious leaders of the nation rejected Him (v. 19), and so His death became inevitable. The Triumphal Entry on Sunday marked the beginning of Passion Week. For Jesus it was the beginning of the end, as far as His earthly ministry was concerned. His "hour" had now come.

And so instead of repeated denials that His hour had come, we find repeated affirmations that it had. The story of the Last Supper begins in John's Gospel with the statement; "Now before the feast of the passover, when Jesus knew that his hour was come that he should depart out of this world unto the Father, having loved his own which were in the world, he loved them unto the end" (13:1). Jesus was very much aware of the fact that His days on earth were numbered.

Men were about to hold Jesus up to scorn and ridicule. Only a few hours later they would mock Him, spit on Him, slap His face, whip Him with the cruel Roman scourge, and then climax this with the disgraceful death on a cross. He would be the One who above all others would be "despised and rejected of men; a man of sorrows, and acquainted with grief" (Isaiah 53:3).

It was on the eve of His crucifixion, facing ignominy and shame, that Jesus prayed to His Father: "Glorify thy Son." But it was not a selfish prayer, for He added: "That thy Son also may glorify thee."

The Father had given Him "power [literally, "authority"] over all flesh, that he should give eternal life to as many as thou hast given him." Regard-ing Christ's authority, Westcott writes: "He received a legitimate authority (*exousia*) over humanity as its true Head, and this could only be exercised in its fulness after the Ascension. At the same time the exaltation of the Son as Saviour carried with it the glorification of the Father, as the spring of the eternal life which Christ sent through the Spirit from heaven" (*John*, p. 238). As "the last Adam," Christ is the federal head of the human race (I Corinthians 15:45). But He actually becomes the Savior of only those who believe. Westcott comments further: "The contrast implied in *all flesh* and *all that has been given* marks a mystery of the divine working which we cannot understand. The sovereignty is universal, the present blessing is partial" (p. 239).

What is eternal life? Here John defines it this way: "And this is life eternal, that they might know thee the only true God, and Jesus Christ whom thou hast sent" (v. 3). Knowledge of God means life. But this is more than knowledge *about* God. It is knowing Him personally as our Father and knowing Jesus Christ as our own Savior and Lord. Such intimate, vital fellowship *is* eternal life. For one cannot know God this way and at the same time be lost.

2. The Restoration to Glory: vv. 4-5

As He came to the end of His ministry, Jesus could say to the Father: "I have glorified thee on the earth; I have finished the work which thou gavest me to do." Will we be able to say this when *we* come to the end of life's trail down here? It is a sobering thought.

Then Jesus prayed: "And now, O Father, glorify thou me with thine own self with the glory which I had with thee before the world was" (v. 5). What was this glory? Probably the best answer to this is given in Philippians 2:5-11. Christ "emptied himself" (KJV, "made himself of no reputation") of the divine splendor He enjoyed in heaven in order that He might come down into this world of sorrow,

---

DISCUSSION QUESTIONS

1. In writing his Gospel, what were some of the advantages that John had over Matthew, Mark, and Luke?
2. What did an early church father mean when he said that after the other three wrote "bodily Gospels" of Jesus, John wrote a "spiritual Gospel"?
3. What is the importance of right belief?
4. What does it mean to believe in Jesus?
5. What kind of life do we find in Jesus?

suffering, and sordid sin. So He was praying that the glories of the heavenly realm might be restored to Him. That this prayer was answered is plainly declared by Paul when he writes: "Wherefore God also hath highly exalted him, and given him a name which is above every name" (Philippians 2:9). Jesus received a royal welcome on His return to heaven!

B. For His Disciples: vv. 6-19

In a few hours Christ was to give His life for the salvation of sinners of all time and every place. But in this great prayer as High Priest He was representing especially His own—those who believe on Him. So He says: "I pray for them: I pray not for the world, but for them which thou hast given me; for they are thine" (v. 9). He is leaving the world, but the disciples must remain in it, with all its danger, hardship, and temptation. And so the Master prays that His own may be kept. While He was with them He had kept them, and not one of them was lost except "the son of perdition" (v. 12)—Judas Iscariot. Christ did not pray for His disciples to be taken out of the world but to be kept from its evil—or "the evil one" (v. 15).

Twice Jesus declares of His disciples: "They are not of the world, even as I am not of the world" (vv. 14, 16). We are to be *in* the world but not *of* it. Every genuine Christian knows what this means. We still live in the midst of selfish, sinful men, who want their own way rather than God's way, but we do not share their spirit.

Verse 15 contains an important truth for us as Christ's disciples. He does not want us to isolate ourselves from society. In a very real sense we can only win people to the Lord as we become involved with them in love and helpfulness. Jesus was constantly involved with people. This was the only way He could have a redemptive ministry toward them, and it must be so with us.

C. For His Church: vv. 20-26

The third division of the prayer begins with these words: "Neither pray I for these alone, but for them also which shall believe on me through their word" (v. 20). Jesus was concerned for His church that was to come into being at Pentecost.

There are three main petitions that Jesus made for His own. Twice He prayed for their *preservation* (vv. 11, 15). "Keep them" was His cry to the Father. Having lived on earth, He knew the dangers that faced His followers.

Next, He prayed for their *sanctification* (vv. 17, 19). They were to be sanctified "through thy truth: thy word is truth." True sanctification is always related to the Word of God; it is conformity to that Word. Christ continues: "And for their sakes I sanctify myself, that they also might be sanctified through the truth." Christ consecrated Himself to death on the cross to make possible our sanctification.

It is very significant that Christ prayed five times for the *unification* of His church—in verses 11, 21 (twice), 22, and 23. This was one of His greatest concerns as He faced the cross. May we help to see that that prayer is answered!

CONTEMPORARY APPLICATION

We have taken a preliminary look at "The Gospel According to John," as it is called in the early Greek manuscripts. It is John's portrayal of Jesus Christ, under the inspiration of the Holy Spirit. Through this Gospel men can see Jesus as the Son of God and the Savior of men.

Now the question confronts us: What is the Gospel according to me and according to you? How do we portray Jesus in our daily lives? Do people, looking at us, see the true Jesus reflected in our actions and attitudes?

December 9, 1973

WHO IS THIS JESUS?

DEVOTIONAL READING	John 1:35-45

ADULTS

Topic: *Who Is This Jesus?*

Background Scripture: John 1:29-51; 10:22-39

Scripture Lesson: John 10:22-39

Memory Verse: *I and the Father are one.* John 10:30

YOUTH

Topic: *Who Is This Jesus?*

Background Scripture: John 1:29-51; 10:22-39

Scripture Lesson: John 10:22-39

Memory Verse: *I and the Father are one.* John 10:30

CHILDREN

Topic: *Come and See*

Background Scripture: John 1:19-46

Scripture Lesson: John 1:35-46

Memory Verse: *We have found the Messiah.* John 1:41

DAILY BIBLE READINGS

Mon., Dec. 3: "The Lamb of God," John 1:35-42.
Tues., Dec. 4: The One of Whom the Prophets Wrote, John 1:43-51.
Wed., Dec. 5: "The Good Shepherd," John 10:22-30.
Thurs., Dec. 6: Doing the Works of the Father, John 10:31-42.
Fri., Dec. 7: The Manifestation of Life, I John 1:1-5.
Sat., Dec. 8: The Son of God, I John 5:1-5.
Sun., Dec. 9: A Living Hope, I Peter 1:3-9.

LESSON AIM

To see who Jesus is, as portrayed in the Gospel of John.

LESSON SETTING

Time: Jesus' teaching, as recorded in John 10:22-39 took place in December of A.D. 29.

Place: In the temple at Jerusalem

LESSON OUTLINE

Who Is This Jesus?

I. The Lamb of God: John 1:29-39
   A. The Sacrifice for Sin: vv. 29-34
   B. The New Leader: vv. 35-39

104

II. The Messiah: John 1:40-45
   A. The Testimony of Andrew: vv. 40-42
   B. The Testimony of Philip: vv. 43-45

III. The Son of God: John 1:46-49

IV. The Son of Man: John 1:50-51

V. One with the Father: John 10:22-30
   A. The Demand of the Jewish Leaders: vv. 22-24
   B. The Answer of Jesus: vv. 25-29
   C. The Declaration of Deity: v. 30

VI. The Miracle Worker: John 10:31-39
   A. Accused of Blasphemy: vv. 31-33
   B. Defended by Scripture: vv. 34-36
   C. Proved by Miracles: vv. 37-39

SUGGESTED INTRODUCTION FOR ADULTS

Who and what is Jesus? This is the most crucial question in Christian theology today as it has always been. If Jesus of Nazareth was merely a man, then Christianity is only one of many world religions and may be compared with them for relative strengths or weaknesses. But if Jesus was what He claimed to be, the Son of God and the only Savior of mankind, then Christianity is utterly unique and the only true religion. For no other great religion claims that its founder was divine—whether Confucius, Gautama the Buddha, Mohammed, or any other. Christianity stands alone in being founded by One who is the Creator of all life and the eternal Son of God.

How do we know that Jesus Christ is the Son of God? The New Testament declares this over and over again, from Matthew to Revelation. History supports the claim, for acceptance of Christ and His salvation has transformed millions of lives and changed many nations for good. Wherever vital Christianity has gone, society has been elevated to higher heights morally and spiritually.

But there is another witness, besides the New Testament and history. That is the inner witness of the Holy Spirit to our own consciousness. This is the final and undoubted confirmation.

One cannot be absolutely certain of the deity of Jesus because of anything he has heard or read. Full certainty comes only by the conviction of the Spirit of God, speaking to our inmost soul. His witness leaves no doubt, no uncertainty.

SUGGESTED INTRODUCTION FOR YOUTH

Young people today are reading all kinds of philosophies. Many have become enamored of Jean Paul Sartre and his nihilistic existentialism. Too often the result is that they are left without any faith in God or man. Such a plight is a living death, far worse than physical death.

Can there be any certainty in our philosophical, scientific age? For those to whom this question is crucial we would propose a simple procedure. Get down on your knees in honest humility and say: "Jesus, if you are the Son of God, speak to my heart and show it to me." Many have done this and contacted reality. We can *know* that Jesus Christ is the Son of God and our Savior.

| CONCEPTS FOR CHILDREN | 1. Jesus has a special love for children.
2. He wants them to know Him as their friend.
3. If we pray to Him, He will speak to our hearts.
4. Jesus is God's Son and wants to be our Savior. |

THE LESSON COMMENTARY

I. THE LAW OF GOD:
John 1:29-39

A. The Sacrifice for Sin: vv. 29-34

John the Baptist was having a tremendous ministry. Large crowds of people were coming from far and near to hear him, as we learn from the accounts in the Synoptic Gospels (cf. Matthew 3:5; Mark 1:5). The Jewish leaders at Jerusalem became concerned about this. So they sent priests and Levites to ask him, "Who are you?" (John 1:19).

John did not procrastinate or prevaricate. His immediate reply was, "I am not the Messiah" (v. 20). When asked if he was Elijah (cf. Malachi 4:5-6), he said, "I am not" (v. 21). Was he "that prophet" (cf. Deuteronomy 18:15)? His simple answer was "No." Then they said: "Well, who are you? We have to give an answer to those who sent us. What do you say about yourself?" He said, "I am the voice of one crying in the wilderness," as predicted by Isaiah (v. 23).

The investigating committee probed a bit further. "Why are you baptizing if you are not the Messiah, Elijah, or that Prophet?" (v. 24) Then John told them about One who "coming after me is preferred before me" (v. 27). This is the One we are studying about in today's lesson.

It was the next day that John saw Jesus coming toward him. At once he made the astounding announcement: "Behold the Lamb of God, which taketh away the sin of the world" (v. 29).

The reference is undoubtedly to the fifty-third chapter of Isaiah. There we read of the Suffering Servant of the Lord: "He is brought as a lamb to the slaughter, and as a sheep before her shearers is dumb, so he openeth not his mouth" (v. 7). Westcott comments: "But the idea of vicarious suffering endured with perfect gentleness and meekness, which is conveyed by the prophetic language (compare Jer. xi.19), does not exhaust the meaning of the image. The lamb was the victim offered at the morning and evening sacrifice. (Exod. xxix.38ff), and thus was the familiar type of an offering to God. And yet more, as the Passover was not far off (ii.12, 13), it is impossible to exclude the thought of the Paschal Lamb, with which the Lord was afterwards identified (xix.36. Cp. I Pet. i.19). The deliverance from Egypt was the most conspicuous symbol of the Messianic deliverance (Rev. xv.3; Heb. iii.3 ff.; Ezek. xx.33 ff); and 'the lamb' called up all its memories and its promises" (*John*, p. 20). John introduced Jesus as God's sacrificial Lamb that would take away the world's sin.

Then the Baptist went on to declare the preexistence of Jesus. Though John was six months older, he identified his relative from Nazareth as the one about whom he had already said (v. 15): "He that cometh after me is preferred before me: for he was before me" (v. 30). The last clause in Greek is particularly striking. Literally it reads: "because he was first of me." Westcott says of this clause: "It expresses not only relative, but (so to speak) absolute priority. He was first altogether in regard to me, and not merely former as compared with me" (*John*, p. 13) Perhaps the simplest translation is: "He was first of all and before me." Later Jesus Himself declared: "Before Abraham was, I am." John testified to the preexistence of Christ.

John admitted that he did not at first know who was the Messiah. But when God called him to his baptismal ministry, He told him: "Upon whom thou shalt see the Spirit descending, and remaining on him, the same is he which baptizeth with the Holy Ghost" (v. 33). This sign was fulfilled: "I saw the Spirit descending from heaven like a dove, and it abode upon him" (v. 32). So John testifies: "And I saw, and bare record that this is the Son of God" (v. 34). John was not left in doubt. Now he was certain that Jesus of Nazareth was the Messiah.

B. The New Leader: vv. 35-39

The next day John was standing with two of his disciples. Seeing Jesus walking nearby, he once more said, "Behold the Lamb of God!" When the two disciples heard this they turned and followed Jesus. It would appear that this was what John wanted them to do; perhaps he had already given them instructions to do so if Jesus appeared again.

Turning to the two men, Jesus asked them what they were looking for (v. 38). Courteously they addressed Him by the Hebrew title "Rabbi," which means "Teacher" (KJV, "Master"). Then they asked, "Where do you live?"

His reply was brief and to the point: "Come and see" (v. 39). They went with Jesus to the place where He was staying "and abode with him that day: for it was about the tenth hour." Unfortunately we are not certain what this means. Although the Jewish day extended from sunset to sunset, the hour of the day was usually reckoned from sunrise. This would make the tenth hour four o'clock in the afternoon, implying that the two stayed that night. But the Roman day began at midnight, as ours does. That would mean ten o'clock in the morning, implying that they remained with Jesus for the rest of the day. We cannot be sure which is meant. What we do know is that these men left John to follow a new leader, Jesus.

II. THE MESSIAH: John 1:40-45

A. The Testimony of Andrew: vv. 40-42

"One of the two which heard John speak, and followed him, was Andrew, Simon Peter's brother." Who was the other, who is unnamed? The obvious answer is that it was John, the writer of the Gospel, who never mentions himself by name.

Andrew "first findeth his own brother Simon, and saith unto him, We have found the Messiah, which is being interpreted, the Christ, And he brought him to Jesus." This was the finest thing that Andrew ever did. Little did he dream that his brother would become the leader of the apostles and would preach a sermon on the day of Pentecost that would result in three thousand people being saved. We need today more Andrews who will bring more Peters to the Master. In heaven Andrew will share in the rewards of Peter's great ministry. Just so today a quiet, unassuming layman, perhaps an obscure Sunday school teacher, can lead to Christ someone who will become an internationally known evangelist with multiplied thousands of converts. So it was with the Sunday school teacher, whose name few know, who contacted young D. L. Moody. Moody is credited with having won more souls to Christ than any other man up to that time. One of the thrills of bringing people to the Savior is that we never know what potential may be wrapped up in them. This is the great challenge not only to pastors and evangelists, but also to

Sunday school teachers and humble laymen. It is Opportunity Unlimited.

When Jesus saw Andrew's brother, He said to him: "Thou art Simon the son of Jona [rather, "John"]: thou shalt be called Cephas"—the Aramaic word for "stone." This man is better known as "Peter," from *petros* the Greek word for stone.

B. The Testimony of Philip: vv. 43-45

Because the religious climate of Jerusalem was not friendly to Jesus, He started out for Galilee. Finding Philip—we are not told where—He said to him, "Follow me." This means: "Become my disciple." It is the expression Jesus used in calling each of His disciples.

Those whom Jesus finds are to find others and bring them to Him. That is what Philip did. He found Nathanael and said to him: "We have found him of whom Moses in the law, and the prophets, did write, Jesus of Nazareth, the son of Joseph" (v. 45). In other words, "We have found the Messiah, about whom our Scriptures prophesy."

III. THE SON OF GOD: John 1:46-49

That Nazareth was held in low repute is shown by the response of Nathanael: "Can there any good thing come out of Nazareth?" It was part of the *kenosis* (self-emptying, Philippians 2:5-8) that Jesus should have His home in a little, despised village of Galilee.

Philip's answer was wise: "Come and see." That is all we can say today to those who doubt that Jesus is what we claim He is.

As Nathanael approached, Jesus greeted him as a sincere Israelite. Surprised, Nathanael asked, "How do you know me." Jesus said, "I saw you under the fig tree"—probably meditating and worshiping. Amazed at this evidence of divine knowledge Nathanael exclaimed: "Rabbi, thou art the Son of God; thou art the King of Israel."

IV. THE SON OF MAN: John 1:50-51

Jesus assured Nathanael that what had surprised him was only a small matter—"You will see greater things than these." Then He said, "Verily, verily" ("truly truly"). In the original Greek this is *Amen, amen.* This double expression is found only in John's Gospel (25 times) and is used for special emphasis with important statements. The Synoptic Gospels all have this single "verily" (*amen*) many times. In the rest of the New Testament the word is simply transliterated as "Amen" in the same way that we use the term today, usually at the end of doxologies or benedictions. An exception is Revelation 3:14: "These things saith the Amen." Jesus is God's "Amen" to us, the assurance that the divine promises are true.

What was the important statement in this case? "Hereafter ye shall see heaven open, and the angels of God ascending and descending upon the Son of man." The expression "the Son of Man" was one of the several titles for the Messiah, as Ethelbert Stauffer and others have shown. In the Gospels Jesus refers to Himself by this designation over eighty times.

The statement here is an echo of Jacob's vision at Bethel (Genesis 28:12). God's "angels"—the word means "messengers"—are "ascending and descending." They are already down here, ministering to us (Hebrews 1:14). The expression "ascending and descending upon the Son of man" suggests the great truth that Jesus Christ is the only bridge between God and man. He is the one whom Jacob saw as a ladder reaching from heaven to earth. It is only through Christ that any human being can come into God's presence.

In the narrative of this first chapter of John's Gospel, Jesus has been revealed successively as the greater Successor of John the Baptist (vv. 26-27), the Lamb of God (vv. 29, 36), the Son of God (vv. 34, 49), the Messiah (vv. 41, 45), the King of Israel (v. 49). And now He reveals Himself as the Son of man (v. 51), the One who had come in human form to reveal the Father.

V. ONE WITH THE FATHER: John 10:22-30

A. The Demand of the Jewish Leaders: vv. 22-24

In the first part of this tenth chapter we find two of the ten "I Am's" of John's Gospel—one of its distinctive features. Here we read: "I am the door of the sheep" (v. 7) and "I am the good shepherd" (vv. 11, 14). We shall note the other "I am's" in connection with Lesson 6.

Jesus declared that He was the only doorway into the kingdom of God. There is no other entrance. Those who refuse to come through Christ will find themselves forever outside the fold of God.

Two beautiful statements occur here. One is found in verse 9: "I am the door, by me if any man enter in, he shall be saved, and shall go in and out, and find pasture." Here is freedom of movement and a happy, contented life. These are found only in Christ.

The other statement is in verse 4: "And when he putteth forth his own sheep, he goeth before them, and the sheep follow him: for they know his voice." When we follow Him as obedient sheep, we find that our Good Shepherd always goes before us, leading us in the right way and protecting us from all danger.

Jesus also declared that as the Good Shepherd He would give His life for His sheep (v. 11). He made the significant assertion: "No man taketh it from me, but I lay it down of myself" (v. 18). Jesus' death was not forced on Him; He voluntarily gave Himself as the Sacrifice for our sins.

The reaction of the Jewish leaders, as usual, was one of unbelief and scorn. They said: "He has a demon and is crazy, why do you listen to him?" (v. 20). Others protested: "These are not the words of a demon-possessed person. Can a demon open the eyes of the blind?" So there was a division (v. 19).

Verse 22 gives us the setting for the discussion that followed. It took place in Jerusalem and it was at the time of the Feast of Dedication, in the winter. This is not one of the seven annual Jewish festivals described in Leviticus 23. In fact, it is not mentioned in the Old Testament. To find its origin we have to go to the intertestamental period.

In 168 B.C. Antiochus Epiphanes, king of Syria, decided to put an end to the Jewish religion. To the great horror of the Jews, he desecrated the altar of sacrifice in the Temple by offering on it a pig, the outstandingly unclean animal in the eyes of God's people. The result was the Maccabean revolt. The Maccabees finally defeated the Syrian soldiers and regained possession of the Temple area. In December of 165 B.C. they cleansed the Temple ceremonially and rededicated it. In the time of Christ this significant event was commemorated annually in the Feast of Dedication. Today this festival, held each December by the Jews around the world, is called Hanukkah, or the Feast of Lights.

Jesus was walking in the Temple, in Solomon's "porch," or colonnade. This was on the east side of the Temple area, just inside the outer wall. It had a roof supported by columns. It is later mentioned as a meeting place of the early Christians (Acts 3:11).

Here the Jewish leaders surrounded Jesus and demanded: "How long do you hold us in suspense? If you are the Messiah, tell us plainly" (v. 24). They wanted Him to commit Himself definitely in public.

B. The Answer of Jesus: vv. 25-29

Christ chided the Jews: "I told you, and ye believed not." Already He had applied to Himself Messianic terms. Then, too, the miracles that He performed were a witness to the fact that He was God's chosen Messiah. The reason the Jewish leaders did not believe in Him was that they were not His sheep. Then the Good Shepherd declared: "My sheep hear my voice, and I know them, and they follow me: and I give unto them eternal life; and they shall never perish, neither shall any man pluck them out of my hand" (vv. 27-28). Nor can anyone pluck them out of the Father's hand. As long as we remain in Christ, by faith and obedience, we are eternally secure.

C. The Declaration of Deity: v. 30

It is difficult to imagine a stronger statement of the deity of Jesus than His declaration here: "I and my Father are one." This means more than unity of purpose and aim; it means oneness of essential being. It is clearly indicated that the Jews understand it this way, and Jesus did not "correct" their interpretation, as some modern theologians would try to do. Jesus asserted unequivocally that He was God just as truly as the Father was. This doctrine of the deity of Jesus is the touchstone of orthodoxy. There is no true Christianity without a divine Savior. We can be saved only through faith in Jesus as the Son of God.

VI. THE MIRACLE-WORKER: John 10:31-39

A. Accused of Blasphemy: vv. 31-33

Shocked by Jesus' declaration of full deity, the Jewish leaders "took up

stones again to stone him." (The "again" refers back to 8:59.) Jesus reminded them that he had done many "good works," such as healing the impotent man at the Pool of Bethesda and giving sight to the man born blind. For which of these miracles were they stoning Him?

Their reply was that it was not for any good work, "but for blasphemy; and because that thou, being a man, makest thyself God" (v. 33). This shows that they understood Jesus' statement in verse 30 to be a claim to full deity. In the Mosaic law it was enjoined that anyone who was guilty of blasphemy should be put to death by stoning (Leviticus 24:16).

B. Defended by Scripture: vv. 34-36

In reply to their accusation, Jesus quoted from Psalm 82:6: "I said, Ye are gods." These words were said about the judges of Israel, who were divinely appointed to their office and represented God in judging the people. If they are called "gods," why did the present leaders accuse Jesus of blasphemy when He claimed to be the Son of God? It is an argument from the lesser to the greater. Because Jesus had been sent directly from the Father, He could claim to be God's Son in a unique sense. The leaders should have weighed His claims carefully instead of hastily condemning Him.

C. Proved by Miracles: vv. 37-39

Now Jesus directly challenged them: "If I do not the works of my Father, believe me not. But if I do, though ye believe not me, believe the works." If they refused to believe Jesus' words, they still had no right to reject the evidence of His works. These miracles were evidence of His deity. Jesus called them "works of my Father." They demonstrated not only divine power, but also divine love and compassion. "God is love" (I John 4:8, 16), and so Christ's acts of love were godly in the highest sense. He did not perform miracles in a sensational

---

DISCUSSION QUESTIONS

1. In what ways was Jesus "the Lamb of God"?
2. What is the meaning of *Messiah*?
3. Why did Jesus call Himself "the Son of man"?
4. In what sense is He "the Son of God"?
5. What was the purpose of Jesus' miracles?
6. What does it mean to believe in Jesus?

way, to draw attention to Himself. But when He saw a lame man, He healed him; when He saw a blind man, He gave him sight. These were all deeds of mercy, of compassionate love. But they were also proof of His deity.

Instead of accepting the evidence, the Jewish leaders once again rejected it. They simply refused to believe that Jesus was what He claimed to be, the Son of God. So again they tried to take Him, "but he escaped out of their hand" (v. 39). Because the opposition was so heavy in Jerusalem and His life was in constant danger there, Jesus left that area and went back to the east side of the Jordan River, where He would be relatively safe. There He could carry on His preaching, teaching, and healing ministry without interruption. It was not the time yet for His crucifixion.

But in that more isolated area "many resorted unto him" (v. 41). Their comment was: "John did no miracle: but all things that John spake of this man were true." John the Baptist had done a good job of preparing the way for Jesus by calling the people to repentance. Then he had introduced Jesus as the Messiah and stepped aside, letting Christ take the center of the stage.

The result of Jesus' ministry in Perea (across the Jordan) was that "many believed on him there" (v. 42). This is the twelfth time in the Gospel of John that we are told of people believing in Jesus. This has rightly been called "The Gospel of Belief" (see Dr. Merrill Tenney's book with that title).

The first time was after Jesus turned the water into wine (2:11). Again it is said that the disciples believed on Him (2:22). While He was at the Passover in Jerusalem "many believed in His name" (2:23). At the village of Sychar many Samaritans believed on Jesus because of the report of the woman and many more believed after hearing Him themselves (4:39, 41). When Jesus told the nobleman that his son was healed, the man believed His word; and later when he was informed that the healing had actually taken place, he and his whole house believed in Christ (4:50, 53). The eighth time was when people were forsaking Jesus because of His strong teaching. Turning to His disciples, He asked them if they were also going to leave Him. Peter rose to the occasion and declared the faith they had in their Master (6:69). At the Feast of Tabernacles "many of the people believed on Him" because of His miracles (7:31). After Jesus had declared that He was the Light of the world "many believed on him" (8:30). The eleventh time is in 9:38, where we read that the man born blind, when he learned that the One who had healed him was the Son of God, said, "Lord, I believe." Is this our response to Christ as He confronts us today?

CONTEMPORARY APPLICATION

On page 311 of his book *Jesus in the Gospels*, Saunders writes that man "either lives out of the emptiness of false existence or the fulness of true existence. The intolerant claim of the New Testament is that there is no authentic living that is not life in relationship to the One acknowledged to be the Maker and Master of his being. To live with God now is to move out of graceless subsistence into graceful existence."

In this lesson Jesus has been revealed as "God brought near." In Him, and only in Him, we can find our true existence in redemptive relationship to the eternal God.

December 16, 1973

BELIEF OR UNBELIEF?

<table>
<tr>
<td>DEVOTIONAL
READING</td>
<td>John 12:20-36a</td>
</tr>
<tr>
<td>ADULTS</td>
<td>Topic: Belief or Unbelief?

Background Scripture: John 3:16-21; 5:30-47; 12:37-50

Scripture Lesson: John 12:37-50

Memory Verse: He who believes in the Son has eternal life; he who does not obey the Son shall not see life, but the wrath of God rests upon him. John 3:36</td>
</tr>
<tr>
<td>YOUTH</td>
<td>Topic: What Difference Does It Make?

Background Scripture: John 3:16-21; 5:30-47; 12:37-50

Scripture Lesson: John 12:37-50

Memory Verse: He who believes in the Son has eternal life, he who does not obey the Son shall not see life, but the wrath of God rests upon him. John 3:36</td>
</tr>
<tr>
<td>CHILDREN</td>
<td>Topic: What Difference Does Trust Make?

Background Scripture: John 4:46-53; 5:30-47

Scripture Lesson: John 4:46-53

Memory Verse: All things are possible to him who believes. Mark 9:23</td>
</tr>
<tr>
<td>DAILY BIBLE
READINGS</td>
<td>Mon., Dec. 10: "Whoever Believes in Him," John 3:16-21.
Tues., Dec. 11: Belief and Salvation, Romans 10:1-10.
Wed., Dec. 12: Prayer and Belief, Luke 11:1-10.
Thurs., Dec. 13: Some Greeks Seek Jesus, John 12:20-26.
Fri., Dec. 14: "When I Am Lifted Up," John 12:27-36a.
Sat., Dec. 15: The Tragedy of Unbelief, John 12:36b-43.
Sun., Dec. 16: No Need to Remain in Darkness, John 12:44-50.</td>
</tr>
<tr>
<td>LESSON AIM</td>
<td>To show the supreme importance of faith in Jesus Christ as Son of God and Savior and to note the results of belief and unbelief.</td>
</tr>
<tr>
<td>LESSON SETTING</td>
<td>Time: The events described probably took place shortly before the Passover of A.D. 30, that is, in March.

Place: Bethany, two miles from Jerusalem</td>
</tr>
</table>

Belief or Unbelief?

I. The Results of Belief and Unbelief: John 3:16-21
   A. Belief Brings Life: vv. 16-17
   B. Unbelief Brings Condemnation: vv. 18-21

II. Witnesses to Jesus: John 5:31-47
   A. John the Baptist: vv. 31-35
   B. Jesus' Works: v. 36
   C. The Father: vv. 37-38
   D. The Scriptures: vv. 39-47

III. The Unbelief of the Jewish Rulers: John 12:37-41
   A. Refusal to Accept the Evidence: v. 37
   B. Description by Isaiah: vv. 38-41

IV. Secret Believers: John 12:42-43

V. Faith in the Father and the Son: John 12:44-46

VI. The Basis of Judgment: John 12:47-50

In a previous lesson we noted that John's Gospel can be called "The Gospel of Belief." But it can also be called "The Gospel of Belief and Unbelief." As we read it we can trace two contrasting consequences of Jesus' teaching and working miracles. His disciples and many of the common people believed on Him. At the same time, the leaders of the nation disbelieved. We note a steady increase of belief in Jesus on the part of the disciples and a corresponding increase of unbelief on the part of the religious leaders. The disciples' faith found its fruition at Pentecost. The unbelief of the Jewish leaders hardened into a hatred that resulted in Jesus' death. Both belief and unbelief still manifest themselves in reaction to hearing the gospel.

The fact is that when people are confronted with Christ they have to make a decision either for or against Him. They either accept Him in faith or reject Him in unbelief. No one can be neutral about Christ, no one can ignore Him. He demands a decision, and everyone has to respond in some way.

Religious indifference is the mood of the hour in many countries. Millions of young people simply ignore God and the church. Religion seems to them irrelevant. They are building secular lives.

At the same time there is evidence of a great spiritual hunger on the part of thousands of youth today. The "Jesus People" are proof of this. The great gathering of mission-minded young people at Urbana is eloquent proof of this, as well as the more recent Explo-72 at Dallas. These are heartening signs that many young people feel the need of a stabilizing faith in God. May this trend increase!

Each young person, as each older one, has to make his own decision about Jesus Christ. What is yours going to be?

<table>
<tr><td>CONCEPTS FOR CHILDREN</td><td>

1. Faith is taking Jesus at His word.
2. The Roman official had a simple, sincere faith in Jesus.
3. Boys and girls can have that same kind of faith.
4. Jesus never lets us down when we really believe in Him.
</td></tr>
</table>

THE LESSON COMMENTARY

I. THE RESULTS OF BELIEF AND UNBELIEF: John 3:16-21

A. Belief Brings Life: vv. 16-17

John 3:16 is commonly referred to as the Golden Text of the Bible. What was the setting for this great evangelistic utterance?

It was Jesus' interview with Nicodemus that formed the occasion for it. That prominent religious teacher and member of the Sanhedrin came to Jesus by night. He wanted to have a quiet, uninterrupted conversation with the prophet from Nazareth. He soon found that Jesus had one message for him: "You must be born again" (v. 7).

Nicodemus was slow to understand spiritual truth. And so Jesus used a familiar illustration from the books of Moses that this Jewish rabbi taught. He said: "And as Moses lifted up the serpent in the wilderness, even so must the Son of man be lifted up: that whosoever believeth in him should not perish, but have eternal life" (vv. 14-15). God requires only one thing of us for salvation, and that is faith in Jesus. But, as we have noted in a previous lesson, genuine faith involves obedience. "Trust and obey" belong together and cannot actually be separated in experience.

There has been considerable discussion as to whether verses 16-21 are to be taken as a continuation of Jesus' conversation with Nicodemus, or whether they are John's inspired interpretation of verses 14-15. It should be recognized that the value and authority of these words are not at all affected by the decision we reach on this matter. For if we believe in the divine inspiration of the Scriptures, the passage carries equal weight either way. Many good and godly Bible scholars are ranged on both sides of this question. It must be conceded, however, that most Christians prefer to think of verses 16 and 17 as containing the actual words of Jesus.

John 3:16 has also been called "the gospel in a nutshell." It is certainly that. It begins by emphasizing the divine initiative—God. True religion is God reaching down to man, and only then man reaching up to God. If it were all, or even first of all, man's search for reality—as some claim it is—it would be utterly empty and futile. But because God makes the first move, it is effective.

What was the motive for God taking the initiative in man's salvation? the answer is divine love: "For God so *loved*." It is all a proof and expression of the great truth, "God is love" (I John 4:8, 16). Because God is love—pure, holy, unselfish love—He had to act. He had to do something about man's sad plight. He could not leave mankind lost in its sin and hopelessness. He had to provide a remedy.

The third truth we note is that "God so loved *the world*." What kind of a world? It was a world of sinners who had broken His laws and rejected His love again and again. But God *so* loved that He reached out a hand of compassionate help to those who had many times spurned His call. It is easy to love those who are lovely and loving. But to love the unlovely, the hateful, the rebellious—that is something else.

In the fourth place, "God so loved the world that he *gave*." True love is always giving. It is outflowing, outgoing—outgiving others. *Agape* love described here, is never self-seeking, but always seeking the best good of others. You say you are poor and have nothing to give? The greatest gift you can offer anyone is your sincere love. That is what the world needs most— real love.

In the fifth place, "God so loved the world that he gave his only begotten *Son*." This was His most precious possession. No material wealth, which God could create in endless supply, could meet the real need of man. What men need most is a Savior. Only God's Son could qualify to fill the role of a sacrifice for the sins of the world. So God gave His own Son. It was a costly gift! For it seems reasonable to hold that God, who is All-Love, suffered infinitely as He saw His Son writhing in agony on the cross.

What was the purpose of this all? "That whosoever believeth in him should not perish, but have everlasting life." Salvation means eternal life. And this is available only to those who are believing in Jesus. God did not send His Son to condemn the world, "but that the world through him might be saved" (v. 17). The provision is for all. If any who hear are lost, it is because they have not accepted God's offer of salvation.

B. Unbelief Brings Condemnation: vv. 18-21

"He that believeth on him is not condemned"--as long as he is believing. That is the force of the present tense in the Greek: it emphasizes continuous action. "But he that believeth not is condemned"—as long as he is believing. he hath not believed in the name of the only begotten Son of God." To refuse to believe in Jesus Christ as Savior is the greatest sin anyone can commit, (cf. 16:9) because it is the supreme sin against love—the love that Jesus showed in dying on the cross in our place.

Men are condemned for rejecting light, for preferring darkness rather than light. This is because "their deeds were evil," and evil likes to hide in the dark (v. 19). The one who is doing "truth" is not afraid of the light; rather, he welcomes it (v. 21).

II. WITNESSES TO JESUS: John 5:31-47

A. John the Baptist: vv. 31-35

Jesus had healed the impotent man at the Pool of Bethesda (5:1-9). When the man walked away with his bedroll on his back, the Jewish leaders challenged him: "It is the sabbath day: it is not lawful for thee to carry thy bed" (v. 10). His reply was: "The man who healed me told me to pick up my bed and walk" (v. 11).

The result of this incident was that Jesus again came into conflict with the religious leaders of the nation, for we read: "And therefore did the Jews persecute Jesus, and sought to slay him, because he had done these things on the sabbath day" (v. 16).

But the worst was yet to come. Jesus said to them: "My Father worketh hitherto, and I work." His hearers caught this point and reacted as before: "Therefore the Jews sought the more to kill him, because he not only had broken the sabbath, but said also, that God was his Father, making himself equal with God" (v. 18). It was the old charge of blasphemy appearing again.

There is one more verse in the earlier part of chapter 5 that is definitely pertinent to the main thrust of this lesson. It is verse 24: "Verily, verily, I say unto you, He that heareth my word, and believeth on him that sent me, hath everlasting life, and shall not come into condemnation; but is passed from death unto life." Again we would note that "believeth" is in the present tense of continuous action. As long as one is believing—trusting and obeying—he has eternal life and will not come into condemnation. This is the glorious heritage of all those who are in Christ.

Then in verse 31 we read: "If I bear witness of myself, my witness is not true." What He evidently means is: "You will say that my witness is not true," or, "My witness would not stand up in court," for two or three witnesses were required by the law (Hebrews 10:28).

So Jesus proceeded to summon the witnesses—not just two or three, but four in all. The first was John the Baptist. He had definitely witnessed that Jesus was the Son of God (1:34).

B. Jesus' Works: v. 36

The miracles that Jesus performed were first of all acts of compassionate mercy, but they were also evidences that He was the Son of God. But probably "works" here takes in all the active ministry of Jesus, for He refers to them as "the works which the Father hath given me to finish." His deeds and words and attitudes of love were all "works" that witnessed to His divine character.

C. The Father: vv. 37-38

Jesus cites as the third witness His Father. How had the Father witnessed? At Jesus' baptism the voice had come from heaven: "This is my beloved Son, in whom I am well pleased" (Matthew 3:17).

D. The Scriptures vv. 39-47

"Search the scriptures" should probably be rendered, "You search the Scriptures." In the second person plural of the Greek exactly the same form is used for the indicative and the imperative. Since these Jewish scribes were constantly studying the Scriptures, it seems best to take the words

here as a statement of fact rather than a command. What Jesus meant was: "You are always searching the Scriptures. Why don't you find me there, for they witness about me." The tragedy was: "And ye will not come to me, that ye might have life" (v. 40). This shows that the unbelief of these religious leaders was moral rather than mental. They refused to believe in Jesus. The trouble was that they did not have the love of God in their hearts (v. 42).

Then Jesus added this pathetic statement: "I am come in my Father's name, and ye receive me not: if another shall come in his own name, him ye will receive" (v. 43). This may refer to the revolt of the false Messiah, Bar Cochba, which caused the final destruction of Jerusalem in A.D. 135, or it may be a veiled reference to the appearance of the Antichrist at the end of this age. It is tragic to reject the true and accept the false.

The Jews gave high honor to Moses as the founder of their nation and the one who had given them their law. Jesus scored a heavy point when He declared: "Had ye believed Moses, ye would have believed me: for he wrote of me" (v. 46). He must have made these teachers of the Law wince when He added: "But if ye believe not his writings, how shall ye believe my words?" (v. 47). The Pharisees and Sadducees, especially the latter, considered the five Books of Moses (Genesis—Deuteronomy) to be the most sacred and authoritative part of their Scriptures (our Old Testament). Jesus said in effect: "When you reject Me you are rejecting Moses." It was a rapier-like thrust.

III. THE UNBELIEF OF THE JEWISH RULERS: John 12:37-41

A. Refusal to Accept the Evidence: v. 37

Again we see the stubborn refusal of the religious leaders of the nation: "But though he had done so many miracles before them, yet they believed not on him." The evidence was right before their eyes, for several of Jesus' outstanding miracles—the healing of the impotent man (chap. 5) and of the man born blind (chap. 9), as well as the raising of Lazarus from the dead (chap. 11)—had happened in or near Jerusalem. The leaders knew all about them, but they stubbornly refused to believe.

B. Description by Isaiah: vv. 38-41

The quotation in verse 38 is from Isaiah 53:1. So far back in Jewish history the prophet had cried out: "Lord, who hath believed our report?" It is significant that Jesus cited this passage, for the fifty-third chapter of Isaiah is the greatest description in the Old Testament of the Suffering Servant of the Lord—the role which Jesus filled. In other words, Isaiah was really predicting that the Servant of the Lord would be rejected when He came to earth to be the divine Sacrifice for men's sins. This point should have struck home with much force.

In verse 40 Jesus quotes from Isaiah 6:10. The truth that needs to be recognized is that the blinding of men's eyes and the hardening of their hearts was not the arbitrary dictum of an adamant dictator. Rather, it was the inevitable moral consequence of a stubborn refusal to believe. Because men *would* not see, they *could* not see. God blinded their eyes and hardened their hearts by letting the moral results of their unbelief appear in a distortion of their vision and a warping of their minds. It is always so.

Jesus adds the striking statement: "These things said Isaiah, when he saw his glory and spoke of him" (v. 41). It will be remembered that this quotation comes right after Isaiah's vision of the holiness of God (Isaiah 6:1-8), when he saw "the Lord sitting upon a throne, high and lifted up" (v. 1) and heard the seraphim cry: "Holy, holy, holy, is the Lord of hosts: the whole earth is full of his glory" (v. 3). But this glory was rejected by Israel.

IV. SECRET BELIEVERS: John 12:42-43

Surprisingly, we read that "among the chief rulers also many believed on him; but because of the Pharisees they did not confess him, lest they should be put out of the synagogue." The sad comment is added: "For they loved the praise of men more than the praise of God." This is a tragic appraisal to have to make of religious leaders. But unquestionably there have been such in every generation, not only of Hebrew history, but also of Christian history. Were Nicodemus and Joseph of Arimathea among these? Perhaps so, for we read of the latter that he was "a disciple of Jesus, but secretly for fear of the Jews" (19:38). Their joint burial of Jesus attested to a change in this cowardly attitude.

V. FAITH IN THE FATHER AND THE SON: John 12:44-46

Jesus declared: "He that believeth on me, believeth not on me, but on him that sent me." This expresses an important truth. We cannot really believe in God without believing in Jesus, for to believe in Him is to believe in the Father. This is a needed antidote to the altogether too common attitude in religious circles that we should believe in God, but we don't need to believe in Jesus; that He was simply a great religious leader whose obedience to God we should emulate. Here it is stated clearly that to believe on Jesus *is* to believe in God.

Then Jesus made a startling claim: "He that seeth me seeth him that sent me" (v. 45). He repeated this in 14:9: "He that hath seen me hath seen the Father." For anybody but Jesus to have uttered these words would have been the sheerest idiocy or the most blatant blasphemy. But on His lips they seemed perfectly natural and carried conviction to those who were willing to believe. The centuries have confirmed the truth of His claim. To know Jesus is to know God.

We have already seen that Jesus declared Himself to be "the Light of the world" (8:12, 9:5). Now He repeats and expands this: "I am come a light into the world, that whosoever believeth on me should not abide in darkness" (v. 46). John is especially fond of contrasts, as, for instance, between life and death. But one of his favorites is light and darkness (cf. 1:5). So here he quotes Jesus as saying that He is the one who brings spiritual light to men. No one who believes in Jesus will dwell in darkness. Faith turns on the light in the human soul. Sin is sickness. Sin is slavery. Sin is death. Sin is darkness. All of these are meaningful figures. They, and many others, can only suggest the terrible negativeness of sin in its various aspects.

Anyone who has experienced the New Birth can testify that when he was converted he moved from the realm of darkness into the realm of light. Satan wants to keep his victims in darkness. But Christ came to give them light. The only way that one can explain the unbelief of those who hear the gospel but refuse it is to recognize that sin is blindness and darkness.

DISCUSSION QUESTIONS

1. What does it mean to "believe in the Son"?
2. What are the results of belief and unbelief?
3. Can one really be "a secret believer" in Jesus?
4. How did Jesus describe His relationship to the Father?
5. What will be the basis of Christ's judgment of men?
6. How can we nurture faith and avoid unbelief?

VI. THE BASIS OF JUDGMENT: John 12:47-50

The last part of verse 47—"I came not to judge the world, but to save the world"—is in line with what has already been stated in 3:17—"for God sent not His Son into the world to condemn the world; but that the world through him might be saved." The purpose for which Jesus came was not that of judgment but of salvation.

But what about the first part of the verse? It reads: "And if any man hear my words, and believe not, I judge him not." Jesus was presenting Himself as Savior in His first coming. At His return in glory He will act as Judge of all men.

Christ went on to say: "He that rejecteth me, and receiveth not my words, hath one that judgeth him: the words that I have spoken, the same shall judge him in the last day" (v. 48). While Christ was refraining from pronouncing the judgment of doom on unbelievers at the time, He warned that His words would ultimately judge those who heard them. This is a solemn warning to all who hear the gospel preached or who read the Word of God. The words of Jesus which we hear and read will finally judge us. The only way to escape this judgment is to constantly repent and live in obedience to the divine Word. Westcott warns: "The word may be refused, but it cannot be banished. It still clings to the hearer as his judge. Its work is even now begun as it shall hereafter be fully revealed" (*John*, p. 187).

Jesus said that His word would judge His hearers "in the last day." This phrase is found only in John's Gospel, where it occurs six times. Jesus declared that He would "raise up" (resurrect) every believer "at the last day" (6:39, 40, 45, 54). This obviously refers, in the light of other passages of Scripture, to the time of His second coming. In 11:24 Martha says of her dead brother Lazarus: "I know he shall rise again in the resurrection at the last day." These five passages all point to the time of the resurrection of all true believers in Christ. But the expression "the last day" seems to include the Judgment as well. It takes in the whole end time of God's dealing with humanity.

Many times Jesus asserted that He lived under the authority of the Father. He was equal to the Father in essence, or being, but subordinate in office. This seems to be the clear teaching of the New Testament. So here He says: "I have not spoken of myself," or "from myself as ultimate source and authority." He had already declared, "The Son can do nothing of himself, but what he seeth the Father do: for what things soever he doeth, these also doeth the Son likewise" (5:19).

Yet the Father had delegated much authority to the Son. For we find Jesus saying that "the Father judgeth no man but hath committed all judgment unto the Son" (5:22). He who now offers Himself to us as our Lawyer to represent our case at the Father's throne will eventually be the Judge of all those who reject this offer.

Jesus also said that the Father had "given him authority to execute judgment also, because he is the Son of man" (5:27). This conveys a striking truth. Because Jesus has experienced human life on earth He is qualified to act as Judge. He knows our weaknesses and temptations; so He will be fair and merciful. But He also knows that the Father's power and presence are available at all times to God's children. When Jesus was tempted in the wilderness, He used only one weapon—the sword of the Spirit, which is the Word of God (cf. Ephesians 6:17). And that very weapon is available to all His followers. With it He defeated Satan; with it we can do the same. It is altogether fitting that the Son of Man will be the final Judge of all men.

Jesus concludes this discourse by saying: "But the Father, which sent me, he gave me a commandment, what I should say, and what I should speak. And I know that his commandment is life everlasting: whatsoever I speak therefore, even as the Father said unto me, so I speak" (vv. 49-50). Jesus lived in complete submission to the Father's will. In so doing He showed us the path of life—for God's commandment brings "life everlasting."

CONTEMPORARY APPLICATION

The memory selection for this lesson is John 3:36: "He that believeth on the Son hath everlasting life: and he that believeth not the Son shall not see life; but the wrath of God abideth on him." The verb *believe* is in the present tense (continuous action) both times. What the verse says is, "He who is believing on the Son is having eternal life (as long as he is believing)); and he who is not believing the Son shall not see life. . . ." It is faith that unites us to God, and that union is sure and certain as long as faith is operative. There *is* eternal security in Christ.

THE WORD DWELT AMONG US

DEVOTIONAL READING	I John 1:1-4

ADULTS

Topic: *The Word Dwelt Among Us*

Background Scripture: John 1:1-5, 14-18

Scripture Lesson: John 1:1-5, 14-18

Memory Verse: *The Word became flesh and dwelt among us, full of grace and truth; we have beheld his glory, glory as of the only Son from the Father.* John 1:14

YOUTH

Topic: *Jesus Was Here*

Background Scripture: John 1:1-5, 14-18

Scripture Lesson: John 1:1-5, 14-18

Memory Verse: *The Word became flesh and dwelt among us, full of grace and truth; we have beheld his glory, glory as of the only Son from the Father.* John 1:14

CHILDREN

Topic: *Jesus Is Born*

Background Scripture: Luke 2:1-20; John 1:1-18

Scripture Lesson: Luke 2:1-7

Memory Verse: *For to you is born this day in the city of David a Savior, who is Christ the Lord.* Luke 2:11

DAILY BIBLE READINGS

Mon., Dec. 17: "God with Us," Isaiah 7:10-14.
Tues., Dec. 18: "To Us a Son Is Given," Isaiah 9:1-7.
Wed., Dec. 19: "Good Tidings to the Afflicted," Isaiah 61:1-4.
Thurs., Dec. 20: The Lord's Servant, Isaiah 52:13—53:3.
Fri., Dec. 21: The Servant's Suffering, Isaiah 53:4-12.
Sat., Dec. 22: The Source of All Life, John 1:1-5.
Sun., Dec. 23: God Incarnate, John 1:14-18.

LESSON AIM

To try to understand the significance of the eternal Word coming to earth in human form.

LESSON SETTING

Time: John's Gospel was written about A.D. 95.

Place: It was written in Ephesus.

120

The Word Dwelt Among Us

LESSON OUTLINE

I. The Eternal Word: John 1:1-5
   A. One with God: vv. 1-2
   B. Creator of All Things: v. 3
   C. Source of Life: v. 4
   D. Source of Light: v. 5

II. The Incarnate Word: John 1:14-18
   A. Full of Grace and Truth: v. 14
   B. Witnessed To by John: v. 15
   C. Giver of Grace: v. 16
   D. Bringer of Reality: v. 17
   E. Revealer of God: v. 18

SUGGESTED INTRODUCTION FOR ADULTS

Each of the four Gospels begins in a very different way. Matthew, writing to the Jews, starts out with a Jewish genealogy of "Jesus Christ, the son of David, the son of Abraham." The first question his readers would ask about the One whom Matthew presents as King of the Jews is this: "Is He the son of David, and so heir to the throne?"

Mark has practically no introduction. The first verse is the title of the book: "The beginning of the gospel of Jesus Christ, the Son of God." Then after only a dozen verses covering briefly the ministry of John the Baptist and the baptism and temptation of Jesus, he plunges immediately into the public ministry of the Master.

Luke, who was a well-educated, widely traveled physician and artist, begins his Gospel with a literary preface (1:1-4) in which he dedicates the book to a Roman official named Theophilus. This was in keeping with the best literature of that period. He also has a genealogy (3:23-38). But instead of beginning with Abraham as Matthew does, he goes back past the father of the Israelites to Adam, "who was the son of God."

But John goes still farther back. He begins with a theological prologue which presents Jesus Christ as the eternal Logos. The One who appeared on earth had from all eternity lived in fellowship with the Father. Jesus of Nazareth was actually the eternal Son of God.

SUGGESTED INTRODUCTION FOR YOUTH

"Are you for real?" This was a question which Cathy Jones was asked by her senior classmates in high school. It made her stop and think: "Am I actually for real?"

Fortunately Cathy was a consecrated Christian and her answer was a sincere yes. What would be your reply? John tells us that "grace and truth," or "grace and reality," come through Jesus Christ (1:17).

What is an unreal person? An unreal person is one who is playing a role instead of being himself or herself. Some young people today think that every person over thirty years of age is a hypocrite—especially the conformists. So thousands of youth have struck out on a path of non-conformity, hoping to find reality that way. But non-conformists can be just as guilty of role-playing as conformists. Someone has said of the hippies: "They want so desperately to be different, but they end up being so pitifully alike."

CONCEPTS FOR CHILDREN

1. Christmas should mean more than toys and Santa Claus; it celebrates the coming of Christ.
2. At this season we should think about His birth.
3. He became very humble and was born in a manger.
4. Jesus wants to come into our hearts, not as a baby, but as our King.

THE LESSON COMMENTARY

I. THE ETERNAL WORD: John 1:1-5

A. One with God: vv. 1-2

The Gospel of John has a very striking opening verse, similar to that of Genesis, where we read: "In the beginning God created the heaven and the earth." Here we find a statement that goes back far beyond that: "In the beginning was the Word, and the Word was with God, and the Word was God." This takes us back to the eternity of the past, long before there was any creation.

"Word" is a translation of *logos*, a familiar term among the Greeks. W. F. Howard, in his book *Christianity According to St. John*, says: "It was in this very city of Ephesus, some six centuries before that date, that Heraclitus first made use of the Logos idea. With him it was 'the rational principle, power, or being which *speaks* to men both from without and from within'" (p. 34).

Plato used *Logos* for the divine force creating the world (cf. John 1:2). With Aristotle it meant "insight."

The first systematic exposition of the doctrine of the Logos was made by the Stoics. Alexander (*International Standard Bible Encyclopedia*, p. 1912) writes: "It is the key to their interpretation of life. They held that the primordial source of all things is eternal fire and they called this Logos or God." It will be seen that they were groping in the right direction, but without reaching the truth.

Alexander points up the difference between the Hellenistic and Hebrew concepts. He says: "In the Hellenistic usage the doctrine was substantially a doctrine of Reason, while in Jewish literature it was more especially the outward expression or word that was emphasized" (pp. 1912-13). This is in keeping with the Hebrew emphasis on active, concrete concepts, in contrast to the Greek emphasis on abstract ideas.

Philo was a Jewish philosopher of the time of Christ (30 B.C.–A.D. 45). Living in Alexandria, Egypt, he tried to harmonize Greek philosophy with the Hebrew Scriptures. So he took the Greek emphasis on Logos as a rational principle and combined it with the Hebrew idea of the Logos as a mediating agent of the Divine Being. The Greeks thought of Logos as Reason, the Jews thought of it as Word. Philo made a synthesis of the two concepts, and this became the prevailing view.

Philo uses the term *Logos* thirteen hundred times. Many scholars have argued that John's Gospel derived its concept of the Logos from him. But while Philo approached the Johannine idea, he never reached it. For instance, Philo wrote: "The principle existence is God, and next to him is the Logos of God." But that leaves the Logos less than Deity. Again, "The image of God is the Logos, through whom the whole universe was framed." That comes nearer, but still does not arrive. W. F. Howard (*Christianity According to St. John*) makes the significant observation that in Philo's writings "though the Logos is often personified, it is never truly personalized" (p. 38). He also declares: "In no writings outside the New Testament is there any true parallel to the statements made about the Logos in the Johannine Prologue" (p. 41).

It is interesting to note that the term *Logos* is used for Christ only in John 1:1, 14; I John 1:1; and Revelation 19:13. In the New Testament it is uniquely and exclusively a Johannine concept.

Now we want to look a little more closely at what John says here. First, he declares the eternality of the Logos, who existed from "the beginning." Second, he says that the Logos was "with God." The Greek expression suggests that He was "face to face with God," in close fellowship.

But the third statement is the most striking one: "and the Word was God." The word order is reversed in the Greek. "God" is first for emphasis. Here we have the strongest possible statement of the full deity of Jesus. He was *God* in the highest and most definite sense.

Verse 2 ties together the first two clauses of verse 1: "The same was in the beginning with God." The Logos not only existed from all eternity, but He was eternally in face-to-face fellowship with the Father. Any attempt to make Jesus Christ less than God in the fullest sense of that term is an outright denial of what John declares here. We have to accept this or deny the divine inspiration of the Scriptures.

B. Creator of All Things: v. 3

Four times in the first two verses we find the verb *was*. In the Greek this is in the imperfect tense and expresses the idea of "continual timeless exis-

tence" (Bernard, *International Critical Commentary*).

In striking contrast to this is the verb in verse 3 translated "were made." In the first place, a different verb is used, the verb "to become" instead of "to be" as in the first two verses. In the second place, it is in the aorist tense of punctiliar action rather than the imperfect of continuous existence. The Logos always existed; matter came into existence at a point in time.

Verse 3 is very striking in the Greek. Literally it reads: "All things came into being through Him, and apart from Him not even one thing came into being." This states unequivocally the fact that Christ was the Creator of everything.

This same emphasis on Jesus as fully divine and as the Creator of all things is found in Colossians 1:15-17 and Hebrews 1:2-3. It is interesting to note also that in all three of these places Christ's redemptive work is put alongside His work in creation.

C. Source of Life: v. 4

John says about the Logos: "In him was life"—not derived, but inherent. He not only *had* life, He *is* life and *gives* life.

The term *life* is one of the key words of John's Gospel. It occurs thirty-six times, eleven of these with the adjective *eternal*. It is also used eighteen times in John's First Epistle. Always it means "spiritual life."

As we noted before, John is not interested in belief for its own sake. He is always concerned that men may have *life* as a result of believing (20:31). Faith is not the end; it is only a means to the end. The goal of it all is eternal life, which man finds only in the eternal Logos. In Him we are alive, spiritually and eternally.

But we should realize that even our physical life is derived from our Creator. Without Him we would not be alive. Paul expresses it graphically in Colossians 1:17: "By him all things consist." The original Greek says, "In

Him all things hold together." Christ is not only the Creator; He is also the Sustainer of all life. An eminent scientist said years ago: "If the creative force in the universe should be withdrawn for even a moment, the whole universe would collapse." The Bible declares that that creative force is Christ. In Him the whole universe holds together; without Him it would fall apart.

And what is true of the universe is also true of our individual selves. Why do so many people go to pieces today? Because they are not held together in Christ. We need to live each day in the consciousness that we are *in Him*, and sustained by His presence.

D. Source of Light: v. 5

In the latter part of verse 4 John writes: "And the life was the light of men." *Light* is another key word in this Gospel, occurring twenty-three times. Spiritual life brings intellectual illumination. We can only see spiritual truth as we have spiritual life. And this life is found only in Christ. The eternal Logos is both the life and light of men.

John goes on to say: "And the light shineth in the darkness; and the darkness comprehended it not." Today *comprehend* means "understand." It is not at all certain that this is the correct meaning here. The Greek verb literally means "take hold of, seize." The margin of the American Standard Version (1901) has "overcame," with "apprehended" in the text. The latter has the advantage of going both ways. To "apprehend" may mean to understand, but it is also a technical term for arresting someone. The fact is that we cannot be sure which is intended here. Arndt and Gingrich conclude: "Most Greek commentators since Origen take *katalambano* here as *overcome, suppress*. . . . But perhaps John intended to include both meanings here . . . and some such translation as *master* would suggest this." That is probably the best solution.

"The darkness" is the spiritual darkness of men's hearts and minds resulting from the Fall. As the light of the eternal Christ penetrates this darkness, two things are true: most men do not grasp the light for their own salvation, but neither can their darkness arrest the light. It still shines on, coming from Him who declared, "I am the light of the world" (8:12).

II. THE INCARNATE WORD:
   John 1:14-18

A. Full of Grace and Truth: v. 14

In verse 14 John moves from the eternal Logos, who has always been the life and light of men, to the incarnate Logos, who came into the world for man's redemption. This is what the gospel is all about.

We find here one of the great theological statements of Scripture: "The Word was made flesh." Again we note the change of verb from the first two verses of this prologue. There it was the continuous imperfect of the verb "to be"—Christ was eternally one with the Father; He was God. But here, as in verse 3, it is the aorist tense of the verb "to become." The Logos always was divine; He became human in the Incarnation. Now He is both.

The term *incarnation* is from the Latin, as are most of our theological terms. This is simply because Latin was the dominant academic and ecclesiastical language of Europe during the Middle Ages, when theological formulations were being made. The word literally means "enfleshment." It refers to the act of Christ in coming in the flesh.

This does not simply mean that the eternal Logos took on a body of flesh. It is not a matter of the divine nature being encased in a physical body. It says, "The Word *became* flesh." Christ not only took a human body; He took on Himself human nature. Across the pages of the Old Testament we see God invading *history*—at the Red Sea, at Sinai, and at a hundred other points. But now a new thing happened: God invaded *humanity*. In the person of Jesus Christ, He actually entered the human race. The Son of God became the Son of man. The Incarnation is the highest possible expression of divine love. In fact, Christ is Divine Love Incarnate.

Every normal person loves a baby. Perhaps most of us have been in a group of adults when someone said the wrong thing. Suddenly the atmosphere became tense. The situation was embarrassing. Everyone sat there silent, "uptight." We all wished we were somewhere else!

Then the awkward silence was broken by a sound. A baby laughed, or cried, or gurgled. No matter which, it did the trick. Everybody—almost with a sigh of relief—turned to look at the baby. Faces relaxed, smiles appeared, and soon the adults were not only smiling at the baby but smiling at each other. The whole atmosphere of the room was transformed—by the presence of a baby!

It was thus at the Incarnation. God could have sent His Son into the world as a full-grown adult, who would have preached and taught, and then died on a cross as Savior. But instead, in His infinite love and wisdom, He gave Himself to humanity in the form of a newborn babe. The eternal Logos, one with the Father, became one with us. He who fills the universe became a baby in a manger at Bethlehem.

Behold the wonder of it! The *Eternal One* caught in a moment of time. *Omnipresence* corralled in a cave manger. *Omnipotence* cradled in a helpless infant, who couldn't even lift His head from the straw. *Omniscience* confined in a baby who could not say a word. *The Christ* who created the heavens and the earth cradled in a manger in a cave stable.

This is the Christmas story! It is more than tinsel and toys, than green trees and glittering lights. Christmas is Christ!

We remember when our little son was just learning to talk. We were driving home on Christmas Eve, after a Sunday night service. Everywhere we could see the bright evidences of Christmas. But we were thrilled when he suddenly said: "Pretty lights; Jesus come." That's what it's all about.

The eternal Logos, who became flesh, "dwelt among us." The Greek literally says, "tented among us." That is, He camped in our midst for a short time, perhaps thirty-three years, and then went back to heaven.

The phrase could also be translated as "tabernacled among us." The verb is used that way in the Septuagint (Greek translation of the Old Testament), where we read that God "dwelt" in the midst of His people. This was symbolized by the Tabernacle (Greek, "tent"), which was pitched in the very middle of the congregation of Israel, with the twelve tribes grouped around it. God's presence was manifested in the Tabernacle on various occasions.

So Christ camped among us, as proof of God's interest in us and desire to be one of us. That is why Jesus was called Emmanuel, the Hebrew for "God with us" (Matthew 1:23). He came to earth for a brief time in order that He might come into each of our hearts as "God with us," making the divine presence real to us. Christ had to be born at Bethlehem before He could be born, in the New Birth, in individual hearts.

John goes on to say: "And we beheld his glory, the glory as of the only begotten of the Father." Even though that eternal glory was veiled by human flesh, some of it still shone through. Specifically, His was "the glory as of the only begotten of the Father" because He manifested in His life and ministry the divine characteristics of holiness, compassionate love and supernatural power. So we, who call ourselves Christians should manifest the nature and spirit of Christ in our daily living, or we are denying His name that we bear.

The verb *beheld* is much stronger than *saw*. The Greek word is one from which we get our term *theater*. It suggests the idea of looking at someone or something at length, of contemplating what we are viewing. So John is reminding his readers that he did not get just a fleeting glimpse of Jesus. He and his fellow disciples had watched the Master day after day for some three years. They had had abundant opportunity to see His reaction to various situations, to sense His spirit, and evaluate His character. They had viewed His "glory" over and over again. In his commentary on John's Gospel, R. H. Lightfoot writes: "The seeing is neither physical only, nor spiritual only, but the seeing which arises from belief" (p. 85).

They had seen clearly that He was "full of grace and truth." Every student of the New Testament is aware of the fact that "grace" is a great Pauline concept, a favorite word in his vocabulary. Paul uses it a hundred times in his Epistles. But John uses it only three times in his Gospel, all in this passage (vv. 14, 16, 17). Aside from that he uses it three times in formal benedictions (II John 3; Revelation 1:4, 22:21). *Grace* is decidedly a Pauline emphasis.

But *truth* is one of the great Johannine terms, used by him twenty-five times. It is one of his absolutes. God is absolute truth, and so is Christ. In fact, John is the only one who quotes Jesus as saying, "I am the Truth" (14:6). The writer of this Gospel was interested not only in propositional truth, which bulks larger

in Paul's Epistles, but in personal truth. Jesus Christ embodies all truth in His own Person. He is ultimate truth. That is what we have when we have Him! The pathetic thing is that many people search for truth all their lives and never find it. The search can be ended in the glorious discovery of the One who is the Truth.

B. Witnessed To by John: v. 15

We have already noted in another lesson, that *witness* is a favorite Johannine term. The verb form of this word occurs thirty-three times and the noun form fourteen times. John the Baptist was a witness to Christ. This has already been told (vv. 7, 8). Now it is reiterated: "John bare witness of him." He told the people, "This is the One I was talking about." And then he used language which is repeated in verse 30: "He that cometh after me is preferred before me: for he was before me." As we noted in connection with that verse, the Greek implies: "He was first of all and prior to me." John recognized the preexistence of Jesus. Though younger than John in human age, the One who now came was the eternal Logos, the Light of mankind since the beginning of history.

With regard to the word *cried* here, Westcott comments: "The voice of the Baptist was more than that of a witness. It was the loud, clear voice of the herald who boldly proclaimed his message so that all might hear" (p. 13). There was no uncertainty as John announced that the Messiah had come.

C. Giver of Grace: v. 16

"And of his fulness have all we received, and grace for grace." The best Greek text reads: "Because out of his fulness we have all received." This looks back to verse 14: "full of grace and truth." That is, we know that He is full of grace and truth because we have been the recipients of that fulness in our own lives. It is only as we receive Christ into our hearts that we can really know His character. It is not

---

DISCUSSION QUESTIONS

1. How can we make Christmas more effective?
2. Could John's prologue (1:1-18) be used as a Christmas story?
3. What is the meaning of "Only-begotten God"?
4. What does John mean by calling Jesus "the Word"?
5. Why does John not tell the birth stories as Luke does?
6. How can Christ be more real to us this Christmas?

a matter of hearing about Him, but of experiencing Him within.

It would seem that verse 15 is parenthetical. As we have noted, verse 16 follows out of verse 14. Furthermore it seems clear that verses 16-18 are not connected with verse 15 as a part of John's witness. Westcott says on verse 16: "These words and those which follow are certainly the words of the Evangelist and not of the Baptist. This is shown not only by their general character, but by the phrase *we all*." John the Apostle is joining his testimony with those of his fellow Christians.

"Grace for grace" is literally "grace instead of grace." In the life of the true followers of Christ there is always a higher grace superseding our present grace. As it were, it is one grace after another.

D. Bringer of Reality: v. 17

In this verse John contrasts law and grace. He says that the law was given by Moses (at Sinai), "but grace and truth came by Jesus Christ." This might well be rendered: "But grace and reality came through Jesus Christ." The law was a shadow of good things to come (Hebrews 10:1). Westcott comments: "Grace and Truth are now presented under the aspect of their complete embodiment" (in Christ). He goes on to say: "The Gospel is spoken of as 'grace,' so far as it is the revelation of God's free love, and as 'truth,' so far as it presents the reality and not the mere images or shadows of divine things. . . . In both

respects it was contrasted with the Law" (p. 14).

Reality in life can only be found in Jesus Christ. So John tells us, and so millions who have received Him can testify. What every normal person wants more than anything else is reality. It is the consuming quest of young people today. What they need is to be pointed to Christ, so that they may have their needs of heart and mind fully met in Him.

E. Revealer of God: v. 18

"No man hath seen God at any time." God is spirit (4:24) and can never be seen with physical eyes. Only with our spiritual eyes can we discern Him.

But God's only, beloved Son, who came into the world, has revealed Him. In Christ we see God, and in no other way.

Instead of "only begotten Son," the oldest and best Greek manuscripts have "only begotten God." This makes this verse one of the strongest passages in the New Testament on the deity of Jesus. The "Only Begotten One, who is God" is now the Savior of men. With joy we sing: "Hallelujah! What a Savior!"

No one has seen God. But the Only Begotten One, who is truly God and is "in the bosom of the Father in eternal fellowship," He has "declared him"— literally, "led Him forth," so that we can see Him. The verb is *exegesato*, from which we get "exegesis." Christ has exegeted God so that through Him we know the Father.

CONTEMPORARY APPLICATION

Every Christmas we face the question as to what is a proper way to celebrate the birth of Christ. Too often we settle for a celebration that is secular, if not downright worldly.

What we need to do is to realize that Christmas means the Incarnation. If we take time to meditate on the

truths that have been presented in this lesson, Christmas this year can be a high point of spiritual experience, instead of a wearisome nightmare, as it sometimes proves to be.

Let us begin by putting Christ into Christmas. This can be done by reading the significant parts of the

Christmas story in Luke, the second chapter, as a family. Then there should be a prayer of thanksgiving to God for the great gift of His Son. This will make Christmas come alive for us and our children.

WATER FOR THE THIRSTY

DEVOTIONAL READING	Psalm 42

ADULTS

Topic: *Water for the Thirsty*

Background Scripture: John 4:1-42

Scripture Lesson: John 4:7-15

Memory Verse: *Whoever drinks of the water that I shall give him will never thirst; the water that I shall give him will become in him a spring of water welling up to eternal life.* John 4:14

YOUTH

Topic: *Water That Satisfies*

Background Scripture: John 4:1-42

Scripture Lesson: John 4:7-15

Memory Verse: *Whoever drinks of the water that I shall give him will never thirst; the water that I shall give him will become in him a spring of water welling up to eternal life.* John 4:14

CHILDREN

Topic: *Jesus Offers Life*

Background Scripture: John 4:1-42

Scripture Lesson: John 4:7-14, 28-29

Memory Verse: *We have heard for ourselves, and we know that this is indeed the Savior of the world.* John 4:42

DAILY BIBLE READINGS

Mon. Dec. 24: God Has Visited His People, Luke 1:68-79.
Tues., Dec. 25: "O Holy Child of Bethelem," Luke 2:8-20.
Wed., Dec. 26: The Living Water, John 4:1-15.
Thurs., Dec. 27: God Is Spirit, John 4:16-26.
Fri., Dec. 28: Deep Inner Satisfaction, John 4:27-38.
Sat., Dec. 29: "We Have Heard for Ourselves," John 4:39-42.
Sun., Dec. 30: "So Longs My Soul for Thee," Psalm 42.

LESSON AIM

To show how Jesus is the Water of Life, to satisfy the deepest desires of the human heart.

LESSON SETTING

Time: Shortly after the Passover, probably in A.D. 27

Place: Jacob's Well near Mt. Gerizim, in Samaria, which was the central part of Palestine in Jesus' day, between Judea to the south and Galilee on the north

129

Water for the Thirsty

LESSON OUTLINE

SUGGESTED INTRODUCTION FOR ADULTS

The lesson today covers John 4:1-42. While only a small central portion of this is designated as the Scripture lesson, it is necessary to study the entire passage if the lesson is to be meaningful. This highlights the fact that all members of adult and youth classes should be encouraged to bring their Bibles or Testaments to class. It will also create much added interest if half a dozen different versions are in the hands of various pupils. Have specific persons agree to bring certain translations. Most helpful will be The New American Standard Bible New Testament (nearest to the Greek), the Revised Standard Version and The New English Bible. Three others are free paraphrases, but give some helpful insights: Phillips, The Living Bible and Good News for Modern Man. It must be realized of course, that these should not be used for settling theological arguments or for precise points of exegesis. They are highly interpretive, rather than exact translations. But they do serve as commentaries, and throw fresh light on many passages. Anyone who uses the King James Version alone, without any additional helps, will be decidedly limited in his understanding of the Bible.

SUGGESTED INTRODUCTION FOR YOUTH

The Samaritan woman at the well is a typical example of many people in modern society. She wanted the larger life and thought she could find it through promiscuous living is real freedom! But those who adopt this way of have a good time with all of them?

That is the way many persons reason today. Permissive living is real freedom! But those who adopt this way of life soon find that the worst slavery of all is that of being a slave to sinful habits. True freedom is found only in commitment to Christ. He brings the larger life—yes, the largest life! For Jesus Himself said, "I have come that they might have life, and that they might have it more abundantly" (John 10:10). Not less life, but more life. Not a smaller life, but a larger one. Not less pleasure, but more pleasure—in pleasing Him. Actually, the freest, happiest, most thrilling life is that which is lived in the center of God's will. Those who have tried it have found it so.

CONCEPTS FOR CHILDREN

1. The woman at the well wanted happiness in life, as every normal person does.
2. She tried to find it in sinful pleasure, but this left her unhappy.
3. Jesus promised to give her "living water," which would satisfy her soul.
4. In accepting Christ as her Savior, she finally found her goal.

THE LESSON COMMENTARY

I. A WEARY CHRIST:
John 4:1-6

Jesus had been carrying on a very busy ministry in Judea. But the Pharisees were evidently becoming concerned about the fact that He was baptizing so many people—though His disciples were doing the actual baptizing (v. 2). Probably they thought He was winning converts to Himself, and this they could not tolerate. To avoid a clash with them, Jesus left for Galilee.

Verse 4 says, "And he must needs go through Samaria." This is an interesting statement. It was not a geographical necessity that compelled Him to go that way. True, the route through Samaria was by far the shortest one. But many of the Jews of Galilee, when they came down to Jerusalem for the feasts, crossed over the Jordan River and came down the east side, returning the same way. This was to avoid going through the "unclean," unfriendly territory of the Samaritans.

Probably the necessity in Jesus' case was an inner compulsion to go this way in order that He might minister to a lost sinner from the village of Sychar. He *had* to go by Jacob's Well to meet her need.

Finally Jesus reached Jacob's Well, near Sychar, and sat down on the low wall surrounding it. It was "about the sixth hour." As we have already noted in another lesson, in connection with 1:39, we cannot be sure whether John is using Roman time, beginning at midnight and noon, or Jewish time, beginning at sunset and sunrise.

II. A THIRSTY WOMAN:
John 4:7-9

A. Jesus' Request: vv. 7-8

A woman was walking across the fields, dragging her heels. She was all at six's and seven's inside, out of fix with herself and everybody else.

As she approached the well, she said to herself, "I hope there's nobody there." But to her consternation she saw a stranger sitting there and she resented His presence.

She tried to hurry past Him to draw water. But a kind voice said, "Pardon me, lady, but may I have a drink of water?" That's the way we would say it now. Jesus was thirsty but had no way of getting water from the well. His disciples had gone to the nearby town to buy some food. So He turned to the woman, who had a water pot she could let down into the well by a rope lying there—as one can still see beside wells near Jerusalem.

B. The Woman's Response: v. 9

Instead of giving Jesus a drink of water, the woman asked Him a question: "How is it that thou, being a Jew, askest drink of me, which am a woman of Samaria?" This was a double wonder. In the first place, she was a woman, and no self-respecting Jewish man would ever be seen talking with a woman in public—not even his own wife, mother, or sister. It just wasn't done. In the second place, she was a Samaritan and, as the writer of the Gospel informs us, "the Jews have no dealings with the Samaritans."

Who were the Samaritans? To find the answer to that question we have to go back to the eighth century B.C. The northern Kingdom of Israel had descended into idolatry and immorality. So God sent the Assyrians to punish the people for their sins. In 722/21 B.C. the Assyrian armies conquered Samaria, the capital of Israel, and took many people into captivity—never to return to their land. But we also read that "the king of Assyria brought men from Babylon, and from Cuthah, and from Ava, and from Hamath, and from Sepharvaim, and placed them in the cities of Samaria instead of the children of Israel and they possessed Samaria, and dwelt in the cities thereof" (II Kings 17:24). This was a deliberate policy on the part of the Assyrians to break down any nationalistic spirit and so avoid all danger of a revolt. The result, inevitably, was that the people intermarried and thus produced a race of half-breeds. And half-breeds are usually despised by people on both sides.

There was not only a biological and cultural mixture of divergent peoples, but also a religious one. The newcomers brought with them the worship of pagan gods. A strange combination resulted: "They feared the Lord, and served their own gods" (II Kings 17:33).

At the time of Christ the Jews would have nothing to do with the Samaritans, because they considered them unclean. We can see why the woman at the well was surprised that Jesus would speak to her. Most Jews would have refused a drink from this woman, considering her water pot to be contaminated.

III. THE WATER OF LIFE: John 4:10-15

A. Jesus' Offer of Living Water: v. 10

It would seem that the woman's response (v. 9) may have been voiced with some annoyance, indicating that she didn't want to talk to Jesus. For the Master did not answer her question. Instead He said: "If you knew the gift of God, and who it is that is asking you for a drink, you would have asked him, and he would have given you living water."

Jesus does not directly call Himself the Water of Life, as He does the Bread of Life (chap. 6). But we are probably justified in saying that He is presented here in that capacity. He can satisfy the thirst, as well as the hunger, of every human heart.

If the woman had recognized "the gift of God"—His only Son sent for the salvation of the world—she would have been the petitioner. Westcott says about *gift*: "The word here used (*dorea*) occurs only in this place in the Gospels. It carries with it something of the idea of bounty, honour, privilege; and is used of the gift of the Spirit (Acts ii.38, viii.20, x.45, xi.17) and of the gift of redemption in Christ (Rom. v.15; II Cor. ix.15), manifested in various ways (Eph. iii.7, iv.7; Hebr. vi.4) . . . 'The gift of God' is all that is freely offered in the Son" (p. 69).

While Jesus asked the woman for a drink of ordinary water, He wanted to give her "living water"—"that is, perennial, springing from an unfailing source, ever flowing fresh" (Westcott p. 69). The phrase "living waters" is found in Zechariah 14:8; Jeremiah 2:13; 17:13. In the last two passages the Lord is called "the fountain of living waters." That is what Jesus wanted to be to this needy woman and to all of us today. Too many, as in Jeremiah's day, prefer "broken cisterns that can hold no water."

B. The Woman's Reaction: vv. 11-12

Again the woman seems to be protesting against what Jesus is saying. Her reply was: "Sir, thou hast nothing to draw with, and the well is deep." Jacob's Well is about one hundred feet deep, and normally has about twenty feet of water in it. It is still an important supply of water for that area. We have had a drink from Jacob's Well, and the water was cool and clear.

But Jesus had nothing with which to draw water. How then could He give her "that living water"? One of the greatest problems Jesus had, as reflected frequently in John's Gospel, was to get people's minds off material things and centered on the spiritual truths He was trying to teach. The woman should have known that He was not talking about ordinary water.

Then the woman asked, "Art thou greater than our father Jacob?" It almost sounds like, "Who do you think you are, anyhow?"

C. Jesus' Explanation: vv. 13-14

Now Christ sought to make clear to this woman what He was talking about. So He made one of the great declarations of John's Gospel: "Whosoever drinketh of this water shall thirst again: but whosoever drinketh of the water that I shall give him shall never thirst; but the water that I shall give him shall be in him a well of water springing up into everlasting life." This was surely a clear indication that He was not talking about ordinary water.

The word for "well" here is a different one from that used by the woman in verse 11. There it is *phrear*, which basically means a hole in the ground. That is all the religion many people have—just a form with no spiritual content, a hole with no living water in it. But Jesus used here the word *pege*, which means a "fountain." What Jesus was saying to this woman, and still says to everyone, is this: "If you will let me, I will put a bubbling fountain of living water in your soul that will satisfy all the thirsty longings of your heart. It will keep bubbling up into eternal life."

There is another passage that might well be related to this one. On the last day of the Feast of Tabernacles, Jesus called out: "If any man thirst, let him come unto me, and drink. He that believeth on me, as the scripture hath said, out of his belly [heart] shall flow rivers of living water." Lest there should be any question as to what was meant, John the writer adds this word of explanation: "But this spake he of the Spirit, which they that believe on him should receive" (7:37-39). Jesus not only wants us all to have a bubbling fountain in our souls that will completely satisfy the deepest longings of our being. He also desires that out of our Spirit-filled hearts there shall flow *rivers* of living water to bless other lives about us.

D. The Woman's Request: v. 15

What was the woman's reaction to Christ's profound statement about living water? She said: "Sir, give me this water, that I thirst not, neither come hither to draw."

Now, if this woman thought that Jesus was going to put within her an endless supply of physical water, she was certainly stupid. But any woman that could wind five men around her fingers probably wasn't that "dumb." It seems likely that this woman's intuition told her that Jesus was moving in on her territory, and it wouldn't bear inspection! It looks as though she was trying to turn Him off by making the ridiculous request for ordinary water, when she could hardly help knowing that He was talking about spiritual water.

IV. A SINNER AND THE SAVIOR: John 4:16-26

A. Exposure of Her Guilt: vv. 16-18

One reason that we feel justified in adopting this interpretation is that Jesus abruptly changed the conversation. Dropping the topic of water, which seemed to have reached an impasse, he suddenly said to the woman, "Go, call thy husband."

This command must have hit the woman with a heavy thud, "Husband— how I hate that word!" Almost sullenly she probably snarled at him, "I have no husband."

Looking at her with a soul-piercing gaze, Jesus said, "Thou hast well said, I have no husband [Huh, he doesn't know, does he!] for thou hast had five husbands; and he whom thou now hast is not thy husband."

B. The Woman's Evasion: vv. 19-25

We can well imagine the terrible shock the woman sustained when she heard Jesus' words. All her life of sin and sham and shame was suddenly revealed in the white light of divine judgment. It was a shattering moment for this woman of casual morals—a moment of truth.

For a few moments she must have been like a scared rabbit looking for a way of escape. What could she do or say?

Suddenly it came to her. Turning to Jesus with all the composure she could muster, she said to Him: "Sir, I see that you are a prophet. Now I have a big theological problem that I would like to have you help me solve."

Regaining her self-control, she explained what the problem was. Pointing to Mount Gerizim, in plain sight less than a mile away, she said: "Our fathers worshipped in this mountain; and ye say, that in Jerusalem is the place where men ought to worship." The Samaritans had built a temple on Mount Gerizim, a rival to that in Jeru-

salem, and claimed that here was where God was to be worshiped. Even today the Samaritans hold their Passover each spring on the top of Mount Gerizim, with most of the two hundred or so survivors of the sect present. (They all now live in the same country, Israel.)

Probably she hoped to turn Jesus' attention away from her sinful life by involving him in an endless theological argument. But Jesus was not to be sidetracked into a profitless discussion of Jerusalem vs. Gerizim. He came right to the point: "God is Spirit [omit "a"] and they that worship him must worship him in spirit and in truth" (v. 24). That is one of the greatest statements about true religion to be found anywhere, and its message needs to be sounded afresh in every generation. Real religion is not a matter of outward trappings and ceremonies; it is entirely spiritual.

The woman tried her last tactic— putting off a decision. To the man in front of her she said: "I know that Messiah is coming, the one who is called Christ: when he comes, he will tell us all things." Perhaps what she was thinking was: "You have told me plenty already, and a little too much!"

C. The Messiah's Disclosure: v. 26

What a shock it must have been to her to hear Jesus calmly reply: "I that speak unto thee am he." The woman had no escape. She finally capitulated. How do we know? Because she left her waterpot, hurried back to the town and said to the people: "Come, see a man who told me all I ever did; can this be the Messiah?" (v. 29).

V. A RIPENED HARVEST: John 4:27-38

While Jesus was concluding His conversation with the woman at the well, the disciples returned with the provisions they had purchased. They "marvelled that he talked with the woman." But the Greek says they marveled that He was talking with "a woman." The amazing thing to them was that He would be caught talking with any woman in public. The rabbinic rule was: "Let no one talk with a woman in the street, no not with his own wife." Jacob's Well was almost as public a place as a city street. It wasn't very proper for Jesus to be conversing with a woman!

Meanwhile the woman left, and the disciples begged, "Master, eat" (v. 31). Probably they had put off eating until He asked a blessing on the food, but now they were hungry and anxious to eat.

Jesus' reply was one of those spiritual statements that the disciples, as well as the crowd, seemed never to understand. He said, "I have food to eat that you don't know about." Perplexed, they asked each other, "Has someone brought him something to eat?" As usual, the Master had to explain the spiritual meaning to His disciples: "My food is to do the will of the One who sent me, and to finish his work." Spiritual sustenance comes from spiritual living.

Still concerned about spiritual rather than material matters, Christ continued: "You say it will be four months to harvest. But I tell you, 'Lift up your eyes, and look on the fields: for they are white already to harvest.' " It has been suggested that a crowd of people dressed in white Oriental garments was approaching. Verse 30 has already told us that the people of the village of Sychar "went out of the city, and came unto him." But the Greek clearly says that they "went out [aorist tense] and were coming [imperfect] to Him." They had not yet arrived.

What Jesus was saying was: "Here is a large crowd of people hungry for the Bread of Life. I must give Myself to them, rather than think about My own wants."

Verse 38 states a truth that every Christian worker should keep in mind. Jesus said to His disciples: "I sent you to reap that whereon ye bestowed no labour: other men laboured, and ye are entered into their labours." No

man works absolutely alone in the Kingdom. We are all the heirs of centuries of Christian service. We often reap where others have sowed. There is no room for exclusive pride in these matters.

VI. A REAPED HARVEST: John 4:39-42

Many of the Samaritans of Sychar believed on Jesus because of the testimony of the woman. So they begged Him to stay with them. He acceded to their request and remained there for two days. The result was that "many more believed because of his own word" (v. 41). They told the woman: "We have heard him ourselves, and know that this is indeed the Christ, the Saviour of the world." This was a tremendous testimony, coming from these despised Samaritans. In spiritual apprehension and faith they were far ahead of the religious leaders in Jerusalem! Jesus had almost been driven out of the Holy City; He had to escape to save His life. His message, rejected at Jerusalem, was eagerly received and believed at Sychar.

Rejection at Jerusalem and a revival in Samaria. How incredible! But that is exactly the kind of thing that often happens today. Too often the Spirit cannot move the hearts of people in the church.

DISCUSSION QUESTIONS

1. How should one begin a conversation with a spiritual "prospect"?
2. What are the dangers of theological arguing?
3. Should we ever sharply contradict people when we are doing personal work?
4. What should we do when people try to put us off?
5. How is morality related to religion?
6. What is the greatest secret of successful soul-winning?

CONTEMPORARY APPLICATION

The incident of today's lesson is the greatest example for personal soul-winning that can be found in the Bible. It will pay us to look at it closely.

First, Jesus began on a plane of common interest. He and the woman were both thirsty. She had the means of obtaining water; He did not. So He courteously asked her for a drink.

But Jesus did not waste time talking endlessly about material things. He moved over into the spiritual realm by offering the woman "living water."

When the woman sought to sidetrack Him, the Master came right to the point of the woman's need. He offered to put in her heart a bubbling fountain of water, to satisfy her deepest need.

When she insisted on pulling the conversation back down to the material level (v. 15), Christ suddenly changed the subject and confronted her with her life of sin. Since she refused to see the spiritual issues He was raising, He challenged her in the moral realm, where there was no escape.

Her last tactic was delay. How often we have heard it! "Yes, I know I need to surrender my life to Christ—but not tonight." And so people try to put if off.

The main lessons to be learned here are clear. We must keep bringing the conversation back to the spiritual realm, even though the other person repeatedly tries to pull it down to the material realm.

One of the most important lessons is this: Avoid theological arguments when doing personal work. People are not won to Christ by arguing, but by witnessing. You may win an argument and lose a soul.

Perhaps one more point needs to be made: Press for a decision. Jesus persisted with this woman, in spite of all her attempted evasions, until she finally surrendered.

BREAD FOR THE HUNGRY

(Temperance)

DEVOTIONAL READING	John 6:52-65

ADULTS

Topic: *Bread for the Hungry*

Background Scripture: John 6

Scripture Lesson: John 6:35-51

Memory Verse: *The bread of God is that which comes down from heaven, and gives life to the world.* John 6:33

YOUTH

Topic: *Bread That Fills*

Background Scripture: John 6

Scripture Lesson: John 6:35-51

Memory Verse: *The bread of God is that which comes down from heaven and gives life to the world.* John 6:33

CHILDREN

Topic: *Jesus Shows Concern*

Background Scripture: John 6:1-51

Scripture Lesson: John 6:5-13

Memory Verse: *Be watchful, stand firm in your faith, be courageous, be strong. Let all that you do be done in love.* I Corinthians 16:13-14

DAILY BIBLE READINGS

Mon., Dec. 31: Feeding the Five Thousand, John 6:1-14.
Tues., Jan. 1: Rejection of a Revolutionary Plot, John 6:15-21.
Wed., Jan. 2: Food Which Perishes, John 6:22-34.
Thurs., Jan. 3: Food Which Endures, John 6:35-40.
Fri., Jan. 4: Living Bread from Heaven, John 6:41-51.
Sat., Jan. 5: The Living Bread Rejected, John 6:52-65.
Sun., Jan. 6: "Will You Also Go Away?" John 6:66-71.

LESSON AIM

To see what Jesus meant when He spoke of Himself as the Bread of Life, and how we may feed our souls on Him.

LESSON SETTING

Time: Shortly before the Passover (in March or April) of, probably, A.D. 28

Place: The Feeding of the Five Thousand seems to have taken place on a hillside near the northeast corner of the Lake of Galilee, south of Bethsaida Julias. The great discourse on the Bread of Life was given in the synagogue at Capernaum (6:59).

137

Bread for the Hungry

SUGGESTED INTRODUCTION FOR ADULTS

Once again we need to look at the whole chapter if we are going to understand the lesson. Without seeing the background in the miracle, we cannot understand the discourse. And unless we follow right through to Jesus' explanation in the last part of the chapter, we shall miss the real meaning of what He was saying. It should be noted that the whole chapter comprises the lesson proper. And once more it is evident that the members of the class must all have Bibles or Testaments if they are going to get much help from the discussion.

In an earlier lesson we noted that John gives only seven of the many miracles performed by Jesus and that he always calls these miracles "signs," because they "signified" some spiritual truth. Nowhere is this striking feature more obvious than in the chapter we are studying today. Jesus first performed the miracle of feeding the five thousand. Then He gave His great discourse on the Bread of Life, which explained the spiritual significance of the miracle. In other words, He furnished the illustration first and then the exposition. We shall find the reversal of this in chapters 8 and 9, where He first expounds and then illustrates.

SUGGESTED INTRODUCTION FOR YOUTH

The great search of life is for something that will satisfy. Everyone is engaged in this search; there are no dropouts here.

And this quest is perfectly natural and normal. We *should* want the deepest longings of our hearts to be satisfied. What we should realize is that a loving God wants us to find complete satisfaction. The main point of this lesson is that the highest satisfactions in life can only be found in Christ.

There is nothing more pitiful than the substitutes that people are trying. They seek satisfaction through nicotine, alcohol, drugs, sex, pleasure—anything but Christ. But just as we know that nicotine, alcohol, and drugs will not take the place of wholesome food in giving health and strength to our physical bodies, so we must realize that worldly pleasures will never satisfy the soul.

CONCEPTS FOR
CHILDREN

1. Jesus is concerned for all our needs.
2. He wants children to be happy.
3. Only by letting Jesus have His way in our hearts and lives can we be truly happy.
4. Jesus wants to use all of us to help others.

THE LESSON COMMENTARY

I. FEEDING THE FIVE THOUSAND:
John 6:1-14

A. The Setting: vv. 1-4

Again Jesus left the throng of people—those who kept Him busy preaching, teaching, and healing—on the west side of the Lake of Galilee and sought a quiet vacation with His disciples on the east side of the lake. He was probably almost worn out physically and needed some rest.

Here and in 21:1—and nowhere else in the New Testament—the Lake of Galilee is called "the sea of Tiberias." This reflects the late date of John's Gospel. The city of Tiberias, the only city now remaining on the shores of the Lake of Galilee, was built by Herod Antipas, ruler of Galilee, as his capital. It was founded in about A.D. 25, just before Jesus began His public ministry, and named in honor of the ruling Roman Emperor, Tiberius. Because part of it was built over an old cemetery, the Jews considered it defiled and largely refused to live in it. There is no record in the Gospels that Jesus ever visited Tiberias. But by the time John wrote his Gospel (about A.D. 95) the city had given its name to the lake on which it stood.

On the relatively uninhabited east shore of the lake Jesus hoped to find seclusion with His disciples. But a large crowd followed Him, eager to see more miracles of healing (v. 2). By the time He was settled on a hillside with His disciples, many people began to throng around Him again. We read that the Passover was nearing and this may account for the great crowds that came to Him. The people were beginning to flock together in preparation for going to Jerusalem.

The traditional site for the feeding of the five thousand is at the location of the present Church of the Loaves and Fishes, on the west shore of the Lake of Galilee, south of Capernaum. Here tourists are shown an ancient mosaic in the floor, depicting Christ feeding the multitude. But there would have been no problem in getting food if this event had taken place on the northwest shore, where there were several big cities nearby. The picture given in the Gospel accounts clearly favors the eastern shore.

Incidentally, the Feeding of the Five Thousand is the only miracle recorded in all four Synoptic Gospels. John relates it because it suggests a great spiritual truth.

B. The Problem: vv. 5-9

When Jesus saw the big crowd out in front of Him, He turned to Philip and said, "Whence shall we buy bread, that these may eat?" He knew what He was going to do, but He wanted to test Philip, to see what he would say.

Philip evidently had a calculating mind, for he replied: "Two hundred pennyworth of bread is not sufficient for them, that every one of them may take a little." The Greek word for "pennyworth" is *denaria*. The denarius was a Roman silver coin, worth about twenty cents. But at that time it represented a day's wages, as indicated in the Parable of the Workers in the Vineyard (Matthew 20:2). So two hundred denarii would be equivalent to wages for eight months, allowing for Sabbaths and feast days. Obviously, this was a large amount in the thinking of that day. Some have suggested that Philip mentioned this figure because that was the amount of money in the apostolic treasury at the moment. But this seems rather unlikely.

Overhearing the conversation, Andrew, who as usual is identified here as Peter's brother, offered a suggestion: "There is a lad here, who has five barley loaves and two small fish." Then apologetically he added: "But what are they among so many?" It was obviously ridiculous to think of feeding five thousand people with one boy's lunch! And the boy was from a poor family, for only the poorest people ate barley. Those who were better off ate wheat, which cost twice as much (II Kings 7:1).

The lesson to be learned from this passage is that we should not apologize for the smallness of our assets in doing Christian work. As the old saying is, "Little is much if God is in it." Faith can bring divine power to bear on any situation, changing poverty to plenty. For God is able to multiply what little we have and make it enough to go completely around and meet every need.

C. The Miracle: vv. 10-14

The Master gave just one simple order: "Make the men sit down." John notes that "there was much grass in the place." Mark makes it even more specific. He says that the people sat down on the "green grass" (6:39). This agrees with John's statement that it was shortly before the Passover. Palestine is a dry country much like the southwestern part of the United States. Normally the grass is green only in March, April, and May, after the winter rains. The Passover, based on a lunar calendar, came in March or April.

Then we read: "So the men sat down, in number about five thousand." In the Greek the word translated "men" in the early part of verse 10 is *anthropoi*, which means "human beings." But in the latter part of the verse it is *andres*, which refers specifically to male individuals. Matthew, writing to Jews, says that Jesus fed "about five thousand men, beside women and children" (14:21). This reflects the fact that Jewish men never ate in public with women and children. The latter would be by themselves, separated from the men. This custom is still followed in some countries.

Jesus took the five barley "loaves," each about the size of a small pancake or a flat biscuit, gave thanks and "distributed to the disciples, and the disciples to them that were set down." He did the same with the two small fish, "as much as they would," that is, until everybody had eaten all he wanted. There was plenty to go around.

At what point did the miracle of multiplying the loaves and fish take place? Apparently as Jesus was breaking them in His hands the supply became endless. We can imagine the astonishment of the disciples as they kept coming back for more. It must have taken a long time to feed that big crowd.

When everybody was "filled," Jesus said to His disciples: "Gather up the fragments that remain, that nothing be lost." Though He had provided plenty of food, it was not to be wasted. This should be a lesson for us. If God, in answer to believing prayer, supplies an abundance of money for a project of the Kingdom, we should not become careless in the handling of the funds.

So the disciples gathered the broken pieces of food that were left over and filled twelve baskets with them. These were probably the lunch baskets, that the disciples, like all devout Jews, carried with them when traveling. So each disciple got his "tip" for waiting on the crowd.

When the people saw the miracle which Jesus had performed they said: "This is of a truth a prophet that should come into the world" (v. 14). We have already had a reference to "that prophet" (1:21, 25). Later we read of the people saying, "Of a truth this is the Prophet" (7:40). Peter in the Temple and Stephen before the Sanhedrin both quoted Deuteronomy 18:15: "A prophet shall the Lord your God raise up unto you of your brethren, like unto me; him shall ye hear," and applied this prophecy to Christ (Acts 3:22; 7:37). This is evidently the prophecy that the people had in mind.

II. WALKING ON THE WATER:
John 6:15-21

The statement in verse 15 is found only in John's Gospel, though it fits in well with the Synoptic accounts. The people wanted to "take him by force, to make him a king." Anyone who could miraculously supply all their needs would make a wonderful king to take care of them! How many of those people were identifying Him as Messiah we do not know. But in any case it would have been extremely dangerous for Jesus to have been acclaimed King of the Jews at this time. The results would have been disastrous not only for Him but for the nation, as the Romans would have answered such a revolt with wholesale massacre.

So Jesus went off to a mountain to pray, while the disciples returned to their boat—under His orders (Mark 6:45)—and set off across the lake for the western shore. We are told that "it

was now dark, and Jesus was not come to them"—a statement with obvious application to some experiences in our lives.

That night there was a heavy wind blowing against them, making the rowing very difficult. By early morning (Mark 6:48) they had only gone twenty-five or thirty "furlongs"—about three or four miles. So they were only halfway across the Lake of Galilee, which is about thirteen miles long and seven miles wide.

Suddenly they saw Jesus approaching. Thinking Him to be a ghost (Mark 6:49) "they were afraid." But He immediately called out to them: "It is I; be not afraid." What a comfort that must have been! They gladly welcomed Him into the boat, and in no time at all they arrived safely at the other shore. How often has Christ come to us in dark, stormy hours and brought us safely and quickly to solid ground again!

III. THE INQUISITIVE CROWD:
John 6:22-27

Meanwhile the crowd that Jesus fed had camped somewhere for the night. In the morning the people wondered where Jesus was. They had seen His disciples leave by boat without Him. Not being able to find Him, they set off across the lake, perhaps using some boats that had come from Tiberias (v. 23).

When they found Him at Capernaum, they asked, "Rabbi, when camest thou hither?" Jesus ignored their inquisitiveness and reproved them for their selfish motives in following Him. They were not seeking Him because of His miracles, but only because they wanted more free food. He urged them not to work simply for physical food, but for that "which endureth unto everlasting life, which the Son of man shall give unto you" (v. 27). In love and mercy He had ministered to their needs physically on the other shore. Now He wanted to give them the far more important spiritual food for their souls.

IV. THE INQUIRING CROWD:
John 6:28-34

Jesus had told them not to "work" (Greek *ergazomai*) for perishing physical food. His listeners picked up the same verb and asked: "What shall we do, that we might work the works of God?" The Master's answer is profound in its implications: "This is the work of God, that ye believe on him whom he hath sent" (v. 29). There is no way that we can "work works" that will bring about our salvation. The only "work" that a sinner can do that will please God is to *believe* on Jesus Christ. Any other works are useless. We have to trust in the finished work of Christ on the cross for us. That is the only basis of our acceptance with God.

Still in an inquiring frame of mind the people asked: "What sign showest thou then, that we may see, and believe thee?" (v. 30). And they had just witnessed the feeding of the five thousand! What more did they want?

Then the people made reference to the manna with which God had fed the Israelites in the desert of Sinai (v. 31). Jesus replied: "Moses gave you not that bread from heaven [it was God who had given it] but my Father giveth you the true bread from heaven. For the bread of God is he which cometh down from heaven, and giveth life unto the world." Just as Jesus had labored with the woman at Jacob's Well to turn her attention from ordinary water to living water, so now He tries to get these people to understand that their real need was not more loaves and fish but spiritual food for life eternal.

They replied: "Lord, evermore give us this bread." Probably they were more sincere and discerning in their request than was the Samaritan woman (4:15). Yet they still had ahead of them a long journey in spiritual understanding, as the rest of the chapter shows. People seem to be incurably materialistic.

V. THE BREAD OF LIFE:
John 6:35-51

A. The Message of Jesus: vv. 35-40

Finally Jesus came to the heart of His discussion about the true bread from heaven. He said, "I am the Bread of Life."

This is the first of ten "I am's" in the Gospel of John—a very striking and unique feature of this "spiritual Gospel." The second is found in 8:12 and 9:5 "I am the Light of the World." The third, in 8:58, is in absolute form, when Jesus said, "Before Abraham was, I am." Here He identified Himself with the One who revealed Himself to Moses at the burning bush as, "I AM." No wonder the Jews tried to stone Him (8:59)!

The fourth is in 10:7: "I am the Door of the Sheep." The fifth follows closely: "I am the Good Shepherd" (10:11, 14). The sixth is in 11:25: "I am the Resurrection." The seventh, eighth, and ninth are found together in 14:6: "I am the Way, the Truth and the Life." The tenth is in 15:1: "I am the True Vine." Taken together, these present some of the many facets of Jesus' Person and work, and yet they do not begin to portray the fullness of who and what He was. Human language cannot adequately describe Him.

To the woman at the well Jesus had said, "Whosoever drinketh of the water that I shall give him shall never thirst" (4:14). Here He adds to this: "I am the bread of life: he that cometh to me shall never hunger; and he that believeth on me shall never thirst." Jesus has promised to satisfy completely all those who accept Him as the Living Water and as the Bread of Life. To have one's deepest longings satisfied is the richest treasure anyone can have here on earth.

Verse 36 sounds a pathetic note. Christ's listeners had seen Him for some time, but they still did not believe in Him.

Verse 37 contains one of the most frequently quoted of evangelistic promises: "Him that cometh unto me I will in no wise cast out." What a comfort to know that He has already given His word that if we come to Him sincerely He will receive us as His own. No repentant heart will ever be turned away by a loving Savior.

In the previous chapter Jesus had declared: "I seek not mine own will, but the will of the Father which hath sent me" (5:30). Here (6:38) He says: "For I came down from heaven, not to do mine own will, but the will of him that sent me." In this Jesus set an example for all who follow Him.

The idea that Jesus' disciples had been given to Him by the Father is expressed several times in John's Gospel (6:39; 10:29; 17:2, 6). Here He declares it is the Father's will that none of these should be lost. He goes on to say (v. 40): "And this is the will of him that sent me, that every one which seeth the Son, and believeth on him, may have everlasting life: and I will raise him up at the last day." Here we find sounded again the keynote of John's Gospel: eternal life through believing in Jesus Christ (cf. 20:31).

B. The Misunderstanding of the People: vv. 41-42

The Jews "murmured," or "muttered," against Jesus because He claimed to be the bread which had come down from heaven. "Is not this Jesus the son of Joseph," they asked, "whose father and mother we know?" How then could He say that He came down from heaven? Their knowledge of His humanity prevented their believing in His deity. And this is a stumbling block to many today. But believing in Jesus as the Son of God is a step of faith. One cannot take this step by sheer reasoning.

C. The Explanation by Jesus: vv. 43-51

Jesus told the people to stop their muttering among themselves. Then He uttered an important truth: "No man can come to me, except the Father which hath sent me draw him: and I will raise him up at the last day." We have to recognize the divine initiative in our salvation. Probably the warning here is especially directed toward those who feel God speaking to them and drawing them to faith in Christ, but put it off by saying, "Some day I'll get saved." Such people have no assurance that God will ever speak to them again, and they cannot be converted any time they get ready. "Now is the day of salvation" (II Corinthians 6:2). God has given us no promise of tomorrow. But those who listen to His voice today will come and be saved (v. 45).

In 1:18 we read: "No man hath seen God at any time." Here (v. 46) we have an echo of that: "Not that any man hath seen the Father, save he which is of God, he hath seen the Father." Westcott comments (p. 105) "He alone who is truly God can naturally see God. The voice of God came to men under the old Covenant, but in Christ the believer can now see the Father (xiv.9) in part, and will hereafter see God as He is (I John iii.2)."

Then with a double "Verily" Jesus declared: "He that believeth on me hath everlasting life" (v. 47). Again we would note (cf. 3:36) that the Greek says: "He who is believing on me is having (right now) eternal life." The life is dependent on the believing.

Once more Jesus announced the text of this discourse: "I am the bread of life" (v. 48). (The Greek does not say "that bread," as KJV has it.) He had been trying to explain what He meant by this, but His hearers had been slow to understand. So now He tries again. He reminds them that though their forefathers ate the life-giving manna in the desert, they finally died. But He was the bread that had come down from heaven. Then comes a meaningful elaboration of His text: "I am the living bread which came down from heaven: if any man eat of this bread he shall live for ever: and the bread that I will give is my flesh, which I will give for the life of the world" (v. 51). That is, only by His death on the cross could Christ become the Bread of Life to a starving (spiritually) world. He would be the Bread broken for every man.

VI. THE NECESSITY OF FEEDING ON CHRIST:
John 6:52-59

Not surprisingly the Jewish leaders reacted sharply to Jesus' words. "How can this man give us his flesh to eat?" they asked.

As if to confound them further, Jesus made His previous statement still more explicit: "Except ye eat the flesh of the Son of man, and drink his blood, ye have no life in you. Whoso eateth my flesh, and drinketh my blood, hath eternal life; and I will raise him up at the last day" (vv. 53-54). And for several more verses (55-58) we find Jesus continuing to talk about the necessity of eating His flesh and drinking His blood.

What did He mean? Several Christian denominations give a very easy answer: "It obviously means eating His flesh and drinking His blood in the communion service." Without any desire to enter into argument about the Real Presence, we would simply say

that nothing material can produce spiritual life.

In verse 59 we are told that this discourse on the Bread of Life was given at the synagogue in Capernaum. This was probably the greatest message that Jesus gave in the place that was, in a sense, His "home church" at this time.

VII. THE SPIRITUAL MEANING OF THIS:
John 6:60-65

When His disciples complained that what He had said was a "hard saying," Jesus made a profound statement that sets all the previous discourse in a clear light. He said: "It is the spirit that quickeneth; the flesh profiteth nothing: the words that I speak unto you, they are spirit, and they are life" (v. 63). How may we feed on Christ? By meditating on His Word with the help of the Holy Spirit. It is thus that our souls are fed and we have eternal life. God's Word is the spiritual food we need. And we can and must feed on this Word every day.

VIII. THE CRISIS OF DISCIPLESHIP: John 6:66-71

Jesus had come to the very heart of what Christianity is: not a church or a creed, but Christ! But this was too much for some of His hearers. We read the sad statement: "From that time many of his disciples went back and walked no more with him." With perhaps a tinge of sorrow Jesus turned to His disciples and said, "You do not wish to go away also, do you?" (v. 67, literal Greek). Peter rose magnificently to the occasion and replied: "Lord, to whom shall we go? thou hast the words of eternal life. And we believe and are sure that thou art that Christ, the Son of the living God"; or, as the best Greek text says: "that you are the Holy One of God." What comfort those words must have brought to the heart of Jesus!

DISCUSSION QUESTIONS

1. Why is the Feeding of the Five Thousand related in all four Gospels?
2. What are some lessons we can learn from this incident?
3. What is the importance of "bread"?
4. How may we feed on Christ?
5. How can Christ satisfy our deepest needs?
6. What role does the church have in feeding the hungry?

CONTEMPORARY APPLICATION

The Feeding of the Five Thousand presents a real challenge to us today. "Little is much if God is in it." That can be the secret of our success. Our natural assets may not seem to amount to any more than the lad's lunch. But in Christ's hands they can be multiplied into enough to meet the need.

Another important lesson is that Christ actually fed the five thousand people by using His disciples as waiters. He could multiply the loaves and fishes but He could not very well serve all those people individually. It was a task for the Twelve. So Christ today wants to feed the hungry multitudes on the Bread of Life—through us. He needs our hands and feet to do the job.

LIGHT FOR THE BLIND

DEVOTIONAL READING	John 9:24-33

ADULTS

Topic: *Light for the Blind*

Background Scripture: John 8:12-30; 9

Scripture Lesson: John 9:1-7, 35-41

Memory Verse: *I am the light of the world; he who follows me will not walk in darkness, but will have the light of life.* John 8:12

YOUTH

Topic: *Now I See!*

Background Scripture: John 8:12-30; 9

Scripture Lesson: John 9:1-7, 35-41

Memory Verse: *I am the light of the world; he who follows me will not walk in darkness, but will have the light of life.* John 8:12

CHILDREN

Topic: *Jesus Gives Courage*

Background Scripture: John 8:12-30; 9

Scripture Lesson: John 9:1-11, 24-25

Memory Verse: *All things are possible to him who believes.* Mark 9:23

DAILY BIBLE READINGS

Mon., Jan. 7: Light for All People, Luke 2:25-32.
Tues., Jan. 8: Jesus, the Light of Life, John 12:27-36.
Wed., Jan. 9: The Light of the World, John 8:12-20.
Thurs., Jan. 10: The Man Born Blind, John 9:1-17.
Fri., Jan. 11: "One Thing I Know," John 9:18-25.
Sat., Jan. 12: Jesus and Judgment, John 9:26-41.
Sun., Jan. 13: "The Lord Is My Light." Psalm 27:1-6.

LESSON AIM

To show how Christ is the Light of the World and how He may enlighten each of our hearts.

LESSON SETTING

Time: Probably in the late fall of A.D. 29

Place: Apparently in or near Jerusalem

LESSON OUTLINE

Light for the Blind

    I. The Disciples' Question: John 9:1-2
       A. The Man Born Blind: v. 1
       B. A Strange Question: v. 2

II. The Master's Answer: John 9:3-5
   A. Manifestation of God's Power: v. 3
   B. The Light of the World: vv. 4-5

III. The Master's Miracle: John 9:6-7
   A. The Symbolical Preparation: v. 6
   B. The Miracle of Healing: v. 7

IV. The Neighbors' Inquiry: John 9:8-12

V. The Pharisees' Investigation: John 9:13-17

VI. The Parents' Fear: John 9:18-23

VII. The Pharisees' Opposition: John 9:24-34

VIII. The Master's Challenge: John 9:35-38
   A. Presentation as Messiah: vv. 35-37
   B. Acceptance and Worship: v. 38

SUGGESTED INTRODUCTION FOR ADULTS

In the last lesson we saw how Jesus performed the miracle of feeding the five thousand and then gave the discourse on the Bread of Life. In this lesson we find the reverse. Jesus declared, "I am the light of the world" (8:12) and then He illustrated this saying by healing the man born blind (chap. 9). The connection between the two is shown by the repetition of "I am the light of the world" in 9:5, followed immediately by the miracle.

Sin is spiritual blindness and darkness. The man born blind is a symbol of the fact that all men are born in sin and so are spiritually blind from birth. Only Christ can open their eyes.

One of the interesting features of this chapter is the indication of the step-by-step progress of the healed man in his understanding of Christ. He is a striking example of walking in the light, which always results in spiritual progress. The man started out with practically no knowledge of Jesus. All he knew about Him was His name. He ended up by worshiping Jesus as the promised Messiah and the Son of God.

SUGGESTED INTRODUCTION FOR YOUTH

Who is Jesus? That is the most important question confronting every person. This is the question that is discussed in chapter 9 of John's Gospel.

It is thrilling to see how the man who had been born blind not only was given his physical sight but also grew in spiritual insight. He was alert, eager, and quick to learn.

As indicated in this chapter, argument and opposition only sharpened the man's understanding of what was true. It was so with Martin Luther, and it has been true with many others. If we are willing to think clearly and honestly on the question as to who Jesus is we will come out with a definite faith in Him as Son of God and Savior. With hearts and minds open to the truth, we will grow in grace.

CONCEPTS FOR
CHILDREN

1. The man Jesus healed wanted to know the truth.
2. He had courage enough to stand up for what he believed.
3. As he followed what he knew his knowledge increased.
4. Because he was honest and open, he found Jesus as Lord.

THE LESSON COMMENTARY

I. THE DISCIPLES' QUESTION: John 9:1-2

A. The Man Born Blind: v. 1

Jesus had been teaching in the Temple but, as usual in Jerusalem, His message had been rejected by the religious leaders of the nation. The previous verse in this Gospel says: "Then took they up stones to cast at him: but Jesus hid himself, and went out of the temple." Now we read: "And as Jesus passed by, he saw a man which was blind from birth." Driven from the sacred Temple by threat of death, He gave His attention to a poor blind beggar (cf. v. 8). This is typical of Jesus' ministry. He was rejected by the religious establishment, but He found needy individuals everywhere.

B. A Strange Question: v. 2

The disciples asked Jesus: "Master, who did sin, this man or his parents, that he was born blind?" As soon as one begins to analyze this question, it appears very strange. That a person could be born blind because of a sin of his parents is clear enough. This has often happened. Certain types of disease caused by sinful living can cause congenital defects at birth. But how could one be born blind because of his own sin?

Three suggestions have been offered: (1) the man was punished in advance for sins that God knew he would commit; (2) the unborn infant sinned; (3) the man had sinned in a previous existence. The first can be dismissed at once as unreasonable. But how about the other two?

W. J. Howard writes: "There are also sayings in the Targums and in the Talmud [Jewish writings of the early Middle Ages] which seem to show that some rabbis thought it possible that a child could sin while in its mother's womb. It is hardly likely that belief in the pre-existence of souls had penetrated into Palestinian Judaism, but since it is found in Philo's writing ... and at a later period in the Hermetic tracts, it may have been known in the world for which this Gospel was written" (*Interpreter's Bible*, VIII, 613-14).

Westcott says: "There are traces of a belief in the pre-existence of souls, at least in later Judaism (Wisdom 8:20)." Some recent scholars have questioned this. But we do know that the idea of the preexistence and reincarnation of the human soul was widely held at that time. Plato had taught it, and it is a basic doctrine of Hinduism and other religions and philosophies. It was obviously formulated as a proposed solution to the inequities of human birth—a problem that has plagued thoughtful people from time immemorial. Why are some people born in such unfortunate circumstances? It must be that they sinned in a previous existence! It would seem to us that the question of the disciples implies that such ideas were circulating in Palestine in Jesus' day.

II. THE MASTER'S ANSWER: John 9:3-5

A. Manifestation of God's Power: v. 3

The first part of Jesus' answer provides a good opportunity for sounding a much-needed word of caution. He said, "Neither hath this man sinned, nor his parents." Taken by themselves, these words are a flat contradiction of the teaching elsewhere in the Bible that "all have sinned" (Romans 3:23). But every statement in the Scriptures must be read in the light of its context. What Jesus obviously meant was: "It was not a sin of this man or his parents that caused him to be born blind." We must always be careful not to quote a few words from the Bible and then apply them in a way that is not in accordance with their context— both the immediate context of the passage and the larger context of the general teachings of the Scriptures.

The second part of Jesus' answer poses another problem: Was He saying that this man was born blind "in order that the works of God should be made manifest in him?" It is true that the Greek conjunction *hina* usually indicates purpose—"in order that." But it is also used sometimes to express result—"with the result that." This is the way it should be taken here. The man's blindness furnished the occasion for a demonstration of divine power, which was soon to take place.

B. The Light of the World: vv. 4-5

Jesus felt the urgency of His task: "I must work the works of him that sent me, while it is day: the night cometh, when no man can work." We should follow Him in this. History gives many examples of the importance of this warning. In the early part of this century the vast country of China was being evangelized by thousands of missionaries from Europe and America. Buddhists and Confucianists were being won to Christ in large numbers. Then suddenly the sun set and the darkness of atheistic Communism descended on the most populous country in the world. Before long there was not a single foreign missionary left in China, and the bamboo curtain has been closed for a generation. And now the second most populous country, India, is threatening to close its doors to Christian missionaries. We must work

"while it is day," before the darkness of night puts an end to the opportunities for evangelism. Meanwhile we thank God for the reports of great revivals in Indonesia and a few other countries. We must pray and work that this may increase.

Jesus had already declared that He was the Light of the World (8:12). Now He repeats it: "As long as I am in the world, I am the light of the world" (v. 5).

Some have insisted that the first part of this verse implies that Jesus is no longer the Light of the World, since He is no longer in it. This is another example of the danger of taking a Bible statement out of its context. John 1:4-9 teaches the great truth that the eternal Logos has been the Light of the World since the dawn of creation. But He became the Light of the World in a larger and more effective way in His incarnation. He continues to light the world through the ministry of the Holy Spirit. And His light shines today mostly through us as Christians, since we are now "the light of the world" (Matthew 5:16).

III. THE MASTER'S MIRACLE: John 9:6-7

A. The Symbolical Preparation: v. 6

Jesus "spat on the ground, and made clay of the spittle, and he anointed the eyes of the blind man with the clay." This was perhaps intended as an aid to the man's faith. The next verse may also suggest that it was involved in testing the man's obedience. A third possible meaning is offered by W. F. Howard: "By making a paste of dust and spittle, Jesus may have symbolized the creative act of Gen. 2:7." The Creator was now the Re-creator, the Restorer of His creation.

B. The Miracle of Healing: v. 7

Having put clay on the man's eyes, Jesus now told him to go to the Pool of Siloam and wash the mud plaster off his eyes. The blind man obeyed and immediately was able to see—for the first time in his life. We can hardly imagine how this must have revolutionized his whole life. He had never seen a blossoming flower or a glorious sunset. He had never seen the faces of his loved ones. What an overwhelming experience it must have been suddenly to see thousands of objects that he had previously known only by touch or sound. He lived in a new world!

We are told that Siloam means "sent." The name was probably given to it originally because the water in the pool is discharged from a tunnel that leads from the Virgin's Fountain, the only spring of fresh water near the city. Possibly the meaning is noted because the blind man was sent there to wash. But in view of John's penchant for giving spiritual significance to little items like this, we may assume that he mentions it to remind his readers that Jesus was "sent" from the Father (cf. 17:3).

The visitor to Jerusalem today should by all means see the Pool of Siloam, one of the few undisputed sites around that city. There can be no question about its identification. The pool is fifty-eight feet long, eighteen feet wide and nineteen feet deep, though the water is shallow. Today it is used mainly by the neighborhood women who do their laundry there.

One can still walk through the tunnel when the water is low. At the Siloam end there was discovered in 1880 an inscription cut in the wall, written in the Hebrew of Old Testament times. The inscription reads "The boring through is completed. And this is the story of the boring through while yet they plied the drill, each toward his fellow.... And on the day of the boring through the stone-cutters struck ... drill upon drill; and the water flowed from the source to the pool for a thousand and two hundred cubits, and a hundred cubits was the height of the rock above the heads of the stone-cutters."

The finding of this inscription settled one issue. Among scholars there had been considerable dispute as to the length of the "cubit" mentioned frequently in the Bible. When the tunnel was measured, it was found to be 1780 feet long, almost 1800 feet. So the 1200 cubits must have each equaled a foot and a half, or eighteen inches—not twenty-two as some had claimed.

The reason for the building of this tunnel is given in II Chronicles 32:30. When the Assyrians approached Jerusalem and threatened to take it, the main problem was to preserve a water supply for the city in case of siege. So Hezekiah had this tunnel cut through solid rock to bring fresh water inside the city walls from "Gihon," now called Virgin's Fountain. Then he covered up the spring, so that it would not be found by the enemy. This happened about 700 B.C.

IV. THE NEIGHBOR'S INQUIRY: John 9:8-12

In the lengthy section between the two portions listed as the Scripture passage for today's lesson we find a very interesting account of the increasing opposition of the Jewish leaders to Jesus, and at the same time the growing understanding of the healed man as to who Jesus was.

It began with the inquisitive neighbors. When they saw this man walking freely around, they asked, "Is not this he that sat and begged?" Some voiced their opinion: "This is he." Others weren't sure. "He is like him," they said. But the man himself flatly asserted, "I am he!"

So they asked him, "How were your eyes opened?" His answer was clear and simple: "A man that is called Jesus made clay, and anointed mine eyes, and said unto me, Go to the pool of Siloam, and wash: and I went and washed, and received my sight" (v. 11). This is the first step in the man's knowledge of the one who healed him. It was "a man called Jesus." That is all he knew—but it was more than the cripple healed at the Pool of Bethesda had been able to say (5:12-13).

But when the neighbors asked, "Where is he?" the man could only reply, "I don't know." Jesus had disappeared. Probably the man was so excited about seeing everything and everybody that he forgot to go back and report to his Healer.

V. THE PHARISEES' INVESTIGATION:
John 9:13-17

For some unstated reason the neighbors of the blind man brought him to the Pharisees. Probably they thought that the religious leaders should know about this miracle.

Verse 14 sounds a frequent note in both the Synoptic Gospels and especially in the Fourth Gospel—Jesus coming into conflict with the Pharisees because He healed someone on the Sabbath day. This was considered work and was forbidden by the rabbinical rules.

When the Pharisees asked the man how he had been healed, he gave a straightforward answer (v. 15). Immediately some of them voiced their criticism: "This man is not of God, because he keepeth not the sabbath day." But others asked, "How can a man that is a sinner do such miracles?" This difference of opinion caused a "division" (Greek, *schism*).

Since they couldn't agree among themselves, they once more questioned the man before them. "What do you say about him, since he opened your eyes?" His reply shows definite progress: "He is a prophet" (v. 17). This is the second stage in the man's understanding of Jesus and shows clear, logical thinking. Certainly only a prophet of God could do what Jesus had done.

VI. THE PARENTS' FEAR:
John 9:18-23

The stubborn unbelief of these religious leaders is seen in the fact that they rejected the man's testimony. Surely he ought to have known what happened! But they wouldn't believe his story.

So they summoned the man's parents. It was a serious matter to be called in before the local Sanhedrin that acted as a judicial court. Without doubt the parents came with fear and trembling.

When the Pharisees questioned them, the parents made a twofold reply. First they said, "We know that this is our son, and that he was born blind" (v. 20). There was no question about those two facts. Then they quickly added: "But by what means he now seeth, we know not; or who hath opened his eyes, we know not: he is of age, ask him: he shall speak for himself" (v. 21). The reason for their refusal to get involved is clearly stated by the writer: "These words spake his parents, because they feared the Jews: for the Jews had agreed already, that if any man did confess that he was the Christ, he should be put out of the synagogue." The last five words are all one word in Greek, equivalent to our "unchurched." So the die was cast. Anyone who followed Jesus and accepted Him as the Messiah would be expelled from the religious community. It was a drastic step, but they had already made the ruling.

So the parents refused to take any responsibility in relation to their son. He was old enough to answer for himself. Older people are naturally conservative, and this couple did not want to be expelled from the synagogue. But we could wish that they had stood courageously with their son!

VII. THE PHARISEES' OPPOSITION:
John 9:24-34

The religious leaders again summoned the healed man to stand before them. This time they said, "Give God the praise"—Greek, "glory." In the light of what they went on to say, this seems like cruel hypocrisy. Actually it was a formula used for putting a man under oath to tell the truth. We have a striking Old Testament example of this in Joshua 7:19: "And Joshua said unto Achan, My son, give, I pray thee, glory to the Lord God of Israel, and make confession unto him; and tell me now what thou hast done: hide it not from me."

So the first clause of what they said was perfectly proper. But the next statement they made was not: "We know that this man is a sinner." To say the least, this was prejudging the case.

The man's answer is typical of his forthrightness. He said: "Whether he be a sinner or no, I know not: one thing I know, that, whereas I was blind, now I see." A witness is supposed to tell what he actually knows and nothing else. This man shows up as an admirable, honest witness at every point. He simply told what he knew.

The persistence of the Pharisees in pressing the issue reveals them in a very bad light. They ought to have been rejoicing with the man in his marvelous healing, and praising God for it. Instead they criticized the Healer and berated the man who had been healed. With stubborn unreasonableness they asked him again: "What did he to thee? how opened he thine eyes?"

By this time the man was justifi-

DISCUSSION QUESTIONS

1. What part did obedience play in the man's healing?
2. Does God ever use human props, as Christ seemed to do in using the clay?
3. How should we react to unbelief and opposition that we meet?
4. What part did opposition have in leading this man in his knowing Christ?
5. What is the relation between understanding and commitment?
6. How does a closed mind hinder spiritual understanding?

---

ably disgusted with their lack of fairness and reasonableness. It was obvious that they were not looking for information but for some way of punishing Jesus, whom they had already condemned in their minds. So the healed man said to them: "I have told you already, and ye did not hear: wherefore would ye hear it again? will ye also be his disciples?" The "also" implies that he considered himself a disciple of Jesus.

The last question was well deserved but not exactly diplomatic! The Pharisees reacted predictably: "Then they reviled him, and said, Thou art his disciple; but we are Moses' disciples" (v. 28). This was a false antithesis, as Jesus had already pointed out (5:45-47). The leaders added: "We know that God spake unto Moses: as for this fellow, we know not from whence he is." It will be noted that *fellow* is in italics, indicating that it is not in the original Greek. But it is entirely clear in the Gospels, that the pronoun *this* is used several times by Jesus' opponents in a contemptuous sense, and so "this fellow" is a good translation.

Doubtlessly shocked by the closed minds of the religious leaders of the nation and their complete lack of either fairness or reason, the healed man blossomed out into a bit of a theologian. First, he expressed his surprise at their ignorance concerning a prophet who could perform such a miracle of healing. Then he went on to give them a needed lesson in logic: "Now we know that God heareth not sinners: but if any man be a worshipper of God, and doeth his will, him he heareth" (v. 31). For good measure, he added: "Since the world began was it not heard that any man opened the eyes of one that was born blind. If this man were not of God, he could do nothing" (vv. 32-33). This marks the third step in the man's progress in knowledge about Jesus: the Healer must be a man of God.

The man's logical, theological speech didn't do any good! Thoroughly enraged, his religious leaders turned on him and said: "You were altogether born in sins, and do you teach us?" Whereupon they "cast him out"— excommunicated him from the synagogue.

VIII. THE MASTER'S CHALLENGE: John 9:35-38

A. Presentation as Messiah: vv. 35-37

When Jesus heard of this action, He went in search of the man and found him. Here was a devout Jew who was suddenly thrown out of his "church" because he was honest and truthful. He needed a friend! Jesus knew it, and with the thoughtful compassion that always characterized Him, He went to the man's rescue at once.

When Jesus found the man, He said to him, "Dost thou believe on the Son of God?" The earliest Greek manuscripts have "Son of man." But both these expressions mean essentially the same thing: "the Messiah." In Matthew 16:16 and John 20:31 we find "the Christ" (Messiah) and "Son of God" joined together. And "Son of man" was a Messianic title among the Jews of Jesus' day. So what Jesus was asking was: "Do you believe on the Messiah?"

With typical honesty and openness the man replied: "Who is he, Lord, that I might believe on him?" Some people are troubled by the fact that recent translations of the New Testament use "sir" in a few places where the King James Version has "Lord." The Greek word here, *Kyrios,* is translated "sir" in Matthew 13:27; 21:30; 27:10. The term is also used frequently in both the Gospels and Epistles for "masters" of slaves. But the most striking fact is that Jesus Himself is addressed as "Sir" in the King James Version by the Samaritan woman at the well (John 4:11, 15, 19), by the nobleman (4:49) and by the impotent man at the Pool of Bethesda (5:7). The basis for deciding between "sir" and "Lord" is simply this: Did the one addressing Jesus think of Him as the Son of God? If so, then "Lord" is the proper translation; if not, it should be "sir." Since it is not until verse 38 that this man believes in Jesus as the Messiah, a good case could be made for using "sir" in verse 36.

Jesus had a definite answer for the man's question. He said: "You have both seen Him, and it is He who is talking with you."

B. Acceptance and Worship: v. 38

The man did not hesitate in his response. Joyfully he cried, "Lord, I believe [Certainly this should be "Lord"!]. And he worshipped him." Now his understanding and faith had reached their goal in his acceptance of Jesus as his Messiah and Lord. It was worth all the long, rough road to arrive finally at this destination.

CONTEMPORARY APPLICATION

There are many sincere people around us who will follow the light that leads to faith in Christ, if only that light is shown to them. We need to watch for opportunities to point such people to Christ. All they need is a guide; they will follow the star when they see it. This man's growth in understanding and faith is a beautiful picture, and it should be duplicated in many lives today.

LOVE AMONG BELIEVERS

| DEVOTIONAL READING | I John 3:11-18 |

ADULTS

Topic: *Love Among Believers*

Background Scripture: John 13:1-20, 31-35

Scripture Lesson: John 13:1-5, 12-14, 34-35

Memory Verse: *By this all men will know that you are my disciples, if you have love for one another.* John 13:35

YOUTH

Topic: *Love Is the Thing*

Background Scripture: John 13:1-20, 31-35

Scripture Lesson: John 13:1-5, 12-14, 34-35

Memory Verse: *By this all men will know that you are my disciples, if you have love for one another.* John 13:35

CHILDREN

Topic: *Jesus Asks Us to Love*

Background Scripture: John 13:1-20, 31-35

Scripture Lesson: John 13:3-12, 34-35

Memory Verse: *A new commandment I give to you, that you love one another, even as I have loved you, that you also love one another. By this all men will know that you are my disciples, if you have love for one another.* John 13:34-35

DAILY BIBLE READINGS

Mon., Jan. 14: Washing the Disciples' Feet, John 13:1-11.
Tues., Jan. 15: "I Have Given You an Example," John 13:12-20.
Wed., Jan. 16: "A New Commandment," John 13:31-35.
Thurs., Jan. 17: "A More Excellent Way," I Corinthians 12:31—13:13.
Fri., Jan. 18: "Love One Another," I John 3:11-18.
Sat., Jan. 19: "This Is His Commandment," I John 3:19-24.
Sun., Jan. 20: "Love Your Enemies," Matthew 5:43-48.

LESSON AIM

To see the importance of brotherly love among believers in Christ, and the witness that it gives to the world.

LESSON SETTING

Time: Thursday evening of Passion Week, the night before the Crucifixion, which perhaps took place on the 6th of April, A.D. 30

154

Place: The upper room—a large guest room in a private home in Jerusalem

Love Among Believers

LESSON OUTLINE

SUGGESTED INTRODUCTION FOR ADULTS

The Gospel of John divides itself quite naturally into two parts. Chapters 1—12 give Jesus' ministry to the world, and chapters 13—21 describe His minstry to His own disciples. As He neared the end of His life on earth, Christ realized that the most important thing He could do was to prepare His disciples to carry on His work after He went back to heaven. So he cloistered Himself with them in the upper room. No less than five chapters (13—17) are devoted to what went on in the few hours of that last evening before His crucifixion. The world was shut out and the Master was alone with His disciples.

Chapter 13 tells us what took place at the Last Supper. (This must be supplemented by the Synoptic accounts of the inauguration of the Lord's Supper at that time). Chapters 14—16 give us what is commonly termed "The Last Discourse." Chapter 17 consists of the great high-priestly prayer of Jesus, which we have already looked at in a previous lesson. Then chapters 18 and 19 tell of His arrest, trials, and crucifixion. The final two chapters (20—21) describe several of the postresurrection appearances of Jesus.

So now we move from the public ministry of Jesus to His private ministry. With chapter 13 we enter into the shadow of the cross.

SUGGESTED
INTRODUCTION
FOR YOUTH

"Love Is the Thing." This is the youth topic for today's lesson. What does it mean?

Sometime ago we read in the newspaper that the dirtiest word in the hippie vocabulary is *love*. When hippies talk about "doing their thing" and call it *love*, they mean something a million miles removed from what Jesus was talking about in our lesson today. They are thinking of love on a purely physical level—sensual self-indulgence. Jesus commanded us to love each other with holy love—a love that is unselfish and seeks the highest good of others. There is nothing more needed today than a proper understanding of what Christian love is. Let us ask Christ to show us how to carry out His commandment.

CONCEPTS FOR
CHILDREN

1. Jesus showed His love for His disciples by an act of humble service to them.
2. We can show our love to others in the same way.
3. Jesus wants to help us in doing this day by day.
4. We show that we are God's children when we really love each other.

THE LESSON COMMENTARY

I. THE FINAL HOUR OF FELLOWSHIP:
John 13:1-3

A. Jesus' Love for His Own: v. 1

The final Passover of Jesus' ministry took place probably on April 5, A.D. 30. It will be remembered that the Jews used a lunar calendar, in which each month began with the new moon. Because the Passover was held on the fifteenth of the month Nisa, it always came at the time of full moon. Hence astronomers can calculate the exact date for the Passover of A.D. 30, in terms of our day.

We have noted that in John's Gospel it is stated several times that Jesus' hour had not yet come. But now we read, "When Jesus knew that his hour was come that he should depart out of this world unto the Father. . . . " There were three stages in that departure: His death, His resurrection, and His ascension. All three together comprise His appointed hour that had now come. What was the dominant thought and feeling of Christ as He faced this hour? It was love! John records: "Hav-

ing loved his own which were in the world, he loved them unto the end." Paul wrote: "Love never fails" (I Corinthians 13:8).

B. Judas's Treachery Toward His Master: v. 2

Finally they came to the end of the supper, the last fellowship meal that Jesus would have with His disciples before He went to the cross. But Satan was already stalking his prey, eager for the kill. He had persuaded one of the Master's own chosen apostles to betray his Lord. It was to be one of the saddest experiences of Jesus' life.

C. Jesus' Knowledge of His Mission: v. 3

The combination of the human and divine natures in the Person of Jesus Christ is a secret too profound for our finite minds. In the Gospel accounts we find Him professing ignorance concerning the time of His return (Mark 13:32). In other passages His supernatural knowledge is clearly indicated (e.g., John 4:18). Here we are told that He knew "the Father had given all things into his hands, and that he was come from God, and went to God." In other words, He was sure of His divine origin and of the fact that He would soon be returning to His Father's side. His life on earth had been brief—perhaps thirty-four years. But He accomplished more in that time than anyone else who has ever lived.

II. THE FINAL ACT OF SERVICE: John 13:4-5

A. The Symbol of the Towel: v. 4

In those days a man's clothing apparently consisted of a sleeveless tunic which he wore next to his skin, and a long flowing robe or cloak with full sleeves. When it says that Jesus "laid aside his garments," the reference is to the outer cloak and perhaps to a prayer shawl over it. He put these off so that He could work without hindrance.

Then He "took a towel." Everyone is familiar with the cross as the most widely used symbol of Christianity. Nor would we want to substitute anything for this! The Crucifixion is at the very center of the story of redemption. And the cross is a symbol of our death with Christ to our own will, and our complete submission to God's will.

But we should like to add another significant symbol. While the cross is the symbol of *sacrifice*, the towel is a symbol of *service*. And the former without the latter would not become fully effective for the salvation of men. There are some, we fear, who would proudly carry the cross but are unwilling to take the towel.

Looking at this passage we can see that the towel really carries a threefold significance. It was: (1) The Symbol of Love (v. 1); (2) The Symbol of Service (vv. 2-11); (3) The Symbol of Humility (vv. 12-15). We should be willing, with Jesus, to take the towel in humble, loving service to others.

Several times in the New Testament we read that a person "girded" himself. Here it simply means that Jesus fastened the towel at or around His waist. In other places it sometimes means putting on one's clothes and tightening the sash around the middle.

B. Washing the Disciples' Feet: v. 5

After Jesus had poured water into a basin, He proceeded to wash the disciples' feet. In those days men wore open sandals, with no socks. When they came in from the dusty roads and streets their feet would often be grimy. The first thing they did on entering a house was to take off their shoes and wash their feet—or let a servant wash them. But there was no servant to do it here, and not one of the disciples volunteered for the job. So Jesus played the part of a humble slave and washed their feet.

Incidentally, a word needs to be said about the arrangement of the room. Leonardo da Vinci's famous painting, *The Last Supper*, is a thing of beauty and has often been carved in wood. But it portrays the disciples sitting around the table according to the custom in Italy in the Middle Ages, not as they did in Palestine in the first century!

One thing should be apparent at once. If the disciples were seated with their feet under the table, how could Jesus have reached those feet to wash them?

The true picture is something different. The Roman custom widely followed in Palestine at that time was to place couches around the table, with soft pillows on the couches. "Sat at meat" in the King James Version of several passages is really "reclined at the table." Reclining on their left elbows, the disciples would eat with their right hands. Meanwhile their feet were all at the outer edge of the couches, where Jesus could easily wash them and then dry them with the towel.

III. THE CONVERSATION WITH PETER:
John 13:6-11

Not a word was said as Jesus worked His way silently around the table. But by the time He reached Peter, the big fisherman was feeling pretty small at the sight of what was happening. At once he protested: "Lord, are you going to wash my feet?"

Jesus replied: "What I am doing you do not understand now, but you will know later."

In response to this, impulsive Peter cried out: "You will never wash my feet!"

He was probably a bit shocked at his Master's answer: "If I do not wash you, you have no part with me."

Peter's immediate reaction was typical of him: "Lord, not my feet only, but also my hands and my head." If he had to let Jesus wash his feet in order to belong to the Master, he wanted to be in all over! Peter really loved his Lord and wanted to belong fully to Him. Anything that would tie him more tightly to Christ he wanted to have.

But Jesus in effect replied: "No I don't need to wash your hands and face." He spelled it out this way: "He that is washed needeth not save to wash his feet, but is clean every whit" (v. 10). What this translation does not indicate is that the word *wash* occurring twice in this verse actually renders two different Greek words. The first is used for washing the whole body, the second only for washing part of it. So the correct translation is: "He who has bathed only needs to wash his feet."

The reference is to a man taking a bath and putting on clean clothes. Then he goes to the market place to do some buying. When he comes back he does not need to take another bath, but simply to wash his feet, which have become dirty.

The application is especially important for young people and new converts. The newborn Christian rejoices in the consciousness that his sins have been washed away. Then he goes to school, to his business, or to his job. After being with sinners all day, he may come home at night feeling almost defiled by what he has seen and heard. But he doesn't have to go again through "the bath of regeneration" (Titus 3:5). All he needs to do is to wash the contamination from his mind. This can be done in a very few minutes of time simply by sitting down and reading prayerfully a few choice verses of Scripture. Meditation on the Word of God is the quickest way to wash our minds from any contaminating thoughts.

Jesus added: "And ye are clean, but not all." Verse 11 explains what He meant. As a group the disciples were "clean"—cleansed by the presence of the Christ they had accepted as "the Lamb of God, which taketh away the sin of the world" (1:29). But one of them, Judas Iscariot, had let Satan take possession of his heart and was already plotting to betray his Master.

IV. THE EXAMPLE OF HUMBLE SERVICE:
John 13:12-17

A. A Needed Lesson: vv. 12-14

When Jesus finished washing their feet, He put on His outer cloak again, sat down and said to His disciples, "Do you know what I have done to you?" Did He then reprove them for calling Him "Master" (Greek, "Teacher") and "Lord"? No, He commended them for it: "And ye say well, for so I am." He continued: "If I then, your Lord and Master, have washed your feet; ye also ought to wash one another's feet." They should follow their Master in humility and service to others.

B. A Pointed Example: vv. 15-17

Do verses 14 and 15 mean that Christians should literally wash each other's feet? This is the practice among some religious groups, and we offer no criticism. We would simply call attention to the fact that foot-washing was a regular custom of that day, with no relation to religion. With our modern custom of wearing shoes and socks, it has lost its relevance. Probably what Jesus primarily meant was that we were to follow His example in humble, loving service to those about us, even to the lowliest of people. The particular application is to our treatment of fellow Christians.

"The slave is not greater than his master," said Jesus, "nor the one sent on an errand greater than the one who sent him" (v. 16). The expression "he that is sent" (KJV) is all one word in Greek, *apostolos* ("apostle"), which comes from the verb *apostello*, "send on an errand." So an apostle is one sent on a mission.

What Jesus is saying here, of course, is that as the Sender He was greater than His apostles. Yet He stooped to wash their feet, doing the work of a common slave. Then He said to His disciples: "If you understand these things I am saying, you will be happy in doing them" (v. 17). Obedience to Christ always brings joy to the Christian.

V. THE TRAGEDY OF BETRAYAL: John 13:18-30

A. The Hint of Warning: vv. 18-20

In what He had just said, Jesus did not include Judas Iscariot. For that apostle, chosen by the Master, had already by his inner attitude excluded himself from the fellowship.

As horrible as was the betrayal of Jesus by one of His chosen Twelve, it had been predicted in the Scriptures centuries before. Christ proceeded to quote the passage from Psalm 41:9: "He that eateth bread with me hath lifted up his heel against me." The seriousness of this crime can hardly be appreciated by the modern Occidental reader. But among the ancient Orientals—and it is still the practice among Arabs in the Middle East—to eat with a person meant that you were giving your word of honor that you would

not harm him. If you were not willing to furnish that guarantee, then you refused to eat with him. In that case he would be well advised to get out of your territory as quickly as possible! The people of that culture considered it unspeakably despicable for anyone to eat with a supposed friend and then to injure him. To bring about his death would be worse than murder; it would be a terrible crime against society.

Jesus was warning His disciples of what was to happen, so that they would not be caught off guard when it came. The fact that He predicted it would increase their faith in Him as the Son of God (v. 19).

Then He made an interesting double statement. To receive His messengers is to receive Him; and to receive Him is to receive the Father who sent Him. This underscores the importance of a right attitude toward genuine servants of the Lord.

B. Judas the Betrayer: vv. 21-30

No wonder that Jesus was "troubled in spirit." After having spent the whole of one night in prayer for the Father's guidance, He had carefully chosen twelve apostles (Luke 6:12-13). They were to be His messengers to the world. Now one of them was actually going to betray Him to death. The Master could not keep still any longer. To His shocked disciples He said: "Verily, verily, I say unto you, that one of you shall betray me." The apostles looked incredulously at one another. This couldn't be!

Only in John's Gospel do we find the narrative that follows. This is perfectly logical if we accept the conclusion that John was himself the one about whom he was speaking when he wrote: "Now there was leaning on Jesus' bosom one of his disciples, whom Jesus loved" (v. 23). The early church held that John the apostle was the "beloved disciple" of the Fourth Gospel, and this seems the most reasonable view today.

Simon Peter signaled—the German Bible (1956) says *winkte*—to John to ask Jesus whom He was talking about. So the beloved disciple, leaning his head back on Jesus' chest, said: "Lord, who is it?" From verse 28 it is obvious that this was all done quietly, the other disciples did not know what was said.

Jesus made a definite reply: "He it is, to whom I shall give a sop, when I have dipped it" (v. 26). He then dipped a piece of bread or meat in the dish of sauce—as one can still see people doing in Palestine—and handed it to Judas Iscariot. It was the custom for a host to dip a choice piece of meat in the sauce and then hand it, in his fingers, to the guest of honor. This was the way Jesus was treating the one He knew was planning to betray Him!

When Judas accepted the "sop" from the hand of his Master, it was tantamount to his saying aloud: "I give you my word of honor that I will never hurt you." No greater act of diabolical duplicity could have been committed by Judas than to take the proffered gift when he was right then planning to betray Jesus to death. No wonder we are told that "after the sop Satan entered into him" (v. 27). Judas Iscariot had sold himself completely to the devil, who now took possession of him.

Why did Jesus sound such definite and repeated warnings at the table? The logical deduction seems to be that He was making His final appeal to Judas, trying to turn him back from the suicidal road he was taking. When Judas took the sop he sealed his decision, and so sealed his doom. It was his last chance, and he missed it.

Then Jesus said to Judas, "That thou doest, do quickly." He might as well finish his atrocious deed.

Verse 28 tells us that no one at the table knew why Jesus said these words. Some thought that because Judas was the treasurer of the group the Master was telling him to buy supplies for the Passover Feast or to give something to the poor.

Verse 30 is a very familiar passage and illustrates well John's love for words with a twofold meaning, one literal and one spiritual. We are told that as soon as Judas had made his final, irrevocable decision by accepting the sop, he went "out"; "and it was night." It was late in the evening and dark outside in the street. But these words also have terrible spiritual significance. Judas deliberately "went out" from the presence of Him who was the Light of the World, and into eternal spiritual darkness.

VI. THE NEW COMMANDMENT: John 13:31-35

A. The Glorification of Christ: vv. 31-33

Jesus had reserved the cream of His teaching until Judas left. Now He turned to the eleven who were left. It would seem that tragedy had struck. The Master said that He, the Son of man, was now glorified, and God was glorified in Him. How could this be? Westcott suggests: "Perfect self-sacrifice even to death, issuing in the overthrow of death, is the truest glory."

The time had come for the Master to share some disturbing news with His disciples. Tenderly He said to them: "Little children, yet a little while I am with you" (v. 33). He had already told the religious leaders that He was soon going away and that they would not be able to go where He was going (7:33-36). But this was different. Now He was making it personal and definite with His close associates. It was a sad hour for them.

DISCUSSION QUESTIONS

1. What are some ways in which Jesus showed His love for His disciples?
2. How may we acquire this love for others?
3. How may this love be increased?
4. In what ways can we show this love to each other?
5. What is the relationship between love and service?
6. What is the importance of love?

B. The Commandment of Love: v. 34

This verse contains one of the greatest pronouncements of Jesus: "A new commandment I give unto you, That ye love one another; as I have loved you, that ye also love one another." This is the most important instruction to Christians. We are not living under the law, but under grace. And grace comes from love. If grace is to continue, it must in turn issue in love to others. It is by loving one another that we demonstrate the fact that we have God's love in our hearts.

C. The Badge of Discipleship: v. 35

This title has been given to the statement of this verse for many years. How will people recognize us as Christ's disciples? Because we show His spirit of love! When we show sincere love toward each other we are bearing effective witness to the fact that we belong to Him.

What was the purpose of Jesus' washing the disciples' feet? To answer that question we have to look at the immediate background.

On the way up to Jerusalem the disciples had been quarreling with one another as to who was going to be the greatest. Two of the inner circle of the three closest to the Master—James and John, the sons of Zebedee—had come to Jesus with the request that in His kingdom they might sit in the places of greatest honor and authority, one on either side of Him (Mark 10:35-37). The other ten apostles resented the fact that James and John had asked first! Luke tells us that even at the table in the upper room while they were eating the Passover and Jesus was about to inaugurate the Lord's Supper (22:15-20), the disciples were still carrying on the quarrel as to which of them should be considered the greatest (22:24).

Jesus wanted to talk to His disciples about the Holy Spirit, who would be their Comforter and Counselor when He left. But the atmosphere of the upper room was so filled with tension, envy, and ill will that it was impossible to speak effectively about the precious truths of the Holy Spirit. Something had to be done to change the situation.

One reflection of the selfishness and jealousy of these disciples of Jesus is that they were all reclining at the table with dirty feet. Actually they felt as uncomfortable as we would if we went to the table with dirty hands! Yet not one of them would offer to wash the others' feet. Each one thought someone else should do it.

Their saddened Master gave them plenty of time to volunteer. Finally at the end of the meal He did something drastic to change the atmosphere of the place. Rising from His place He girded Himself with a towel, took a basin of water, and washed the disciples' feet.

When He finished the whole tone of the room was completely changed. Instead of each one feeling proud and egotistical, they were all filled with shame and embarrassment at the exposure of their selfishness. Instead of feeling envious and jealous of each other, they now felt that they were worthless and unworthy of any honor.

With the atmosphere thus changed, Jesus was able to give His superb message on the Holy Spirit. And by the self-exposure that took place, the disciples were being prepared to receive the Holy Spirit on the day of Pentecost.

CONTEMPORARY APPLICATION

Samuel Logan Brengle was an eloquent orator in college days. At Boston University School of Theology, studying under Dr. Daniel Steele in Greek New Testament, he saw the selfishness of his heart and surrendered himself completely to the Holy Spirit.

Then the Lord seemed to say to

him definitely, "I want you to join the Salvation Army." He traveled to London to see General Booth, who tried to put him off. The Chief of Staff, Bramwell Booth, was even more opposed to taking him in. But young Brengle persisted.

His first orders were to "black the boots"—shine the shoes—of the Army Corpsmen. He walked down into a dingy basement and faced eighteen pairs of muddy boots on a bench. He was tempted to feel that he had made a mistake. "Lord God, am I burying my talent? Is this the best they can do for me in the Salvation Army? Have I followed my own fancy three thousand miles to come here to black boots?"

And then in his imagaination, he saw a scene from long ago: Jesus washing His disciples' feet. Bowing his head, Brengle prayed: "Dear Lord, Thou didst wash their feet; I will black their boots!"

That was in 1887. Years later he wrote: "I had fellowship with Jesus every morning for a week while down in that cellar blacking boots. It was the best training I could have had. . . . My new prayer was: Dear Lord, let me serve the servants of Jesus. That is sufficient for me."

LIFE IN CHRIST

DEVOTIONAL
READING

John 14:1-14

ADULTS

Topic: *Life in Christ*

Background Scripture: John 14:1-7; 15:1-17

Scripture Lesson: John 15:1-11

Memory Verse: *I am the way, and the truth, and the life; no one comes to the Father, but by me.* John 14:6

YOUTH

Topic: *Living in Christ*

Background Scripture: John 14:1-7; 15:1-17

Scripture Lesson: John 15:1-11

Memory Verse: *I am the way, and the truth, and the life; no one comes to the Father, but by me.* John 14:6

CHILDREN

Topic: *What Love Demands*

Background Scripture: John 15:1-17

Scripture Lesson: John 15:9-17

Memory Verse: *Greater love has no man than this, that a man lay down his life for his friends.* John 15:13

DAILY BIBLE
READINGS

Mon., Jan. 21: The True Way of Life, John 14:1-7.
Tues., Jan. 22: Jesus and the Father, John 14:8-14.
Wed., Jan. 23: Fellowship with God, John 14:15-24.
Thurs., Jan. 24: Christ's Peace, John 14:25-31.
Fri., Jan. 25: The Life-giving Vine, John 15:1-11.
Sat., Jan. 26: New Intimacy in Christ, John 15:12-17.
Sun., Jan. 27: Abiding in Love, I John 4:13-21.

LESSON AIM

To explore the meaning of "life in Christ" and to see how we may experience that life.

LESSON SETTING

Time: The night before the crucifixion, in April of A.D. 30

Place: The words of chapter 14 seem clearly to have been given by Jesus in the upper room in Jerusalem. Some think that chapters 15 and 16 were uttered on the way to the Garden of Gethsemane.

Life in Christ

LESSON OUTLINE

SUGGESTED INTRODUCTION FOR ADULTS

The main topic of the Last Discourse in the upper room, as we shall see in next week's lesson, is the coming of the Holy Spirit as Comforter. But this long discourse (chaps. 14—16) begins with an emphasis on Christ as the source of our life. Unless we are in Christ we cannot have the Holy Spirit.

In fact, the opening verse of today's lesson emphasizes the close relationship of the Trinity. Throughout church history two opposing tendencies have had to be avoided: either separating the Persons of the Trinity until there seem to be three gods, or confusing the Persons as one until it borders on Unitarianism, making Christ and the Holy Spirit simply manifestations of the one Person, God.

Constantly we have to remember that our finite minds cannot encompass or comprehend infinity. To hold that there are three Persons in the Trinity and yet that they are one God is an act of faith, based on the teaching of God's Word. In his Gospel, John underscores especially the unity of Father and Son. It is in Christ and through the Holy Spirit that we know the Father.

SUGGESTED INTRODUCTION FOR YOUTH

Where can we find life, real life? That is one of the most important questions that young people have always asked.

Many answers have been given. The most popular one is "pleasure." Millions of young people have hunted for real life through the pursuit of pleasure. But this is a dead-end street. Paul wrote to Timothy: "She who lives in pleasure is dead while she lives" (I Timothy 5:6). This is not the road to life.

Others have thought that making lots of money brings the larger life. But this is also a mirage in the desert, leading only to disillusionment and death. Some years ago a man said to a leading evangelist: "I am reputed to be the richest man in Texas. But I want to tell you that I am the most miserable man in Texas." A few weeks later he committed suicide.

What is the true answer, then? It is simply this: Real life is found in Christ. Millions of young people can testify to that fact.

CONCEPTS FOR CHILDREN

1. Love is the real secret of life.
2. The more we truly love people, the happier we are.
3. God is love. We must be in Him in order to love.
4. Jesus will teach us the way of life as we live in Him.

THE LESSON COMMENTARY

I. FAITH IN FATHER AND SON: John 14:1

Jesus had just told His disciples that He was leaving them, and they could not go with Him (13:33). He had also said to Peter: "The rooster will not crow, before you have denied me three times" (13:38). No wonder their hearts were "troubled." So Jesus sought to comfort them. He said: "Ye believe in God, believe also in me." Since "ye believe" and "believe" are exactly the same in the Greek this verse can be translated: "Believe in God; believe also in me." In view of the fact that they were troubled rather than trusting, either way makes perfectly good sense.

As we have noted before, one cannot really believe in the Father without believing in the Son. But in this transitional stage from Judaism to Christianity, the King James rendering fits very well, for as Jews the disciples believed in God.

II. PROMISE OF CHRIST'S RETURN: John 14:2-3

A. Christ Going to Prepare a Place: v. 2

C. H. Dodd of England emphasized the idea that whereas in the Synoptic

Gospels we have a futuristic eschatology, in John's Gospel we find only a "realized eschatology." The main basis for this theory is that in the Fourth Gospel the Last Discourse of Jesus takes the place of the Olivet Discourse in the other three. In the Last Discourse Jesus says that He will come to the disciples in the person of the Holy Spirit, who will be "another Comforter." The promise "I will not leave you comfortless: I will come to you" (14:28) was fulfilled on the day of Pentecost.

We would agree fully with this last interpretation. But we cannot agree that John thought only of the Second Coming in terms of an inner experience of Christ "realized" in our hearts in this life. For the verses we are now studying clearly indicate a futuristic eschatology.

Jesus said, "In my Father's house are many mansions." The word for "mansions" simply means "dwelling places." Probably the best translation here is "rooms." Then He assured His disciples: "I go to prepare a place for you."

B. Christ's Coming Again: v. 3

This verse definitely points beyond any coming of Christ to our hearts in this life. Jesus promised His disciples: "And if I go and prepare a place for you, I will come again, and receive you unto myself; that where I am, there ye may be also." His coming again in this passage is the same as the Second Coming in the Olivet Discourse. It is Jesus coming to take His church to be with Him forever. So John's Gospel is not in conflict with the Synoptic Gospels, the Pauline Epistles, the General Epistles, and Revelation in teaching that Christ will personally return to gather His own to Himself.

III. CHRIST THE LIFE: John 14:4-7

A. Thomas's Problem: vv. 4-5

Jesus assured His disciples: "And you know the way where I am going" (literal Greek). Thomas protested: "Lord, we don't know where you are going; how can we know the way?" Poor Thomas! He seems to have been a perennial pessimist (11:16) and chronic doubter (20:24-25), taking somewhat of a negative approach to life.

B. Jesus' Answer: vv. 6-7

But we may be glad that Thomas raised the question here. For it called forth one of the most sublime statements Jesus ever made: "I am the way, the truth, and the life." Here we find in one place three of the ten "I am's" of John's Gospel.

Liberal scholars have said that Jesus shows us the way to God; that He found that way for Himself and now He wants to share the great discovery. If we follow His example of prayer and devotion, of sacrifice and service, we too can find our way to God.

But Jesus said, "I *am* the Way." He does not *point* the way, He *provides* the way. Lest His disciples should fail to get the full implication of this, He added: "No man cometh unto the Father, but by me." This is in line with what we found in 10:7-9. Jesus is the only Door into the sheepfold; we cannot enter the Kingdom except through Him. He is also the only Way

to God; there is no other. Jesus said: "No man cometh unto the Father, but by me."

In our day of eclecticism in religion—of synthetic religions—this note needs to be sounded clearly. There is no way to God except through Christ. To try some other, man-made way will only end in frustration and failure— and final death. Christ is *the* Way, the only way, to God. It is sinful pride that makes men search endlessly for some other way. We can never find God by any of our own human efforts; we can only let Him find us through Christ. Humility is the first step toward God. We have to confess that we cannot ourselves find the way, that all our own efforts are evidences of pride and self-will; and then humbly submit to enter the only door that is open, and trust Him for our salvation.

Christ also declared, "I am the Truth." Again, many people spend their lives searching for truth. And many of them confess at the end that they have not found it. They want some insight, some philosophy, some proverb that they can feel summarizes "the truth."

But Truth is more than a proposition; it is a Person—Jesus Christ. On the intellectual side we have Paul's description of Him: "In whom are hid all the treasures of wisdom and knowledge." But when Jesus said, "I am the Truth," He meant more than that. For He is Truth embodied, incarnate. One could say that in an ultimate sense all truth is found in Christ.

But even more important than these is His statement, "I am the Life." As we noted in our study of the prologue to this Gospel, Jesus is the Source of life. This is indicated in the assertion that He created all things (1:3). He is the Source of all physical life, all intellectual life, and all spiritual life. The main emphasis here, without doubt, is on the fact that He is Eternal Life. Outside of Him no one has eternal life, but all who are in Him have this life here and now.

Once more Christ affirms the close relationship between Himself and the

Father. "If ye had known me, ye should have known my Father also." It is obvious that *known* here means more than being acquainted with. It means understanding the nature of. In spite of their close association with Jesus for three years, the disciples still did not really "know" Him. But Christ went on to say: "And from henceforth ye know him, and have seen him." To what was He referring? Chapters 14—16 indicate that He had reference to the coming of the Holy Spirit, who would guide them into all truth (16:13). The startling fact is that by the help of the indwelling Holy Spirit, after Pentecost, the disciples would have a clearer spiritual vision of God than they had acquired in three years of watching Jesus while He was physically present with them.

It takes the Spirit of God to give spiritual understanding. Paul stated this categorically in I Corinthians 2:11: "Even so the things of God knoweth no man, but the Spirit of God." The Holy Spirit is our greatest Teacher. He alone can enable us to understand the spiritual truths of God's Word.

Eager to know more, Philip said to Jesus: "Lord, show us the Father, and that will be sufficient for us" (v. 8).

In His answer, Jesus portrays the sadness He felt at the disciples' lack of spiritual perception. He asked: "Have I been so long time with you, and yet hast thou not known me, Philip?" How little understanding they had received in all those months! Today we marvel at their spiritual dullness. But we have the Holy Spirit to help us, and they did not.

And then Jesus made another one of those startling statements of His full deity. He declared, "He that hath seen me hath seen the Father." For anyone else to say that would have been sufficient proof of insanity. But on the lips of Jesus it reflected His clear consciousness of the fact that He was one with the Father.

If they had trouble in believing His "words," then they should believe His "works" (vv. 10-11). That is, they should believe in Him because He had given clear evidence of His deity in the many cases of healing incurable diseases, and even raising the dead—as Lazarus (chap. 11). The disciples had no excuse for not believing.

Then Jesus made a tremendous prediction and gave a tremendous promise. The prediction was this: "He that believeth on me, the works that I do shall he do also; and greater works than these shall he do; because I go unto my Father." How could this possibly be? Jesus healed hundreds of people and even raised the dead. Greater works than these?

Yes; Christ's prediction was fulfilled abundantly. He had only a few converts, relatively speaking, during His earthly ministry. But on the day of Pentecost three thousand souls were saved. That had never happened before. The spiritual victories of the church across the centuries are greater works in God's sight than the miracles that Jesus performed.

And then for the promise: "And whatsoever ye shall ask in my name, that will I do, that the Father may be glorified in the Son. If ye shall ask anything in my name, I will do it" (vv. 13-14). This reads like a blank check, a carte blanche. But there is one important, repeated condition: "in my name." As every student of the Bible knows, this means "in my nature." Whatever we ask in the spirit of Christ, we shall have. It is something far more than parroting at the close of the prayer: "in Jesus' name." It means praying in the Spirit, and He knows what is best for us (Romans 8:26-27).

IV. THE VINE AND THE BRANCHES: John 15:1-8

A. The True Vine: v. 1

There have been many false vines—false religions on which people have pinned their hopes—but there is only one "true vine," and that is Jesus Christ. This vine is cared for by the

Father, who is the "husbandman," or gardener.

B. Fruitful and Unfruitful Branches: vv. 2-3

"Every branch in me that beareth not fruit he taketh away." Some have held that this should be translated "takes up." We once heard a preacher on the radio give this meaning and then explain: "It means that God will take up to Himself in heaven any branch that is unfruitful." But Arndt and Gingrich's *Lexicon* gives for this passage, "cuts off." The context suggests that this is the proper sense here. An unfruitful branch will not be tolerated on the vine. It will be cut off and thrown away.

On the other hand, "every branch that beareth fruit, he purgeth it, that it may bring forth more fruit." As a good gardener, God will prune the branches, trimming off any useless shoots, so that all the energy may go to bearing more fruit. The verb translated "purgeth" means to make clean. This passage underscores the fact that cleansing is an important factor in growth in grace and increasing fruitfulness.

More cleansing will take place, but the disciples are already clean in a measure. Jesus told them, "Now ye are clean through the word which I have spoken unto you." A very significant cleansing of these same disciples took place at Pentecost. We have Peter's testimony to this fact. Speaking at the Council of Jerusalem (A.D. 48) he said "And God, which knoweth the hearts, bare them witness, giving them the Holy Ghost, even as he did unto us; and put no difference between us [Jews] and them [Gentiles], purifying their hearts by faith" (Acts 15:8-9). Peter declared that the same thing happened at the house of Cornelius (Acts 10) as happened to the 120 in the upper room at Pentecost (Acts 2). In both cases they were filled with the Holy Spirit and their hearts were cleansed from sin.

C. The Necessity of Abiding in Christ: vv. 4-6

One of John's favorite words is *abide* (cf. 14:16). The Greek word for this occurs no less than twelve times in this chapter. The most important single secret of living a victorious, fruitful Christian life is found in the admonition here: "Abide in me, and I in you." In Christ we have everything; apart from Him we have nothing.

Jesus goes on to spell this out in terms of the horticultural figure He is using: "As the branch cannot bear fruit of itself, except it abide in the vine; no more can ye, except ye abide in me." Everybody knows that a branch has no life in itself, apart from the vine. It is the sap flowing into it from the vine—the Greek word means "grapevine"—that gives life to the branch and enables it to bear fruit.

Now Jesus makes the case more explicit: "I am the vine, ye are the branches" (v. 5). If we abide in Him and He in us, we will bear "much fruit." Note the progression: "fruit" and "more fruit" in verse 2, and now "much fruit." This is God's will for us. As the Divine Gardener, this is what He desires. Are we bearing "much fruit"?

This leads us to a necessary question: What is meant by *fruit* here? The answer is twofold. We may think of it either in terms of the fruit of the Spirit or in relation to bringing others to Christ. Probably a majority of Bible readers take it in the latter sense. But the former is important, too. We would do well to meditate on each of "the fruit of the Spirit" in Galatians 5:22-23—love, joy, peace, patience, gentleness, goodness, faithfulness, humility, self-control—and then ask ourselves if these nine virtues are appearing abundantly in our lives as "much fruit." If we did this, the result would be real growth in grace.

The last clause of verse 5 underscores a vital truth we have already noted: "For without me ye can do nothing." Severed from the vine, a branch is absolutely powerless to bear fruit. We have no life in us except that which we derive constantly from Christ. The moment we are separated from Him we are spiritually dead. A branch may still look green and have grapes on it for a while after it is cut off from the vine. But death has already set in and this will soon become apparent. So we may still look like Christians for some time after we lose vital union with Christ, but it will soon become apparent that we are dead.

The seriousness of this is depicted graphically by Jesus in verse 6: "If a man abide not in me, he is cast forth as a branch, and is withered; and men gather them, and cast them into the fire, and they are burned." This passage clearly speaks of branches that were once in the vine but somehow became separated from it. As a result they wither and are useless. So they are gathered up and burned. The lesson is crystal clear: A man may be in Christ and then may be severed from Him by his own disobedience.

D. The Results of Abiding in Christ: vv. 7-8

"Ask whatever you wish, and it will be done for you." That is a sweeping promise that certainly every Christian would like to claim. But two very important conditions are attached. The first is: "If you abide in me." It is only as we abide in close fellowship with Christ that we can expect our prayers to be answered. That means that we do not rush to Him and ask for this and that and the other. Rather, we wait in His presence thanking Him for what He has already done for us, worshiping Him and expressing our love and gratitude to Him. Then, in that kind of an atmosphere, we can expect to receive whatever we wish. For when we are that close to Christ we want only what He wishes.

But there is also a second condition, somewhat more objective in nature: "And my words abide in you." This means that we study carefully the Word of God, and particularly the teachings of Jesus, to see how our Master wants us to live. Someone has well said: "His words abide in us when they beget in us conduct conforming to those words." It is not enough to read a few verses, or even a whole chapter, of the Bible each morning in our private devotions. We should pray: "O Lord, help me to walk today according to Your Word." Specifically, we should ask the Holy Spirit to call our attention to the truths we especially need to notice, and then show us how we can apply them in our daily living. Yes, and ask Him to help us make that application! That is why Jesus said He would send the Holy Spirit—"to lead us into all truth," not only in spiritual understanding but also in practical application.

When we live in accordance with God's Word, abiding in Christ, our prayers will be answered, the Father will be glorified, and we will bear "much fruit" (v. 8). And thus we will truly be Christ's disciples, and people will know that we are. The statement "so shall ye be my disciples"—coming as it does at the end of these many admonitions—shows that true discipleship is more than signing a card, joining a church, or even making a genuine commitment to Christ and being born again. It is a daily walk in obedience to our Lord.

V. ABIDING IN LOVE: John 15:9-11

A. The Secret of Abiding in Love: vv. 9-10

"As the Father hath loved me, so have I loved you." The love that Christ has for us is the same *agape* love that binds the Trinity together. "God is love" (I John 4:8, 16)—limitless, infinite, eternal. That love comes through Christ to us.

Jesus said: "Continue ye in my love." The Greek word for "continue" is the one that is translated "abide" in the preceding verses. It occurs ten times in the first ten verses of this chapter and is the keynote of this section.

Now we are told the secret of abiding in love: "If ye keep my commandments, ye shall abide in my love; even as I have kept my Father's commandments, and abide in his love." The real test of love is obedience, and it is also the proof of love and the condition of continuing in love. That is, as soon as we cease to obey Christ, we are no longer in His love. This is a sobering thought. Obedience is the condition of abiding!

B. Love and Joy: v. 11

Love brings joy. This is a truth that anyone can see. People whose hearts are filled with genuine, unselfish love are happy people. The more love we show to others the more joy we feel within. The way to be happy is to make others happy.

Because Christ was constantly expressing His love to others in kind words and deeds, He was supremely joyful. His highest joy was to do His Father's will. Now He tells His disciples that He wants *His* joy to be theirs, and He wants that joy to be "full." Fullness of joy—that is what we can have in Christ. What more would anyone want?

VI. THE CENTRALITY OF LOVE: John 15:12-17

In 13:34 Jesus declared: "A new commandment I give unto you, That

ye love one another; as I have loved you, that ye also love one another." Now He repeats it in more summary form: "This is my commandment, That ye love one another, as I have loved you." John picks up this strong emphasis of Jesus and elaborates it in his First Epistle (4:7-21). This passage in I John might well be read in this connection. It is the best commentary on these words of Christ.

The supreme expression of love would be for a man to lay down his life for his friends (v. 13). Then Jesus said, "Ye are my friends, if ye do whatsoever I command you." Note the condition of friendship with Jesus: If we do not obey Him we are not His friends.

Then comes a beautiful note in the teaching of Jesus. He tells His disciples that henceforth He will not call them servants but friends. For He is sharing with them the secrets His Father tells Him. As His friends, they are "in," belonging to the fellowship.

The divine initiative is stressed in verse 16: "Ye have not chosen me, but I have chosen you, and ordained you, that ye should go and bring forth fruit, and that your fruit should remain." The last clause is especially comforting to all who are engaged in Christian work. We not only want fruit—new converts to Christ—but fruit that will remain. We want people to be full, forever-Christians.

The results of this fruit-bearing will be "that whatsoever ye shall ask of the Father in my name, he may give it to you." Those who are busily engaged in winning people to Christ can testify to many answers to prayer.

This section closes with a reiteration of Jesus' main emphasis in His closing session with His disciples: "These things I command you, that ye love one another." This was His supreme concern for His first disciples, and it is still His heart cry for His followers today.

DISCUSSION QUESTIONS

1. What does John's Gospel say about the Second Coming?
2. How do we obtain life in Christ?
3. How do we maintain it?
4. What is the main secret of answered prayer?
5. How may we show our love to each other?
6. What lessons do we learn from the vine and branches?

CONTEMPORARY APPLICATION

We should face realistically the fact that Christ's main concern for His disciples was that they should love one another. Are we helping to see that His desire is fulfilled in His church today, as far as we are concerned? Are we seeking to foster love, rather than misunderstanding and suspicion?

February 3, 1974

PROMISE OF THE COUNSELOR

<table>
<tr><td>DEVOTIONAL
READING</td><td>John 16:16-24</td></tr>
<tr><td>ADULTS</td><td>Topic: Promise of the Counselors

Background Scripture: John 15:18—16:15

Scripture Lesson: John 16:4c-15

Memory Verse: The Counselor, the Holy Spirit, whom the Father will send in my name, he will teach you all things, and bring to your remembrance all that I have said to you. John 14:26</td></tr>
<tr><td>YOUTH</td><td>Topic: You Have a Counselor

Background Scripture: John 15:18—16:15

Scripture Lesson: John 16:4c-15

Memory Verse: The Counselor, the Holy Spirit, whom the Father will send in my name, he will teach you all things, and bring to your remembrance all that I have said to you. John 14:26</td></tr>
<tr><td>CHILDREN</td><td>Topic: God's Love Without End

Background Scripture: Luke 15:11-32; John 15—16:15

Memory Verse: He who does not love does not know God; for God is love. In this the love of God was made manifest among us, that God sent His only Son into the world, so that we might live through him. I John 4:8-9</td></tr>
<tr><td>DAILY BIBLE
READINGS</td><td>Mon. Jan. 28: In a Hostile World, John 15:18-27.
Tues., Jan. 29: Comfort for Christian Outcasts, John 16:1-6.
Wed., Jan. 30: The Spirit's Ministry in the World, John 16:7-11.
Thurs., Jan. 31: A Counselor at Your Side, John 16:12-15.
Fri., Feb. 1: Life in the Spirit, Romans 8:1-11.
Sat., Feb. 2: Following the Spirit's Lead, Romans 8:12-17.
Sun., Feb. 3: "The Spirit Helps Us," Romans 8:26-30.</td></tr>
<tr><td>LESSON AIM</td><td>To discover what the promised Holy Spirit can be to us in our daily lives.</td></tr>
<tr><td>LESSON SETTING</td><td>Time: Thursday evening, perhaps the 5th of April, A.D. 30</td></tr>
</table>

172

Place: The upper room in Jerusalem, where Jesus had just eaten the Passover with His disciples

Promise of the Counselor

I. A Personal Comforter: John 14:15-18

II. A Personal Companion: John 14:19-24

III. A Personal Counselor: John 4:25-27

IV. A Personal Co-Witness: John 15:18-27
   A. The World's Hatred of Christians: vv. 18-21
   B. The World's Hatred of Christ: vv. 22-25
   C. The Holy Spirit as Co-witness: vv. 26-27

V. A Personal Convictor: John 16:4c-11
   A. The Need for the Spirit: vv. 4c-11
   B. The Advantage of Having the Spirit: v. 7
   C. The Conviction by the Spirit: vv. 8-11

VI. A Personal Conductor: John 16:12-15
   A. Guiding into All Truth: vv. 12-13
   B. Glorifying Christ: vv. 14-15

LESSON OUTLINE

SUGGESTED INTRODUCTION FOR ADULTS

The Scripture lesson for today is taken entirely from chapter 16 (vv. 4c-15). The background Scripture reaches back into the last part of chapter 15 (beginning with v. 18). But the lesson topic is "Promise of the Counselor." To treat that at all adequately, one must go back to the fourteenth chapter. For Jesus' Last Discourse, in which He told His disciples about the Holy Spirit, covers chapters 14—16. This whole passage needs to be considered in the lesson for today.

The last sentence of chapter 14—"Arise, let us go hence"—poses a bit of a problem. Did they leave the upper room at this point? If so, where were the words of chapters 15 and 16 spoken?

There has been a great deal of difference of opinion on this point. Westcott thinks they left the house and went to the Temple area, where Jesus continued His discourse. Martin Luther, Adam Clarke, and others have suggested that the words were uttered on the way from the upper room, that Jesus walked as He talked. But we would agree with Meyer that this is "psychologically improbable." And how about chapter 17? Certainly Jesus was not moving around when He prayed that majestic prayer!

So we would agree with the large number of commentators who hold that after Jesus said, "Arise, let us go hence," He continued His discourse in the upper room. Someone has suggested that this sentence was a "spontaneous and irrepressible expression of the deep earnestness of His spirit to get into the conflict." At any rate, Hendriksen points out, the rest of the discourse would take only about ten minutes to deliver. We agree with Tenney's comment about the discourse: "The exact location is less important than its unity." Jesus is talking about one topic in chapters 14—16, and it seems to us that all three belong together. That is the way we have treated them.

SUGGESTED INTRODUCTION FOR YOUTH

"You Have a Counselor." That is a word that young people need to hear today. In recent years the role of the counselor in high school has assumed major proportions. It is not many years ago that such a person as a high school counselor was unheard of. Probably few schools would try to function without one today. Large city high schools often have four or more counselors. The lives of young people today are so complex that oftentimes counseling is desperately needed.

To all young people we would say, "You have a Counselor who is always available. If you will receive Him into your heart, He will give you the guidance you need."

CONCEPTS FOR CHILDREN

1. The story of the Prodigal Son shows God's forgiving love.
2. Even though we disobey Him, God still loves us and wants to save us.
3. If we go away from God, we should come back; when we do we will experience His love again.

THE LESSON COMMENTARY

I. A PERSONAL COMFORTER: John 14:15-18

Verse 15 sums up what is repeatedly emphasized in this section of John's Gospel: "If ye love me, keep my commandments." Obedience is the real test of love. Then Jesus went on to say: "And I will pray the Father, and he shall give you another Comforter, that he may abide with you forever" (v. 16). He was leaving them, but the Comforter would come to stay. The word *another* suggests someone else of the same kind. The Holy Spirit would take Jesus' place with them.

The Greek word translated "Comforter" is *paracletos*, which has been taken over into English as Paraclete. It comes from the verb *paracaleo*, which means "call alongside to help." So the basic meaning of the word is "helper." It is found in the New Testament only five times—four times in the Gospel of John (14:16, 26; 15:26; 16:7) and once in his First Epistle (2:1).

F. C. Grant *Nelson's Bible Commentary*) writes: "In first-century Greek the word *Paraclete* has a variety of meanings—advocate,' 'advisor,' 'defender,' 'intercessor'—all legal terms." In I John 2:1 it is correctly translated "advocate" in the King James Version. There it refers to Jesus Christ, who is our Lawyer or Attorney representing us at the court of heaven. As Intercessor, He pleads for us. On the other hand, the Holy Spirit, as Intercessor, pleads *through* us for others (Romans 8:26).

There are some who think that we ought to translate *paracletos* as Advocate here in John 14—16. But we feel that this is a mistake. In the First Epistle it is Christ in heaven. In the Gospel it is the Holy Spirit on earth. The persons, spheres, and functions are all three different and should be represented differently.

How then should *Paraclete* be translated in John 14—16? The King James Version uses "Comforter." The

Revised Standard Version has "Counselor," and that is the reason for the title of our lesson. Actually, the only English term that adequately describes this word in all its ramifications is "Helper," and that is what the New American Standard Bible has. This seems a rather colorless term, but it is the most comprehensive one.

Because of the many facets of the word and the many functions of the Person, we are presenting the Holy Spirit in this lesson as our personal Comforter, Companion, Counselor, Co-witness, Convictor, and Conductor. These are six functions of the Spirit that are suggested in these three chapters on the Paraclete.

In verse 17 the Paraclete is identified as "the Spirit of truth," or Holy Spirit. About Him it is stated: "whom the world cannot receive, because it seeth him not, neither knoweth him." Jesus clearly indicates here that the Holy Spirit is not for sinners but for believers. To His disciples He said: "But ye know him, for he dwelleth with you, and shall be in you." The Holy Spirit had come down upon Jesus at His baptism. And so in their association with their Master they had the Holy Spirit *with* them. But it was not until Pentecost that the Spirit came to fill their hearts and dwell *in* them.

Jesus continued: "I will not leave you comfortless: I will come to you" (v. 18). The Greek word for "comfortless" is *orphanous*, from which we get "orphans." The Master said to His sorrowing disciples, who had been saddened by the news that He was soon to leave them (13:33), "I will not leave you as orphaned children; I will come to you." This last clause was fulfilled on the day of Pentecost, when Jesus came to them in the person of the Holy Spirit.

II. A PERSONAL COMPANION:
John 14:19-24

The Holy Spirit is not only our personal Comforter in times of sorrow, but also our personal Companion in times of joy. He wants to share all life's experiences with us. Probably most of us have found ourselves at sometime enjoying an unusual experience and have wished that some loved one was with us to share it. The truth is that the joys of life are doubled when we share them with someone else. That is one of the real blessings of marriage. But there may be times when no human friend is present, and then the Holy Spirit is always there to share *every* experience of life with us.

Once more the connection between love and obedience is stressed: "He that hath my commandments and keepeth them, he it is that loveth me: and he that loveth me shall be loved of my Father, and I will love him and will manifest myself to him" (v. 21). Coming, as this does, between two great passages on the Paraclete (vv. 16, 26), it seems reasonable to assume that Jesus meant He would "manifest" Himself to His followers through the Holy Spirit. That is the way He shows Himself to us today. It is the Spirit who makes Christ's presence real to us.

When Judas (not Iscariot) asked Jesus how it was that He would manifest Himself to them and not to the world, the Master again underscored the necessity for obedience: "If a man love me, he will keep my words: and my Father will love him, and we will come unto him, and make our abode with him" (v. 23). The reason He could not manifest Himself to the world is given in the next verse: "He that loveth me not keepeth not my sayings"—and so shuts himself out from the divine fellowship.

III. A PERSONAL COUNSELOR:
John 14:25-27

Jesus had much more that He wanted to say to His disciples. But the rest would have to wait until the Holy Spirit could reveal it to them. And so He ways: "But the Comforter, who is the Holy Spirit, whom the Father will send in my name, he shall teach you all things, and bring all things to your remembrance, whatsoever I have said unto you." Jesus' time for teaching had been very limited. Now the Holy Spirit would continue to teach them endlessly. This is one of the most important functions of the Spirit in the life of the Christian. The Holy Spirit is the Teacher *par excellence*.

Verse 27 contains a beautiful promise: "Peace I leave with you, my peace I give unto you." The peace in Jesus' heart, that kept Him in perfect poise before Pilate, He says He will share with us.

IV. A PERSONAL CO-WITNESS: John 15:18-27

A. The World's Hatred of Christians: vv. 18-21

Jesus felt obligated to warn His disciples that the world would hate them just as it had hated Him. The reason they would be hated was that they did not belong to the world, did not share its spirit (v. 19). Jesus had already warned them of this inevitable conflict. The reference in verse 20 is primarily to 13:16 and secondarily to Matthew 10:24-25. Persecution of some kind is inevitable.

B. The World's Hatred of Christ: vv. 22-25

Jesus declared that in His life the world had "both seen and hated both me and my Father" (v. 24). The Scripture (Psalm 35:19) was fulfilled, "They hated me without a cause."

C. The Holy Spirit as Co-witness: vv. 26-27

To get the picture of the Holy Spirit as Co-witness we need to see the action of verse 27 as proceeding from the action in verse 26. (Note the punctuation which indicates this.) The Holy Spirit would witness about Jesus—"testify" in verse 26 is the same Greek word as that translated "bear witness" in verse 27—and the disciples would also witness to Him. In Acts 1:8 Jesus said to His disciples: "You will receive power, when the Holy Spirit

has come on you and you will be my witnesses" (the best Greek text). The glory of witnessing for Christ is that when we witness, the Holy Spirit witnesses with and through us, making our witness effective.

V. A PERSONAL CONVICTOR: John 16:4c-11

A. The Need for the Spirit: vv. 4c-6

The first three verses of chapter 16 pick up again the theme of the world's hatred of Christians. Jesus said to His disciples: "These things have I spoken unto you, that ye should not be offended"—rather, "trapped," or "caused to stumble." Then He warned them about specific persecutions. They would be put out of the synagogues, as the man born blind had already experienced. People would think that they were doing God's work when they condemned Christians to die. The reason would be that they did not really know Christ or the Father.

Jesus had not told them these things before, because He was with them (v. 4c). But now He was going back to the Father, and He knew that they needed to be forewarned in order to be forearmed.

The news that their Master was leaving them made the disciples very sad. For three years they had depended on Him for guidance and support in what they did. Now it seemed that suddenly they were being left leaderless.

B. The Advantage of Having the Spirit: v. 7

Solemnly Jesus affirmed: "It is expedient [advantageous, or profitable] for you that I go away." Why? "For if I go not away, the Comforter will not come unto you; but if I depart, I will send him unto you." Christ's ascension had to precede Pentecost.

The significance of Jesus' statement is easily apparent. In His human body He could be in only one place at one time. If some of His followers were in Judea when He was in Galilee, or vice versa, they could not enjoy His presence. Not so with the Holy Spirit. He can be with all of God's people everywhere all the time! No wonder Jesus said it was better for His disciples that He go away.

Some people say they wish they had lived when Jesus was here on the earth. This is hardly a Biblical point of view. Paul probably never met Jesus during His earthly ministry. But the Holy Spirit enabled the apostle to understand the Person and work of Christ better than any of those who walked with Him on earth, with the possible exception of John, the writer of this Gospel. The disciples could have fellowship with Jesus only at some places and at certain times. We today can, through the Spirit, have fellowship with Christ at any time, wherever we may be. In the loneliest spot on earth, the Christian can sense Christ's presence and hear His voice.

C. The Conviction by the Spirit: vv. 8-11

"When he is come, he will reprove the world." But the translation "reprove" is very weak. The Revised Standard Version has "convince." This is better, but still not strong enough. The Greek verb *elencho* was a technical judicial term in the first century. It was used for convicting a person in court. And that is the force here. Personally I can testify that when the Holy Spirit spoke to me definitely about my spiritual need, He did not just "reprove" me. It was not a matter of saying: "Now you really shouldn't have done that. It isn't nice." No! The Spirit, as it were, pointed His finger in my face and said, "You are a low-down, lost sinner." He *convicted* me of the fact that I stood condemned before God and must repent if I hoped to be saved.

Incidentally, it is often said that the King James Version is written in strong language and other versions are weak. This is true in some passages. But there are other passages where the King James Version gives a weak ren-

dering of the Greek. The New American Standard Bible has "convict" here, and that is what the word obviously means in this context.

Of what will the Holy Spirit convict the world? The answer is: "of sin, and of righteousness, and of judgment." These three items are then spelled out in the next three verses.

He will convict the world of *sin*—because people lie, cheat, and steal? rob, rape, and murder? No, it does not say that here. "Of sin, because they believe not on me." The greatest sin that anyone can commit in God's sight is to refuse to believe in His Son whom He sent to be the Savior of the world. This is the greatest sin because it is the sin against divine, infinite, eternal love. When we realize the enormous price that Christ paid to redeem us from the slavery of sin, the infinite agony of soul through which He passed as He took the world's sins upon Himself, then we can see why rejection of His sacrifice for us is the most diabolical sin a person can commit. We need to face the fact that "love is the measure of all things." With this criterion, the exceeding sinfulness of unbelief in Jesus becomes apparent. It is the ultimate crowning sin of the human heart.

What about the second area of conviction? He says: "Of righteousness, because I go to my Father, and ye see me no more" (v. 10). The connection with the stated cause is not as easy to see as in the previous case. But Tenney offers this helpful suggestion: "The return of Jesus to the Father was the ultimate proof that He was the perfect pattern for righteousness, accepted by the Father" (*The Gospel of Belief*, p. 236). The Holy Spirit will convince the world of Christ's righteousness and of the righteous sacrifice He made for the sins of all men, as attested by the fact of His ascension to the Father's right hand. This verse could also be interpreted as meaning that men will be convicted for the lack of the righteousness that they could have in Christ. That is, they will be convicted "in relation to" or "in regard to" righteousness.

The third item is somewhat easier to understand: "Of judgment, because the prince of this world is judged" (v. 11). Since Satan has been already judged and condemned, those who follow Him can be certain that their fate will be the same.

Jesus said that the Holy Spirit would convict the world of sin. But when will this happen? The answer is: "When he is come." The first application of this is obviously to the coming of the Spirit on the day of Pentecost. And this prediction was fulfilled in abundant measure that very day, for three thousand people were convicted and converted.

But this suggests a secondary application. When the Holy Spirit comes in His fullness on Christians, He will convict the world. We have often seen this happen, as God's people opened their hearts fully to the Spirit, one could sense the gracious moving of the Spirit. The result has many times been a spontaneous surrender of sinners to Christ. "When he is come" to us, the unsaved world will be convicted. The greatest need in our church services is for the presence of the Holy Spirit, blessing the saints and convicting the sinners.

VI. A PERSONAL CONDUCTOR: John 16:12-15

A. Guiding into All Truth: vv. 12-13

Jesus had many things to say to His disciples before He left them, "but ye cannot bear them now." We have already seen how dull they were in spiritual understanding. This limited what He could say to them.

Then He went on: "Howbeit when he, the Spirit of truth, is come, he will guide you into all truth." He would not speak "of himself [Greek "from himself"] but whatsoever he shall hear, that shall he speak." That is, the Father would tell Him what to say. "And he will show you things to come." This is one of the ministries of the Holy Spirit: He alerts us at times as to the future. The greatest fulfill-

ment of this promise is perhaps to be seen in the Book of Revelation, where John records the visions of the future that he received when he was "in the Spirit" on the Lord's Day.

B. Glorifying Christ: vv. 14-15

Still more important is Christ's next assertion: "He shall glorify me: for he shall receive of mine, and shall shew it unto you." One of the main functions of the Holy Spirit is to reveal Christ to the Christian. He is the One who makes our Lord real to us. He enables us to have spiritual vision so that we see the things of God. The only way that we as human beings can have spiritual understanding is for us to have the Holy Spirit enlighten us.

This truth is so important that Jesus repeated it: "All things that the Father hath are mine: therefore said I, that he shall take of mine, and shall shew it unto you" (v. 15).

Jesus said of the Holy Spirit: "He shall glorify me." The implications of this statement are far reaching. It means, for one thing, that if we are being guided by the Spirit, what we do will glorify Christ. If it glorifies man rather than God, it is not of the Spirit, but of the flesh. This is a very probing test. We should check our motives at this point. Are we seeking to glorify ourselves, or glorify God?

Tenney has pointed out another application: "Any movement which purports to be led by the Spirit, and which focuses interest on its phenomena rather than on the person of Christ belies its own claims" (*Gospel of Belief*, p. 239). If the Holy Spirit is directing a service, Christ will be exalted. If man is exalted instead, then the Spirit of God is not in it.

What is our main concern in doing Christian work? Is it to enhance our own reputation? Is it to bring glory to some institution? Or are we genuinely concerned for the salvation of souls and for the glory of God? That is the real test.

The Holy Spirit is our "Personal Conductor," if we will let Him be that to us. It means much to have a conductor to guide a group of tourists. We once talked with a woman who was returning from a trip to the Holy Land. It was at the airport in Rome and we were on our way to Palestine for the third time. "You had a wonderful trip, I am sure," we said. To our surprise she said no. Then we asked, "Who was your conductor?" "Oh," she said, "I didn't have any conductor. I went alone." On further inquiry we found that she had missed the most important sights in the Holy Land and their significance. If we are going to get the most out of our journey through life, we need the Holy Spirit as our Conductor.

The Bible is our road map for living. If we follow it carefully, we will surely make it safely to heaven. But often there are decisions to make for which we find no specific guidance in the Word of God. The Bible lays down principles, but it does not tell us what woman to marry or what job to take or what home to buy! For these decisions, and many others, we need a Personal Conductor to show us the way to go.

The last words of loved ones are always especially precious. We remember our own father's words to us the night he died at the age of seventy-five: "Son, the anchor holds." What a thrill to know that as he changed worlds he was not taking a leap into the dark or a plunge into the vast unknown, but that he felt the anchor chain holding him fast as he came to rest in the harbor of the Lord he had loved and served those many years.

In John 14—16 we have the last words of Jesus to His disciples before He went to the cross. They ought to be especially precious to us, and we should study them carefully and prayerfully.

His main concern was to tell us what the Holy Spirit could be to us. The question is, "Are we letting the Spirit be all these things to us?"

Let us review them briefly. In times of sorrow do we mourn and weep, or do we let the Holy Spirit comfort our hearts? We need to realize

that no sorrow is too deep to be reached by His healing balm. Are we turning to Him as our *Comforter*, rather than depending on ourselves?

And how about the Holy Spirit as our constant *Companion*? "That he may abide with you forever," said Jesus. That means all the time, everywhere. Do we treat Him as a companion? We are warned not to grieve the Spirit. When we pay no attention day after day to His presence, we grieve Him, as we would any human friend whom we ignored.

Then we need the Holy Spirit as *Counselor*. Life is so complicated these days that it is very difficult to avoid compromise. We constantly need the Spirit's counsel and advice as to what will please the Lord. Jesus said that He would "teach" us. But we have to be teachable in order to be taught. We must listen if we would learn. One of the greatest secrets of successful Christian living is that of listening daily to the Spirit's voice and obeying it.

Every true Christian should be a witness for Christ. But we need the Holy Spirit as our *Co-witness* if our witness is to be effective.

Are we letting the Holy Spirit come to us so fully that He is able to fulfill His role as a *Convictor* of the world?

And lastly, are we letting the Spirit be our *Conductor* day by day, guiding us surely in God's will?

DISCUSSION QUESTIONS

1. When may we properly ask the Holy Spirit to comfort us?
2. What are some conditions for being taught?
3. How may we find closer companionship with the Spirit?
4. What are some ways by which we may create greater awareness of His presence?
5. How can we glorify Christ in our daily lives?
6. What was Jesus' greatest concern for His disciples?

CONTEMPORARY APPLICATION

Why is it that there is more religion in America than ever before and at the same time more crime in this country than ever before? How can we put these together?

The answer seems to be that we have the wrong kind of religion. People want comfort, but not correction. They want to *feel* good, but not to *be* good. All they want religion to be is a bottle of aspirin tablets, to ease the aches and pains of life. They want religion to make them feel *comfortable*; however, it is only after convic-

tion of sin has made them *uncomfortable* enough to ask for God's forgiveness that the Holy Spirit can comfort them with the promise that all who come in faith will be accepted.

But the Holy Spirit comes to us not only as Comforter, but as Counselor. He comes to "teach" us, and sometimes teaching is not easy to take. What He asks us to do is to submit ourselves completely to Him and let Him make us true Christians worthy of the name.

VICTORIOUS IN DEFEAT

DEVOTIONAL READING	John 18:1-11

ADULTS

Topic: *Victorious in Defeat*

Background Scripture: John 18:12—19:15

Scripture Lesson: John 18:33-38; 19:7-11

Memory Verse: *For this I was born, and for this I have come into the world, to bear witness to the truth.* John 18:37

YOUTH

Topic: *Victorious in Defeat*

Background Scripture: John 18:12—19:15

Scripture Lesson: John 18:33-38; 19:4, 7-11

Memory Verse: *For this I was born, and for this I have come into the world, to bear witness to the truth.* John 18:37

CHILDREN

Topic: *Courage in Defeat*

Background Scripture: John 18:12—19:15

Scripture Lesson: John 18:23-38

Memory Verse: *For this I was born, and for this I have come into the world, to bear witness to the truth.* John 18:37

DAILY BIBLE READINGS

Mon., Feb. 4: Jesus Betrayed, John 18:1-6.
Tues., Feb. 5: Jesus Apprehended, John 18:7-11.
Wed., Feb. 6: Jesus Examined, John 18:12-23.
Thurs., Feb. 7: Jesus Before Caiaphas, John 18:24-28.
Fri., Feb. 8: Jesus Before Pilate, John 18:29-41.
Sat., Feb. 9: Jesus Innocent, Yet Condemned, John 19:1-16.
Sun., Feb. 10: Jesus Crucified, John 19:17-24.

LESSON AIM

To see how God can bring eternal victory out of cosmic defeat.

LESSON SETTING

Time: Probably April 6, A.D. 30. The arrest in the Garden took place around midnight of the previous night, the trial before Pilate that morning.

Place: Jerusalem

181

Victorious in Defeat

LESSON OUTLINE

SUGGESTED INTRODUCTION FOR ADULTS

In last week's lesson we were in the upper room in Jerusalem. After Jesus had fininshed His high-priestly prayer (John 17), He and His disciples went out the eastern gate of the city and down across the Kidron Valley to the lower slopes of the Mount Olives. There they entered a "garden," or olive grove. From the other Gospels we learn that this was called Gethsemane, which means "oil-press." Olive oil has always been in important production in Palestine. Judas knew that this was a place where Jesus often liked to go with His disciples. So when he did not find the Master still in the upper room, he proceeded on to the olive grove. With him was "a band of men and officers from the chief priests and Pharisees . . . with lanterns and torches and weapons" (18:3).

Jesus knew that the time of His arrest had come. So He went out to meet them and asked, "Whom are you looking for?" They answered, "Jesus of Nazareth." Boldly Christ informed them, "I am he." The shock was so great that the armed men fell to the ground. When the same question and answer had been repeated, Peter drew his sword and swung it at the neck of the high priest's servant. The man "ducked" and lost only the lobe of his right ear, instead of his head. (The word for "ear" literally means "little ear.") Peter loved his Lord and was not going to see Him captured without putting up a fight. He was Jesus' self-appointed bodyguard!

But Jesus told Peter to put up his sword. Then He added these significant words: "The cup which my Father hath given me, shall I not drink it?" He willingly submitted to death for our sins.

The arrest of Jesus in Gethsemane, which immediately precedes our lesson, furnishes an example for us today. Peter swung his sword to try to keep the "officers" (Temple police) from taking Jesus. But his Master told him to sheath his sword; then He submitted to arrest.

In other words, Jesus practiced what He preached. He had told His followers to submit to authority and not to resist evil. Now He set a consistent example. Though He knew He would not get a fair trial, He permitted Himself to be taken.

Violence is never Christian, no matter under what name or for what cause it is employed. Better to be wronged, said Jesus, than to do wrong. If we follow Christ we must adopt the same attitude.

1. Jesus was mistreated. Sometimes we will be mistreated, also.
2. He did not strike back at those who wronged Him.
3. He was willing to suffer wrong, but refused to do wrong.
4. We should follow His example.

THE LESSON COMMENTARY

I. JESUS BEFORE ANNAS: John 18:12-23

A. Annas and Caiaphas: vv. 12-14

"Then the band and the captain and officers of the Jews took Jesus, and bound him." "The officers of the Jews" would be the Temple police.

The Greek word for "band" was used for the Roman cohort, which was a tenth part of a legion. Since the Roman legion consisted of six thousand men, the cohort would normally have about six hundred men, with perhaps two hundred or so on duty. In any case, this was a large detachment of soldiers that came to arrest Jesus. The word for "captain" literally means the leader of a thousand soldiers, but was used at this time for the commander of a cohort—perhaps equivalent to a major or colonel today. Judas

Iscariot must have thought that Jesus' disciples would put up a big fight!

The soldiers arrested Jesus and "bound" Him. He was handcuffed like a common criminal. This was part of the humiliation He endured for us! This was the reward He received for going about doing good, healing the sick, giving sight to the blind, and comforting the broken-hearted. Was there ever love like this?

John alone tells us that they first took Jesus to Annas for preliminary questioning. We are told that Annas was the father-in-law of Caiaphas, who "was the high priest that same year." In Luke 3:2 we find an even stranger expression: "Annas and Caiaphas being the high priests." There was supposed to be only one high priest at a time!

The explanation is that the Roman governor appointed the high priests. If his appointee was not cooperative, he would take him out and put in another man. Annas had been the high priest for about ten years (A.D. 6-15). He was followed by five of his sons and his son-in-law Caiaphas (A.D. 18-36). But Annas kept control of the situation; he was the power behind the throne. So the office of high priest, the most sacred position among the Jews, had become the pawn of politicians. According to our count, in the seventy-five years between the birth of Christ (5 B.C.) and the destruction of the Temple (A.D. 70)—when the office of high priest came to an end—there were no less than twenty-five high priests, or an average of one every three years in an office that was supposed to be held for life! It can readily be seen that this position would not be held in very high respect in Jesus' day.

We are reminded here that Caiaphas was the one who had advised that it was best for one man to die for the people (v. 14). Being high priest he had made this statement prophetically (11:49-52).

B. Peter's First Denial: vv. 15-18

Poor Peter! He loved Jesus and couldn't leave Him. So he followed the procession of soldiers—at a safe distance (Mark 14:54). John alone tells us that "another disciple" also followed. The most natural deduction is that this other disciple was John, the writer of this Gospel. In the early chapters of Acts, Peter and John are mentioned several times as being together (Acts 3:1, 3, 11; 4:13, 19).

We are told that the other disciple was "known to the high priest." So he went right in with Jesus to the high priest's palace. This has raised some eyebrows. How would a Galilean fisherman know this official? But James and John were in partnership with Peter and Andrew (Luke 5:10), and John may well have been the one who took care of the sale of their fish in Jerusalem.

Meanwhile Peter was standing outside the door. So "that other disciple" (v. 16) went out and asked the servant girl at the door to let him in. John of course intended this as a kindness to his fellow disciple, but it actually got Peter into trouble. For the girl at the door asked him, "Aren't you one of this man's disciples?" Flatly he declared, "I am not."

Did Peter love Jesus? Most certainly! Why then did he deny Him? Obviously it was a quick, spontaneous reaction. Peter usually acted impulsively, and sudden impulses are often wrong.

The palace servants and guards were standing in the large courtyard, around which the palace was built. It was a cold night (v. 18). Jerusalem is at an elevation of about twenty-five hundred feet above sea level, and in April the nights would still be chilly. So the servants had made a fire and were warming themselves. Peter joined the crowd.

C. First Questioning of Jesus: vv. 19-23

"The high priest"—it is not certain whether this is Annas or Caiaphas—asked Jesus about His disciples and His teaching. Christ's reply was specific and to the point: "I have spoken openly to the world. I always taught in a synagogue or in the Temple, where all the Jews come together; I said nothing in secret. Why do you ask me? Ask those who heard, what I told them. Certainly they know the things I said" (vv. 20-21). This answer may seem a little blunt. But we must remember that the Sanhedrin had been checking up on what Jesus was saying and doing. Most of the miracles and teaching of Jesus recorded in John's Gospel took place in Jerusalem. The high priest had plenty of information about this.

The immediate reaction to Jesus' words was vigorous, if not violent. One of the guards hit Him with his fist, or perhaps slapped His face "with the palm of his hand." As he did so, he said, "Are you answering the high priest this way?" (v. 22). Calmly Jesus replied, "If I have spoken wrongly, testify about the wrong; but if well, why are you hitting me?" (v. 23). The act of the guard was certainly illegal.

II. JESUS BEFORE CAIAPHAS: John 18:24-27

A. Jesus Still Bound: v. 24

The King James translation of this verse, "Now Annas had sent him bound unto Caiaphas the high priest," is obviously due to the fact that verse 19 says the high priest questioned Jesus. But the Greek here is literally: "Annas therefore sent Him bound to Caiaphas the high priest." It is altogether possible that Annas and Caiaphas had different apartments in the same large palace surrounding the center courtyard, and the transfer was easily made.

B. Peter's Second Denial: v. 25

Peter was warming himself at the wrong fire. Perhaps its light caused someone to recognize him as an associate of Jesus. In any case, he was asked, "You are not one of his disciples, are you?" (The Greek indicates that a negative answer was expected.) Again he denied it: "I am not."

C. Peter's Third Denial: vv. 26-27

When Peter swung his sword in the Garden of Gethsemane, it is a wonder that he escaped being seized by the soldiers. He was now taking a big risk in standing with them around the fire. How dangerous it was is shown by what followed. For right there in the group was a relative of Malchus, whose ear Peter had severed. He asked a question that must have scared Peter half to death: "Didn't I see you in the garden with him?" For the third time, Peter denied his Lord. Just then the rooster crowed. The other Gospels tell us how the disciple remembered his Master's warning and went out and wept bitterly.

III. JESUS BROUGHT TO PILATE: John 18:28-32

The Roman government had deprived the Jewish Sanhedrin of the right to administer capital punishment, except in the case of a Gentile who entered the sacred Temple (beyond the Court of the Gentiles). So the Jews had to turn Jesus over to Pilate if He was to be put to death.

Christ was led from Caiaphas's palace to "the hall of judgment." This is one word in the original, *praitorion*, the Greek form of the Latin *praetorium* that we have taken over into English. It was early in the morning, and the Jews did not enter the Praetorium. They did not want to be "defiled" ceremonially, and so disqualified from eating the Passover (v. 28).

This poses a problem. The Synoptic Gospels seem clearly to state that Jesus ate the Passover meal with His disciples the night before His crucifixion. How is it, then, that the next morning the Jews wanted to keep themselves ceremonially clean so that they "might eat the Passover"?

Massey H. Shepherd, of the Church Divinity School of the Pacific, writes: "In that particular year the Jews in Palestine observed Passover on Saturday; those in the Dispersion observed it on Friday" (*Journal of Biblical Literature*, LXXX, 125). The Synoptics give it one way, John the other; both are right, he says. This would mean that Jesus and His disciples followed the Dispersion calendar, eating the Passover on Thursday evening (Jewish Friday) and the leaders on Friday evening (Jewish Saturday). Admittedly, no solution is universally acceptable to scholars. Many insist that the writer of John's Gospel was primarily concerned to make Jesus die when the Passover lamb was slain. But Shepherd declares: "It is in any case unconvincing to affirm that the Fourth Gospel has deliberately altered the tradition in the interest of a theology that associated the death of Jesus with the slaughter of the paschal lamb" (p. 129).

Pilate went out to the Jews, since

they would not come into the Praetorium, and asked them, "What accusation do you bring against this man?"
(v. 29). The tension that existed between the Roman governor and the
Jewish leaders is shown by the latters'
surly reply: "If this man was not doing
wrong, we would not have turned him
over to you" (v. 30). When Pilate told
them to take Jesus and judge Him according to their law, they answered,
"It is not lawful for us to put any man
to death" (v. 31). This was, no doubt,
a sore point with them.

The meaning of verse 32 is that
Jesus had said He would be lifted up
on the cross (12:32-33). Now the Jewish method of capital punishment was
by stoning. So Jesus had to be turned
over to the Romans to be crucified, as
that was their method.

IV. JESUS QUESTIONED BY PI-
LATE:
John 18: 33-40

A. Are You the King of the Jews?:
vv. 33-38a

Since he was getting nowhere
talking with the Jewish leaders, Pilate
went back into the Praetorium, summoned Jesus and said to Him, "Are
you the King of the Jews?" Jesus in
turn asked, "Do you say this from
yourself, or did others tell you this
about me?" With evident anger, resentment, and contempt, Pilate replied,
"Am I a Jew" (v. 35). Then he demanded, "What have you done?"

Instead of answering the question
directly, Jesus explained to the governor that His was not an earthly kingdom. If it were, His servants would
have fought in His defense (v. 36). His
kingdom was not a political kingdom,
but a spiritual one. So Jesus was no
threat to Roman rule.

Even though Jesus had not answered Pilate's first question—"Are
you the King of the Jews?"—He had
three times used the expression "my
kingdom" (v. 36). So Pilate asked,
"Are you a king then?" (v. 37). Jesus'
answer was: "You say that I am a

king." F. C. Grant would translate this:
"You say it because I am a king." He
was a king, but not in the sense that
Pilate was thinking, as verse 36 clearly
indicates. Then Jesus went on to say
that He had come into the world to
witness to the truth. Truthful people
would listen to Him.

Pilate had had enough of this talk.
So he said to Jesus, "What is truth?"
(v. 38). F. C. Grant comments that this
was "not a profound philosophic
query, but an expression of the disgust
and resentment of a 'practical' Roman
over what seemed to him to be merely
the quibbling of a religious fanatic or
dreamer" (Nelson's Bible Commentary).

B. Pilate's Effort to Release Jesus:
vv. 38b-40

The governor evidently had no desire to continue the conversation. He
was satisfied in his own mind that
Jesus was not a dangerous political
threat, but only a harmless religious
fool and fanatic. He was ready to drop
the case.

So he went out and said to the
Jews: "I find in him no fault at all."
The word "fault" is obviously not the
most appropriate translation. Pilate
was not passing on Jesus' character.
The Greek word aitian means "cause
or reason." At that time it was a technical legal term, meaning a "charge"
that could be brought in court. All
that Pilate was saying was this: "I find
in this man no cause for a court case.
There is no real legal charge against
him."

Then he tried a new tactic to get
Jesus' case dismissed. He said: "You
have a custom that I should release
someone to you at the Passover. Is it
your will that I release to you the King
of the Jews?" (v. 39).

He could not have said a worse
thing! The very mention of "King of
the Jews" was a red flag in the face of
these religious leaders. Immediately
they shouted, "Not this fellow, but
Barabbas!" (v. 40).

We are told that Barabbas was a

"robber." The Greek word here was used for an "insurrectionist" or a "revolutionist." And that is what Barabbas was. Mark 15:7 says that he had "committed murder in the insurrection." The Jewish leaders preferred to have a murderous revolutionary let loose in their midst, rather than the compassionate Jesus who went around healing the sick and ministering to the needs of humanity. But people are still making that same kind of choice today.

The ironical thing about it was the meaning of Barabbas' name. The Aramaic word for "son" is *bar*, and the Aramaic word for "father" is *abba*. So Barabbas means "son of the father." The religious leaders rejected the true Son of the Father and demanded to have a false "son of his father." Doubtless Barabbas continued to foment the rebellion of the Jews against the Roman government, a rebellion that finally brought about the destruction of Jerusalem in A.D. 70.

V. JESUS MOCKED AND RE-JECTED:
John 19:1-6

A. The Scourging: v. 1

It is difficult to understand why Pilate scourged Jesus. He had just declared that He was innocent of any crime. And yet he subjected the compassionate Christ to one of the most cruel punishments imaginable. The Roman scourge was a whip made of leather thongs with sharp pieces of metal or bone attached to the end. The victim had his body pulled taut over a low stone pillar, with his hands and feet fastened on opposite sides. Then this cruel scourge was brought down again and again on the naked back, leaving it lacerated and bleeding. Many a man died under the Roman lash.

B. The Mockery: vv. 2-3

After the scourging came the mocking by the soldiers. They wove a crown of thorns and placed it on His head. Then they clothed Him in a "purple robe"—perhaps a legionnaire's old, faded scarlet cloak. At any rate, it was intended as a sort of ragged symbol of royalty. They cried out, "Hail, King of the Jews!" But as they did so they slapped His face in utter contempt and mockery. It was a sad revelation of the depths of depravity in the human heart.

C. The Rejection: vv. 4-6

Again Pilate went out to the Jews, who were still waiting outside the Praetorium. And once more he declared, "I find no crime in him." Then he brought Jesus out to them, still wearing the crown of thorns and the purple robe. Probably he hoped that the sight of this pitifully abused prophet would excite some feelings of sympathy. Certainly they would take pity on Him now! Their hatred of Him would be satisfied. Pointing toward Jesus, Pilate said, "Behold the man!"

But it did no good. When the chief priests and the Temple police saw Him, they yelled: "Crucify him, crucify him!" Disgusted, Pilate said: "You take him and crucify him, for I do not find in him any cause for punishment" (v. 6). It was the third time that the governor had declared Jesus' innocence. Pilate will forever stand condemned before the bar of social conscience as well as his own conscience for having put to death a man he three times declared to be innocent.

VI. JESUS AND PILATE:
John 19:7-11

A. The Jewish Charge Against Jesus: v. 7

When Pilate declared that he found in Christ no crime, no grounds for condemnation in court, the Jews were fearful that they might be losing out. So they took a new turn—bringing a specific charge against Jesus. They said: "We have a law, and by our law he ought to die, because he made himself the Son of God." To them this was blasphemy, and it was on this charge that the Sanhedrin had condemned Him to death (Mark 14:64).

Here is where Pilate especially shows up in a bad light. He was a Roman governor and as such was supreme judge over Judea. But it was his responsibility to judge people according to Roman law, not Jewish law. His was a civil court, not a religious tribunal. Jesus had not broken any Roman law, and Pilate had three times asserted this. The only honorable thing he could have done would have been to dismiss the case as having no place in a Roman court. That is what Gallio did at Corinth (Acts 18:14-16). But Gallio was a man of honorable character as the Roman records of that day show. He was the brother of Seneca and a person held in high repute. Unfortunately, Pilate was of a different stripe. He was a selfish politician, interested mostly in his own welfare.

B. An Angry Pilate: vv. 8-10

In addition to his other faults, Pilate was evidently superstitious, as were many Romans of that day. For when he heard that Jesus claimed to be the Son of God, "he was the more afraid" (v. 8). He wondered what kind of a person he had on his hands, and what might be the consequences. If only he had sincerely asked Jesus, "What is truth?" If he had been sincere, and had been willing to listen, Christ would gladly have told him.

Once more Pilate came back into the Praetorium. This time he asked Jesus, "Where did you come from?" By this time Jesus knew that there was no use in trying to talk to the governor, so He did not answer his question. This enraged Pilate. Angrily he said to Christ: "Are you not going to speak to me? Don't you know that I have authority to release you and that I have authority to crucify you?" (v. 10). In other words, he said: "Your life is in my hands! You had better be careful how you act in my presence. If you don't do what I say, I can have you put to death."

C. A Calm Christ: v. 11

The governor was all flustered with anger and was storming at Jesus. But Christ stood there—a pitiful sight for physical eyes, but actually in all His eternal, royal majesty. It was He who was master of the situation, not Pilate. Quietly He replied to the angry, blustering governor: "You would not have any authority at all over me, unless it had been given you from above. So the one who delivered me to you has the greater sin." In other words, Jesus let Pilate know that the governor's authority did not come ultimately from his Roman overlords, but from heaven. God could cut off that authority, and even Pilate's life, in a moment of time. Pilate was on trial that day, not Jesus.

The words sank in. "And from henceforth Pilate sought to release him" (v. 12). But the religious leaders were by now desperate about the matter. They shouted: "If you let this man go, you are not Caesar's friend; whoever makes himself a king speaks against Caesar."

The Gospels agree that when the leaders of the Jewish nation saw that they were getting nowhere with Pilate by talking about Jesus being guilty of blasphemy, they switched from a religious charge to a political one. By claiming to be king, Christ was setting

---

DISCUSSION QUESTIONS

1. Why was Peter defeated (in his denials)?
2. How can we avoid permanent defeat?
3. How did Jesus react to persecution?
4. What lessons may we learn from His conduct before Pilate?
5. What is sometimes the price of ultimate victory?
6. What lessons do we learn from Jesus' arrest?

himself up against the emperor at Rome.

The expression "Caesar's friend" was a technical designation at that time. Only a few fortunate Roman officials had this high honor. Apparently Pilate had managed to get sufficiently in the good graces of the aging Tiberi- us at Rome to gain this much-coveted title. The Jews were now blackmailing Pilate: "If you don't crucify Jesus, we will see that you lose your status as Caesar's friend." And then Pilate "caved in." (See Paul Maier's excellent book, *Pontius Pilate*.)

CONTEMPORARY APPLICATION

Jesus' arrest in the garden, His Jewish trial, His Roman trial, the scourging and mockery—all these must have seemed to be serious defeats for Him. But they were all steps on the path to the greatest victory of all time, the provision of redemption for all mankind.

Sometimes our seeming defeats turn out to be victories. What the final outcome is depends largely on our attitude. Any defeat can be turned into ultimate victory if we accept it as a part of God's will for us. Usually it is the hard things in life that prove to be the greatest blessings, not the easy things. Pain, sickness, financial failure, disappointment, even seeming tragedy—all these can bring us into closer fellowship with Christ, and that is the greatest blessing in life. Sometimes lessons learned in temporary defeats make possible larger victories than we would otherwise have had.

VICTORIOUS IN DEATH

DEVOTIONAL READING

John 2:13-22

ADULTS

Topic: *Victorious in Death*

Background Scripture: John 19:16-42

Scripture Lesson: John 19:17-22, 28-30

Memory Verse: *Jesus ... said, "It is finished"; and he bowed his head and gave up his spirit.* John 19:30

YOUTH

Topic: *Victorious in Death*

Background Scripture: John 19:16-42

Scripture Lesson: John 19:17-22, 28-30

Memory Verse: *Jesus ... said, "It is finished"; and he bowed his head and gave up his spirit.* John 19:30

CHILDREN

Topic: *Jesus Gave His Life*

Background Scripture: John 19:16-42

Scripture Lesson: John 19:16-19, 40-42

Memory Verse: *God so loved the world that he gave his only Son, that whoever believes in him should not perish but have eternal life.* John 3:16

DAILY BIBLE READINGS

Mon., Feb. 11: Jesus Foretells His Death, John 2:13-22.
Tues., Feb. 12: Our King Crucified, John 19:16-22.
Wed., Feb. 13: "Behold Your Mother," John 19:23-27.
Thurs., Feb. 14: "It Is Finished," John 19:28-37.
Fri., Feb. 15: The Burial of Jesus, John 19:38-42.
Sat., Feb. 16: He Endured the Cross, Hebrews 12:1-10.
Sun., Feb. 17: Christ Died for Us, Romans 5:1-8.

LESSON AIM

To see how God can bring life out of death, and victory out of defeat.

LESSON SETTING

Time: The sixth of April, A.D. 30

Place: Jerusalem

LESSON OUTLINE

Victorious in Death

I. The Crucifixion: John 19:16-18
   A. Pilate's Final Decision: v. 16
   B. Christ Carrying the Cross: v. 17
   C. Christ on the Cross: v. 18

190

II. The Inscription Above the Cross: John 19:19-22
   A. The Inscription Itself: v. 19-20
   B. The Protest of the Jews: v. 21
   C. The Answer of Pilate: v. 22

III. The Distribution of His Clothes: John 19:23-24

IV. Jesus' Care of His Mother: John 19:25-27

V. Final Moments and Death: John 19:28-30
   A. "I Thirst": vv. 28-29
   B. "It is Finished": v. 30

VI. The Piercing of Jesus' Side: John 19:31-37
   A. Breaking the Criminals' Legs: vv. 31-32
   B. Piercing Jesus' Side: vv. 33-35
   C. Fulfilling Scripture: vv. 36-37

VII. The Burial of Jesus: John 19:38-42
   A. Joseph of Arimathea: v. 38
   B. Nicodemus: vv. 39
   C. Preparation for Burial: v. 40
   D. The Garden Tomb: vv. 41-42

SUGGESTED INTRODUCTION FOR ADULTS

About the turn of the century a significant book was written by a man who later became famous as a great musician, philosopher, theologian, and medical missionary to Africa. His name was Albert Schweitzer.

When translated into English this volume carried the title, *The Quest of the Historical Jesus.* Its main thesis was that Jesus expected the kingdom of God to come during His lifetime. When that did not happen, He died a disappointed man, crying out: "I'm done for, finished; its all over now!"

Was that what Jesus meant when He said, "It is finished"? This question lies at the very heart of our lesson today. If the answer is yes, then the story of the cross ends in defeat. But we know that this is not the correct interpretation. Instead, Jesus was victorious even in death.

How do we know? We know it not only because the Bible clearly teaches this, but also because history proves it. The death of Christ, instead of being the greatest tragedy of all time, is the greatest victory in human history. It was truly a cosmic victory.

SUGGESTED INTRODUCTION FOR YOUTH

A great deal is said about following Jesus as our Example. But we cannot follow Him until we have found Him. And the only place we can find Him is at the foot of the cross. He cannot be our Example until He has first become our Savior.

Which means that His death is of primary importance to us. If He had not died for us, we could not have a new life in Him. Much as we dislike the thought of death, we must realize that our eternal life depends on Christ's death in time.

Jesus was victorious in death, and we can only be victorious as we identify ourselves in His death. We have to die to live. This is one of the great paradoxes of Christianity. But it is a secret that every victorious Christian knows to be true. In His death we find our life. And it is life everlasting.

Unless we are willing to die, we cannot live. This is the main message of Romans 6—8. Crucified with Christ, we begin a new life of resurrection victory in Him.

CONCEPTS FOR CHILDREN

1. Jesus gave His life for us.
2. Because He was willing to die for us, we should be willing to live for Him!
3. Jesus was victorious in death, and we can be victorious through Him.
4. Jesus' death was an expression of divine love.

THE LESSON COMMENTARY

I. THE CRUCIFIXION: John 19:16-18

A. Pilate's Final Decision: v. 16

Pilate seems to have been thoroughly cowed by the Jewish threat to end his friendly relations with the Roman emperor (v. 12). So he brought Jesus out for final trial. He himself sat down on "the judgment seat." The Greek word is *bema*, which one can see inscribed on the wall in old Corinth where Gallio sat on his judgment seat. It is claimed that a Roman governor could give legal sentence only when he was seated on the *bema*. This judgment seat was in the place known as "the Pavement"—literally "stone pavement."

North of the Temple area today visitors are taken some dozen feet below the street level to an old Roman pavement which may well have been the very "Gabbatha" where this took place. On the pavement are carved games that were played by the Roman soldiers of that day.

We are told that Pilate's trial of Jesus took place on "the preparation of the passover" (v. 14). The Greek word for "preparation" is the regular name for Friday in the Greek world. There seems to be little question that

Jesus was crucified on Friday, in spite of some modern arguments in favor of a Wednesday crucifixion. Mark 15:42 is conclusive for Friday.

The statement that it was about the sixth hour is difficult to harmonize with the Synoptic indication that Jesus was crucified at "the third hour" (Mark 15:25). We have already noted in an earlier lesson that probably John is using Roman time, which here would mean after six o'clock in the morning, while the Synoptics are employing Jewish time, in which the third hour would be nine o'clock. We would have to assume that the "sixth hour" refers to the time when the trial before Pilate began.

Presenting Jesus to the assembled crowd of Jews, Pilate said, "Behold your King!" It is probable that these words were more sarcastic than his utterance in verse 5. Evidently the governor was disgusted with the whole affair and wanted to show his contempt for the Jews.

The answer of the crowd (v. 15) was an echo of verse 6, only with more vehemence and violence. The Jewish leaders didn't want to see Jesus any more. So they yelled: "Take him away, take him away; crucify him!"

Pilate got in one last insulting thrust: "Shall I crucify your King?"

Enraged, the leaders answered: "We have no king but Caesar." In view of the Pharisees' opposition to Roman rule, this was a rather hypocritical remark.

Pilate had had enough. In compliance with the Jewish demands, he turned Jesus over to the soldiers, who led Him away to be crucified (v. 16). The governor had showed the weakness of his character in giving in to unjust pressure.

B. Christ Carrying the Cross: v. 17

John says: "And he bearing his cross went forth." Some have tried to find a contradiction between this statement and the one in the Synoptics that a man named Simon was compelled to carry the cross for Christ (Matthew 27:32; Mark 15:21; Luke 23:26). But it is evident from the Synoptic accounts that it was outside the city gate that Simon was impressed into service—he was on his way in from the country. It appears that Jesus started out carrying His cross—or the crossbeam, as some think—but was so weakened by the events of the night and especially the scourging, that He was unable to carry it far. So it was placed on the shoulders of Simon. Incidentally, Simon was from Cyrene, in North Africa, and so was probably not a black man.

The soldiers took Jesus to a place called "Skull Place." The Greek for "skull" is *cranion* (cf. *cranium*, the Latin form which we have taken over into English). We are told here that the Hebrew (or Aramaic) was *Golgotha*.

We cannot be sure of the exact site of the crucifixion. The reason for this is explained by F. C. Grant: "It is not surprising that no trace of the location survives, for in the siege of Jerusalem in A.D. 68-70 the whole area north of the city was swept bare and made into a huge ramp so that the Roman battering-rams, towers, and other artillery could be moved up against the walls" *(Nelson Bible Commentary)*.

Today there are two sites that are pointed out to visitors. The traditional place is the Church of the Holy Sepulcher. This is now well within the walls of Jerusalem, but in Christ's day may have been outside the north wall of that time. A favorite location with many Protestants is Gordon's Calvary, named after General Gordon of the British Army, who chose this site because of a large, skull-shaped rock north of the present wall of Jerusalem. One can easily pick out the appearance of the forehead, eyes, nose, and chin. Archaeologists are more impressed with the claims of the Church of the Holy Sepulcher, since that site was chosen by Queen Helena, the mother of Constantine, the first "Christian" Roman emperor. Suffice it to say that if one wants to relive the scenes of the crucifixion and resurrection he can do so much more satisfactorily at Gordon's Calvary and the Garden Tomb than he can in the Church of the Holy Sepulcher. In the latter place the sights and sounds and smells are often repulsive.

C. Christ on the Cross: v. 18

Jesus started out for Calvary (Latin for "skull") carrying His cross. He ended by being nailed to it. As all four Gospels state, Jesus was crucified between two others. These are identified in Matthew 27:38 and Mark 15:27 as "thieves" (KJV). But the Greek clearly says "robbers," which we have noted was a term used for insurrectionists. Without any doubt Barabbas was scheduled to die on that middle cross between his two colleagues in the revolution, but Jesus took his place. This makes the whole narrative all the more poignant.

II. THE INSCRIPTION ABOVE THE CROSS: John 19:19-22

A. The Inscription Itself: vv. 19-20

Pilate wrote a "title" (Greek, *titlos*) and placed it at the top of the cross. This was an inscription or "notice" as to why the man was being crucified. Naturally, passersby would be curious to know what crime the criminals had committed.

If one compares the four Gospel accounts of this inscription, he will find variations in wording. Matthew has: THIS IS JESUS THE KING OF THE JEWS (27:37). Mark has the shortest: THE KING OF THE JEWS (15:26). Luke has: THIS IS THE KING OF THE JEWS (23:38). John has the longest form: JESUS OF NAZARETH THE KING OF THE JEWS (19:19).

Two or three observations can be made. The first is that they all agree that the inscription included Mark's brief wording: "The King of the Jews." The second is that all four accounts can be combined into what may have been the complete inscription: "This is Jesus of Nazareth the King of the Jews." Each writer chose the part that he wanted to emphasize. A third factor is that the inscription was written in three different languages, as John tells us, and it may have differed in these three. For instance, the Hebrew alphabet has only consonants, no vowels. The same words in Hebrew, then, would take less space than the same words in Latin or Greek. So the Hebrew inscription may have contained more. In the light of these observations, it will appear evident that it is not justifiable to talk about "contradictions" between the accounts.

The place of crucifixion was near the city, consequently many people read the inscription. It was written in Hebrew, Greek, and Latin. Hebrew was the language of the Scriptures (our Old Testament) and so especially sacred to the Jews. Greek was the language of commerce and international communication at that time. Latin was the Roman official language. Many scholars think that "Hebrew" here means "Aramaic," the popular language of Palestine in the time of Christ.

B. The Protest of the Jews: v. 21

The expression "the chief priests of the Jews" shows that John was writing at a later time, when there were no longer any of "the chief priests" mentioned in the Synoptic Gospels. When the Temple was destroyed in A.D. 70, the priests had no place to function and soon disappeared from the scene. This Gospel was probably written about twenty-five years later, around A.D. 95.

These religious leaders were not at all pleased with Pilate's identification of Jesus as "The King of the Jews." They asked him to change the inscription to say that this was only what He claimed to be, not what He was. They did not want people to think that they had actually condemned the King of the Jews!

C. The Answer of Pilate: v. 22

Pilate was sick and tired of the Jewish leaders who had haggled with him for hours. Now he was taking his revenge on them. They had pressured him into crucifying an innocent man. So he announced officially that this one they had condemned and demanded the death sentence for was actually their king. It was a bitter pill for them to swallow. When they protested, he asserted his authority—which he should have done hours before—by making the memorable declaration: "What I have written I have written."

Unfortunately for Pilate, these words have boomeranged on him. "What I have written" included more than the inscription. In the preceding hours of that fateful morning he had written, in his actions, a record which has stood against him for nineteen centuries and will face him at the Judgment. "What I have written I have written" is a solemn warning to every human individual. We are all writing the record of our lives each day and can never unwrite it. But thank God it can be erased, as far as guilt is involved, by the blood of Christ.

III. THE DISTRIBUTION OF HIS CLOTHES:
John 19:23-24

All the Gospels mention the fact that the soldiers took Jesus' clothes (Matthew 27:35; Mark 15:24; Luke 23:34). This was evidently the Roman custom. But only John tells us about the seamless robe, or tunic. The soldiers each took one fourth of His other clothes. But when they looked at His robe and saw that it was woven in one piece from top to bottom, they decided not to tear it into four pieces for the cloth. It was evidently an expensive garment, probably provided by some woman of means who wanted to show her appreciation to Jesus. So they "cast lots" for it, in fulfillment of the Scripture found in Psalm 22:18. (Psalm 22 is the most vivid description of the Crucifixion to be found in the Old Testament.) It should perhaps be noted that the word translated "coat" in the King James Version is *chiton,* which means the undergarment or tunic, not the outer cloak.

IV. JESUS' CARE OF HIS MOTHER:
John 19:25-27

Standing by the cross were four women. The first was Jesus' mother. The second was her sister, whom some think was Salome, the mother of James and John, the sons of Zebedee. This would help to explain John's close connection with Jesus and also why he does not name Salome, since she was his mother. The third was "Mary the wife of Cleophas," or rather, Clopas. The fourth was Mary Magdalene (from Magdala in Galilee), who was the first to see Jesus after His resurrection (20:11-18).

Also standing there was "the disciple whom He loved"—John the apostle, the writer of this Gospel. Jesus said to His mother: "Woman, behold thy son!" Then looking at John, He said, "Behold thy mother." (These are treated together as one of the "Seven Sayings from the Cross.") John immediately caught the point. Jesus did not want His mother to suffer longer, watching His agony. So John led her away to his home, where she remained after that.

This tender care of His mother when Jesus was dying on the cross for the sins of the whole world ought to serve as a lesson for us. We should never become so busy in the affairs of the Kingdom that we neglect our proper responsibilities to our loved ones. On the one hand, we are told that we must love them less than we love Christ; He must have our supreme devotion (Matthew 10:37). But on the other hand, it should be said that when we love Christ supremely we also love our family and friends more than ever before. Our capacity for loving people unselfishly is increased when Christ comes in.

V. FINAL MOMENTS AND DEATH:
John 19:28-30

A. "I thirst": vv. 28-29

Jesus was aware that the end was coming near. He had "accomplished" all that His Father had sent Him to do. And so, in fulfillment of Scripture, He said, "I thirst."

In this utterance He was not playing a role on the stage. His body had become dehydrated by intense suffering and by hours of exposure on the cross. His agony of soul only deepened the irresistible longing for water. So He cried, "I thirst."

Nearby was a jar filled with "vinegar." This was probably the cheap "sour wine" that the Roman soldiers drank. Someone filled a sponge with the sour wine, put it on a reed, and held it up to Jesus' mouth.

B. "It is Finished": v. 30

When Jesus had tasted the sour drink, He said, "It is finished." Then He bowed His head and "gave up the ghost"—rather, He "dismissed His spirit." He died voluntarily, as He had said He would (10:17-18). "I thirst" emphasizes His humanity; "It is finished," His deity.

We have already noted that when Jesus uttered these words He was not saying, "I'm done for; it's all over now!" What did He mean?

The declaration, "It is finished," might be taken as indicating three things. The first is that *the Old Testament types and prophecies had been fulfilled.* We can go all the way back to Genesis 22, and see Abraham offering Isaac, his beloved son. (There is a double type here, for a lamb was substituted.) In Exodus we find many types of Christ and His redemptive ministry clearly pictured in the Tabernacle, every part of which was a symbol of His work. In Leviticus the same thing can be said about the various offerings and sacrifices. In Numbers we read of the "Star out of Jacob, and a Sceptre . . . out of Israel" (24:17). In Deuteronomy 18:15 we find the prophecy that is quoted by both Peter and Stephen (Acts 3:22; 7:37): "The Lord thy God will raise up unto thee a Prophet from the midst of thee, of thy brethren, like unto me."

We could go on through the various books, but we skip over to the Psalms. As we have already noted, Psalm 22 gives a graphic portrayal of Christ's crucifixion. There are many other Messianic Psalms, which we do not have space to mention.

Turning to the Prophets, in Isaiah 9:6 we have a beautiful prediction of Christ's first coming and in Isaiah 53 a picture of His sacrificial death for the sins of all the lost sheep of humanity. In Micah 5:2 we find a prophecy of His birth at Bethlehem. And finally in Malachi 4:2, in the last chapter in the Old Testament, we read these beautiful words: "But unto you that fear my name shall the Sun of righteousness arise with healing in his wings." A thousand fingers in the Old Testament point to Christ, the One that should come.

In the second place, "It is finished" means that *the righteous demands of the Law had been satisfied.* Christ lived the only perfect life ever lived on earth. The three greatest Old Testament characters are Abraham, Moses, and David; yet Scripture is almost frighteningly honest in depicting the faults of each of these. Jesus alone was without sin.

We can never *achieve* righteousness, we must *accept* it from Christ. Theodore Cuyler once said: "When thought advances beyond the cross on Calvary, it goes over a precipice."

The third and most specific thing that "It is finished" means is that *the basic work of redemption is completed.* Christ's sacrificial death on the cross was adequate to atone for all the sins of all mankind for all time. It was a finished work for us. Nothing is lacking in the provision for our salvation. This is the glorious declaration that Jesus made in His dying moments on the cross. And we can take great comfort in those words.

VI. THE PIERCING OF JESUS' SIDE: John 19:31-37

A. Breaking the Criminals' Legs: vv. 31-32

It was "the preparation," which we have already noted means Friday. The Jews did not want the Sabbath desecrated by leaving the bodies on the cross over that day, which began at sunset Friday night, especially since this Sabbath was a "high day"—that is, both a Sabbath day and a feast day. So they asked Pilate to have the criminals' legs broken, to induce death quickly by having the bodies slump down on the cross, causing respiratory failure. So the Roman soldiers came and broke the legs of the robbers on either side of Jesus.

B. Piercing Jesus' Side: vv. 33-35

When they came to the Man on the middle cross, they found that He was already dead. This no doubt surprised them, for the people usually hung on the cross for twenty-four to forty-eight hours before they expired from pain and weakness. But Jesus, as we have noted, had voluntarily dismissed His spirit.

Still, they were responsible to see that these men died. So, to make doubly sure that Jesus was actually dead, one of the soldiers jabbed a spear through His side and into His heart. Blood and water flowed out. Some say this shows that He died of a ruptured heart.

John affirms that he himself actually saw this with his own eyes. As Barrett says in his commentary on this Gospel, "John intended to provide evidence that Jesus was a real man and that he really died. . . . The real death of Jesus was the real life of man." We learn from John's First Epistle that one of the main heresies he had to combat in Ephesus was Docetic Gnosticism, which held that Jesus only *seemed* to be human; that He did not really have a physical body, only the appearance of one.

C. Fulfilling Scripture: vv. 36-37

The fact that Jesus had already died so that His legs were not broken, was in fulfillment of the prophecy in Psalm 34:20: "He keepeth all his bones: not one of them is broken." This, in turn, is connected with the regulation in the Mosaic law that not a bone of the Passover lamb was to be broken (Exodus 12:46; Numbers 9:12). Paul tells us: "For even Christ our Passover is sacrificed for us" (I Corinthians 5:7). As our Passover Lamb, it was important that Jesus should fulfill all the requirements of the Law.

Another Scripture was fulfilled: "And they shall look upon me whom they have pierced" (Zechariah 12:10). This is also cited by John in Revelation 1:7 and applied to Christ's second coming: "Behold, he cometh with clouds; and every eye shall see him, and they also which pierced him."

VII. THE BURIAL OF JESUS: John 19:38-42

A. Joseph of Arimathea: v. 38

This man, from Arimathea about twenty miles northwest of Jerusalem, was a member of the Sanhedrin, the Supreme Court of Israel, for Mark (15:43) calls him "an honourable counsellor." He also says that Joseph went in "boldly" to Pilate and begged for the body of Jesus. In view of all that had happened, it took real courage for Joseph to do this—an indication that he was no longer "a disciple of Jesus, but secretly for fear of the Jews."

B. Nicodemus: v. 39

This man was also a member of the Sanhedrin, "a ruler of the Jews" (3:1). He is identified as the one who "came to Jesus by night." This happened "at the first," that is, at the beginning of Jesus' ministry. Being a man of means, he brought a large amount of expensive aromatic ointments.

C. Preparation for Burial: v. 40

Joseph and Nicodemus, with loving care, took the body of Jesus. In accordance with Jewish custom, they wrapped His body in long strips of linen cloth, sealing each fold with the aromatic ointment—a sort of partial embalming. Though Jesus died as a condemned criminal, He was given an expensive burial by two rich men (cf. Isaiah 53:9).

D. The Garden Tomb: vv. 41-42

Right by the place of crucifixion was a garden, in which was located a

---

DISCUSSION QUESTIONS

1. What is the importance of the cross in Christianity?
2. Why did Christ have to die?
3. Why did Jesus have to be both Son of man and Son of God?
4. Why did John emphasize the reality of the human body?
5. What is the symbolism of the piercing of Jesus' side?
6. Why was it important that Jesus' burial be witnessed?

new, unused sepulcher. Because it was nearly sunset, when the Jewish Sabbath would begin and no burden could be carried, the two men laid Jesus' body to rest in this place. As we have noted "preparation" means Friday, which with the Jews ended at sunset.

CONTEMPORARY APPLICATION

We are told that the great Cathedral at Cologne, Germany, was five centuries in building. This means that many hundreds of people, covering fifteen generations, had worked on this massive and magnificent structure.

It seemed that it would never be finished. But finally the day of completion arrived. A large crowd was gathered for the occasion. Then came the last act. As the cross was lifted and put in place at the top of the towering spire, the thousands of people below united in shouting, 'Es ist vollendet!"—"It is finished."

For untold centuries, God had been building the house of redemption for His people. But it was not completed until Christ on the cross uttered those words, "It is finished." We are the recipients of that blessing.

February 24, 1974

THE RESURRECTION VICTORY

DEVOTIONAL READING	John 11:17-27

ADULTS

Topic: *The Resurrection Victory*

Background Scripture: John 20—21

Scripture Lesson: John 20:19-29

Memory Verse: *Blessed are those who have not seen and yet believe.* John 20:29

YOUTH

Topic: *New Meaning for Life*

Background Scripture: John 20—21

Scripture Lesson: John 20:19-29

Memory Verse: *Blessed are those who have not seen and yet believe.* John 20:29

CHILDREN

Topic: *Victory in Life*

Background Scripture: Mark 16:1-8; John 20:1-21

Scripture Lesson: Mark 16:1-8

Memory Verse: *God so loved the world that he gave his only Son, that whoever believes in him should not perish but have eternal life.* John 3:16

DAILY BIBLE READINGS

Mon., Feb. 18: The Empty Tomb, John 20:1-10.
Tues., Feb. 19: "I Have Seen the Lord," John 20:11-18.
Wed., Feb. 20: "Peace Be with You," John 20:19-23.
Thurs., Feb. 21: "My Lord and My God!" John 20:24-30.
Fri., Feb. 22: "It Is the Lord!" John 21:1-14.
Sat., Feb. 23: "Do You Love Me?" John 21:15-19.
Sun., Feb. 24: "Follow Me!" John 21:20-25.

LESSON AIM

To show how through death with Christ we may come into a resurrection life of victory in Him.

LESSON SETTING

Time: The Resurrection probably took place on Sunday morning, April 8, A.D. 30. Jesus appeared to Mary Magdalene that morning and to ten disciples that evening. A week later He appeared to the eleven (Thomas present). The incident in chapter 21 happened within forty days of the Resurrection (cf. Acts 1:3).

Place: The events of chapter 20 took place in or near Jerusalem, those of chapter 21 in Galilee.

The Resurrection Victory

LESSON OUTLINE

**SUGGESTED
INTRODUCTION
FOR ADULTS**

The cross is usually thought of as the central emphasis in Christian theology. But Floyd Filson wrote a helpful book on New Testament Theology, *Jesus Christ the Risen Lord*, in which he suggests that the Resurrection is the keynote of New Testament teaching. He has made an impressive case for this point of view.

Anyone who reads the opening chapters of Acts carefully will soon discover that the Resurrection had the primary place in early apostolic preaching. In his great sermon on the day of Pentecost, Peter devoted far more space to his discussion of the resurrection of Jesus (Acts 2:24-32) than he did to His life (v. 22) and His death (v. 23) put together. The first persecution of the apostles is introduced with the statement that the Sadducees arrested them, "being grieved that they taught the people, and preached through Jesus the resurrection from the dead" (Acts 4:2).

Why was this the central emphasis in apostolic preaching? The answer is that if Jesus had not risen from the dead, He was not the Messiah; He was just another misguided martyr. But if He did actually rise from the dead, this was evidence that He was what He claimed to be—the Son of God. In preaching to the Jews, the Resurrection was of paramount importance.

Paul gives the same emphasis in his Epistles. In I Corinthians 15 he lists half a dozen postressurection appearances of Jesus and then declares that if Christ has not risen, "then is our preaching vain, and your faith is also vain" (v. 14). In Romans 4:25 he says that Jesus "was delivered for our offences, and was raised again for our justification." The Resurrection was the divine declaration that Christ's sacrifice for our sins had been accepted and validated in the court of heaven. It is our assurance of salvation.

SUGGESTED
INTRODUCTION
FOR YOUTH

The resurrection of Jesus gives "New Meaning for Life"—the youth topic for today. Jesus died for us, and that death atoned for all our sins. All we have to do is to accept its provisions by faith.

But His resurrection means that the Risen Christ wants to live in our hearts. It is not only what He did *for* us back at Calvary; it is what He wants to do *in* us now. Jesus said: "Because I live, you will live also" (John 14:19). Our life of victory is really His living His life in us. That is what the Resurrection should mean to us.

CONCEPTS FOR
CHILDREN

1. Jesus showed His love not only in dying for us, but also in rising again to live in our hearts.
2. We do not worship a dead Christ, but a living Savior.
3. With Jesus in our hearts we can live as He wants us to live.

THE LESSON COMMENTARY

I. APPEARANCE TO MARY MAGDALENE:
John 20:1-18

A. Mary Comes Early to the Tomb: v. 1

We are told that on "the first day of the week" Mary Magdalene came "early, when it was yet dark," to the tomb. Since she saw "the stone taken away from the sepulchre," it was evidently daylight when she arrived, though dark when she started.

It is not difficult to reconstruct the picture. She was perhaps staying out at Bethany, half an hour's walk away. She had not slept much that night. Her mind was haunted by the horrible sight of seeing her Lord crucified (19:25)—the One who had delivered her from the dominance of seven demons (Luke 8:2). She could never sufficiently show her love and gratitude to Him. And now He was dead! She rolled and tossed, her heart bleeding for Him.

Finally it was early morning. She rose and dressed in the darkness, then headed out over the Mount of Olives for the garden tomb, north of the city wall.

As she hurried along in the dim light of dawn, the birds were chirping their good morning songs and the spring flowers were blooming along the path. But Mary had no eyes to see or ears to hear. All she could think of was Jesus. She would never see Him alive again!

When she came near she discovered to her consternation that the stone had been rolled back from the door of the sepulcher. What had happened?

B. Peter and John Visit the Tomb: vv. 2-10

Mary was perplexed and probably a bit frightened. So she decided to go and report the matter to Peter and John (v. 2).

The two men immediately ran together toward the tomb. John, being younger and fleeter of foot, outran Peter and arrived first at the open sepulcher. He stooped down and looked in but, with a becoming sense of awe and reverence, he did not enter.

Then came the Big Fisherman, panting and out of breath. Typically, he "barged" right into the tomb. There he saw the linen clothes, and the cloth that had been around Jesus' head lying by itself. What did it all mean?

Meanwhile John stepped quietly and reverently inside. We read that "he saw, and believed" (v. 8). The two men saw exactly the same things with their physical eyes. But John looked with eyes of faith. He noted how the clothes were arranged. If someone had stolen the body, the clothes would have been gone, too. But here they were, just as if the body had slipped out of its cocoon and left it there. It wasn't a robbery; it was a resurrection! He *saw* and *believed*. Do we look, as he did, with the eyes of faith?

In spite of the fact that Jesus had three times told His disciples that He would die and then rise on the third day (Mark 8:31; 9:31; 10:34), they had not understood. Nor did they realize that the Scriptures foretold the Resurrection.

Since there was nothing more to do, the two disciples went home. There was no use in staying there!

C. Mary Meets Jesus: vv. 11-18

"But Mary." These words are filled with dramatic significance. "But Mary stood without the sepulchre weeping." Our capacity for suffering is measured by our love. Those who love deeply suffer keenly. Mary's hurt was deep down inside. Because she loved Jesus more than most of His followers did— He had completely transformed her life—His death had caused her the greatest agony.

"But Mary." The men could go away but Mary was held there by love. She stayed and suffered. She waited and wept—waited to see Jesus. Without Him life held no meaning for her. She couldn't leave.

As she wept, she stooped down and looked into the tomb. There she saw two angels dressed in white. One was sitting at the head of the stone slab where Jesus' body had been placed, the other at the foot.

The angels said to her, "Woman, why are you crying?" With a wail in her voice she replied: "Because they have taken away my Lord, and I know not where they have laid him" (v. 13) It has often been pointed out that these words could well be echoed today by those who have been robbed

of their faith in Jesus Christ as Lord and Savior.

As Mary turned away from the tomb, she saw a Man standing there, but she did not recognize Him as Jesus. Probably she was so bowed down with grief that she hardly looked up. Then, too, her eyes were so full of tears that she could not see clearly.

This Man repeated the question of the angels: "Woman, why are you crying?" (v. 15). Then He added: "Whom are you looking for?"

She thought He was the gardener, the only one that would be around that early in the morning. So she said to Him: "Sir, if you have carried him away, please tell me where you have put him, and I will take him away."

Then it happened. Suddenly her heart felt! Her ears heard! Her eyes saw! A familiar voice uttered just one word: "Mary." She wheeled around and looked Him full in the face. It was Jesus! Spontaneously she cried out, "Rabboni"—"My Master!" It had been well worth the waiting!

Probably she threw herself impulsively at His feet, wrapped her arms around His ankles, and held on to Him with all her strength. She would never let Him go again! Now that she had found Him, she would never leave Him. Never!

Then a kind voice said, "Touch me not" (KJV). All scholars, as far as we know, agree, with the modern versions, that the correct translation is, "Do not cling to me." She must let Him go in the flesh that she might receive Him in the Spirit at Pentecost. Then He *would* never leave her. Through the Holy Spirit dwelling in her heart He would be with her every moment everywhere, for the rest of her life. No wonder Jesus said, "Don't hold on to me." It was for her best good that He should leave again and go back to heaven (v. 17). For then He would send the Holy Spirit to make His presence continually real to her heart.

There is a real sense in which Easter is a prelude to Pentecost. Without Pentecost, Easter would have been just another dream castle dissolved in the rising sun of hard reality. It was Pentecost that made the risen Christ available to all Christians through the Holy Spirit. Just as the Crucifixion would have been incomplete without the Resurrection, so the Resurrection would have been incomplete without Pentecost. The story of redemption in the New Testament does not end with the empty tomb. It goes on to the outpouring of the Spirit on the day of Pentecost. This is the real birthday of the Christian church.

It is typical of literalistic Biblical interpretation that some people claim that Jesus ascended to heaven during the first week after His resurrection. What is the basis for this? Simply that on that first Sunday morning He said: "Touch me not, for I am not yet ascended to my Father" (v. 17), whereas on the next Sunday evening He told Thomas to touch Him (v. 27). This proves that in the meantime He had gone to the Father!

As we have already noted, Jesus did not tell Mary not to touch Him. He urged her not to hold on to Him, but to let Him go. It was forty days later when He ascended to the Father, and then ten days after that the Holy Spirit filled the hearts of the 120 believers in the upper room. After that Mary could hold on to Him all she wanted to—in the Spirit. This is what this passage clearly means.

A significant expression occurs in verse 17: "I ascend unto my Father, and your Father: and to my God, and your God." Jesus taught His disciples to pray: "Our Father." But the passage here clearly indicates Christ's consciousness that God was His Father in a distinctly different sense from which He was the Father of others. We dare not blur this distinction!

Apparently Jesus disappeared as mysteriously as He had suddenly appeared. Mary hurried off to tell the disciples that she had seen the Lord. She also reported to them what Jesus had instructed her to tell them.

Mary came to the tomb to weep, but she found it a temple where she worshiped her Risen Lord. The place of death became the place of a great discovery.

II. APPEARANCE TO TEN DISCIPLES:
John 20:19-25

A. "Peace Be unto You": vv. 19-23

On that first Sunday evening the disciples were gathered in a room, with the doors locked for fear of the Jews. Was this the same upper room where the Last Supper took place? Perhaps so.

Suddenly Jesus stood in their midst. How did He come through those closed doors? We do not know. The nature of Christ's resurrected body has been the subject of much debate—which too often, perhaps, is only shared ignorance. Was it His glorified body, or did He receive that at His ascension? The answers differ. We do know that He appeared in a visible body and that He ate food as proof that He was not a ghost (Luke 24:36-43). But He could also appear and disappear at will and could go through locked doors. Probably this problem will remain unsolved, one of those mysteries we have to live with in this period of our partial knowledge (I Corinthians 13:9, 12).

Undoubtedly the disciples were frightened at the sudden appearance of their Master. So the first words He said to them were, "Peace be unto you"— the equivalent of the Hebrew greeting, "Shalom." To prove that it was really He and not some strange spirit, He showed them His hands and side. There they could see the nail holes and the wound made by the spear. When the disciples were sure that it was the Lord, they rejoiced to see Him again.

Again Jesus said, "Peace be unto you" (v. 21). But now He added a commission: "As my Father has sent me, even so send I you." The last four words have been made into a very moving missionary song. Its challenge has sent many people across the seas with the gospel of Christ.

When Jesus had said this, He breathed on them and said to them, "Receive the Holy Spirit." As might be expected, liberal critics have seized on this as a contradiction of the second chapter of Acts. They claim that the Johannine tradition is that the disciples received the Holy Spirit on the evening of the Resurrection, not fifty days later on the day of Pentecost. The reasonable way to treat this is as a prophetic prediction and promise of what was soon to take place. John R. W. Stott, one of the great evangelical preachers of our day, calls it "a dramatic anticipation of Pentecost." That describes it well.

Jesus then made the astounding pronouncement: "Whose soever sins you remit, they are remitted unto them; and whose soever sins you retain, they are retained" (v. 23). Some have taken this as divine authorization for the church to grant absolution to penitent sinners. It is admittedly difficult to be sure just what Jesus meant. This much can be said: By the preaching of the gospel or by personal soul-winning we can contribute to people's sins being remitted (forgiven), and by failure in such testimony we contribute to those sins being retained.

B. Doubting Thomas: vv. 24-25

Some people feel that we are being a bit harsh with Thomas when we give him this title. But he earned it! He was not there the evening of the Resurrection, when Jesus appeared to the other disciples. Where was he? What was he doing? We do not know. But he is a good type of those today who fail to go to church some Sunday, and it turns out to be just the time when there is a gracious visitation of the Spirit. We have known this to happen. We cheat ourselves when we don't go to church.

Thomas was "one of the twelve" apostles. He was called Didymus, which means "the Twin." When the other disciples told Thomas joyfully, "We have seen the Lord," he refused to believe it. In fact he became very specific in laying down the only conditions on which he would be willing to believe: "Except I shall see in his hands the print of the nails, and put my finger into the print of the nails, and thrust my hand into his side, I will not believe." This comes very close to stubborn unbelief. And this man was confusing seeing with believing. These are two very different things. Thomas would join the illogical unthinkers who say, "Seeing is believing." True faith is believing when there is nothing to see!

III. APPEARANCE TO ELEVEN DISCIPLES: John 20:26-29

A. Jesus Challenges Thomas: vv. 26-27

We shall have to give Thomas credit for one thing: The next Sunday evening he was on hand! So he was opening himself to the possibility of seeing Jesus, if the Master returned.

Jesus' tender compassion is shown in the fact that He *did* return that second Sunday. Again the doors were locked, but Jesus suddenly appeared in the room. And again He addressed them with "Peace be unto you."

Of course Christ knew what Thomas had said earlier that week. So He gave His whole attention at first to this doubting disciple. He invited Thomas to fulfill the conditions he had insisted on. In fact, he could do more. He could not only see the nail holes in Jesus' hands, but feel them. And he could thrust his hand into the riven side. Then Jesus gently chided him: "Be not faithless, but believing."

B. Thomas Believes: vv. 28-29

It was enough for Thomas. His doubts all dispelled, he cried, "My Lord and my God." The evidence was overwhelming, and he accepted it.

Then Jesus made a significant statement: "Thomas, because you have seen me, you have believed:

blessed are those who have not seen, and yet have believed." This takes in all Christians today. Jesus pronounced a special blessing on us who are willing to believe in Him without any visible evidence. His spiritual presence in our hearts is proof enough.

IV. APPEARANCE TO SEVEN DISCIPLES:
John 21:1-17

A. Failure in Fishing: vv. 1-3

We noted when studying John 6:1 that the Sea of Galilee is called the Sea of Tiberias only in John's Gospel. This agrees with the late date of this Gospel as compared with the Synoptics.

Seven of the twelve disciples were together one day. Probably Jesus had not appeared to them for some time, and Peter was getting restless. So he announced, "I'm going fishing." The others said, "We'll go with you." So off they started at once in a "ship"—rather, a "boat"! That night they caught nothing. It just wasn't the right time.

B. The Big Catch: vv. 4-8

Morning came and still no fish. In the dawning light they saw a man standing on the shore, but nobody recognized that it was Jesus.

He called out, "Boys, have you anything for eating?" Disconsolately they answered, "No."

Then He said to them, "Throw the net out on the right side of the boat." To their utter astonishment, when they did this the net immediately filled with so many fish that they couldn't haul it in.

John had a keener spiritual sensitivity than the other disciples. He turned to Peter and said, "It's the Lord!"

Peter had taken off his outer garment—that's what "naked" means. Now he quickly pulled it on, jumped into the water and waded to shore. He was so glad to see Jesus again that he didn't even wait to help the others haul in the net. But the half dozen who were left managed to drag it the last hundred yards ("two hundred cubits") to shore.

C. Breakfast by the Lake: vv. 9-14

On the beach they found a fire already burning, with fish cooking on it and bread nearby. But with seven hungry men, who had been out on the lake all night, more food was needed. So Jesus said, "Bring some of the fish you have caught." Always impulsive, the Big Fisherman grabbed the net and hauled it ashore. To everyone's surprise, it contained 153 big fish. But in spite of the heavy weight, the net had not broken.

Then they heard a welcome invitation, "Come and have breakfast" (v. 12). By this time they all knew that it was the Lord who was feeding them. He gave each of them a big helping of bread and fish. It was a happy reunion by the Lake of Galilee, where they had often eaten with Him. We are told this was the "third time" Jesus appeared to His disciples after His resurrection. We have already studied the other two in today's lesson (20:19-25; 20:26-29).

D. Jesus and Peter: vv. 15-17

This is one of the most interesting incidents in John's Gospel. It is worth studying closely.

When they had finished breakfast, Jesus turned to Peter. We shouldn't miss the thoughtfulness of the Master in waiting until they had eaten before He questioned His disciple.

Jesus addressed him as "Simon." Was this because he had failed to live up to his name "Peter," which means "rock"? Or was it only that Christ wanted to use the more familiar Jewish name as a sign of affection? Perhaps it was both.

The question Jesus asked was a very penetrating one: "Simon, son of John, do you really love me more than these?" What did he mean by "more than these"? He could have meant, "more than you love these other disciples," but that is very unlikely. Or He could have been saying: "Do you love me more than these other disciples love me?" This interpretation fits well with Peter's vigorous assertion: "Although all shall be offended, yet will not I" (Mark 14:29). A third possibility is: "Do you love me more than these fishing materials you once left?" Perhaps the second suggestion is most likely, though the third cannot be ruled out.

Peter replied, "Yes, Lord, you know that I am your friend"—or, "I care for you." In Jesus' question, He used the verb *agapao*, which means to love with an unselfish love of loyalty, a love that seeks the best good of its object. It is used in the command to love the Lord with all our heart, soul, mind, and strength (Matthew 22:37). It is the verb used in John 3:16: "God so loved the world." In fact, it occurs about 125 times in the New Testament. The cognate noun, *agape*, occurs over a hundred times.

By way of contrast, the verb that Peter used in his reply is found only 25 times. It is *phileo*, which means to have affectionate love or friendship love. In fact, the noun *philos* (about 30 times) is regularly translated "friend." The cognate noun *philia* is found only once (James 4:4) and is translated "friendship." That *phileo*

indicates affectionate love is shown by the fact that this verb is rendered "kiss" in Matthew 26:48 and Mark 14:44.

Why did Peter respond with the lesser word, *phileo?* The answer seems clear. He knew that His denials of his Lord had proved that he did not have that loyalty-love that Jesus asked him if he had.

In response to Peter's assertion of friendship-love, the Master said, "Feed my lambs." Peter did later feed Christ's lambs on many occasions.

A second time Jesus asked the same question: *"Agapas me?"* And again Peter replied, *"Philo se."* This time the Great Shepherd said to His under-shepherd, "Shepherd my sheep" (literal Greek).

But the third time (v. 17) Jesus dropped down to the lower verb that Peter had used. He asked: "Phileis me?"—"Are you even my friend?" We read that Peter was "grieved"— not because Jesus questioned him the third time, but rather because on that third time He said, "Do you actually care for me?" This is what broke Peter's heart. He knew he could not honestly profess the *agape* love of full loyalty; his denials would not let him. But he did have real affection for Jesus. And so, with tears in his voice, he replied: "Lord, you know everything. You know that I care for you." Jesus seemed satisfied, and said, "Feed my sheep."

It has often been pointed out that just as Peter had three times denied his Lord the night before the Crucifixion, so he now was asked to declare his love three times. As F. C. Grant says, "The three denials are now matched by three protestations of love and three pastoral Commissions." Doubtless Peter thought of this.

Some commentators and translators feel that *agapao* and *phileo* are used interchangeably. In fact, one prominent New Testament scholar a few years ago went so far as to say that these three verses prove that *agapao* and *phileo* mean the same thing. To us the case seems just the

DISCUSSION QUESTIONS

1. Why was Mary Magdalene the first to see Jesus after His resurrection?
2. Why did the two disciples leave without seeing Jesus?
3. How can one overcome tendencies to doubt?
4. What are some means of strengthening faith?
5. What lesson may we learn from the different settings of the postresurrection appearances of Jesus?
6. Why did Jesus take time to talk to Peter as He did?

opposite. We feel that the whole point of the passage turns on the fact that Jesus in His third question adopted Peter's lesser word and so jolted the disciple into realizing that he needed to have a love he did not possess. It was only after Pentecost that Peter could say "*Agapao se*"—"I love you, Lord, with full loyalty and devotion." After that he never deviated in his loyalty to Christ.

In his classic work, *Synonyms of the New Testament*, Trench writes: "The passing of the original from one word to the other is singularly instructive, and should by no means escape us unnoticed" (p. 42). We would agree completely with Westcott's comment on this passage. Speaking of Peter, he says: "He lays claim only to the feeling of natural love (*philo se*, Vulgate *amo te*), of which he could be sure. He does not venture to say that he has attained to that higher love (*agapan*) which was to be the spring of the Christian life. . . . So *Peter was grieved* not only that the question was put again, but that this *third time* the phrase was changed" (p. 303). The best treatment of this passage is found in William Hendriksen's commentary, *John.*

CONTEMPORARY APPLICATION

In the Home Moravian Church in Winston Salem, North Carolina, there are four stained-glass windows in the rear of the sanctuary. On the two windows at the left are pictured Gethsemane and Calvary. To the right of the entrance the windows portray the Resurrection and Ascension. By an unplanned coincidence, we were told, the sun never shines on the two left windows, because of a nearby college building. But each afternoon in clear weather the sunshine lights up the two windows on the right.

Gethsemane and Calvary were dark hours. But morning dawned at the empty tomb and the full light of day broke forth at Pentecost, following the Ascension.

THE CHURCH EMPOWERED

DEVOTIONAL READING	Isaiah 6:1-8

ADULTS

Topic: *Power for Growth*

Background Scripture: Acts 1—2

Scripture Lesson: Acts 2:1-4, 16-17, 36-42

Memory Verse: *You shall receive power when the Holy Spirit has come upon you.* Acts 1:8a

YOUTH

Topic: *"Power!"*

Background Scripture: Acts 1—2

Scripture Lesson: Acts 2:1-4, 17, 36-42

Memory Verse: *You shall receive power when the Holy Spirit has come upon you.* Acts 1:8a

CHILDREN

Topic: *How God Helps the Church to Grow*

Background Scripture: Acts 1—2

Scripture Lesson: Acts 1:8; 2:14, 22-24, 41-42

Memory Verse: *You shall receive power when the Holy Spirit has come upon you.* Acts 1:8a

DAILY BIBLE READINGS

Mon., Feb. 25: Wait for the Spirit, Acts 1:1-5
Tues., Feb. 26: "You Shall Be My Witness," Acts 1:6-11.
Wed., Feb. 27: A New Apostle, Acts 1:12-26.
Thurs., Feb. 28: The Coming of the Spirit, Acts 2:1-13.
Fri., Mar. 1: Joel's Prophecy Fulfilled, Acts 2:14-21.
Sat., Mar. 2: Lord and Christ, Acts 2:22-36.
Sun., Mar. 3: "What Shall We Do?" Acts 2:37-47.

LESSON AIM

To discover the secret of the sudden growth of the early church and see how we can have this same power today.

LESSON SETTING

Time: The first chapter of Acts covers the fifty days between the Resurrection and Pentecost, from April to June of A.D. 30. The second chapter describes the events of the day of Pentecost.

Place: Except for the Ascension, which took place near that city, all the events described here happened in Jerusalem.

The Church Empowered

LESSON OUTLINE

SUGGESTED INTRODUCTION FOR ADULTS

Today we begin our study of thirteen lessons covering most of the Book of Acts. Since there are twenty-eight chapters, each lesson usually includes about two chapters. Even then there are some gaps, but the outstanding themes of Acts are all noted.

The purpose of this study is to discover the factors which contributed to the rapid growth of the early church and see how those principles may be applied to our day. The first and most significant factor was the power of the Holy Spirit, and this is the subject of the first lesson. Without Pentecost the Book of Acts would never have been written.

The greatest need of the church of our day is for a fresh outpouring of the Holy Spirit. When we read what happened in the Roman Empire in the first generation after Jesus' death, it makes us realize that we are certainly not matching that performance. Filled with the Spirit, the 120 in the upper room exploded on to the streets of Jerusalem and 3,000 people were converted that day. Soon the Gospel reached throughout Palestine and then to the ends of the empire. Within a generation the vast Roman Empire had been rather well evangelized. The Book of Acts stands as a constant reminder of what can be done when the church is filled with the power of the Holy Spirit.

**SUGGESTED
INTRODUCTION
FOR YOUTH**

We live in an age of power. It started largely with the discovery of electric power, which has revolutionized the life of almost the entire world. There are very few areas left that electricity has not reached. Even remote villages in seemingly undeveloped countries often have electric lights. And beyond where power lines have gone one can find transistor radios with electric batteries.

But now it is the age of nuclear power, which conceivably can do away with the need for depending on the diminishing resources of coal and oil. Power unlimited—that seems to be the wave of the future.

But there is a greater power than any or all of these put together—the power of the Holy Spirit. That is being released in the lives of many Spirit-filled young people today. What we need is more of our youth surrendered to the Spirit of God, to let Him work through them.

**CONCEPTS FOR
CHILDREN**

1. God uses people who are filled with the Holy Spirit to help the church to grow.
2. The Holy Spirit can come into the lives of children today.
3. He will help us to live as Jesus wants us to.
4. Even children can help the church to grow, by inviting others.

THE LESSON COMMENTARY

I. THE PRELUDE:
Acts 1:1-26

A. The Command: vv. 1-4

The Book of Acts begins with a reference to "the former treatise" that the author had written. There is no question but what this means the Gospel of Luke. In the first place, both books are addressed to Theophilus (cf. Luke 1:3). In the second place, many of the emphases of both books are the same, especially the emphasis on the Holy Spirit. In the third place, some fifty words found in Luke and Acts, are found nowhere else in the New Testament. The early church is unanimous in saying that these two books were written by "Luke, the beloved physician" (Colossians 4:14).

The author tells us that in his previous volume he had written about "all that Jesus *began* both to do and teach"—that is, His works and words.

The implication is that in Acts he is telling us what Jesus *continued* to do and teach through His disciples by the power of the Holy Spirit. And that is what we find in this Book.

The first volume ended with the Ascension—"until the day in which he was taken up" (v. 2). It also recorded some of the postresurrection appearances: "to whom also he showed himself alive after his passion by many infallible proofs" (v. 3). The last two words are one in the Greek, a term used for convincing evidence that will stand up in court.

We often hear references to the "ten days" that the 120 waited in the upper room. How do we know that it was that long a period? The answer is that here, and only here, we are told that Jesus was seen by the disciples, off and on, for "forty days." Subtracting forty from the fifty days between the Resurrection and Pentecost (see comments on p. 212, II, A) leaves ten days of waiting.

What was the command that Jesus gave His disciples? "That they should not depart from Jerusalem, but wait for the promise of the Father, which you have heard from me" (v. 4). This was the promised Holy Spirit.

B. The Promise: vv. 5-8

John the Baptist had said: "I indeed baptize you with water unto repentance: but he who comes after me . . . will baptize you with the Holy Spirit and fire" (Matthew 3:11). Jesus now picks this up: "For John truly baptized with water; but you will be baptized with the Holy Spirit not many days from now."

Unfortunately, there was another matter that the disciples were more interested in. They asked Jesus: "Lord, will you at this time restore again the kingdom to Israel?" (v. 6). While their Master was concerned about the coming of the Holy Spirit to establish the spiritual kingdom of God in the hearts of men, His disciples were thinking about an earthly political kingdom and their places of honor with Him. It shows how much they needed Pentecost!

Jesus' answer was firm: "It is not for you to know the times or the seasons, which the Father has put in his own power" (v. 7) God has His appointed time, but Jesus said that even He did not know the time of the Second Coming (Mark 13:32).

Instead of predicting the date when the kingdom would be restored to Israel, Christ promised the Holy Spirit: "And you will receive power, after the Holy Spirit has come on you" (v. 8). The Holy Spirit not only *gives* power; He *is* power. Personal power is greater than impersonal power, for all physical force comes from creative Personality. When we have the Holy Spirit, we have power—power adequate for all our needs.

Empowered by the Holy Spirit the disciples would be Christ's witnesses—the best Greek text has "my witnesses," rather than "witnesses unto me"—"both in Jerusalem, and in all Judea and Samaria, and unto the uttermost part of the earth."

Acts 1:8 gives us two significant insights. First, it reveals both the power and the program of the church of Jesus Christ. The *power* is the Holy Spirit. The *program* is world evangelization. People who are not interested in missions prove thereby that they are not filled with the Holy Spirit. For the Spirit of God will generate a concern for world missions in every heart that He indwells.

Acts 1:8 also gives us the outline of the Book of Acts which describes the witness of the church: (1) in Jerusalem (chaps. 1—7); (2) in Judea and Samaria (chaps. 8—12); (3) in all the world (chaps. 13—28). (For the sake of simplicity, we have included chapter one, which is introductory, in the first division.)

C. The Ascension: vv. 9-11

One of the significant points of connection between Luke's Gospel and Acts is that the Ascension is described in the last chapter of Luke and the first chapter of Acts, and nowhere else in the New Testament. The former account says that Jesus led His disciples out toward Bethany, "and he lifted up his hands, and blessed them. And it came to pass, while he blessed them, he was parted from them, and carried up into heaven" (Luke 24:50-51). Here in Acts we read that "while they beheld, he was taken up; and a cloud received him out of their sight" (v. 9).

But a very important addition is found here. While the disciples were gazing heavenwards, two angels appeared with the comforting announcement: "This same Jesus, who was taken up from you into heaven, will so come in the same way as you saw Him going into heaven" (v. 11). His ascension was visible to believers, and so will be His return. This is one of the most significant prophecies of the Second Coming.

D. The Upper Room: vv. 12-14

Apparently the Ascension took place on the Mount of Olives, out toward Bethany, which is on its eastern slope. For we read that they returned to Jerusalem, which is west of the hill, "from the mount called Olivet, which is from Jerusalem a Sabbath day's journey"—a little over half a mile. That is the approximate distance from the eastern gate of Jerusalem to the top of the Mount of Olives.

Arriving in the city, "they went up into an upper room," where the eleven apostles were now living. It is tempting to believe that this was the same upper room in which the Last Supper was held. There the apostles "continued with one accord in prayer and supplication, with the women, and [that is, "including"] Mary the mother of Jesus, and with his brethren" (v. 14). It is comforting to learn that Jesus' brothers, who had formerly not believed in Him (John 7:5), were in the upper room and received the Holy Spirit. It is probable that Jesus' appearance to His brother James after His resurrection (I Corinthians 15:7) was responsible for this result.

E. The Election of Matthias: vv. 15-26

The rest of the chapter is taken up with this incident. One important piece of information is given in verse 15: There were about 120 in the upper room, who were filled with the Holy Spirit on the day of Pentecost.

It will always be a debated question as to whether Peter did the right thing in leading the people in electing the twelfth apostle at this time. Jesus had told His disciples He was sending them the Holy Spirit, who would "guide" them (John 16:13). Would it not have been better to have waited until the promised Holy Spirit came and then have sought His guidance in the matter? They decided the election by casting lots (v. 26). We never read of their using this method after Pentecost. From then on it was

the Holy Spirit who guided them. At any rate, Matthias was elected, and we hear nothing more of him.

II. THE POWER:
Acts 2:1-4

A. The Appointed Day: v. 1

In the Old Testament *Pentecost* is called the Feast of Weeks (Exodus 34:22; Deuteronomy 16:10), because it came seven weeks after the offering of the first sheaf of the barley harvest during the Passover season (Leviticus 23:15). The Greek-speaking Jews called it Pentecost (Greek "fiftieth") because it fell on the fiftieth day from the Feast of Firstfruits (Leviticus 23:16), which was celebrated in connection with the Feast of Unleavened Bread that immediately followed the Passover. Since the Mediterranean was still rough for sailing at the Passover time (March—April), the Jews from the provinces preferred to come to Jerusalem for Pentecost in June. That is why we read of so many nationalities in verses 9-11. When the day of Pentecost finally came, the believers were "all together in one place"—so the best Greek text reads (v. 1). They were still waiting, in accordance with Jesus' command.

B. The Sound of Wind: v. 2

Suddenly the house was filled with a roaring sound, as of a rushing wind. The purpose of this may have been partly to make sure that everyone was wide awake, alert to see clearly what took place next. After being gathered together in prayer for about ten days, some of them may have been a bit sleepy. We read that they were "sitting," which suggests that they had finished their praying and were now simply waiting. Frightened by the violent noise, all the people were sitting with eyes wide open.

C. The Tongues of Fire: v. 3

So they all saw the flame of fire that moved into the room. "Cloven tongues" is literally "tongues being distributed." Lenski comments: "Perhaps we may say that the flamelike tongues appeared in a great cluster and then divided until a tongue settled on the head of each one of the disciples" (*The Interpretation of the Acts of the Apostles*, p. 59). This signified that each person there was to be individually filled with the Spirit.

D. The Filling with the Spirit: v. 4

The central experience of Pentecost is stated here: "They were all filled with the Holy Spirit." All else was mere accompaniment. The sound and sight, the roar and fire—these were just associated signs, given for the moment and then disappearing. The all-important thing is that the Holy Spirit came into their hearts to abide forever (John 14:16).

We are also told that the believers "began to speak with other tongues, as the Spirit gave them utterance." Apart from this passage, speaking in tongues is mentioned only twice in Acts (10:46; 19:6). Numbers of other times we read of people being filled with the Spirit, but nothing is said about speaking in tongues. The topic is discussed at length in I Corinthians 12—14. But none of the other twenty-five books of the New Testament makes any mention of it. (Mark 16:17 is not in the oldest Greek manuscripts.)

The three accompanying signs of wind, fire, and speaking in tongues are all significant. The wind was a symbol of *power*, the fire of *purity*, and the speaking in other tongues, was a symbol of *worldwide evangelism*. The coming of the Holy Spirit was to effect these three things. There is no purity without power, and there is no power without purity. The two come to us simultaneously when we are filled with the Holy Spirit. And the power is not for us to enjoy selfishly. We are empowered by the Spirit for the specific purpose of witnessing. And the speaking in fifteen intelligible languages (vv. 6-11) symbolized the fact that this witness is to be worldwide.

But aside from the symbolism why did these spectacular events take place? There seems to be a clear answer to this question. The Jews held that the Feast of Pentecost was a commemoration of the giving of the Law at Sinai (F. J. Foakes-Jackson, "Acts" in *Moffatt New Testament Commentary*, p. 10). What happened then? We read that "there were thunders and lightnings, and a thick cloud upon the mount, and the voice of a trumpet exceeding loud. . . . And mount Sinai, the whole of it smoked, because the Lord descended upon it in fire . . . and the whole mount quaked greatly" (Exodus 19:16-18, ASV). Why all this divine pyrotechnic display? Because God wanted His people to realize that this was an epochal event: a new era was being inaugurated. God was making a covenant with the people and giving them His law.

It was a similar thing at Pentecost. That day marked the beginning of a new era, the dispensation of the Holy Spirit. It was important that the disciples should realize the supreme significance of the occasion. And so there was a tornado-like roar, with tongues of fire, and speaking in languages that were strange to the Galilean disciples.

It was the birthday of the new church, and a celebration was in order. Or, to use another figure, it was the inauguration day for the new regime of the Holy Spirit. On inauguration day there are big parades and speeches, and a lot of fanfare. But we do not expect this to be repeated every time the president appears after that.

III. THE PERPLEXITY:
Acts 2:5-13

There were dwelling in Jerusalem "Jews, devout men." The latter term has sometimes been taken as referring to Gentiles. But the Greek word here is used in the New Testament only by Luke, and in its other three occurrences (Luke 2:25; Acts 8:2; 22:12) it clearly describes Jews. So most scholars feel that this is the meaning here. These men came from "every nation under heaven."

"Now when this was noised abroad" (v. 6) is literally "when this sound happened." What sound? Among the best scholars there is a difference of opinion as to whether the reference is to the roar of verse 2 or the speaking in tongues of verse 4. There is no way of being sure which is intended.

As any rate, a large crowd gathered. But the people were all perplexed, because "every man heard them speak in his own language." The last word is *dialectos*, from which we get "dialect." It means "language."

The listeners were all "amazed and marvelled" (v. 7). These are both strong words in the Greek, indicating shocked surprise. The astonished people said, "Are not all these who speak Galileans? And how hear we every man in our own tongue, wherein we were born?" There follows a list of fifteen different geographical areas from which these people had come. The names reach all the way from beyond the Mesopotamian valley in the east to North Africa and Italy in the west.

The whole crowd was composed of two groups: "Jews and proselytes" (v. 10). The latter were those who had accepted Judaism and had become members of its religious community.

Verses 6, 8, and 11 all indicate clearly that those who spoke in tongues on the day of Pentecost employed intelligible languages that were in use at that time in fifteen different nations. It appears to have been for the purpose of evangelizing more effectively these "foreigners" by speaking in their native tongues. This, and this alone, is what took place when the disciples were filled with the Holy Spirit in the upper room.

Still amazed, the crowd asked, "What does this mean?" (v. 12). The mocking answer of some was: "These men are full of new wine"—or, "sweet wine." Since people could not nor-

mally get drunk on *gleukos*, it would appear that this remark was sarcastic.

IV. THE PREACHING: Acts 2:14-36

A. The Prophecy of Joel: vv. 14-21

Peter is a model for preachers in the pulpit. The Greek says that he "stood up," "lifted his voice" and "spoke out." Everybody could hear him.

The first thing he did was to deny the charge of drunkenness. It was only nine o'clock in the morning, too early to be drunk.

Then he proceeded to tell what it was: "But this is that which was spoken by the prophet Joel" (v. 16). The quotation that follows (vv. 17-21) is from Joel 2:28-32.

In view of Peter's application of this prophecy to what had just taken place, it is obvious that "the last days" in this passage refers to the entire Christian age. It is equivalent to the Jewish phrase "the days of the Messiah."

The outpouring of the Spirit would be on "all flesh"—Gentiles as well as Jews. The result would be that not only their sons, but also their daughters would "prophesy"—that is, "preach." The exclusion of women from the preaching ministry is clearly contrary to God's Word. Even male and female servants would preach.

The apocalyptic language of verses 19-20 has caused some comment. Is this all figurative, or will there take place some literal fulfillment? We know that apocalyptic speech is highly symbolical. But in this atomic age one should probably be cautious in denying all possibility of literal interpretation.

Verse 21—"And it shall come to pass, that whosoever shall call on the name of the Lord shall be saved"—has been called "the gospel in a nutshell." Though coming from the Old Testament, it definitely anticipates the New Testament gospel.

B. The Presentation of Jesus: vv. 22-23

Peter declares that Jesus of Nazareth was a man "approved" by God. The word may mean "appointed" or "attested." It is used frequently in the papyri of that time for "proclaiming" an appointment to public office. The meaning here is that the miracles which Jesus performed attested Him as God's appointed Messiah.

But in spite of this, His Messianic claims were rejected by the Jewish leaders and He was condemned to death. This was according to the "determinate counsel and foreknowledge of God." Yet, as free moral beings, they were responsible and guilty for what they did. Peter accuses them of having "crucified and slain" their Messiah though they did it "by wicked hands." The Greek says "by the hands of lawless men." This means the Romans, for the Jews held that all Gentiles were "lawless" because they were without the Mosaic law.

C. The Importance of the Resurrection: vv. 24-32

Peter spoke only briefly about the life of Christ (v. 22) and His death (v. 23), but it takes nine verses here to record what he said about Christ's resurrection. This is because it was necessary to establish the fact of Jesus' resurrection if He was to be accepted as the Messiah. The death of Jesus, especially by shameful crucifixion, was a strong barrier against the Jews' acceptance of Him as their Messiah. Only His resurrection could validate His claims.

Because of this Peter labors the point. He quotes at length Psalm 16:8-11 (in vv. 25-28). David said that God would not allow "His Holy One" to suffer corruption. The Jews commonly applied this Scripture to David. But Peter points out the fact that David's body did undergo corruption. David's tomb was right there near Jerusalem—"his sepulchre is with us unto this day" (v. 29). So David was not speaking of himself. He was prophesying about the coming Messiah— "Christ" in verse 30 means "Messiah." It was His resurrection that David was talking about.

Then Peter climaxed his argument with the assertion: "This Jesus has God raised up, whereof we all are witnesses." The "all" would refer to the 120 who had been filled with the Spirit, all of whom were probably among the "above five hundred brethren" who saw the resurrected Christ at one time (I Corinthians 15:6).

D. The Ascension: vv. 33-35

The ascension of Jesus means that He is exalted at the right hand of God. The proof of this is that He has sent the promised Holy Spirit. David has not yet ascended to heaven (v. 34). When he wrote the words of Psalm 110:1 (quoted in verse 34), he was speaking of God the Father asking the resurrected Son to sit at His right hand.

E. Jesus Is the Messiah: v. 36

This is the climax of Peter's sermon. All the Jews should realize that "God has made that same Jesus, whom you have crucified, both Lord and Christ." The last word, as we have seen, means "Messiah." Jesus is the Messiah, Peter declares. But "Lord" is perhaps even more significant. For in the Septuagint (Greek translation of the Old Testament) the word here for

---

DISCUSSION QUESTIONS

1. Do we have the power the early church had? If not, why not?
2. Are conditions today any harder than in the first century?
3. Is the Holy Spirit any less powerful?
4. Do we have less of the Spirit?
5. How may we recover the power of the Holy Spirit?

"Lord" is used to translate "Jehovah" (or "Yahweh"). So Peter was declaring that Jesus was Jehovah of the Old Testament. To the Jews this was sheer blasphemy.

V. THE IMPACT:
Acts 2:37-42

A. Conviction by the Spirit: vv. 37-40

It was only the Holy Spirit who could have given Peter the boldness to make the twofold declaration we have just noted: "You murdered your Messiah, Jesus, who is the Lord." But the same Holy Spirit convicted Peter's hearers, so that instead of persecuting Peter, they cried out: "Men, brethren, what shall we do?" (v. 37). Jesus had promised that the Holy Spirit would witness with them (John 15:26-27), and now He was fulfilling His roles as Co-witness and Convictor.

Peter's answer was, "Repent, and be baptized every one of you in the name of Jesus Christ for the remission of sins, and you will receive the gift of the Holy Spirit" (v. 38). The promise was to them and their children, and also "all that are afar off, even as many as the Lord our God shall call." The salvation that Christ had provided was to reach around the world. "With many other words" Peter exhorted his hearers to save themselves from their "untoward" (or "crooked") generation.

B. Conversion of Many: vv. 41-42

Many "gladly received his word." They repented and were baptized, as he had instructed them. Then comes the amazing statement: "And the same day there were added unto them about three thousand souls." Peter without the Holy Spirit had been an abject failure. Now, filled with the Spirit, he had preached a sermon that resulted in three thousand being saved and joining the Christian community. And it was no passing emotional experience. For we read that "they continued steadfastly in the apostles' doctrine and fellowship, and in breaking of bread and in prayers" (v. 42). The word translated "doctrine" means "teaching." Breaking bread probably refers to taking communion. And "prayers" means public prayers. The three thousand converts were fruit that remained (John 15:16).

CONTEMPORARY APPLICATION

A missionary society was holding the annual meeting of its directors. The report from one station in Africa was: "No converts." This had gone on year after year. One of the directors moved that the Lone Star mission be discontinued. But another man suggested they pray about it overnight.

That night this man was burdened in prayer. The Lord gave him a poem with the refrain, "Shine on, Lone Star." He read it the next morning. The board was moved by it and voted to give the work one more year.

During that year there was a gracious outpouring of the Holy Spirit, with many people saved. On one day, 2,222 converts were baptized between sunrise and sunset with six preachers working in relays at the river's edge. The power of the Spirit had accomplished the impossible.

WHEN THE SPIRIT FILLS A LIFE

DEVOTIONAL READING	Isaiah 61:1-4

ADULTS	Topic: *When the Spirit Fills a Life* Background Scripture: Acts 3—4 Scripture Lesson: Acts 3:1-6; 4:31-37 Memory Verse: *With great power the apostles gave their testimony to the resurrection of the Lord Jesus, and great grace was upon them all.* Acts 4:33

YOUTH	Topic: *Turned On by the Spirit* Background Scripture: Acts 3—4 Scripture Lesson: Acts 3:1-6; 4:31-37 Memory Verse: *With great power the apostles gave their testimony to the resurrection of the Lord Jesus, and great grace was upon them all.* Acts 4:33

CHILDREN	Topic: *The Company of Believers* Background Scripture: Acts 3—4 Scripture Lesson: Acts 4:32-37 Memory Verse: *Now the company of those who believed were of one heart and soul.* Acts 4:32

DAILY BIBLE READINGS	Mon., Mar. 4: A Lame Man Healed, Acts 3:1-10. Tues., Mar. 5: "To This We Are Witnesses," Acts 3:11-16. Wed., Mar. 6: Repent and Turn, Acts 3:17—4:4. Thurs., Mar. 7: "By What Power?" Acts 4:5-12. Fri., Mar. 8: "They Had Been with Jesus," Acts 4:13-22. Sat., Mar. 9: A Prayer for Boldness, Acts 4:23-31. Sun., Mar. 10: All Things in Common, Acts 4:32-37.

LESSON AIM	To see how the Spirit-filled person can meet all of life victoriously.

LESSON SETTING	Time: Apparently a few days or weeks after Pentecost, in June of A.D. 30 Place: Jerusalem

217

When the Spirit Fills a Life

I. Healing of a Lame Man: Acts 3:1-11
   A. Peter and John Going to the Temple: v. 1
   B. The Lame Beggar: vv. 2-3
   C. Peter's Command: vv. 4-6
   D. The Miracle of Healing: vv. 7-8
   E. The Amazement of the People: vv. 9-11

II. Peter's Second Sermon: Acts 3:12-26
    A. The Murder of the Messiah: vv. 12-15
    B. The Source of Healing: vv. 16-18
    C. Repentance and Salvation: vv. 19-21
    D. The Promised Messiah: vv. 22-26

LESSON OUTLINE

III. The First Persecution: Acts 4:1-22
     A. The Arrest: vv. 1-4
     B. The Public Hearing: vv. 5-14
     C. The Private Conference: vv. 15-17
     D. The Public Injunction: vv. 18-22

IV. The Prayer Meeting: Acts 4:23-30
    A. Divine Sovereignty Recognized: vv. 23-28
    B. Divine Power Requested: vv. 29-30

V. The Fellowship of Believers: Acts 4:31-37
   A. Fresh Filling of the Spirit: v. 31
   B. Unity in Community: vv. 32-33
   C. Sharing of Funds: vv. 34-35
   D. Example of Barnabas: vv. 36-37

SUGGESTED
INTRODUCTION
FOR ADULTS

The devotional reading for today, Isaiah 61:1-4, is one of the greatest Messianic passages in the Old Testament. That is shown by the fact that Jesus read the first one and a half verses of this in the synagogue of His hometown, Nazareth, and then declared: "This day is this scripture fulfilled in your ears" (Luke 4:21). It was a description of the work that He as the Messiah was already engaged in.

The Holy Spirit had descended as a dove upon Jesus at His baptism, and we read that after His baptism and temptation He "returned in the power of the Spirit into Galilee" (Luke 4:14). So He could rightly say, "The Spirit of the Lord God is upon me." We read further: "The Lord has anointed me to preach good news to the poor. He has sent me to proclaim release to the captives and recovering of sight to the blind, to set at liberty those who are oppressed, to proclaim the acceptable year of the Lord."

These words had special application to the ministry of Christ. But they should also characterize the ministry of His followers. Our hearts should be so filled with the Holy Spirit, who is the Spirit of Christ, that we show His compassionate love to needy souls around us. As Christians we should have a redeeming, healing ministry to broken hearts and broken lives.

SUGGESTED
INTRODUCTION
FOR YOUTH

A university student was asked to speak to the first gathering of the "Jesus people" on a state university campus in the Midwest. He first spoke of the evidences for the deity of Jesus and for Christianity as the true religion. When he finished they asked for more. Then he talked about being filled with the Spirit. About 150 responded to the invitation. Finally, he said, almost the whole crowd moved forward on the shore of the lake where he was speaking.

There is a hunger for the Holy Spirit on the part of many young people today. We should pray that this seeking will be directed into dedicated Christian living on a high and holy level. That is the need of the hour among the young. A movement that is of the Spirit will show itself primarily and most prominently in holy lives. Today young people are being turned on by drugs and sex. They need to be turned on by the Holy Spirit. He alone can give them the full satisfaction they are longing and looking for.

CONCEPTS FOR
CHILDREN

1. Peter and John gave something more important than money or things, for by showing the lame man the way to Christ they gave him healing for both body and soul, so that even when he died he had eternal life. That is what we do when we tell others about Jesus.
2. Peter did not take any honor for the good deed he did but gave all the glory to God.
3. Peter was no longer a frightened man but was brave and courageous now that the Spirit had come into his heart.
4. The members of the early church had only one purpose—to praise God and bring others to know Christ as their Lord and Savior. This should also be our goal.

THE LESSON COMMENTARY

I. HEALING OF A LAME MAN: Acts 3:1-11

A. Peter and John Going to the Temple: v. 1

Peter and John are not named this way together in the Gospels, except when they were sent to prepare the Passover meal the night before Jesus' crucifixion (Luke 22:8). But in the first part of Acts we find them working as a pair (cf. 8:14).

These two disciples were going up to the Temple at the hour of prayer. The "ninth hour" would be three o'clock in the afternoon. This was the time of the evening sacrifice each day, as nine in the morning was the hour for the morning sacrifice. Scheurer says that incense was offered on the golden altar in the Holy Place before the lamb was sacrificed on the brazen altar in the morning and after the evening sacrifice, "so that the daily burnt offering was, as it were, girt around with the offering of incense." He also says: "While this was going on the people were also assembled in the temple for prayer" (*History of the Jewish People in the Time of Jesus Christ*, II, i, 290).

B. The Lame Beggar: vv. 2-3

A certain man who had been lame from birth was placed daily at the Beautiful Gate of the Temple to beg for alms. This gate is said by Josephus to have been seventy-five feet high, with doors sixty feet in height. It is also claimed that it was made of Corinthian brass and overlaid with silver and gold. No wonder it was called Beautiful! It appears that this was the main entrance to the Court of the Women, where the Temple treasury was located. Perhaps these two facts together form the background for Peter's remark, "Silver and gold have I none" (v. 6). But it was certainly a prize location for a needy beggar.

When the man saw Peter and John about to enter the Temple, he "asked to receive alms" (v. 3)—so the oldest Greek manuscripts. In the light of what is stated in verse 7, someone has suggested that the beggar "asked for alms and got legs!"

C. Peter's Command: vv. 4-6

There were really two commands. First, Peter, looking intently at the man, got his undivided attention by commanding him to look at them. The man complied, apparently expecting a generous gift of money. It must have been something of a disappointment when Peter continued: "Silver and gold have I none." But the beggar was not left in low spirits very long. For the second command followed quickly: "In the name of Jesus Christ of Nazareth, rise up and walk." What a challenge to a man who had never walked!

D. The Miracle of Healing: vv. 7-8

Peter assisted the man's faith. He "took him by the right hand and lifted him up." But obviously the man cooperated, or Peter could not have lifted him. And it is that way in our relation to God. When he commands us to repent and believe, our first reaction may be that we can't. But as we respond to His command, we find that He gives enabling grace.

And so as the man exerted his will to obey Peter's order, "immediately his feet and ankle bones received strength." It is always so as we respond in obedience. Our only obligation is to obey God's commands. It is His obligation to enable us to carry them out.

The man "leaped" to his feet, displaying instant obedience. He "stood" there with new strength in his feet and ankles that had been paralyzed since birth. Then he began to "walk." He didn't hurry away. Instead he entered into the Temple with Peter and John. He was headed in the right direction. So excited was he that he was "walking and leaping, and praising God." If anyone ever had a right to carry on in this way, it was this healed beggar! He rejoiced in his newfound freedom.

E. The Amazement of the People: vv. 9-11

The Temple was crowded with many worshipers at this hour. So the man's actions received wide attention. The people quickly recognized him as the familiar beggar at the Beautiful Gate. When they saw him walking and praising God, "they were filled with wonder and amazement at what had happened to him."

The lame man was clinging to Peter and John in gratitude. The whole affair created so much excitement that people came running to the place where the apostles now stood, in "the porch that is called Solomon's"—the Colonnade of Solomon on the east side of the Court of the Gentiles, just inside the outside (east) wall of the Temple area.

II. PETER'S SECOND SERMON: Acts 3:12-26

A. The Murder of the Messiah: vv. 12-15

Peter was never one to lose a good opportunity. When he saw the crowd gather, he decided it was time to preach! So he called out, "Ye men of Israel." Having gained their attention, he continued: "Why do you marvel at this? Or why do you look so earnestly at us, as though by our own power or piety we had made this man walk?"

Then he proceeded to tell his audience who was really responsible for the miracle. The God of their fathers had "glorified his Son Jesus" (v. 13). Then Peter moved in with a sweeping accusation. He reminded these Jerusalem Jews that they had arrested Jesus and denied Him before Pilate, when the governor was "determined to let him go."

Closing in with still greater precision, Peter affirmed: "But ye denied the Holy and Righteous One [two Messianic titles] and asked for a murderer to be granted unto you; and killed the Prince of life" (vv. 14-15, ASV). These words are full of dramatic significance. Every sinner is holding on to a murderer, Sin, while at the same time he rejects the Prince of Life. What greater folly could be imagined! The absurdity of sinning shows up powerfully in this contrast. Though not in such an open, startling way as the Jewish leaders, yet everyone who turns his back on Jesus Christ is rejecting life and welcoming death. How can intelligent men do this? The answer is that Satan has blinded their eyes so that they cannot see the truth.

But God had raised the crucified Christ. Peter and others had seen their risen Lord. There was no doubt about the Resurrection.

B. The Source of Healing: vv. 16-18

It was through the name of Jesus—the One they had killed and God had raised—and through faith in that name, that this man had been healed. Yes, faith in the name of Jesus had "given him this perfect soundness in the presence of you all." It was not a halfway healing; the man was completely well and strong. The Jewish nation had rejected the Author of life, and soon would find death as a nation.

The man had accepted Jesus as the Messiah ("Christ," v. 6) and now was perfectly whole. We all decide our destiny on the basis of our attitude toward Jesus Christ.

In a kind tone Peter now addressed his hearers as "brothers" (v. 17) and assured them: "I wot [old English for "I know"] that through ignorance you did this, as did also your rulers." That is, they had not fully realized that Jesus was the Messiah. Yet they had had ample evidence in His miracles and teaching, so that they were morally responsible for their rejection of Him, as the four Gospels, especially John's, clearly indicate. For three years Jesus had taught in their synagogues and Temple. They had criticized Him for associating with sinners and offering them forgiveness. It was their narrow-minded legalism that had made them oppose Him.

Then Peter sounded a note that recurs frequently in Acts in connection with preaching to Jews: the Old Testament Scriptures teach that the Messiah would suffer. Peter declared that God had announced beforehand "by the mouth of all his prophets that Christ [the Greek says "His Christ" (Messiah)] would suffer," and this had now been "fulfilled" in the death of Jesus of Nazareth. The thing the Jews stumbled over in accepting Jesus as their Messiah was that they expected the Messiah to reign in glory and triumph, whereas Jesus' career had ended in defeat and death. What they failed to realize is that their own Scriptures, especially Psalm 22 and Isaiah 53, clearly taught that the Messiah would suffer and die. Peter emphasizes this point, as does Paul (17:3).

C. Repentance and Salvation: vv. 19-21

The keynote of John the Baptist's preaching was "Repent!" (Matthew 3:2). Jesus began His ministry with the same demand (Matthew 4:17). Now we find it as the central thrust of early apostolic preaching. Peter sounded this note in both of his sermons (cf. 2:38).

Here he says, "Repent . . . and be converted." The last word means "turn again." That is what the Jews needed especially to do at this time, after rejecting their Messiah.

The result would be that their sins would be "blotted out." The Greek word means to "wipe out" or "erase." When we repent and believe in Jesus Christ as Savior, all the record of our sins of the past is erased, as far as God is concerned. What a consolation!

This will happen "when the times of refreshing shall come from the presence of the Lord." It is especially in "times of revival"—as Lake and Cadbury translate the phrase—that people's sins are blotted out.

These times of revival will culminate in the Second Coming—"And he shall send Jesus Christ, who before was preached unto you" (v. 20). That this refers to the return of Christ is clearly indicated by verse 21: "Whom the heaven must receive until the times of restitution of all things, which God has spoken through the mouth of all his holy prophets since the world began." Universalists have eagerly seized upon the phrase "restitution [or "restoration"] of all things" to prove their claim that ultimately all people will be saved. But, typically, they ignore the qualifying clause "which God has spoken through the mouth of all his holy prophets." What kind of a restoration has God promised? Many feel—and we would agree—that it includes a restoration of the Jews to the land that God promised to Abraham: "For all the land which thou seest, to thee will I give it, and to thy seed for ever" (Genesis 13:15). There is no record that this promise was ever abrogated. And we have to face the fact that in our own day, for the first time in nineteen hundred years, the Jews have been restored in large numbers to their own land.

D. The Promised Messiah: vv. 22-26

Then Peter quoted (v. 22) from Deuteronomy 18:15, as Stephen did

later before the Sanhedrin (7:37). When Moses was getting old and about ready to die, he told the people: "A prophet shall the Lord your God raise up unto you of your brethren, like unto me." The first reference was to Joshua, who would succeed Moses as the leader of the Israelites. But both Peter and Stephen give the passage a Messianic interpretation. Christ was the Prophet who was predicted. This twofold application—first, a limited fulfillment in the time of the prophet, and secondly a complete fulfillment in Christ—is one of the most important principles to observe in understanding the Old Testament Scriptures. It is called "the telescopic principle of prophecy"—a near and partial fulfillment as well as a distant and complete fulfillment. (Verse 23 is from Deuteronomy 18:19.)

Peter went on to say: "Yea, and all the prophets from Samuel and those that follow after, as many as have spoken, have likewise foretold these days." While there is a sense in which Moses and Joshua are both called "prophets," as we have just seen, it is usually considered that Samuel was the first of a long line of prophets that stretches through the rest of the Old Testament down to Malachi.

Peter concluded his sermon by saying: "Unto you first God, having raised up his son Jesus, sent Him to bless you, in turning away every one of you from his iniquities" (v. 26). It was the resurrected Christ whom the apostles preached as Savior.

III. THE FIRST PERSECUTION: Acts 4:1-22

A. The Arrest: vv. 1-4

While Peter was still preaching, "the priests, and the captain of the temple, and the Sadducees came upon them, being grieved that they taught the people, and preached through Jesus the resurrection from the dead." The priests were all Sadducees, as was the captain of the Temple guard. In the Gospels we find that the main op ponents of Jesus were the Pharisees, who taught the Scriptures in the synagogues. But after Christ cleansed the Temple, the Sadducees were infuriated (Mark 11:15-18, 27-28). It was the chief priests (Sadducees) who were most responsible for pressuring Pilate into crucifying Jesus (Mark 25:1, 3, 11).

In the early chapters of Acts it is definitely the Sadducees who led in the persecution of the Christians. This was due, in large part, to the emphasis on the Resurrection in early apostolic preaching. The Sadducees did not believe in any resurrection, nor in the existence of angels or spirits (23:8). So they were the ones who were "grieved"—better, "indignant" or "upset"—because the apostles preached "through Jesus [rather "in the case of Jesus"] the resurrection of the dead." That is, they proved by the well-attested resurrection of Jesus that the Sadducees were wrong in denying any resurrection. Of course the chief priests could not tolerate this!

So "they laid hands on them [arrested the two apostles] and put them in hold [better, "placed them in custody"] unto the next day"—because it was evening. This is the first persecution of the infant church.

Verse 4 consists of a summary statement of the growth of the Christian community up to this time: "Howbeit many of them which heard the word believed; and the number of the men was about five thousand." Some have supposed that this means that five thousand more were converted at this time, in addition to the three thousand on the day of Pentecost. But the Greek says: "The number of the men became about five thousand." This was the total number at this point.

B. The Public Hearing: vv. 5-14

The next day there was a meeting of the Great Sanhedrin at Jerusalem, the Supreme Court of the Jewish nation. It had seventy-one members, corresponding to Moses and the seventy elders of Israel. Three groups of men comprised this august body. The first was the "rulers," probably equivalent to the "chief priests" (Mark 14:53). They were the leading members of the Sanhedrin. Next were the "elders"— Greek, *presbyteroi*—a general term for members of the *presbyterion*, as the Sanhedrin was sometimes called (22:5; Luke 22:66). Then came the "scribes," who were mainly Pharisees. They were the teachers of the Law in the synagogues.

"Annas" is mentioned as "the high priest" (cf. Luke 3:2). Actually "Caiaphas" (A.D. 18-36) was in office at this time, but his father-in-law Annas, who had been high priest A.D. 6-15, still kept the reins of power. In calling him the high priest, Luke simply reflected the popular opinion of the Jews in Jerusalem.

The Sanhedrin called in Peter and John. The seventy judges were sitting in a semicircle so that they could all see the defendants clearly and also see the reactions on each other's faces. Now these justices asked: "By what power or in what name have you done this?" (v. 7).

Peter had wilted before the accusing voice of a servant girl in the courtyard of the high priest. As he now faced a semicircle of scowling faces, knowing that he might well be condemned to death, surely he would quail with fear!

But this time it was a different Peter—"filled with the Holy Spirit" (v. 8). This is the key phrase of Acts, occurring some forty times. This was the main secret of the success of the early church. Pentecost had made Peter a new man!

Courteously he addressed the judges as "rulers of the people, and elders of Israel." Then he came right to the point. He and John were not criminals. They were being examined about a "good deed done to the impotent man," who had been "made whole" (v. 9).

The next words of Peter are astonishing. Facing that semicircle of seventy judges plus the high priest, he said:

"Be it known to you all, and to all the people of Israel, that by the name of Jesus Christ of Nazareth, whom you crucified, whom God raised from the dead, even by him this man stands here before you whole" (v. 10). The prisoner at the bar had turned prosecuting attorney! Instead of trying to defend himself, Peter charged the leaders of the nation with the most serious crime they could have committed. Peter went on to say: "This is the stone which was rejected by you builders, but which has become the head of the corner" (v. 11). And then he made one of the greatest evangelistic utterances in the Book of Acts: "Neither is there salvation in any other; for there is no other name under heaven given among men by which we must be saved" (v. 12). This was a startling statement to make to a Jewish audience.

The judges were amazed at the boldness of Peter and John, realizing that they were "unlearned and ignorant men." The probable meaning of these two adjectives is that the apostles were without training in the rabbinical schools and were merely laymen. How then could they talk this way? The answer was, they had "been with Jesus" (v. 13).

There was one argument that the judges could not answer. Standing with the apostles was the man who had been healed, a living demonstration of divine power. The result was that the rulers "could say nothing against it" (v. 14). The miracle was unquestioned.

C. The Private Conference: vv. 15-17

The apostles were asked to step outside the meeting place of the Sanhedrin ("council"). Then the judges conferred among themselves. They could not deny that a notable miracle had taken place, for all Jerusalem knew about it. But they must not let this "heresy" spread any further! So they decided to threaten the apostles not to speak any more in "this name"

(v. 17). They themselves would not even repeat the hated name "Jesus."

D. The Public Injunction: vv. 18-22

The Sanhedrin called in again the two apostles and commanded them not to be speaking or teaching at all in the name of Jesus. But once more, filled with the Spirit, Peter and John showed holy boldness. They replied: "Whether it is right before God to listen to you more than to God, you judge" (v. 19). Meanwhile they could not keep still: "For we cannot but speak the things which we have seen and heard" (v. 20).

The judges threatened them further and then let them go, for there was obviously no case against these preachers! The rulers were aware that the people were on the side of the apostles, "for all men glorified God for that which was done" (v. 21). The reason this miracle made such an impression was due to the fact that the man was over forty years old when he was healed. By that time his condition was beyond human hope.

IV. THE PRAYER MEETING: Acts 4:23-30

A. Divine Sovereignty Recognized: vv. 23-28

As soon as Peter and John were released, they went to their own group and reported what had happened. Immediately a significant prayer meeting took place. The basis of belief is our concept of God. These men prayed: "Lord, thou art God, who made heaven and earth, and the sea, and all that is in them" (v. 24). He was the Almighty Creator. Although both Jews and Gentiles conspired against the Messiah (v. 27), yet they only accomplished what "thy hand and thy counsel determined before to be done" (v. 28). In other words, the One to whom they were praying was the Sovereign Lord of the universe. Such a concept raised their faith.

B. Divine Power Requested: vv. 29-30

This is an amazing prayer. The disciples did not ask for protection against their persecutors, but for power to preach—and take the consequences! Sure enough, in the next chapter we find them back in jail. All they cared about was that "the name of thy holy child Jesus" should be glorified through miracles of healing.

V. THE FELLOWSHIP OF BELIEVERS: Acts 4:31-37

A. Fresh Filling of the Spirit: vv. 31

The unselfish prayer they had made was abundantly answered: "And when they had prayed, the place was shaken where they were assembled together; and they were all filled with the Holy Spirit, and they spoke the word of God with boldness." It was the kind of prayer God delights to answer. And so the work went on.

B. Unity in Community: vv. 32-33

No better description of Christian unity could be given than what we find here: "And the multitude of those that believed were of one heart and one soul" (v. 32). So united were they that they did not emphasize the rights of private ownership. Instead "they had all things in common." The first clause of this verse indicates a unity of fellowship; the second and the third clauses suggest a community of goods. But the latter idea must be interpreted in the light of the context, which we shall soon note.

The result of this unity and unselfish generosity is expressed beautifully: "And with great power gave the apostles witness of the resurrection of the Lord Jesus: and great grace was upon them all" (v. 33). The forbidden subject of the Resurrection was still the keynote of their preaching, and the Lord honored it. Above all, "great grace was upon them all." If only the church had stayed that way!

C. Sharing of Funds: vv. 34-35

Verses 34-35 (which should be read at this point) sound very much like a complete system of community of goods. But there is one important factor found here and also in the parallel passage in 2:44-45. This is the use of the imperfect tense, which signifies not a once-for-all act of putting everything into a common treasury, but rather repeated acts of selling property and bringing money to meet needs as they arose. Acts 2:45 has three of these imperfects and might be paraphrased thus: "And from time to time they were selling their possessions and goods and were parting them to all, according as from time to time any man had need."

In 4:34 we find two imperfects, plus two present participles of continuous or repeated action. It should read: "For as many as were possessors of fields or houses, selling them were bringing the prices of the things that were being sold." Verse 35 has three imperfects. It says: "And they were placing them at the feet of the apostles, and distribution was being made to each even as any one was having a need." This does not indicate a mass sale of all property and everything put into a common treasury. Rather, it

---

DISCUSSION QUESTIONS

1. What is the greatest need of all men?
2. What do we have to offer for that need?
3. How should we react to persecution?
4. What is the relation of prayer and power?
5. What lessons in stewardship may we learn from the early church?
6. What is the Christian attitude toward material possessions?

describes occasional selling of property to meet needs that arose. In other words, the early church in Jerusalem practiced real Christian stewardship.

D. Example of Barnabas: vv. 36-37

The last two verses of the chapter support this view. Special mention is made of the fact that Joseph, who is better known as Barnabas, a Levite from Cyprus, sold some land and gave the proceeds to the church. This ac-

count would make no sense if everybody sold all he had and placed the money in the church treasury.

One of the great needs of the church of our day is for the unity in the Spirit that is described here. The church should first of all be a fellowship. What is needed is not unification or uniformity, but a true spiritual unity in Christ. Only the Holy Spirit can bring this about. We should by prayer and our own attitude help in this.

CONTEMPORARY APPLICATION

"What I have I give to you" (3:6). These were the words of Peter to the poor beggar, and then he fully met the man's need.

What do we have to give to people who are in spiritual need? We may be as penniless as Peter, but if we are filled with the Spirit we have something far better than money. We have Christ's presence to share, His forgiveness to offer, the power of His Spirit to meet every human need.

It is selfish of us to say, "I can't do anything." Regardless of our own mea-

ger resources, the divine resources are adequate.

During the Middle Ages the great Christian scholar Thomas Aquinas was visiting Pope Innocent IV at Rome. After showing his visitor the fabulous treasures of the papal see, the pontiff proudly declared: "No longer does the church have to say, *Silver and gold have I none*." "Yes," replied the Angelical Doctor, "and no longer can she say to the lame man, *Rise up and walk*." Could this incident be paralleled today?

OVERCOMING HINDRANCES TO CHURCH GROWTH

DEVOTIONAL READING	Psalm 24:3-6
ADULTS	Topic: *Overcoming Hindrances to Church Growth* Background Scripture: Acts 5:1—6:7 Scripture Lesson: Acts 5:1-4; 6:1-7 Memory Verse: *Religion that is pure and undefiled before God and the Father is this: to visit orphans and widows in their affliction, and to keep oneself unstained from the world.* James 1:27
YOUTH	Topic: *Do I Really Count?* Background Scripture: Acts 5:1—6:7 Scripture Lesson: Acts 5:1-4; 6:1-7 Memory Verse: *We are witnesses to these things, and so is the Holy Spirit whom God has given to those who obey him.* Acts 5:32
CHILDREN	Topic: *What Keeps the Church from Growing?* Background Scripture: Acts 5—6 Scripture Lesson: Acts 5:27-32 Memory Verse: *We must obey God rather than men.* Acts 5:29
DAILY BIBLE READINGS	Mon., Mar. 11: Ananias and Sapphira, Acts 5:1-11. Tues., Mar. 12: A Ministering Church Grows, Acts 5:12-16. Wed., Mar. 13: Obedience in Spite of Opposition, Acts 5:17-26. Thurs., Mar. 14: "We Must Obey God," Acts 5:27-32. Fri., Mar. 15: Beware of Opposing God, Acts 5:33-42. Sat., Mar. 16: How Christians Solved a Problem, Acts 6:1-7. Sun., Mar. 17: Those Who Seek the Lord, Psalm 24:1-6.
LESSON AIM	To see how the early church overcame hindrances to its growth and how we may apply those principles today.
LESSON SETTING	Time: A few weeks or months after Pentecost of A.D. 30 Place: Jerusalem

227

Overcoming Hindrances to Church Growth

LESSON OUTLINE

SUGGESTED INTRODUCTION FOR ADULTS

Sometimes we are tempted to think that we have many problems in the church today. And we do! But the church has always had problems and always will until Jesus returns. The reason is that the church is composed of human beings and wherever there are human beings there will be problems! We should realize that while the church is divinely ordained, the church on earth is actually a human institution.

In the last lesson we found that the church was faced with persecution. But this was an external problem and was met successfully by prayer and a fresh infilling of the Holy Spirit. Problems from the outside are always easier to meet than problems originating inside.

In today's lesson we have two internal problems. The first was hypocrisy within the church membership. This was dealt with summarily and severely by sudden divine judgment on the guilty parties.

The second problem was far more serious and required careful consideration to arrive at a solution. There were two distinct groups even in that earliest church community in Jerusalem, which we found in the last lesson was so beautifully united in love. One group lodged a complaint against the other. This could easily have led to a schism in the church. But the apostles dealt with the matter promptly, and the problem was solved.

"Do I Really Count?" That is the young people's topic for today. We learn from this lesson that everyone in the church is important.

Unfortunately, Ananias and Sapphira counted for evil in the church. But their sin of hypocrisy was taken care of by God's hand of judgment, for their influence could have had dire consequences for the Christian community.

The second problem was that of a minority group within the church membership. Today we are very much aware of minority groups in society that are understandably sensitive to any evidence of discrimination. But that this should happen in the church—and especially so soon after Pentecost—seems a bit shocking. How could Christians be careless about such matters?

The answer, of course, is that human prejudices are often deep-seated, and sometimes the guilty ones are not as aware of these attitudes as they should be. Deeply ingrained prejudices die slowly. What we all need to do is to be stern with ourselves in facing any wrong attitudes we may discover in ourselves, but generous and understanding in our treatment of offenders at this point.

SUGGESTED INTRODUCTION FOR YOUTH

CONCEPTS FOR CHILDREN

1. When church members are selfish in looking out for their own interests, it keeps the church from growing.
2. Disagreement among members also hinders church growth.
3. When we take a good attitude toward everybody we help the church to grow.

THE LESSON COMMENTARY

I. HYPOCRITES IN THE CHURCH: Acts 5:1-10

A. Conspiracy of Ananias and Sapphira: vv. 1-2

The "But" at the beginning of this chapter points up the contrast with the preceding paragraph (4:36-37). There we read that Barnabas sold some land and gave the proceeds of the sale to the church. Evidently Ananias and Sapphira wanted to get public recognition for doing the same thing. So they sold a possession; verse 3 indicates that it was land, as in the case of Barnabas.

But here the parallel ends. This man and his wife "kept back part of the price." The verb here is a strong one that was sometimes used to indicate the misappropriation of public funds by state officials. It is the same verb that is used in the Septuagint for Achan's sin, when he "took of the devoted thing" (Joshua 7:1). It will be remembered that he was put to death.

"Being privy to it" is literally "sharing the knowledge of," Sapphira was in on the deal, and so was equally guilty with her husband. Her name (cf. "sapphire") means "beautiful," and was perhaps given her because she was a beautiful baby. But she was not beautiful in character. Just as pitiful was the distortion of the name Ananias (Hebrew, Hananiah), which means "Jehovah is gracious." God is gracious to all of us, but Ananias was not gracious to God.

B. Exposure of Guilt: vv. 3-4

When Ananias brought "a certain part" of the selling price and "laid it at the apostles' feet," Peter challenged him: "Ananias, why has Satan filled your heart to lie to the Holy Spirit, and to keep back part of the price of the land?" Ananias might have protested: "I did not tell a lie; I never said this was what we sold it for." But Peter's words underscore an important truth: a lie is an intention to deceive. One can tell a lie without saying a word. On the other hand, a person may make a statement which is factually untrue and not be guilty of lying—if he thought he was telling the truth.

Verse 4 is another conclusive evidence that the members of this early church were not required to sell all their private possessions and place the proceeds in a common treasury. In fact either question by itself would prove this. For Peter asked: "While it remained, was it not your own? And after it was sold, was it not in your authority?" Ananias had not been under any obligation to sell the land, nor to give all the proceeds to the church. All this was voluntary. What, then, was his sin? Simply that he intentionally gave the impression that he was putting it all into the treasury. He had conceived this deliberate deception in his heart.

Peter concluded with the words: "You have not lied to men, but to God." Two observations might be made. The first is that Peter obviously meant: "You have not lied *only* to men, but also to God." Whenever we lie to people, we are lying to God. The second is that a comparison of verses 3 and 4 shows that the Holy Spirit is here declared to be God.

The reality of Satan as the chief tempter of humanity is also underscored in verse 3. The word *Satan* means "adversary." The word has come from the Hebrew through Aramaic and Greek into English. Satan is the great adversary of God and men. In the New Testament he is the equivalent of "the devil"—*diabolos*, which means "slanderer."

C. Death and Burial of Ananias: vv. 5-6

When Ananias heard his sin of hypocrisy exposed, he fell down and "gave up the ghost." This phrase is all one word in Greek, meaning "expired." Some strong young men "wound him up"—better, "wrapped him round," probably with cloth, as was the custom then—and carried out his body and buried it.

D. Deeper in Deception: vv. 7-8

About three hours later Sapphira, not knowing what had happened, came in. Probably she expected to be received with honor because of the generous gift they had made to the church. Instead Peter said to her: "Tell me, did you sell the land for so much?"—naming the amount Ananias had given. She replied, "Yes, for so much"—naming the same amount. So she actually spoke a lie.

E. Death and Burial of Sapphira: vv. 9-10

Peter's next words must have come as a terrible shock: "How is it that you have agreed together to test the Spirit of the Lord? Look, the feet of those who have buried your husband are at the door and will carry you out." She likewise fell down and expired, and soon was buried beside her husband. It was a terrible price to pay for hypocrisy.

Several questions come to mind. Did Peter kill Ananias and Sapphira? There is nothing whatever in the narrative to indicate this. He did not even pronounce a curse on them. Ananias expired when Peter exposed his sin. Peter did predict Sapphira's death, but there is not even a hint that he brought it about.

Did they die by direct divine judgment or by psychological shock? Though some recent commentators have opted for the latter, the older standard writers affirm the former. In his third commentary on Acts, F. F. Bruce takes this position.

Why did these two meet such sudden, severe punishment? The answer seems to be that God wanted to sound a strong note of warning right at the beginning, that hypocrisy was one sin He could not tolerate in His church. Of course, if all the hypocrites in the church since that time had been suddenly struck dead, some church rolls would have been "cleaned" in radical fashion!

II. OVERCOMING THE HINDRANCE: Acts 5:11-16

A. Fear and Respect of People: vv. 11-13

The first effect of these two shocking deaths was to bring fear on all the church, as well as all who heard about them. No insincere people dared to join the Christian community for fear of being struck dead. Outsiders viewed the church with respect, if not awe (v. 13). The apostles continued to work miracles as their Lord had done (v. 12). Apparently their main meeting place was Solomon's Portico, inside the east wall of the Temple area. There great crowds could gather in the spacious Court of the Gentiles.

In verse 11 the word *church* (*ecclesia*) is found for the first of twenty-one times in the Book of Acts. It occurs only three times in the Gospels, all in Matthew (16:18; 18:17 twice). In Paul's Epistles it is found some sixty-two times, and twenty times in Revelation.

As is well known, the noun comes from the verb meaning "to call out." So it refers to an assembly of "called out ones." The word was first used for an assembly of the free citizens of a Greek city, who were "called out" by a herald. This usage is found three times in Acts (19:32, 39, 41), where the word is translated "assembly." The use of *ecclesia* in the New Testament comes from the Septuagint, where the word is used for the "congregation" of Israel. In Acts and Paul's Epistles the term is used mostly for local churches, but also for the general Church of Jesus Christ, the true body of believers who have been called out of the world.

B. Large Additions to the Church: v. 14

In spite of the fact that no one dared to join the believers carelessly (v. 13), we yet read the amazing statement: "And believers were the more added to the Lord, multitudes both of men and women." It usually works this way. When God's presence and power are manifested in the church, people are attracted to it. On the surface, verses 13 and 14 almost seem to contradict each other. But the obvious meaning of verse 13 is that no insincere people dared to join, for fear of death.

C. Miracles of Healing: vv. 15-16

The apostles continued their Master's ministry of healing the sick. As in the case of Jesus, we read that "they were all healed" (v. 16).

A thoughtful reader of verse 15 might well ask whether Peter's shadow actually healed people. Probably the correct answer is that people were healed through faith in Jesus Christ (cf. 4:9-10), but that Peter's shadow may have been a symbolical aid to their faith, as is the Scripturally prescribed use of oil today (James 5:14).

III. SECOND PERSECUTION: Acts 5:17-42

A. Arrested by the Sadducees: vv. 17-18

Again we find the Sadducees—the high priest and his colleagues—heading up the opposition to the new movement, which they probably felt was threatening their hold on the people. They were filled with indignation—the Greek says "jealousy" (cf. Matthew 27:18).

The Sadducees are here called a "sect." Josephus, the famous Jewish historian of the first century, says that there were four "sects," or parties, in the Judaism of that day: Pharisees, Sadducees, Essenes, and Zealots. The *Pharisees* were the Separatists of that period, who majored on meticulous observance of all the ceremonial requirements of the law, so that they would be separated from the world around them. Their scribes taught the Scriptures in the synagogues, which were found everywhere. The *Sadducees* furnished the priests, who had control of the one Temple, which was in Jerusalem. The *Essenes* are not mentioned in the New Testament, but we now have a wealth of material about them from the Dead Sea Scrolls. They had a semimonastic community at Qumran on the west shore of the Dead Sea. The scrolls were found in caves in the nearby hills. The Essenes were even stricter than the Pharisees. The *Zealots* were the radical opponents of Roman rule. One of Jesus' disciples, "Simon the Zealot" (Luke 6:15; Acts 1:13), was perhaps a member of this group.

The leaders at the Temple arrested the apostles and put them in jail (v. 18). They couldn't afford to let this new movement spread any further.

B. Released by an Angel: vv. 19-20

The prisoners didn't stay long in confinement. That very night "the angel [Greek, "an angel"] of the Lord" came and opened the prison doors and let them out. He then told them to go back to the Temple and speak to the people "all the words of this life"—a beautiful expression for the gospel message.

C. Perplexity of the Council: vv. 21-24

In obedience to the angel's command the apostles entered the Temple "early in the morning"—probably as soon as the doors were opened—and began to teach. They could not afford to waste any of their "free" time.

Meanwhile the high priest had convened a meeting of the Sanhedrin. It is referred to here by two names: "council" (*synedrion*, Sanhedrin) and "senate" (*gerousia*, assembly of older men). Both terms indicate the same group.

The council sent "officers" (Temple police) to bring the apostles from prison. But when the police arrived, the jail cells were empty. The officers returned and reported to their superiors: "We found the prison all safely locked up and the guards standing at the doors, but when we opened them we found nobody inside" (v. 23). Understandably the high priest and his associates were perplexed and wondered what this would turn out to be. They were not used to having to deal with the supernatural!

D. Arraignment of the Apostles: vv. 25-28

About that time someone came hurrying in to report: "The men you put in jail are in the temple and teaching the people." This time the "captain" of the Temple went with his officers to get the apostles and brought them "without violence." These policemen were actually afraid that the people might stone them! This shows how popular the new movement had become with the masses.

Once again the apostles stood before the Sanhedrin. Probably with partially controlled anger the high priest said to them: "Didn't we strictly charge you not to teach in this name, and look, you have filled Jerusalem with your teaching, and intend to bring this man's blood on us" (v. 28). When Peter and John were arraigned the first time they had been ordered "not to speak at all nor teach in the name of Jesus" (4:18). Clearly they were guilty of blatant disobedience of the Sanhedrin, and this was a serious crime!

E. The Apostles' Defense: vv. 29-32

As usual, Peter acted as the chief spokesman for the apostles. Their answer to the high priest was this: "We ought to obey God rather than men." This had been Peter and John's previous reply to the Sanhedrin (4:19). And this must still be—and still is, in hundreds of cases—the basic answer of the consecrated Christian to the orders of those who would prohibit the preaching of the gospel. Thank God for those courageous souls like Brother Andrew, "God's Smuggler," who carry on in spite of persecution and threats against their lives.

And once more Peter charged the religious leaders of the nation with the death of Jesus, at the same time emphasizing the Resurrection as the validation of His Messiahship. Linked with Jesus' death and resurrection (v. 30) is His ascension (v. 31), which was His exaltation—"Him has God exalted at His right hand to be a Prince and a Savior, to give repentance to Israel, and forgiveness of sins." The Resurrection and Ascension are valid proof of Jesus' deity, proof that He did not die merely as a human martyr.

The apostles went on to say that they were "witnesses of these things [(v. 32) they had seen Christ after His resurrection and had witnessed His ascension] and so is the Holy Spirit, whom God has given to those who obey Him." This combination again reminds us of John 15:26-27. Knowling comments: "Here we have also the twofold witness—the historical witness borne to the facts—and the internal witness of the Holy Ghost in bringing home to men's hearts the meaning of the facts" (Expositor's Greek Testament, II, 155).

Another truth is highlighted here: obedience is the price of having the Holy Spirit. A professed faith which is not accompanied by obedience does not produce results.

F. Gamaliel's Plea: vv. 33-40

The apostles not only pictured Jesus as exalted Lord and Savior; in addition, they once again charged the religious leaders with being guilty of His death. This was more than the latter could take. We read that "they were cut to the heart." This is all one word in the Greek, a strong verb which literally means, "they were sawed in two." Knowling comments: "Here we have not the pricking of the heart, ii. 37, which led to contrition and repentance, but the painful indignation and envy which found vent in seeking to rid themselves of the disciples as they had done of their Master" (Expositor's Greek Testament, II, 155). We read that they "took counsel to slay them."

One member of the Sanhedrin came to their defense. He was a "Pharisee." This word, which occurs here for the first time in Acts, literally means "separated one." The Pharisees had separated themselves from those Jews they felt were worldly or compromising.

The man's name was Gamaliel. He was a grandson of the great Rabbi Hillel. Like his grandfather, he was a "doctor of the law"—Greek, "teacher of the Law." (The original meaning of the English word doctor was "teacher.") We are also told that he was held in high esteem by the people.

Gamaliel gave good advice. He cited the case of two mistaken revolutionists who had been killed. We do not know the date of the rebellion under Theudas, but the one under Judas of Galilee occurred in A.D. 6. It was at the time of "taxing (v. 37)—rather, "enrollment" or "census"—made by Quirinius, legate of Syria, in A.D. 6.

Gamaliel's conclusion was: "Leave these men alone. If this work is of men, it will come to nothing. If it is of God, you cannot overthrow it, and you would be fighting against God." The members of the Sanhedrin agreed. But they did not release the apostles until they had first beaten them and once more commanded them not to speak in the name of Jesus (v. 40).

G. Continued Preaching: vv. 41-42

Though beaten for disobeying the previous orders (4:18), the apostles did not leave dejected and discouraged. Rather they were "rejoicing that they were counted worthy to suffer shame for his name." People like that can't be defeated!

Did the beating and further threatening stop the apostles from preaching? Hardly! We read: "And daily, in the temple and at home, they did not stop teaching and preaching the Messiah, Jesus." These were the Spirit-filled Christians of that day. And they have had many successors during the ensuing centuries.

IV. SECOND PROBLEM:
Acts 6:1-7

A. Charge of Discrimination: v. 1

Although in our expositions we have used the term *disciples* several times, the word does not actually occur in Acts until this point. The Greek word is *mathetes*, which means "learner." In the Gospels it is the most common designation for the followers of Jesus, occurring 74 times in Matthew, 45 in Mark, 38 in Luke and 81 in John. Aside from that it occurs only in Acts, where it is found 28 times, making a total of 266 times in the New Testament. From this point on it becomes the characteristic name for believers in Acts.

The number of disciples was increasing rapidly. The result was problems. The first serious internal problem and its solution are described in this paragraph. It started with a "murmuring." The sound of the Greek word *gongysmos* suggests the buzzing of bees. And when bees begin to swarm, it's time to look out for trouble. Perhaps there was a whispering campaign—buzz, buzz.

The murmuring came from the Hellenists ("Grecians," or Greek-speaking Jewish Christians). They complained against the "Hebrew," the Hebrew or Aramaic-speaking Christians. The cause of the complaint was that the Hellenists felt their widows were being "neglected," or "overlooked," in the daily distribution of food (or money).

It was the old familiar problem of a minority group feeling that it was being discriminated against. This was not exactly a racial problem, since probably all those involved were Jews. But it was a similar sort of thing, since the "Hebrews" doubtless looked down on the "Hellenists" as being somewhat less loyal to the Jewish traditions. It seems to be a general rule that majority groups tend to discriminate against minority groups in any society—including, unfortunately, the church community, because it too is composed of sinful human beings.

B. Recommendation of the Apostles: vv. 2-4

Fortunately "the twelve"—the eleven apostles (besides Judas Iscariot) that Jesus appointed, plus Matthias (1:26)—had their ears to the ground, heard the murmuring, and acted at once. They called together the church—"the multitude of the disciples"—and told them: "It is not desirable for us to forsake the Word of God and wait on tables" (v. 2). The apostles had been trained by Jesus to preach and teach the Word, which at that time meant our Old Testament. It would be a tragic waste of their talents, time, and training if they waited on tables—a function that others could just as efficiently perform.

In recent years there has been an increasing tendency among scholars to interpret "tables" here as meaning money tables. It is true that the Greek word here, *trapeza*, is used of the tables of money-changers in Matthew 21:12 and that it can be seen over the entrance of about every bank in Athens today. So some think the idea here is that of financial administration. But the earliest meaning of the verb *diaconeo* ("serve") was to wait on somebody at the table. The problem is that we do not know whether the "ministration" (diaconia) of the first verse was serving food or distributing money. Both methods were probably used in the Jewish synagogues and the early church, and perhaps both are included here. In either case, the supplying of material needs should be done by consecrated laymen, not by men who have been ordained to preach the Word.

So the apostles recommended that the church choose seven men to take care of this matter. It is important to note that even for this employment they specified three rigid requirements. The men chosen for this task must be: (1) of good reputation; (2) full of the Holy Spirit; and (3) full of wisdom, or tact. All of these qualifications were essential. It is of supreme importance that men who handle church money should have in their community a high reputation for honesty. In the second place, in dealing with the discontented Hellenists, it was necessary that these seven "deacons," as they are often called (but not in Acts) should be filled with the Spirit so that they would have patience and love in dealing with this difficult situation. And finally, they would need all the tact they could muster in order to keep everybody happy.

Meanwhile the apostles would give themselves continually to: (1) "prayer," that is, public worship; (2) "the ministry of the word"—preaching and teaching. As Christ's ordained ministers, they would devote their full time to these spiritual tasks.

C. Appointment of Seven Helpers: vv. 5-6

The church gladly accepted the recommendation of the apostles and chose seven men. The first and most prominent of them was *Stephen*. Not only did he meet the three qualifications specified by the apostles, he is specifically singled out as "a man full of faith and of the Holy Spirit." He became a minister and finally the church's first martyr. Chapters 6 and 7 are devoted almost entirely to his doings. The next man is *Philip*, to whom chapter 8 is given over. These two men graduated from waiters to preachers, doing both jobs well! The last man on the list was a "proselyte" (Gentile convert to Judaism) from Antioch in Syria.

One observation should be made about the men: they all had Greek names. The congregation showed great wisdom in selecting seven Hellenists to wait on the Hellenists. This sensible reasoning paid good dividends.

It is interesting to note that the apostles ordained these seven men to their task of handling the material business of the church: they "prayed" and "laid their hands on them." It was very important that the problem that had risen be taken care of in the fullest possible way.

D. Prosperity of the Church: v. 7

Some people decry all organization. But the alternative to proper organization is chaos and confusion. People rush around in all directions, bumping into each other, spinning wheels, and causing general confusion. There is no efficiency in any sphere without careful organization.

When the apostles organized the work of the church and eliminated the complaints of the Hellenists, the result was threefold: (1) "the word of God increased"; (2) "the number of the disciples multiplied in Jerusalem greatly"; (3) "a great company of the priests were obedient to the faith." The church moved forward along all lines: spiritually, numerically, and socially.

DISCUSSION QUESTIONS

1. What are some causes of misunderstanding in a church?
2. How does greed for money hinder church growth?
3. How may discrimination hurt a church?
4. What kind of leadership does a church need?
5. How may wrong attitudes toward others cause trouble?
6. What are some rules for dealing with problems?

The conversion of "a great company of priests" (Josephus claims there were in all about twenty-thousand priests at that time) probably shows that the priests were favorably impressed with the new organization of church work. They were used to functioning in an orderly way themselves, and they gained new respect for the church. The division of labor insti-tuted by the apostles was similar to what they had: the priests ministering at the altar and the Levites taking care of the more menial tasks.

When hindrances are removed, the church grows. This is always true. We should seek to discover these hindrances and with prayer and wisdom eliminate them.

CONTEMPORARY APPLICATION

One of the most important secrets for dealing successfully with problems is to handle them while they are small, before they grow too big to grapple with. That is what the apostles did at Jerusalem. When they heard the low sound of "murmuring," they did something about it promptly. Soon the problem was solved, everybody was happy, and the church rapidly grew in size.

This secret is much needed today. If two people in a church have a disagreement, they should be brought to-gether and the thing ironed out immediately. If not, the disagreement may become a quarrel. Then other members of the church begin to take sides. The next step is that what was a private quarrel becomes a church quarrel, and this too often ripens into a church split. When this takes place, it is usually too late to solve the problem, for church splits are not healed easily. Usually a congregation is permanently damaged when this happens. The secret is to deal promptly with problems while they can be handled.

GIVING ONE'S BEST

DEVOTIONAL READING	Matthew 16:21-26

ADULTS

Topic: *Are You Willing to Take a Risk?*

Background Scripture: Acts 6:8—8:3

Scripture Lesson: Acts 6:8-11; 7:54-60

Memory Verse: *Let us run with perseverance the race that is set before us, looking to Jesus the pioneer and perfecter of our faith, who for the joy that was set before him endured the cross, despising the shame, and is seated at the right hand of the throne of God.* Hebrews 12:1-2

YOUTH

Topic: *Are You Willing to Take a Risk?*

Background Scripture: Acts 6:8—8:3

Scripture Lesson: Acts 6:8-11; 7:54-60

Memory Verse: *Let us run with perseverance the race that is set before us, looking to Jesus the pioneer and perfecter of our faith, who for the joy that was set before him endured the cross, despising the shame, and is seated at the right hand of the throne of God.* Hebrews 12:1-2

CHILDREN

Topic: *When a Christian Gives His Best*

Background Scripture: Acts 6:8—8:3

Scripture Lesson: Acts 6:8-14

Memory Verse: *Be watchful, stand firm in your faith, be courageous, be strong.* I Corinthians 16:13

DAILY BIBLE READINGS

Mon., Mar. 18: A Man Full of Grace and Power, Acts 6:8-15.
Tues., Mar. 19: Moving Out in Faith, Acts 7:2-8.
Wed., Mar. 20: Using Opportunities for Service and Training, Acts 7:9-22.
Thurs., Mar. 21: Accepting God's Assignment, Acts 7:30-38.
Fri., Mar. 22: Faithfulness Under Persecution, Acts 7:54—8:3.
Sat., Mar. 23: Persevering Toward the Goal, Hebrews 11:32—12:2.
Sun., Mar. 24: Take Up Your Cross and Follow, Matthew 16:21-26.

LESSON AIM

To show the importance of complete consecration to God's will and work regardless of the consequences.

| Time: Probably a few months after Pentecost, A.D. 30

Place: Jerusalem

Giving One's Best

I. Stephen's Debate: Acts 6:8-11
   A. Full of Grace and Power: v. 8
   B. Full of Wisdom and the Spirit: vv. 9-10
   C. Falsely Accused: v. 11

II. Stephen's Arrest: Acts 6:12-15
   A. Brought Before the Council: v. 12
   B. Accused of Blasphemy: vv. 13-14
   C. Reacting in Love: vv. 15

LESSON OUTLINE

III. Stephen's Defense: Acts 7:1-53
   A. Abraham and the Promised Land: vv. 1-8
   B. Joseph in Egypt: vv. 9-16
   C. Moses the Leader of Israel: vv. 17-44
   D. No Temple Can Hold God: vv. 45-50
   E. Resistance to the Spirit of God: vv. 51-53

IV. Stephen's Death: Acts 7:54-60
   A. Rage of the Sanhedrin: v. 54
   B. Stephen's Vision of Jesus: vv. 55-56
   C. Stoning of Stephen: vv. 57-60

V. **Saul's Persecution of the Church: Acts 8:1-3**

**SUGGESTED
INTRODUCTION
FOR ADULTS**

Someone has well said: "The church is looking for better methods; God is looking for better men." He found such a man in Stephen.

Stephen was appointed to "serve tables." He might have complained that this job was beneath his dignity, that it did not give proper recognition to his talents. He might have slighted his work, feeling that it was not worthy of his time and energy. Men who take that kind of an attitude soon find themselves unwanted.

Instead, Stephen overflowed his job. He did his tasks so well that soon he was promoted to preaching. Some people never learn that the way to get promotion in the kingdom of God is not to seek it but to earn it.

The same devotion that Stephen showed in taking care of the material needs of the Hellenistic widows he carried over into his new task of preaching. Jesus said, "He that is faithful in that which is least is faithful also in much" (Luke 16:10). If we do not do our lesser tasks well, we cannot hope to be given greater ones.

Stephen gave his best to his Master. What reward did he get for this? Just looking at this life, one would say, "Death." But beyond that was the martyr's crown of eternal life.

SUGGESTED
INTRODUCTION
FOR YOUTH

"Are You Willing to Take a Risk?" In many ways following Christ means taking a risk. It means risking the loss of friends; of position; and, in extreme cases, of life itself. If any one wants an easy way, if he wants to "play it safe," he shouldn't risk following Jesus.

But the risks are only for this life and only relate to secondary matters. Actually, if we take the way with Christ, we take the safest way, the only sure way. The risk of hell is far more serious than the risk of death. The risk of losing Christ's friendship is of more importance than the risk of losing earthly friends. Actually we are better off without those "friends" who drop us when we follow Christ.

Stephen took a risk when he witnessed boldly for his Lord. Few of us will ever be called on to risk our lives for Jesus. But he did. Is he sorry now? To ask the question is to answer it.

Are we ready to put our hand in His hand, and let Him lead where He will? This is life worth living.

CONCEPTS FOR CHILDREN

1. Stephen gave his best to his Master.
2. Because he did so, God used him greatly.
3. God needs strong leaders today.
4. God gave His best, His beloved Son, for us. We should give our best to Him.

THE LESSON COMMENTARY

I. STEPHEN'S DEBATE: Acts 6:8-11

A. Full of Grace and Power: v. 8

Instead of "faith and power" the best Greek text has "grace and power." This is a wonderful combination. Some people are gracious but not powerful, and as a consequence they do not seem to accomplish much. Others are powerful but not gracious, and as a result they offend people. The winning combination is grace and power together.

The term *grace* is one of the great words of the New Testament. Luke is especially fond of it, using it eight times in his Gospel and sixteen times in Acts. It occurs over one hundred times in Paul's thirteen Epistles, being one of the keynotes of his theology.

The Greek word (*charis*) first meant "gracefulness." Then it came to mean "graciousness." In the New Testament it is used mainly for the grace of God, His gracious favor to us in Christ. But F. F. Bruce comments on this passage: "It is possible that *charis* has here its earlier sense of 'charm,' i.e., spiritual charm" (*Acts*, p. 155). This is a real asset in a Christian worker.

God enabled Stephen to do "great wonders and miracles among the people." Presumably these were miracles of healing the sick and casting out demons (cf. 5:12-16).

B. Full of Wisdom and the Spirit: vv. 9-10

Though the term *synagogue* is common in the Gospels (34 times) this is the first of twenty times we find it in Acts. The English word is a transliteration of the Greek *synagoge*, which literally means a gathering together. As

in the case of "church," it first meant
a congregation and then the building
in which the worshipers met. It is the
earlier meaning that fits here.

It is uncertain how many synagogues are mentioned in this verse.
Different scholars champion the idea
of one, two, three, four, or five synagogues. The word *Libertines* here does
not mean morally unrestrained people,
as it does today, but rather "freed
men"—that is, those who had formerly been slaves or whose parents had
been slaves. So the reference may well
be to one synagogue, or Jewish congregation, in Jerusalem, composed of
freedmen from these four geographical
areas. But the Greek construction
lends some support to the idea of two
groups, one from Africa (Cyrene and
Alexandria) to the west, and the other
from Asia (Cilicia and Asia) to the
east. It must be remembered that the
term *Asia* in the New Testament always refers to the Roman province of
Asia, at the west end of Asia Minor
(modern Turkey).

The mention of Cilicia here is of
special interest, because that was
Paul's home province. It is commonly
thought that young Saul may have
been involved in the arguments with
Stephen, and that this might be one
factor in his later conversion.

These freedmen were "disputing"
with Stephen. The word literally
means "questioning together," and so
"debating" or "discussing." We are
told that these debators "were not
able to resist the wisdom and the Spirit by which he spoke." (Probably
"spirit" in King James Version should
be capitalized.) It was the Holy Spirit
giving Stephen supernatural wisdom
which made his words irresistible. And
that is our only hope today.

C. Falsely Accused: v. 11

Stephen's opponents "suborned"
men, who brought false charges against
him. The verb is found only here in
the New Testament. As to its meaning,
Lake and Cadbury write: "It applies to
the secret instigation of persons who

are supplied with suggestions of what
they are to say, much as in a modern
'frame-up' " (*Beginnings of Christianity*, IV, 68-69). The Revised Standard Version correctly translates it,
"secretly instigated." The charge they
brought against Stephen was: "We
have heard him speak blasphemous
words against Moses and against God."
Of course there was no truth to this
whatever.

II. STEPHEN'S ARREST:
Acts 6:12-15

A. Brought Before the Council: v.
12

This false report naturally created
a stir, for there was nothing that
would horrify Jews more than this. So
the people and their leaders ("elders"
and "scribes") seized Jesus and
brought Him before the "council," or
Sanhedrin. It was here that Jesus had
been arraigned and condemned to
death on similar charges (Mark 14:58,
64). Now Stephen was following his
Lord.

B. Accused of Blasphemy: vv.
13-14

When Jesus was before the Sanhedrin, "many false witnesses" testified
against Him (Matthew 26:60). The
same fate was now overtaking His servant. Again they accused Stephen of
blasphemy, this time against "this holy
place and the law." In the eyes of the
Jews it was almost as bad to speak
against the Temple as to speak against
God, and "the law" would be equivalent to "Moses" (v. 11). Stephen was
in deep trouble!

These false witnesses also claimed
they had heard him say that "this
Jesus of Nazareth shall destroy this
place, and shall change the customs
which Moses delivered us" (v. 14). Was
there any truth to this? Perhaps so.
Jesus Himself had been accused of
saying "I will destroy this temple that
is made with hands, and within three

days I will build another made without hands" (Mark 14:58). What He had actually said was: "Destroy this temple of His body (John 2:19-21). The up." But He was speaking of the temple of HIs body (John 2:19-21). The false witnesses had simply garbled the words of Jesus.

But later Jesus had predicted the destruction of the Jewish Temple (Matthew 24:1-2). It is possible that Stephen may have alluded to this. But the charge that Jesus would destroy "this place" was clearly untrue. As was the case in Jesus' trials, the report against Stephen was a garbled version.

Again, Stephen might have said that Jesus would change the customs which Moses had prescribed, although Christ made no such announcement. Being a Hellenist, Stephen may have been more free from bondage to the law than were the "Hebrews" (6:1). But the charge of blasphemy was completely unfounded.

C.   Reacting in Love: v. 15

In the face of false accusation, Stephen showed a Christlike spirit. Instead of reacting in anger, he reacted in love to the cruel hatred of his opponents. This is being "more than conquerer" (Romans 8:37). We read that all who sat in the Sanhedrin, looking intently at him, "saw his face as it had been the face of an angel." The witnesses had accused Stephen of speaking blasphemous words against Moses. But now his face was shining as Moses' face had when he came down from forty days with God on Mount Sinai (Exodus 34:29), or as Jesus' face had on the Mount of Transfiguration. It was a divine vindication of Stephen, but hate and prejudice so blinded the eyes of these religious rulers that they failed to see the clear implications of this.

As with the Jewish trial of Jesus, it was really the Sanhedrin that was on trial that day, not Stephen. God vindicated him; his opponents, however, stood condemned for framing a false charge.

III. STEPHEN'S DEFENSE:
Acts 7:1-53

A. Abraham and the Promised Land: vv. 1-8

As Chief Justice of the Supreme Court, the high priest asked the defendant, "Are these things so?" The answer comprises the next fifty-two verses which we have labeled "Stephen's defense." It is a defense in the most effective form: a clear statement of what he had actually been teaching. Early apostolic preaching emphasized the history of God's dealings with Israel (cf. 13:16-41) and warned against following Israel's example in the past.

The false witnesses had accused Stephen of speaking against the holy Temple and saying that Jesus was going to destroy it. They also accused him of blasphemy against the law. So Stephen's speech has two main arguments: (1) God is not restricted to "holy" places, such as the Temple of the land of Palestine, for the patriarchs were blessed in worshiping God without Temple and in various countries; (2) the Jewish nation had always been rebellious against God and His prophets and it was now rejecting the Messiah and His servants.

Courteously Stephen addressed the members of the Sanhedrin as "brethren and fathers." His next words were: "The God of glory." Far from blaspheming God (6:11), he wanted to glorify Him.

He then scored his first point: God had appeared to Abraham in Mesopotamia. The word is compounded of two Greek words: *mesos*, "between," and *potamos*, "river." So it means "the land between the rivers" (the Tigris and Euphrates). Ur of the Chaldees, the birthplace of Abraham, was in the Tigris-Euphrates Valley.

God said to Abraham, "Leave your country and your kindred, and come to a land I will show you" (v. 3). This is a quotation of Genesis 12:1. There the call of Abraham is placed after he had left Ur of the Chaldees and moved

to Haran (Greek, "Charran"). But it is
altogether reasonable to hold that the
call of Abraham first took place in Ur.
That is why he moved to Haran, which
was a partway stop. Then the call was
renewed in Haran, with greater inten-
sity and Abraham went on to Canaan,
where he was supposed to go. This is
the way it is described here, and there
is no contradiction between this and
the Genesis account.

At first Abraham didn't own a foot
of land in Canaan, and yet God promised that it would all belong to him
and his "seed" (descendants). This
promise was made "when as yet he
had no child" (v. 5).

But God also warned Abraham
that his descendants would sojourn for
several generations in a "strange"
("foreign") country, where they
would be subjected to slavery and
treated cruelly. But divine judgment
would subsequently come on the oppressors and God's people would escape and "serve me in this place" (v.
7). God also gave to Abraham "the
covenant of circumcision," which set
apart his descendants as God's people
(v. 8). The sons of Jacob, from whom
the twelve tribes descended, are here
called "the twelve patriarchs."

B. Joseph in Egypt: vv. 9-16

"The patriarchs"—actually ten of
Joseph's brothers—became jealous of
him. This was due in part to the favor-
itism that Jacob showed and in part to
Joseph's dreams. So they "sold Joseph
into Egypt: but God was with him, and
delivered him out of all his afflictions,
and gave him favour and wisdom in
the sight of Pharaoh king of Egypt;
and he made him governor over Egypt
and all his house" (vv. 9-10). The
point that Stephen is making is that
God was with Joseph *in Egypt* and
blessed him there. God's presence was
not restricted to Canaan. Any place
where God dwells is holy because of
His presence.

Not only did God bless Joseph in
Egypt, He also made Joseph a blessing
to others. For it was Joseph who fed

many thousands of people through
seven years of famine.

The statement that "at the second
time Joseph was made known to his
brethren" (v. 13) may have a prophetic significance. It may well be that
just as Joseph was rejected by his
brothers at his first coming to them
but accepted the second time (in
Egypt), so the nation of Israel, which
rejected Christ at His first coming will
accept Him when He comes again at
the close of this age. Even Lake and
Cadbury say: "It is possible that the
author is thinking of the first and
second 'comings' of Jesus" (*Beginnings*, IV, 73).

C. Moses the Leader of Israel: vv. 17-44

God is never late. As the hour approached for the Israelites to return to
Canaan, "another king arose, who
knew not Joseph" (v. 18). Actually it
was a new dynasty. Joseph was prime
minister of Egypt when that country
was ruled by Hyksos kings, who were
Semitic, like the Israelites. That is one
reason that Joseph and his brothers
were treated with so much kindness.
But when a native Egyptian dynasty
expelled the Hyksos, it can easily be
seen why the Israelites would be oppressed. So the new king "dealt sub-
tilly"—rather, "exploited"—the people
of Israel. Josephus says that the Egyptians made the Israelites dig canals and
build city walls and pyramids, "and by
all this wore them out" (*Antiquities*,
II, 9, 1).

At this time Moses was born, the
future deliverer of his people. First he
received a thorough training in king-
ship at the court of Pharaoh. We read
that he "was learned in all the wisdom
of the Egyptians, and was mighty in
words and deeds" (v. 22). This helped
to prepare him for the difficult task of
forging a crowd of many thousands of
slaves into a nation and also writing
the Pentateuch.

At forty years of age Moses struck
a blow for freedom. But it was a very
weak blow, and it backfired. Moses

had to flee for his life! The next forty years he spent in the land of Midian (v. 29) as a shepherd. In leading sheep he learned some of the lessons of patience he would need in leading the Israelites through that same desert region.

But the most important thing that happened to him was his experience at the burning bush (vv. 30-34). God met him there and revealed Himself as "the God of thy fathers, the God of Abraham, and the God of Isaac, and the God of Jacob." And then comes a significant statement: "Take off your shoes, for the place where you are standing is holy ground" (v. 33). Holy ground outside of Palestine? Yes, right there in the desert of a pagan land. The point that Stephen was making was that the Jewish Scriptures (our Old Testament) clearly taught that God manifested His presence in many places outside the Temple and even the land of Palestine, and thereby made those places holy.

Then Stephen quoted (v. 37) the prophecy of Deuteronomy 18:15, which Peter had already used (3:22). Moses had predicted the coming of the Messiah.

With verse 39 the second main argument of Stephen's speech comes into focus. Though Moses had led the children of Israel out of Egyptian bondage and safely through the wilderness, yet they rebelled against him and wanted to return to Egypt. Right at the time when Moses was on Mount Sinai receiving the Law from God, the people gave themselves over to idol worship. They were continually disobeying God and rejecting His will. Over and over again they turned away into idolatry.

Once more Stephen sounds the note that God's presence is not restricted to one "holy place" (6:13). He said that the early Israelites had "the tabernacle of the testimony" (v. 44), which is what the Septuagint has for "the tent of meeting" (Exodus 33:7, etc.). This was not the Temple. Furthermore, it was "in the wilderness," not in the Holy Land. Yet God

manifested His presence there. And God had met Moses at Mount Sinai and given him the instructions for building the Tabernacle.

D. No Temple Can Hold God: vv. 45-50

"Jesus" in verse 45 obviously should be "Joshua." The reason for this anomaly in the King James Version is that "Jesus" is the Greek word for the Hebrew "Joshua" (or, *Yehoshua*). But when familiar Old Testament characters are mentioned in the New Testament, they should always be given their well-known Old Testament names. Otherwise the reader or listener does not get the connection. The same unfortunate translation occurs in Hebrews 4:8. It was Joshua not "Jesus," who led the Israelites into Canaan.

The greatest king of Israel was David. One of the Messianic terms applied to Jesus in the Gospels is "the Son of David." Stephen reminded his audience that David wanted to build God's house. But through the prophet Nathan the Lord told him that he could not build it; instead his son Solomon would build the Temple, which he did.

Then Stephen stated the case in plain, straightforward language: "But the Most High does not dwell in temples made with hands" (v. 48). Idols can be placed in temples, but not God. How can a man-made building contain the God who says, "Heaven is my throne, and earth is my footstool" (v. 49)? God has made the vast universe (v. 50); He cannot be confined to a few square feet of space.

E. Resistance to the Spirit of God: (vv. 51-53).

Verse 51 marks a rather radical break with what precedes. There is a sudden change of tone and shift of approach. It may well be that Stephen was interrupted at this point or that he sensed the growing opposition to what he was saying and wanted to get in this final thrust before he was silenced.

He charged his hearers with being "stiffnecked," a term that is found only here in the New Testament, though it occurs several times in the Old Testament. "Uncircumcised in heart" is another Old Testament expression (Leviticus 26:41; Ezekiel 44:7). The idea of being uncircumcised in ears is suggested in Jeremiah 6:10.

Before the Sanhedrin, Stephen had been charged with blasphemy. Now he turned the tables, just as Peter had done (4:10; 5:30), and charged the religious leaders of the nation with rebelling against God: "You always resist the Holy Spirit; as your fathers, so are you."

He went on to remind them that their forefathers had persecuted the prophets and killed the ones who predicted the coming of the Messiah ("the Righteous One," see 3:14). But now his very hearers were guilty of being the "betrayers and murderers" of the Righteous One, Jesus Christ. It was a telling blow.

But Stephen did not stop there. The false witnesses had accused him before the Sanhedrin of speaking blasphemous words against the law (6:13). Now he says to these solemn judges: "You received the law . . . and have not kept it" (v. 53). This was a very serious and solemn charge to bring against these leaders who prided themselves on being perfect examples of law observance. But the unjust attitude they were taking against him was a denial of the emphasis in the law of Moses on justice and fairness. They were motivated by jealousy in opposing both Jesus and Stephen.

IV. STEPHEN'S DEATH: Acts 7:54-60

A. Rage of the Sanhedrin: v. 54

Again the members of the Sanhedrin were "cut to the heart" (see comments on 5:33). This time they "gnashed on him with their teeth" in uncontrollable rage. On the day of Pentecost Peter had charged his hearers with the crime of having crucified Jesus (2:23, 36). They were "pricked in their heart and asked, 'What shall we do?'" As a result of this contrite attitude, three thousand of them were saved. But the reaction of the religious leaders was quite different. They were "cut to the heart" with anger and hatred against this man who had told them the truth.

B. Stephen's Vision of Jesus: vv. 55-56

Again we find the key phrase of Acts. Stephen, "full of the Holy Spirit," looked steadily into heaven. There he saw the glory of God, and Jesus standing at God's right hand. Was Jesus standing up to greet His first martyr? Perhaps so. It was certainly worth all Stephen's persecution and suffering to be given this glorious vision of his Lord awaiting him in heaven. No wonder he met his death so calmly.

The heavens had been opened to give him a glimpse inside. Stephen testified to what he saw: the "Son of man" standing at God's right hand. This is the only place outside the Gospels where this designation is used for Jesus, and there it is always used by Christ (81 times) as His principal way of referring to Himself.

DISCUSSION QUESTIONS

1. What are some lessons we can learn from Stephen's life?
2. How should we react to false accusation?
3. Why did Stephen discuss Old Testament men?
4. Why was it important to prove that God was not confined to the Holy Land?
5. What lessons can we learn from Joseph's life?
6. Is there danger of disobedience among God's people today?

C. Stoning of Stephen: vv. 57-60

Stephen's vision of the Son of man standing at the right hand of God proved that Jesus, who called Himself by this title, was actually the Messiah. This was more than the listeners could take. They "cried out with a loud voice, and stopped their ears, and ran upon him with one accord" (v. 57). Then they "cast him out of the city, and stoned him" (v. 58). This sounds like a description of mob action. In any case, the assailants acted very unreasonably. The mention of "witnesses" suggests a formal execution, since the law required that the witnesses who testified in court should cast the first stones at the condemned person (Deuteronomy 17:7).

It is in this verse that Saul first comes into the picture. We are told that the witnesses "laid down their clothes at a young man's feet, whose name was Saul." It is probable that this scene, and especially Stephen's radiant face under persecution, made a lasting impression on Saul.

The wording of verse 59 in the King James Version is not logical, for grammatically "calling upon God" would refer back to "they." The Greek clearly reads: "They stoned Stephen as *he* was calling upon God." He prayed, "Lord Jesus, receive my spirit." And then, as death drew near, he echoed Jesus' prayer on the cross, as he said, "Lord, lay not this sin to their charge." Then he "fell asleep" in Jesus.

This scene was probably one of the main factors leading finally to Saul's conversion on the road to Damascus. Someone has well said: "Had Stephen not prayed, Paul had not preached."

V. SAUL'S PERSECUTION OF THE CHURCH:
Acts 8:1-3

"Saul was consenting to his death." Evidently this young Pharisee had already attained a place of influence among the religious leaders.

The original Greek of "at that time" means literally "on that day." It appears that a violent persecution of the church began immediately after Stephen's death. Instead of inducing a reaction of shame and regret for the violent, illegal act—for the Roman government had deprived the Sanhedrin of the right of capital punishment—the murder of this innocent man provoked an outburst of cruel persecution. The result was that the members of the church of Jerusalem were all scattered abroad through Judea and Samaria, "except the apostles." Since these leaders of the church were evidently still worshiping in the Temple and observing the law, it may be that they were not the object of opposition as much as the Hellenists, to whom Stephen belonged. It is also possible that the apostles felt it their duty to stay in Jerusalem to hold things together.

Devout men buried Stephen with great mourning (v. 2), but Saul "made havock of the church." The verb means "laid waste." It is used in the Septuagint for a wild boar tearing up a vineyard. Saul was violent, if not actually vicious, in his persecution of Christians. He even entered private houses, "haling" (rather, "hauling") men and women off to jail. Fortunately, after he was converted he preached and propagated the faith just as intensely and vigorously as he had formerly persecuted it.

CONTEMPORARY APPLICATION

It has often been said that the blood of the martyrs is the seed of the church. And this has many times proved true in history. One phenomenon that has often been observed is

that the church thrives better in times of persecution than in times of prosperity. Self-complacency is the death of devotion.

The Church in Korea is a shining

example of how a people of God grow stronger during times of persecution. At one time it seemed that the Communists would kill every Christian pastor in South Korea, and many of them did die. But the church grew both numerically and spiritually because of this.

We should be true to God regardless of the cost. Stephen was, and his death resulted not only in greater persecution, but also in greater preaching of the gospel, as we shall see in the next lesson.

March 31, 1974

OVERCOMING HUMAN BARRIERS

DEVOTIONAL READING	I John 5:1-5

ADULTS

Topic: *Overcoming Human Barriers*

Background Scripture: Acts 8:4-40

Scripture Lesson: Acts 8:18-31

Memory Verse: *There is neither Jew nor Greek, there is neither slave nor free, there is neither male nor female; for you are all one in Christ Jesus.* Galatians 3:28

YOUTH

Topic: *Who's Accepted?*

Background Scripture: Acts 8:4-40

Scripture Lesson: Acts 8:18-31

Memory Verse: *There is neither Jew nor Greek, there is neither slave nor free, there is neither male nor female; for you are all one is Christ Jesus.* Galatians 3:28

CHILDREN

Topic: *The Gospel Makes Us One*

Background Scripture: Acts 8:4-40

Scripture Lesson: Acts 8:26-31, 35-40

Memory Verse: *You are all one in Christ Jesus.* Galatians 3:28b

DAILY BIBLE READINGS

Mon., Mar. 25: Overcoming Barriers of Religion, Acts 8:4-13

Tues., Mar. 26: Overcoming Barriers of Race, Acts 8: 26-39.

Wed., Mar. 27: Overcoming Barriers of Jealousy and Strife, I Corinthians 3:1-11.

Thurs., Mar. 28: Overcoming Barriers of Nationality, Galatians 2:1-10.

Fri., Mar. 29: Overcoming Barriers of Social Status, Philemon 8-20.

Sat., Mar. 30: "Let Us Love One Another," I John 4:7-12.

Sun., Mar. 31: Children of God, I John 5:1-5.

LESSON AIM

To show that God is interested in people of all countries and cultures and also to see the diverse way that the Holy Spirit works in the various situations.

LESSON SETTING

Time: Perhaps two or three years after Pentecost

Place: A city of Samaria; the road to Gaza, in southern Palestine

247

Overcoming Human Barriers

I. Philip in Samaria: Acts 8:4-8
   A. Laymen's Missionary Movement: v. 4
   B. Preaching Christ: vv. 5-7
   C. Great Joy in the City: v. 8

II. Simon the Sorcerer: Acts 8:9-13
   A. An Impostor: vv. 9-11
   B. A Professing Believer: vv. 12-13

III. The Apostles in Samaria: Acts 8:14-17
   A. Peter and John Sent from Jerusalem: v. 14

LESSON OUTLINE
   B. Samaritans Receive the Holy Spirit: vv. 15-17

IV. Simon the Seeker: Acts 8:18-25
   A. Seeking Power: vv. 18-19
   B. Rebuked by Peter: vv. 20-23
   C. Seeking Immunity: v. 24

V. Evangelizing the Samaritans: Acts 8:25

VI. Philip and the Ethiopian Eunuch: Acts 8:26-40
   A. The Meeting in the Desert: vv. 26-28
   B. Making Contact: vv. 29-31
   C. Interpreting the Scriptures: vv. 32-35
   D. Baptizing the Eunuch: vv. 36-38
   E. Evangelizing the Coastal Cities: vv. 39-40

**SUGGESTED
INTRODUCTION
FOR ADULTS**

In our first lesson of this quarter we noted that Acts 1:8 gives a logical outline for the Book of Acts in three parts: (1) Witnessing in Jerusalem (chaps. 1—7); (2) Witnessing in Judea and Samaria (chaps. 8—12); (3) Witnessing in All the World (chaps. 13—28). It will be seen that with today's lesson we enter the second division of the book.

This is highlighted by the statement in the first verse of chapter 8: "They were all scattered abroad throughout the regions of Judea and Samaria." This is followed by the account of Philip's preaching in Samaria (vv. 5-25). It is true that Saul's conversion (9:1-22) took place near Damascus, far to the north. But in the last verses of chapter 9 we read about Peter ministering in Lydda and Joppa (vv. 32-43). Lydda was near the Mediterranean coast and Joppa right on the sea, both of them cities of Judea. In chapter 10 we find Peter ministering in the house of Cornelius at Caesarea, the northernmost Judean city also situated on the coast. In chapter 11 Peter reports in Jerusalem on what took place in Cornelius' house. Verses 19-30 of this chapter describe what happened in Antioch, in northern Syria. But in chapter 12 we are back in Jerusalem and Caesarea. So most of the events described in these five chapters took place in Judea and Samaria.

"Who's Accepted?" Our memory text declares: "There is neither Jew nor Greek, there is neither bond nor free, there is neither male nor female: for you are all one in Christ Jesus" (Galatians 3:28). All are accepted in Christ, but are they all accepted in the church?

Let's take a look at the matter. We say that we have done better than the Jews of Jesus' day: we do not classify the rest of mankind as Gentiles ("Greek"). And we have got rid of slavery. But how about "neither male nor female"? Many denominations do not accept women on an equal status with men; they are barred from ordination into the ministry. But Paul says there is no distinction between them in Christ; they are all one—men and women alike.

Jesus accepted the despised Samaritans, as we know from the fourth chapter of John's Gospel and the Parable of the Good Samaritan (Luke 10:25-37). Philip followed His example. Do we?

1. Philip obeyed the Lord and won an African to Christ.
2. If we want people to accept Christ, we must accept them.
3. The Lord used Philip to help break down racial barriers.
4. The gospel makes all Christians one in Christ.

THE LESSON COMMENTARY

I. PHILIP IN SAMARIA:
Acts 8:4-8

A. Laymen's Missionary Movement: v. 4

In the first verse of this chapter we read that the members of the church at Jerusalem "were all scattered abroad . . . except the apostles." Now we have the statement: "Therefore those that were dispersed went about preaching the Word" (v. 4). It wasn't the apostles doing the preaching. So this is sometimes referred to as "the laymen's missionary movement of the first century."

The word for "preaching" is the verb *euangelizo*, which we have taken over into English as "evangelize." Luke is especially fond of this word, using it ten times in his Gospel. It occurs only once in the other Gospels (Matthew 11:5) and fifteen times in Acts. It literally means "announce good news"—a very appropriate missionary word to describe preaching the gospel to people who had never heard it before.

B. Preaching Christ: vv. 5-7

Philip was one of the seven who had been appointed to wait on tables, taking care of the needs of the Hellenistic widows (6:1-6). But, like Stephen, he had gone beyond his assignment and was preaching the gospel. Now he went northward to "the city"—or possibly, "a city"—of Samaria. There he "preached Christ."

The word for "preached" here is a different one from that in the previous verse. This is *kerysso*, from *keryx*, "herald." So it means to "herald" or "proclaim." Philip proclaimed to these people the Messiah ("Christ"). We know from John 4:25 that the Samaritans had Messianic expectations. Philip now brought the good news that the Messiah had come in the person of Jesus of Nazareth.

The Samaritans gave Philip a receptive audience—"with one accord gave heed"—impressed by the "miracles" (Greek, "signs") which he did. Jesus commissioned His apostles to carry on a miraculous healing ministry (Matthew 10:8), and this continued after His ascension (Acts 3:1-8). But these "signs" were not restricted to the apostles, for we are told that Stephen "did great wonders and miracles [signs] among the people" (6:8). So it is not surprising to read that his colleague, Philip, was doing the same.

The miracles performed by Philip included casting out many "unclean spirits," or demons. Also, many who were paralyzed or lame were healed. These miracles no doubt attracted much attention and also served to validate the authority of the message preached.

C. Great Joy in the City: v. 8

When people are being converted to Christ there is always great joy. Sin brings sorrow and suffering. Salvation brings joy and gladness.

The greatest thing that can happen to any city today is to have a spiritual revival. It will solve more problems and eliminate more troubles than anything else that can happen. History records many instances when the atmosphere of an entire community was transformed by God's saving presence in Christ.

II. SIMON THE SORCERER: Acts 8:9-13

A. An Impostor: vv. 9-11

Before Philip arrived to proclaim Christ and His salvation, a faker had worked the city for his own profit. His name was Simon, the most common Jewish name of the first century. This man is usually referred to as Simon Magus—the "magician" or "sorcerer." For some time he had "used sorcery"—*mageuon*, from which we get "magic." So he was one who practiced magic. In this way he had "bewitched"—better, "amazed" or "confounded"—the people of Samaria, claiming to be "some great one." To him they all "gave heed," as they later did to Philip (same word in verses 6 and 10). So astonished were they by his magic that they said, "This man is the great power of God" (v. 10). The best Greek text says: "This man is that power of God which is called Great." They evidently deified this magician, believing that he was divine. For a long time he had amazed them with his "sorceries" (*magia*, "magic").

In times of religious decline, fakers and impostors multiply. When people reject the true God they take up with false gods. Superstitious credulity is a poor substitute for faith!

B. A Professing Believer: vv. 12-13

The power of the Holy Spirit in Philip's preaching proved to be greater than the magical powers of Simon, so that the people "believed." Philip was "preaching the things [literally "announcing the good news" (one word in Greek, *euangelizomeno*)] concerning the kingdom of God." This emphasis on the kingdom of God goes all the way back to the preaching of John the Baptist (Matthew 3:3) and the early preaching of Jesus (Matthew 4:17).

But a new note occurs here: they believed in "the name of Jesus Christ." Peter had already sounded this note when he declared: "Neither is there any other name under heaven given among men by which we must be saved" (4:12). Emphasis on the name of Jesus is prominent in early apostolic preaching.

As a result of their faith, people were baptized, "both men and women." This was as it should be, for both are needed in the church. Water baptism was especially important for these people, as it was a public testimony that they had accepted the new faith and had transferred their loyalty to it. Even today public baptism has special significance for new converts to Christianity.

But there was one fly in the ointment—Simon Magus. We are told that he "himself believed also" (v. 13). The same verb is used as for the genuine converts in the previous verse. But it is hard to accept the idea that Simon's faith was genuine, in the light of what soon follows. If he was converted, he backslid very quickly!

Some think that Simon's believing was sincere but superficial. Knowling thinks that Simon's faith "rested on the outward miracles and signs." He comments further: "He may have believed in the Messianic dignity of Christ, and in His Death and Resurrection . . . but it was a belief about the facts, and not a belief in Him whom the facts made known, a belief in the *power* of the new faith, but not an acceptance of its *holiness*" (*Expositor's Greek Testament*, II, 215). That is, Simon's faith was a matter of mental assent but not one of moral consent, a matter of the head rather than the heart. He may have accepted everything with his mind, but his will did not submit to the will of God.

III. THE APOSTLES IN SAMARIA: Acts 8:14-17

A. Peter and John Sent from Jerusalem: v. 14

The apostles at Jerusalem were still the highest earthly authority in the church. When they heard what had happened in Samaria, they decided that they needed to investigate the matter. It would appear that this was the first time since Pentecost that people outside the fold of Judaism had professed faith in Jesus Christ as their Savior. For the defiled, despised Samaritans to do this was a bit shocking! Could this indeed be a genuine work of God? They must find out. So they sent the two leading apostles, Peter and John, to check up on the situation. We have already found these two men working together in the early church (Acts 3:1, 3, 4, 11; 4:13, 19). John, however, does not appear again in the Book of Acts. Fortunately, his record here ends on a high note.

B. Samaritans Receive the Holy Spirit: vv. 15-17

We may be thankful that it was Peter and John who comprised the investigating committee. Instead of raising questions about what right the Samaritans had to be baptized into the Christian church, they obviously gave their blessing to the work. Perhaps they remembered how the people in the village of Sychar, in this same geographical area, had believed in Jesus when they heard Him some years earlier (John 4:39-42). Could there possibly be some connection between these two events?

In any case, Peter and John were evidently satisfied that these new converts were genuine believers. So they "prayed for them, that they might receive the Holy Spirit." This was the most important contribution these two apostles could make to the life of the new community.

Verse 16 gives us an interesting explanation: "For He had not yet fallen upon any of them; they were only baptized in the name of the Lord Jesus." The account continues: "Then they laid their hands on them and they received the Holy Spirit" (v. 17).

There is no denying the fact that these Samaritans were converted under the preaching of Philip and filled with the Spirit under the ministry of Peter and John. Some have held that it was some special gift or gifts of the Spirit that is intended here. But Knowling takes definite issue with this idea. He says: "In a book so marked by the working of the Holy Spirit . . . it is difficult to believe that St. Luke can mean to limit the expression *lambanein* [receive] here and in the following verse to anything less than a bestowal of that divine indwelling of the spirit which makes the Christian the temple of God" (*Expositor's Greek Testament*, II, 216).

"In the name of the Lord Jesus" (v. 16) is literally "into the name of the Lord Jesus." F. F. Bruce makes this helpful comment: "The expression *eis to onoma* is common in a commercial context: some property is paid or transferred 'into the name' of someone, i.e., into his account. So the person baptized *eis to onoma tou kyriou Iesou* bears public testimony that he has become Christ's property" (*Acts*, p. 187).

IV. SIMON THE SEEKER: Acts 8:18-25

A. Seeking Power: vv. 18-19

When Simon saw that the Holy Spirit was given to people through the apostles laying their hands on them, he decided that he would like to have this miraculous power. Here was something that outshone all his magical tricks! So he offered Peter and John a sum of money if they would give him the authority to bestow the Spirit on people by laying his hands on them. He probably figured that this would be a good investment; he would get his money back many times over from grateful patrons. Simon's idea of buying ecclesiastical authority is the origin of our word *simony*.

B. Rebuked by Peter: vv. 20-23

Such a greedy, selfish attitude brought a sharp rebuke from Peter. He said to Simon: "Thy money perish with thee, because thou hast thought that the gift of God may be purchased with money" (v. 20). The first clause reads literally: "May your silver be with you for perishing." Some people have felt that these words are overly harsh. But Knowling writes: "The words are no curse or imprecation, as is evident from verse 22, but rather a vehement expression of horror on the part of St. Peter, an expression which would warn Simon that he was on his way to destruction" (*Expositor's Greek Testament*, II, 218). Basically, Peter was saying that he wished Simon's money, which was threatening to drag the man down to destruction, might perish. If Simon was ever to be saved, he would have to loosen the

greedy grasp he had on his money That Peter's ultimate desire and prayer was for Simon's salvation is shown clearly by verse 22. Peter was not cursing this man to hell, as some have unwisely assumed.

The real nature of Simon's condition is declared unequivocally by Peter in verse 21: "You have neither part nor lot in this matter; for your heart is not right before God." The apostle exposed the real nature of sin. It is wanting things for ourselves, rather than seeking God's will and His glory. Basically, sin is selfishness, self-will, self-centeredness.

But Peter did not want Simon to be lost. So he urged him: "Repent therefore, of this wickedness of yours, and petition the Lord, if perhaps the thought of your heart may be forgiven" (v. 22). Evidently Peter believed that it was not too late for Simon to repent and be saved.

The Greek word translated "thought" is found only here in the New Testament. It literally means "design" or "plot." Simon had contrived a wicked design, which in God's sight was a serious sin. Yet he could have been forgiven if he had repented. Unfortunately, there is no indication that he did. He evidently continued in the pitiful state described in verse 23: "in the gall of bitterness, and in the bond of iniquity." He was a slave to his own selfish sinful desires, and he was not willing to let the Savior free him from his sin.

C. Seeking Immunity: v. 24

It is sad to read Simon's reaction: "Pray to the Lord on my behalf that none of these things you have mentioned may come on me." This reveals the deep-seated selfishness of this man's heart. He was not asking for the forgiveness of his sins, but only for escape from their consequences. There is no evidence whatever of any conviction for the wrongness of his sin, or any repentance.

Too many people today have the

same attitude. They do not want to be lost forever, but they are not willing to forsake their sin! They do not have that godly sorrow that produces genuine repentance. Paul spells it out clearly in II Corinthians 7:10: "For godly sorrow works repentance to salvation not to be repented of: but the sorrow of the world works death." Simon had worldly sorrow. He was sorry because he was caught in wickedness, sorry about the consequences that threatened him. But godly sorrow is sorrow for the sin itself. It is being sorry for the ingratitude of our hearts that has hurt the heart of God. This kind of sorrow produces real repentance, a hatred of sin itself because it is sin and a turning away from all sin to follow God's will. There is nothing more needed in our world today than sincere repentance for sin.

Superficial repentance produces superficial conversions. It is more than a matter of saying we believe in Jesus. Repentance is the necessary condition for faith. When we have truly repented of our sins, we can believe in Christ for forgiveness.

V. EVANGELIZING THE SAMARITANS:
Acts 8:25

After testifying and preaching for a time in the city where Philip was, Peter and John returned to Jerusalem with a good report of what they had seen. But on the way back they "preached the gospel in many villages of the Samaritans." The Greek says that they "evangelized many villages."

As already noted in connection with verse 5, we do not know the name of the city where Philip was ministering. If the correct reading is "the city" (v. 5), it would probably be Sebaste (modern Sebastiyeh) on the striking hilltop where the capital city, Samaria, was located in Old Testament times. If "a city" is correct, it would probably be Neapolis (modern Nablus), located near ancient Shechem. In any case, the two apostles evangelized their way back to Jerusalem. They did not pass by the opportunity of preaching the gospel to those needy people.

The Samaritans formed a "halfway house between Judaism and the Gentile world." So the evangelization of this area was an important step in the transition of Christianity from the Jews to the Gentiles.

VI. PHILIP AND THE ETHIOPIAN EUNUCH:
Acts 8:26-40

A. The Meeting in the Desert: vv. 26-28

The expression "the angel of the Lord" seems to be used in the Old Testament for God Himself appearing or speaking to men. But here the Greek text says "an angel of the Lord." A comparison with verses 29 and 39 would almost suggest that it is the Holy Spirit who spoke to Philip.

The orders were: "Arise, and go toward the south to the road that goes down from Jerusalem to Gaza; this is desert." There were two roads that went down from Jerusalem. One went almost straight south to Hebron (20 miles) and on to Beersheba. The other one, mentioned here, went southwest to Gaza, on the coast. Both these roads are busy highways today and they do lead through desert areas.

It is not clear from the Greek whether "this is desert" refers to the road or the city, since both "road" and "Gaza" are feminine, as is the pronoun "this." Eminent scholars are ranged on both sides of the question. One argument against the city is that the Gaza of that time was on the coast. But the old Gaza, which was two and a half miles inland from the Mediterranean, had been destroyed by Alexander the Great in 332 B.C. and was deserted at this time. So the reference may be to this.

When Philip heard the command, "Arise, and be going" (v. 26), "he arose and went" (v. 27). These last two verbs are both in the aorist tense, suggesting immediate action. Prompt obedience to the Spirit's guidance is one of the main secrets of success in the Christian life. If Philip had dallied around for a few hours, he would have missed his divinely made appointment in the desert.

Philip could well have stopped to argue: "But Lord, it isn't reasonable for me to leave this big city-wide revival with all these new converts who need attention, and go out into the desert where nobody lives!" Fortunately, he didn't do this. He obeyed at once, without quibbling, and the result was that he found his man. How often do we miss God's appointments for us because we do not obey promptly?

Now we are introduced to the man Philip was to meet. He was an Ethiopian. Scholars are generally agreed that this is not modern Ethiopia, also known as Abyssinia, with its capital Addis Ababa, but a kingdom on the Nile River between modern Aswan and Khartoum. The Ethiopians were dark-skinned but not blacks.

The man was also a eunuch. According to the Mosaic law (Deuteronomy 23:1) a eunuch was barred from the congregation of the Lord. But it appears that this ban was later lifted (Isaiah 56:3-5).

He was also a man "of great authority." This phrase is one word in the Greek—*dynastes*, from which we get "dynasty." The word means "prince, ruler, potentate." So the eunuch was probably the leading official, or prime minister, under "Candace." This word is not a personal name, but a title like *Pharaoh*. Eusebius says that Ethiopia was ruled by queens in his day (fourth century). Furthermore, this man had charge of all the queen's treasure. To win him to Christ would be to influence a whole nation.

The Ethiopian eunuch had come up to Jerusalem to worship, probably at one of the annual Jewish feasts. He was a man who had accepted the true God of Judaism. On his way home now, he was "sitting in his chariot and reading Isaiah the prophet" (v. 28). Because all the scrolls at that time were written by hand, they were expensive; but the eunuch was a wealthy man and could afford them. Some scholars hold that all reading in that day was out loud. At any rate, the rabbis taught that the Scriptures should be read aloud when they were read as one traveled. We know that the eunuch was reading aloud, because Philip heard him (v. 30).

B. Making the Contact: vv. 29-31

The Spirit now told Philip to go and be joined to the chariot. Eagerly God's messenger "ran" obediently toward the moving vehicle. As he approached, he heard the man reading from Isaiah, and he asked him, "Do you understand what you are reading?" In the Greek this is a play on words: *ginoskeis ha anaginoskeis.* (In the 1930s when we studied at Boston University School of Theology these three words were on a plaque fastened to the door of the classroom where Dr. Daniel Steele used to teach Greek New Testament. They formed a fitting challenge to every student who entered that room.)

The eunuch's reply was appropriate: "How can I unless someone guides me?" (v. 3). Then he asked Philip to get into the chariot with him. Here was a man who was eager to learn the Scriptures. And God's messenger was there to teach him.

DISCUSSION QUESTIONS

1. Do we have "hang-ups" about witnessing to some people?
2. Does God have to justify to us His seemingly strange orders?
3. What were some secrets of Philip's success?
4. Why do we sometimes hesitate to obey?
5. How can we know that it is God who is speaking?
6. Are numbers the most important criterion for decisions?

C. Interpreting the Scriptures: vv. 32-35

The Ethiopian pointed out to Philip the passage he was reading, Isaiah 53:7-8. Then he asked: "Is the prophet speaking of himself or of some other person?"

This was all the opening that Philip needed. What an opportunity! Here was a high-class official who wanted to know the meaning of one of the greatest Messianic passages in the Old Testament. The fifty-third chapter of Isaiah is the leading description of the Suffering Servant of the Lord, a role that Jesus filled on the cross as He became the Propitiatory Sacrifice for our sins. At once Philip "opened his mouth, and began at the same scripture, and preached unto him Jesus" (v. 35). This was the answer to the eunuch's question. The prophet was predicting the coming of the Messiah, and this Messiah was Jesus.

D. Baptizing the Eunuch: vv. 36-38

As the two men rode along in the chariot, they came to a spring or brook of water by the roadside. The eunuch requested baptism, and Philip gladly administered it. Gentiles had to be baptized in water to become proselytes to Judaism, and doubtless the Ethiopian assumed it would be true for a convert to Christianity.

Verse 37 is not in the oldest Greek manuscripts. It was added by a later scribe as a familiar baptismal formula.

"Went down into the water" (v. 38) and "came up out of the water" (v. 39) both suggest that the baptism took place in a pool or running brook. This was the custom in the early church (*Didache* 7:1).

E. Evangelizing the Coastal Cities: vv. 39-40

The Spirit of the Lord caught away Philip, and the eunuch went on his way rejoicing. What a beautiful way for this striking incident to end.

Philip found himself at Azotus (v. 40), the old Philistine city of Ashdod about twenty miles north of Gaza. Making his way northward he preached in "all the cities" along the coast. This would include Joppa and Lydda, where we find believers in the next chapter (9:32-42). Finally he arrived in Caesarea, near Mount Carmel. This city had been rebuilt by Herod the Great about 13 B.C. and named Caesarea in honor of the emperor. It became the Roman capital of the province of Judea.

CONTEMPORARY APPLICATION

Philip obeyed promptly and met the Ethiopian eunuch, who was converted and carried the Christian gospel back to his own land. Suppose Philip had procrastinated for a few hours. Only God knows how many souls would have been lost as a result.

A godly Quaker lady was visiting with friends in a large city. One day she was impressed that she should go to a certain street and number. She told her host, who immediately objected that this address was in a notoriously wicked neighborhood; it would not be safe for her to venture there.

But when she insisted she was going, he finally ordered his horses and carriage, and they were driven to the end of the specified street.

Here the man told her he dared not go farther. After much persuasion a policeman agreed to walk down the street with her, gun in hand. Finally they arrived at the number that had been impressed on her mind by the Holy Spirit. While the burly policeman stood fearfully out in the street, she walked up to the front door and opened it. Through the swirling tobacco smoke she saw a frightened girl sitting in the midst of the hubbub. Quickly the woman beckoned, and the girl ran out to her.

Back at the host's home she told her story. A handsome young man had come to her little town. After some acquaintance he asked her to go to the city with him. He turned out to be a white slave trader. Horrified to find herself in the clutches of the gang, but as yet unmolested, she was desperately looking for a way of escape when the Christian lady suddenly appeared. A happy and wiser girl soon found herself safely home again. But the timing had to be perfect.

IMPORTANCE OF SUPPORTIVE ROLES

DEVOTIONAL READING	I Corinthians 12:4-11
ADULTS	Topic: *Serving in Supportive Roles* Background Scripture: Acts 9:1-43 Scripture Lesson: Acts 9:10-17, 23-30 Memory Verse: *As in one body we have many members, and all the members do not have the same function, so we, though many, are one body in Christ, and individually members one of another.* Romans 12:4-5
YOUTH	Topic: *Here I Am, Lord* Background Scripture: Acts 9:1-43 Scripture Lesson: Acts 9:10-15, 22-30 Memory Verse: *As in one body we have many members, and all the members do not have the same function, so we, though many, are one body in Christ, and individually members one of another.* Romans 12:4-5
CHILDREN	Topic: *God's Helpers* Background Scripture: Acts 9:1-43 Scripture Lesson: Acts 9:10-15 Memory Verse: *Through love be servants of one another.* Galatians 5:13b
DAILY BIBLE READINGS	Mon., Apr. 1: Saul the Persecutor Meets the Lord, Acts 9:1-9 Tues., Apr. 3: Ananias Ministers to Saul, Acts 9:10-19a. Wed., Apr. 3: Believers Help Saul Escape, Acts 9:19b-25. Thurs., Apr. 4: Barnabas Speaks for Saul, Acts 9:26-31. Fri., Apr. 5: Dorcas, Doer of Good Works, Acts 9:36-43. Sat., Apr. 6: Every Member Is Needed, I Corinthians 12:14-27. Sun., Apr. 7: Members of One Body, I Corinthians 12:4-13.
LESSON AIM	To show that each member of the body of Christ has some function to perform and that all members must function together.
LESSON SETTING	Time: Saul's conversion probably took place in A.D. 34, four years after Pentecost. Place: Damascus and Jerusalem

Serving in Supportive Roles

LESSON OUTLINE

**SUGGESTED
INTRODUCTION
FOR ADULTS**

Without any question, the coming of the Holy Spirit on the day of Pentecost is the most important single event in the Book of Acts. Apart from this, the Book would never have been written. The first chapter of Acts, which is introductory, shows the disciples still looking for an earthly Messianic kingdom (1:6) instead of a spiritual kingdom in the hearts of men (1:7-8). At best they were waiting (1:14), not working or witnessing.

Pentecost changed all of that. Immediately the disciples became powerful, effective witnesses. The church in Jerusalem grew phenomenally—by the thousands (2:41; 4:4; 5:14). But Jesus' statement that the apostles would be His witnesses to "the uttermost part of the earth" (1:8) was not being fulfilled.

It took "a great persecution against the church which was at Jerusalem" (8:1) to shake the home nest and start the Christians fulfilling Christ's commission to evangelize the world. As a result of that persecution, the church members "were all scattered abroad" (8:1) and "went everywhere preaching the word" (8:3). But that "everywhere"—which over-translates the Greek—was limited to "the regions of Judea and Samaria" (8:1). Philip became the evangelist to the latter territory.

It is an interesting coincidence that Saul, who was the main persecutor that scattered the early church in Jerusalem, became the great apostle to the Gentiles, the one most responsible for carrying the gospel to the far reaches of the Roman Empire—which was the world of that day. So it seems reasonable to hold that Saul's conversion is the second most important event in the Book of Acts. This is supported by the fact that over half the Book (chaps. 13—28) is devoted almost entirely to the story of Paul's labors in the Gentile world.

SUGGESTED INTRODUCTION FOR YOUTH

"Here I am, Lord." Those were the words of the young Samuel when the Lord first called him (I Samuel 3:4-10). And he became the first of the great succession of prophets that lasted through the kingdom period of Israel's history.

They were also the words of Ananias when the Lord spoke to him in Damascus (9:10), over a thousand years later. They should be our response to God's call to us today.

God had a great work for Saul, later called Paul, to carry out. Paul was without doubt the greatest missionary and theologian of the early church. He wrote thirteen of the twenty-seven books of the New Testament.

But Paul would never have accomplished what he did had it not been for Ananias and Barnabas. The lesson today gives us some hint of the tremendous importance of the supportive role of lesser characters. Ananias is mentioned only in this one place. Barnabas did become a missionary, but he drops out of sight after he accompanied Paul on that first journey. Paul, however, went on to accomplish great things for Christ. Yet it was because Ananias ministered to Saul in Damascus and Barnabas sponsored him in Jerusalem that he was able to play this great role in establishing churches among the Gentiles. Each of us, however humble we may be, can have a significant part to play in the support of those who carry on the public work of the church. If *we* fail, the whole project suffers.

CONCEPTS FOR CHILDREN

1. Ananias felt weak and afraid.
2. God told him to go anyway.
3. Ananias obeyed, and by doing so made it possible for Paul to become a great missionary.
4. God wants boys and girls to be His helpers in the church.

THE LESSON COMMENTARY

I. SAUL'S CONVERSION: Acts 9:1-9

A. Commission from the High Priest: vv. 1-2

Saul was "breathing out" threatening and slaughter against the disciples of the Lord. The Greek says "breathing in." So the best translation is simply "breathing," as in the Revised Version. Murder of Christians seemed to be the very breath of Saul's life. He himself tells us that he was "exceedingly mad against them"

(26:11). He also says: "I persecuted this way unto the death" (22:4). Paul had a real "hang-up" about this new sect!

This arch-persecutor was not satisfied with making havoc of the church at Jerusalem (8:3). He went to the high priest, Caiaphas—the one who had condemned Christ—and asked for letters to the synagogues of Damascus, authorizing him to arrest any Christians he might find there and bring them in chains to Jerusalem. Rome had granted to the high priest the authority to demand the extradition of Jews who broke their law. Saul may have been mainly interested in bringing back Christians who had fled from Jerusalem to Damascus. He was determined that none of these "heretics" should escape being punished or put to death.

The fact that "synagogues" is in the plural implies a sizable community of Jews in Damascus. Josephus says that at the time of the Jewish War (A.D. 66-70) the Damascenes killed 10,500 Jews, or 18,000 including women and children.

Christianity is here referred to as "the Way" (not "this way" as King James Version has it). This is one of the earliest designations for the new religion, and its use here implies an early date for Acts. In China, Christianity used to be called "the Jesus Way."

Three times in the Book of Acts we find specific mention of Saul's persecution of women (8:3; 9:2; 22:4). It took the Spirit of Christ to soften this man's harsh spirit and give him a fine appreciation for women in the Christian church (Romans 16:1-3, 6, 12, 13, 15). Christianity has done much to ameliorate the unkindness of men to women that was the rule rather than the exception in the ancient world.

B. A Light from Heaven: v. 3

Damascus is about two hundred miles from Jerusalem. So it would have taken Paul at least the full six days between Sabbaths to have made the trip. This would give him plenty of time to think about this new "heresy."

We can imagine him stopping for the night and trying to sleep. It may well be that the face of Stephen, shining with the glory of God (6:15), haunted his dreams at night. These followers of the Nazarene must be wrong! Their worship of Jesus was sheer blasphemy. The heretics must be destroyed and the heresy rooted out. On to Damascus!

By the time they neared Damascus Saul's mind was probably in a turmoil. Could the Christians perhaps be right? Perish the thought! Saul was kicking against the ox goad (26:14). And it was hurting.

Just then it happened. A light from heaven, like a lightning flash, blinded him and he fell to the ground. He later said that this took place at "midday" and that the light was "above the brightness of the sun" (26:13). (The verb translated "shined round" if translated literally would be "flashed around.")

C. A Voice from Heaven: vv. 4-7

As Saul lay prostrate on the ground, he heard a voice asking; "Saul, Saul, why are you persecuting me?" Saul's answer was: "Who are you, Lord?" Since exactly the same word in Greek is used for "lord" and "sir," it may be that the best translation here is: "Who are you, sir?" Had Saul yet acknowledged Jesus as Lord? The answer, of course, is no. And it is also obvious from his question that he did not know whose voice was calling his name. Saul is on the verge of being converted, but it has not yet taken place.

The answer from heaven must have shocked Saul: "I am Jesus, whom you are persecuting." The implication of this is crystal clear. The true church is the body of Christ; He is the Head. A blow anywhere on our physical body is immediately registered in our head as pain. So it is with Christ's spiritual body. When we hurt any of His own, we hurt Him. This is one of the most important lessons for Christians to learn. When we realize that every time we hurt a fellow believer we hurt our Lord, it will certainly make us more careful what we say and do. We sometimes see the hurt look in the eyes of a friend or loved one; if only we could see it in His eyes!

All the Greek manuscripts omit the last clause of verse 5—"It is hard for thee to kick against the pricks" (goad)—and the first half of verse 6—"And he trembling and astonished said, Lord, what wilt thou have me to do? And the Lord said unto him." There is no question but that this is a later addition. The last part of verse 5 was inserted here by some scribe from 26:14, where it is found in the Greek. The first part of verse 6 has no support anywhere in the Greek; it comes from the Latin Vulgate.

The prostrate young Pharisee was then commanded by the voice from heaven to get up and go into the city; there he would be told what to do. Saul was now taking orders from the recently hated Jesus! It was a quick and radical switch.

We are told that "the men which journeyed with him stood speechless, hearing a voice, but seeing no man" (v. 7). On the surface this seems to be in flat contradiction to the statement in 22:9: "And they that were with me saw indeed the light . . . but they heard not the voice of him that spake with me." How can these two assertions possibly be reconciled?

The answer lies in a point of Greek grammar. In 9:7 the verb "hearing" is followed by the genitive case of "voice," which suggests only an audible sound. In 22:9 "voice" is in the accusative case, indicating the intelligible content of what was said. (This distinction is supported by the leading British *Grammar of New Testament Greek*, by J. H. Moulton.) So Paul's companions heard a voice, but didn't

catch what was said. We have a good example of this in John 12:29. The Father's voice from heaven spoke a message of reassurance to the Son. But those who stood by and heard it said that it thundered! The message was lost on them.

D. Three Days of Fasting and Prayer: vv. 8-9

In obedience to Jesus' command Saul got to his feet. But when he opened his eyes, he discovered that he was blind. He had to be led by the hand into Damascus, like a helpless child. It wasn't exactly the way this proud young Pharisee had planned to enter that city, carrying official letters from the high priest! Those letters were never delivered.

One often hears it said that the flash of lightning knocked Saul off his horse to the ground. This is doubtful. In the first place, the Jews traditionally did not like to ride horses, which were symbols of the hated rule of their Roman conquerors. In the second place, if Saul had been riding, it would seem natural for his companions to put him back on his horse, instead of leading him by the hand.

Saul spent the next three days in fasting and prayer (v. 9; cf. v. 11). Almost without warning he had suddenly been plunged into the greatest crisis in his life. To accept Jesus of Nazareth as Messiah and Son of God would take a drastic revamping of his thinking. This sort of thing takes time. Saul needed three days of quiet, uninterrupted meditation to make sure that the heavenly vision had not been an hallucination. His whole future depended on it. And God is always willing to give His children the time they need to understand His will. He never expects us to make major decisions without being sure this is "it." The raging young persecutor, who had been chasing the Christians relentlessly, needed to sit still and listen to a new voice within—the same voice that had spoken to him from heaven.

II. SAUL AND ANANIAS:
Acts 9:10-18

A. Command from the Lord: vv. 10-12

The Lord knew that Saul after three days alone in the dark needed a human touch. So he tenderly provided it by sending Ananias to minister to him. Aside from this human comfort there were two very important purposes served by Ananias's visit. The first was that Saul would be made to feel that he was accepted into the Christian community. The second was that this would be assured by Ananias vouching for him, because he had seen him.

Ananias was the first one to play a supportive role in Saul's new Christian life. He is described very simply here as "a certain disciple at Damascus, named Ananias." Paul later speaks of him as "a devout man according to the law, having a good report of all the Jews which dwelt there" (22:12). Yet this obscure Christian formed a vital link in the transition Saul had to make.

The Lord appeared to Ananias in a vision, calling his name. Promptly this godly man replied, "Here I am, Lord." It was the same response that Samuel had made long ago, and it is the response we must make today when God speaks to us.

Because of Ananias's openness, God was able to give him a message. He was to go to Straight Street—still the main street across the city of Damascus from east to west—and ask at the house of Judas for Saul of Tarsus. Instead of persecuting the Christians, Saul was now praying. And he also had received a vision—a man named Ananias coming in and laying his hands on Saul, so that Saul's sight might be restored. Thus both men were prepared for meeting each other.

B. Hesitation of Ananias: vv. 13-14

Though a consecrated Christian, Ananias was a bit concerned about this matter of ministering to Saul. He had "heard" how Saul had been persecuting the saints at Jerusalem. This shows that Ananias was not a recent refugee from that city. He also knew the purpose of Saul's trip to Damascus. Evidently some Christians in Jerusalem had learned about the letters from the high priest and had sent word to the believers in Damascus to be on their guard. Ananias did not want to get caught!

C. Assurance from the Lord: vv. 15-16

There was no denying what Ananias said. But something else had happened that apparently Ananias did not know about. The picture was different now: "He is a chosen vessel unto me, to bear my name before the Gentiles, and kings, and the children of Israel." Paul's primary ministry was to the Gentiles, as the order here suggests. He did witness before "kings"—Herod Agrippa II (chap. 26) and probably Nero (27:24). But he also preached to "the children of Israel" in the synagogues of most of the cities where he went.

Saul was God's "chosen vessel" and well prepared for the massive role he filled in the first century. He was born in the Gentile city of Tarsus (in Asia Minor) and so was well acquainted with Greek culture. As a young man he had studied the Scriptures at the feet of Gamaliel in Jerusalem—a rather more liberal rabbi than the average, a man who would expose his students to a wide range of thought. Then, too, Tarsus was the third greatest educational center in the Roman Empire, after Athens and Alexandria. No man was better prepared to carry out Christ's commission to be "the Apostle of the Gentiles" (Romans 11:13; cf. Galatians 2:7).

But this was a costly honor. The Lord added: "For I will show him how great things he must suffer for my name's sake" (v. 16). Paul was sometimes given intimations of these beforehand (20:23; 21:11). And in II Corinthians 11:23-28 we have an unparalleled chronicle of human suffering that makes most of our trifling annoyances in life look like a Sunday school picnic by comparison.

D. Obedience of Ananias: vv. 17-18

When this faithful servant of the Lord was sure of his instructions, he lost no time in carrying out his commission. He went to the designated house and entered. Saul had been in physical darkness for three days. What a comfort it must have been to him to feel kind hands laid on his head! And then this comfort was doubled when he heard the greeting in familiar Hebrew: "Brother Saul." This man whom he had come to arrest and hopefully see killed was now calling him "Brother." It must have been a wonderful revelation to Saul of the grace of God that would enable a Christian to love his former enemy. The term *Brother* also indicated that Saul was accepted into the Christian fellowship.

The expression, "the Lord, even Jesus" becomes doubly significant when we remember that the Greek word for "Lord" was used in the Septuagint (Greek Old Testament) to translate Jehovah (Yahweh). So the combination here is a strong assertion of the deity of Jesus. Three days before this Saul would have wanted to kill Ananias for using such a blasphemous expression! Now he heard it gladly, for Jesus had become his Lord also.

It was Jesus who appeared to Saul on the road to Damascus. Now He had sent Ananias for the follow-up, to give Saul his sight again, and to be the human instrument in Saul's being filled with the Holy Spirit (cf. 8:17). This would help to tie Saul into the Christian community.

Immediately flakes or a scaly substance fell from Saul's eyes, and he could see again. He got to his feet and Ananias baptized him as a new member of the Christian church.

III. SAUL PREACHING: Acts 9:19-22

A. Christ the Son of God: vv. 19-20

For the first time in three days, Saul ate—"meat" in the King James Version simply means "food"—and was "strengthened." Anyone who has fasted for three days knows how weak one feels at the end of that time.

A new Saul entered a new fellowship: "with the disciples who were at Damascus." He also entered a new occupation: "Straightway he preached Christ in the synagogues, that he is the Son of God." These were the very synagogues to which Saul had planned to come with letters from the high priest authorizing him to arrest Christians and take them in chains to Jerusalem to be punished. Now he is in these same synagogues seeking to make converts to Christianity!

Some have wondered how verse 20 can be harmonized with Paul's statement in Galatians 1:17 that after his conversion he went into Arabia and then returned to Damascus. But there is no conflict here. It would be perfectly natural for Saul to start preaching "straightway" and then to feel the need for more meditation and a "thinking through" of his new Christian theology.

The basic doctrine in Christianity that the Jews have always objected to, right down to the present, is the deity of Jesus. But this was the central emphasis of Saul's preaching after his conversion. For him it was a complete reversal of thinking.

B. Persecutor Becomes Preacher: vv. 21-22

Those who heard Saul preach "were amazed"—literally, "stood out of themselves" in astonishment—and inquired as to whether this was not the same man who had ravaged the church in Jerusalem. The distinctively Jewish reference to those "who call on this name" (of Jesus) is found here and in verse 14. To the Jews, worshiping Jesus was blasphemy.

In spite of the skeptical attitude of many of his hearers, "Saul increased the more in strength, and confounded the Jews which dwelt at Damascus, proving that this is very Christ" (v. 22). The main message that the Jews needed to hear was an exegesis that proved from their own Scriptures that Jesus was the Messiah ("Christ"). Until the Jews accept Jesus as their Messiah and the Son of God, they cannot receive Him as their Savior. This intermediate step, which the Gentile listeners do not need to take, is the great stumbling block in Jewish evangelism.

IV. SAUL PERSECUTED:
Acts 9:23-25

A. The Preacher Persecuted: vv. 23-24

It is not surprising that the Jewish listeners to such preaching soon had enough of it. They now "took counsel to kill him." To make sure that Saul didn't flee from the city they "watched the gates day and night to kill him." Alerted to this, Saul stayed out of sight.

B. Rescued by the Disciples: v. 25

Finally it was clear that it was not safe for Saul to stay any longer in Damascus. He was apt to be assassinated any time. So "the disciples took

---

DISCUSSION QUESTIONS

1. What did Ananias actually contribute to Saul?
2. What was Barnabas's contribution?
3. What happens to people who are not accepted?
4. How can we show our acceptance?
5. How can we be like Barnabas?
6. How can our local church have a more redemptive role?

---

him by night and let him down by the wall in a basket." In II Corinthians 11:33 Paul writes: "And through a window in a basket was I let down by [rather, "through"] the wall." Today near the East Gate at the end of Straight Street in Damascus one can see houses built in the outside wall of the city, with windows through which one could be lowered by a rope to the ground. So both these accounts agree with the conditions.

V. SAUL AND BARNABAS:
Acts 9:26-28

When Saul escaped safely from Damascus, he made his way back to Jerusalem. Instead of reporting to the high priest with a string of Christian prisoners, Saul tried "to join himself to the disciples." To his consternation, "they were all afraid of him." They thought he was a wolf in sheep's clothing, ready to scatter the flock again. They couldn't believe that he had been converted, he had been such a fanatical persecutor.

Then it was that Barnabas came to his rescue. This is the same Barnabas, "son of consolation," that we met back in 4:36-37. There he appears as a man who was dedicated and generous. Here he appears further as large-hearted and kind. He took Paul and brought him to the apostles, the leaders of the church. He told them how Saul had met Jesus on the road, and that the young convert had been preaching boldly at Damascus "in the name of Jesus" (v. 27). How Barnabas had learned all this, we don't know. More difficult to understand is why the apostles at Jerusalem had not heard of Saul's conversion three years earlier (cf. Galatians 1:18). Evidently communications between believers in Damascus and Jerusalem were not very good.

The result of Barnabas' sponsorship was that Saul was able to mingle freely with the disciples at Jerusalem (v. 28). Barnabas had saved Saul from rejection and whatever consequences might have followed. One trembles to think what might have happened if Barnabas had not lived up to his name and functioned lovingly and effectively in this supportive role.

VI. SAUL IN JERUSALEM: Acts 9:29-31

A. Persecuted by Hellenists: v. 29

Saul was strong-willed and vigorous. It was impossible for him to be passive and placid. So here in Jerusalem, the hot-spot of persecution, he spoke "boldly in the name of the Lord Jesus, and disputed against the Grecians" (the Hellenists who had opposed and killed Stephen). The predictable result was that "they went about to slay him." This must have brought to Saul's mind sad memories of his own crusades in earlier days in this same city.

B. Sent Home: vv. 30-31

Poor Saul! It seemed that wherever he went he got into trouble. Now his life was in danger. His vigorous preaching was probably also threatening to bring more severe persecution to the already scattered church in Jerusalem. So "the brethren" brought him down to the seaport, Caesarea, and shipped him home to Tarsus. We can be pretty sure they bought him a one-way ticket!

The result of Saul's departure was that the churches "throughout all Judea and Galilee and Samaria"—Palestine proper—had rest. There was no rest when Paul was around! But perhaps it was the wise thing at this stage to give the churches of that area a little respite from persecution, and a chance to grow. We are told that they were "edified ["built up"] and walking in the fear of the Lord, and in the comfort of the Holy Spirit, were multiplied." The work prospered with God's blessing when everyone was in his proper place. Meanwhile, Saul was evangelizing his home province of Syria and Cilicia (Galatians 1:21).

CONTEMPORARY APPLICATION

In this lesson we see the importance of serving in supportive roles. Suppose Ananias and Barnabas had not helped young Saul at crucial points in his life, what would the story have been? One trembles to think about it. But they did *not* fail Saul, and we must not fail those who need us.

THE COVENANT
AND THE RESURRECTION

EASTER

DEVOTIONAL R ADING	Luke 24:1-7

ADULTS

Topic: *The Covenant and the Resurrection*

Background Scripture: Genesis 12:1-3; Deuteronomy 26: 5-9; Joshua 24:1-28; Acts 11:19-26; 13—14

Scripture Lesson: Acts 13:16-23, 26-31

Memory Verse: *We bring you the good news that what God promised to the fathers, this he has fulfilled to us their children by raising Jesus.* Acts 13:32-33

YOUTH

Topic: *The Covenant and the Resurrection*

Background Scripture: Genesis 12:1-3; Deuteronomy 26: 5-9: Joshua 24:1-28; Acts 11:19-26; 13—14

Scripture Lesson: Acts 13:16-23, 26-31

Memory Verse: *We bring you the good news that what God promised to the fathers, this he has fulfilled to us their children by raising Jesus.* Acts 13:32-33

CHILDREN

Topic: *God Keeps His Promises*

Background Scripture: Acts 11:19-26; 13:1-4, 21

Scripture Lesson: Acts 13:26-33

Memory Verse: *We bring you good news that what God promised . . . he has fulfilled . . . by raising Jesus.* Acts 13:32-33

DAILY BIBLE READINGS

Mon., Apr. 8: Good News for All Men, Acts 11:19-26.
Tues., Apr. 9: A Savior from the Chosen People, Acts 13:16-23.
Wed., Apr. 10: The Savior Rejected and Killed, Acts 13:24-29.
Thurs., Apr. 11: Forgiveness Through the Risen Savior, Acts 13:30-39.
Fri., Apr. 12: Christ Is Victor over Death, I Corinthians 15:20-28.
Sat., Apr. 13: The Prophecies Fulfilled in Christ, Luke 24:13-27.
Sun., Apr. 14: Christ Is Risen, Luke 24:1-9.

LESSON AIM

To show how God always keeps His promises and fulfills the covenant He has made with His people.

LESSON SETTING

Time: The covenant with Abraham was made about two thousand years before Christ. The events in Deuteronomy and Joshua occurred around 1400 B.C. The probable date of the beginning of Paul's first missionary journey (Acts 13) is A.D. 47.

The Covenant and the Resurrection

LESSON OUTLINE

I. Christians at Antioch: Acts 11:19-26
   A. Preaching to Gentiles: vv. 19-21
   B. Investigation by Barnabas: vv. 22-24
   C. Barnabas and Saul: vv. 25-26

II. Inauguration of Foreign Missions: Acts 13:1-3

III. Ministry on Cyprus: Acts 13:4-13
   A. At Salamis: vv. 4-5
   B. At Paphos: vv. 6-13

IV. Ministry in Pisidian Antioch: Acts 13:14-52
   A. Reception in Synagogue: vv. 14-15
   B. Paul's Sermon: vv. 16-41
   C. Response to the Message: vv. 42-43
   D. Reaction of the Jews: vv. 44-47
   E. Expulsion of Missionaries: vv. 48-52

V. Ministry in Iconium: Acts 14:1-7
   A. Preaching of the Apostles: vv. 1-3
   B. Persecution by the Jews: vv. 4-7

VI. Ministry in Lystra: Acts 14:8-20
   A. Healing a Cripple: vv. 8-10
   B. Hailed as Gods: vv. 11-18
   C. Stoned by the People: vv. 19-20

VII. Confirming the Congregations: Acts 14:21-28

SUGGESTED INTRODUCTION FOR ADULTS

From the beginning of human history God has been making covenants with His people. Adam broke his covenant with God by disobedience. After the Flood, the Lord made a covenant with Noah that the earth would not again be destroyed by a deluge (Genesis 9:8-17).

But it is with Abraham that we have the beginnings of the covenant people. The Lord told Abraham to leave his country and kindred, and go to a land that He would show him. If Abraham obeyed, God said He would "make of thee a great nation, and I will bless thee, and make thy name great and thou shalt be a blessing . . . and in thee shall all the families of the earth be blessed" (Genesis 12:1-3). This last sweeping promise has, of course, been fulfilled in Christ.

The next great covenant was at Sinai, after the Israelites had been delivered from slavery in Egypt. The Lord instructed Moses to tell the people: "Now therefore if ye will obey my voice indeed, and keep my covenant, then ye shall be a peculiar treasure unto me above all people . . . and ye shall be unto me a kingdom of priests, and a holy nation" (Exodus 19:5-6). The last clause is applied to Christians in I Peter 2:9. God's obedient people are his "precious treasure." (The word translated "peculiar" in the King James Version should be translated "precious.")

The lesson passage in Deuteronomy 26:5-9 stresses the fact that God had brought the Israelites out of Egypt and into a land flowing with milk and honey. This was in fulfillment of God's promise to Moses: "And I am come down to deliver them out of the hand of the Egyptians, and to bring them up out of that land unto a good land and large, unto a land flowing with milk and honey" (Exodus 3:8). This was the Promised Land, the land that God had promised to Abraham and his descendants forever: "For all the land which thou seest, to thee will I give it, and to thy seed forever" (Genesis 13:15).

The promise to Abraham that the land of Canaan would belong to his "seed" was first given to him at Shechem (Genesis 12:7). It was there that Joshua gathered the people of Israel after the conquest of Canaan (Joshua 24:1). There he challenged them to serve the Lord (vv. 14-15). We read further: "So Joshua made a covenant with the people that day, and set them a statute and an ordinance in Shechem" (v. 25).

All these Old Testament covenants find their fulfillment in Christ—partially at His first coming, and fully at His second coming. We may rejoice that we are heirs of these God-given covenants.

SUGGESTED INTRODUCTION FOR YOUTH

Our memory verse for today tells us that "what God promised to the fathers, this he has fulfilled to us their children by raising Jesus." The resurrection of Jesus is God's guarantee to us that all His covenant promises will be fulfilled, for they can only be fulfilled to us in the risen, living Lord. When we are "in Christ" we are in the covenant, and all its gracious provisions are ours. The only responsibility we have is to see that we are continually and fully *in Christ*.

CONCEPTS FOR CHILDREN

1. Jesus' resurrection is the good news that God's promises have been kept.
2. This good news gave new life to the early church.
3. It also gives life to the church today.
4. We do not worship a crucifix; we worship a risen, living Christ.

THE LESSON COMMENTARY

I. CHRISTIANS AT ANTIOCH:
Acts 11:19-26

A. Preaching to Gentiles: vv. 19-21

Verse 19 begins with exactly the same words in the Greek as 8:4: "Therefore they that were scattered abroad." So here, after considerable intervening material, we follow again the progress of "the laymen's missionary movement."

Some of those who had to flee from Jerusalem to escape Saul's violent persecution went to Phoenicia (on the coast north of Palestine), Cyprus (a large island in the eastern Mediterranean), and Antioch (far north in Syria, near the coast). These lay preachers were "speaking the Word" (literal Greek) to the Jews only.

However, some of these lay missionaries had originally come from Cyrene in North Africa and from the Island of Cyprus. Having been brought up in a Hellenistic culture, they felt more free than the Jerusalem Jews. So when some of these came to Antioch, they began to speak to the Greeks, "preaching the Lord Jesus" (v. 20). This was one of those vital steps taken in this period of transition of the gospel from the Jewish people to the Gentile world.

In doing this they were obeying Christ's instruction in Matthew 28:19 and Acts 1:8. Since all the original leaders in the church were Jews, the new movement was a little slow in launching its Gentile mission. But when they branched out, God blessed them. We read: "And the hand of the Lord was with them: and a great number believed, and turned to the Lord" (v. 21). God prospers those who obey Him.

B. Investigation by Barnabas: vv. 22-24

When the church at Jerusalem heard about all this, there were probably mixed reactions. Some may have wondered it things were "getting out of hand" in Antioch. In any case, Barnabas was sent to check up on the situation.

It was a most fortunate choice. This "son of consolation" was a man with a large heart. When he saw the many new Gentile converts and recognized the grace of God among them, he "was glad, and exhorted them all, that with purpose of heart they would cleave to the Lord" (v. 23). We are told that the reason Barnabas showed such a beautiful spirit was that he was "a good man, and full of the Holy Spirit and of faith" (v. 24). The result was that "much people was added to the Lord." Instead of criticizing the work, Barnabas encouraged it. (His name may also be translated "son of encouragement.")

C. Barnabas and Saul: vv. 25-26

Barnabas was one of those rare persons who recognize that they have a job that is too big for them and so enlist the help of someone with greater talent and ability. It takes real humility to do this, but as a Spirit-filled man Barnabas had this. He realized that the growing Gentile work at Antioch needed a man with a Hellenistic background and yet a thorough training in the Scriptures.

Fortunately Barnabas knew a man who could exactly meet these requirements. So he went to Tarsus, "to seek Saul" (v. 25). This implies that Saul was not sitting at home, "sucking his thumb," or sulking because the Jerusalem church had sent him home to Tarsus. Instead he was busy evangelizing his home province of Syria and Cilicia (Galatians 1:21). But finally Barnabas located him and brought him to Antioch. There the two men carried on a very profitable partnership in the ministry in this metropolitan area, the third largest city in the Roman Empire (after Rome and Alexandria).

One of the most interesting statements in this chapter is found at the end of verse 26: "And the disciples were called Christians first in Antioch." Hitherto they had been known as "believers," "saints," "brethren," and the like. Here for the first time they are identified as followers of Christ. The term "Christian" occurs only three times in the entire New Testament (here; 26:28; I Peter 4:16). It quite obviously was a name given by outsiders. Up to this point the new movement had been considered another sect within Judaism (28:22). In fact, Paul was called by the Jews "a ringleader of the sect of the Nazarenes" (24:5).

But in Antioch the situation was different. It appears that most of the converts there were Gentiles and probably had no contact with the Jewish synagogue. The community of believers had become so large that there had to be some way of referring to its members. So they were called "Christians" because they claimed Christ as their leader. The name may have been given in derision, but not necessarily so. There is no evidence that the name became a common designation for believers until near the end of the first century.

II. INAUGURATION OF FOREIGN MISSIONS:
Acts 13:1-3

The great world missionary enterprise began in a prayer meeting, as has almost every important kingdom development since. We are told that in the church at Antioch there were five men who were "prophets" (preachers) or "teachers." Barnabas and Saul are listed among them. As they waited on the Lord in fasting and prayer, the Holy Spirit said to them: "Separate for me Barnabas and Saul for the work to which I have called them" (v. 2).

A further time of fasting and prayer was held—possibly by the whole church. Then "they"—the other apostles?—laid their hands on them and sent them away (v. 3). But the first clause of verse 4 says: "they,

being sent out by the Holy Spirit." This is the ideal combination. They were called and sent by the Spirit. But the church—or at least its leaders—recognized this call, ordained the two missionaries to this special task, and sent them on their way. This is God's plan.

III. MINISTRY ON CYPRUS:
Acts 13:4-13

A. At Salamis: vv. 4-5

The missionaries probably walked the fifteen miles to Seleucia, which was the seaport for Antioch. From there they sailed about a hundred miles to Cyprus, an island about 150 miles long by 40 miles wide. It was noted for its production of copper, which gave it its name.

They landed at Salamis, on the east end of the island. There they "preached the word of God in the synagogues of the Jews" (v. 5). The fact that there was here more than one synagogue shows that there was a large Jewish colony in this chief city of the island.

We are told at this point that "they had also John to their minister." The last word can be misleading, as "minister" now usually designates a preacher. The Greek word means "servant" or "attendant." John was not the one who did the preaching. Rather, he took care of the material needs of the two missionaries. This "John" is John Mark, the writer of the Second Gospel. Both Paul and Peter refer to him in their Epistles as "Mark." John was his Jewish name, Mark (Marcus) his Roman name.

B. At Paphos: vv. 6-13

Sir William Ramsay notes that the Greek verb translated "gone through" (v. 6) was "the technical term for making a missionary progress through a district" (*St. Paul the Traveller*, p. 384). Luke's use of this word would suggest that he means that they evangelized their way across "the whole island"—as the Greek says. Ramsay goes so far as to say: "The word 'whole' is probably intended to bring out clearly that they made a complete tour of the Jewish communities in the island, preaching in each synagogue" (p. 73).

At the west end of the island they came to Paphos, the new Roman capital. There they found "a certain sorcerer [or "magician"] a false prophet, a Jew, whose name was Bar-jesus." (It will be remembered that the prefix *bar* means "son of.") It is a bit shocking to read of Jewish magicians such as this man and Simon Magus (8:9) going around deceiving the people.

The "deputy"—rather, "proconsul," the governor of a senatorial province—was a man names Sergius Paulus. He called for Barnabas and Saul "and desired to hear the word of God" (v. 7). But "Elymas the sorcerer" (magician)—another name for Bar-jesus—opposed the preaching of the missionaries.

The phrase "then Saul (who is also called Paul)" introduces us to an interesting transition in Paul's life. His father had given the baby boy a good Jewish name, "Saul," but, being a Roman citizen (22:27-28), had also given him a Roman name, "Paul" (Paulus). Up to this time Paul had worked mostly among Jews, so he went by his Jewish name. But now he was launching out on his mission to the Gentiles. His meeting with Sergius Paulus was an appropriate moment for him to use his Roman name, the same name the proconsul bore. This is the first time he is called "Paul" in Acts, but after this the name occurs 132 times in this Book (plus 30 times in the Epistles).

Another change also took place. Up to this point it has been "Barnabas and Saul." Hereafter it is almost always "Paul and Barnabas." He became the natural leader of the party (cf. "Paul and his company," v. 13).

Paul predicted that the false magician would become blind, which happened immediately (vv. 9-11). The result of this divine judgment was that

the proconsul became a believer (v. 12).

Leaving Paphos, the missionary party sailed about 170 miles to Perga in Pamphylia (v. 13), on the mainland of Asia Minor. Here John Mark left to go back home to Jerusalem. He was a young man and may have become homesick. Or he may have been unhappy about the fact that Paul had become the leader of the party. John Mark was a cousin of Barnabas—in Colossians 4:10 "sister's son" should be "cousin"—and he may have thought his relative should continue to have first place. A third possible motive may have been that he disagreed with the idea of going up over the mountains to the central plateau of Asia Minor. Whatever the reason, he went home.

IV. MINISTRY IN PISIDIAN ANTIOCH:
Acts 13:14-52

A. Reception in Synagogue: vv. 14-15

Paul and Barnabas left Perga and went up over the mountains to "Pisidian Antioch." This is the correct reading, rather than "Antioch in Pisidia," for Antioch was in Phrygia at this time, not Pisidia. The oldest Greek manuscripts all have "Pisidian Antioch"; that is, the Antioch near Pisidia, to distinguish it from Syrian Antioch—the home base for Paul's missionary journeys.

The reason for going up into the mountains was probably that Paul was suffering from an attack of chronic malaria and had to get away from the swampy lowlands of Pamphylia on the coast. Pisidian Antioch was at an elevation of thirty-six hundred feet. Later Paul wrote to the churches of that area. "You know that it was on account of [not "through"] a weakness of the flesh that I preached the gospel to you at the first" (Galatians 4:13).

As was their custom, the missionaries on the Sabbath day went into the synagogue and sat down. The most important part of every Sabbath service was "the reading of the law and the prophets" (our Old Testament). Then the rulers of the synagogue invited these strangers to speak. This was customary at that time.

B. Paul's Sermon: vv. 16-41

Paul "stood up." The Jewish custom, followed by Jesus (Luke 4:16-21), was to stand while reading the Scripture and then sit down to preach. But Paul, in this Gentile city, followed the Greek custom of standing while speaking, as we do today.

Paul had probably been impressed by Stephen's sermon (7:2-53), which was a digest of God's dealings with His people; he adopted the same pattern here. He started with the exodus from Egypt (v. 17), and then went on to talk about the wandering in the wilderness (v. 18), the conquest of Canaan (v. 19), the period of the Judges (v. 20), the reign of Saul (v.21), and the reign of David (v. 22). He devoted the central part of his sermon to Jesus: His life (vv. 23-26), His death (vv. 27-28), His burial (v. 29), and His resurrection (vv. 30-37). (Again it will be seen that the Resurrection received the dominant place in apostolic preaching.) He ended his sermon (vv. 38-41) by talking about the salvation which Jesus provides.

Today's lesson consists of the introductory historical background (vv. 16-23) and the central emphasis on Jesus (vv. 26-31). We shall concentrate on these two passages.

The Exodus (v. 17) marked the beginning of Israel's history as a nation. God "exalted the people" from slavery to national status. The Israelites always looked back to the Exodus as God's great redemptive act of delivering them from Egyptian bondage and choosing them to be His people. It was the focal point in all their history.

Paul passes quickly over the unhappy period of forty years' wandering in the wilderness (v. 18) when Moses was their leader. (Some Greek manuscripts have a verb meaning "endured"—"suffered he their manners" [KJV]—while others have a verb that means "nourished." This accounts for differences in translation of this verse in modern versions.) He next speaks of the time of Joshua (v 19), who led the people in the conquest of Canaan (Joshua 1—12) and in the division of the land among the tribes (Joshua 13—24). The "seven nations in the land of Canaan" are listed in Deuteronomy 7:1.

Paul devoted just one sentence to the period of the Judges (v. 20). But we run into a problem here. The King James Version says that God "gave unto them judges about the space of four hundred and fifty years." This conflicts with the statement in I Kings 6:1 that the fourth year of Solomon, when he began to build the Temple, was 480 years after the Exodus. Fortunately, the problem is in the King James Version, not the Greek text. All the best Greek manuscripts place the "four hundred and fifty years" with verse 19, not verse 20. This period would then include the 400 years' sojourn in Egypt, the 40 years of wandering in the wilderness, and about 10 years spent in the conquest of Canaan. This is best expressed by The New International Bible: "All this took about 450 years."

Samuel (v. 20) was the last of the judges and the first of a long succession of prophets. That is why he is called here "Samuel the prophet." The people wanted a king (v. 21), so Samuel anointed Saul, of the tribe of Benjamin, as their first king. He ruled for about forty years.

Saul sinned, so God "removed him" (v. 22). The point Paul is making is that God's choices are conditioned on man's obedience. God chose Saul as the first king of Israel. But when he disobeyed, God removed him. The same thing happened to Israel—they were "removed" by the Babylonian captivity. Paul was sounding a note of warning. The Jews' rejection of Jesus resulted in the destruction of Jerusalem in A.D. 70.

In Saul's place God "raised up" David (v. 22). Of him He said, "I have found David the son of Jesse, a man after my own heart, who will fulfill all my will." Interestingly, this brief quotation is in three parts, taken from three places in the Old Testament (Psalm 89:20; I Samuel 13:14; Isaiah 44:28).

From David's "seed" God has "according to his promise raised unto Israel a Saviour, Jesus" (v. 23). This is the heart of Paul's message. As "the Son of David," Jesus is the rightful King of Israel. But more importantly He is the Savior of the world.

Skipping over the brief reference to John the Baptist's ministry (vv. 24-25), we now come to the second part of this lesson (vv. 26-31). Paul addressed himself to the two groups in his audience. It was composed mainly of Jews—"children of the stock of Abraham." But there were also present many Gentile worshipers in the synagogue—"whosoever among you feareth God." To both of them "is the word of this salvation sent," the salvation that Jesus had now provided.

Because the people at Jerusalem (v. 27), and especially their leaders, did not recognize Jesus and did not understand the message of the prophets read every Sabbath day in the synagogues, they had fulfilled these very prophecies in condemning Christ. Though they found in Him no cause for the death penalty, yet they had demanded that Pilate have Him executed.

When they had "fulfilled all that was written of him"— (v. 29) as the Gospels point out—they took Him down from the cross and buried Him in a tomb. Paul is emphasizing the fulfillment of Scripture in the life and death of Jesus. The Jews should therefore accept Him as their promised Messiah.

But Jesus' death and burial did not end His life, for "God raised him from the dead" (v. 30). This is the central emphasis of the apostolic preaching. It was Christ's resurrection that validated His sacrifice for our sins and assures us of our justification before God (Romans 4:25).

How do we know that Jesus actually rose from the dead? Because He was seen "many days" (v. 31)— actually forty days—by those who had come up with Him from Galilee to Jerusalem. They were reliable witnesses to the reality of the Resurrection.

The memory verse for today climaxes this thought: "We bring you the good news that what God promised to the fathers, this he has fulfilled to us their children by raising Jesus" (vv. 32-33, RSV). Then Paul quoted from three Old Testament passages—Psalm 2:7 in verse 33, Isaiah 55:3 in verse 34, and Psalm 16:10 in verse 35. He showed that these prophecies were not fulfilled in David, but in Christ. David's body did decay. But Jesus' body was raised from the dead before decay had set in.

The next two verses (38-39) present the offer of salvation to the Jews: "through this man is preached unto you the forgiveness of sins; and by him all that believe are justified from all things, from which you could not be justified by the law of Moses." This was the essential message that Paul wanted to get across to his hearers.

The conclusion of the sermon (vv. 40-41) is a warning to the Jews not to reject this salvation. If they did, the fate predicted in Habakkuk 1:5 would overtake them. And it did, in A.D. 70, when Jerusalem was destroyed by the Romans. This was only about twenty years after Paul sounded this warning in A.D. 47 or 48.

C. Response to the Message: vv. 42-43

When the Jews left the synagogue, the Gentiles begged the missionaries to tell them more of this on the next Sabbath. Also many of the Jews and "religious proselytes" followed Paul and Barnabas, receiving further encouragement from these messengers.

D. Reaction of the Jews: vv. 44-47

What had happened in the synagogue was the talk of the town during the ensuing week. The result was that on the next Sabbath day "almost the whole city" gathered "to hear the word of God." This made the Jews jealous—as had happened in other places (cf. 5:17). So they raised public objection to what Paul was saying, "contradicting and blaspheming." They were so enraged that they went to extremes in their opposition, probably blaspheming the name of Jesus.

The two missionaries thereupon made an important announcement. It was necessary that the gospel should first be preached to the Jews. But "since you put it from you and do not judge yourselves worthy of eternal life, we now turn to the Gentiles" (v. 46). The messengers found support for this decision in Isaiah 49:6: "I have set you as a light for the Gentiles."

E. Expulsion of the Missionaries: vv. 48-52

Naturally the Gentiles were very happy to hear that they were to be the recipients of salvation through Christ, and "as many as were ordained to eternal life believed" (v. 48). Adam Clarke suggests that this means those who had

---

"the disposition or readiness of mind" to accept the message.

The "word of the Lord" spread throughout that area. But this very success provoked opposition. The Jews "stirred up the devout and honorable women, and the chief men of the city, and raised persecution against Paul and Barnabas, and expelled them from their borders" (v. 50). The missionaries "shook off the dust of their feet" as a sign of God's rejection (cf. Matthew 10:14) and walked the sixty miles to Iconium. The chapter ends on a note of triumph: "And the disciples were filled with joy, and with the Holy Spirit"—the former because of the latter.

V. MINISTRY IN ICONIUM: Acts 14:1-7

A. Preaching of the Apostles: v. 1-3

As always where there was a synagogue, the missionaries began there, sure of having an audience. We read that they "so spake that a great multitude both of the Jews and also of the Greeks believed" (v. 1). In spite of the opposition of "unbelieving Jews," who "stirred up the Gentiles" against the apostles (v. 2), the Word of God prospered, accompanied by attesting miracles (v. 3).

B. Persecution by the Jews: vv. 4-7

As before, the apostles' success brought about their persecution. And as almost always happens when the gospel is preached, there was a division: "part held with the Jews, and part with the apostles" (v. 4). Finally things became violent. The Jewish leaders assaulted the missionaries, insulted them, and tried to stone them (v. 5). So the Lord's messengers moved on to Lystra and preached the gospel there. Persecution only pushed the work into new areas.

DISCUSSION QUESTIONS

1. What is the importance of Christ's resurrection?
2. How is Easter related to our worship on Sunday?
3. What covenant does God make with us in Christ?
4. What were the main emphases of Paul's preaching?
5. What part does prayer have in world missions?
6. How can we share in the great missionary enterprise?

VI. MINISTRY IN LYSTRA:
Acts 14:8-20

A. Healing a Cripple: vv. 8-10

At Lystra there was a man who was "impotent"—literally "power-less"— n his feet. He had never walked. Paul looked intently at him and saw that he had faith to be healed, so he said to him in a strong voice: "Stand up on our feet!" (v. 10). Immediately the man leaped to his feet and began walking.

B. Hailed as Gods: vv. 11-18

When the people saw this miracle, they decided that these two strangers in their midst must be divine beings. Because Barnabas was the larger man, they called him "Jupiter" (Latin for the Greek "Zeus"). Because Paul was the chief spokesman, they called him "Mercury" (Latin for the Greek "Hermes"). In Oriental cultures, the one who does the talking is the subordinate, acting for his superior.

As soon as Paul and Barnabas discovered that the people planned to worship them as gods, they protested and put a stop to it (vv. 13-18). They told them in Greek—which the people understood, though when excited they jabbered in Lycaonian (v. 11)—that they were mere men and wanted them to "turn away from these vanities [idols] to the living God" (v. 15).

C. Stoned by the People: vv. 19-20

Not content with having driven the missionaries out of their cities, Jews from Antioch (100 miles away) and Iconium (40 miles) walked those long distances to Lystra. There they "persuaded the people, and, having stoned Paul, drew him out of the city, supposing he had been dead" (v. 19). This is a good example of the fickleness of people. One day they wanted to worship these messengers as gods; a few days later they stoned one of them. But Paul revived and left town (v. 20).

VII. CONFIRMING THE CONGREGATIONS:
Acts 14:21-28

These missionaries were not satisfied simply to evangelize and win converts. They were concerned about the follow-up, the shepherding of these new lambs in Christ. So they returned through Lystra, Iconium, and Antioch—risking their lives to do so—"confirming the souls of the disciples" and organizing the churches by appointing elders in every congregation (vv. 22-23). Then they returned to Antioch to report (vv. 26-28).

CONTEMPORARY APPLICATION

In this day of death and violence, the message of Christ's resurrection needs to be sounded again. In spite of death, life can come—but only in Christ! He is alive today, and He is here! If people will turn to Him, they will find that all the covenant promises of God's Word will be fulfilled in their lives. This is the good news of Easter, and we should share it with them.

THE SPIRIT TRANSCENDS INSTITUTIONS

DEVOTIONAL READING	Romans 8:35-39

ADULTS	Topic: *The Spirit Transcends Institutions* Background Scripture: Acts 11:1-18; 15:1-35 Scripture Lesson: Acts 15:1-12 Memory Verse: *He is our peace, who has made us both one, and has broken down the dividing wall of hostility.* Ephesians 2:14

YOUTH	Topic: *When to Change Your Mind* Background Scripture: Acts 11:1-18; 15:1-35 Scripture Lesson: Acts 15:1-12 Memory Verse: *He is our peace, who has made us both one and has broken down the dividing wall of hostility.* Ephesians 2:14

CHILDREN	Topic: *The Spirit Guides Us* Background Scripture: Acts 11:1-18; 15:1-35 Scripture Lesson: Acts 15:1-10 Memory Verse: *When the spirit of truth comes he will guide you into all truth.* John 16:13

DAILY BIBLE READINGS	Mon., Apr. 15: Peter's Vision in Joppa, Acts 11:1-10. Tues., Apr. 16: The Spirit Comes to Cornelius, Acts 11:11-18. Wed., Apr. 17: Saved by Law or Grace? Acts 15:1-11. Thurs., Apr. 18: God Has Visited the Gentiles, Acts 15:12-21. Fri., Apr. 19: A Letter to Gentile Christians, Acts 15:22-29. Sat., Apr. 20: A Happy Outcome, Acts 15:30-35. Sun., Apr. 21: "More Than Conquerors," Romans 8:31-39.

LESSON AIM	To see the supreme importance of following the leadership of the Holy Spirit, especially in matters relating to the church.

LESSON SETTING	Time: The Council of Jerusalem probably took place in A.D. 48. Place: Jerusalem

276

The Spirit Transcends Institutions

LESSON OUTLINE

SUGGESTED INTRODUCTION FOR ADULTS

Legalism has been a stifling influence in the church from its earliest days. And it is still with us, continually threatening the freedom in Christ which is the rightful heritage of every Christian.

Actually, the Holy Spirit and legalism are antithetical forces. Wherever there is a gracious moving of the Spirit, as in the early church, legalists are sure to appear and voice their criticisms. Without realizing it, they assert their own authority as if it were divine authority. In so doing, they take God's place as judge. When such an attitude is analyzed carefully, it is seen to border on blasphemy.

Legalists are usually sincere in thinking they are right, and this makes them all the more dangerous, for people fear to oppose them lest they be found fighting against God.

There is an aura of righteousness about legalists that easily degenerates into self-righteousness. They usually find support for their rigorous demands in two ways. One is by taking Biblical texts out of their context and applying them as they wish. The other is by giving a very literalistic interpretation to certain Scripture passages, rather than seeing the spiritual principles that are being enunciated.

SUGGESTED INTRODUCTION FOR YOUTH

The old adage says: "Wise men seldom change their minds, but fools never." But when should a person change his mind?

We need to distinguish—if we can!—between conviction and opinions. Convictions come from God, through the Holy Spirit. Opinions come from our own minds, or from other human sources. But people often become confused as to which is what.

When we refuse to change our opinions, we are stubborn. And when we demand that others shall govern their lives by our opinions, we are dogmatic legalists.

Flexibility in thinking, without any compromise of basic convictions, is what we should all desire. This means that we are willing to listen to the other person, and perhaps learn from him. But it also means that we do not lower our moral standards, no matter what happens. Above all, our discussion of differences should be dominated by love. And we should always keep our hearts and minds open for the Holy Spirit to lead us in new paths.

CONCEPTS FOR CHILDREN

1. The Holy Spirit comes into our hearts to be our Guide.
2. We should ask Him to show us how to live.
3. We should seek His help in showing the right spirit toward others.
4. We should pray for His presence when we meet together.

THE LESSON COMMENTARY

I. PETER'S DEFENSE AT JERUSALEM:
Acts 11:1-18

A. Criticism by Judaizers: vv. 1-3

The background of chapter 11 is chapter 10. There we read that in Caesarea—a seaport city built by Herod the Great and later the Roman capital of Judea—there was a centurion named Cornelius. As the word indicates, a "centurion" was an officer in charge of a hundred soldiers. Though a Gentile, Cornelius was "a devout man, one who feared God with all his house, gave much alms to the people, and prayed to God alway" (v. 2). An angel appeared to him in a vision and told him to send to Joppa for a man called Peter; "he will tell you what you ought to do" (v. 6).

Before the messengers arrived, God had prepared Peter by giving *him* a vision. This showed him that he should not think of the Gentiles as "unclean"; God makes no such distinctions (v. 28).

So Peter had gone to Cornelius's house and preached to the group assembled there. He had ended up by having many of the Gentiles baptized, after which he stayed for some days at Cornelius's home (v. 48). All this Peter had done in good faith, under the Lord's clear leading.

Before Peter got back to Jerusalem, "the apostles and brethren throughout Judea heard that the Gentiles had also received the word of God" (11:1). Philip had preached the gospel to the Samaritans (8:5), who were part Jew and part Gentile. But Peter was apparently the first to present Christ to a purely Gentile audience, without any connection with the Jewish synagogue.

When Peter arrived in Jerusalem he was challenged by the Judaistic party in the church—"they of the circumcision" (v. 2). They said to him: "You went in to uncircumcised men and ate with them" (v. 3). Eating with Gentiles was strictly forbidden by the rabbis, for this was thought to render a person ceremonially unclean.

B. Peter's Account of What Happened: vv. 4-15

If a person knows he is right, his best defense is simply to tell the facts. That is what Peter did, and it worked. We are told specifically that he "expounded," or "exposed" the whole thing to them in order (v. 4).

He began with his vision on the housetop at Joppa, when he was praying at the noon hour. He saw what looked like a large sheet being let down by its four corners from heaven. Inside were animals, birds, and reptiles of all kinds. A voice called to him: "Arise, Peter; slay and eat" (v. 7). He immediately replied that no unclean food had ever entered his mouth (v. 8). But the voice answered: "What God has cleansed you must not call unclean" (v. 9). (In Jewish thinking "common" was used as equivalent to "unclean.") For emphasis, to make sure that Peter didn't fail to catch the point, the vision came to him three times (v. 10).

As soon as the vision ended, Peter learned that three men from Caesarea were at the door, inquiring for him. The Holy Spirit told him to go with them, "nothing doubting" (v. 11). A better translation is "making no distinction." His vision had shown him that in God's sight there was no distinction between Jews and Gentiles. So Peter, as a Jew, must never again discriminate against a Gentile.

Peter did one thing which proved to be very wise. He says, "Moreover these six brethren accompanied me." They were right there now and could vouchsafe for everything he was about to relate. This was the best protection Peter could have.

When they arrived at Cornelius's house, he greeted them gladly. He told about his vision and the instructions that he was to send to Joppa for Peter, "who shall tell thee words, whereby thou and all thy house shall be saved" (v. 14). Though Cornelius had heard about Jesus' work (10:37), it seems evident that he had not yet received the gospel message of salvation through the death and resurrection of Christ.

Then came the central fact of Peter's defense: "As I began to speak, the Holy Spirit fell on them, as on us at the beginning" (v. 15). Peter wasn't responsible for this; it was God who did it.

C. Peter's Conclusion: vv. 16-17

When he saw this happen, Peter was reminded of Jesus' words: "John indeed baptized you with water; but you will be baptized with the Holy Spirit." These words are quoted from 1:5, where Jesus said them to His disciples after His resurrection. In the Gospels the statement is attributed to John the Baptist, but Jesus repeated it Himself.

Now comes Peter's grand finale. Since God had given to the people in the house of Cornelius the same gift of the Holy Spirit as the disciples had received on the day of Pentecost, "What was I, that I could withstand God?" In other words, "I couldn't stop Him from blessing the Gentiles, could I?" It was an unanswerable question.

D. Critics Satisfied: v. 18

What *could* they say? We appreciate the fact that when the evidence was presented these Judaizers recognized its validity: "When they heard these things, they held their peace, and glorified God, saying, Then God has also to the Gentiles granted repentance unto life." It is difficult for us to place ourselves in their shoes. They had been taught that salvation was for the Jews, not the Gentiles.

II. DISSENSION CAUSED BY JUDAIZERS: Acts 15:1-5

A. Judaizers Invade Antioch: v. 1

Some men "came down" from Judea to Antioch. They went north for hundreds of miles—"up" on the map, but one always went "down" from Jerusalem to any other place.

When these men from Jerusalem arrived in Antioch they began to teach the Gentile Christians there: "Unless you become circumcised after the custom of Moses, you cannot be saved." This was shocking to hear. It was bad news, not "good news"! One can almost see the startled, puzzled looks on the faces of these joyful believers.

B. Opposed by Paul and Barnabas: v. 2

There were two men who were watching this, and taking it all in. The men in the congregation were mostly the converts of these men. The apostles had seen them come out of the darkness of paganism into the bright light of Christianity. They had witnessed the joy and peace that came with forgiveness of sins simply through believing in Jesus Christ as Savior. And now these Judaizers would place these happy Christians into bondage to the law.

Paul was not the kind of person to take a thing like this "lying down," and apparently Barnabas stood right beside him. The two men had "no small dissension and disputation" with the Judaizers. It is evident that the men from Jerusalem were stubborn in pushing their legalistic propaganda.

It seems clear also that the church stood by its two main leaders. It was finally decided to send Paul and Barnabas, and some others to Jerusalem to consult with the apostles and elders about the matter. This precipitated the Jerusalem Council of A.D. 48.

C. Emissaries Sent to Jerusalem: vv. 3-4

"Being brought on their way by the church" probably means that the congregation at Antioch paid the expenses of these representatives who were sent on this important mission. The party passed through Phoenicia (modern Lebanon, on the coast) and Samaria (central Palestine). On the way Paul and Barnabas were "de-claring the conversion of the Gentiles." They didn't have to wait until they saw the leaders at Jerusalem to find out whether or not Gentiles could be saved through faith in Jesus. They knew that already. And they kept preaching it! We admire the courage and consecration of these first two foreign missionaries.

When they reached Jerusalem they were apparently given a cordial welcome by the leaders of the church— "the apostles and elders." This was a good opportunity for Paul and Barnabas to report to the headquarters church about their first missionary journey, when they had evangelized new territory in Asia Minor and founded several good churches there. It was all what "God had done with them." They gave Him the glory.

D. Opposed by Christian Pharisees: v. 5

This report of God's marvelous working among the Gentiles ought to have caused universal rejoicing among the Christians. Unfortunately, it did not. "There rose up certain of the sect of the Pharisees who believed, saying, 'It is necessary to circumcise them and command them to keep the law of Moses.'" Maybe it was all right to preach Christ to these Gentiles but they must at once be instructed that if they were going to be God's covenant people they must be circumcised and observe all the Mosaic law! It is clear that to these Pharisaic Christians the new movement was really a sect of Judaism. Outside of Judaism there was no salvation.

What was the matter with these Jewish Christians? Didn't they know that salvation was only through Christ? It is easy for us to sit in judgment on them. But we must remember that they had been taught all their lives that the descendants of Abraham were God's chosen people. Salvation was only within the covenant. They did not yet have any New Testament to read, with its references to "the new covenant" in Christ. Deeply ingrained ideas are hard to change. We live in the light of nineteen hundred years of Christian history.

III. PETER AT THE JERUSALEM COUNCIL: Acts 15:6-12

A. No Difference Between Jews and Gentiles: vv. 6-9

It would have been too time-consuming and inefficient for the whole church to deal with the problem in a plenary session. So "the apostles and elders," the leaders of the church in Jerusalem, met together "to see about this matter." It was the greatest problem which had yet confronted the church, for it involved the whole future of Christianity, not just a temporary schism.

After much disputing, Peter got up. He would be listened to with respect, for it was he who had preached the great sermon on the day of Pentecost that resulted in three thousand souls being saved. He began by saying: "You know that in the early days God made a choice among you that through my mouth the Gentiles should hear the word of the gospel and believe." Peter was referring to the fact that he was the first one in the early church to preach the gospel to a purely Gentile audience. This took place in the house of Cornelius, as we have just noted. It seems a providential choice that Peter, who was often thought of as a leader in the Jewish sector of the church, and who was probably claimed as a supporter by the Judaizers, should be the one to introduce Christianity to the Gentiles. (This is the last time that Peter is mentioned in Acts.)

Verses 8 and 9 make a significant identification. There are many people who recognize and emphasize the need of being filled with the Spirit for victorious Christian living, but they say nothing about cleansing in connection with it. But here Peter forcefully combines the two. He declares that his listeners in the house of Cornelius were filled with the Holy Spirit, just as the original disciples were on the day of Pentecost. (Peter here says, "giving them the Holy Spirit," but in 2:4 it is "filled with the Holy Spirit.") He also says that their hearts were purified by faith. It is obvious that when one is filled with the Spirit, his heart is cleansed from sin. Power and purity go together. We cannot have one without the other. The Holy Spirit both purifies our hearts from sin and empowers us for life and service. Neither aspect should be over-emphasized to the neglect of the other.

But in relation to the dispute going on at the Council of Jerusalem, and the purpose for which it met, the important statement here is: "And put no difference between us and them" (v. 9). Peter was speaking as a Jew to his fellow Jews. He said: "In God's sight there is no difference between us Jews and those Gentiles." They were one in Christ.

It is difficult for us to realize now what a revolutionary concept this was for these Jews. They had always been taught that they were *the* people of God. The Old Testament seemed to support this. Peter himself would never have made this statement had he not had that vision on the housetop at Joppa. He had already shared that vision with the Jerusalem church, as we saw in the early part of this lesson. But now he has to make the implications crystal clear.

B. Salvation Equally for All: vv. 10-11

Peter's conclusion from all of this was forcefully stated: "Now why therefore do you put God to the test by placing on the neck of the disciples a yoke that neither our fathers nor we have been able to bear?" The yoke was a familiar figure with the Jewish rabbis. They talked about "the yoke of the Torah" (the law). By this they meant the obligation to keep the commandments.

Some have objected to Peter's description of the Mosaic law as an unbearable yoke. But Schuerer says:

"Life was a continual torment to the earnest man, who felt at every moment that he was in danger of transgressing the law; and where so much depended on the external form, he was often left in uncertainty whether he had really fulfilled its requirements" (*History of the Jewish People in the Time of Jesus Christ*, II, ii, 124).

Peter wound up with this pointed statement: "But we believe that through the grace of the Lord Jesus we shall be saved in the same way as they" (v. 11). There was not one way of salvation for Jews and another way for Gentiles. There was only one way, equally for all—"through the grace of the Lord Jesus" ("Christ" is not in the oldest Greek manuscripts).

C. Speech by Barnabas and Paul: v. 12

Peter's speech made a strong impression on his listeners, so that "all the crowd became silent," with no further opposition. The expression used here seems to suggest a larger group than just the apostles and elders, though the same phrase is used to describe the Sanhedrin in 23:7. (It had seventy-one members.) However that may be, we do find a reference to "the whole church" in verse 22. It would seem that somewhere in the prolonged discussion the apostles had called the church congregation together for a decision (cf. 6:2). Rackham says: "Though the initiative rested with the apostles, the consent of the whole church was required" (*Acts*, p. 249).

Meanwhile "Barnabas and Paul"—note the order here in a Jewish setting in Jerusalem—had shown good sense in keeping still. If they had made their report at the first, it would probably have provoked considerable reaction. But because Peter had prepared the way so beautifully for what they wanted to say, now the whole group "gave audience" in respectful silence while the two missionaries related "what signs and wonders God had done among the Gentiles through them." Here was plenty of proof that

the Lord wanted to save the Gentiles as well as the Jews. It would have taken considerable time to tell the story of the first missionary journey, but probably the session was unhurried.

IV. DECISION EXPRESSED BY JAMES: Acts 15:13-21

Finally the speeches had all been made and the arguments presented. Then James, the brother of Jesus—who was evidently head pastor of the Jewish-Christian church, and now acted as moderator of this first church council—gave the decision. He said, "Listen to me" (v. 13). Then he called attention to Peter's speech. Symeon ("Simeon") is the Septuagint form in the Old Testament (e.g., the tribe of Simeon) and is closer to the Hebrew than the more common form "Simon." It would be the natural name for Jewish Christians in Jerusalem to use in referring to Peter. James repeated the fact that God had visited the Gentiles, "to take out of them a people for his name" (v. 14). The Jews were not the only people of God. James then showed that what happened in Cornelius's house was the fulfillment of prophecy, by quoting (in vv. 16-17) from Amos 9:11-12. The heart of this Scripture was: "That the residue of men might seek after the Lord, and all the Gentiles, upon whom my name is called, saith the Lord, who doeth all these things" (v. 17).

Then the moderator expressed the decision of the meeting: "Wherefore I for my part judge that we should stop annoying those Gentiles who are turning to God" (v. 19). The Greek could mean either "I decree" or simply "I recommend." He further recommended that the church "write"— "literally, "send a message by letter" —to the Gentile Christians, putting on them only four restrictions. They were to abstain from: (1) "pollutions of idols"—the Greek says only "pollutions," but verse 29 shows that it was "food offered to idols" that is meant;

(2) "fornication," including violations of Jewish marriage laws; (3) "things strangled," reflecting the pagan custom of eating meat with the blood still in it, which was particularly obnoxious to Jews and forbidden in the Mosaic law; (4) "blood," which could mean "bloodshed," or murder. Some manuscripts (Western text) omit the third and so give just three moral prohibitions—against idolatry, immorality, and murder. Assuming that all four are genuine, we would say that James was concerned that the Gentile Christians should not unnecessarily offend their Jewish brothers.

After giving his specific recommendations, James added one note of comment: "For Moses from ancient generations has in every city those who proclaim him, being read in the synagogues every sabbath" (v. 21). There are at least three possible interpretations of this verse. One is that the Gentiles who attended the Jewish synagogues would be familiar with the Mosaic law and would not object to these four restrictions. Another is that since there were Jews everywhere, their scruples should be respected. The third, which appeals to us, is this: Moses would continue to be read in the synagogues every Sabbath, so that Jewish Christians could still hear the Law. The greater liberty given to Gentile converts would not in any way imperil the continued worship in the synagogues.

V. LETTER SENT TO GENTILE CHRISTIANS: Acts 15:22-29

"Then pleased it" is literally, "Then it seemed good." But Lake and Cadbury claim that the verb here (*edoxe*) "is the technical term in Greek of all periods for 'voting' or 'passing' a measure in the assembly." So they translate it here, "It was voted" (*Beginnings of Christianity*, IV, 178).

In any case, "the apostles and elders, with the whole church" sent two of their best men, Judas Barsabas

and Silas, along with Paul and Barnabas as these two missionaries returned to Antioch. They also sent with them a gracious letter of greeting. It was addressed to "the brethren who are of the Gentiles in Antioch, Syria and Cilicia."

The body of the letter got right down to business. The Jerusalem church had heard that some of its members had gone down to Antioch and "troubled you with words, subverting your souls" (v. 24). This is followed immediately in the Greek by a strong disclaimer: "to whom we gave no commandment." (The phrase "Ye must be circumcised, and keep the law" is not found here in the oldest manuscripts, cf. vv. 1, 5.) The word "such" in verse 24 is a good example of the King James Version inserting a word in italics that makes the statement weaker and less accurate. The Jerusalem church had given the Judaizers *no* authority.

It is refreshing to read here the gracious way the Jerusalem Jewish Christians referred to "our beloved Barnabas and Paul, men who have hazarded their lives for the name of our Lord Jesus Christ" (vv. 25-26). This further discredited the Judaizers, who were especially critical of Paul and his preaching to Gentiles.

The wording of verse 28 is significant: "For it seemed to the Holy Spirit and to us . . . ." The leaders at Jeru-

---

DISCUSSION QUESTIONS

1 How may the church find the leadership of the Spirit?
2. In what spirit should we share our disagreements?
3. Is there room for "give and take" in church discussions?
4. What should be our attitude when decisions have been made?
5. What is the danger of too much emphasis on tradition?
6. What problems face the church today?

salem had a firm conviction that the Spirit of God had led them to the decision they had made: to lay upon the Gentile converts "no greater burden than these necessary things" (v. 28)—that is, the things necessary for good fellowship between Jewish and Gentile Christians. Then the letter spelled out the "four decrees" of the Jerusalem Council (v. 29).

It would be difficult to overestimate the importance of this decision of the Council of Jerusalem. Perhaps the force of this statement can be better appreciated if we contemplate the results had a different judgment been reached. Suppose the leaders in Jerusalem had agreed with the Judaizers that all Gentile converts must be circumcised and keep the law of Moses. In that event Christianity would have been merely another sect within Judaism. It would have been strangled in the swaddling cloths of legalism. Never could it have become a world religion, marching in conquest around the globe, entering every country and culture. Judaism is tied pretty much to one people, the Jews. Christianity is for all people of the world. But it could not have fulfilled its divinely ordained function as a way of salvation for all mankind had it not broken loose from the legalistic bond-

age of Judaism. For the position of the Judaizers was in effect a denial of the central message of Christianity: salvation only through faith in Jesus Christ.

VI. CONTINUED BLESSING AT ANTIOCH: Acts 15:30-35

The four men mentioned above journeyed far north to Antioch. There they gathered the congregation together and delivered the official letter from Jerusalem. When the Antioch Christians read it, "they rejoiced for the consolation" (v. 31). There had doubtless been considerable concern and prayer about what would take place in Jerusalem. Now these Gentile converts were much relieved to find that they were not being asked to keep the Jewish law. There was nothing in the four decrees that posed any problems for them.

Judas and Silas were also preachers ("prophets"). So they "exhorted," or "encouraged," the "brethren" with many words and "strengthened" them (v. 32). Paul and Barnabas stayed in Antioch again for some time, "teaching and preaching the word of the Lord, with many others also" (v. 35). With the right decision made, the work of God prospered.

CONTEMPORARY APPLICATION

How did the early church solve this very serious problem of the agitation and unrest that was being caused by the Judaizers? Several things the church did then are very significant for us today.

First, they faced the problem, instead of ignoring it or running away from it. The Antioch church, plagued with this problem, sent representatives to "headquarters" to get a decision in the matter.

In the second place, a conference was called at which everyone was allowed to have his say. One of the quickest ways to solve problems is to

get them out in the open. Fairness in letting people express different opinions is important in human relationships.

In the third place, the church sought divine guidance. Jesus said that the Holy Spirit would guide His own into all truth. When the council was ended, its members could say, "It seemed good to the Holy Spirit and to us." This is the ideal.

Moderation prevailed over extremism. This is the great need everywhere and at all times. Extremists are the ones who create difficulties in every area of life.

A STRATEGY FOR MISSION

DEVOTIONAL READING	Psalm 51:10-17

ADULTS	Topic: *A Strategy for Mission* Background Scripture: Acts 15:36—16:40 Scripture Lesson: Acts 15:39—16:10 Memory Verse: *I heard the voice of the Lord saying, "Whom shall I send, and who will go for us?" Then I said, "Here I am! Send me."* Isaiah 6:8
YOUTH	Topic: *You're Calling Me, God?* Background Scripture: Acts 15:36—16:40 Scripture Lesson: Acts 15:39—16:10 Memory Verse: *I heard the voice of the Lord saying, "Whom shall I send, and who will go for us?" Then I said, "Here I am! Send me."* Isaiah 6:8
CHILDREN	Topic: *A Man Asks for Help* Background Scripture: Acts 15:36—16:40 Scripture Lesson: Acts 16:9-15 Memory Verse: *Through love, be servants of one another.* Galatians 5:13
DAILY BIBLE READINGS	Mon., Apr. 22: Conflict in the Fellowship, Acts 15:36-41. Tues., Apr. 23: Paul Takes Timothy with Him, Acts 16:1-5. Wed., Apr. 24: The Call of Macedonia, Acts 16:6-15. Thurs., Apr. 25: Opposition and Imprisonment, Acts 16:16-24. Fri., Apr. 26: A Jailer Hears About Jesus, Acts 16:25-34. Sat., Apr. 27: A Dignified Departure, Acts 16:35-40. Sun., Apr. 28: Prayer for Healing and Renewal, Psalm 51:10-17.
LESSON AIM	To show how the early church enlarged its missionary outreach in spite of problems and difficulties, and how we can do the same today.
LESSON SETTING	Time: Perhaps the spring of A.D. 49, after sailing on the Mediterranean had been resumed, following the winter storms Place: Antioch in Syria to Philippi in Macedonia

285

A Strategy for Mission

I. A Missionary's Concern for His Converts:
   Acts 15:36

II. Two Missionary Parties Formed: Acts 15:37-41
    A. A Sharp Disagreement: vv. 37-39
    B. Paul's New Colleague: vv. 40-41

III. Completing the Personnel: Acts 16:1-3

IV. Strengthening the New Churches: Acts 16:4-5

V. The Guidance of the Spirit: Acts 16:6-8

VI. The Call to a New Area: Acts 16:9-12
    A. Come Over into Macedonia: v. 9
    B. A New Missionary Associate: v. 10
    C. The Trip to Philippi: vv. 11-12

VII. Paul in Philippi: Acts 16:13-40
     A. The First Convert: vv. 13-15
     B. A Demon Cast Out: vv. 16-18
     C. The Missionaries Beaten and Imprisoned:
        vv. 19-24
     D. The Conversion of the Jailer: vv. 25-34
     E. The Exoneration of the Missionaries: vv. 35-40

We saw in our study of Acts 13 how the great world mission enterprise of the church began in a special time of prayer at Antioch. In our last lesson we observed how the crucial problem of the relation of Jewish and Gentile Christianity was solved satisfactorily. The result was that all the churches—Jewish and Gentile alike—were prospering.

The new movement was on the move. It had spread, as we have seen, from Jerusalem to all of Judea and then north to neighboring Samaria—the halfway house on the road to the Gentile world. It found a new home base for operations in Antioch, far north in Syria. This was a Gentile metropolis, and it became the launching pad for foreign missions. The third largest city in the Roman Empire, it had a world outlook. From here Christianity could move across Europe to Rome.

Problems always arise in the case of such rapid expansion. Many adjustments have to be made. We saw in our last lesson that the most difficult and crucial adjustment was that between Jewish and Gentile Christians, with their almost totally different backgrounds. Fortunately an amicable agreement was reached at the Council of Jerusalem (see Acts 15:1-29).

But the church had not yet faced its task of evangelizing Europe; it had gone only as far as Asia Minor. It actually took a disagreement between the two leading missionaries of the church and the consequent formation of two missionary parties to release Paul for his greatest work, the planting of the gospel seed in Macedonia and Greece. So the work went on!

SUGGESTED
INTRODUCTION
FOR YOUTH

"You're Calling Me, God?" The answer was yes for Samuel, for Saul, and now for three men in our lesson today. Because Silas was on hand at the right place and time, he became Paul's associate in the launching of the Christian crusade in Europe. Because Timothy had proved to be an earnest, conscientious young Christian, he was chosen as the attendant for these two adult missionaries. This resulted in a lifelong association with the prince of apostles, Paul, so that two letters of the New Testament are addressed to him. What honors he received because of his obedience to God's call! The third one to receive a call was Paul, who heard the cry, "Come over into Macedonia and help us." He went, and it revolutionized his life and outlook. Are you answering God's call to you?

CONCEPTS FOR
CHILDREN

1. God calls even young children for life service.
2. We should ask God what He wants us to do.
3. When the call comes we should say, as Isaiah did, "Here am I, send me."
4. God needs more helpers.

THE LESSON COMMENTARY

I. A MISSIONARY'S CONCERN FOR HIS CONVERTS:
Acts 15:36

Paul and Barnabas were busy in their home church at Antioch, "teaching and preaching the Word of the Lord" (v. 35). No doubt they were both very happy in doing this and would have enjoyed continuing there indefinitely.

But one day Paul began thinking about their new converts in the province of Galatia, as well as on the Island of Cyprus. So he said to the one who had been his colleague on that first missionary journey: "Let us go and visit our brethren in every city where we have preached the word of the Lord, and see how they do." Too often those who win people to the Lord are careless about shepherding the newborn lambs, with the result that many of those lambs die. We have already seen, in a previous lesson, how

these two missionaries retraced their steps (14:21). They had done this to strengthen their recent converts (14:22-23). Now Paul feels that it is time to go back and check up on them.

II. TWO MISSIONARY PARTIES FORMED:
Acts 15:37-41

A. A Sharp Disagreement: vv. 37-39

Barnabas "determined" to take along John Mark, who had started out with them on the first journey (13:5). Perhaps this translation is a little too strong. The best Greek text suggests "wished" or "wanted." We have already noted (lesson 7) that Barnabas was John Mark's cousin. It was only natural that he would want to take the young man again as their attendant to look after their material needs. "But

Paul thought best not to take with them one who had withdrawn from them in Pamphylia, and had not gone with them to the work" (v. 38).

The Bible is very frank in depicting the faults of its greatest characters—only Jesus Christ lived a perfect life. So here we read of the two leading missionaries of the early church—both of them Spirit-filled men—that "there arose a sharp contention, so that they parted asunder one from the other" (v. 39, ASV). The expression "sharp contention" is one word in Greek—*paroxysmos*, from which we get "paroxysm." Perhaps the English rendering is a little too strong. Arndt and Gingrich translate it "sharp disagreement." At any rate, it was a sufficient provocation to separate these two companions of many years.

It is not difficult to reconstruct the scene. Barnabas said, "Let's take John with us again." "No" said Paul, "he's a quitter, a coward."

"But he's older now, Let's give him another chance. I think he will stay with it this time."

"No, I don't want to be bothered again. Once is enough! When I look at him, all I can see is a big yellow streak. This work is too important to be hindered by someone who is not dedicated."

The discussion finally came to an impasse. Barnabas would not go without John Mark, and Paul would not go with him. So the two leaders parted company.

Which was right? We would probably have to agree that in this case Paul was wrong. He was so utterly dedicated that he simply could not understand or appreciate any lack of dedication in others. But suppose Paul and Barnabas had both rejected John Mark and left him behind. Would he have become the writer of the Second Gospel? Or would he have become discouraged and quit?

There is one thing for which we must admire Paul: he could recognize his mistakes and rectify them. Languishing in prison at Rome and facing the death which soon overtook him,

Paul wrote to Timothy: "Take Mark and bring him with you; for he is profitable to me for service" (II Timothy 4:11). The young man who had failed made good in the end.

Now let us look at the other side of the coin—the side of divine providence. Perhaps the Lord permitted this disagreement to take place in order that His purpose might be carried out. It was time for Paul to move across to Europe and establish churches there. Would Barnabas have fitted into this new situation perfectly? We know that he was more closely related to the Jewish Christians in Jerusalem than Paul was. It is true that Barnabas had come from the Island of Cyprus (4:36), and so had something of a Hellenistic outlook (cf. 11:20). But it is very doubtful if he had the broad background of Greek culture and learning that Paul had. The latter was brought up in Tarsus, third greatest intellectual center in the Roman Empire. Could Barnabas have reasoned with the Epicureans and Stoics in the Agora at Athens or have made a speech before the Areopagus? Probably not. It may well be that the Lord knew Paul needed a new associate for the European evangelism.

In any case, "Barnabas took Mark, and sailed for Cyprus" (v. 39), his old home territory and the first place he and Paul had visited on their previous trip together. Here he disappears from the scene. Tradition has it that he was persecuted and put to death on Cyprus. But he had already made a tremendous contribution to the kingdom of God, as is abundantly clear from Acts 4—15. He will always be honored as one of the greatest leaders and helpers in the early church.

B. Paul's New Colleague: vv. 40-41

Jesus had sent His apostles out two by two. The Holy Spirit had called Barnabas and Saul to go together. The divine plan is not for one missionary to go alone, but for at least two to go so that they may help and support each other. The psychology of this is sound.

So Paul had to choose a new associate. He selected Silas, who had come from Jerusalem (15:27, 32). This proved to be a very wise choice. While Silas never rose to great prominence, he was a faithful companion and co-worker. He is mentioned several times in Paul's Epistles under his Latinized name Silvanus (II Corinthians 1:19; I Thessalonians 1:1; II Thessalonians 1:1). He is also probably the Silvanus who wrote Peter's First Epistle for him (I Peter 5:12). He made a real contribution to the ongoing of the church.

We are told that when Paul and Silas left Antioch they were "recommended by the brethren unto the grace of God." Did the church take the side of Paul in his dispute with Barnabas? Perhaps so. At any rate, it is clear that the church endorsed Paul's mission. Just as Barnabas had gone to his home territory, Cyprus, so Paul headed for his native province of *Syria et Cilicia,* "confirming the churches."

III. COMPLETING THE PERSONNEL:
Acts 16:1-3

Probably Paul stopped briefly at his hometown, Tarsus. Then he went up through the Cilician Gates over the Taurus Mountains on to the high plateau of the province of Galatia. His first stop was at Derbe, the farthest point to which he and Barnabas had gone on their first journey (14:20).

It is not clear from our common English version whether Timothy lived at Lystra or Derbe. But the best Greek text says Paul came "to Derbe and to Lystra." So he found Timothy at the latter place.

Timothy's mother was a Jewess "and believed." That is, she had been converted to Christianity. His father was "a Greek," which implies that he was neither a proselyte to Judaism nor a Christian. Evidently the father was indifferent to religion and so allowed his son to have a pious upbringing by the boy's mother Eunice and his

grandmother Lois (II Timothy 1:5; 3:14, 15).

Paul addresses Timothy as "my own son in the faith" (I Timothy 1:2). This implies that the young man had been converted under Paul's ministry at Lystra as described in 14:8-19. He may very well have been among the disciples who stood around Paul as he lay apparently dead on the ground after being stoned, and who rejoiced when the apostle stood to his feet (14:20). This may help to explain Timothy's great love for his spiritual father.

This young convert was also "well reported of by the brothers at Lystra and Iconium" (v. 2). It is obvious that he had been an unusually devoted, conscientious Christian, so that the congregations in nearby cities knew about him.

Timothy was repaid for his faithfulness to the Lord by one of the highest honors he could have received—an invitation by Paul to accompany him, a veteran missionary, in his travels. Probably Timothy never dreamed that the itinerary would include Greece and Macedonia, over in Europe.

Paul had Timothy circumcised because all the Jews in that area knew that his father was a Greek. The apostle realized that this young man, who had been brought up in the synagogue but kept from circumcision by his Greek father, would not be accepted in Jewish circles without being circumcised. Paul always tried to do what was best for the kingdom of God. He wanted nothing in his program to hinder the salvation of souls.

IV. STRENGTHENING THE NEW CHURCHES:
Acts 16:4-5

As they went through the cities of Galatia, Paul and Silas delivered to the Christian congregations "the decrees" (Greek, *dogma*) that had been "ordained," or decided on, by the apostles and elders at Jerusalem. The happy result was that the churches were "established in the faith, and increased in number daily" (v. 5). One of the hindrances to Gentiles becoming proselytes to Judaism was the rigid legalism of that religion. Many thoughtful Greek-speaking people were disillusioned with idolatry and wanted to worship the true God. Christianity, with its freedom from legalistic requirements, was much more acceptable. But if the Council of Jerusalem had imposed the Mosaic law on the Christian church, as the Judaizers were demanding, this would not have been true. The decision at Jerusalem had massive implications for the whole future of Christianity.

V. THE GUIDANCE OF THE SPIRIT:
Acts 16:6-8

The missionaries went "throughout Phrygia and the region of Galatia"—more accurately, "the region of Phrygia and Galatia." According to Ramsay, this means "the Phrygian region of *the province* Galatia." The term *Phrygia* applies to an area where the Phrygian language was spoken, an ethnic territory. Galatia, on the other hand, was a Roman province that included part of Phrygia.

They were headed west, toward Ephesus. But they were "forbidden by the Holy Spirit to preach the word in Asia." As we have noted before, the term *Asia* in the New Testament never refers to the continent, as now, but only to the Roman province of Asia at the west end of Asia Minor (modern Turkey).

Since the missionaries were forbidden to go west, they turned northward. Finally they came "over against Mysia" (v. 7)—that is, opposite the eastern border of Mysia, which was the northwest part of the province of Asia. At that point they "assayed"—"were trying"—to go into Bithynia, a Roman province northeast of the province of Asia. But once again "the Spirit did not permit them to." The oldest Greek manuscripts all say "the Spirit of Jesus," a striking phrase that is not found elsewhere in the New Testament.

Since the missionaries were not allowed to preach in either of these northern areas, there seemed to be only one thing to do—turn westward to Troas, on the coast. "Passing by" probably means going through without stopping to preach, for they could not reach Troas without going through Mysia.

VI. THE CALL TO A NEW AREA:
Acts 16:9-12

A. Come Over into Macedonia: v. 9

When Paul got to Troas, he was probably in severe perplexity. The missionaries had tried to preach in the provinces of Asia and Bithynia but had been forbidden to do so. Here they were in Troas at land's end! What were they to do? Probably the apostle went to bed that night feeling deeply distressed in his mind. It seemed that every door was closed.

But during the night the whole matter was cleared up. In a vision Paul saw "a man of Macedonia"—whom he probably recognized by his distinctive dress—saying, "Come over into Macedonia, and help us." Now the apostle could understand why the Holy Spirit had said, "Not Asia," and "No, not Bithynia either." It was because God had a greater task for him to do—in Europe!

B. A New Missionary Associate: v. 10

A very significant item enters the Book of Acts at this point. Hitherto we have been reading about what was done by Peter, Stephen, Philip, Paul, and Barnabas—always in the third person. The pronoun *we* has occurred only in speeches, never in the narrative. Here, for the first time, we find the *narrator* saying "we." It shows that Luke, the writer of the Book, joined Paul's missionary party at this point. This "we-passage" continues through verse 17. Then the third person is resumed. We find "we" appearing again in 20:6, when Paul left Philippi for Jerusalem on his third journey. This implies that Luke stayed as pastor of the new church at Philippi until Paul finally passed through that city again, perhaps half a dozen years later.

The language of verse 10 shows that Luke joined heartily in the plans for entering Europe. How did he happen to meet Paul in Troas? We know from Colossians 4:14 that Luke was "the beloved physician." Did Paul have another attack of chronic malaria and have to seek the services of a physician? Or there is another possibility. One of the leading medical schools of that day was at Tarsus. Could Paul and Luke possibly have been students together at the "university" of Tarsus and perhaps known each other? This is not altogether impossible.

C. The Trip to Philippi: vv. 11-12

The missionary party, now consisting of four, set sail from Troas. "We came with a straight course" (v. 11) is all one word in Greek, meaning "we sailed before the wind." That they actually were sailing before the wind is shown by the fact that they made the 140 miles from Troas to Neapolis in two days. Going in the opposite direction on a later trip took them five days (20:6).

The first day out from Troas they came to Samothrace and probably anchored there for the night. (Ships in those days had no compass.) This was a mountainous island, with an elevation of five thousand feet, and so served as an important landmark for sailors. At the end of the next day they landed at Neapolis ("New City"), the seaport of Philippi.

From there the missionary party walked about ten miles over the hills and down into Philippi, which was an important Macedonian city and a "colony." This word, found only here in the New Testament, was a Latin term. A Roman colony was often located on the outskirts of the empire and populated with veteran soldiers, so that it served as a sort of garrison. People living in these colonies had the same legal privileges as those living in Italy.

VII. PAUL IN PHILIPPI:
Acts 16:13-40

A. The First Convert: vv. 13-15

Perhaps partly because it was a Roman colony, there were not enough Jews (ten men) there to found a synagogue. So Paul and his associates "went out of the city"—best Greek text, "went outside the gate"—to a riverside, where they thought there might be a place of prayer. (Because of ceremonial washings, the Jews liked to meet by a river.) There they sat down and spoke to the women who had gathered for prayer.

And so Paul's first convert in Europe was a woman. Her name was Lydia. She was "a seller of purple." This is a compound word in the Greek. The "purple" part of the word was first used as the name for a "purple fish," then for the expensive "purple dye" derived from that fish, and finally as here, for the "purple fabrics" made with this dye. Lydia was a prosperous lady merchant.

She is further described as one who "worshiped God." This implies that she was a Gentile who had come to believe in the true God. We know that there was a large colony of Jews in Thyatira (in the province of Asia) and she had evidently worshiped in the synagogue there.

Lydia was baptized, along with her "household" (v. 15), which probably means her servants. (Nothing is said about her having a husband.) Then she asked all the missionaries to stay at her house. Evidently they demurred at first, for she "constrained them." Someone has said that this word indicates "the vehement urgency of the feeling of gratitude." The fact that Lydia could take care of the missionary party shows that she had a large home with plenty of servants. It was probably her kind generosity as well as the thoughtfulness of Pastor Luke that resulted in the church at Philippi sending more love offerings to the apostle Paul than any other church (Philippians 4:15-16).

B. A Demon Cast Out: vv. 16-18

As the missionaries were going to the place of prayer by the riverside, a slave girl "having a spirit of divination" met them. The Greek word for "divination" is *pythona* (python). Plutarch uses this term for ventriloquist soothsayers. It appears evident that this girl was a demon-possessed ventriloquist. She brought her masters much "gain" ("work," or "business") by her "soothsaying"—her practice of divination.

She kept following the missionaries and crying out: "These men are the servants of the Most High God, who show us the way of salvation" (v. 17). Paul finally got tired of this free advertising from such an undesirable source. He turned and said to the spirit: "I command you in the name of Jesus Christ to come out of her" (v. 18). Immediately the spirit obeyed.

C. The Missionaries Beaten and Imprisoned: vv. 19-24

When the slave girl's masters saw that the hope of their business—the python spirit—had gone out, they seized Paul and Silas and dragged them off to the Agora (the marketplace).

DISCUSSION QUESTIONS

1. Can good sometimes come out of what seems bad?
2. What part does homelife play in the preparation of a missionary?
3. How may a young person prepare himself for useful service?
4. How can we recognize the Spirit's leading?
5. How important is proper personnel in the Lord's work?
6. What preceded Isaiah's saying, "Here I am; send me"?

There they brought a very serious accusation against them before the magistrates: "These men, being Jews, do exceedingly trouble our city" (v. 20). There was double dynamite in this charge. In the first place, there was an appeal to racial prejudice—the Jews were not liked by the Romans. In the second place the one thing that Rome would not tolerate was a disturbance of the peace—upsetting Pax Romana. To add further force to this the accusers went on: "and teach customs that are not lawful for us to receive or observe, being Romans" (v. 21). This painted the situation in about as bad a light as it could be. These men were in trouble!

The wild charges had the desired effect. The crowd in the Agora rose up against these Jewish missionaries. The magistrates had the defendants' clothes ripped off them and gave orders for them to be beaten on their bare backs. After "many stripes" had been laid on them, they were thrown into prison, with orders to the jailer to "keep them safely," as if they were dangerous criminals. Having received such orders, the jailer put them in the inner prison and fastened their feet in the stocks. This was a very painful position, and it was often made worse by spreading the legs far apart for days at a time. It was a cruel world!

D. The Conversion of the Jailer: vv. 25-34

Paul and Silas were in too much pain to sleep. So they prayed—aloud, as was the custom of that day. This raised their faith until finally at midnight they were singing. What a triumph of faith! They sang so loudly and joyously that the prisoners heard them (v. 25). This was something different! And they were not singing a mournful dirge. It says that they "sang praises to God." What did they have to praise God for? Answering that question will help us through the hard times in our lives.

Their prayers and praises produced results. Suddenly there was a great earthquake, which shook the foundations of the prison. All the doors opened and the chains and stocks fell off hands and feet.

The earthquake also shook the jailer awake. When he looked out of his quarters and saw the prison doors wide open, he assumed that of course all the prisoners had escaped. So he grabbed his sword and was about to commit suicide. He knew that before the Roman government it was his life for theirs, and it was more honorable to take his own life.

But Paul saw what the jailer was preparing to do and called out, "Don't harm yourself; we are all here." Hardly daring to believe his ears, the jailer called for a light and rushed into the prison. There he fell down before Paul and Silas. Bringing them out of their cell, he earnestly inquired, "What must I do to be saved?" The answer was simple and straightforward: "Believe on the Lord Jesus Christ and you will be saved, and your house." The missionaries then gave to the household the message of the gospel.

In contrition and gratitude the jailer washed the bleeding backs of the beaten missionaries. Then he and all his household were baptized as a testimony to their faith in God.

Paul had seen a "man" of Macedonia calling to him to come over. He had come. But what he found was a group of devout women. His first convert was Lydia. He may well have asked the Lord, "Where's my man?" He finally found him—by going to jail.

E. The Exoneration of the Missionaries: vv. 35-40

Probably the earthquake at midnight wakened the magistrates. Being superstitious, maybe they said, "We shouldn't have beaten those Jews!" So when morning came they sent some officers to the jailer with the order: "Let those men go" (v. 35). The jailer conveyed this message to the prisoners; then Paul stood on his rights as a Roman citizen. The magistrates had acted illegally in beating a Roman citizen, uncondemned. They could be summoned to Rome and severely punished for this. So when Paul said, "Let them come themselves and escort us out of prison," the magistrates hurriedly came in person, brought the missionaries out of prison, and begged them to leave town.

Why did Paul stand on his rights here? Not for personal reasons, but because he wanted the new Christian community exonerated publicly—that it had not been started by two foreign criminals. He did all for the sake of the gospel.

CONTEMPORARY APPLICATION

God's leadings are not always easy to understand at the time. Sometimes it may seem to us, as it did to Paul, that all the doors are closing in our faces. We are tempted to be distressed and discouraged.

But if we hold steady and obey the voice of the Spirit, the Lord will always open a better door for us. And God knows what is best. But we must wait for Him.

This truth could be documented a thousand times. One illustration: The seminary where I teach had its eye on what seemed a nice property in a good location. But the neighbors objected to having an institution in that lovely residential area. One member of the faculty, especially, was almost crushed with disappointment.

But the Lord opened up a much larger property in what was actually a better location. As the seminary expanded to over three hundred students we realized that we never could have functioned properly on the restricted area we had wanted. The Lord knew what we would need in the future, we didn't. He closed the door in order to open a larger and better one for us.

VARIED RESPONSES TO THE GOSPEL

DEVOTIONAL READING	Acts 17:22-34

ADULTS	Topic: *Varied Responses to the Gospel* Background Scripture: Acts 17 Scripture Lesson: Acts 17:1b-5, 8-18 Memory Verse: *They received the word with eagerness, examining the Scriptures daily to see if these things were so.* Acts 17:11
YOUTH	Topic: *Is Anybody Listening?* Background Scripture: Acts 17 Scripture Lesson: Acts 17:1b-5, 8-17 Memory Verse: *They received the word with all eagerness, examining the Scriptures daily to see if these things were so.* Acts 17:11
CHILDREN	Topic: *Eager to Learn About Jesus* Background Scripture: Acts 17:1-34 Scripture Lesson: Acts 17:1-3, 10-13 Memory Verse: *Ask, and it will be given you; seek and you will find; knock, and it will be opened to you.* Matthew 7:7
DAILY BIBLE READINGS	Mon., Apr. 29: Jewish Opposition in Thessalonica, Acts 17:1-9. Tues., Apr. 30: Receptivity of the Beroeans, Acts 17:10-15. Wed., May 1: The Skepticism of the Athenians, Acts 17:16-32. Thurs., May 2: The Parable of the Soils, Matthew 13:3-8 Fri., May 3: Listening with Understanding, Matthew 13:18-23. Sat., May 4: Responding to God's Call, Isaiah 6:1-8. Sun., May 5: "Give Me Understanding," Psalm 119:33-40.
LESSON AIM	To show the different responses that hearers make to the preaching of the gospel, and the consequences of this.
LESSON SETTING	Time: A.D. 49 Place: Thessalonica and Beroea, in Macedonia; Athens in Achaia (Greece)

Varied Responses to the Gospel

LESSON OUTLINE

SUGGESTED INTRODUCTION FOR ADULTS

Jesus one day told the Parable of the Sower (Matthew 13:3-8) and interpreted it (13:18-23). The seed is the Word of God (Luke 8:11). The differences in results of the sowing are due to differences in the soil—the hearts of men. Some have hard hearts and do not accept the gospel at all. Some have shallow hearts and so are superficial and short-lived in their Christian experience. Others make a good start, but the thorns of life choke out the Word. Even in the case of "good ground" there is a wide variation in bearing fruit.

Paul's ministry illustrates the truth of this parable. Almost everywhere he went the record is that some believed his message and some did not believe. And that is still true today.

There is always a tendency to blame the preacher when there are not large accessions to the faith. But even Jesus did not always meet with success in His preaching. Few people in Jerusalem accepted His message. As in the case of Paul, we see in Jesus' ministry that results varied a great deal with different localities. Galilee was far more receptive than Judea. And so the results of preaching today differ widely. The three cities in today's lesson furnish good examples of such variation.

SUGGESTED INTRODUCTION FOR YOUTH

"Is Anybody Listening?" Sometimes the preacher is tempted to wonder! The truth is that almost invariably some in the audience are listening and some are not.

In the lesson today we see varied responses to the preaching of the gospel. In Thessalonica it was mostly *hostility*. Conversely, in Boroea it was *receptivity*. And at Athens it was largely *skepticism*. So we may expect all those reactions today.

As young people, the most important question that faces us is this: "Are we listening?" Do we go to Sunday school class and to church services asking the Lord to speak to us through the Word? Do we ask Him to make clear to us what particular message He has for us at that time? And then do we listen carefully to catch that message? This is our responsibility.

CONCEPTS FOR CHILDREN

1. People who listen are "more noble."
2. We should always listen carefully to our pastor and our Sunday school teacher.
3. If we listen we will learn some things that will help us to live a better life.
4. We need to learn all we can about Jesus.

THE LESSON COMMENTARY

I. ACCEPTANCE AND REJECTION IN THESSALONICA: Acts 17:1-9

A. Preaching Jesus in the Synagogue: vv. 1-3

From Philippi the missionaries took the Via Egnatia (Egnatian Way) that stretched over five hundred miles from the Hellespont to Dyrrachium on the Adriatic. It was the main highway connecting the eastern part of the empire with Rome.

On this famous road they "passed through" Amphipolis and Apollonia, apparently without preaching. These cities were something over thirty miles apart, with the total distance from Philippi to Thessalonica being a hundred miles. One interesting implication of this is that if Amphipolis and Apollonia were the only two places Paul stopped on the way to Thessalonica, he must have used horses for his party. On foot people usually traveled only fifteen to twenty miles per day.

Thessalonica was the largest city in Macedonia, and the third main port (after Ephesus and Corinth) on the Aegean Sea. The mention of a Jewish synagogue here may imply that there was none in either Amphipolis or Apollonia and that this was the reason Paul did not stop to preach there. It was the synagogue that usually gave him an opening in each new city.

As was his custom, Paul went into the synagogue and for three Sabbath days "reasoned with them out of the scriptures." The verb here is a favorite with Luke, occurring ten times in Acts, and only three times elsewhere in the New Testament. It means to "discourse, discuss, argue." Paul was an expository preacher. He presented the Christian message out of its background in the Old Testament.

Verse 3 gives us a very significant summary of Paul's preaching to the Jews: "Opening and alleging, that Christ had to suffer and rise from the dead, and that this is the Messiah, Jesus, whom I am announcing to you." The first verb, "opening," is another favorite with Luke; he uses it six out of the eight times in the New Testament. It means "opening up completely." Paul was opening up to the Jews their own Scriptures, so that they could see Jesus there. "Alleging" is literally "placing beside." The apostle placed the Old Testament Scriptures alongside the life and ministry of Jesus and showed the agreement. The verb also means "bring forward, quote as evidence." Paul quoted from the Old Testament prophets to prove that these taught a suffering Messiah. There were two points that Paul had to make, and in this order: (1) the Scriptures teach that the Messiah must suffer; (2) this Jesus, who did suffer on the cross, is the Messiah.

Perhaps this is the place at which to note that the Greek expression, "the Christ" and the Hebrew "the Messiah" both mean "the Anointed One." The Jews were looking for their promised Messiah to come, but they expected Him to reign in glory. They failed to understand their own Scriptures, which taught that the Messiah would suffer for the sins of the people. Paul doubtless spent much time expounding such passages as Isaiah 53 and Psalm 22. It was necessary for the Jews to recognize this important truth in their Scriptures before they could accept Jesus as the Messiah.

B. Some Jews and Many Greeks Believe: v. 4

Some of Paul's listeners in the synagogue believed the gospel message and accepted Jesus as Messiah and Savior. The word translated "believed" is literally "were persuaded." These Jews "consorted with" ("joined") Paul and Barnabas.

We are told that "a great crowd" of "devout Greeks"—Gentiles who worshiped the true God, and attended the Jewish synagogue—and "not a few" of the "chief women"—probably "wives of the chief men"—also believed. So there was already the nucleus of a good congregation.

The clear indication of this verse is that the church at Thessalonica was composed mainly of Gentiles. This agrees perfectly with the picture we find in Paul's First Epistle to the Thessalonians. He says to his readers: "You turned to God from idols to serve the living and true God." (1:9). Because most of the Jews at Thessalonica rejected the gospel, a strong Gentile congregation was formed.

We do not know how long Paul and his party stayed in Thessalonica. But it was evidently much longer than the three weeks mentioned in verse 2. For the apostle wrote to the Philippians: "Even in Thessalonica you sent once and twice to my needs" (Philippians 4:16). This would suggest a period of several weeks, if not months.

C. Persecution by the Jews: vv. 5-9

The Jews were jealous of the success of these new missionaries in winning so many converts. It would appear that numerous Gentiles who had moved from idolatry to worshiping in the synagogue now took the further step of accepting Jesus as their Messiah and Savior. This incited the Jews to action. They took some "lewd fellows"—better, "worthless men." These were "of the baser sort." The Greek for this is: "of those in the Agora." The Jews went to the Agora, or central plaza, of the city and rounded up the ones who were lounging there. Lake and Cadbury translate the whole expression "bad men of the lower class." It was pathetic that religious leaders would enlist the help of such people to carry out their designs against the missionaries!

It says that they "gathered a company"—literally, "having made a crowd." That is, they organized a mob. Then "they set on an uproar" the whole city. The single word in the Greek means "threw into confusion." This is the tactic of Communism today. Again we say that it is a pity the worshipers of the true God would stoop to employ such a despicable method in their opposition to the Christians.

A mob, once aroused, soon gets out of hand. After having thrown the town into confusion, the mobsters assaulted" the house of Jason, where they thought the missionaries were staying. They wanted to bring Paul and his associates "out to the people." The word for "people" is *demos* (cf. democracy); sometimes this meant "a public meeting." But Lake and Cadbury think that the attackers wanted to subject the missionaries "to the violence of the crowd."

Fortunately Paul, Silas, and Timothy were not in the house at the time. So the rabble "drew"—the Greek says "dragged," indicating the violence of the mob—"Jason and certain brethren to the rulers of the city" (v. 6). They were determined to put an end to the work of the preachers.

"Rulers of the city" is one word in Greek, *politarchas*, found only here and in verse 8. In the nineteenth century it was popular to point out "inaccuracies" in the Book of Acts. This was one. The Greek word had not been found anywhere else. So the writer of Acts must have made it up out of his own head! But in 1898 E. D. Burton in an article in the *American Journal of Theology* (pp. 598-632) called attention to seventeen inscriptions that had been discovered containing this word, and "of these, thirteen [now fourteen] are referred to Macedonia, and of these again five to Thessalonica, extending from the beginning of the first to the middle of the second century, A.D." So once again archaeology has proved the Bible to be right and its unfriendly critics wrong.

The missionaries were accused to the politarchs of having "turned the world upside down." Deissmann says that the verb means "incite to tumult, stir up sedition, upset" (*Light from the Ancient East*, p. 80).

The prosecutors went on to say that Jason had "received" these troublemakers (v. 7). The compound verb means "to receive under one's roof, receive as a guest, entertain hospitably." In so doing he had harbored dangerous criminals—for these missionaries "do contrary to the decrees of Caesar, saying that there is another king, Jesus." The opponents were smart enough to bring against Paul and Silas the serious political charge of treason. This was perhaps the worst sin in the eyes of Rome.

Finally the politarchs "took security" from Jason and the rest, and released them. This was similar to our present custom of posting bond. In fact, the Greek phrase used here is "a literal rendering of the Roman legal term . . . and means to take security or a bond which can be forfeited if the offence be repeated" (*Beginnings*, IV, 206). Perhaps the bond was a guarantee of peace and included the promise that Paul would not return to Thessalonica. This may be what the apostle was referring to when he said that Satan had hindered him from visiting this church again (I Thessalonians 2:18).

II. ACCEPTANCE AND INTERFERENCE IN BEROEA: Acts 17:10-15

A. Daily Examination of Scripture: vv. 10-11

Perhaps one condition of Jason's bond was that these preachers should leave town at once. Or there may have been a threat of further rioting that would make it unsafe to stay. In any case, "the brethren immediately sent away Paul and Silas by night to Beroea (best spelling). This city was about fifty miles southwest of Thessalonica. It is called Verria today.

As in most of the cities that he visited, Paul began his work in the synagogue. It is difficult for us to realize now what a tremendous advantage this was. It gave the missionaries a "pulpit" from which to preach and a sure audience, beginning with their first Sabbath day in town. This would be an exceedingly rare situation today in foreign missionary work. When one adds to that the fact that Paul could preach in Greek in every country he entered, and that all these "nations" were under one government, the Roman Empire, it becomes apparent that the stage had been set for the rapid spread of Christianity.

Verse 11 is a familiar passage to most Bible readers: "These were more noble than those in Thessalonica, in that they received the word with all readiness of mind, and searched the scriptures daily, whether these things were so." The adjective translated "noble" is literally "well-born," but here it is used metaphorically in the sense of "noble-minded." Its Latin equivalent means "free from prejudice." The Beroean Jews were open-minded in the right sense of that term—open to receive more light. They accepted the Word as preached with all "readiness"—literally, "eagerness." They were eager to learn more truth, as every honest person should be. The word translated "searched" is better translated "examined." The verb was used at that time for a judicial investigation. These Jews checked Paul's messages against the Scriptures, which should be done by every careful Christian today. And when these listeners examined the Scriptures, they found that Paul was really preaching the Word, giving them the truth.

B. Many Jews and Some Greeks Believe: v. 12

The results of daily examining of the Scriptures could have been predicted: "Therefore many of them believed." These were the Jews. In addition, "not a few" of the Greek "honourable women," or "women of high standing," accepted the gospel. We are happy to read that also some Greek "men" believed. This did not happen very often and Luke takes care to report it. Careful examination of the Scriptures really paid off!

C. Interference by Jews from Thessalonica: vv. 13-15

One of the striking features of Acts is the way the Jews who rejected Jesus as Messiah hounded Paul's footsteps wherever he went. On his first missionary journey we found them following him the one hundred miles from Pisidian Antioch (reinforced by a contingent from Iconium) to Lystra and trying to kill him there. Now they pursued him fifty miles from Thessalonica to Beroea. They seemed almost as eager in opposing the gospel as Paul was in preaching it!

When the people of Beroea had been stirred to opposition by the Jews from Thessalonica, the "brethren" felt that the only safe thing to do was to get Paul out of town. He was the center of the agitation. It was all right for Silas and Timothy to stay in Beroea, but Paul must leave. So the believers "immediately" (v. 14) "sent away Paul to go as it were to the sea" (the Aegean). This language sounds as though it might have been a ruse: they actually conducted Paul by land to Athens, far to the south. However, some scholars feel that he went by boat.

Although we rightly think of Paul as a rugged individualist, yet no writer in the New Testament gives more emphasis to the matter of "togetherness." (This shows up prominently in the Greek and is an essay in itself.) Actually, Paul craved companionship. This appears in dozens of places in his Epistles. And here it is shown by the statement (v. 15) that when Paul's Beroean escorts had taken him safely to Athens, he sent back instructions by them for Silas and Timothy to "come to him with all speed." He was lonely without them!

It appears from I Thessalonians 3:1-3 that Silas and Timothy did join Paul at Athens but that he was so concerned about the new converts at Thessalonica and Philippi that he sent Silas to Philippi and Timothy to Thessalonica to comfort and establish them in the faith. When they returned with favorable reports, they found that Paul had gone on to Corinth and they joined him there (Acts 18:5).

III. TWOFOLD MINISTRY AT ATHENS: Acts 17:16-21

A. A City Full of Idols: v. 16

While Paul was waiting at Athens for his two associates to join him, "his spirit was stirred [better, "provoked"] in him, when he saw the city wholly given to idolatry." The last four words are one term in the Greek, best translated as "full of idols." Many writers of that day verify this description. It is a sad commentary on the emptiness of merely human philosophy that the leading intellectual city of that day—and at an earlier stage the greatest center of philosophy of all time—should be "full of idols." The pagan world was spiritually bankrupt.

B. Ministry in Synagogue and Agora: v. 17

At Athens Paul had a twofold ministry that is not indicated anywhere else. Each Sabbath day he "disputed"—same Greek verb as "reasoned" in verse 2—with the Jews and God-fearers in the synagogue. During the week he talked daily with Gentiles in "the market." This was the Agora, where Socrates had taught with his inimical method of asking questions. Sir William Ramsay says of Paul's ministry there: "Luke places before us the man who became 'all things to all men,' and who therefore in Athens made himself like an Athenian and adopted the regular Socratic style of general free discussion in the Agora." After noting that "a mere Jew" could not have done this, Ramsay continues: "He was in Athens the student of a great university (Tarsus), visiting an older but yet a kindred university . . . mixing in its society as an equal conversing with men of like education" (*St. Paul the Traveller*, pp. 237-38).

C. Paul and the Philosophers: vv. 18-21

We have noted that Athens was the most famous center of philosophy in human history. The earliest giants were Plato and Aristotle, the idealist and the realist, who founded two great systems of philosophy. But in Paul's day the two most prominent "schools" were the Epicureans and the Stoics. The former was founded by

Epicurus (341-270 B.C.), the latter by Zeno (340-265 B.C.). The Stoics derived their name from the place where Zeno taught, the Stoa Poikile (Painted Porch). Representatives of these two groups "encountered" Paul in the Agora. The verb can be translated "discussed" or "conferred." But it sometimes carries a hostile sense and so could be rendered here "took issue with."

These philosophers were cynical in their attitude toward Paul. They asked "What does this babbler want to say?" The noun they applied to Paul ("babbler") is *spermologos*, which literally means "seed picker." It was first used of birds and then "in Attic slang, of an idler who lives on scraps picked up in the agora" (Abbott-Smith, *Lexicon*, p. 413). So it suggests a "parasite" or "hanger-on." It is difficult to find any English term that adequately translates it. Cadbury suggests "cock-sparrow." The word is found only here in the New Testament.

Some of the philosophers said, "He seems to be a proclaimer of foreign deities." This was because he was preaching "Jesus, and the resurrection." They evidently thought of these as two gods.

So they brought Paul to the Areopagus, demanding to know what this new teaching was (v. 19). He was bringing "strange things" to their ears, and they wanted to know the meaning. Verse 21 gives a character sketch of the Athenians. They always wanted to know the last new idea. This description of them is abundantly corroborated by writers of that period. Idle intellectual curiosity—that was their sin.

IV. SPEECH BEFORE THE AREOPAGUS: Acts 17:22-31

A. The Unknown God: vv. 22-23

"Then Paul stood in the midst of Mar's Hill." These words evoke a picture that is often painted in words, and it is a thrill today to stand on the top of the solid rock which is Mar's Hill in Athens, and to plant one's feet on the bronze plaque that supposedly marks the very spot where the apostle delivered his famous "Sermon on Mar's Hill."

But we need to look at the matter a little more closely. "Mar's Hill" is two words in Greek, *Areios* (Ares or Mars) and *Pagos* (hill). In verse 18 these words are transliterated as one word, "Areopagus"; here they are translated as two words, although the Greek is the same in both places.

The facts of the case are that the supreme Court of Athens used to meet on Mar's Hill and so was given the name Areopagus. But in the first century the Court of the Areopagus met in a portico (stoa) on the northwest side of the Agora, near the foot of Mar's Hill. The majority of scholars today think that Paul stood in the midst of the Court of the Areopagus down in the Agora. But Cadbury favors leaving open the possibility that it might have been on Mar's Hill that Paul spoke.

The King James Version has Paul beginning his speech with the words: "Ye men of Athens, I perceive that in all things ye are too superstitious." But this would have been very undiplomatic, if not positively rude. A better translation is "very religious" or even "extremely religious" (Deissmann). Knowling writes: "It is incredible that St. Paul should have commenced his remarks with a phrase calculated to offend his hearers" (*Expositor's Greek Testament*, II, 370). That seems reasonable.

Paul went on to say that as he went through the streets of Athens, he observed their "devotions" (v. 23). This translation is completely misleading to the modern reader. The Greek word means "objects of worship" (images). Among the idols he found one with the inscription: TO AN UNKNOWN GOD. This was all Paul needed as a launching pad for his message to these Athenians. He declared: "The one therefore whom you unknowingly worship, this one I an-

nounce to you." ("Unknowingly" catches the connection in Greek with UNKNOWN better than "ignorantly.")

B. The God of the Universe: vv. 24-28

The God unknown to these Athenians is the one who "made the world and all things therein." He is "Lord of heaven and earth," and so cannot be contained in man-made temples. Nor is He to be "worshiped" (Greek, "served") with men's hands, "as though He needed anything, for He *himself* [emphatic in the Greek] gives to all people life and breath and all things" (v. 25). This is the true God, in contrast to the pagan gods.

Paul goes on· "And He has made out of one ["blood" is not in the oldest manuscripts] every nation of men to dwell on all the face of the earth, having marked off by boundaries their seasons and the bounds of their dwelling" (v. 26). This emphasis on the unity of the human race is very important in these days of racial discrimination.

What was the purpose of all this? That people might seek God and find Him, for He is not far from any of us (v. 27). Then Paul declares: "In Him we live and move and are" (v. 28). This is thought to be a quotation from an early Greek hymn to Zeus, though some scholars dispute this. But the last

---

DISCUSSION QUESTIONS

1. How did Paul approach his synagogue audiences?
2. How did he deal with the man of the world?
3. How can laymen in the pew contribute to the effectiveness of the preaching in their church?
4. What caused Paul's limited success in Athens?
5. How is the Parable of the Sower related to this?
6. What methods should we use in reaching the lost today?

clause, "for we are also his offspring," is attributed by Paul to one of their poets—Aratus. "His" refers to Zeus, the leading Greek god.

C. The Folly of Idolatry: v. 29

If we are the offspring of God, it is absurd to think that the Deity ("God-head") is like idols of gold, silver, or stone, made by men's hands. This subject of the ridiculousness of idolatry is handled vividly by Isaiah (40:18-25; 44:9-20; 46:5-7).

D. Repentance and Judgment: vv. 30-31

The former times of ignorance God "winked at"(!)—"overlooked." But now he commands all men to repent (v. 30). Why? "Because He has appointed a day in which he will judge the world in righteousness by the Man whom He has ordained, having provided proof of this by raising Him

from the dead" (v. 31). This is a part of the meaning of the resurrection that is usually overlooked at Easter: it is a guarantee of the Judgment.

V. MEAGER RESPONSE AT ATHENS: Acts 17:32-34

The Greeks believed in immortality, but not in a bodily resurrection. So when Paul mentioned God raising Jesus from the dead, some mocked him. Others wanted to hear him again.

The usual pattern when Paul entered a new community was first a revival, then a riot. But here there was neither general acceptance nor any persecution—just indifference. It is true that a few believed. "Dionysius the Areopagite" would be a notable convert, for being a member of the Court of the Areopagus (about thirty persons) was a high honor. But we read of no church being established in Athens.

CONTEMPORARY APPLICATION

Paul used different tactics in different cities and with different groups. This is just common sense. It would have been foolish for the apostle to take the same approach before the Court of the Areopagus that he used in a Jewish synagogue. And at Athens he not only reasoned from the Scriptures on the Sabbath day in the synagogue, on week days he played the role of a peripatetic philosopher, dialoguing with Greeks in the Agora. Paul was flexible in the best sense of the word. He could adjust quickly to varying sit-

uations. He was versatile and adaptable. Thus he was able to minister to all kinds of groups and in varying circumstances.

Adaptability in method is one of the real needs of the church today if it is to survive in this time of change. Our *message* is unchangeable and must be unchanging. But our *methods* must be adjusted to meet the needs of communicating with our present society. We should seek the help of the Holy Spirit in keeping an effective, redeeming contact with people.

THE GOSPEL CONFRONTS CULTURE

(Temperance)

DEVOTIONAL READING	II Corinthians 10:3-8

ADULTS	Topic: *The Gospel Confronts Culture* Background Scripture: Acts 18—19 Scripture Lesson: Acts 19:18-20, 23-29 Memory Verse: *I do not account my life of any value nor as precious to myself, if only I may accomplish my course and the ministry which I received from the Lord Jesus, to testify to the gospel of the grace of God.* Acts 20:24

YOUTH	Topic: *Who Created Your Gods?* Background Scripture: Acts 18—19 Scripture Lesson: Acts 19:18-20, 23-29 Memory Verse: *I do not account my life of any value nor as precious to myself, if only I may accomplish my course and the ministry which I received from the Lord Jesus.* Acts 20:24

CHILDREN	Topic: *The Good News Spreads* Background Scripture: Acts 18:1—19:41 Scripture Lesson: Acts 18:1-4, 24-28 Memory Verse: *"Believe in the Lord Jesus, and you will be saved."* Acts 16:31

DAILY BIBLE READINGS	Mon., May 6: Triumph and Failure in Corinth, Acts 18:5-18a. Tues., May 7: Apollos Grows in Understanding, Acts 18:24—19:7. Wed., May 8: Tempted by the Easy Way, Acts 19:11-20. Thurs., May 9: The Power of Vested Interests, Acts 19:23-24. Fri., May 10: Confidence in God, Psalm 23. Sat., May 11: Substituting Good for Evil, Luke 11:14-26. Sun., May 12: Capturing Every Thought for Christ, II Corinthians 10:3-8.

LESSON AIM	To see how Christianity can triumph even when it confronts pagan cultures.

LESSON SETTING

Time: A.D. 50-54

Place: Corinth in Greece (Achaia) and Ephesus in the province of Asia (west part of modern Turkey)

The Gospel Confronts Culture

I. Ministry to the Jews in Corinth: Acts 18:1-6
   A. Paul Working at His Trade: vv. 1-3
   B. Preaching in the Synagogue: vv. 4-6

II. Ministry to the Gentiles in Corinth: Acts 18:7-11
   A. Preaching in a Home: vv. 7-8
   B. Encouragement from the Lord: vv. 9-11

III. Paul Before Gallio: Acts 18:12-17

IV. Paul's Return to Antioch: Acts 18:18-23

V. Ministry of Apollos at Ephesus: Acts 18:24-28

LESSON OUTLINE

VI. The Ephesian Pentecost: Acts 19:1-7

VII. Paul's Twofold Ministry at Ephesus: Acts 19:8-12
   A. To the Jews in the Synagogue: v. 8
   B. To the Gentiles in a Lecture Hall: vv. 9-10
   C. Miracles of Healing: vv. 11-12

VIII. Exorcism and Magic: Acts 19:13-20
   A. False Jewish Exorcists: vv. 13-17
   B. Burning Magical Scrolls: vv. 18-20

IX. Persecution for Commercial Reasons: Acts 19:21-41
   A. Paul's Purpose to Go to Rome: vv. 21-22
   B. Demetrius and the Silversmiths: vv. 23-29
   C. A Confused Assembly: vv. 30-34
   D. Order Restored by the City Clerk: vv. 35-41

SUGGESTED
INTRODUCTION
FOR ADULTS

On his first missionary journey, Paul, accompanied by Barnabas, evangelized the Island of Cyprus and the southern part of the Roman province of Galatia (chaps. 13—14). This was in the central part of Asia Minor (modern Turkey). In between the first and second missionary journeys the Council of Jerusalem (chap. 15) occurred.

On his second journey, accompanied by Silas and Timothy, Paul revisited the churches of Galatia, crossed over to Europe, and established Christianity in Philippi (chap. 16). Then he pushed on to Thessalonica and Beroea in Macedonia and to Athens in Achaia (chap. 17). In today's lesson we find him spending a year and a half in Corinth (chap. 18). After a brief return to Antioch, he set out on his third missionary journey, spending three years in Ephesus (chap. 19) and three months in Corinth (20:3). From there it was back to Jerusalem, where he was mobbed by the Jews and arrested by the Romans, spending the next four years as a prisoner at Caesarea and Rome. And so the Book of Acts comes to an end.

This bird's eye view will help us to place today's lesson in its proper setting. Paul spent longer in Corinth and Ephesus than anywhere else on his missionary journeys. These were the two leading commercial ports on the Aegean Sea and Paul was wise to concentrate his efforts in establishing a strong church in both of these places. From these two centers the gospel would be carried far and wide by sailors and travelers. (If possible, the teacher should point out these places on a map.)

SUGGESTED INTRODUCTION FOR YOUTH

"Who Created Your Gods?" That is a challenging question. Perhaps our parents created for us our gods of money and pleasure, which are the two main American deities. For some of the older generation, unfortunately, alcohol and tobacco have also been gods to be worshiped daily. This prepared the way for the younger generation to create its own gods of drugs and sex.

But these are all false gods. The only solution to our present situation will be found in turning to the true God. We can rejoice that many are doing it today. But we should pray and work to bring the good news of salvation through Jesus Christ to many more young people. Never was there a greater challenge and opportunity for this than in the exciting seventies. May we not fail God and the youth of our day!

CONCEPTS FOR CHILDREN

1. Priscilla and Aquila were godly laymen who made a large contribution to the Kingdom.
2. We should follow their example of faithful service.
3. There are many ways that we can show our love for Jesus by being kind to others.

THE LESSON COMMENTARY

I. MINISTRY TO THE JEWS IN CORINTH: Acts 18:1-6

A. Paul Working at His Trade: vv. 1-3

Soon after speaking before the Areopagus, Paul left Athens and went some sixty miles to Corinth. He probably walked, as apparently he was not fond of sailing (20:3). The drive today along the old road that follows the coastline from Athens to Corinth is one of the most beautiful in the world.

It would seem that Paul was low on funds when he arrived in Corinth,

for the first thing he did was to inquire for the street of the tentmakers. Even today in such cities as Damascus the people who work at the same trade have their little shops together on the same street.

He "found a certain Jew named Aquila" (Latin for "eagle"). This man had been born in "Pontus," in the northern part of Asia Minor. His wife was named "Priscilla." She was evidently the stronger Christian leader, for her name sometimes precedes his (Romans 16:3; II Timothy 4:19). These two had recently come from Italy because "Claudius had commanded all Jews to depart from

Rome" (v. 2). The Roman historian Suetonius, in his life of Claudius the emperor, says: "He expelled the Jews from Rome, because they were in a state of continual tumult at the instigation of one Chrestus" (*Life of Claudius*, 25, 4). The last word is obviously a misspelling for "Christus" (Latin form of "Christ"). Jews from Rome had been converted on the day of Pentecost (2:10) and had carried the gospel message back to that city and evidently established a strong church there (Romans 1:7-8). Apparently the Jews who rejected the preaching of Jesus as Messiah raised such a "tumult" against the Christian Jews that Claudius told them all to get out of Rome. Probably Aquila and Priscilla were among the converts. The edict of Claudius was made in A.D. 49. It was in A.D. 50 that Paul arrived in Corinth. So these historical notes fit together perfectly.

Tentmaking was the chief manufacture of Paul's native province of Cilicia. Every Jewish boy had to learn a trade, for the rabbinical rule was: "If a man does not teach his son a trade, it is the same as if he taught him to steal." Since tentmaking was Aquila's occupation, Paul moved in with this fine couple. Even today in cities of the Middle East people commonly have their living quarters above their shops, where they both make and sell their goods.

B. Preaching in the Synagogue: vv. 4-6

As at Thessalonica and Athens (17:2, 17), so here in Corinth Paul "reasoned in the synagogue every sabbath, and was persuading both Jews and Greeks" (v. 4). Apparently he was having some measure of success.

Then Silas and Timothy arrived "from Macedonia" (v. 5). As noted in the previous lesson (17:5), Paul had evidently sent Timothy to Thessalonica and Silas to Philippi—both in Macedonia. Now they returned, probably bringing generous love offerings to the apostle, especially from Philippi,

where Luke and Lydia were thoughtful of his needs. Freed from the necessity of working for his living, Paul now perhaps gave his full time to the ministry. It says that he was "pressed in the spirit" (KJV). But the earliest Greek manuscripts all have "constrained by the Word." Ramsay translates this, "wholly absorbed in preaching." His ministry in the synagogue now took on a new note of urgency. We read that he "testified [the Greek says he was "solemnly protesting"] to the Jews that Jesus was Christ" (the Messiah). Evidently he became more definite and vigorous in asserting this truth (cf. 17:3).

The usual result followed (v. 6). Those who refused to accept this message "opposed themselves [rather, simply "resisted"] and blasphemed [probably cried out "Anathema Jesus!"]" In response, Paul "shook his raiment"—"*shook out his lap*, as if he were shaking out their lot from the kingdom of God" (Rackham, *Acts*, p. 325). He warned them: "Your blood be upon your own heads"; that is, "you take the responsibility on yourselves." Then for the second time (cf. 14:46), he declared, "From henceforth I will go unto the Gentiles." This does not mean that after this he ignored the Jews (cf. 19:8), but that his main ministry from now on was to the Gentiles.

II. MINISTRY TO THE GENTILES IN CORINTH: Acts 18:7-11

A. Preaching in a Home: vv. 7-8

Paul's last declaration in verse 6 had an immediate and specific application to Corinth, for "he departed thence" from the Jewish synagogue and spent the rest of his time in that city in preaching mostly to Gentile audiences. This took place in the house of Justus—or "Titus Justus"—a God-fearing Gentile whose home was adjacent to the synagogue and so would be easy to find. In spite of the opposition to Paul, the chief syna-gogue ruler, Crispus, was converted. Also "many of the Corinthians"—presumably Greeks—believed and were baptized. So the work prospered even under adverse circumstances.

B. Encouragement from the Lord: vv. 9-11

Paul had been hounded from city to city on both his first and second missionary journeys. It would appear that now he felt a bit discouraged and fearful for his life. So the Lord spoke to him in a vision at night with words of comfort and command: "Stop be-ing afraid; go on speaking; do not be-come silent" (v. 9). Then came the assurance: "For I am with you, and no one will attack you to hurt you" (v. 10). Attack him they did (v. 12), but did him no harm. The Lord added: "For I have much people in this city." There was a harvest yet to be reaped, and Paul must not run away in fear or discouragement. So he stayed there a year and a half, "teaching the word of God among them" (v. 11). Those were strenuous days that called for strong men, and the apostle met the test. This was the longest he had stayed in one city so far on his journeys.

III. PAUL BEFORE GALLIO: Acts 18:12-17

Apparently toward the end of Paul's stay in Corinth, Gallio became "deputy"—rather, "proconsul," that is, governor—of Achaia. This was the name of the Roman province which included most of Greece (not Mace-donia). An inscription has been found at Delphi, in which the emperor Tiber-ius refers to "Lucius Junius Gallio, my friend, and proconsul of Achaia." The records suggest that Gallio assumed this office in the summer of A.D. 51. Since the narrative in Acts implies that the Jews took advantage of the new governor by immediately presenting Paul's case, and that Paul left town not too long after that, it would seem that

his year and a half in Corinth reached from the spring of A.D. 50 to the fall of A.D. 51. This gives us a central date in the Pauline chronology, from which we can figure backward and forward.

The Jews "made insurrec-tion"—"rose up"—against Paul and brought him to the "judgment seat." In the Greek, *bema*, this is one word. This word can be seen today on the wall at this very spot in ancient Cor-inth. There the Jewish leaders brought their charges against Paul: "This fellow persuades men to worship God con-trary to the law" (v. 13). What they really meant was the law of Moses, but they hoped that Gallio would be naive enough to think they were talking about Roman law. They were trying to catch the new governor off his guard.

But Gallio was too smart for them. He did not even give Paul a chance to defend himself; instead, he made this classic reply: "If it were a civil or criminal case, O Jews, then according to reason I would have to listen to you. But if there are questions about a word and names and the law according to you folk, you yourselves see to them; I will not be a judge of these matters" (vv. 14-15). Ramsay para-phrases this well: "If they are ques-tions of word, not deed, and of names, not things, and of your law, not Ro-man law ..." (*St. Paul the Traveller*, p. 257). And he drove them away from the judgment seat (v. 16).

The King James Version says that "all the Greeks took Sosthenes, the chief ruler of the synagogue, and beat him before the judgment seat" (v. 17). Instead of "all the Greeks" the oldest Greek manuscripts have simply "they all," which would probably mean the Jews (cf. v. 16). It would seem that Sosthenes had been put in place of Crispus when the latter was converted to Christ (v. 8), and the Jews may have been taking their spite out on him because he lost this case in court. If this is the same Sosthenes who is men-tioned in I Corinthians 1:1, then he too became a Christian, perhaps as a result of this beating.

On the basis of the last sentence of verse 17 the proconsul has sometimes been dubbed "the careless Gallio." But this is a slander on the good name of this honorable ruler. He did his duty as a Roman judge in refusing to try a case that did not relate to Roman law.

IV. PAUL'S RETURN TO ANTIOCH:
Acts 18:18-23

Not long after his attempted trial, Paul left Corinth and sailed for "Syria"—Palestine was included in what at that time was called Syria. Apparently he had had his head shaved in Cenchrea, the eastern harbor of Corinth, as part of a temporary Nazirite vow. He took Aquila and Priscilla along with him as far as Ephesus, but left them there (v. 19). The Jews liked his teaching in the synagogue and pressed him to stay. But Paul felt the urge to move on. ("I must by all means keep this feast that is coming in Jerusalem" is not in the oldest Greek manuscripts.) Promising to return—which he did for a lengthy ministry on his third journey—the apostle "sailed from Ephesus" (v. 21).

Landing at Caesarea—the seat of the Roman government of the province of Judea, and the main seaport of Jerusalem—Paul went "up" and "saluted the church," and then "went down to Antioch" (v. 22). There has been a perennial debate as to whether the church he greeted was in Caesarea or Jerusalem. But the New Testament always speaks of "going up" to Jerusalem and "going down" from Jerusalem to any other place. The expression "went down to Antioch" is almost conclusive evidence in favor of Jerusalem, since Antioch is far up the coast to the north of Caesarea.

Verse 23 notes the beginning of Paul's third missionary journey—with no fanfare! As on his second journey, he first revisited the churches in southern Galatia that had been founded on the first journey. The Epistle to the Galatians reflects the apostle's deep concern for these early converts of his.

V. MINISTRY OF APOLLOS AT EPHESUS:
Acts 18:24-28

Apollos is described as a Jew "born at Alexandria, an eloquent man, and mighty in the scriptures" (v. 24). We are further told that he was "instructed in the way of the Lord" and "fervent in spirit," and that he "taught diligently the things of the Lord, knowing only the baptism of John"(v. 25). This probably means that he preached mainly repentance and righteousness, the two chief emphases of John the Baptist's ministry. It is not entirely clear what his relation to Christianity was. When Aquila and Priscilla heard him speak in the synagogue, they took him to their home and "expounded to him the way of God more accurately" (v. 26). Here were laymen instructing the preacher!

Soon after that Apollos left Ephesus for Corinth ("Achaia"), where he had a profitable ministry. It was twofold. He both "helped them much who had believed through grace" (v. 27)—that is, the Christians—and "vigorously confuted the Jews publicly, proving through the scriptures that Jesus was the Messiah" (v. 28). So Apollos helped to carry on the good work that Paul had begun in Corinth. He proved to be a very popular preacher in that city (I Corinthians 1:12; 3:4-6).

VI. THE EPHESIAN PENTECOST:
Acts 19:1-7

This is the name usually given to the event described in these verses. On his third journey Paul finally came to Ephesus, where he labored for about three years (20:31), the longest time in any single place.

In this city he found "disciples." This term in Acts usually designates believers in Jesus. But when Paul asked them if they had received the Holy Spirit, "having believed" (v. 2), they replied: "We have not even heard that there is a Holy Spirit." Surprised, the apostle inquired further: "Into what then were you baptized?" (v. 3). They said, "Into John's baptism." Paul then reminded them that John the Baptist had told the people to believe in Jesus (v. 4). When they heard this, "they were baptized in the name of the Lord Jesus" (v. 15). Rather clearly they now became members of the Christian community for the first time. Then Paul laid his hands on them, and they received the Holy Spirit (v. 6)—"about twelve" of them (v. 7).

Were these men born-again believers before the apostle ministered to them? A dogmatic answer cannot be given. It is obvious that they had never heard of the coming of the Holy Spirit at Pentecost. That is the minimum meaning of verse 2b It is also clear that they had not been a part of the church.

VII. PAUL'S TWOFOLD MINISTRY AT EPHESUS:
Acts 19:8-12

A. To the Jews in the Synagogue: v. 8

When the Sabbath day came, Paul "went into the synagogue and spoke boldly for the space of three months, reasoning and persuading concerning the kingdom of God." In view of his boldness here, it is surprising that he was able to continue in the synagogue for that long period of time. But Josephus informs us that not only was there a large colony of Jews in Ephesus, but that some of them were Roman citizens. It may well be that the Jews in Ephesus were more open-minded than those in other places.

B. To the Gentiles in a Lecture Hall: vv. 9-10

In spite of a measure of tolerance, some of Paul's hearers in the synagogue were "hard and disobedient" (v. 9). They spoke evil of "the Way" (cf. 9:2). So Paul left the synagogue and took "the disciples"—his new converts—with him to the "school" (lecture hall) of Tyrannus. There he carried on a daily ministry of expounding the Word. Some Greek manuscripts say that he did this "from the fifth to the tenth hour" (11:00 A.M.-4:00 P.M.), when business shut down and people took their siesta.

But Paul worked in the early morning at his trade of tentmaking (cf. 20:34) and then, while others rested in the middle of the day, when the lecture hall was not being used, he taught the Scriptures. This is typical of Paul's ardent devotion to the work of the ministry. This went on for two years (v. 10). The result was that "all those living in the province of Asia heard the word of the Lord, both Jews and Greeks." This was Paul's strategy: to evangelize the provincial capitals and build strong churches there and then let the work spread out from these great centers. It still has a lot to commend it!

At Athens Paul had a twofold ministry: on the Sabbath day in the synagogue to the Jews and then on week days to the Greeks in the Agora (17:17). These ministries went on simultaneously. In Corinth he had a twofold ministry: first in the synagogue to the Jews, and then later in the house of Justus (18:4, 7). In Ephesus he also had a twofold ministry: first to the Jews in the synagogue for three months (19:8) and then to the Gentiles in the lecture hall of Tyrannus for two years (19:9-10). Paul set an example of Christian service that comparatively few have duplicated.

C. Miracles of Healing: vv. 11-12

God "wrought extraordinary miracles by the hands of Paul" (v. 11), such as are not described elsewhere in the New Testament.

"Handkerchiefs"—perhaps "sweatbands" worn on the forehead while working—and "aprons" (workmen's aprons) were carried from Paul's body to sick people. The result was that "diseases departed" and "evil spirits went out" (v. 12). It was not the cloth that worked the miracles, however; rather, these articles were used as aids to faith for those who had a poor understanding of the purely spiritual nature of true religion.

VIII. EXORCISM AND MAGIC:
Acts 19:13-20

A. False Jewish Exorcists: vv. 13-17

There were some "vagabond" ("strolling") Jews who were "exorcists." The word occurs only here in the New Testament and literally means "one who administers an oath." But it was used of those who cast out demons by pronouncing a famous name, such as "Solomon." These Jewish exorcists were treading on dangerous ground when they said to the demon-possessed people: "We adjure you by Jesus whom Paul preaches" (v. 13). On a magical papyrus at the Bibliotheque Nationale in Paris there is this striking parallel: "I adjure you by the God of the Hebrew, Jesus" (Deissmann, *Light from the Ancient East*, p. 252)

It is disheartening to read that seven sons of a Jewish chief priest engaged in this kind of performance. But they were appropriately punished for their presumption. The evil spirit answered them: "Jesus I know, and Paul I know, but who are you?" (v. 15). Then the demon-possessed man jumped on all seven of them and beat them up, tearing off their clothes (v. 16). The result was that people were afraid to "toy" with religion, and "the name of the Lord Jesus was magnified" (v. 17).

B. Burning Magical Scrolls: vv. 18-20

The consequence of all this was a large number of conversions. Many of the new Christians had been steeped in the magic and superstition for which Ephesus was noted in that day. They came, "confessing and declaring their deeds" (v. 18). Lake and Cadbury say of the Greek word for "deeds": "The noun also has the technical meaning of 'magic spell,' so that the probable

meaning here is that the former exorcists now disclosed the secret formulae they had used" (*Beginnings*, IV, 242).

Also many who had used "curious arts"—rather, "magical arts"—brought their "books" (papyrus scrolls with magical charms written on them) and burned them publicly (v. 19). This was an expensive bonfire. The cost of these scrolls was counted up and found to amount to "fifty thousand pieces of silver"—about $10,000. In terms of buying power in that day, this would be several times that figure. Evidently these magical papyri sold for fantastic prices.

What was the result of all this? "So mightily grew the word of God and prevailed" (v 20) This is the fifth brief progress report in the Book of Acts (cf. 6:7; 9:31; 12:24; 16:5; 28:36). The power of God won out over all supposedly magical powers in Ephesus. We need to realize that the Holy Spirit is stronger than all other spiritual forces in the universe.

IX. PERSECUTION FOR COMMERCIAL REASONS:
Acts 19:21-41

A. Paul's Purpose to Go to Rome: vv. 21-22

The apostle felt that he needed to go back to Macedonia (Philippi, Thessalonica, Beroea) and Achaia (Corinth) before going to Jerusalem. As we know from the Corinthian Letters, his presence was especially needed in Corinth where things were not going well in the church. After Jerusalem, Paul said, "I must also see Rome" (v. 21). As a Roman citizen he would naturally like to visit the capital of the empire. But far more important was his desire to have a spiritual ministry in that city (Romans 15:22-29).

To prepare the way for his visit to Macedonia, the apostle sent two of his colleagues, Timothy and Erastus, on ahead. For some unstated reason he stayed a little longer in Ephesus (v. 22).

B. Demetrius and the Silversmiths: vv. 23-29

In almost every city where Paul ministered—in the provinces of Galatia, Macedonia, and Achaia—he encountered persecution from the Jews for religious reasons. There was only one exception, Philippi, where the opposition arose from financial causes. Now we have the same thing happening in Ephesus. Demetrius was a silversmith who made silver shrines for Diana (Greek, *Artemis*). He called together the other silversmiths and warned them that if Paul kept on preaching against idolatry, their occupation would be imperiled. Then he made a religious pitch: "So that not only this our craft is in danger to be set at nought, but also that the temple of the great goddess Diana should be despised and her magnificence should be destroyed, whom all Asia and the world worshippeth" (v. 27). The temple of Artemis at Ephesus was considered one of the seven wonders of the ancient world.

It might seem a far-fetched hyperbole for Demetrius to say that all the world worshiped Artemis. But his assertion is well attested. Lily Ross Taylor writes: "Not only was the cult the most important of the province of Asia: it had a fame throughout the Greek and Roman world that probably no divinity except Apollo of Delphi could surpass" (*Beginnings*, V, 251).

When the silversmiths heard these words of Demetrius, "they were full of wrath, and cried out, saying, Great is Diana of the Ephesians" (v. 28). The result was that "the whole city was filled with confusion" (v. 29). Two of Paul's traveling companions from Macedonia were caught and carried along in a grand rush into the theater. This was a magnificent building 340 feet long by 160 feet wide, with 100 columns over 55 feet high.

C. A Confused Assembly: vv. 30-34

Paul, always courageous, wanted to go into the crowd. But the Christians would not permit this. They knew his life would be in danger. Even some of the Asiarchs ("chief of Asia"), who were Paul's friends, sent word to him not to venture into the theater. The mood of the crowd is shown by the fact that the people shouted for two hours, "Great is Diana of the Ephesians." This is a significant revelation of the usual intelligence of a mob!

D. Order Restored by the City Clerk: vv. 35-41

The city clerk entered the theater and finally managed to quiet the crowd. Then he reproved the people for their senseless "howling," as Lake and Cadbury call it. He reminded them that everyone knew about the Ephesian worship of Artemis and of "the image which fell from Jupiter" (v. 35)—rather, "the sacred stone that fell from the sky" (RSV). This was a black meteorite that the Ephesians accepted as a goddess.

The city clerk said that if Demetrius and his fellow craftsmen had any complaints, they should bring them to court or have them settled in a "regular assembly" (v. 39). He warned the people that they were in danger of being "called in question" by the Roman government for this wild uproar. Then he dismissed the assembly.

DISCUSSION QUESTIONS

1. Why did Paul always begin in the synagogue?
2. What was his main message there?
3. Why did the Jews not receive it?
4. What do you think of Paul's policy of concentrating his efforts on the big cities?
5. Why are magical cults increasing today?
6. What place does greed have in hindering the work of God?

CONTEMPORARY APPLICATION

Paul's courage in facing danger, and even the threat of death, is a constant challenge to us. Also his untiring devotion to the spread of the gospel and to the salvation of souls should put most of us to shame. Paul had one passion in life. He expresses it this way: "The love of Christ constraineth us." David Livingstone adopted this as the explanation for his unparalleled devotion: "The love of Christ compelled me."

BOLD WITNESS PROVOKES CONTROVERSY

DEVOTIONAL READING	John 15:18-23

ADULTS

Topic: *Bold Witness Provokes Controversy*

Background Scripture: Acts 21—22

Scripture Lesson: Acts 21:10-14, 17-24a

Memory Verse: *I am ready not only to be imprisoned but even to die at Jerusalem for the name of the Lord Jesus.* Acts 21:13b

YOUTH

Topic: *Tell the Good News*

Background Scripture: Acts 21—22

Scripture Lesson: 21:10-14, 17-24a

Memory Verse: *I am ready not only to be imprisoned but even to die at Jerusalem for the name of the Lord Jesus.* Acts 21:13b

CHILDREN

Topic: *Paul, a Brave Man*

Background Scripture: Acts 21—22

Scripture Lesson: 21:10-14, 30-33

Memory Verse: *Be strong and of good courage.* Joshua 1:6a

DAILY BIBLE READINGS

Mon., May 13: Paul Warned, Acts 21:1-6.
Tues., May 14: God's Will Be Done, Acts 21:7-14.
Wed., May 15: Paul at Jerusalem, Acts 21:15-26.
Thurs., May 16: Paul Arrested, Acts 21:27-40.
Fri., May 17: Paul's Testimony, Acts 22:1-11.
Sat., May 18: Paul's Commission, Acts 22:12-21.
Sun., May 19: Paul's Roman Citizenship, Acts 22:22-29

LESSON AIM

To explore some of the problems connected with witnessing and to see how God works it all out for good.

LESSON SETTING

Time: A.D. 56

Place: Tyre, Ptolemais, Caesarea, Jerusalem

Bold Witness Provokes Controversy

LESSON OUTLINE

SUGGESTED INTRODUCTION FOR ADULTS

In our last lesson we studied Paul's ministry of a year and a half in Corinth (chap. 18) and three years in Ephesus (chap. 19). After that he moved rather quickly from place to place. First he went through Macedonia, probably stopping to preach in Philippi, Thessalonica, and Beroea (20:1-2). But his main goal was Corinth in Greece, where he spent three months with the church (v. 3). He had planned to sail from there to "Syria" (Palestine), but when he learned that the Jews were plotting to seize him, he returned on foot through Macedonia. Luke (cf. "we") joined the party at Philippi (v. 6).

Paul spent a week with the church at Troas. Planning to leave on Monday morning, he met with the disciples on Sunday evening for a communion service and preached until midnight. A young man grew drowsy and fell out a window on the third floor where Paul was speaking. Paul restored him to life (v. 10) and then, nothing daunted, he preached until daybreak!

From Troas the missionary party sailed to Miletus. Paul sent for the elders of the church at Ephesus to meet with him there, as he himself did not have time to go to Ephesus. The apostle's speech to the Ephesian elders at Miletus (20:17-35) is one of the most moving passages in the Book of Acts. The memory verse for the last lesson (20:24) was taken from it. Paul apparently expected to die at Jerusalem, for he told these people they would not see him again (v. 25). This caused a sad parting, a touching scene as the people tearfully said good-bye to the aging apostle they had learned to love.

"Tell the Good News." Yes, but sometimes this can be costly and dangerous. It was for Paul. It was for the five martyrs at the hands of the Auca Indians. It has been for thousands of other witnesses across the centuries.

There are still places in the world where a faithful Christian witness may result in death. However, for most of us it will not be physical persecution but unfavorable reactions and controversy.

In spite of this we must be willing to witness, no matter what the dangers or difficulties. And always we should seek the guidance of the Spirit as to how and where to witness. "Where God guides, He provides." When we are in His will, we know that in spite of hardships and setbacks the Word will finally triumph.

1. Paul was a brave man, willing to face death, if necessary, to carry on his ministry.
2. Some people thought Paul had made the wrong decision.
3. God worked everything out for the best good of His kingdom.

THE LESSON COMMENTARY

I. WARNINGS TO PAUL AT TYRE: Acts 21:1-7

A. Sailing from Miletus to Tyre: vv. 1-3

After the sorrowful parting at Miletus, Paul and his party sailed to Patara. There they found a ship about to leave for Phoenicia (modern Lebanon). They boarded it and finally landed safely at Tyre, the main seaport of Phoenicia.

B. Concern of Disciples at Tyre: vv. 4-6

"Finding disciples" suggests one of two things: Either Paul did not know there were Christians at Tyre, or he had to look around to find them. We cannot be sure which it was. In any case, the party stayed at Tyre for a week.

These disciples "said to Paul through the Spirit that he should not go up to Jerusalem" (v. 4). On the surface this seems like a clear direction from the Holy Spirit given through the Christians at Tyre that the apostle must not go on with his plan to visit Jerusalem. Why then did he go?

"Through the Spirit" could mean "through a revelation by the Spirit." That is, the Holy Spirit revealed to these disciples that Paul's life would be in danger if he went to Jerusalem. Their natural reaction would be to urge him not to go. In any case, we know that Paul was sincere in believing that it was his duty to carry out his original purpose. He certainly was not deliberately disobeying God!

At the end of the week, "we departed and went on our way" (v. 5). The concern of the Christians is shown by the fact that they, even including their wives and children, escorted Paul to the ship. On the beautiful beach at Tyre they knelt down with the apostle and prayed. Then they bade him a sad farewell.

C. One Day at Ptolemais: v. 7

This city was situated on the Bay of Acre, where the town of Acre is today (across the bay from Haifa). There Paul and his party "saluted the brethren" and stayed one day.

II. FURTHER WARNINGS AND PLEAS AT CAESAREA: Acts 21:8-14

A. Philip and His Four Daughters: vv. 8-9

After the single day in Ptolemais the party left for Caesarea, some forty miles to the south. This trip would take two days on foot, but less than one by boat. There is no indication here as to which method was used.

At Caesarea the travelers stayed in the home of "Philip the evangelist." This man started out waiting on tables as one of "the seven" (6:1-5). Later he evangelized a city of Samaria (8:5). The verb *euangelizomai* is used for Philip's preaching there (8:12). After Philip had converted the Ethiopian eunuch (8:26-31), he evangelized (*euangelizomai*) "all the cities" along the coast from ancient Ashdod to Caesarea (8:40). Because of his work he was known as "the evangelist." *Euangelistes* occurs only here and in Ephesians 4:11 and II Timothy 4:5.

Philip had "four daughters, virgins who prophesied" (v. 9). More than twenty years (A.D. 33-56) had elapsed since Philip had reached Caesarea (8:40). It appears that he had settled down there and raised a family. The word "prophesied" in the New Testament usually means "preached." Some people do not believe in women preachers, but the Lord blessed Philip with four of them! At that time they

were unmarried, but Clement of Alexandria says that two of them did marry later.

B. Prophecy of Agabus: vv. 10-11

Paul evidently enjoyed the fellowship in Philip's home, for Luke says that the party stayed there "many days." During that time a prophet named Agabus "came down from Judea," that is, Jerusalem. In a symbolical act he took Paul's "girdle [belt], bound his own hands and feet, and said, Thus says the Holy Spirit, So will the Jews at Jerusalem bind the man who owns this girdle, and will deliver him into the hands of the Gentiles" (v. 11). Earlier this same Agabus had predicted a famine throughout the Roman Empire, which happened just as he said it would (11:28). So he had probably gained a reputation for having a special gift of prophecy, and people took his predictions seriously.

C. Pleas of Paul's Friends: v. 12

Understandably all the Christians, both those in Paul's party and the ones who lived at Caesarea, begged him not to go up to Jerusalem. They loved him and did not want to see him suffer persecution. Then, too, he was much needed in the missionary work among the Gentiles, where he had done more than anybody else. Why should he go on to Jerusalem and be imprisoned there? He had better turn around and go back to the provinces of Asia Minor or Europe.

D. Purpose of Paul: vv. 13-14

It is clear that Paul felt he *must* go through with his planned visit to Jerusalem. We do not know all the thoughts that were going through his mind. But in the light of all we know about this great apostle, we may be sure he was convinced that it was God's will for him to go ahead with his plans.

Paul was not a man to be moved to action by mere emotions. So he answered his friends' pleas by saying: "What are you doing, crying and breaking my heart? I am ready not only to be bound, but also to die at Jerusalem for the name of the Lord Jesus" (v. 13). He felt that they were trying to weaken his purpose, and this he could not allow. So his friends gave in saying, "The will of the Lord be done." F. F. Bruce calls this an "echo of the Lord's own prayer in Gethsemane" (Luke 22:42).

III. JOURNEY TO JERUSALEM: Acts 21:15-16

Luke records: "After this we took up our carriages, and went up to Jerusalem" (v. 15). In our century a "carriage" has been something that carried people; in 1611 it meant what people carried! Today we would call it "baggage," not "carriages." Actually, "we took up our carriages" is all one word in Greek, a participle meaning "having prepared ourselves." Probably the simplest translation here is: "having packed up, we went on up to Jerusalem."

Some "disciples" from Caesarea went along. The phrase translated "brought with them one Mnason" is more accurately translated "bringing us to Mnason" (RSV). Apparently what happened is that they stopped overnight at the house of Mnason, who lived in some village on the way. Since the distance from Caesarea to Jerusalem is about sixty miles, they would have to stop twice for the night if they walked. Mnason is described as an "old disciple." A better translation would be "an early disciple." He was perhaps one of the 120 in the upper room at Pentecost.

IV. REQUEST OF JAMES AND THE ELDERS: Acts 21:17-25

A. Good Reception at Jerusalem: v. 17

We are glad to read that when the party arrived in Jerusalem, "the brethren received us gladly." By this time Paul seems to have established himself in the good graces of the mother church.

B. Paul's Report to James and the Elders: vv. 18-19

The next day "Paul went in with us to James; and all the elders were present" (v. 18). It is obvious that James was considered the head of the Jewish Christian community in Jerusalem (cf. 12:17; 15:13). Probably the reason the elders had gathered for this occasion was that Paul and his companions were bringing the large offering they had collected in the Gentile churches of Macedonia and Achaia for the poor saints at Jerusalem (Romans 15:25-28; I Corinthians 16:2-4; II Corinthians 9:1-5). It does seem strange that no mention is made here of this offering being presented to the Jerusalem church. A logical possibility seems to be that Luke was himself active in raising the money and in bringing it to Jerusalem, and his modesty led to his silence on this point.

What we are told here is that Paul reported to James and the elders "what things God had wrought among the Gentiles through his ministry" (v. 19). He gave God all the credit for what he had been able to do.

C. The Judaizers' Mistrust of Paul: vv. 20-21

The elders as a whole did rejoice at Paul's report and "glorified the Lord" (v. 20). But then they went on to say: "You see, brother, how many myriads [Greek, *myriades*, "tens of thousands"] of Jews there are who have believed, and they are all zealous of the law." These Jewish Christians had been told that Paul was teaching the Jews out in the provinces "to forsake Moses, saying that they ought not to circumcise their children nor live by the customs." There is no evidence that Paul did this. What he did do was to tell the *Gentile* Christians that they should not be circumcised nor keep the law of Moses (Galatians 5:1-4). Unfortunately the Judaizers were in the habit of maligning Paul, putting the worst construction on what he said and did.

D. Suggestion of James and the Elders: vv. 22-25

The leaders of the church were anxious to avoid any disturbance because of Paul's presence in Jerusalem. So they suggested that in order to silence his critics and satisfy all the Jewish Christians, he should join four men who were under a vow (v. 23). This was probably a temporary Nazirite vow, which usually lasted for thirty days. Paul was to "purify" himself ceremonially with them and "be at charges with them," that is, pay the expenses of their vows (v. 24). Josephus tells how Herod Agrippa I paid the expenses of some men who were Nazirites. Perhaps Paul did this out of the offering he had brought with him. These men would "shave their heads" at the close of the period they had pledged to observe with their hair uncut.

The reason for the elders making this request was that "all may know that the things they were told about you are nothing, but that you yourself also walk in an orderly way, keeping the Law." As far as the Gentile Christians were concerned, their status had already been settled at the Jerusalem Council, and the leaders assembled there had written them that they need "observe no such thing" (v. 25), but just obey the four restrictions against things offered to idols, blood, strangled animals, and immorality.

In view of the consequences of Paul's complying with this request, one cannot help asking why he insisted on going to Jerusalem at this time, when he knew he would get into trouble. Not only was his life endangered in the Temple (v. 31), but he spent the next four years in prison, unable to travel, thus limiting the witnessing he could do. That was a long time for Paul to be tied up!

Two things should probably be said about this problem. The first is regarding Paul's reason for pushing on to Jerusalem in the face of many warnings not to. His consuming passion at this time was to unite the Jewish and Gentile churches, so that there would be just one church of Jesus Christ, made one in Him. This was apparently the chief reason he gave major attention to raising in the Gentile churches the offering for the Jewish Christians at Jerusalem. In his First Epistle to the Corinthians he stressed this in the last chapter. In the Second Epistle he devoted the heart of his letter to this subject (chaps. 8—9). After successfully raising a large offering, he wanted to go to Jerusalem himself to make sure that it was well received there as a token of love from the Christian Gentiles. Paul's passion for the unity of the church is clearly revealed in his Epistle to the Ephesians (4:3-6). So at this time he felt he must see that the project did not fail in its conclusion.

A second fact should be noted. While Paul spent those four years in enforced quiet he had more time to meditate than when he was busy traveling and preaching. We might say that his thinking had time to settle and that he skimmed off the cream and gave it to us in his four Prison Epistles. It was while a prisoner at Rome that he wrote his richest letters, especially Ephesians, Colossians, and Philippians. We might be tempted to think that Paul's ministry to his own generation would have been greater if he had remained free. But his contribution to the succeeding centuries is richer because he was laid aside in prison.

V. PAUL MOBBED AND ARRESTED: Acts 21:26-40

A. Seized by the Jews: vv. 26-30

Dutifully Paul took the four men, went through the ceremony of purification with them, and accompanied them into the Temple. He paid for the offering that each one had to give—one male lamb, one ewe lamb, and one ram, with their meal and drink offerings (Numbers 6:13-15). This may have consumed four days, one day for each of the men.

The "seven days" (v. 27) probably refers to Numbers 6:9. It was the time required for purification from defilement. Paul had a rather long ordeal caring for the needs of these men.

James had been concerned about the attitude toward Paul on the part of Christian Jews in Jerusalem. But it was actually non-Christian Jews from "Asia" (Ephesus) who caused trouble. They saw Paul in the Temple and recognized him as the one who had preached Christ in their city for three years, and especially in their synagogue for the first three months (19:8). So they "stirred up all the people, and laid hands on him." Shouting for help, they brought serious charges against Paul: "This is the man that teaches all men everywhere against the people [Israel], and the law [Mosaic law], and this place [the Temple]; and furthermore he brought Greeks into the Temple and defiled this holy place" (v. 28).

The last accusation was a particularly dangerous one. For the Roman government had deprived the Jewish Sanhedrin of the authority to enforce capital punishment, except in the case of a Gentile entering the sacred area of the Temple. So Paul was under the threat of death.

What was the basis of this false charge? These Asian Jews had earlier seen Paul walking along a street in Jerusalem with "Trophimus an Ephesian"—probably a Gentile convert, whom the apostle had won to Christ while in Ephesus. Now they see Paul in the Temple and assume that he brought this Gentile there. It is a typical example of an utterly unfounded accusation.

The Temple was the center of life in Jerusalem. If anything exciting happened there, it affected the whole town. We read that "all the city was moved, and the people ran together" (v. 30). The last expression is used by such writers as Aristotle to describe the forming of a mob. The people seized Paul and dragged him out of the Temple. Then the doors were shut to prevent further defilement.

B. Rescued by the Romans: vv. 31-36

Not content to wait for legal action, the mob was going to kill Paul then and there. Word of this got to "the chief captain of the band"—"the tribune of the cohort." He heard that "all Jerusalem was in an uproar." So he immediately took "soldiers and centurions" (v. 32). Since each centurion had a hundred soldiers under him, it is evident that the tribune considered this a serious matter. The officers and soldiers "ran down to them" from the Tower of Antonia, the Roman garrison at the northwest corner of the Temple area (in the Court of the Gentiles). When the people saw the hundreds of soldiers rushing toward them, they stopped beating Paul. His life was saved.

The tribune arrested Paul and ordered that he be bound with two chains (v. 33). This was perhaps for two reasons: to prevent Paul's escape if he was a dangerous criminal and to protect him if he was an innocent victim of the mob. Then he inquired who he was and what he had done. Some were shouting one thing, and some another. When the tribune saw that there was nothing but irrational confusion, he ordered that Paul should be carried into "the castle"—rather, "the barracks." The violence of the mob was such that the prisoner had to be carried up the stairs by the soldiers. Following hard after him was the crowd, yelling, "Away with him!"

C. Paul's Request to Speak to the People: vv. 37-40

As Paul was about to be carried inside the barracks, he said to the tribune, "May I speak with you?" Surprised, the centurion asked, "Do you know Greek? Are you not the Egyptian who before these days stirred up an insurrection and led into the desert four thousand men of the Assassins?" (v. 38). The Egyptians were looked down on by Romans, Greeks, and Jews alike. They were often thought of as inhuman barbarians. Josephus tells about this particular insurrectionist. He had come to Jerusalem, claiming to be a deliverer of the Jews. Gaining a following, he led his band to the top of the Mount of Olives and declared that the walls of Jerusalem would fall at his command and the Roman garrison would be defeated. But Felix, the governor, killed many of his followers, though the Egyptian himself escaped. Now the tribune thought he had returned.

To the question asked him, Paul gave a straightforward answer: "I am a Jew from Tarsus in Cilicia, a citizen of no mean city. I beg you, let me speak to the people" (v. 39). When the tribune gave his consent, Paul stood on the stairs and beckoned for silence. Then he addressed the people "in the Hebrew tongue"—that is, Aramaic, the language of Palestine at that time.

When the people heard the prisoner speaking to them in Aramaic they listened to hear what he would say. They kept quiet long enough for him to make a speech.

DISCUSSION QUESTIONS

1. How do we know when persistence is a result of the guidance of the Holy Spirit?
2. Is controversy a sign that we are wrong?
3. What role did the Roman government play in Paul's fortunes at Ephesus and then at Jerusalem?
4. What are some ways in which Paul is an example to us?
5. How do we ascertain the leading of the Spirit?
6. How did Paul exemplify the command to "seek first the Kingdom"?

VI. PAUL'S SPEECH TO THE JEWS: Acts 22:1-21

The first thing Paul did was to identify himself. As we have noted before, if one knows that he is innocent, the best defense he can offer is the simple truth. So Paul declared: "I am a Jew born in Tarsus of Cilicia, but brought up in this city at the feet of Gamaliel and instructed according to the exactness of the law of the fathers, being zealous for God, just as you all are today" (v. 3). He went on to tell how he had persecuted "the Way" even to death, "binding and delivering into prisons both men and women" (v. 4). Paul's tenderness in dealing with people is all the more remarkable in view of his harsh cruelty before his conversion. He reminded his hearers that the high priest and his colleagues could vouch for his story (v. 5).

Then Paul recounted his conversion (vv. 6-16). The account is in close accord with the historical narrative of it in 9:3-18 and the recital of it again before King Agrippa (26:12-18).

Paul went on to tell what happened on his first visit to Jerusalem after his conversion. He was praying in the Temple when he found himself in a trance (v. 17). He saw the Lord saying to him: "Hurry up, and get quickly out of Jerusalem, because they will not receive your testimony concerning me" (v. 18). Paul had protested: "Lord, they know that I imprisoned and beat in every synagogue those who believe on you. And when the blood of your martyr Stephen was poured out, I myself was standing there and consenting, and guarding the clothes of those who killed him" (vv. 19-20). But the voice from heaven had answered: "Go, for I will send you far away to the Gentiles" (v. 21).

VII. PAUL IN THE ROMAN GARRISON: Acts 22:22-30

The audience listened attentively until the word "Gentiles" was uttered. When these Jews heard Paul say that the Lord had told him to go to the Gentiles, they broke into a frenzy, yelling: "Away with such a fellow from the earth, for it is not fit that he should live!" (v. 22). Typical of a senseless mob they "cried out, and cast off their clothes, and threw dust into the air" (v. 23).

It looked to the tribune as if he had a notorious character on his hands. So he ordered Paul taken into the barracks and "examined by scourging" (v. 24). This was the "third degree" of that time, a very cruel method of forcing a prisoner to confess his misdeeds.

As they were tying Paul over a low post to make his bare back taut for laying on the Roman scourge—a whip made of leather strips with sharp metal or bone fastened to the ends—the apostle felt that he had had enough. He said to the centurion standing by in charge: "Is it lawful to scourge a man who is a Roman and uncondemned?" (v. 25).

Immediately the centurion hurried to the tribune with the warning: "Watch out what you are doing: this man is a Roman!" (v. 26). The tribune rushed to Paul. "Tell me, are you a Roman?" The answer was one word, "Yes" (v. 27). Almost stunned, the tribune said wonderingly: "With a great sum I obtained this citizenship" (v. 28). Paul replied, "I was born a citizen." This shows that his father was a Roman citizen, who had either purchased it, or more likely had been honored thus for some outstanding service to the Roman government. This gave him commercial as well as personal advantages.

Immediately the tribune gave orders for Paul to be untied. He was "afraid" (v. 29), for he knew that it was against the law for a Roman citizen to be bound unless he had been tried in court and convicted of a crime. He was doubtless relieved that he had discovered Paul's status before the actual scourging took place, for under no circumstances could a Roman citizen be scourged. This cruel punishment was reserved for slaves and aliens.

The question naturally presents itself: Why did Paul not plead his Roman citizenship at Philippi and escape the severe beating he suffered there (16:22-23)? The answer probably is that there was such noisy confusion that day that Paul could not be heard above the din of the crowd. There is another possibility: If Silas was not a Roman citizen it would be just like Paul to refuse to claim any exemption from suffering that his colleague could not also claim. However, the plural "Romans" (16:37) would seem to indicate that Silas also had this status. In any case, Paul now made good use of his citizenship to escape the cruel scourging.

CONTEMPORARY APPLICATION

Witnessing can be dangerous business. One thinks of the five missionaries to the Aucas, who were murdered. Were they foolhardy to so expose themselves to danger? Was their death an unmitigated tragedy?

These questions can only be answered in the light of the consequences of their murder. The facts are that as a result an entrance was gained to this wild tribe. All informed Christians are aware of the reception that the gospel finally received. Would this evangelization and conversion of many have taken place without the martyrdom? Only God knows.

Another factor should not be forgotten. Hundreds of young people have been challenged to a deeper consecration by the example of these dedicated missionaries. And much publicity has been given to the words Jim Elliott wrote in his diary: "He is not a fool who gives up what he cannot keep to gain what he cannot lose."

WHEN IS A MAN REALLY FREE?

DEVOTIONAL READING	Psalm 118:6-9

ADULTS	Topic: *When Is a Man Really Free?* Background Scripture: Acts 25—26 Scripture Lesson: Acts 26:19-32 Memory Verse: *. . . if the Son makes you free, you will be free indeed.* John 8:36

YOUTH	Topic: *No Fear of Death* Background Scripture: Acts 25:1—26:32 Scripture Lesson: Acts 26:19-32 Memory Verse: *While we live we are always being given up to death for Jesus' sake, so that the life of Jesus may be manifested in our flesh.* I Corinthians 4:11

CHILDREN	Topic: *Paul, a Free Man* Background Scripture: Acts 25—26 Scripture Lesson: Acts 25:1-12 Memory Verse: *You shall love the Lord your God with all your heart and with all your soul, and with all your mind, and with all your strength.* Mark 12:30

DAILY BIBLE READINGS	Mon., May 20: Paul Appeals to Caesar, Acts 25:1-12. Tues., May 21: Charges Against Paul, Acts 25:13-27. Wed., May 22: Paul's Background, Acts 26:1-12. Thurs., May 23: Paul's Witness, Acts 26:12-23. Fri., May 24: Agrippa's Decision, Acts 26:24-32 Sat., May 25: "Called to Freedom," Galatians 5:1-11. Sun., May 26: Freedom from Fear, Psalm 118:5-9.

LESSON AIM	To see how and why Paul faced death without any fear.

LESSON SETTING	Time: A.D. 58, at the end of Paul's two-year imprisonment at Caesarea Place: Caesarea, the seat of the Roman government of the province of Judea

When Is a Man Really Free?

LESSON OUTLINE

SUGGESTED INTRODUCTION FOR ADULTS

At the close of our last lesson we noted that the Roman tribune brought Paul before the Sanhedrin to find out what the Jews really had against this man (22:30). Paul stood there as a prisoner at the bar, facing a semicircle of seventy unfriendly faces. He spoke first. Courteously addressing them as "Brethren," he declared, "I have lived in all good conscience before God until this day" (23:1). Before his conversion he had been a conscientious Jew, doing what he believed was God's will, and after his conversion he had been a conscientious Christian.

Knowing that the Sanhedrin was composed of both Pharisees and Sadducees, Paul decided to divide his enemies. So he asserted: "I am a Pharisee, the son of a Pharisee: concerning the hope and resurrection of the dead I am being judged" (23:6). Immediately the two groups in the Sanhedrin got into such a heated fight that the tribune was afraid Paul would be pulled to pieces (23:10). So he took him back to the barracks.

The next day more than forty Jewish men made a solemn pact under oath that they would not eat or drink until they had killed Paul (23:12). When the tribune was informed of this he realized that he had a bigger problem on his hands than he had thought. Hastily he got Paul out of town by night, and sent him down to Caesarea, sixty miles away, with a military escort of 470 armed men. He was taking no further chances.

Chapter 24 describes Paul's trial in Caesarea before

Felix, the Roman governor. Paul made an excellent defense. Felix knew he was innocent. But he wanted to get a bribe out of Paul, and so he very unjustly kept him in prison for two years. When his term of office expired, he left Paul in detention. The new governor, Festus, inherited his problem.

SUGGESTED INTRODUCTION FOR YOUTH

Are you afraid to die? You need not be. Paul said, "For me to live is Christ, and to die is gain." Instead of saying, as many do today, "I can't win for losing," Paul's philosophy was: "I can't lose for winning." "Life or death, either way I win." Death will not separate the Christian from Christ; in fact, it will bring him right into the unveiled presence of his Lord. So death is nothing to be afraid of. Paul set us a good example of unflinching faith and undaunted courage in the face of death.

CONCEPTS FOR CHILDREN

1. Paul did not blame God for his imprisonment.
2. Even in prison, Paul was a free man in spirit.
3. Loving God with all our hearts makes us free.
4. When we are free, we want others to share our freedom.

THE LESSON COMMENTARY

I. PAUL IS ACCUSED TO FESTUS: Acts 25:1-5

A. Jewish Plot to Kill Paul: vv. 1-3

In A.D. 58 Felix was recalled to Rome by Nero, and Festus took his place as procurator of the province of Judea. Three days after he arrived in Caesarea, the seat of the Roman government in Judea, he went up to Jerusalem, the religious capital of the nation. This was a courteous and diplomatic act on his part.

In spite of the fact that Paul had been in prison and out of sight and circulation for two years, the high priest and Jewish leaders had not forgotten him. When they met the new governor, "they brought formal charges against Paul" (v. 2). They asked as a special favor that he would send orders down to Caesarea for Paul to be brought up to Jerusalem. But they were plotting to kill him on the way.

B. Festus Refuses to Comply: vv. 4-5

Had Festus been told about the previous plot to assassinate Paul (23:12)? Perhaps so. It seems reasonable that he might have heard about the heavy protection Claudius Lysias gave Paul when he sent him from Jerusalem down to Caesarea (23:23). In any case, he informed the Jewish leaders "that Paul was being kept at Caesarea, and that he himself would be going there soon" (v. 4). He added: "Let them therefore which among you are able go down with me, and accuse this man" (v. 5). This sounds as if he meant that those who could stand the trip should go. But this expression is used by Josephus for the "principal men" of the Jews, and that is what it means here.

II. PAUL IS TRIED BEFORE FESTUS:
Acts 25:6-12

A. Jewish Charges Against Paul: vv. 6-7

Festus stayed in Jerusalem "more than ten days" (v. 6)—but the Greek text says, "not more than eight or ten days." Then he went down to Caesarea. The day after he arrived there he sat down on "the judgment seat" and commanded Paul to be brought in. We noted in a previous lesson (in connection with Pilate's trial of Jesus, John 19:13) that a governor's decision had no legal authority unless he was sitting on the *bema.* Josephus writes this about Herod the Great's son Philip: "He used to make his progress with a few chosen friends; his tribunal also, on which he sat in judgment, followed him in his progress; and when anyone met him who wanted his assistance, he made no delay, but had his tribunal set down immediately, wherever he happened to be, and sat down upon it, and heard his complaint: he there ordered the guilty that were convicted be punished, and absolved those that had been accused unjustly" (*Antiquities,* XVIII, 4, 6).

When Paul was brought in, the Jews from Jerusalem "stood round him, bringing against him many weighty charges, which they could not prove" (v. 7). These were probably the same as in 24:5-6.

B. Paul's Defense: v. 8

The apostle did not need any longer to defend himself. He simply answered with a flat denial of the false charges: "Neither against the law of the Jews, nor against the Temple, nor against Caesar, have I committed any sin."

C. Paul's Appeal to Caesar: vv. 9-12

It must be said that the Roman governors of Judea do not show up very well in the New Testament. Pilate, Felix, Festus—they all lacked the courage to do what they knew was right. Festus, "willing to do the Jews a pleasure"—the same phrase as with Felix in 24:27—asked Paul: "Are you willing to go up to Jerusalem and there be judged by me concerning these things?" (v. 9).

By this time Paul was heartily "fed up" with the cowardice, selfishness, and injustice to these Roman governors. He knew that if he was taken to Jerusalem, his life would not be worth a penny. So he stood on his rights as a Roman citizen, at the same time reproving Festus for his dishonesty and lack of integrity. Boldly he declared, "I stand at Caesar's judgment seat, where I ought to be judged, as you very well know" (v. 10). He was not afraid to die if he had committed a capital offense, but if he was not guilty of the things the Jews had accused him of, "no man"—not even Festus—"can give me to them. I appeal to Caesar" (v. 11). Paul knew what he was talking about. The moment he made his appeal to the emperor, his case was out of the governor's jurisdiction. Festus could not hold a trial of Paul either in Caesarea or Jerusalem. He now had only one responsibility in the matter: to see that Paul was sent safely to Rome to be tried by the emperor. The case was now completely in the emperor's hands.

This change of events probably shocked Festus into realizing that he had made a bad blunder right at the beginning of his administration. The emperor would not be pleased to have an innocent man sent up to him. But it was too late for Festus to do anything about it. Due to his selfish desire to please the Jewish leaders he had missed his chance to acquit Paul and establish himself, in contrast to Felix, as an honorable judge.

He conferred with his council. But there was only one possible answer now. He announced to Paul: "To Caesar you have appealed; to Caesar you will go" (v. 12).

III. FESTUS CONFERS WITH AGRIPPA:
Acts 25:13-27

About that time Herod Agrippa II, the great-grandson of Herod the Great, came with his sister Bernice to pay a state visit to the new governor. (She was a profligate woman, and they were reputed to be living together as man and wife.) But Festus had a problem on his hands—Paul. Since Agrippa knew a lot more about the Jews than did the Roman governor, Festus asked his advice. He recounted the story of how his predecessor, Felix, had left Paul in prison. The Jewish leaders had asked for Paul to be brought to trial (v. 15). To Festus' surprise, they named no criminal acts, "but had against him some questions concerning their own religion [or, perhaps, "superstition" (KJV)] and concerning a certain Jesus who was dead, but who Paul said was alive" (v. 19). To Festus this all sounded like foolish nonsense.

The governor went on to say that he had asked Paul if he was willing to go up to Jerusalem to be tried. Since Paul had "appealed to be kept for the decision of the emperor, I commanded him to be kept until I could send him to Caesar" (v. 21). When Agrippa heard this he said, "I would like to hear the man myself" (v. 22). And so arrangements were made for him to do this the next day.

Typical of the Herods, Agrippa and Bernice came in "with great pomp" (v. 23), along with many military and civil dignitaries. Then a poor, shackled prisoner was brought in. But today Paul stands tall across the centuries, and the Herods are execrated for their shameful lives.

After Festus had informed the group as to why Paul was there, he revealed his problem: He had nothing certain to write to the emperor ("my lord"), and wanted this informal hearing to give him "somewhat to write" (v. 26). Then he added, almost plaintively: "For it seems unreasonable to me to send a prisoner and not to indicate the charges against him" (v. 27).

IV. PAUL SPEAKS BEFORE AGRIPPA:
Acts 26:1-29

A. His Early Life: vv. 1-5

Festus had introduced Paul to Agrippa and the assembled dignitaries (25:24). So now King Agrippa took over, saying to the prisoner, "It is permitted you to speak." Stretching out his right hand in a gesture of greeting—perhaps the left hand was chained to a soldier—Paul "answered for himself" (literally, "made his defense"). While this was not a legal trial (see above), the apostle felt the need of defending himself for the sake of the church.

Before Felix, the hired lawyer Tertullus had made a flattering and untrue introduction (24:2-4). Not so Paul. He spoke very courteously and expressed his appreciation for the fact that Agrippa, who was part Jew, was knowledgeable in all the customs and questions of the Jews, as Festus was not. So he could expect a good hearing before the king.

Paul began his speech proper by calling attention to the fact that all the Jews knew of his early life. They were well aware that "after the strictest sect of our religion I lived as a Pharisee" (v. 5). The two main sects of Judaism were the Pharisees and the Sadducees, and the former was by far the most strict of the two. Josephus writes of the Pharisees: "These are a certain sect of the Jews that appear more religious than others, and seem to interpret the laws more accurately" (*War*, VII, 5, 2). Agrippa would understand full well what it meant for Paul to say that he was a strict Pharisee and kept the law.

B. The Real Problem: vv. 6-8

Weymouth translates verse 6 this way: "And now I stand here impeached because of my hope in the promise made by God to our fathers." Paul is showing the unreasonableness of his being attacked for holding the very hope that was the basis of Jewish worship.

Incidentally, the mention of "our twelve tribes eagerly serving God day and night" (v. 7) sounds an interesting note. It is often assumed that the Jews of today are descended from the tribes of Judah and Benjamin and that the ten tribes of the northern Kingdom of Israel that went into captivity in 721 B.C. have disappeared. But we read that on the day of Pentecost there ws present from Parthia, Media, and Elam (2:9), the very area to which the captives from the northern tribes were taken. F. F. Bruce declares: "Neither Paul nor any other N.T. writer knows anything of the fiction of the ten 'lost' tribes" (*Acts*, p. 489, n. 13).

The hope of which Paul speaks is defined in verse 8. It is the hope of the resurrection. Paul declares that this was the real issue at stake. The Sadducees, who did not believe in any resurrection (23:8), were persecuting him for preaching this doctrine (23:6). Paul here says: "For which hope's sake, king Agrippa, I am accused by the Jews" (v. 7).

C. His Persecution of Christians: vv. 9-11

Paul could understand why the Jewish leaders were persecuting believers in Christ. For he himself had sincerely thought that he "ought to do many things contrary to the name of Jesus of Nazareth" (v. 9). He had been a leader in the persecution of Christians in Jerusalem: "Many of the saints I locked up in prison, having received authority from the chief priests, and when they were put to death, I gave my voice against them" (v. 10). But the Greek word translated "voice" literally means "a small smooth stone or pebble." It has this sense in Revelation 2:17, the only other place in the New Testament where it occurs. Since black and white stones were used for voting in those days—black for no, white for yes—the word came to mean "votes." The correct translation here is, "I gave my vote against them."

This raises the question as to whether young Saul had been a member of the Sanhedrin, for "vote" implies membership in a voting organization. This matter has been debated at length by competent scholars. It is possible that this brilliant, zealous young rabbi had been rewarded with some special privilege or status. The fact that members of the Sanhedrin had to be married men with children is not a decisive factor, for we cannot be certain whether or not Paul had ever been married.

Paul goes on to describe his treatment of the Christians in strong terms. He says: "I punished them often in every synagogue, and compelled them to blaspheme" (v. 11). But the Greek reads: "I *tried* to make them blaspheme" (conative imperfect). There is no evidence that Saul ever succeeded in making people curse the name of Jesus, though he certainly tried. Furthermore, "being exceedingly mad against them, I was persecuting them even to foreign cities." (The term *strange* in the King James Version always means "foreign.") "Being mad" is literally "raging against." Someone has referred to this as the "religious insanity of fanaticism." Unfortunately, this insanity has appeared many times in the history of the church. The blackest chapters of church history are full of this mad rage against the true followers of Jesus Christ.

D. His Conversion: vv. 12-18

Probably Saul's conversion would be considered the outstanding one in Christian history. It is described three times in Acts (9:3-18; 22:6-16; 26:12-18). It gave the church its greatest missionary and theologian.

Saul was journeying to Damascus "with authority and commission" ("full power") from the chief priests at Jerusalem when suddenly at noontime he saw "a light from heaven, above the brightness of the sun" (v. 13). He and his companions all fell to the ground (v. 14), though the latter soon staggered to their feet again (cf. 9:7). Then Saul heard a voice speaking to him "in the Hebrew tongue." This probably means the Aramaic language, which was the main language of Palestine at that time. The rabbinical writings actually assert that the voice from heaven preferred Aramaic to Hebrew and liked to use the double vocative, as we find here: "Saul, Saul."

The voice asked, Why are you persecuting me?" Then it added (only here in the best Greek text): "It is hard for you to kick against the goads." Saul was only hurting himself when he kicked back, like a stubborn ox, against the goads of conscience. The "wisdom and the spirit" with which Stephen out-argued his opponents in the synagogue (6:10), plus that unforgettable sight of Stephen's face shining like an angel (6:15), followed by a victorious death scene such as the young Pharisee had never witnessed (7:55-60)—these had all left a lasting impression on Saul's mind. Doubtless on that long trip to Damascus his mind had been plagued with the nagging question, "Could it possibly be that these followers of Jesus are right?" But he had kicked against these goads, these pricks of conscience, and pushed madly on to persecute.

When the Speaker had identified Himself as Jesus (v. 15; cf. 9:5), He gave Saul his commission. He was to be a servant and a witness "both of things you saw and of the things in which I will appear to you" (v. 16). In this ministry Paul would be rescued from "the people" (the Jews) and from the Gentiles (v. 17). It was to the latter especially that Christ was sending him. He was "to open their eyes to turn them from darkness to light and from the authority of Satan to God, so that they might receive forgiveness of sins and an inheritance among those who are sanctified by faith in me" (v. 18). The reference to the Gentiles was what had enraged the Jews (23:22). But it was Christ's special commission to Paul; he was to be the apostle to the Gentiles.

E. His Preaching and the Opposition: vv. 19-21

Verse 19 is one of the great statements of Paul's consecration to his task: "Whereupon, O king Agrippa, I was not disobedient to the heavenly vision." This stands as a constant challenge to every Christian. We have all had some vision of what our Lord wants us to do. Perhaps in some high moment of prayer that vision has been clarified and enlarged. Have we been true to the vision, obedient to the will of God as revealed to us? Or has the vision faded and our obedience become only partial?

The new convert began at once to p

he "announced first to those in Damascus and Jerusalem and then to all the country of Judea and to the Gentiles, that they should repent and turn to God, doing deeds worthy of repentance" (v. 20). Paul says in Galatians 1:22 that he was "unknown by face to the churches of Judea that were in Christ." But the reference here is evidently to a later ministry in Palestine.

It was because of all this that the Jews had seized him in the Temple and tried to kill him (v. 21; cf. 21:27-31). They were enraged at him for two things: (1) that he preached Jesus of Nazareth as the Messiah and resurrected Lord; (2) that he claimed God had sent him to proclaim salvation to the Gentiles.

F. The Suffering and Risen Messiah: vv. 22-23

But divine intervention had caused the Romans to rescue Paul from the mob in the Temple, so that he could say: "Having therefore obtained help [the Greek word means "assistance from an ally"] from God, I have stood until this day" (v. 22). He was "testifying to both small and great, saying nothing except what Moses and the Prophets said would come." Paul was careful to "preach the Word," as he admonished Timothy to do (II Timothy 4:2). He insisted that "Moses and the prophets"—the two main parts of the Jewish canon, sometimes used for the entire Old Testament—taught what he was preaching. He especially had to mention Moses, since the Sadducees placed the Pentateuch on a higher level than the prophets.

Primarily and specifically he had reference to the death and resurrection of Christ. We have noted before that the first point that had to be demonstrated in preaching to the Jews was the fact that their Scriptures taught "that the Messiah would suffer and, as the first to rise from the dead, would proclaim light to his own people and to the Gentiles." It is mainly in type and symbol that the death and resurrection of the Messiah are taught in the Pentateuch. The greatest passage on the suffering Messiah is, of course, Isaiah 53.

While other people had been raised from the dead, Christ was "the first to rise from the dead" in an actual resurrection. The others who were raised, in both Old and New Testament times, died again in due time. But Jesus was resurrected, never to die again. And the result of His resurrection was that new "light," the light of salvation from the dark dungeon of sin, came to "the people" [the Jews], and to the Gentiles." His death alone, without His resurrection, would have left the world in darkness. It was His rising again that brought hope to mankind. And it is as the risen, living Lord that He is now "the Light of the world." In our primary emphasis on Christ's death for our salvation we sometimes neglect the supreme importance of His resurrection. We were redeemed by His death, but we live in His life.

G. Festus and Paul: vv. 24-26

As Paul was "making his defense" (v. 24), Festus shouted in a loud voice: "You are raving mad, Paul! Your great learning is turning you to madness." Perhaps he had observed Paul's studious habits in prison. Or it may simply be that he was overwhelmed with the profound thought and fervent speech

of his prisoner. In any case, to a Roman this talk about a resurrection sounded like pure nonsense.

Courteously Paul replied: "I am not mad [insane], most noble Festus— [the proper address to a governor, not a verdict on Festus's character!]—but am uttering words of truth and soberness" (v. 25). Paul was not crazy; he was sober. What he had said was true and reasonable.

Paul continued: "For the king knows about these things, and I am speaking freely to him" (v. 26). This was a gentle reproof to Festus, who had turned the session over to Agrippa. Paul reminded his rude interrupter that he was talking to the king, not to the governor. As far as the record goes, Festus did not say another word. It was "the perfect squelch."

Paul was persuaded that King Agrippa knew what had been going on, "for this thing was not done in a corner." The last clause is a common proverb of that time, occurring in the teaching of such men as Plato and Epictetus. There is considerable evidence in the New Testament that Paul may have read the Greek philosophers. Two factors probably contributed to this. The first is that Paul was born and raised in Tarsus, the third greatest center of Greek learning in his day. The second is that Gamaliel, under whom he studied, was a liberal rabbi who encouraged his students to read Greek literature.

DISCUSSION QUESTIONS

1. Is there such a thing as absolute freedom?
2. Are there any limitations on God's freedom?
3. What are some limitations of human freedom?
4. What do we mean by man being really free?
5. How did Paul's freedom in Christ show itself?
6. What are some things from which a Christian is free?

H. Paul and Agrippa: vv. 27-29

It was easily apparent that nothing would be gained by a further conversation with Festus, who simply could not understand what Paul was talking about. But perhaps Agrippa might be open to the truth. So Paul turned abruptly to him and asked, "King Agrippa, do you believe the prophets?" Perhaps seeing a look of hesitation on the king's face and not sure what he might say, Paul quickly volunteered: "I know you believe!"

Herod Agrippa II was part Jew and part Idumean (Edomite, descended from Esau). When his father, Herod Agrippa I, died of divine judgment in A.D. 44 at Caesarea (12:23), the son was only seventeen years old. So he was not given the whole of Palestine, which his father had ruled, but only some less important areas north of Galilee. He was, however, responsible for the Temple treasury and the appointment of the high priest, as well as the garments that the high priest wore only on the Day of Atonement. So he knew full well what was going on in Palestine.

The reply of Agrippa has always been of special interest to evangelists. The invitation hymn "Almost Persuaded" is based on the words: "Almost thou persuadest me to be a Christian" (v. 28). The Greek literally says: "In a little you are persuading me to make [or, do] a Christian." But what does this mean? Hackett writes: "Agrippa appears to have been moved by the apostle's earnest manner, but attempts to conceal his emotion under the form of a jest" (*Acts*, p. 289). He feels that the translation "almost" is "unphilological." Lechler comments: "It is indeed possible that for a moment a serious impression was made on the king; still he immediately replies in derisive terms." We cannot be sure whether Agrippa's answer was serious or sarcastic. The Greek text seems to favor a cynical attitude on his part.

In any case, we know that Paul's response was utterly sincere: "I could pray to God that both in a little and in much not only you but also all who hear me today might become as I am, except for these bonds" (v. 29). He was bound physically, but was free spiritually. His listeners were free physically but were bound spiritually. He wished for them the same freedom in spirit that he enjoyed, the same peace and salvation.

V. THE CONCLUSION OF THE HEARING: Acts 26:30-32

A. Paul Exonerated: vv. 30-31

At this point "the king rose," not wanting to be embarrassed by any more personal questions or preaching. No one, of course, would dare to move until the king stood up. The governor was next in rank, and he stood. Bernice had to wait until third place, and then the others followed.

Away from Paul, a brief conference was held. There was general agreement that Paul was innocent of anything deserving death or even imprisonment.

B. Agrippa's Verdict: v. 32

King Agrippa put the conclusion in its legal setting: "This man could have been set at liberty, if he had not appealed to Caesar." But since he had made his appeal, there was nothing the governor could do except to send him to Rome. The only advantage of the hearing was that it gave Paul an opportunity to witness to King Agrippa.

CONTEMPORARY APPLICATION

"When is a man really free?" That is the topic of today's lesson, and the answer is: When he is the love-slave of Jesus Christ. Augustine said something like this: "Love God and do as you please." That is either a dangerous doctrine or a profound truth, depending on our understanding of it.

But what about our relationship to others? Martin Luther put it this way: "A Christian man is a perfectly free lord of all, subject to none. A Christian man is a perfectly dutiful servant of all, subject to all."

THE THESSALONIAN WITNESS

DEVOTIONAL READING	I Peter 1:13-25

ADULTS	Topic: *A Church's Witness* Background Scripture: I Thessalonians 1 Scripture Lesson: I Thessalonians 1 Memory Verse: *We give thanks to God ... remembering ... your work of faith and labor of love and steadfastness of hope in our Lord Jesus Christ.* I Thessalonians 1:2-3
YOUTH	Topic: *Your Life Talks* Background Scripture: I Thessalonians 1 Scripture Lesson: I Thessalonians 1 Memory Verse: *We give thanks to God ... remembering ... your work of faith and labor of love and steadfastness of hope in our Lord Jesus Christ.* I Thessalonians 1:2-3
CHILDREN	Topic: *Spreading the Good News* Background Scripture: Acts 17:1-7; I Thessalonians 2:1-10 Scripture Lesson: I Thessalonians 2:1-10 Memory Verse: *We speak not to please men, but to please God.* I Thessalonians 2:4
DAILY BIBLE READINGS	Mon., May 27: The Gospel with Power, I Thessalonians 1:1-5. Tues., May 28: The Gospel Joyfully Received, I Thessalonians 1:6-10. Wed., May 29: "Treasure in Earthen Vessels," II Corinthians 4:1-12. Thurs., May 30: An Unashamed Witness, II Timothy 1:8-14. Fri., May 31: Suffering for Christ, II Timothy 2:1-13. Sat., June 1: "Born Anew to a Living Hope," I Peter 1:3-9. Sun., June 2: Our Hope in Christ, I Peter 1:13-21.
LESSON AIM	To see how a church congregation can be a vital witness for Christ.
LESSON SETTING	Time: The First Epistle to the Thessalonians was written by Paul in A.D. 50. Place: It was written at Corinth, in Greece (Achaia).

The Thessalonian Witness

This week we begin a new unit of lessons with the general topic, "Letters to Young Churches." This was the title of the first part of the New Testament translation published by J. B. Phillips, and the use of his translation will add freshness to the reading of these Letters.

Specifically we shall be studying the First and Second Epistles to the Thessalonians and the Epistles to the Ephesians, Philippians, and Colossians. Because these five Letters are rather brief, all twenty-two chapters will be included in the lessons. Special attention will be given to Paul's relationship to each of the four churches. Four lessons are devoted to the Epistles to the Thessalonians, and four to the Letter to the Colossians, since the latter has not been studied closely in our lessons in recent years.

Some scholars have thought that the Epistle of James is the earliest book of the New Testament to be written. In recent times many have favored Galatians for this

SUGGESTED INTRODUCTION FOR ADULTS

place. But probably a majority of New Testament scholars today hold that the first book of the New Testament to be written was I Thessalonians. It was written at Corinth, during the year and a half that Paul preached there (Acts 18:11). The apostle wrote it in A.D. 50. The Second Epistle to the Thessalonians was probably written in the next year, A.D. 51. The three Prison Epistles—Ephesians, Philippians, and Colossians—were written during Paul's first imprisonment at Rome, A.D. 59-61.

The thing that should be recognized is that these Epistles are not textbooks in systematic theology. They were written as "occasional letters," that is, letters sent by Paul to meet certain occasions that arose in these churches. It is thrilling to realize that the earliest Books of the New Testament were missionary letters, written by the veteran missionary of the first century to churches founded as a result of his three missionary journeys. They are not formal treatises, but letters of life—living letters. It is hoped that during this quarter of study they will come alive for us and for our day.

SUGGESTED
INTRODUCTION
FOR YOUTH
"Your Life Talks." That is a truth we cannot escape. It talks every day! But what does it say?

Paul thanked God for the lives of the Thessalonian Christians. In the memory verse we are told that he was thankful for their "work of faith and labor of love and steadfastness of hope in our Lord Jesus Christ" (I Thessalonians 1:3, RSV). Do we exhibit these? What do our lives tell our friends and schoolmates about Jesus? About reality?

CONCEPTS FOR
CHILDREN
1. Paul was a missionary, writing letters to his recent converts.
2. He was concerned for their spiritual welfare.
3. He was thankful for their Christian witness.
4. We should be witnesses for Jesus.

THE LESSON COMMENTARY

I. GREETING:
I Thessalonians 1:1

The first word of all thirteen of Paul's Epistles is *Paulos*. When we analyze this, it seems very wise. The first thing we need to know when we read a letter is who wrote it; otherwise the letter will not make sense. The ancients had the good judgment to realize this so they always began with their own name, and then the name of the person to whom they were writing. We now have hundreds of papyrus letters from the first century, dug up from the dry sands of southern Egypt, all of which begin with the name of the writer. This is obviously much more logical than our practice today.

Paul associated with himself in the writing of this Epistle his two colleagues on his second missionary journey, Silvanus and Timotheus. The former of these is better known as Silas. He was the one Paul selected to take the place of Barnabas as his companion in travel (Acts 15:40). The latter is more familiar to us by his shorter name, Timothy. He had joined Paul and Silas at Lystra (Acts 16:1-3). We have in our New Testament two letters written to him at a later time.

After the addressor comes the addressee. In this case it is "the church of the Thessalonians in God the Father and the Lord Jesus Christ." Thessalonica was in Macedonia, in the northern part of Greece today. It is still an important port, now under the name Salonika.

This church was in God and in Christ. Today we think of a local congregation as being in a certain denomination. Perhaps we need to recover the first-century emphasis on the church as being in God. The Greek word for "church," *ecclesia*, means "an assembly of called out ones." That is what every Christian congregation should be—called out of the world to belong to Christ.

In the regular pattern of letters in that day, following the addressor and the addressee comes the greeting. In all of his Epistles Paul greets his readers with "Grace . . . and peace."

All the papyrus letters have *chairein*, "greetings." But Paul uses a different form, *charis*, "grace." It is not just "Hello," but "God bless you." The word *grace* is one of the great theological terms of the New Testament. As often defined, it means "God's unmerited favor."

To refresh our memories, let us review the origin of this word. The first meaning of *charis* was "gracefulness," which is largely physical. Then it came to mean "graciousness," which is mainly psychological. Paul gave it the higher spiritual sense of divine favor or blessing. Perhaps God's grace is shown in our lives by our being gracious, if not also graceful. One reason that people are not attracted to the church is that the lives of the members are not attractive enough to attract anyone. We sometimes fail to win people to the Lord because our personalities are not winsome enough. If we repel people by rudeness and crudeness, we do not draw them to Christ.

The other greeting is "peace." (In the Greek this is *eirene*, from which comes "Irene." So Irene should be a peaceful person!) This is the Greek equivalent of the Hebrew *shalom*, which is still the characteristic Jewish greeting today. The Oriental greeting "Salaam" is just a modification of *shalom*. There is no more beautiful greeting than "Peace." It is what the world needs, and it is what individuals need.

In all his Letters Paul combines the Greek and the Hebrew greetings. He was writing to both Jews and Greeks, and he greets both. This underscores the fact that Christianity had both a Greek and a Jewish background. Recognition of this truth is essential to all intelligent study of the New Testament.

Speaking in the abstract, it could be said that peace is God's greatest gift to the world and to us as individuals. There is nothing that the human heart longs for more than for peace. It is the quest of the ages. But, as every Christian knows, it can be found only in Christ. We should share this important secret with others.

The emphasis on God as "our Father" is prominent in the teachings of Jesus. He came to reveal *His* Father and to make Him *our* Father. This was the greatest expression of love that Christ could give to a lost world.

Paul's favorite name for Jesus is the full, threefold expression, "Lord Jesus Christ." Each part of this is significant, and the whole is a theological creed in itself.

The Greek for "Lord" is *Kyrios*. In the Greek translation of the Old Testament (the Septuagint, 250-150 B.C.), *Kyrios* is the translation of Jehovah, or Yahweh. So this term, as applied to Jesus, means Deity. It was this clear connection in the preaching of the apostles that enraged the Jewish leaders. They could not stand to have Jesus called "Lord." It was also the watchword of the early Christian martyrs. When they were commanded to say "Lord Caesar" they replied, "Lord Jesus"—and died for their faith.

The word *Jesus* (Hebrew: *Joshua* or *Yehoshuah*) means "Savior." An angel of the Lord told Joseph: "You are to call his name Jesus, for he will save his people from their sins (Matthew 1:21).

We have previously noted that *Christ* means "Anointed One." The Greek *christos* is the equivalent of the Hebrew *messia*. Jesus is the Messiah, the fulfillment of Old Testament prophecy. So when we say, "Lord Jesus Christ," we are confessing the deity of Jesus and His lordship in our lives. We are also declaring that He is the Savior from sin, the only Savior of the world. And we are saying that He is the Messiah, in whom all the promises and prophecies of the Old Testament are fulfilled. No wonder Paul was fond of using this expression.

II. THANKSGIVING:
I Thessalonians 1:2-4

A. Remembrance in Prayer: vv. 2-3

In all of Paul's Epistles, except that to the Galatians, the greeting is followed by a thanksgiving. In that Letter the apostle was so distressed over the conditions in the churches of Galatia that he didn't even stop to thank God, but plunged right into the subject at hand.

In this Letter to the Thessalonians he follows his usual custom of thanking God "for you all, making mention of you in our prayers." In the Greek, "for you all" can be taken with "making mention in our prayers." Paul had a large prayer list (cf. Philippians 1:4). He had a real pastor's heart, and it was large enough to take in all his converts.

We ought to follow Paul's example in thanking God for our friends and fellow church members. This practice is altogether too rare among Christians.

The apostle goes on to say that he unceasingly remembers three things about these Thessalonian believers. The first is their "work of faith." This could mean their work produced by faith (subjective genitive). Or it could be the work that is faith (appositional genitive). This would be in line with what we read in John's Gospel where the people asked Jesus: "What shall we do, that we might work the works of God?" The Master's reply was: "This is the work of God, that you believe on the One He has sent" (John 6:28-29). Perhaps we should allow both interpretations, as they both make good sense.

What is faith? It is essentially a trust in God as absolute Power, absolute Love, and absolute Knowledge. Since He is all of these, we can safely trust ourselves completely to Him.

The second thing Paul remembered about his readers was their "labor of love." Again, it is labor prompted by love, or it is love showing itself in laboring for the Lord and for others. The more we read the New Testament the more we realize that only work done in love merits God's approval. Elsewhere Paul declares: "Though I bestow all my goods to feed the poor, and though I give my body to be burned, and have not love, it profits me nothing" (I Corinthians 13:3). Those are strong words. Nothing we do is of any value unless we do it in love. That is why we need to ask the Holy Spirit, who alone can fill our hearts with divine love, to monitor our motives. Why do we work hard in the church? Is it to gain the approval of men? Is it to get a better position of leadership? Is it even to salve our conscience? Or is it for love of Christ? Everything we do should be motivated by love—supreme love for God and unselfish love for others. This is the

Christian ideal, taught by the Scriptures, and we should make this our goal in life.

The third virtue of the Thessalonians that Paul mentions is their "patience of hope." But "patience" is too tame a translation. Patience is a passive thing—it means keeping quiet, not saying anything, refraining from anger or impatience. It is largely negative in connotation.

On the other hand, the Greek word used here is positive in its thrust. It means "steadfast endurance." One does not win a race by being patient, by sitting down, doing and saying nothing. He wins by *endurance*, by keeping on running when his muscles and his nerves are taut. And that is the way we win the race of life. This is the message of Hebrews 12:1 where the same Greek word is translated "patience" as it usually, and incorrectly, is in the King James Version.

Again we find a genitive case with more than one possible meaning. Is it the endurance that comes from hope (subjective genitive)? Or is it the endurance that expresses our hope? Probably both. Hope must remain steadfast if we are going to emerge as victors at the end of life.

There is a striking parallelism between verse 3 and verses 9-10. Speaking to the Thessalonian Christians, Paul indicated that their "work of faith" was that "you turned to God from idols," to accept Jesus Christ as Savior. Their "labor of love" was "to serve the living and true God." And their "steadfastness of hope" was "to wait for his Son from heaven." The "blessed hope" is the hope of His second coming (Titus 2:13). This is the only thing that will hold us steady in a worsening world of sin and suffering.

But we can only have this hope "in our Lord Jesus Christ." The outlook is often dark and dismal and discouraging. But the uplook is always glorious. When we let our eyes dwell on circumstances around us—the winds and the waves—we begin to sink, as Peter did (Matthew 14:30). But as long as we keep our eyes on Jesus we can walk safely on the troubled waters of this world. Hope in human individuals or institutions is sure to be disappointed at times. Hope in Jesus Christ will never let us down. For "Christ is not a disappointment."

And all this is "in the sight of God and our Father." It is before Him that we live our lives daily, and the consciousness of this will both spur us to faithfulness and strengt every need.

B. A Chosen People: v. 4

The King James translation of this verse is a bit ambiguous: "Knowing, brethren beloved, your election of God " When we speak of the "election of the president," we mean the act of the people in electing their leader. Obviously that is not the sense here; it is not our electing God, but His electing us. The correct translation is: "your election by God." The King James Version uses the preposition "of" in hundreds of places in an inexact way, contrary to correct English today.

What is meant by "election"? The Greek word means "the act of choosing." God has chosen us; this is the glorious truth of this passage. As we shall notice in a few moments, the readers of this Epistle were mainly Gentiles. So a special significance here would be: "Not only have the Jews been God's chosen people, but you Gentiles are now chosen by Him for salvation."

III. AN EXEMPLARY CHURCH:
I Thessalonians 1:5-7

A. Paul's Powerful Ministry: v. 5

"Our gospel" was the glorious good news of salvation through Jesus Christ. Paul says that this gospel did not come to the Thessalonians "in word only, but also in power, and in the Holy Spirit"; that is, in the power of the Holy Spirit. The Spirit-anointed preacher is not only saying words; he is uttering God's truth in the power of the Spirit. That is what makes his preaching effective. Not only do sound waves carry the message to the listeners' ears, but the Holy Spirit carries it to their hearts, so that saints are comforted and sinners are convicted. (Sometimes the saints also need to be convicted!)

The Greek word for "power" is *dynamis,* from which we have the English words *dynamite* d *y* universe is the Holy Spirit. There is no

Spirit-filled believer should be dynamic; if he is not, he belies his profession.

Paul's gospel also came to the Thessalonians "in much assurance."

strong compound that literally means "fullness." It also means "full assurance" or "complete conviction." When we add to this the adjective *much*, it makes a powerful statement. It suggests an abundance of full certainty. Faith is not wishful thinking. The gospel does not offer a "hope so" salvation. To those who accept it there is full assurance of God's grace.

The last part of this verse should be read in the context of the first part. Paul is evidently saying more than that he lived a godly life while at Thessalonica. He means that his readers know he lived not only a pure life but a powerful life. He was so filled with the Spirit that his messages carried conviction to his hearers.

B. Imitators of Paul and of the Lord: v. 6

The Greek word for "followers" is stronger than its English translation here. It is *mimetai,* which means "imitators." Only Paul would dare to say: "Become imitators of us and of the Lord." Of course he was doubtless including his colleagues in "us." But it was because the apostle imitated the Lord carefully and closely that he could write this way.

The people at Thessalonica had "received the word in much affliction [or, "persecution"], with the joy of the Holy Spirit." It is only the Holy Spirit who can give joy in the midst of persecution and suffering (cf. Acts 13:50-52). Evidently Paul's converts there had suffered persecution after he left, and that is one reason he wrote this Letter to them.

C. Examples to All Believers: v. 7

Paul declares that the Thessalonian Christians became "examples to all that believe in Macedonia and Achaia." The other believers in Macedonia would be chiefly at Philippi and Beroea. Those in Achaia would be at Athens and Corinth. It appears that in spite of the difficult time Paul had at Thessalonica, his converts were unusually fine Christians, setting a good example to others.

IV. A WITNESSING CHURCH:
I Thessalonians 1:8

It is not enough for us to live exemplary lives. We must witness to others by lip as well as life. That is what these Thessalonian believers had done. From them the "word of the Lord" had "echoed" not only as far as Macedonia and Achaia, "but also in every place your faith toward God is spread abroad." Here was a witnessing church that was having a powerful influence far beyond its own commu-

nity. Its example was affecting nearby congregations, and its witness was reaching far and wide. Paul's preaching was being multiplied. The apostle didn't need to say anything about what had happened under his ministry at Thessalonica, for the report had gone out everywhere.

V. A TRANSFORMED CHURCH:
I Thessalonians 1:9

So Paul could write: "For they themselves report what kind of reception you gave us" (New International Bible). What had happened? His hearers had "turned to God from idols to serve the living and true God." This shows that they were Gentiles, for the Jews did not relapse into idolatry after the Babylonian captivity. And this indication is confirmed by what we read of the founding of the church at Thessalonica. We are told that only a few Jews accepted Paul's preaching in the synagogue but that "a great multitude" of Greeks believed (Acts 17:4). The result was a largely Gentile congregation in that city. These former idolaters now worshiped the true God. We shall notice later in this Epistle that their Gentile traits are in the apostle's mind as he writes his admonitions to them.

VI. A WAITING CHURCH:
I Thessalonians 1:10

The witnessing, working church was also a waiting church, expecting the return of its Lord. What assurance did these believers have that He would come back to reign in glory? The answer is: the Resurrection. Without the resurrection of Jesus there would be no salvation for us—for a dead Savior cannot save. And without His resurrection there would be no hope of His second coming. The empty tomb is as important as the cross. We are "rescued" because Christ paid the penalty of our sins, and we have spiritual life only in the living Christ, who rose again to live in our hearts.

DISCUSSION QUESTIONS

1. What does the word *grace* mean to you?
2. How would you define the term *peace*?
3. How wide should our prayer interests be?
4. What is the value of having a prayer list?
5. What is the relationship between exemplary living and effective witnessing?
6. What part should the hope of the Second Coming play in our lives?

CONTEMPORARY APPLICATION

The Thessalonian church is a constant challenge to us today. Most of us have a Christian background, at least a nominal one. If we were not brought up in a godly home and taken to a spiritual church, we still had considerable general knowledge about Christianity. It was not something entirely foreign to us.

How about these Thessalonians? They had a pagan background of idolatry and immorality. And yet they lived exemplary lives and witnessed widely and effectively. Should we do less?

PASTOR AND PEOPLE

DEVOTIONAL READING	Ezekiel 34:11-16

ADULTS

Topic: *The Ministry of Pastor and People*

Background Scripture: I Thessalonians 2—3

Scripture Lesson: I Thessalonians 2:1-13

Memory Verse: *May the Lord make you increase and abound in love to one another and to all men, as we do to you.* I Thessalonians 3:12

YOUTH

Topic: *Working with the Pastor*

Background Scripture: I Thessalonians 2—3

Scripture Lesson: I Thessalonians 2:1-13

Memory Verse: *May the Lord make you increase and abound in love to one another and to all men, as we do to you.* I Thessalonians 3:12

CHILDREN

Topic: *Timothy, Faithful Helper*

Background Scripture: Acts 16:1-5; I Thessalonians 3:1-10

Scripture Lesson: Acts 16:1-5

Memory Verse: *May the Lord make you increase and abound in love to one another and to all men.* I Thessalonians 3:12a

DAILY BIBLE READINGS

Mon., June 3: A Faithful Pastor, I Thessalonians 2:1-6.
Tues., June 4: An Exemplary Pastor, I Thessalonians 2:7-12.
Wed., June 5: A Pastor's Hope and Joy, I Thessalonians 2:13-20.
Thurs., June 6: A Pastor's Longing, I Thessalonians 3:1-13.
Fri., June 7: A Pastor's Work, Ezekiel 34:11-16.
Sat., June 8: A Pastor's Qualifications, I Timothy 3:1-7.
Sun., June 9: A Pastor's Responsibility, I Peter 5:1-5.

LESSON AIM

To show the proper relationship between pastor and his people and how this relationship may be fostered today.

LESSON SETTING

Time: A.D. 50

Place: Paul was writing to the Thessalonian Christians from Corinth.

Pastor and People

I. A Persecuted Pastor: I Thessalonians 2:1-2

II. A Faithful Pastor: I Thessalonians 2:3-6
  A. A Sincere Preacher: vv. 3-4
  B. A Selfless Apostle: vv. 5-6

III. A Devoted Pastor: I Thessalonians 2:7-9
  A. Gentle: v. 7
  B. Loving: v. 8
  C. Sacrificial: v. 9

LESSON OUTLINE

IV. A Godly Pastor: I Thessalonians 2:10-13
  A. A Holy Life: v. 10
  B. A Fatherly Care: vv. 11-12
  C. A Divine Message: v. 13

V. Pastor and People: I Thessalonians 2:14-20
  A. Persecuted Christians in Thessalonica: v. 14
  B. Opposition to Paul's Ministry: vv. 15-20

VI. A Concerned Pastor: I Thessalonians 3:1-5

VII. A Comforted Pastor: I Thessalonians 3:6-9

VIII. A Praying Pastor: I Thessalonians 3:10-13

SUGGESTED INTRODUCTION FOR ADULTS

Paul was not only the leading missionary and theologian of the first century, he may well have been its best pastor as well. In this lesson he uncovers his heart a bit and shows us his concern for a congregation he pastored briefly.

He also carried a prayer burden for all the churches he had founded in the provinces of Galatia, Asia, Macedonia, and Achaia. At the end of a heartrending recital of the many hardships and sufferings he had endured in the work of the ministry, Paul adds this: "Beside those things that are without, that which cometh upon me daily, the care of all the churches" (II Corinthians 11:28).

In his Epistle we catch a few glimpses of the tremendous burden of concern for his converts that the apostle carried. We can only guess what was included in the complete picture. The full story will never be told until Paul gets his citation in heaven.

The lesson today reveals a beautiful relationship between a pastor and his people. God took first place in Paul's life and God's children the next place. His own interests came last. His dedication poses a challenge to all of us.

SUGGESTED INTRODUCTION FOR YOUTH

Working with the pastor is one of the finest ways for a young person to develop spiritually. While he is helping, he will be learning. And being busy in the Lord's work is one of the surest guarantees against backsliding, and one of the best ways to grow in grace.

The relationship between pastor and people is a two-way street. If the pastor has to make all the advances, things can never be ideal. A consecrated young person should ask his pastor what he can do to help, thereby making his services available. There is always plenty of work for willing hands to do.

Some young men have developed beautiful working relationships with their pastors, relationships that have been mutually helpful. Young ladies can find plenty of work to do, too. There is a tremendous satisfaction in the consciousness that one is making a worthwhile contribution to life. This is the surest way to be happy.

CONCEPTS FOR CHILDREN

1. Paul's care for his converts was like that of a gentle nurse for her children.
2. We should try to help others by showing our love to them.
3. There is work in the church for all ages.

THE LESSON COMMENTARY

I. A PERSECUTED PASTOR:
I Thessalonians 2:1-2

When Paul arrived in Thessalonica he had just come from Philippi. There he had been beaten publicly and imprisoned. He had not only suffered physically, he had been insulted—"treated shamefully"—as well.

In spite of this, the apostle did not cease his preaching nor "soft-pedal" his message. He says: "We were bold in our God to speak unto you the gospel of God with much contention." This last phrase could be misunderstood. It sounds as if Paul preached contentiously. The correct translation is: "in the face of strong opposition." The "contention" came from others, not from Paul.

Because of his bold preaching, his "entrance in unto you [better, "our visit to you"] was not in vain," that is, not a failure. If Paul had been afraid, he would have failed. But his courage resulted in further conquest for Christ.

II. A FAITHFUL PASTOR:
I Thessalonians 2:3-6

A. A Sincere Preacher: vv. 3-4

The apostle asserted that he had not had any ulterior purpose in his preaching at Thessalonica. As the New International Bible puts it, "For the appeal we make does not spring from error or impure motives, nor are we trying to trick you" (v. 3). He had been perfectly sincere in his "exhortation," seeking only the highest good of his hearers.

An important test of anyone's ministry is this: Are we trying to please God or men? Paul passed this test with flying colors. He had only one desire and that was to please his Master.

Men-pleasers are not only undedicated but also irrational. For the preacher who tries to please the people will always be in trouble. When he pleases some, he offends others. Thus he is constantly "in hot water." The honest thing to do, and the thing that pays off in the long run, is to have just one purpose and goal in life and that is to please God. When we have a "single eye," Jesus said, our whole body will be full of light (Matthew 6:22).

The important thing to remember is that God tests our hearts. The verb rendered "trieth" was used in those days for testing metals to see if they were pure. They were tested in the fire, and any dross in them was separated by the intense heat of the furnace. Just so God monitors our motives. He not only observes all our actions, but also examines all our attitudes. He weighs our thoughts in his scales, to see if they are solid gold— unselfish, sincere, kind. Our motions may be pleasing to men, but are our motives pleasing to God? Our outward actions may pass the test of human surveillance, but do our inner attitudes pass the test of divine scrutiny? What we need to remember is that at the final judgment we will not face a jury of fallible men but the Judge who knows all the thoughts and intents of our hearts. Only as we pass His examination in our daily lives are we qualified to enter heaven. There will be no Ananias or Sapphira over there.

A. A Selfless Apostle: vv. 5-6

Flattery is a common form of insincerity. What is the difference between sincere compliments and "flattering words"? Sometimes the margin is narrow. And at times the motive may be the same for both: to encourage the other person or boost his sagging morale. Nevertheless flattery is wrong. It is strongly condemned in the Old Testament. Why? Because we are to tell the truth. Flattery is saying something about a person that you know—and often your listeners know—is not true. The end does not justify the means. The alternative is *not* demeaning or denouncing someone, but rather saying only those kind things that can be said honestly. Neither did Paul use a mask to cover up any greed—"a cloak of covetousness." He had not preached for

money, nor to win the applause of men—"nor of men sought we glory" (v. 6). Love of money and love of praise are two of the most serious snares that threaten the soul and the service of Christian workers. Paul was immune to both because of his complete dedication to God.

Paul, Silas, and Timothy could all be called "apostles of Christ." For the word *apostle* literally means "one sent on an errand," and so "a messenger." These three could have "been burdensome" to the Thessalonians, expecting financial support from the fledgling flock. Instead they had earned their own living.

III. A DEVOTED PASTOR: I Thessalonians 2:7-9

A. Gentle: v. 7

Gentleness is one characteristic of the fruit of the Spirit (Galatians 5:22). But it is a virtue that is not too common among Christians. Some men confuse roughness with ruggedness. They try to prove their loyalty to truth by being offensively outspoken, riding roughshod over the feelings of people. If there is any unfavorable reaction to this, they are being "persecuted for righteousness' sake." There is nothing much more self-satisfying than a martyr complex!

We are apt to think of the apostle Paul as being a rugged individualist— strong, a bit stern, not much given to sociability. But here he declares: "We were gentle among you, even as a nurse cherishes her children." What greater picture of gentleness could we have than this? The thing that many men need to learn is that gentleness is a sign of strength, not of weakness. It is a beautiful sight to see a powerful athlete being tender with a little child. And that is the picture we have here of the great apostle.

B. Loving: v. 8

Paul showed affection—"being affectionately desirous of you." But

love is more than affection. The proof
of our love is what we are willing to do
for those we profess to love. Paul went
all the way in this. He wrote to the
Thessalonian converts: "We were willing to have imparted to you, not the
gospel of God only, but also our own
souls, because you were dear to us."
Jesus said: "Greater love has no man
than this, that a man lay down his life
for his friends" (John 15:13). Paul was
ready to do exactly this. In fact he
went further than this when he wrote:
"I could wish that I myself were ac-
cursed from Christ for my brethren,
my kinsmen according to the flesh"
(Romans 9:3).

C. Sacrificial: v. 9

True love is always sacrificial love.
Paul reminds his readers of the toil and
hardship ("labour and travail") he had
endured at Thessalonica in order to
minister to them. Then he spells out
what this involved: "working night
and day in order not to be a burden to
any of you, we preached to you the
gospel of God." The apostle had
worked with his own hands to support
himself, so that he would not be a
financial burden to these new converts. He had worked "night and day,"
perhaps weaving goats' hair into tent
cloth by the dim light of an olive oil
lamp, then preaching during the day-
time. Paul was in the work—body,
soul, and spirit.

Some people have the idea that a
minister of the gospel has a soft job. If
he is a truly dedicated man of God,
this is far from true. Having been born
on a dairy farm, as a teen-ager I had to
be out in the barn milking the cows at
4:45 in the morning. The hours were
long and the work hard. But I can
testify that I have worked longer hours
and carried greater burdens in the ministry than I did on the farm. There is
no work that takes more out of a
person than preaching with a passion
for souls.

IV. A GODLY PASTOR:
I Thessalonians 2:10-13

A. A Holy Life: v. 10

The apostle could say that both
the Thessalonians and God—with His
all-knowing eye—were witnesses that
he had lived a holy, righteous, and
blameless life among the believers. In
another place Paul testified that he
sought always to have a "conscience
void of offence toward God and toward man" (Acts 24:16). That is the
way a Christian is supposed to live.
And a minister of the gospel must be
especially careful to conduct himself
in such a way as to avoid bringing any
reproach on the cause of Christ. One
cannot be too careful in such matters,
for a lifetime of preaching can be canceled out by one act of indiscretion.
Greek society in that day had much
the same type of loose permissiveness
in morals as we find today in America
and Europe. At such times extra care
is needed in setting a high example of
Christian conduct.

B. A Fatherly Care: vv. 11-12

Paul declared that he had dealt
with each one of his converts as a
father does with his children. They
were his spiritual children, and he
watched over them with the care of a
loving father (v. 11).

In the Greek text the three verbs in
the middle of verse 11 are found at the
beginning of verse 12, where they appear in participial form: "encouraging,
comforting, and imploring you to walk
worthy of God, who calls you into His
kingdom and glory." Paul had a fatherly concern for all his converts.

C. A Divine Message: v. 13

Again the apostle thanks God
"without ceasing" (cf. 1:2). This time
it was because his readers had received
the Word of God as divine, and not as
human. Paul affirms that it is indeed
and in truth God's Word, not the word

of men. Backed by divine power, it "effectually works also in you that believe." The apostle has already declared that his preaching at Thessalonica was in the power of the Holy Spirit (1:5). The reason we must preach the Word of God is that the same Spirit who inspired the writing of it will empower the preaching of it. There is a power in the Word of God that cannot be found in the opinions of men. Every preacher should seek to emulate Paul in proclaiming God's Word, which is the only seed that, planted in the human heart, will grow up to life eternal. And every listener should try to follow the example of the Thessalonians who "received" the Word of God.

V. PASTOR AND PEOPLE:
I Thessalonians 2:14-20

A. Persecuted Christians in Thessalonica: v. 14

As new Gentile converts to Christianity, the Thessalonian believers had become "followers [Greek, "imitators"] of the churches of God which in Judea are in Christ." The Jews had higher moral standards than did the Gentiles of that day. They also diligently studied the Scriptures. So the Christians with a pagan background and still living in pagan surroundings needed to follow the example of their Jewish brethren.

But just as the Christians in Judea had suffered persecution from their fellow Jews, so these new converts at Thessalonica had been persecuted by their own countrymen.

This probably gives us a clue as to one reason why Paul wrote this First Epistle to the Thessalonians. He had heard that they were undergoing persecution and he was writing to encourage and comfort them, and to strengthen them in the faith. As their spiritual father, he was concerned not only about their new birth but also about their Christian growth. He

wanted to make sure that they did not become discouraged and fall by the wayside. The people and their (absentee) pastor were experiencing a fellowship in suffering.

B. Opposition to Paul's Ministry: vv. 15-20

Paul has rather stern words here for his opponents. He says that they "both killed the Lord Jesus, and their own prophets, and have persecuted us; and they please not God, and are contrary to all men: forbidding us to speak to the Gentiles that they might be saved, to fill up their sins alway: for the wrath is come upon them to the uttermost" (vv. 15-16). This seems like a severe stricture. But it is well documented by the four Gospels and the Book of Acts. One of the greatest tragedies of human history was the Jews' rejection of Jesus as their Messiah, and their persecution of the early Christians. If they had only accepted Christ, their lot would have been very different.

Paul had been separated for a short time from his spiritual children at Thessalonica (v. 17). But it was in body only; his heart was still with them. He had eagerly, and with great longing, wanted to see their faces again. Several times he would have gone to see them, "but Satan hindered us" (v. 18). In our study of Acts 17:9 we noted that this may have been a guarantee that Jason had to give to the rulers of Thessalonica that Paul would not return to that city.

Verse 19 is typical of Paul's attitude toward his children in the Lord. They were his hope, joy, and crown of rejoicing. Probably the apostle had no wife or children. His spiritual children were his greatest joy and comfort in life. And they would especially be this "before our Lord Jesus at his coming."

The Greek word for "coming" is *parousia*. Literally it means "a being beside," and so "presence." In the first century this was "the official term for a visit of a person of high rank, especially of kings and emperors visiting a province. [In the New Testament it is used for Christ] and nearly always of his Messianic Advent in glory to judge the world at the end of this age" (Arndt and Gingrich, *Lexicon*, p. 635).

This is the most common word in the New Testament for the Second Coming. It is used this way four times in the Olivet Discourse (Matthew 24:3, 27, 37, 39) and once in I Corinthians (15:23). It is used six times by Paul for the literal "coming" or "presence" of human beings. But it is in the Thessalonian Letters that we find it most frequently—four times in the First Epistle (2:19; 3:13; 4:15; 5:23) and three times in the Second Epistle (2:1, 8, 9). This underscores the fact that the main emphasis in the two Letters to the Thessalonians is on the second coming of Christ, so that they are sometimes called the Advent Epistles. (The term *parousia* also occurs six times in the General Epistles, always for the return of Christ.)

VI. A CONCERNED PASTOR:
I Thessalonians 3:1-5

Paul could not personally visit the church at Thessalonica, perhaps for the reason noted above, but he became deeply concerned for his recent converts. The phrase "wherefore when we could no longer forbear" (v. 1), or "so

---

DISCUSSION QUESTIONS

1. How did persecution affect Paul's relations with the church at Thessalonica?
2. How did he overcome these difficulties?
3. In what ways may a pastor foster close relations with his people?
4. What should the congregation do to help this?
5. What part can we as individuals play in this?
6. Why are pastors needed?

---

when we could stand it no longer," reveals something of the intense love that the apostle felt for his children in the faith. Although he craved the companionship of his colleagues, he was willing "to be left at Athens alone." So he sent Timothy back to Thessalonica to see how things were going there. Though only a young man, he is described by Paul as "our brother, and minister of God, and our fellow labourer in the gospel of Christ" (v. 2). Timothy was more than simply an "attendant," as John Mark had been at the start of the first journey. This young associate was taking an active part in the ministry of the gospel. His assignment at Thessalonica was "to establish you and to comfort you concerning your faith." Establishing new converts in the Lord is just as important as winning them to Christ.

The apostle does not want any of the Thessalonian Christians to be "moved ["shaken" or "disturbed"] by these afflictions" (v. 3). The reference is evidently to the persecutions that the Gentile converts at Thessalonica were still undergoing. All Christians are "appointed" (or, "destined") to such for their own good. It is in the conflicts of life that we develop spiritual strength. Paul had faithfully warned his new converts that they would be persecuted, and so they were prepared for it (v. 4).

But now he could "stand it no longer" (v. 5)—same expression as in verse 1. So he sent Timothy "to know your faith." Paul had seen some of his other converts fall by the wayside, and he was concerned for these Thessalonians, "lest by some means the tempter have tempted you, and our labor be in vain" (v. 5).

VII. A COMFORTED PASTOR:
I Thessalonians 3:6-9

Timothy had just returned from Thessalonica. He brought good news of their "faith and love" (v. 6) and of the fact that the Christians there were remembering Paul and were longing to see him—as he also was to see them. There was a real bond of love between these people and their first pastor even though he was compelled by unfortunate circumstances to be away from them. Everything we read in this Epistle speaks well of the devotion and faithfulness of this young congregation.

The good report that Timothy brought from Thessalonica was like a breath of fresh air from heaven. The situation in Athens had been very discouraging, and Paul had moved on to Corinth before Timothy returned. The work there was not easy. He apparently arrived in Corinth "dead broke" and had to go to work immediately at his trade of tent-making (Acts 18:1-3). Corinth was a very wicked city. It was dominated by a pagan temple that was said to have a thousand sacred prostitutes. For a man brought up in the strict morality of Judaism, this must have been extremely depressing. Now Paul was comforted in his "affliction and distress" (v. 7) by Timothy's report of the Thessalonians' faith and faithfulness—the Greek word *pistis* means both.

How deeply Paul felt about the spiritual condition of his converts is shown by the amazing statement in verse 8: "For now we live, if you stand fast in the Lord." The apostle felt that he could hardly keep going if his spiritual children failed. They were a vital part of his very life.

Paul had started his Letter, after the greetings, by saying: "We give thanks to God always for you all" (1:2). Now he writes: "For what thanks can we render to God again for you, for all the joy with which we rejoice on account of you before our God" (v. 9). The report of Timothy had filled the apostle's heart to overflowing with joy and rejoicing. He was really living, now that he knew they were keeping alive in Christ.

VIII. A PRAYING PASTOR: I Thessalonians 3:10-13

Paul was still concerned about the spiritual growth of the believers, as every true pastor must be. He expressed it this way: "Night and day praying exceedingly that we might see your face, and might perfect that which is lacking in your faith" (v. 10). The word translated "exceedingly" is a strong double compound in Greek, literally "abundantly beyond above." Paul was a man of deep feelings and intense consecration. The verb *perfect* means "put into proper condition, complete."

What was it that was lacking in their faith? The apostle does not specify. Some feel that 4:3 and 5:23 suggest the need of a deeper work of sanctification in their hearts. The last two verses of this third chapter may suggest that they needed to have more love abounding in their lives. In any case Paul felt that there was some gap that he wanted to see filled.

The pastor's desire was that the Lord would make the Thessalonians "increase and abound in love one toward another, and toward all men, even as we do toward you." Christians should have a special love for each other as brothers and sisters in the Lord. But they should also love "all" people, regardless of who or what they are. Only thus are we truly the children of the great God of love, who "loved the world."

Those who abound in love will have their hearts established "unblameable in holiness before God, even our Father, at the coming [*parousia*] of our Lord Jesus Christ with all his saints" (v. 13). This is the final goal of Christian living.

CONTEMPORARY APPLICATION

The relationship between pastor and his people is very important for both. The progress of any church depends a great deal on this. If there is a happy, harmonious spirit, the church will grow. If there is misunderstanding and tension, the work will retrogress.

Both pastor and people carry a responsibility in this matter. It is not a one-way street. The two things that are essential are love and thoughtfulness. A common devotion to the Christ is also a binding force. The greatest factor in unity, however, is the Holy Spirit. He alone can unite all our hearts in love.

CHRIST'S COMING, OUR HOPE

DEVOTIONAL READING	Psalm 13

ADULTS	**Topic:** *Christ's Coming, Our Hope*
	Background Scripture: I Thessalonians 4—5
	Scripture Lesson: I Thessalonians 4:13—5:6
	Memory Verse: *Beloved, we are God's children now; it does not yet appear what we shall be, but we know that when he appears we shall be like him, for we shall see him as he is.* I John 3:2

YOUTH	**Topic:** *What of the Future?*
	Background Scripture: I Thessalonians 4—5
	Scripture Lesson: I Thessalonians 4:13—5:6
	Memory Verse: *Beloved, we are God's children now; it does not yet appear what we shall be, but we know that when he appears we shall be like him, for we shall see him as he is.* I John 3:2

CHILDREN	**Topic:** *A Helpful Letter*
	Background Scripture: I Thessalonians 1:1-10; 2:13; 3:1-4, 6; II Thessalonians 3:1
	Scripture Lesson: I Thessalonians 1:1-4; 2:13; 3:1-4, 6
	Memory Verse: *Rejoice always, pray constantly, give thanks in all circumstances.* I Thessalonians 5:16-18

DAILY BIBLE READINGS	Mon., June 10: Waiting for God to Act, Psalm 13.
	Tues., June 11: Practical Christian Living, I Thessalonians 4:1-12.
	Wed., June 12: The Coming of the Lord, I Thessalonians 4:13-18.
	Thurs., June 13: Ready for His Coming, I Thessalonians 5:1-11.
	Fri., June 14: "Kept Sound and Blameless," I Thessalonians 5:12-24.
	Sat., June 15: "Our Blessed Hope," Titus 2:1-13.
	Sun., June 16: "We Shall Be Like Him," I John 2:28—3:3.

LESSON AIM	To show the importance of our hope that Christ will return for His own.

LESSON SETTING	Time: A.D. 50
	Place: Corinth

Christ's Coming, Our Hope

LESSON OUTLINE

SUGGESTED INTRODUCTION FOR ADULTS

Many Christians today shy away from any discussion of the Second Coming. This is because they have heard so many wild speculations concerning it that they have been "turned off." It seems to them that every religious crackpot has some new crazy ideas on the subject.

This attitude is unfortunate. Teaching about the return of Christ bulks large in the New Testament. It is the subject of the only long discourse found in all three Synoptic Gospels, the Olivet Discourse. It is the main topic of Paul's two earliest Epistles, I and II Thessalonians. It is referred to a number of times in the later Letters. And it is the focal point of the last Book of the Bible, Revelation. To ignore this subject is to be less than Scriptural in our study or in our preaching. No Christian has the right to neglect the doctrine of the Second Coming.

What, then, is to be our attitude? The answer always is: "See what the Bible says about it." This must be our basic approach to all problems. What we need to do is not to turn off the light, but to turn it on more brightly by careful study of the Scriptures. If we always did this we would be saved from going to either the extreme left or the extreme right. The First Epistle to the Thessalonians is a good place for one to begin this study of the second coming of Christ.

SUGGESTED
INTRODUCTION
FOR YOUTH

What of the future? That is almost a universal question among young people today. What is going to happen next? Where do we go from here? This is what young people want to know.

The truth is that God is the only one who knows with certainty anything about the future. We do not know what will happen tomorrow, to say nothing of years from now.

So we are utterly dependent on God's Word for our knowledge of the future. In the New Testament we find several indications as to future events. The most definite thing we are told is that Christ will return to earth. This is repeated over and over again in different Books of the New Testament. It is an emphasis that many young people have recaptured.

CONCEPTS FOR
CHILDREN

1. The Thessalonian Christians were loyal to Paul.
2. We should be loyal to our pastor, not criticizing him, but encouraging him.
3. We should be always ready for Jesus' return.

THE LESSON COMMENTARY

I. THE PRIORITY OF HOLINESS: I Thessalonians 4:1-7

A. Living to Please God: vv. 1-2

Paul was not a "bossy" apostle. He always preferred entreaty to command. However, when the occasion demanded it he could be firm in giving orders.

But here he says, "We beseech you, brethren and exhort you." This could just as accurately be translated, "We request you, brothers, and beseech you." He does not command them as subordinates, but beseeches them as brothers.

He had already told his converts at Thessalonica how they should "walk." The verb *peripateo* (cf. English "peripatetic") literally means "walk around." But it is used frequently in the New Testament in a figurative sense for the walk of life, with the

meaning "live" or "conduct oneself." Arndt and Gingrich say: "In the N.T. this use of the word is decidedly Pauline ... elsewhere it is reasonably common only in the two small Johannine letters" (*Lexicon*, p. 655).

In this first verse the apostle urges us that we should live "to please God." This is really what it means to be a Christian. A sinner is one who lives basically to please himself. A genuine, born-again Christian is one who lives to please his Lord. This is the test we can apply to ourselves each day.

The verb *abound* is a favorite with Paul. He did not believe in barely getting by, in hardly keeping his head above water. He believed in the abundant life. He uses the verb *perisseuo* twenty-six times and it is used only fourteen times in all the rest of the New Testament. Jesus said, "I came in order that they might have life, and have it in abundance" (John 10:10).

The apostle reminds his readers that he had already given them such "commandments." A better translation is, "instructions." These he had evidently imparted to them when he was with them.

B. Sanctification, the Will of God: vv. 3-6

The custom in the King James Version of inserting words in italics that are not in the original is unfortunate. For instance, here we have "*even* your sanctification." It is simpler and clearer to say, as the Greek does, "For this is the will of God, your sanctification." It should be recognized that these words were written to people who are described in chapter 1 (vv. 7-10) as converted Christians who were leading exemplary lives and propagating their faith. The exhortations to sanctification are addressed to believers, not to sinners.

What is meant by sanctification? The noun is formed from the perfect passive participle of the verb *hagiazo*, which means "make holy." So this passage can be translated: "For this is the will of God, that you should be made holy." It is the clear teaching of the New Testament that this is what God wants to do. A holy God must have a holy people. This is the emphasis of the so-called Holiness Code in Leviticus 17—27. There the keynote is: "Ye shall be holy: for I the Lord your God am holy" (19:2). Again we read: "Sanctify yourselves therefore, and be ye holy: for I am the Lord your God" (20:7). It is true that much of the emphasis in Leviticus is on ceremonial holiness. But all scholars are agreed that in the New Testament the dominant idea of *hagiazo* is that of moral and spiritual holiness.

Some people confuse the terms *consecrate* and *sanctify*. But a check of *Webster's Unabridged Dictionary* will show that while the two terms have much in common there is one unique feature which belongs to

sanctify and not to *consecrate*, and that is the definition "to cleanse." Sanctification is a cleansing of the heart by the Holy Spirit. It is the Holy Spirit's indwelling presence that makes us holy. It is *His* work, not ours.

Holiness means purity. This is indicated emphatically in this section (vv. 3-6). It is God's will that we be sanctified, made holy, so that we will "abstain from fornication." Paul was writing to people who had recently come out of pagan idolatry and immorality (1:9), and they were still surrounded by these seductive influences. They needed to be purified within in order to withstand the impurities all around them.

Paul goes on to say, "That every one of you should know how to possess his vessel in sanctification and honour" (v. 4). What is meant here by "vessel?" This is a much debated question. The two main alternatives are "body" and "wife." The strongest argument for the latter is the fact that the verb translated "possess" is literally "procure for oneself, acquire, get." A man does not acquire his body, but he does acquire a wife. Arndt and Gingrich prefer the latter meaning, while allowing the possibility of the former: "*take a wife for himself* (or: *gain control over his own body*)" (p. 456). Obviously both meanings are relevant and logical and so probably both applications should be made.

Paul continues: "Not in the lust of concupiscence, even as the Gentiles which know not God" (v. 5). The old Latinism "concupiscence" is not a current term in the English language. The Greek word used here simply means "desire." It was originally neutral, being used for good and bad desires. We find both uses in the New Testament, though clearly the bad sense prevails. Perhaps the best translation here is, "not in passionate desire." This was the prevailing sin of the Gentile world of that day. The Jews had strict moral standards. But these Gentile converts with a pagan background and open immorality all around them needed to be especially well fortified.

The apostle warned "that no man go beyond and defraud his brother in any matter" (v. 6). It should be noted that the word "any" is in italics, indicating that it was inserted by the translators. But this distorts the true sense of the passage. The Greek says "the matter," which could just as accurately be translated "this matter." (The definite article is often used as a demonstrative pronoun.) He is talking about the particular matter of passionate desire that would cause a man to sin against his fellowman. God will punish all those who are guilty of this, and will avenge the wrong. Paul had evidently warned the Thessalonian converts about this previously.

C. God's Call to Holiness: v. 7

The basic characteristic of holiness is purity. This is implied in the statement: "For God has not called us to uncleanness, but in sanctification" (same word as in verse 3). There is no such thing as an unclean holiness. We demonstrate the sanctification of our hearts by living holy lives. This is the *sine qua non* of Christianity.

II. THE IMPORTANCE OF BROTHERLY LOVE: I Thessalonians 4:8-12

A. Taught by God: vv. 8-9

The one who rejects ("despiseth") what Paul is saying does not reject man alone, but also God; for the truth is from the Holy Spirit. This underscores the seriousness of rejecting Spirit-inspired messages delivered by men of God.

The apostle goes on to say that it should not be necessary for him to write them about "brotherly love [Greek, *philadelphia*], for you yourselves are taught by God to love one another" (v. 9). Jesus said that the Holy Spirit would "teach you all things" (John 14:26), and one of the most important things He teaches us is to love our brothers and sisters in the Lord.

B. Practiced by the Thessalonians: v. 10.

Indeed they were showing this love to their fellow Christians in Macedonia but Paul wants them to "increase" ("abound," same word as in 3:12 and 4:1) more and more. It is obvious that we cannot have too much of genuine holy love in our hearts and lives. There is never an oversupply of unselfish love.

C. Demonstrated in Daily Life: vv. 11-12

In these days of hurry and worry and flurry, verse 11 carries a timely message for us all. Paul admonished the Thessalonian Christians to "study ["aspire"] to be quiet, and to do your own business, and to work with your own hands." Quietness of soul is one of the greatest needs of people in this jittery Aspirin Age. Many consecrated Christians have too many "irons in the fire." A sensible focus of our time and energies will sometimes produce more lasting good. But we must also be careful to "walk honestly" in relation to those outside the church.

III. THE RAPTURE OF THE SAINTS: I Thessalonians 4:13-18

A. Concern About Believers Who Had Died: vv. 13-14

It would seem that one of the reasons Paul wrote this First Epistle to the Thessalonians was that a real problem had risen in the minds of the people in that congregation. The apostle had told them that Christ was coming back for His church; they could expect His return at any time. Now some months had passed, and still the Lord had not come. Meanwhile some of the Thessalonian believers had died. The loved ones left behind were concerned about this. Would the deceased Christians have a share in the blessings of the Second Coming? From the way Paul writes here we infer that the problem had become rather acute for some. He says that he does not want his readers to be ignorant about the fate of those who "are asleep" in Jesus, so that they will not sorrow "even as others who have no hope." When unbelievers lose their loved ones, there is often the feeling of being separated forever. Not so with Christians whose believing loved ones leave this world. For them the separation is only for a time.

If we believe in the resurrection of Jesus (v. 14), we should also believe in the resurrection of those who "sleep in Jesus." God will bring "with him"— that is, with Christ—all those who are asleep in Christ. If they are in Him, we need not be concerned about their fate. Jesus will not forget or forsake His own.

The concept that deceased Christians "sleep in Jesus" is a beautiful one. It suggests a place of quiet rest and security, after the trials and dangers of this life. But we must be on guard against reading too much into the expression. There are some that emphasize the idea of "soul-sleep"— that the dead are in a state of unconsciousness between death and the resurrection.

The facts of the case are that the Scriptures tell us very little about what is commonly referred to as "the intermediate state"; and where the Bible is silent we do well to be silent, too. But Paul does speak of "having a desire to depart, and to be with Christ" (Philippians 1:23). This and some other passages of Scripture seem clearly to teach that the spirits of deceased Christians go immediately into the presence of God.

B. Resurrection and Rapture: vv. 15-17

The apostle goes on to tell his readers "by the word of the Lord"— that is, by divine authority—that "we who are alive and remain until the coming [parousia] of the Lord will not precede [old English, "prevent"] those who are asleep." God will take care of them first; so we need have no concern about them.

Then comes a vivid description of what is commonly called "the Rapture," the transporting of the saints from earth to heaven. We read: "For the Lord himself [the One Paul elsewhere refers to as "Jesus Christ our Lord"] shall descend from heaven with a shout, with the voice of the archangel, and with the trump of God" (v. 16). This suggests a sudden, victorious coming. In the Old Testament times the trumpet was used to sound an alarm of war, but also to signal a victory won.

Christ came the first time in humility, as a helpless baby in a stable manger. He lived the life of a servant and died the death of a criminal. But when He comes again it will be in glorious triumph, marked by a shout of command, the announcing voice of the archangel and a blast from God's trumpet.

The language of this passage finds a striking parallel in I Corinthians 15:52: "In a moment, in the twinkling of an eye, at the last trump: for the trumpet shall sound, and the dead shall be raised incorruptible, and we shall be changed." Both these passages suggest a sudden, unexpected coming. But they certainly do not picture a secret, silent return of Christ. And we have to take the words of Scripture as we find them.

Who will be the first to hear the trumpet call of God? We are told that "the dead in Christ shall rise first." And next? "Then we who are alive and are left will be caught up with them in the clouds to meet the Lord in the air: and so we will be with the Lord forever" (v. 17). Doubt and discouragement will be left behind. Hardship and danger will never be experienced again. Sadness and sorrow will have no place in Christ's presence. The greatest reward and blessing that can come to any human individual is to be forever with the Lord. It will be well worth all the trials and tests of this life to enjoy this eternal bliss.

One is saddened to think of what sorry substitutes people choose in place of this. A few moments of thrills, a few days spent in worldly pleasure, a few dollars saved up for someone else to spend—are these worth more than Christ's presence forever?

C. A Comforting Hope: v. 18

The beautiful passage on the Rapture closes with this admonition: "Wherefore comfort one another with these words." The verb *parabaleo* literally means "call alongside" (to help). It can be translated either "comfort" or "exhort." Both of these renderings fit the context very well. The coming of Christ is a comforting hope. But since it is important that we be ready for His return, the idea of exhorting is also appropriate. In view of the language of verse 13, it seems probable that Paul meant "comfort" here. The sorrowing Christians were to be comforted with the assurance that they would one day be reunited with their departed loved ones.

IV. WATCHING FOR THE SECOND COMING:
I Thessalonians 5:1-6

A. The Times and Seasons: v. 1

Paul tells his readers that he does not need to write them about "the times and the seasons." The first of these nouns is *chronos* (cf. "chronology"). It refers to the passing of time, to periods of time. The second is *kairos*, which means "the right, proper, favorable time," or a definite, fixed time. Arndt and Gingrich note that it is "one of the chief eschatological terms [and means] the time of crisis, the last times" (p. 396). It is recognized by scholars as being a technical term in some New Testament passages, carrying prophetic significance. It seems in some places, as here, to mean God's appointed time.

The rather obvious meaning of this verse is that Christians should be able to recognize some of the "times and seasons" that point the way to Christ's return. But we need to handle carefully and cautiously the interpretation of such phenomena. For Jesus warned His disciples: "It is not for you to know the times or the seasons, which the Father has put in His own power" (Acts 1:7). Date-setting has always been the bane of speculative lectures and books on what is commonly called "prophecy."

B. As a Thief in the Night: vv. 2-3

The emphasis of the New Testament is not on the date of the Second Coming but on the fact that it will be sudden and unexpected. "The day of the Lord" will come "as a thief in the night." This is in line with the words of Jesus in the Olivet Discourse: "Watch therefore: for you know not what hour your Lord will come. But know this, that if the owner of the house had known in which watch the thief would come, he would have been on the alert, and would not have allowed his house to be broken into. Therefore, you be ready; for in such an hour as you do not think, the Son of Man will come" (Matthew 24:42-44).

Paul's extended warning here seems especially appropriate in our times. He says that when people say, "Peace and safety," then "sudden destruction comes on them" like labor pains to an expectant mother, "and they shall not escape" (v. 3). Many times in our generation we have heard people talk about "world peace" or "peace in our time." But always when such talk is most optimistic, we are plunged into fresh fighting. The facts are that world peace will never be achieved until the return of "the Prince of Peace." We cannot afford to pin our hopes on anyone or anything else.

C. Watching and Waiting: vv. 4-6

The apostle assures his readers that they are not in the dark so that the day of Christ's coming should "over-take [them] as a thief." The Christian need not be caught unawares. If we are ready to meet Jesus at any time, "with our lamps all trimmed and burning," we will not be caught off guard. We are "children of light" and "children of the day" (v. 5). In view of the constant imminence of our Lord's return, "let us not sleep, as do others; but let us watch and be sober" (v. 6).

V. THE HOPE OF SALVATION:
I Thessalonians 5:7-11

People sleep or get drunk at night. We Christians, who belong to the day, should be sober and alert, "putting on the breastplate of faith and love" to protect our hearts, and, to protect our heads, the helmet of "the hope of salvation." By means of these we can keep ourselves safe until the Lord comes. God has not appointed us to eternal wrath, "but to obtain salvation by our Lord Jesus Christ." This was made possible for us by Jesus' death on the cross, so that "whether we wake or sleep [are alive or dead] we shall live together with him." Anyone who is spiritually in Christ will not be separated from Him by life or death.

Again we are told: "Wherefore

DISCUSSION QUESTIONS

1. What arguments are raised against Christ's return?
2. What are the strongest arguments in favor of it?
3. How may we be ready for His coming?
4. What should be our attitude toward long-range plans in the church, and why?
5. What are some "pitfalls of prophecy" that we need to avoid?
6. What phase of our salvation will take place at the Second Coming?

---

comfort yourselves together and edify one another, even as also ye do" (cf. 4:18). We are to build each other up in the hope of His coming.

VI. VARIOUS ADMONITIONS:
I Thessalonians 5:12-22

In this section we have a fairly lengthy series of brief admonitions, all of which are related to our being ready for the Second Coming and so deserve careful meditation and obedience. "Feebleminded" is literally "little-souled" (v. 14). It does not refer to the mentally retarded but rather to the spiritually retarded.

VII. SANCTIFIED THROUGH AND THROUGH
I Thessalonians 5:23-24

Since sanctification is closely related to the Second Coming in this Epistle, we note this significant passage. Paul prays that the God of peace will "sanctify you wholly." The adverb occurs only here in the New Testament. It is a strong compound, meaning "wholly-completely." Martin Luther translated it (1522): "through and through." That is exactly what it means. And the purpose of this sanctification is that our "whole spirit and soul and body" may be "preserved blameless unto the coming of our Lord Jesus Christ." Fortunately, this prayer is followed by the promise: "Faithful is He who calls you, who also will do it" (v. 24).

VIII. CLOSING REMARKS:
I Thessalonians 5:25-28

Paul requests the prayers of his readers, tells them to greet each other in loving fellowship, and charges them to have his Letter read to all the church. Then he signs off with a brief benediction: "The grace of our Lord Jesus Christ be with you."

CONTEMPORARY APPLICATION

Many people today question the doctrine of Christ's return. He has tarried so long! What we need to remember is that the Old Testament saints waited many weary centuries for the coming of the Messiah. But finally, "in the fullness of time," He did come. And just as all the predictions relating to His first coming were fulfilled nineteen hundred years ago, so we believe that all the promises relating to His second coming will be fulfilled in due time.

THE CHRISTIAN'S HOPE AND THE DAILY TASK

DEVOTIONAL READING	Titus 2:11-14

ADULTS

Topic: *The Christian's Hope and the Daily Task*

Background Scripture: II Thessalonians

Scripture Lesson: II Thessalonians 2:1-2; 3:6-16

Memory Verse: *Do not be weary in well-doing.* II Thessalonians 3:13.

YOUTH

Topic: *Don't Just Sit There!*

Background Scripture: II Thessalonians

Scripture Lesson: II Thessalonians 2:1-2; 3:6-16

Memory Verse: *Do not be weary in well-doing.* I Thessalonians 3:13

CHILDREN

Topic: *Guides to Christian Living*

Background Scripture: I Thessalonians 4:1-2, 9-12; 5:12-16

Scripture Lesson: I Thessalonians 5:12-16

Memory Verse: *Always seek to do good to one another.* I Thessalonians 5:15

DAILY BIBLE READINGS

Mon., June 17: Watchful and Faithful, Luke 12:35-48.
Tues., June 18: The Right Use of God's Gifts, Matthew 25:14-30.
Wed., June 19: Steadfast Despite Persecution, II Thessalonians 1:10.
Thurs., June 20: Prayer for God's Chosen, II Thessalonians 1:11-12; 2:13-15.
Fri., June 21: The Lawless One Conquered, II Thessalonians 2:1-12.
Sat., June 22: The Lord Strengthens and Delivers, II Thessalonians 2:16—3:5.
Sun., June 23: Not Idle, but Working, II Thessalonians 3:6-15.

LESSON AIM

To show how our hope of the return of Christ should affect our daily living.

LESSON SETTING

Time: A.D. 51

Place: Corinth

358

The Christian's Hope and the Daily Task

LESSON OUTLINE

SUGGESTED INTRODUCTION FOR ADULTS

Paul wrote his First Epistle to the Thessalonians from Corinth, probably in A.D. 50. Some months later, perhaps in A.D. 51, he wrote the Second Epistle from Corinth.

The purpose of the First Epistle was twofold: (1) to encourage the Thessalonian believers in their time of persecution and (2) to comfort those who had lost Christian loved ones, by assuring them that these would be resurrected at Christ's second coming. The purpose of the Second Epistle was also twofold: (1) to correct a misconception as to the time of the Second Coming and (2) to urge believers to be busily engaged while waiting for Christ to return.

The difference in emphases in the two Epistles has caused considerable comment. Some extreme critics have said that the same man could not have written both. But this is shallow thinking. In his Letters Paul was dealing with problems as they arose in the various churches. Different problems require different instructions for their correction. Here we find different problems in the same church. In the First Epistle, Paul tells his readers that Christ will come as a thief in the night, suddenly and unexpectedly, and will take His faithful ones, both the living and the dead, to be with Him. In the Second Epistle he intimates that some events will precede the Second Coming and believers should be busy while waiting.

"Don't Just Sit There!" That is what Paul was telling his converts at Thessalonica. It would seem that some had become obsessed with the idea that the Second Coming was not only imminent but immediate. They were sitting around doing nothing—just waiting.

There have been such instances in modern times. One group believed its leader's prediction that Christ was coming on a certain day. So the people followed his directions to sell all their property and give the proceeds to the poor. They donned white robes and waited on a hill. The result was rather disillusioning. They were left with only their white robes and a shattered faith.

Paul warned his readers to be busy in the Lord's work while they were waiting. "Occupy till I come"—that is the note sounded by Jesus (Luke 19:13).

1. Being busy is one of the secrets of being happy.
2. We must be sure we are busy doing good things.
3. Doing good to others and making them happy is the way to be happy ourselves.

THE LESSON COMMENTARY

I. INTRODUCTION:
II Thessalonians 1:1-4

A. Address: v. 1

Two interesting observations can be made about the address and greeting. The first is that in the Greek the addresses in the First and Second Epistles are exactly the same, except for the addition in II Thessalonians of "our" before "Father." But in the King James Version we find three words added in italics (not in the Greek) in the first part of I Thessalonians 1:1. These should be omitted. The second observation is that in I Thessalonians the address and greeting are in one verse, whereas in II Thessalonians they are separated into two verses. These inconsistencies show a lack of careful correlation.

In both of these Letters Paul associates with himself in the address his two colleagues, Silas and Timothy. This was a fine gesture of courtesy.

B. Greeting: v. 2

As noted before, all of Paul's Epistles carry the double greeting, "Grace and peace." The first was more Greek, the second Hebrew. And both come from God through Christ.

C. Thanksgiving: vv. 3-4

Paul had received a good report about the progress of the church at Thessalonica. He writes: "Your faith grows exceedingly, and the love you all have for each other abounds" (v. 3). ("Charity" in the modern sense does not fit here at all.) The apostle goes on to say that he boasts in the other churches about the perseverance and faith the Thessalonian Christians have shown in the persecutions and trials they were enduring. The church at Thessalonica was outstanding in its spiritual vigor.

II. CHRIST'S COMING IN JUDGMENT:
II Thessalonians 1:5-12

A. Righteous Judgment: vv. 5-6

The fact that these new converts were able to remain steadfast under persecution was a token of God's righteous judgment. They had shown themselves worthy of the kingdom of God, for which they were suffering. In due time the Lord would balance the account by bringing trouble to those who were troubling these Christians. *Tribulation* and *trouble* (v. 6) have the same root in Greek.

B. Revelation and Destruction: vv. 7-10

A righteous God will give relief to those who are "troubled" (same word), as well as to Paul and his colleagues. This will take place when the Lord Jesus is "revealed from heaven with his mighty angels, in flaming fire taking vengeance on those who do not know God and do not obey the gospel of our Lord Jesus Christ" (vv. 7-8). These will pay the penalty of "everlasting destruction from the presence of the Lord, and from the glory of His power" (v. 9). This will be the fate of all who reject the way of salvation provided in Christ. It will take place at our Lord's return, when He comes "to be glorified in his saints" (v. 10).

It is clear that Paul is speaking here about the return of Christ in glory at the end of this age. Many Bible students hold that the Second Coming will have two phases—the Rapture before the Great Tribulation, when Christ comes *for* His Church; and the Revelation after the Great Tribulation, when Christ comes to earth *with* His church to reign in glory, after defeating His enemies and destroying the forces of evil. Those who hold this view usually identify I Thessalonians 4:13-18 with the Rapture and II

Thessalonians 1:7—2:12, with the Revelation. It must be acknowledged that this interpretation makes it easier to explain the striking differences between these two Letters, since they are then describing two different events.

C. Prayerful Preparation: vv. 11-12

Paul was always praying for his converts. So now he prays that God will count them worthy of their high calling and fulfill every good purpose of theirs. The goal of all this was that "the name of our Lord Jesus Christ may be glorified in you," and they in turn in Him—all through God's grace in Christ (v. 12).

III. EVENTS PRECEDING CHRIST'S COMING:
II Thessalonians 2:1-12

A. False Teaching: vv. 1-2

Paul's favorite name for the Son of God is "our Lord Jesus Christ." It occurs no less than seven times in this short Epistle (1:8; 2:1, 14, 16; 3:6, 12, 18). Added to this we find "the Lord Jesus Christ" three times (1:1, 2, 12). He is Lord, Savior, and Messiah. At His second coming all the saints will be gathered together to Him.

Concerning the Parousia, Paul begs the Thessalonian believers not to be "quickly shaken in mind, or troubled, neither by spirit, nor by word, nor by letter as from us, as that the day of Christ is at hand" (v. 2). The last clause should be translated "as that the day of the Lord has come" (so Arndt and Gingrich's *Lexicon* p. 266, and most commentaries). The heresy that the apostle was combating was the erroneous teaching that the Second Coming had already taken place.

The false teachers were using any and every means to propagate this error. One was "by spirit." This probably means that someone would claim to have a special revelation from the Holy Spirit and would announce it as such in a public service. A second means was "by word"—some special message, report, or rumor. The third way was "by letter as from us." It would appear that these wicked teachers stooped so low as to write a letter setting forth this false doctrine and then presenting the epistle as having been written by Paul and carrying apostolic authority.

It was evidently because of this that he was careful to say at the end of this Letter: "The salutation of Paul with my own hand, which is the distinguishing mark in every epistle; so I write" (3:17). That is, don't accept any letter as from me, unless you see my signature in my own handwriting. As he came to the end of dictating the Letter, the apostle took the quill pen from the hand of his secretary and wrote his own signature, just as we do today to make documents legally valid.

One of the disconcerting things we have to face today is the fanatical zeal with which the followers of a false religion propagate its errors. If evangelical Christians had half the drive that heretics exhibit, the true church would be much farther ahead than it is.

B. The Apostasy: v. 3a

Paul declares that before the return of Christ there would be "a falling away." The Greek says *he apostasia*, "the apostasy."

In the nineteen hundred years of church history there have been many apostasies. But a good case could be made for the claim that only in the past one hundred years have we had "*the* apostasy," and predominantly in the last ten years. The nineteenth century saw the rise of Rationalism, with its denial of the deity of Jesus and of the divine authority of the Scriptures. That was bad enough. But it remained for the last decade to spawn the "death of God" theology. This would seem to be the ultimate in apostasy, especially when we realize that this

baneful note was not sounded by infidels attacking the church from the outside, but by professors in leading theological seminaries in the United States. And this same brood has very logically propagated the New Morality, with its repudiation of any absolute standards of conduct. As far as "the apostasy" taking place before the return of Christ, we don't have to wait any longer.

C. The Man of Lawlessness: vv. 3b-10

Paul pinpointed another event that would precede the day of the Lord: the revelation of "the man of lawlessness" (so the best Greek text, rather than "man of sin"). He is described as "the son of perdition," or the man doomed to destruction. He is the personification of rebellion against God. For he "opposes and exalts himself over every thing that is called God or is worshipped" (v. 4). He even "sits in the temple of God, showing himself that he is God." He sets himself above all the deities, and claims that he is the real God.

Paul reminds his readers that he had warned them about this when he was with them (v. 5). But something is holding back the Man of Lawlessness until the time comes for him to be revealed to the world (v. 6).

Yet "the mystery of iniquity" is already at work (v. 7). The Greek says "the mystery of lawlessness," thus connecting this expression with the Man of Lawlessness of verse 3. Paul goes on to say: "only he who now letteth will let, until he be taken out of the way." But the Greek says very clearly "the one who now holds back," or "hinders." Obviously this is exactly the opposite of the current meaning of "letteth," which means "not hindering." So the uninstructed reader derives precisely the wrong meaning from the passage. There are over two hundred words in the King James Version that have radically changed their meaning since 1611. That is why a good contemporary translation of the Bible is imperative.

Who is this one who holds back the working of the mystery of lawlessness? Some would refer it to the Roman Empire of that time or to any governmental authority that restrains lawlessness today. But since the expression is in the masculine gender in Greek it seems best to identify this one as the Holy Spirit. He is the great restraining influence in a wicked world, and He will continue to restrain until He is "taken out of the way." Many Bible students would refer this to the Holy Spirit's ascent with the church at the Rapture of the saints.

When the Holy Spirit has been taken out of the way, "then shall that Wicked be revealed." Again we lose the connection that is obvious in the original. For instead of "that Wicked," the Greek says, "the Lawless One." The "Lord" (Jesus) will slay this one "with the spirit of his mouth." The Greek language uses the same word, *pneuma*, for "breath" and "spirit." The best translation here is "with the breath of his mouth." Christ will also destroy him "with the brightness of his coming." The Greek word for "coming" is *parousia*, which occurs again in verse 9. "Brightness" is *epiphaneia*.

This is perhaps the logical place to note the three Greek words used in the New Testament for the second coming of Christ. The most common one is *parousia*, which means "presence." It is used eighteen times for the Second Coming. The next in order is *epiphaneia* (six times). Here it is translated "brightness," but in the other five passages it is rendered by its regular meaning, "appearance." The third term is *apocalypsis*, "revelation," which is used five times for Christ's return.

Who is the Man of Lawlessness (v. 3) or the Lawless One (v. 8)? Irenaeus in the second century identified this person and the Beast of Revelation with the Antichrist, a name which occurs only in I John (2:18, 22; 4:3) and II John (v. 7). This view is very widely held today among evangelicals.

D. Powerful Delusion: vv. 11-12

These two verses constitute one of the most solemn warnings in the New Testament. If people wilfully refuse to believe the truth because they want to continue in sinful pleasure, God will send them powerful delusion, so that they will really believe a lie. Belief and unbelief are more moral than mental.

IV. NEED OF STEADFASTNESS:
II Thessalonians 2:13-17

A. Thanksgiving for God's Salvation: vv. 13-14

Paul says, "We ought always to thank God for you, brothers loved by the Lord," because God had chosen them "for salvation in sancitification of the Spirit and belief of the truth" (v. 13). Through the gospel Paul preached to them, God had called them for possession of "the glory of our Lord Jesus Christ." What a rich heritage we have!

B. Holding Fast to Traditions: v. 15

It is popular today to decry all traditions as retrogressive. What we need is something new, not something old!

But civilization makes real progress only as it builds on the traditions from the past. And this is true of the churches. Paul tells his converts at Thessalonica to "stand fast, and hold the traditions you have been taught, whether by word, or our epistle."

C. Comfort and Strength: vv. 16-17

Paul prays that "our Lord Jesus Christ" and God the Father would "comfort your hearts, and establish you in every good word and work." The apostle was always concerned for his converts, that they might be firmly grounded in the Living Word and the Written Word. And that is our need today.

V. PRAYERFUL ASSURANCE:
II Thessalonians 3:1-5

Two related features appear again and again in Paul's Epistles: he is praying for his converts and he asks their prayers for him. This matter of fellowship in prayer was very real to him. And he always felt his need for the prayerful support of others.

This time he requests prayer that "the word of the Lord may have free course." The Greek says, "may run," which probably means "may spread rapidly." And he wants the Word of God to be "glorified [or "honored,"] even as it is with you." He hopes that the gospel will be accepted and believed in other places as it was in Thessalonica.

He also asks his friends to pray that he and his associates will be "delivered from unreasonable and wicked men" (v. 2). The adjective rendered "unreasonable" literally means "out of place." It came to have the moral sense of "wrong" or "improper." Paul had encountered many such men in his missionary work. They had driven him out of city after city and were still hounding his trail. It is no wonder that he asked that they pray that he be delivered from them.

At the same time he assures his readers that the Lord will establish them and keep them from evil (v. 3). And he is confident that they are doing and will do the things he has instructed them to practice. He concludes this brief paragraph by praying: "And the Lord direct your hearts into the love of God, and into the patient waiting for Christ" (v. 5)—literally, "into the perseverance (or, steadfastness) of Christ."

VI. WORKING WHILE WAITING:
II Thessalonians 3:6-16

A. Paul's Example: vv. 6-10

The apostle becomes a bit stern when he thinks of the trouble that is being made by some obstreperous people in the church. He commands the Christians at Thessalonica to separate themselves from any member ("brother") who walks "in a disorderly manner." Arndt and Gingrich say that the adverb has the sense of "insufficient inclination to disciplined work" (p. 119). Here and in verse 11 they would translate the expression "walk disorderly" as "live in idleness." The adverb occurs in the New Testament in only these two places.

Paul reminds his readers of the good example he set them while he was in Thessalonica. They ought to "follow"—literally, "imitate"—him (v. 7). He testifies: "For we did not behave ourselves disorderly among you." The expression "behave ourselves disorderly" is all one word in the Greek, the verb *atakteo* (found only here in the New Testament). Arndt and Gingrich say that "the context demands the meaning *be idle, lazy.*" It is used that way by a number of Greek writers, as well as in the papyri.

The apostle goes on to say: "Nor did we eat anyone's food without paying for it. On the contrary we worked night and day, laboring and toiling so that we would not be a burden to any of you" (v. 8, New International Bible.) This was not because Paul had no right ("power") to such help, but because he wanted to be an example for the Christians to follow. Then he spells out the matter specifically: When he was with them in Thessalonica, he had commanded them "that if any would not work, neither should he eat" (v. 10). In the Greek, "would not" reads: "is not willing to." There are those who cannot work because of handicaps or ill health. There are others who sincerely seek for employment, but cannot find it. All such should have our genuine sympathy. But Paul declares that if an able person is not willing to work he should not be fed.

B. Idle Busybodies: vv. 11-12

Now we come directly to one of the reasons—perhaps the main reason—

why Paul wrote this Epistle. He had heard that some of the members of the congregation at Thessalonica were "walking disorderly [that is, "living in idleness"], working not at all, but are busybodies." These last seven words are only four words in the Greek, literally "not working, but working around." The second verb means "do something unnecessary or useless, be a busybody." Perhaps the best translation here is: "They are not busy; they are busybodies" (New International Bible).

Paul has a word for such people: "Now such people we command and exhort by the Lord Jesus Christ that working quietly they eat their own bread" (v. 12)—that is, the food they have earned by their own labor.

Work is one of the noblest activities in life. Those who want others to wait on them and entertain them deteriorate morally and often physically. Work is one of the most therapeutic agents in life. Idle people are always unhappy people. A proper attitude toward work makes for good health physically, mentally, emotionally, and spiritually.

C. Separation from Such: vv. 13-16

After an admonition not to be "weary in well-doing" (v. 13), Paul tells his Thessalonian converts not to associate with a man who disobeys the teaching of this Letter, so that he will be ashamed of himself and perhaps will repent. Such admonitions as this have sometimes been misunderstood and misapplied by Christians. The apostle did not mean that they were to avoid speaking to him. What he is saying is that they should not count him as a part of their spiritual fellowship while he is living a life of disobedience. Lest his suggestion be carried to the extreme, Paul adds: "Yet count him not as an enemy, but admonish him as a brother" (v. 15). Every effort should be made to turn such a person back from his going astray. The church should always be not only willing but

eager to receive back into fellowship all backsliders who repent.

Paul gives a double benediction at the end of this Epistle. The first is a beautiful farewell: "Now the Lord of peace himself give you peace always by all means. The Lord be with you all" (v. 16). He wishes them peace at both the beginning and the end.

Then he pauses to explain why he is so careful to sign his own name at the end of every Letter. It is the sign of genuineness "in every epistle." So they are not to accept any letter as from him unless it carries his unmistakable signature. He adds: "This is the way I write." As noted earlier (see 2:2) some of the false teachers were evidently writing forged epistles in Paul's name, to deceive the people with erroneous ideas. But Paul, who may have had poor eyesight, probably wrote his name in a large scrawl that could not easily be counterfeited. In Galatians 6:11 he says: "You see with what large letters [not "how large a letter" (KJV)] I have written to you with my own hand." So we may assume that he would here scrawl his name with large letters that his friends would easily recognize.

After carefully making this point Paul added the brief benediction: "The grace of our Lord Jesus Christ be with you all" (v. 18). So we find a blessing of grace and peace at both the beginning and the end of II Thessalonians.

DISCUSSION QUESTIONS

1. What is the harm of living in the future?
2. What are some wrong attitudes we could have in relation to the Second Coming?
3. What is the Christian attitude toward work?
4. What place does work have in character development?
5. How can we best prepare for Christ's return?
6. What is the Christian "work ethic"?

CONTEMPORARY APPLICATION

In recent years there has been a great deal of criticism of "the Puritan work ethic." But this is precisely what Paul teaches in our lesson today. He says that if a person is not willing to work he should not eat.

Unfortunately, this is not the principle on which our present welfare program operates. Anyone who travels around much has had service station managers tell him they can't get fellows to man their pumps. On a busy throughway we have waited for nearly half an hour in a long line of cars leading up to one pump, with the other pumps all idle. A question to the manger brought this reply: "The men would rather cash their welfare checks than come here to work."

As Christians, we must realize that honesty demands we earn our living, if at all possible. Laziness is degrading and demoralizing. Men of God have always been hard workers.

GOD'S REDEEMING GRACE

DEVOTIONAL READING | Ephesians 1:15-23

ADULTS |
Topic: *God's Redeeming Grace*

Background Scripture: Ephesians 1

Scripture Lesson: Ephesians 1:1-14

Memory Verse: *In him we have redemption through his blood, the forgiveness of our trespasses, according to the riches of his grace which he lavished upon us.* Ephesians 1:7-8

YOUTH |
Topic: *God's Purpose for Me*

Background Scripture: Ephesians 1

Scripture Lesson: Ephesians 1:1-14

Memory Verse: *He destined us in love to be his sons through Jesus Christ, according to the purpose of his will.* Ephesians 1:5

CHILDREN |
Topic: *Being a Leader*

Background Scripture: Acts 19:1-8; I Timothy 1:3, 18; 4:11-16

Scripture Lesson: I Timothy 1:3, 18; 14:11-16

Memory Verse: *Let no one despise your youth, but set the believers an example in speech and conduct.* I Timothy 4:12

DAILY BIBLE READINGS |
Mon., June 24: Chosen and Blessed, Ephesians 1:1-6.
Tues., June 25: "Destined and Appointed," Ephesians 1:7-12.
Wed., June 26: How Great It Is, Ephesians 1:13-19a.
Thurs., June 27: Christ over All, Ephesians 1:19b-23.
Fri., June 28: The Gift of Grace, Romans 3:21-26.
Sat., June 29: Free Gift in Christ, Romans 5:12-17.
Sun., June 30: Newness of Life, Romans 6:1-8.

LESSON AIM | To glimpse the greatness of God's redeeming grace through Jesus Christ.

LESSON SETTING |
Time: The Epistle to the Ephesians was evidently written by Paul during his first imprisonment at Rome (A.D. 59-61), probably in A.D. 60.

Place: Rome

God's Redeeming Grace

LESSON OUTLINE

SUGGESTED INTRODUCTION FOR ADULTS

The Epistle to the Ephesians is one of the four so-called Prison Epistles, written by Paul during his first imprisonment at Rome (A.D. 59-61). It would appear that a certain slave named Onesimus had run away from his master Philemon at Colosse and had been converted under Paul at Rome (Philemon 10). The apostle was sending the runaway slave back to his owner, asking him to forgive the culprit. The church at Colosse was meeting in Philemon's house (Philemon 2). So Paul decided to write a letter to that church (the Epistle to the Colossians) and send it by Onesimus and Tychicus (Colossians 4:7-9).

Before the two messengers left, it would seem that the apostle wrote a longer letter, our Epistle to the Ephesians, and had Tychicus take it (Ephesians 6:21). It may have been intended primarily for the congregation at Ephesus, the mother church of the province of Asia (Acts 19:10). But it was also a sort of diocesan letter to all the churches of that province (see discussion under I, A, Address, paragraph 4).

The Epistle to the Ephesians is generally recognized as the most profound and the richest of all Paul's thirteen Letters. Here he plumbs the depths of God's redeeming grace and gives us a glimpse of the vastness of the divine plan of redemption. We must enter the study of it with prayerful hearts and minds.

SUGGESTED INTRODUCTION FOR YOUTH

What is God's purpose for me? That is the most important and most appropriate question that any young person can ask.

Every normal person needs a purpose in life. Without this, life becomes boring and finally unbearable. Could this be why the highest rate of suicide occurs among those of college age? In a recent year in the United States one thousand young people of that age committed suicide and ten thousand more attempted it. These figures should shock us into realizing that we must have a purpose for living.

The Epistle to the Ephesians shows us that God has a purpose for each one of us in Christ. We need to find that purpose and see it fulfilled in our lives. This can happen only as we commit ourselves fully to Jesus Christ as our Savior and Lord.

CONCEPTS FOR CHILDREN	1. Timothy was a good leader because he was a good follower.
	2. We must follow Christ carefully if we want to grow up to be a leader of others.
	3. We must also study hard to prepare ourselves.

THE LESSON COMMENTARY

I. SALUTATION: Ephesians 1:1-2

A. Address: v. 1

As we have noted before, Paul begins all thirteen of his Epistles with his name. (That is one reason why it is very unlikely that Paul wrote the Epistle to the Hebrews.)

He also calls himself an "apostle"—"envoy" or "missionary"—at the start of all but four of his Letters. In the first two, the Epistles to the Thessalonians, he did not feel the need for asserting his apostolic authority. It is obvious why he did not do so in his brief personal note to his friend Philemon. And then the Philippians had been so kind and loving that he did not need to do so with them.

He writes to the "saints." In the Greek this is the plural of the adjective *hagios*, which means "holy." So literally it is "the holy ones." Paul uses it in his Epistles for all Christians, as those who are set apart to God.

The words *en Epheso*, "at Ephesus," are not in the three oldest Greek manuscripts of this Epistle—Papyrus 46 of the second century, and Vaticanus and Sinaiticus of the third century. For this reason it is commonly thought that it was written as a circular letter for all the churches of Asia. Perhaps each copy had the name of a church inserted, and the one addressed to the mother church at Ephesus was most often copied in later times.

The letter is addressed to "the faithful in Christ Jesus." In his book, *Ephesian Studies*, the saintly bishop of the church of England, H. C. G. Moule, said about the term "faithful" that "as a designation of Christians it means not trustworthy, but trustful; *full of faith*, in the Christian sense." The saints are those who put their full trust in Christ Jesus.

B. Greeting: v. 2

As always, Paul says: "Grace ... and peace." *Grace* means "the free and loving favor of God." Someone has defined *peace* as "serenity of soul." Both of these come "from God our Father and the Lord Jesus Christ."

II. CHOSEN BY GOD:
Ephesians 1:3-6

A. Blessed with Every Spiritual Blessing: v. 3

After his address and greeting, Paul regularly has a thanksgiving. Here he begins it with "Blessed be." This can be translated, "Praise be to." We bless God by praising Him.

The apostle declares that God has blessed us with "every spiritual blessing" (so the Greek). He does not promise us every material blessing, for that would ruin us. But he does provide every *spiritual* blessing.

Where do we find these blessings? Paul says, "in the heavenlies in Christ"; that is, in heavenly fellowship with Christ. Spiritual blessings cannot be wrapped and sent in the mail, or delivered in any other way. We receive them only when we are having heavenly fellowship with our Lord. The greatest blessing is His presence.

The expression "in the heavenlies" is perhaps the key phrase of Ephesians. It occurs five times in this Epistle: (1:3, 20; 2:6; 3:10; 6:12). The last of these is a warning to us that even in our times "in the heavenlies" with Christ, wicked forces may seek to invade the privacy of that fellowship.

The last phrase of this verse, "in Christ," is the keynote of Paul's writings. It has often been said that the whole Pauline theology can be summed up in his favorite expression, *en Christo*. Paul's thinking was always Christocentric. And ours should be, too.

B. Chosen to Be Holy: v. 4

God has "chosen us in him," that is, in Christ. Outside of Christ we are not among the chosen ones. All of Paul's Epistles, and especially this one, emphasize the fact that all of God's blessings come to us only because and while we are in Christ.

For what were we chosen in Christ before the foundation of the world? "That we should be holy and without blame before him in love." We cannot be without blame before others. Whatever we do, someone is sure to blame us. But God does not look at our actions only; He sees our attitudes. He is more interested in our motives than in our motions. If He sees that our motives are pure and right, he gladly overlooks our fumbling ways. While others are blaming us, He is comforting us because He knows we meant well.

Some of the newer versions take the closing phrase "in love" with the following verse. In the early Greek manuscripts there are no punctuation marks, so we cannot be certain whether "in love" goes with what precedes or what follows. If we take it in the former way, it underscores the fact that only in the realm of love can we be found blameless before God. If we love Him with all our hearts and love our neighbor as ourselves, He will overlook our faults and failings.

C. Predestined to Be Adopted: v. 5-6

Paul goes on to say that God has "predestinated us unto [literally, "marked us out for"] the adoption of children." This last is all one word in the Greek, literally meaning "a placing as son." In that day it was a technical legal term for the adoption of children. Paul is the only one who uses it in the New Testament (cf. Romans 8:15, 23; 9:4; Galatians 4:5). What a glorious privilege that we, who were alien sinners, should be adopted into the family of God!

But it is only "through Jesus Christ" that we can be adopted. In Him we are in the family; out of Him we are not. God has adopted us "to himself," for precious fellowship with Him as our loving Father. And all this is "according to the good pleasure of his will." Divine sovereignty is stressed strongly in this Epistle, especially in the first chapter.

Typical of Ephesians is the expression, "to the praise of the glory of his grace" (v. 6). Everything will ultimately work out for the praise of

God's glorious grace. What a prospect to look forward to! And in this grace He has made us "accepted in the beloved"; the Greek literally says, "He has graced us in the Beloved." (The Greek for "grace" in this verse is *charitos* and for "made . . . accepted" is *echaritosen.*) It is only in Christ that we are accepted by God. Outside of Christ we have no acceptance, no place with God. It is all of grace, in Christ.

III. REDEEMED BY CHRIST:
Ephesians 1:7-12

A. Forgiveness of Sins: vv. 7-8

In Christ, and in Him alone, we have "redemption." The Greek word originally meant "*buying back* a slave or captive, *making* him free by payment of a ransom" (Arndt and Gingrich, *Lexicon*, p. 95). So Christ paid the ransom price to free us from the slavery of sin. This idea runs through the New Testament. For instance, Jesus said: "For even the Son of man did not come to be served, but to serve, and to give His life a ransom for many" (Mark 10:45). It could well be affirmed that *redemption* is the main theme of the Bible, from Genesis to Revelation. It is the scarlet thread that ties it all together in unity as the Word of God.

What was the price of our redemption? It was "His blood." Peter puts it this way: "Forasmuch as you know that you were not redeemed with corruptible things, as silver and gold . . . but with the precious blood of Christ" (I Peter 1:18).

The first blessing we get through this redemption is "the forgiveness of sins." This alone would be worth it all. To know that every sin of the past is forgiven and forgotten forever—this is a foretaste of heaven.

And this forgiveness is "according to the riches of his grace." God does not forgive halfway; He goes all the way. A beautiful example of this is found in the Parable of the Prodigal Son. The Father did not say to his ragged son, who had wasted every-

thing: "All right, you can live in the barn, and I'll tell the servants to give you something to eat." No, he replaced those rags with "the best robe." He ordered his servants to put shoes on the fellow's bare, sore feet. And then he gave him the signet ring on his finger as a proof of the fact that he was fully accepted back into the family. For with that ring, which bore the family insignia, the son had authority to transact his father's business. That is the way God forgives us, and it is the way we should forgive others!

We have noted before, in our study of Thessalonians, that Paul is fond of the word *abound.* Here he says, "Wherein He has abounded toward us in all wisdom and prudence" (v. 8). God has lavished His grace on us in abundant measure. The Greek word for "prudence" means "understanding, insight, intelligence" (Arndt and Gingrich, p. 874). With His abundant grace He freely gives us wisdom and insight to understand spiritual truths and experiences.

B. The Redemption of All Creation: vv. 9-10

Paul declares that God has made known to us "the mystery of His will." We get our word "mystery" directly from the Greek *mysterion*, which basically means "secret." In the plural it was used as a technical religious term for the secret teaching of the mystery religions. Paul uses it twenty-one times. For him, as for the other writers of the New Testament, it means God's secret plan of redemption, which can never be discovered by human reason but must be disclosed by divine revelation. Primarily in Paul it signifies God's purpose to save the Gentiles as well as the Jews, and out of both to make one church of Jesus Christ.

This is spelled out for us in verse 10: "That in the dispensation of the fullness of times he might gather together in one all things in Christ, both which are in heaven, and which are on earth." Since the neuter "all things" is used, rather than the masculine "all people," it would seem that this takes in the whole of creation. If so, this would be parallel to what Paul wrote in Romans 8:19-22. There he pictures all creation, under the curse because of Adam's sin, groaning for the final day of redemption. Then the curse of sin will be lifted from God's entire creation. What a happy prospect!

We should not miss the Christology of this passage. "According to his good pleasure" (cf. v. 5), God has "purposed in himself"—Greek "in him," perhaps Christ, in line with the rest of this chapter—to carry out His sovereign will. This is to "head up" all things in Christ. Christ is not only the Head of the church, but "head over all things to the church" (v. 22). God will make Him the Head of the "all things" that He created (Colossians 1:16). The main emphasis of the Prison Epistles is Christological, and this is one example. Paul, under the inspiration of the Holy Spirit, gives us a very lofty view of Jesus Christ.

C. The Sovereignty of the Divine Will: vv. 11-12

Paul is constantly reminding us of the high privileges we have "in Christ." So here he writes: "In whom also we have obtained an inheritance." H. C. G. Moule comments: "Better, *were taken into the inheritance*, made part of 'the Lord's portion, which is His people' (Deut. 32:9)." That is, through redemption we have become God's. We are His inheritance, and in Him we find our inheritance.

The verb translated "obtained an inheritance" is based on the noun *kleros*. This was a "lot," that is, a small stone or stick used in "casting lots" (e.g., Acts 1:26). Arndt and Gingrich translate the first clause of verse 11: "in whom our lot is cast" (p. 436). When we cast in our "lot" with God, we get our inheritance. Too many people cast in their lot with the wrong crowd.

Back of our decision is divine sovereignty, always seeking our best good.

Paul says that we are "predestinated according to the purpose of him who works all things after the counsel of his own will." Taken in an extreme, absolute sense this statement would make God responsible for every crime committed by men. We have to balance divine sovereignty with human freedom, for God created man with the privilege of moral choice and He cannot violate His own creation. But through it all and over all God is working out His divine purpose in redemption. All who will accept the divine plan of salvation become a part of it.

"First trusted in Christ" (v. 12) is in the Greek "hoped before in Christ." It is God's will that we who have put our hope in Christ should live "to the praise of His glory" (cf. v. 6).

IV. SEALED BY THE SPIRIT: Ephesians 1:13-14

A. The Seal of the Holy Spirit: v. 13

The apostle says that after the Thessalonians had "heard" the good news of their salvation and had "believed"—both of these are aorist participles, which normally indicate action prior to that of the main verb— they were "sealed with the Holy Spirit of promise." Archaeologists have dug up many cylindrical clay seals from the Assyrian and Babylonian periods. An inscription was made on the soft clay, and then the small cylinder was baked hard in an oven. When a man was sending a bale of goods down the Tigris or Euphrates rivers he would have wax put on the joint of the wrappings. Then a complete rotation of the cylindrical seal would leave a rectangular insignia in the wax, showing to whom the package belonged. In Paul's day the Greeks and Romans used signet rings for the same purpose. But a man could not stamp something with his seal unless it was his property. So God cannot seal us with His Holy Spirit until we give ourselves completely to Him, to be wholly His.

B. The Guarantee of Our Inheritance: v. 14

The Holy Spirit ("which" should be "who") is the "earnest" of our inheritance. The Greek word is *arrabon*. Its first meaning is that of a "down-payment" or "first installment," given as a guarantee that the remainder will be paid. So the Holy Spirit is the down payment of our heavenly "inheritance, until the redemption of God's own possession, to the praise of His glory." What will heaven be like? It will be like those high moments when the Holy Spirit makes the presence of Jesus very real to our hearts. But over there these moments will last forever!

At the time when the New Testament was written the word *arrabon* was used for the bridegroom's betrothal gifts to his bride as a pledge of their marriage. In modern Greek *arrabona* means "engagement ring." Both of these ideas fit in beautifully with the concept here and in 5:25-27. When we are ready to say a full, final yes to Jesus Christ that we will be His forever, He gives us the Holy Spirit to fill our hearts and guide our lives. This is the guarantee that some day we will sit at "the marriage supper of the Lamb" (Revelation 19:7-9).

V. PRAYER FOR GOD'S BLESSING:
Ephesians 1:15-23

Both the first and third chapters of Ephesians end with a long prayer. This one stretches from verse 15 through verse 23. H. C. G. Moule writes: "The recorded prayers of Paul form in themselves one of the richest of Scripture studies." Paul's prayers are intercessory. Moule says again: "He thinks of others, not of self, upon his knees."

A. Thanksgiving: vv. 15-16

It was Paul's custom to begin his prayers with praise to God. This is a very helpful habit. If we start our praying by thanking the Lord for what He has already done for us, it strengthens our faith and encourages us to pray for new blessings. That is why we often ask for testimonies of answered prayer to be given before we begin a period of intercessory praying in a group of Christians. Actually we ought to be courteous enough to say thank you for what the Lord has done before we ask Him for something more. We would be that polite to our friends; why not to our Best Friend? Thanksgiving is always a buoyant force.

Here the apostle thanks God for the good report about the Christians in Asia. In the second century Ephesus was one of the strong Christian centers. Some say that Asia Minor ranked next to Rome in influence during this early period of church history. Paul rejoices in their "faith in the Lord Jesus, and love to all the saints." As we have found in his Letters to other churches he says that he never stops praying for them. In prison the apostle probably had more time to pray than he had been able to find in past years, what with his full schedule of preaching and traveling. Now that he was confined, he could spend hours in prayer. By way of the Throne he could visit the churches in blessing, even though he could not be with them in body. Instead of complaining, he was praying. Instead of pouting, he was praising God. His Prison Epistles are a wonderful tribute to the spirit of this man who refused to be a prisoner in

---

DISCUSSION QUESTIONS

1. Why did Paul make Ephesians such a profound Letter?
2. What does this say about his readers?
3. What are the distinctive roles of Father, Son, and Holy Spirit as suggested here?
4. What does it mean to be "in the heavenlies"?
5. What part do grace and peace play in the Christian life?
6. What example of prayer life did Paul furnish?

his soul. In fact, his imprisonment had actually set him free from a heavy schedule, so that he had leisure to pray.

B. The Hope of His Calling: vv. 17-18

After his thanksgiving to God, the apostle now makes his petitions. In reality it is one long, unbroken petition that reaches to the end of the chapter. We could go a step further and point out that in the original verses 15-23 are all one sentence—a nightmare for translators!

Each of these verses is packed so full of spiritual ideas that it is difficult to pick out separate items for comment. The apostle prays first that these Christians may have "a spirit of wisdom and revelation in the knowledge" of the Lord (v. 17). Then he expresses it another way: "the eyes of your understanding being enlightened" (v. 18). The Greek says, "the eyes of your heart," a beautiful expression. These need to be illuminated so that we may know spiritual truths. With these eyes we see "the hope of his calling."

C. Christ the Head of the Church: vv. 19-23

Verse 19 ought to put strength into any Christian who feels weak. What more could we ask for than "the exceeding greatness of his power toward us who believe"? It is all according to the energizing of "his mighty

power"; literally, "the strength of His might." The very power that was displayed in Christ's resurrection and exaltation is available to us today.

Christ has been exalted to a place far above "all principality, and power, and might, and dominion" (v. 21)— better, "all government and authority and power and lordship." Christ is supreme! Paul was probably writing this as an antidote to the influence of angel worship in the province of Asia. Christ's name is above that of every name in this "world"—rather, "age"— and "also in that which is to come."

Verse 22 asserts a keynote of Ephesians: "And has put all things under His [Christ's] feet, and gave him [and Him alone] to be the head over all things to the church." The word *church* occurs nine times in Ephesians, always referring to the general church of Jesus Christ.

Paul likes concrete figures. Christ is not the head of the church as a man may be president of an organization. For the church is more than an organization; it is an organism. So the church is "His body," "the fullness of him who fills everything in every way" (v. 23). On this verse H. C. G. Moule comments that the body is "a metaphor which suggests not only vital union with the head, but that the will of the head is exercised through the members. They are His *instruments.*" We should carry out Christ's orders as promptly and completely as one's hands or feet obey those sent out by one's head.

CONTEMPORARY APPLICATION

In this modern scientific age, too often only two sources of knowledge are recognized as valid: experimentation and reason. The two sources which alone can give us the highest knowledge are faith and love.

One of the great medieval doctors of learning said: "I *believe* in order that I may know." Back came "the Angelic Doctor" with the significant assertion: "I *love* in order that I may know."

We can have no genuine spiritual knowledge apart from faith. This gives us the knowledge that our sins are forgiven and we are children of God. But the knowledge of God in Christ as a precious friend comes only through love. We never really know people unless we love them. This is even more true if we are to know the God who is love eternal.

GOD'S ETERNAL PURPOSE

DEVOTIONAL READING	Ephesians 2:1-10

ADULTS

Topic: *God's Eternal Purpose*

Background Scripture: Ephesians 2:1—4:16

Scripture Lesson: Ephesians 3:1-13

Memory Verse: *So then you are no longer strangers and sojourners, but you are fellow citizens with the saints and members of the household of God.* Ephesians 2:19

YOUTH

Topic: *When Walls Divide*

Background Scripture: Ephesians 2:1—4:16

Scripture Lesson: Ephesians 3:1-13

Memory Verse: *So then you are no longer strangers and sojourners, but you are fellow citizens with the saints and members of the household of God.* Ephesians 2:19

CHILDREN

Topic: *From Strangers to Friends*

Background Scripture: Ephesians 2:11-22; 4:11-16

Scripture Lesson: Ephesians 2:14-22

Memory Verse: *By this all men will know that you are my disciples, if you have love for one another.* John 13:35

DAILY BIBLE READINGS

Mon., July 1: Once Dead, Now Alive, Ephesians 2:1-10.
Tues., July 2: Made One in Christ, Ephesians 2:11-18.
Wed., July 3: The Mystery Made Known, Ephesians 2:19—3:6.
Thurs., July 4: God's Eternal Purpose, Ephesians 3:7-13.
Fri., July 5: Knowing the Unknowable, Ephesians 3:14-21.
Sat., July 6: Called to Oneness, Ephesians 4:1-10.
Sun., July 7: Growing Up in Christ, Ephesians 4:11-16.

LESSON AIM

To show that God has an eternal purpose for the human race and that this purpose will without fail be carried out in full.

LESSON SETTING

Time: A.D. 60

Place: Rome

God's Eternal Purpose

LESSON OUTLINE

**SUGGESTED
INTRODUCTION
FOR ADULTS**

Human plans often fail. Not so the divine purpose. When God wills a thing it will happen!

Repeatedly we have the disillusionment of seeing human purposes come to nothing. "Five year plans" have flopped. Some years ago one country projected "The Great Leap Forward." When the allotted time for this was finished, it was billed in the news as "The Great Leap Backward." That was what actually happened.

Even in the most progressive nations the twentieth century has witnessed the nonfulfillment of promises and purposes. Without doubt many of these were offered in good faith. But men are neither omniscient nor omnipotent. No matter how well they mean, their performance often falls short. Since this is the common experience of mankind, we ought to be slow to criticize others. Most of us have failed once—or twice!

Sometimes, when we see all the sin and sickness and suffering around us, we are tempted to think that God has failed. But that is because our vision is too narrow and limited. We look at the twentieth century and see how Communism has spread much more rapidly than Christianity and we are tempted to write FAILURE across the record. What we need to do is to take in the sweep of all twenty centuries. Then we see that Christianity has covered every continent and entered every country, becoming a pervasive influence in human society. Communism is just a counterrevolution of man against God in the end time. It will soon be gone, and Christ will reign supreme—and forever.

We live in a world of walls, symbolized by that crowning obscenity, as it has been called, the Berlin Wall. The Iron and Bamboo curtains are actually walls of hate that have divided the whole world into slave and free. This has been one of the tragic phenomena of the twentieth century. It would seem now that those curtains are parting a bit; we hope so. But not until Christ comes will there be one world, united in love.

We need to come closer home. In our own country—whether that be free America, Europe, Asia, Africa, or Australia—there are too many dividing walls. There are walls that divide men from women, old from young, rich from poor, employers from employees, whites from blacks, Catholics from Protestants, the cultured from the uncultured. It is only in Christ that all men can become one. Love Eternal, Incarnate, is the only hope of humanity.

1. God loves all people, not just white Americans.
2. We should show our appreciation for God's love to us by loving others.
3. We should be especially careful to love those who are unloved, and to show a Christlike attitude toward them.

THE LESSON COMMENTARY

I. SALVATION BY GRACE THROUGH FAITH:
Ephesians 2:1-10

A. Dead in Trespasses and Sins:
vv. 1-3

The verb *hath he quickened* (v. 1), which is not in the Greek, is picked up from verse 5. It simply means "he has made alive." All of us were once "dead in trespasses and sins." Christ died that we might live. We are made alive only in Him.

Formerly we lived under the domination of "the prince of the power of the air"—one of the many titles of Satan. He is "the spirit who now works in the children of disobedience" (v. 2). The expression "children of" is a Hebraism for "those characterized

by." All sinners are living in disobedience to God's will.

So Paul reminds his readers that "we all had our conversation [rather, "conduct"] in times past in the lusts of our flesh, fulfilling the desires [Greek, "doing the wishes"] of the flesh and of the mind [Greek, "thoughts"] and were by nature the children of wrath"—subject to God's wrath for our disobediences.

These three verses describe the condition of all men outside of Christ. They are under the twofold domination of Satan and self—that is, the carnal sinful self. To a greater or lesser extent they obey the impulses of their own selfish desires. Where we find genuine altruism and unselfish love on the part of unregenerated people, as we certainly do, it is because of God's prevenient grace that influences all men toward the good.

B. Made Alive in Christ: vv. 4-7

"But God"—this is what makes the difference! Because He is "rich in mercy," and because of "His great love with which He loved us," even when we were "dead in trespasses" (v. 5)—so the Greek—He "has made us alive together with Christ"—the two oldest extant Greek manuscripts have "in Christ." He has also "raised us up together and made us sit together in the heavenlies in Christ Jesus" (v. 6). This is the third time we have had the expression "in the heavenlies" in this Epistle (cf. 1:3, 20). We don't have to wait until the next life to enjoy the blessings of heaven. Right here and now we can sit together in the heavenlies in Christ. What a privilege!

The Greek preposition for "with" is *syn.* When used as a prefix for a verb or noun it is usually translated "together." In verses 5 and 6 we find three of these compound verbs: "made us alive together," "raised us up together" and "made us sit together." Paul is especially fond of compounds with *syn.* Arndt and Gingrich's *Lexicon* has a dozen pages of them, and the vast majority of them are found only in Paul's Epistles. The chief apostle, who is usually thought of as a rugged individualist, stresses *togetherness* more than any other New Testament writer. I once wrote an article entitled, "The Sin of Synlessness." That is what Paul considered it to be.

In this life God shows us the riches of His grace in Christ, so that at times we are almost overwhelmed with His love. What about the next life? Paul challenges our wildest imagination when he writes: "That in the ages to come he might show the exceeding riches of his grace in his kindness toward us in Christ Jesus" (v. 7). How kind can a God who is Infinite Love be? We will spend eternity finding out!

C. The Free Gift of God: vv. 8-10

Ephesians 2:8 is considered one of the leading theological verses in this Epistle. Here the closing parenthetical clause of verse 5 is enlarged upon. Paul declares that it is only "by grace"— God's unmerited favor—that we are saved, and this comes to us "through faith." It must be remembered that saving faith is more than mental assent: it is moral consent. It is not only that the mind believes the teaching concerning Jesus Christ and His salvation, but that the will accepts Him as Savior and Lord.

"That" (v. 8) in the Greek is "this." Paul says that this is "not of yourselves [we did not originate or produce it] it is the gift of God." It is often assumed that the apostle is saying that *faith* is the gift of God. While this is partially true, for only the Holy Spirit can enable us to believe, the Greek does not say this here. For "this" (KJV, "that") is a neuter pronoun, whereas "faith" is in the feminine gender. It is salvation which is the gift of God.

Paul goes on to say that we are God's "workmanship" (v. 10). The Greek word is *poiema*, from which comes "poem." It is a beautiful and, at the same time, a challenging concept to think that we are "God's poem," in which He wants to express His thoughts toward man. People read this poem in our "good works."

II. JEWS AND GENTILES ONE IN CHRIST: Ephesians 2:11-22

A. Gentile Alienation from God: vv. 11-12

The Gentiles were called "Uncircumcision" by the Jews, who prided themselves on being the "Circumcision." Paul notes that the latter was "handmade in the flesh."

The description that Paul gives here of the condition of the Gentiles is indeed a sad one: "without Christ, alienated from the commonwealth of Israel and strangers to the covenants of promise, having no hope and without God in the world" (v. 12). Their case looked completely hopeless.

B. Brought Near in Christ: vv. 13-17

In verse 4 Paul said, "but God." There he was talking about the lost condition of Jews and Gentiles alike and how God has provided salvation for both.

In verse 13 we find another significant "but." Here, however, he is discussing the Gentiles only. Though they were separated from God and His covenants of promise, yet "now in Christ Jesus you who sometimes were far off are made near by the blood of Christ."

Christ is "our peace" (v. 14). He has made both Jews and Gentiles one and has broken down "the middle wall of partition," or "the barrier of the dividing wall." This was the fence that separated the Gentiles from the Jews. The latter were considered to be inside the fold of God, the former outside. But Christ, in His flesh—by His life and death—abolished "the enmity, the law of commandments in ordinances, to make in himself the two into one new man, making peace" (v. 15). Paul goes on: "And that he might reconcile both unto God in one body, through the cross, having killed the enmity in himself." Christ alone could bring about a reconciliation between Jew and Gentile and between both of them and God. And He could do this only through His death on the cross. There was no other way.

The term *cross* occurs in only this one place in Ephesians, but the cross itself can be seen in the background of the entire Epistle. Reconciliation is costly business. The cross was the price that Christ had to pay for reconciling Jews and Gentiles into "one new man." And today it will cost some sacrifice to reconcile the divided groups in our society. But love is measured by love's sacrifice.

By His life, death, and resurrection Christ offers the good news of peace (v. 17) "to you who were far off [the Gentiles], and to those that were near [the Jews]." Both are reconciled to God through Him.

C. Fellow Citizens with the Saints: vv. 18-22

Through Christ both Jews and Gentiles have "access [literally, "the access," or, "our introduction"] in one Spirit to the Father" (v. 18). Here we find the whole Trinity pictured in one sentence. The Holy Spirit leads us through Christ the Door (cf. John 10:7) into the presence of the Father. This statement delineates the function of each member of the Trinity.

Because of this the Gentile believers are no longer "strangers and foreigners," but are "fellow-citizens" with God's holy people, and of "the household of faith." That is, they are new members of God's family. As such they have been "built upon the foundation of the apostles and prophets [New Testament prophets] Jesus Christ himself being the chief corner stone" (v. 20). The last expression, all one word in Greek, literally means the "highest point of the corner." There is considerable debate as to whether this means the capstone or the cornerstone. Actually, Jesus is both. And in Him, "all the building fitly framed together grows into a holy temple in the Lord" (v. 21). The Church is God's sanctuary in this age, the place where He dwells on earth. In Christ both Jews and Gentiles "are being built together for a dwelling of God in the Spirit" (v. 22). What a glorious concept of the church!

III. GOD'S ETERNAL PURPOSE IN CHRIST
Ephesians 3:1-13

A. The Mystery of Christ: vv. 1-7

Paul was a prisoner of the Roman Empire. But by faith he could refer to himself instead as "the prisoner of

Jesus Christ in behalf of you Gentiles." That is, he felt that he was in prison not as the helpless victim of Roman power, but that he had been put there by God to give him more time to minister to the Gentiles by his prayers and Epistles. Even in prison he belonged primarily not to Rome, but to Christ. H. C. G. Moule says of him: "Whatever he is, does, or suffers, it is as Christ's property."

The word "dispensation" (v. 2) does not communicate the correct idea here. This word originally meant "a dispensing," which would fit very well; but now it means a special period of time. This is not what Paul was talking about. The Greek word simply means "stewardship." Paul was God's appointed steward to dispense His grace to the Gentiles (Galatians 2:9).

The phrase translated "as I wrote afore in few words" (v. 3) should probably be translated, "as I have just written in brief." Paul is referring not to a previous letter but to what he had already said briefly in this one (cf. 1:9-10). Now he takes up more fully one of the central emphases of the Epistle to the Ephesians—"the mystery." He declares that by revelation God had made known to him the mystery, and then he calls it "the mystery of Christ" (v. 4).

We have already noted that the word *mystery* in the New Testament means a secret that cannot be discovered by human reason, but only by divine revelation. Now Paul says that in other "ages"—the Greek says "generations"—this mystery was "not made known to the sons of man, as it has now been revealed to His holy apostles and prophets by the Spirit" (v. 5). Hidden for centuries, it had now been revealed in Christ and through the Holy Spirit.

What was this mystery? That the Gentiles should be "fellow heirs, and of the same body, and partakers" (v. 6). This translation obscures the fact that we have here in the Greek three nouns, all beginning with the prefix *syn* (see discussion of 2:5-6). This

should come out in English. A good translation would be: "fellow heirs, fellow members and fellow partakers." Both Jews and Gentiles are equally heirs of and sharers in "the promise in Christ Jesus [best Greek text] through the gospel."

This verse gives us precisely what the "mystery" was. It was God's hidden plan and purpose that the Gentiles should be saved, right along with the Jews. Both would be saved only by faith in Christ, which is what the gospel declares.

Paul goes on to say that he was made a "minister" or "servant" (*diaconos*) of the gospel, "according to the gift of the grace of God that was given to me according to the energizing of His power" (v. 7).

B. The Unsearchable Riches of Christ: v. 8

Paul calls himself "less than the least of all saints." This statement has evoked different reactions. At one extreme are those who think that the words smack of false humility. At the other extreme are those who say that Paul realized he was not living a very godly life. As usual the truth lies somewhere in between. Paul himself tells us what he means: "For I am the least of the apostles, and not fit to be called an apostle, because I persecuted the church of God" (I Corinthians 15:9). No other apostle had done this. It was in the light of his past, not his present, that Paul made these statements about his unworthiness.

But God's grace reached even him, so that he might "preach among the Gentiles the unsearchable riches of Christ." The Greek word for "unsearchable" literally means "not to be tracked by footprints." In the only other place where the term occurs in the New Testament, Romans 11:33, it is translated "past finding out." In our present reference, Arndt and Gingrich suggest "fathomless." H. C. G. Moule comments: "The whole phrase here before us is one of the greatest in holy Scripture. It presents the truths, harmonized into one truth, of the simplicity and infinity of the Gospel. All is centralized in Christ, the Christ of Pauline, of New Testament Theology, the Incarnate Son slain, risen, and glorified; and from that Centre diverge countless lines of application to every need of the human soul."

C. The Manifold Wisdom of God: vv. 9-13

Paul's preaching was "to make all people see what is the fellowship of the mystery" (v. 9). The best Greek text has "the stewardship of the mystery." Knowledge of the mystery involved a responsibility to share that knowledge with others. "From the ages" this mystery was hidden in God, "who created all things by Jesus Christ." That Christ was Creator of all is affirmed again and again in the New Testament (cf. John 1:13; Colossians 1:16; Hebrews 1:2).

What was the purpose of all this? "To the intent that now unto the principalities and powers [the "rulerships and authorities"] might be made known through the church the manifold wisdom of God" (v. 10). The word translated "manifold" literally means "many-sided." There are many facets to divine wisdom and we are to manifest these to the world.

All this is "according to the eternal purpose which He purposed ["made"] in Christ Jesus our Lord" (v. 11). This thought is the title of our lesson today. God's purpose is no sudden notion or brainstorm. It is what He in His omniscience and sovereignty planned from all eternity to do. But all God's purpose for man is "in Christ Jesus." It is only in Christ that we have salvation from sin and the promise of heaven. Outside of Christ we are cut off from divine blessing.

In Christ "we have the boldness and access with confidence through faith in Him" (v. 12). When we know that we are in the Son, we know that we are accepted by the Father. That is the only basis of our acceptance with God. Christ is the One who opens for us the door into heaven. He will do this if we will hear His knocking and open the doors of *our* hearts to Him (Revelation 3:20). When we place ourselves in Christ by faith, we put ourselves in line with God's great eternal purpose in Christ. Then all the glorious provisions of the divine plan become ours. God's eternal purpose does us no good unless we accept it.

Paul closes this part of his discourse by asking his readers not to "faint," or "lose heart," because of his troubles on their behalf. Their steadfastness will be their glory (v. 13). Both Paul and his converts must remain true under testing.

IV. KNOWING THE LOVE OF CHRIST: Ephesians 3:14-21

A. Strengthened by His Spirit: vv. 14-16

In connection with 1:15-23 we noted the value of Paul's prayers in his Epistles. We find another beautiful prayer in this closing paragraph of the third chapter.

Paul begins by saying, "For this cause." There is no greater incentive to prayer and no greater encouragement to faith than a contemplation of God's great eternal purpose. Praying helps to put us in line with that purpose. In fact, that is the main function and value of prayer. God knows what needs to be done, and He has the power to do it. But prayer places us in gear with God in working out His plan.

Paul continues: "I bow my knees unto the Father ["of our Lord Jesus Christ" (KJV) is not in the earliest Greek manuscripts] from whom every family in heaven and on earth receives its name" (v. 15). Then come his petitions. The first is: "That he would grant you, according to the riches of his glory, to be strengthened with power through his Spirit in the inner man" (v. 16). Spiritual "power"—the Greek has *dynamis* here—comes only from the Holy Spirit (Acts 1:8). Power that comes from any other source is not divine power; rather, it is either human or demonic power.

B. Rooted and Grounded in Love: vv. 17-19

Paul's prayer for his readers is "that Christ may dwell [the Greek says "dwell permanently"] in your hearts by faith." This will come as the result of their being spiritually empowered by the Holy Spirit.

Paul is fond of mixed metaphors. Here he has "rooted and grounded." The first figure is that of a plant. It must have an adequate root if it is going to grow. The second figure is that of a building. It must have a firm foundation, or it will not stand. We find exactly the same combination in I Corinthians 3:6-10. If we are to be solid Christians we must be "rooted and grounded in love." These are perfect passive participles in the Greek, suggesting a permanent state. The verb translated "grounded" is literally "having the foundation firmly laid."

Paul's desire is that his readers "may be strong to comprehend with all the saints what is the breadth and length and height and depth" (v. 18). No one person alone can possibly grasp all the divine plan and purpose. We need the help of other Spirit-filled Christians to gain an adequate comprehension. This is true of Bible study. Sometimes, when studying a difficult passage, one must examine as many as

a score of commentaries before finding an explanation that satisfies. It is spiritual pride that makes us think we can know it all ourselves without the help of others. Some people quote I John 2:20: "But ye have an unction from the Holy One and ye know all things." Of course, if this statement is taken literally it makes utter nonsense. Only God is omniscient; no man knows all things. The best Greek text of this passage does not say, "you know all," but "you all know"; that is, all Christians know Christ and His salvation. The essence of fanaticism is the unscriptural attitude of dogmatism in "knowing it all."

The most important thing to know is "the love of Christ" (v. 19). In fact love surpasses knowledge. Then Paul adds a startling climax to his petitions: "that you might be filled with all the fullness of God." This is beyond comprehension. But it is our glorious privilege "in Christ," as we shall see later in our study of Colossians.

C. The Abundant Grace of God: vv. 20-21

Paul closes this prayer with one of his most beautiful benedictions: "Now unto him that is able to do exceeding abundantly above all that we ask or think, according to the power that worketh in us, unto him be glory in the church by Christ Jesus throughout all ages, world without end. Amen." About 90 percent of the times we hear this familiar passage quoted, "can" is inserted before "ask or think." But this is an unjustifiable addition to the Word of God and it distorts the meaning of this sentence. It should be left out.

V. THE CHURCH ONE BODY IN CHRIST: Ephesians 4:1-16

A. The Unity of the Spirit: vv. 1-3

Paul pleads with his readers to "live worthily of the calling with which you were called" (v. 1). It is a

---

DISCUSSION QUESTIONS

1. How long has God planned His purpose in Christ?
2. How is the incarnation related to this purpose?
3. What is Paul's concept of the church of Jesus Christ?
4. How may we help to break down dividing walls?
5. What walls are particularly related to you as an individual?
6. What specifically can you do about them?

high and holy calling and demands a holy life.

True holiness does not foster pride; instead, it fosters "humility and meekness" (v. 2). The Romans looked down on humility as a sign of weakness, and so despised it. But Christ made it the highest virtue in the Christian life. He emphasized it again and again in His teaching and declared that it was the main characteristic of true greatness.

Humility will help us to be "long-suffering, forbearing one another in love, endeavoring to keep the unity of the Spirit in the bond of peace" (v. 3). This was the passionate concern of Paul's heart. It forms one of the keynotes of this Epistle, as we shall see in the following verses.

B. The Unity of the Body of Christ: vv. 4-6

To put a solid foundation under this idea of Christian unity, the apostle now uses the word *one* as an adjective no less than seven times in these three verses. (Seven is the "perfect number.") He declares that there is: "one body ... one Spirit ... one hope ... one Lord, one faith, one baptism, one God." All of these concepts underscore the unity of the church, which is one body unified by one Spirit in one hope. It has one Lord, one faith, one baptism, one God. To divide the church is to deny all these "ones" on

which it is based. Someone has well said: "Where there is disunity, there the Spirit is absent."

At the end of verse 6, "in you all" is in the Greek simply "in all"—a stronger and more absolute statement. God is "above all, through all, and in all." He is infinite.

C. The Unity of Faith and Knowledge: vv. 7-16

Every Christian is "given grace according to the measure of the gift of Christ." That is, our Lord knows how much to give each of us.

Verses 8-10 have caused endless debate. We will not concern ourselves with it here but go on to verses 11-13 which elaborate beautifully on the unity of the church. God has given His church various helpers in the person of apostles, prophets, evangelists, pastors, and teachers. These are "for the equipping of the saints for the work of ministering, for the building up of the body of Christ" (v. 12). More and more today it is being realized that one of the main tasks of the pastor is to equip his "laymen" to go out and witness effectively to masses of people that he himself cannot reach.

The fact that Christ is the Head of the church is stressed again in verse 15. The unity of the church as His body is spelled out in verse 16. This body is to grow up into "a perfect man" (v. 13).

CONTEMPORARY APPLICATION

God's eternal purpose reaches down into the details of our daily life. Some years ago "the worst blizzard in half a century" held me prisoner in a motel for several days. I had just finished speaking at a ministers' conference, and was anxious to get back to my teaching at the seminary—but no planes were flying.

It seemed that I was a prisoner of circumstances, but I finally realized with Paul, that I was a prisoner of

Christ (3:1). When I had finished all the work I had with me and was driven in desperation to fasting and prayer, the Lord brought to mind a young fellow in the city who needed help. I phoned him, and he managed to get to the motel. The son of missionary parents, he had lost his way spiritually. But just before midnight he was ready to kneel and ask God's forgiveness. Then I knew why I was held—in God's purpose.

RENEWED IN MIND AND SPIRIT

(Temperance)

DEVOTIONAL READING	Ephesians 6:10-20

ADULTS	Topic: *Christian Renewal* Background Scripture: Ephesians 4:17—6:24 Scripture Lesson: Ephesians 4:17-32 Memory Verse: *Do not be conformed to this world but be transformed by the renewal of your mind, that you may prove what is the will of God, what is good and acceptable and perfect.* Romans 12:2
YOUTH	Topic: *The New You* Background Scripture: Ephesians 4:17—6:24 Scripture Lesson: Ephesians 4:17-32 Memory Verse: *Do not be conformed to this world but be transformed by the renewal of your mind, that you may prove what is the will of God, what is good and acceptable and perfect.* Romans 12:2
CHILDREN	Topic: *Living with Others* Background Scripture: Ephesians 4:25-32 Scripture Lesson: Ephesians 4:25, 29, 31-32 Memory Verse: *Walk in love, as Christ loved us and gave himself up for us.* Ephesians 5:2
DAILY BIBLE READINGS	Mon., July 8: How Did You Learn Christ? Ephesians 4:17-24 Tues., July 9: Imitate God, Ephesians 4:25—5:2. Wed., July 10: Walk in the Light, Ephesians 5:3-14. Thurs., July 11: "Be Filled with the Spirit," Ephesians 5:15-20. Fri., July 12: Love as Christ Loved, Ephesians 5:21-33. Sat., July 13: Obey, Honor, Serve, Ephesians 6:1-9. Sun., July 14: Armed for the Conflict, Ephesians 6:10-20.
LESSON AIM	To show the importance and possibility of being renewed in mind and spirit, and what this involves in daily living.
LESSON SETTING	Time: A.D. 60 Place: Prison in Rome

384

Christian Renewal

LESSON OUTLINE

Paul's usual pattern in his Epistles is to present doctrine first and then give the practical application to Christian living. That is what he does in the Epistle to the Ephesians. The first three chapters are doctrinal, the last three practical. We might put it this way: 1. The Christian's Worship (chaps. 1—3); 2. The Christian's Walk (chaps. 4—6). We may also have a three-part outline: 1. The Christian's Walk (1:1—3:21); 2. The Christian's Worship (4:1—6:9); 3. The Christian's Warfare (6:10-24).

In the first three chapters of Ephesians Paul takes us up in the airplane of prayer and gives us a vast panoramic sweep of God's great eternal purpose for the world, and for His own redeemed people—those who will accept His Son as their Savior. One has to go high to see far—whether it be from an airplane or from a mountain peak. It is in our mountaintop experiences of prayer that we gain the widest outlook on life. We can look back over the past and see how God was working out His plan in those hard places in our lives. What seemed then like a needless detour was really His guidance around a danger. We can also get glimpses down the road ahead and anticipate some of the divine plan for our future.

But at the beginning of the fourth chapter the apostle brings us abruptly back to earth and says: "Now get out and walk in the light of what you have seen." Five times

SUGGESTED INTRODUCTION FOR ADULTS

in chapters 4 and 5 he says, "Walk" (4:1, 17; 5:2, 8, 15). These five together will give us some idea of what it means to live a Christian life.

We must worship first, if we are going to walk as God wants us to. That is why we worship on the first day of the week in order that we may walk the other six days before our fellowmen as we should. That is also why we need to worship the first thing each morning in our private devotions before we face the day and its demands. This is the only safe pattern for Christian living.

SUGGESTED INTRODUCTION FOR YOUTH

"The New You." Do you want a new you? Certainly every sincere, thoughtful young person does. But how to get it? That is the question we face in this lesson.

Romans 12:1-2 provides the answer. We are first to present ourselves completely to God, to be wholly His. The word translated "present" is in the aorist tense in Greek, suggesting a crisis act of complete commitment to Christ. Then the second verse, our memory selection, says: "Stop being conformed to this world, but go on being transformed more and more by the renewing of your mind." Change your thinking and you change yourself. The new you means a new set of attitudes.

CONCEPTS FOR CHILDREN

1. Learning to live with others is one of the most important lessons of life.
2. Loving others is the basic requirement.
3. Showing a forgiving spirit is also essential.
4. We should treat others as Christ treats us.

THE LESSON COMMENTARY

I. THE NEW MAN:
Ephesians 4:17-24

A. In Contrast to the Corrupt Gentiles: vv. 17-19

In the introduction for adults we noted that in the second half of Ephesians Paul five times says to his readers, "Walk." The first of these five was included in the last lesson: "Walk worthy of the calling with which you were called" (4:1). This walk was to be characterized by humility, loving forbearance, and unity (vv. 2-3). Our high calling is the call to holiness of heart and life, to Christlike living. And humility is of the essence of holiness, as it is also the necessary basis for unity.

In our lesson today we have the other four admonitions to "walk." Here Paul says, "Don't walk any longer as the Gentiles are walking, in the emptiness of their minds" (v. 17). Arndt and Gingrich translate this last part: "walk with their minds fixed on futile things" (p. 496). One of the saddest tragedies in the world today is that masses of people have no real purpose in life. They spend their time with futility and end with frustration.

The apostle delineates further the mental condition of these Gentiles (v. 18) and the moral consequences (v. 19). They have their "understanding darkened" by disobedience. They are "alienated [exactly the same form as in 2:12] from the life of God because of the ignorance that is in them, on account of the hardness of their hearts." The word translated "blind-ness" (KJV) is literally "hardening." In the New Testament it is used always in a figurative sense of "dullness" or "obstinacy." It is a condition brought on by self-will.

The unsaved Gentiles are further described as "being past feeling." This is one word in the Greek, a verb found only here in the New Testament. It means to be calloused, so that one no longer feels pain. Conscience has some-times been described as a sharp-pointed thing inside us that hurts when it is turned by conviction. But if people refuse to pay attention to con-science they become so callous that they do not feel it any longer.

And so, having lost all sensitivity, these Gentiles have given themselves over to sensuality ("lasciviousness"), "to work all uncleanness with greedi-ness." They have a greedy appetite for impurity.

B. In Place of the Old Man: vv. 20-22

Paul reminds his readers that this kind of life is contrary to the teachings of Jesus. Purity of morals is one of the main emphases of the New Testament, from Matthew to Revelation.

So, in relation to our former "con-versation" rather, "manner of liv-ing" we are to "put off [or "lay aside"] the old man." The context suggests that here this expression means the old life. At conversion the old way of living is to be renounced and forsaken.

C. In Mind and Spirit: vv. 23-24

Paul goes on: "And be renewed in the spirit of your mind" (v. 23). As in Romans 12:2, the verb is in the pres-ent tense of continuous action. The renewing of our thinking is a lifelong process. Perhaps "spirit of your mind" refers particularly to the basic atti-tudes we have.

It is not enough to put off the old man; we must "put on the new man" (v. 24), the new way of life. The verb used here is used most commonly of putting on clothes. This new man has been created (aorist passive participle) "in righteousness and true holiness." The language used here suggests that the new man is an inward attitude as well as a basic way of life. There must first of all be a renewal of spirit and thinking before a new life will be lived.

II. THE NEW LIFE:
Ephesians 4:25-32

A. New Attitudes: vv. 25-27

Lying was a way of life for the pagan world. Paul had to admonish his Christian readers to put it aside and "speak every man truth with his neigh-bor." Why? Because "we are members one of another." That is, it is just as unreasonable for a believer to lie to a fellow Christian as it would be to try to deceive himself. As members of the same body, we must be utterly sincere with each other.

What does the apostle mean by saying, "Be ye angry, and sin not"? (v. 26). Is not all anger sinful? The answer is "No." Jesus was angry (Mark 3:5). The meaning clearly is: "Be angry, but in your anger do not sin." That was the case with Jesus. God has a holy wrath against sin, and every holy per-son will be angry with wrong. What is it that makes anger sinful? The answer is "Selfishness." We cannot love the good without hating evil. But selfish anger, anger for our own sakes, is always wrong.

In any case, we are not to let the sun go down on our "wrath." The word here means "angry mood." If we have been angry with anyone, we should ask forgiveness before the day closes. That is, we should never go to bed with any bad feeling at all between us and anyone else. To do so is to "give place to the devil" (v. 27).

B. New Conduct: vv. 28-30

Paul warns not only against lying but also against stealing: "The one who was stealing must steal no more."

To those of us who have been brought up in a more or less Christian culture, it seems odd that in this deeply spiritual Epistle Paul would write that way to believers. But we constantly need to remember the pagan background of these converts, and the low moral level of life all around them still. The habits of a lifetime are not broken easily. First generation Christians often have to be given time to break away completely from their old way of living. The apostle's admonitions here can be understood only in the light of the fact that he was a missionary writing to his recent converts from paganism on a mission field. When we keep this in mind, we can make sense out of these strange commands.

What is the alternative to stealing? "Rather let him labor, doing something good with his own hands, so that he can give to someone in need." Every Christian is a steward. We should seek not only to earn enough for our own living but to have some surplus to share with needy people around us.

After dealing with the basic ethical issues of living and stealing, Paul mentions a less crucial matter, but one that was very important. "Let no corrupt communication proceed out of your mouth" (v. 29) is a rather heavy translation. "Communication" is simply *logos*, "word" or "speech." The word for "corrupt" is *sapros*. It is used in the New Testament of bad fish (Matthew 13:48), trees (Matthew 7:17), and fruit (Matthew 12:33). Here it is used in the figurative sense of "bad," "evil," or at least "unwholesome." We should avoid any talk that is damaging in any way, and should seek rather to say "only what is helpful for building others up according to their needs" (New International Bible).

Verse 30 contains a warning that should be heeded by every Christian: "And do not grieve the Holy Spirit of God, by whom you have been sealed to the day of redemption." How may we grieve the Spirit? The most obvious way is by disobedience. The Holy Spirit comes into our hearts to be our Teacher and Guide (John 14:26; 16:13). If we refuse to obey Him, He will leave.

But we can also grieve Him by sheer neglect. We might use a homely illustration. Suppose I came to your home as an invited guest. I arrived late in the evening and you courteously showed me to my room for the night. The next morning I rose and dressed. Hearing the dishes rattle in the kitchen, I went down to the living room and read the morning paper. Soon I was aware that you were eating breakfast in the kitchen, but nothing was said to me about joining you. And so the morning passed with no recognition of my presence. Probably by that time I would be upstairs packing my bag and getting ready to leave!

It is hard to believe such a thing could take place. Yet that is the way some people treat the Heavenly Guest in their hearts. Ignoring the Holy Spirit's presence is a sure way of grieving Him.

C. New Disposition: vv. 31-32

Another way that we can grieve the Holy Spirit is by taking wrong attitudes and saying unkind things to others. So Paul warns us to get rid of "all bitterness, anger, wrath, clamor, and slander, along with all malice" (v. 31).

It is not enough to put away all these negative things in our hearts and lives. We must adopt new positive attitudes and actions. And so Paul admonishes his readers: "And be kind to one another, tenderhearted, forgiving one another, even as God for Christ's sake has forgiven you" (v. 32). Instead of being bitter toward each other, we should be kind and tenderhearted. Since God has forgiven us for all the many sins we committed against Him, how can we do less than forgive others for the little (or big) things they do that hurt us? The logic of this is unescapable.

The classic example of this truth is the Parable of the Unmerciful Servant

(Matthew 18:23-35). A master called in a servant who owed him ten million dollars. When he pleaded for mercy the master freely forgave him the whole debt. But the forgiven man went out and found a fellow servant who owed him twenty dollars. Taking him by the throat he demanded the money. Turning a deaf ear to the fellow's pleas for time, he threw him into prison. And that same attitude is altogether too common today among professing Christians.

III. THE NEW WALK:
Ephesians 5:1-21

A. Walking in Love: vv. 1-7

We come now to the third "walk" in this letter. Paul asks his readers to be "followers" (literally, "imitators") of God, as dear children (v. 1). Then he says, "Walk in love" (v. 2).

This command takes in a lot of territory. It means that we should apply the principle of *agape* (unselfish love) to every area of life. Love for God and for others must dominate every thought, every attitude, every word, every action, every decision, every deed. It means that love must be the main motive for all we do and say.

Christ has set us the example. He loved us and gave Himself for us as "an offering and sacrifice" to God for "a sweetsmelling savour." Today we use "savour" (if at all) for something we taste, rather than something we smell. The Greek word means "fragrance." The whole phrase is literally "for a fragrance of an aroma." It is a strong double expression trying to communicate something of the indescribable sweetness of Christ's love in giving His life for us on the cross.

Again we find Paul addressing himself to Christian converts living in pagan surroundings. The New International Bible translates verse 3 to read: "But among you there must not be even a hint of sexual immorality, or of any kind of impurity, or of greed, because these are improper for God's holy people." (The word translated

"named" in the King James Version probably means "mentioned.") There should never be any carelessness on the part of the believers that would give occasion for any of these sins to be mentioned.

The Paul came a little closer home, adding: "Neither filthiness, nor foolish talking, nor jesting, which are not convenient, but rather giving thanks" (v. 4). The word for "filthiness" suggests something disgraceful. Such things are not to be discussed by God's children. "Foolish talking" and "jesting" have sometimes been misunderstood. We have known people who insisted that this passage condemned all joking. So they have become as solemn as an owl. But the single Greek word for "foolish talking" means "silly talk," and the third word means "coarse jesting." (All three words are found only here in the New Testament.) What Paul is warning against is not pleasant humor, which is an essential ingredient of any normal life, but silly talk or "dirty" jokes, which are never "proper" in Christian circles. Instead of this there should be thanksgiving. There is no question but that the level of conversation among Christians would be elevated if more time were given to telling about God's blessings and thanking Him for them, and less time to merely frivolous talk! Humor has traditionally been called "the spice of life." A little spice certainly adds a lot of pleasure to eating, but too much spice can be nauseating.

In verses 5 and 6 the apostle warns that no immoral, impure, or greedy person will have any place in the kingdom of God. He goes so far as to say that covetousness is actually idolatry, because it makes money our god. No matter what anyone may say, God's wrath will come on the disobedient people who practice such things. We are not to be partners with people like that.

B. Walking in the Light: vv. 8-14

We now come to Paul's fourth "walk": "Walk as children of light" (v.

8). Those who are disobedient walk in darkness. The obedient are the children of light.

He goes on to say: "For the fruit of the light [so the best text] is in all goodness and righteousness and truth" (v. 9). These are the characteristics of those who walk in the light. "Proving" (v. 10) means "testing," or "finding out." We are to seek carefully to know what is pleasing to the Lord, and practice that. Instead of fellowshiping with "the unfruitful works of darkness," we are to "reprove" them (or "expose" them). Again Paul declares that it is "a shame"—improper or disgraceful—even to mention the things that people do in secret. He continues: "But all things that are reproved are made manifest by the light" (v. 13)—or, as the New International Bible has it, "But everything exposed by the light becomes visible"—for it is the light that exposes. So those who are sleeping in sin are called to waken and "arise from the dead" (v. 14), and Christ will give them light.

C. Walking Carefully: vv. 15-21

We come to the fifth and last of the "walk" passages: "See then that you walk circumspectly [or "carefully"], not as fools, but as wise" (v. 15). The Greek says, "not as unwise, but as wise." We are to "redeem [literally, "buy up" or "buy back"] "the time, because the days are evil" (v. 16). Life today has become so terribly busy for most of us that we must buy up the time if we are going to have enough of it. Stewardship of time is just as vital as stewardship of money. It is a sin to waste time. There is always something good we can do, including rest and recreation at the right time.

The lesson today is labeled a lesson on temperance. Verse 18 is very much to the point: "And don't get drunk on wine, in which is debauchery, but be continually filled with the Spirit." Drunkenness is strongly condemned in both the Old Testament and the New.

It is a sin against the human mind, for drunk men lose their reasoning ability. It is a sin against the will, for it breaks down moral restraint. It is a sin against the human body, for it brings physical deterioration. It is a sin against society, for reasons too numerous to mention. It is a sin against loved ones, who often suffer in many ways from a drunk father, husband, or son. Above all, it is a sin against God, who created man in His own image.

But we must not neglect the second part of this verse: "Be continually filled with the Spirit." Instead of getting drunk to drown our sorrows or escape an unbearable life, we should be filled with the Spirit. That will bring us the relaxation, peace, joy, or whatever we need, with no hangover!

This is spelled out a bit more fully in verses 19-20: "Speaking to yourselves in psalms and hymns and spiritual songs, singing and making melody in your heart to the Lord; giving thanks always for all things unto God and the Father in the name of our Lord Jesus Christ." A Spirit-filled heart should be a singing heart. A Spirit-filled life should live out its thanks to God.

IV. THE NEW RELATIONSHIPS: Ephesians 5:22—6:9

A. Of Wives and Husbands: 5:22-33

Wives are admonished to remember that the husband is the head of the house. But the message to husbands is far more challenging and demanding than that to wives. Paul writes: "Husbands, love your wives, even as Christ also loved the church, and gave himself for it" (v. 25). The husband who sincerely tries to carry out this assignment will not have any time or inclination to "boss" his wife. He will be busy enough fulfilling *his* responsibility!

Christ gave Himself for the church to sanctify it and cleanse it (v. 26).

The Greek says: "sanctify it, having cleansed it." The washing of regeneration (Titus 3:5) called here "the washing of water by the word," precedes sanctification, the purpose of which is the presentation of the church to Christ as His Bride (v. 27).

The combination of the spiritual and the practical, which is a main feature of Paul's Epistles, shows up strikingly in this passage. Paul tells husbands to love their wives, even as Christ loved the church (v. 25). Then he talks about the church as the Bride. Lest someone forget the practical exhortation, he immediately comes back to it: "So ought men to love their wives as their own bodies" (v. 28). Then he declares: "This is a great mystery: but I speak concerning Christ and the church." (v. 32). At once, however, he rejoins: "Nevertheless let every one of you in particular so love his wife as himself" (v. 32).

B. Of Children and Parents: 6:1-4

Children must "obey your parents in the Lord." There have been times when children have had to disobey their parents in order to be loyal to Christ. But this would be a rare thing, especially in Christian countries. The apostle quotes the fifth of the Ten Commandments (Exodus 20:12) and notes that it is the first of these commandments to have a promise attached.

Parents ("fathers") are warned not to provoke their children to anger, by being harsh or unreasonable, but to "bring them up in the nurture and admonition of the Lord" (v. 4). All social relationships must be two-way streets.

C. Of Slaves and Masters: 6:5-9

It is claimed that half the population of the Roman Empire in the first century was composed of slaves. So the relationship of masters and slaves was a vital matter in the church.

Paul dealt with this problem in a very sensible way. He told the slaves to obey their earthly masters "in singleness of your heart, as to Christ" (v. 5). Then he used two interesting compounds: "eye service" and "men pleasers." These are self-explanatory. Instead of having a wrong, selfish attitude, slaves are to act as Christ's, "doing the will of God from the heart" (v. 6) and "as to the Lord and not to men" (v. 7). The Lord will reward all well-doers, "whether bond or free" (v. 8).

But the masters have their responsibility, too. They are to avoid making threats, remembering that their Master is in heaven, and with Him there is no "respect of persons" (v. 9). This phrase is one word in Greek, meaning "receiving of face." It does not mean, of course, that God does not respect persons, but that He shows no partiality. He treats servants just as well as masters, and so should we!

The question has often been raised as to why the New Testament does not condemn slavery. If the New Testament writers had openly opposed this institution, probably the Roman government would have banned Christianity altogether. Instead these writers laid down Christian principles that finally resulted in the abolition of slavery around the world. God's way of attacking corrupt social and political systems is by changing men.

DISCUSSION QUESTIONS

1. How does conformity to the world hinder a Christian?
2. How does our thinking affect our living?
3. What are some ways in which we may renew our thought life?
4. How is reading related to thinking?
5. What are the implications of Paul's twofold concept of the church as the Body and Bride of Christ?
6. In what ways is the Christian's life a warfare?

V. THE NEW WARFARE:
Ephesians 6:10-20

A. Strong in the Lord: v. 10

Paul often uses "finally" in his Letters to introduce his concluding admonitions. Here he says briefly: "Be powerful in the Lord and in the strength of His might." There is no excuse for a Christian being weak, when God's mighty power is available to us all.

B. The Whole Armor of God: vv. 11-17

The word for "whole armor" (vv. 11, 13) is *panoplia* ("panoply"). We are to put this on so that we "may be able to withstand in the evil day, and having done all, to stand" (v. 13)—not as men with their backs to the wall, but as those who have conquered all.

Six pieces of the armor are specified. We are told that the most important one is "the shield of faith" (v. 16). The Greeks had two words for shield. The one used here indicates a large oblong shield (about 2½ by 4 feet) carried by the heavy infantry. We also need the "helmet of salvation" to protect our heads as the "breastplate of righteousness" (v. 14) protects our hearts, and "the sword of the Spirit, which is the Word of God" (v. 17). This last is the only weapon that Jesus used to defeat the devil in the wilderness (Matthew 4:1-11). It is just as available to us today.

C. The Importance of Prayer: vv. 18-20

Since this section is in the sentence describing the panoply of God, it should probably be thought of as a part of that armor. It has been suggested that prayer is the buckle that holds the armor together, so that the wearer is not exposed to danger. It is true that watchful prayer (v. 18) is the price of safety. "Praying always"—this keeps the armor in place.

VI. FAREWELL:
Ephesians 6:21-24

There are no personal greetings at the end of this Epistle. This is another argument for its being a circular letter. Paul mentions only Tychicus, the bearer of the Epistle. As always, he closes with a beautiful benediction.

CONTEMPORARY APPLICATION

The word *renewal* is a very popular one in church circles today. Centers for Renewal are being built. Articles on the subject appear in religious journals. Everybody seems excited about it.

But when we check the meaning of this term as used today, we are somewhat disillusioned. In most cases it means nothing more or less than social action. Too often it means the secularization of Christianity, the identification of the church with society.

Renewal must first be inward before it can be outward. We must be renewed in mind and spirit before we can be renewed in life and conduct. We should not neglect the outer, but we should begin with the inner.

The Christian renewal that is most needed today is an outpouring of God's Spirit on the church in answer to penitent prayer. To be renewed in mind and spirit means to let the Holy Spirit give us the mind of Christ. Then, and then only, we will find ourselves living the life pictured in the Epistle to the Ephesians.

PARTNERSHIP IN THE GOSPEL

DEVOTIONAL READING	James 1:2-15

ADULTS

Topic: *Partnership in the Gospel*

Background Scripture: Philippians 1; 2:19-30; 4

Scripture Lesson: Philippians 1:1-11; 4:10-13

Memory Verse: *I thank my God in all my remembrance of you, always in every prayer of mine for you all making my prayer with joy, thankful for your partnership in the gospel from the first day until now.* Philippians 1:3-5

YOUTH

Topic: *Caring Enough to Be Involved*

Background Scripture: Philippians 1; 2:19-30; 4

Scripture Lesson: Philippians 1:1-11; 4:10-13

Memory Verse: *I thank my God in all my remembrance of you, always in every prayer of mine for you all making my prayer with joy, thankful for your partnership in the gospel from the first day until now.* Philippians 1:3-5

CHILDREN

Topic: *Singing in Jail*

Background Scripture: Acts 16:16-40; Philippians 1:12-18

Scripture Lesson: Philippians 1:12-14

Memory Verse: *Rejoice in the Lord always; again I will say, Rejoice.* Philippians 4:4

DAILY BIBLE READINGS

Mon., July 15: The Challenge of Partnership, Philippians 1:1-6.
Tues., July 16: Partnership of Love, Philippians 1:7-11.
Wed., July 17: Partnership Strengthened by Hardships, Philippians 1:12-14, 27-30.
Thurs., July 18: Partnership Sustained by Courage, Philippians 1:19-26.
Fri., July 19: Partnership in Service, Philippians 2:19-30.
Sat., July 20: Partnership in Faith, Hebrews 11:1-7.
Sun., July 21: Victorious Partnership, Philippians 4:4-13.

LESSON AIM

To show how Christians and their leaders can be in partnership with each other and with the Lord in the work of the gospel.

LESSON SETTING

Time: A.D. 61

Place: Prison at Rome

393

Partnership in the Gospel

LESSON OUTLINE

**SUGGESTED
INTRODUCTION
FOR ADULTS**

We have noted that while Paul was in prison at Rome (A.D. 59-61), Onesimus was converted under him. Paul sent him back with a personal note to his master Philemon, asking forgiveness for the runaway. Along with that he sent a letter to the church at Colosse, which met in Philemon's home. At the same time he sent a longer Epistle to the Ephesians, perhaps as a circular letter to all the Christians in the province of Asia.

Later, toward the end of his first imprisonment, Paul wrote the Epistle to the Philippians. That it was written in the latter part of this period is shown rather clearly by what he says in 2:19-30.

First, he says that he hopes to send Timothy to them as soon as he learns how things are turning out at Rome (vv. 19-23). Timothy has been his junior partner in the work: "as a son with the father, he has served with me in the gospel" (v. 22). Paul hopes to visit them soon (v. 24), which implies that his prison term is nearly ended. It was a rule at that time that no one could be held for more than two years awaiting trial before the emperor. It is altogether possible that the ruling emperor did not consider Paul's case worth bothering with and so he was automatically released at the end of two years. We are specifically told that this was the length of Paul's first Roman imprisonment (Acts 28:30).

A second indication that Philippians was written toward the close of these two years is found in what Paul says about Epaphroditus. The Philippian church had sent this man as its messenger to Paul, with a love offering for the apostle (2:25). While he was in Rome Epaphroditus had taken sick. Then he became sad (v. 26) because he heard that the Philippians were sad because they had heard that he was sick! So Paul was sending him all the more eagerly, in order that they might rejoice when they saw him again in good health (v. 28). All this would consume much time. The journey one way between Philippi and Rome would take some months, and several trips are implied here.

SUGGESTED INTRODUCTION FOR YOUTH

"Caring Enough to Be Involved." This was the case with the Philippian church, with its messenger Epaphroditus, with Paul's messenger Timothy, and preeminently with the great apostle himself.

Do we care enough to be involved with our Sunday school class, our local church, our pastor, our community, our denomination, our missionary responsibility? Or are we sitting on the sidelines, criticizing? Let's not be spectators, but participants!

CONCEPTS FOR CHILDREN

1. Paul sang in prison at Philippi, because he was aware of the Lord's presence.
2. Now he was rejoicing in prison at Rome, for the same reason.
3. Paul wrote this Letter to thank the Philippians for their kind love-offering to him.
4. We should always be careful to thank others for what they do for us.

THE LESSON COMMENTARY

I. INTRODUCTION:
Philippians 1:1-7

A. Salutation: v. 1

Again Paul shows a beautiful courtesy in mentioning his young associate Timothy. They are both "servants" (Greek, "slaves," and so "love-slaves") of Jesus Christ.

The apostle addresses this Letter to the saints at Philippi, "with the bishops and deacons." The Greek word for "bishop" is *episcopos*, from which we get "episcopal." The term was used at that time in a secular sense for an "overseer" of a group of men. So the bishops were to be overseers of the church. It will be noted that there were several "bishops" in the one congregation. In the letters of Ignatius, written early in the second century, we find one bishop for each congregation, with a group of elders and a group of deacons. By the end of the second century we see the appearance of diocesan bishops, as we have today.

The word *deacon* is taken over from the Greek *diaconos*, which originally meant one who waited on table, and so in general a "servant." The deacons in the early church were those who served the congregation by taking care of the material needs as the bishops took care of spiritual matters. Whether either bishops or deacons were officially ordained at this stage is not known.

B. Greetings: v. 2

As in all of Paul's Epistles, we have the twofold greeting, "Grace . . . and peace." Both of these gifts come only from God. (See discussions of the greetings in Thessalonians, pp. 334-35 and Ephesians, p. 369.)

C. Thanksgiving: vv. 3-7

Paul thanks God every time he remembers the Philippian Christians. And well he might, for they were the most thoughtful of his needs. In every prayer for them he makes his prayer with joy ("prayer" and "request" are the same word in Greek.)

He is especially thankful for their "fellowship" in the gospel. The word is *koinonia*, which basically means "having something in common." It may be translated in three ways: "fellowship" (or communion), "partnership," and "participation" (or, "sharing"). Perhaps the best rendering here is that adopted in the lesson title, "Partnership in the Gospel."

Paul was a man of optimistic faith. He was persuaded concerning these Philippians "that he who has begun in you a good work will complete it until the day of Christ Jesus" (v. 6). God will finish what He starts, if we will let Him.

The apostle says it is "meet" (Greek, "right" or "just") for him to think this of them all, "because I have you in my heart." The Greek can also be translated, "because you have me in your heart." Actually, both statements would be true to fact, and because of the uncertainty of the Greek both should be allowed. But probably the traditional rendering is preferable. Paul had a large heart that took in all the Gentile Christians throughout the Roman Empire, as well as his Jewish brethren. The Philippian believers were "partakers of" *(synkoinonous)*, or "sharers in," God's grace along with Paul. They were Paul's partners in both giving and receiving.

II. PAUL'S PRAYER FOR THESE PEOPLE:
Philippians 1:8-11

A. For Spiritual Progress: vv. 8-9

Paul declares: "God is my witness [KJV, "record"], how greatly I long for you all with the tender compassion of Christ Jesus" (v. 8). The use of "bowels" here in the King James Version (as also three times in the short letter to Philemon) is very unfortunate, to say the least. While the Greek word does mean "bowels" and is used in a literal sense in Acts 1:18, yet in the other ten places where it occurs in the New Testament it clearly has the figurative sense. The Greeks considered the bowels to be the center of the affections, but such a concept is very foreign to Western thinking in modern times. So while "bowels" is the literal meaning of the term, this completely distorts the true meaning for the reader today. Certainly, then, one of the newer versions should be substituted in this case.

Paul continues: "And this I pray, that your love may abound still more and more in knowledge and in all judgment" (v. 9). Love abounding, but in accordance with proper knowledge and judgment. This is what is needed.

B. For Spiritual Discernment: v. 10

Paul prays for the Philippians that they may "approve things that are excellent"—or "the things that really matter." Arndt and Gingrich suggest this (p. 189) and also for the whole expression: "approve what is essential" (p. 201). But they also allow the translation: "Discover what is essential" (p. 201). The problem is that the verb has three meanings: (1) test; (2) prove by testing; (3) approve as a result of testing. Perhaps the New International Bible has the best rendering: "discern what is best."

The apostle wants his readers to be "sincere." The Greek word is compounded of the noun *sunshine* and the verb *judge.* So it properly means "that which being viewed in the sunshine is found clear and pure"; that is, "unmixed," "sincere." They are to be "without offence till the day of Christ." This is the way we have to live if we are going to be ready for the second coming of our Lord.

C. For Spiritual Fruit: v. 11

We are also to be filled with the fruit of righteousness." This comes only "through Jesus Christ" and works out for the glory and praise of the Lord. It is not enough to be sincere and blameless. We must be worth something, bearing fruit.

III. PROGRESS OF THE GOSPEL: Philippians 1:12-20

A. Progress Through Opposition: vv. 12-14

Paul is thankful that his arrest and imprisonment had actually worked out for the advance of the gospel (v. 12). While he had been confined and unable to travel, the door was opened for contact with those connected with the imperial court. This would not have been possible otherwise. His "bonds in Christ"—the fact that he was in prison for loyalty to his Lord—had become "manifest in all the palace." In the Greek the last word is *praitorion* (Latin, *praetorium*). The term is used elsewhere in the New Testament only for Pilate's judgment hall (Matthew 27:27; Mark 15:16; John 18:28, 33; 19:9) and for the judgment hall of Herod Antipas (Acts 23:35). Here it apparently means the imperial guard at Rome. We can imagine that Paul was such an unusual prisoner—not the criminal type at all—that his case was widely discussed by the soldiers on guard. Why should this gentle, innocent man be an imperial prisoner? This gave opportunity for the gospel message to be presented in explanation. Many of "the brethren in the Lord" (v. 14) had been encouraged by Paul's circumstances and good spirit to

"speak the Word" more boldly. The result was that there was more preaching of the gospel going on at the imperial headquarters than ever before.

B. Progress in Spite of Insincerity: vv. 15-18

Sad to say, there were some who were preaching about Christ "even of envy and strife" (v. 15), doing it with "contention" (or, "ambitious rivalry"), hoping to stir up trouble for Paul in prison (v. 16). But others were doing it out of love, rejoicing that Paul was set there "for the defence of the gospel" (v. 17). (It should be noted that in the Greek text the order of verses 16 and 17 is reversed, a fact that is reflected in some modern versions.)

The apostle is rejoicing that Christ is being preached, whatever the motive. It would seem that the opposition was presenting the gospel of Christ rather accurately, even though with the motive of getting Paul in trouble. The bigness of his spirit is shown by the fact that, disregarding consequences to himself personally, he could say: "And I therein do rejoice, yea, and will rejoice" (v. 18). All that Paul was concerned about was the Kingdom and the salvation of souls. What happened to him did not matter. It is this kind of spirit that has marked the great missionaries of all time.

C. Paul's Hope of Release: v. 19

The apostle feels confident that all this will turn out for his "salvation" or "deliverance." He believes that the Holy Spirit can bring about his release from prison.

IV. REJOICING IN LIFE OR DEATH: Philippians 1:20-30

A. Paul's Dilemma: vv. 20-26

It was the apostle's "eager expectation and hope" (v. 20) that Christ should be magnified in his body, "whether through life or through death." And then Paul makes this magnificent declaration: "For to me to live is Christ, and to die is gain." If he continued to live on earth, he would be enjoying Christ's presence and blessing every day. If he died, death would be only a momentary tunnel into the unveiled presence of the Lord he had loved and served on earth. Paul's philosophy was: "I can't lose for winning." Whichever way his fortunes went, for him it was up and not down. When a man has that attitude, nothing can defeat him.

So death or life—what difference did it make? But Paul was having a hard time deciding which he preferred. He says, "Which to choose, I don't know" (v. 22). ("Wot" is old-fashioned English for "know.")

Paul was in a dilemma. He had a strong "desire" to "depart" (literally, "unhitch") and "be with Christ; which is far better" (v. 23). Yet he knew that "to abide in the flesh is more needful for you" (v. 24). With the issue thus clarified there was only one decision that a dedicated man like Paul could make: "I know that I shall remain [meno] and remain alongside of [para-meno] you all for your advancement and joy in the faith" (v. 25). All this was in order that "your rejoicing may abound in Christ Jesus on account of me through my coming to you again" (v. 26). The word for "coming" is parousia. We learned in our study of Thessalonians that this is the most common word in the New Testament for the "coming again" of Christ. The apostle was Christ's messenger and envoy to the Gentile churches.

B. Christian Citizenship: vv. 27-28

We have previously noted that three different Greek nouns in the New Testament are translated "conversation," and not one of them means "conversation" in our present use of that term. Here we find one word rendered, "Let your conversation be." It is the verb politeuo. The root is polis, "city." In that day of autonomous city-states, a polites was the "citizen" of a city. Then it came to be used for

citizens of countries. So the verb here literally means "live your life as a citizen" (of the heavenly kingdom). The first part of verse 27 should be translated, "Only live in a manner worthy of the gospel of Christ." So whether Paul was with them or absent from them, he would hear that they were standing steadfast "in one spirit, with one mind contending side by side for the faith of the gospel." By no means were they to be terrified by their adversaries, for, as the New International Bible has, "This is a sign to the latter that they will be destroyed, but you will be saved—and that by God" (v. 28).

C. Partnership in Suffering: vv. 29-30

Partnership in prayer. Partnership in preaching. Partnership in rejoicing. These were all wonderful privileges. But there must also be a partnership in suffering. Paul tells the Philippians: "Because to you it is graciously given [echaristhe; root charis, "grace"] in behalf of Christ, not only to believe on him, but also to suffer for his sake, having the same conflict that you saw in me and now hear to be in me."

What does Paul mean by his "conflict"? The Greek word is agon. It comes from the verb ago, which means "lead" or "bring together." So agon meant a "gathering." But since the largest gatherings of that day, as usually also now, were for sports events, the word agon came to mean a gathering for athletic contests (such as the Olympic Games) and then the contest itself. Finally the word came to be used for any conflict or struggle. Paul is here speaking of the conflict involved in his preaching the gospel, because of opposition.

V. REJOICING IN THE LORD ALWAYS:
Philippians 4:1-23

A. Exhortation to Unity: vv. 1-3

The church at Corinth was split up into four factions (I Corinthians 1:12), so that Paul had to devote the first four chapters of his First Epistle to the problem of divisions in the congregation. It was a sad spectacle indeed.

Very different was the situation at Philippi. The church there was beautifully united in love. With great affection Paul wrote: "Therefore, brothers, you whom I love and long for, my joy and crown, stand thus steadfast in the Lord, dearly beloved" (v. 1). We see here a heart overflowing in love for the believers at Philippi.

There was just one fly in the ointment of fragrant perfume. The apostle writes: "I beseech Euodia and I beseech Syntyche to be of the same mind in the Lord" (v. 2). These two women in the church had evidently had a misunderstanding with each other and were no longer on the same wave length. Paul begs them to get together and think the same thing. We can only hope that they obeyed his admonition.

Then he says, "And I intreat thee also, true yokefellow." The Greek word for yokefellow can be taken as a proper name (Syzygus), as some modern versions do. But probably Paul is addressing the pastor there and giving him some advice. He is to help "those women who labored with me in the gospel," such as Lydia (Acts 16: 14-15, 40), and also Clement (a man) and other fellow workers, "whose names are in the book of life." God is keeping the records, and keeping them faithfully.

B. Praise Instead of Anxiety: vv. 4-9

The keynote of the Epistle to the Philippians is *joy*. Here it is epitomized: "Rejoice in the Lord always; I will say it again: Rejoice!" (v. 4). Not just when you feel like it, but always. Not only when things are going well, but always. This is the secret of a happy life in Christ.

The verb *chairo* has already occurred six times in this brief Epistle. In 1:18 we read: "And therein do I rejoice, yes, and will rejoice." Paul says

to his readers: "I joy, and rejoice with you all" (2:17). The first verb ("joy") is *chairo*, the second *synchairo*, "rejoice together." The same two verbs are found in 2:18. The apostle knows that the Philippians will rejoice when they see Epaphroditus again (2:28). In 3:1 Paul writes: "Finally, my brothers, rejoice in the Lord." No wonder it has been said that the keynote of Philippians is: "I am rejoicing; you rejoice!"

This takes on added significance when we remember two facts: Paul was in prison when he wrote this Epistle, and he was writing to a city in which he had a very painful prison experience (Acts 16:22-24). The apostle was a rare breed: a joyful prisoner.

"Let your moderation be known to all men" (v. 5). Probably most people have heard Matthew Arnold's suggestion for "moderation": "sweet reasonableness." In the Greek the word is an adjective. It means, "yielding, gentle, kind." Arndt and Gingrich suggest: "your forbearing spirit" (p. 292). There are several ways it can be translated, but the central thrust is clear.

Why should we be gentle and kind? Because "the Lord is near." We would not want to be found by Him at His return talking harshly to someone or being unkind in any way. But the fact is that He may come at any moment (I Corinthians 15:52). So the only way to be ready for the Second Coming is to show kindness and gentleness at all times.

We have headed this section: "Praise Instead of Anxiety." This is the way Paul puts it: "Do not be anxious about anything, but in everything, by prayer and petition, with thanksgiving, make known your requests to God" (v. 6). This is the true antidote for the Aspirin Age. We are to pray not with anxiety but with thanksgiving. This steadies our nerves and increases our faith. Thanksgiving should be a prominent ingredient of all our praying, even our times of earnest intercession. We have no right to keep on asking but never saying "Thank You" for the many answers to prayer in the past.

If we pray in this way, "the peace of God, which surpasses all understanding, will guard [our] hearts and thoughts in Christ Jesus" (v. 7). What a consolation! Peace follows prayer and praise.

Verse 8 is a sort of omnibus. Paul tells us to think on the things that are true, noble, right, pure, lovely, "of good report." Arndt and Gingrich note that the single Greek word translated by this last phrase can be interpreted in various ways, as "auspicious, well-sounding, praiseworthy, attractive, appealing" (p. 327). The apostle concludes this verse by stressing two categories, the things that have moral excellence and are praiseworthy.

We have noted in our study of other of Paul's Epistles that he has urged his readers to imitate him even as he imitated Christ. So here he says: "Whatever you have learned and received and heard and seen in me, practice these things. And the God of peace will be with you" (v. 9).

C. Supplying Every Need: vv. 10-23

Epaphroditus had just brought a generous love offering to the apostle from the church at Philippi (v. 18). Paul's typical response is: "I rejoiced greatly in the Lord" (v. 10). He was glad that their care of him had "blossomed again" (literal Greek). He wasn't complaining; he knew they had not had opportunity before.

DISCUSSION QUESTIONS

1. What is the relation of prayer and praise?
2. How can we rejoice in hard circumstances, as Paul did?
3. What should be our attitude toward death?
4. How can we do "all things"?
5. What place does giving have in spiritual growth?
6. How is anxiety a hindrance to prayer?

Then Paul gives an amazing testimony: "I have learned, in whatever state I am, to be content" (v. 11). Once more the word inserted in italics, "therewith," distorts the meaning. Paul had not learned to be content *with* all things; there were many things he wanted to change. But he had learned to be content *in* everything. And this is one of the greatest secrets in life, one that not too many people have learned. To be content wherever God puts us—this is heaven below, on our way to heaven.

Because of this Paul could say, "I can do all things through Christ who strengthens me" (v. 13). When Christ can do everything with us, then we can do everything through Him. Just as the secret of electric power is being properly "plugged in," so the secret of divine power is vital contact with Christ, which is possible only when we are fully committed to Him. The two prongs of the plug are faith and consecration.

In spite of the apostle's sense of self-sufficiency in Christ, he is thankful that the Philippians had shared with him in his affliction (v. 14). This was not the first time they had done it. Theirs was the only church that had contacted Paul about this when he left Macedonia (v. 15). At Thessalonica, his very next stop after Philippi, they had twice sent him a love-offering, even in the short time he was there (v. 16). Paul rejoices in their reward—the spiritual blessing they will get from this (v. 17).

Now Paul can say, "I have all and abound" (v. 18). The large love-offering they had gathered and sent to Rome by Epaphroditus was more than enough to meet the apostle's need. He calls it "a fragrance of sweet perfume, an acceptable sacrifice, well pleasing to God."

Paul gives his kind donors a promise in return: "My God will supply every need of yours, according to his riches in glory in Christ Jesus" (v. 19). Someone has said: "He has promised to supply all our need, but not all our greed."

CONTEMPORARY APPLICATION

Sometimes we feel our lot in life is hard. We have nothing to smile about. And so we go around with a somber face, spreading gloom everywhere we go. And we call this Christianity!

Paul probably had ten times the trials and hardships that any of us have, and a hundred times as many as most of us have. How many days have we spent in prison? Paul wrote this letter that overflows with joy and thanksgiving near the end of four years' imprisonment at Caesarea and Rome. He was not the victim of his circumstances, but victor over them. How about us?

PRESSING ON TOWARD THE GOAL

DEVOTIONAL READING	Philippians 2:1-13

ADULTS

Topic: *Pressing on Toward the Goal*

Background Scripture: Philippians 2:1-18; 3

Scripture Lesson: Philippians 3:4b-16

Memory Verse: *I press on toward the goal for the prize of the upward call of God in Christ Jesus.* Philippians 3:14

YOUTH

Topic: *What's My Goal?*

Background Scripture: Philippians 2:1-18; 3

Scripture Lesson: Philippians 3:4b-16

Memory Verse: *I press on toward the goal for the prize of the upward call of God in Christ Jesus.* Philippians 3:14

CHILDREN

Topic: *Joy in Christian Living*

Background Scripture: Philippians 2:1-4, 14-16; 3:12-14; 4:8-9

Scripture Lesson: Philippians 2:12; 4:8

Memory Verse: *Whatever is true, whatever is honorable, whatever is just, whatever is pure, whatever is lovely, whatever is gracious, if there is any excellence, if there is anything worthy of praise, think about these things.* Philippians 4:8

DAILY BIBLE READINGS

Mon., July 22: Setting the Highest Goal, Philippians 2:1-11.

Tues., July 23: Planning to Reach the Goal, Philippians 2:12-18.

Wed., July 24: Having No Other Goals, Philippians 3:1-11.

Thurs., July 25: Making the Goal My Own, Philippians 3:12-17.

Fri., July 26: Power to Reach the Goal, II Corinthians 4:13-18.

Sat., July 27: Obstacles to the Goal, II Corinthians 6:1-10.

Sun., July 28: Controlled by Christ, II Corinthians 5:11-21.

LESSON AIM

To show the importance of pressing on in our Christian life, not depending on any past experience.

Time: A.D. 61

Place: Prison at Rome

Pressing On Toward the Goal

   I. Progress in Christlikeness: Philippians 2:1-4
      A. Fellowship in the Spirit: v. 1
      B. Unity of Mind: v. 2
      C. Lowliness of Mind: v. 3
      D. Unselfishness Toward Others: v. 4

  II. Working Out Our Salvation: Philippians 2:12-18
      A. God Working in Us: vv. 12-13
      B. Avoidance of Strife: vv. 14-16
      C. Rejoice Together: vv. 17-18

 III. Warning Against Judaizers: Philippians 3:1-4a
      A. Paul's Concern: v. 1
      B. The Concision Party: v. 2
      C. The True Circumcision: vv. 3-4a

 IV. Paul's Jewish Heritage: Philippians 3:4b-6
      A. A Superior Background: v. 4b
      B. A Hebrew of the Hebrews: v. 5
      C. Zealous for the Faith: v. 6

  V. Discounting the Past: Philippians 3:7-11
      A. Gain and Loss: v. 7
      B. Christ Worth More than All Else: vv. 8-9
      C. The Only Thing That Really Counts: vv. 10-11

 VI. Pressing On to the Future: Philippians 3:12-16
      A. Pursuing the Prize: v. 12
      B. Pressing Toward the Mark: vv. 13-14
      C. Perfection the Goal: vv. 15-16

 VII. The Culmination of Redemption: Philippians 3:17-21

Too many evangelical Christians think of their religion in terms of a past experience, when they accepted Jesus Christ as Savior. But Christianity is more than this. It is a life to be lived. And life is never static; it does not stand still. We are always going forward or backward, progressing or retrogressing. We are growing or else deteriorating.

To hold our own we have to press higher. That is a law of life. We might illustrate it this way. Suppose one were to row a boat across a rather rapidly flowing river. If he pointed the bow of the boat toward a spot exactly opposite on the other shore and just rowed straight ahead, he would end up somewhere downstream. In order to hold his own across the river he would have to aim upstream and keep pulling that way. Out on the stream of life we are either rowing upstream or drifting downstream. We cannot stand still.

So Paul warns his readers to keep pressing onward and upward toward the goal of their heavenly calling. Only thus can they maintain their Christian experience successfully.

"What's My Goal?" That is a question that every serious-minded young person should be asking himself. Is it to become a millionaire at forty? What would there be in life that would be worthwhile after that? Is it to make a name for myself? Human glory is a very fickle thing. Is it to become President of the United States? There are many goals much higher than that.

Paul's supreme goal was to become like Christ. This is the highest goal of all. And it is one we shall never reach fully in this life. So there is no anticlimax. Rather there is always the lure, always the pursuit, always the prize still out there in front. This way life becomes a constant adventure. It lures us on every day. There is no boredom, no time for feeling sorry for ourselves. Always there are higher heights ahead. And we never reach the top of this mountain!

To have a goal in life that lures us onward and upward till the day of death—what more could one ask? This is what Paul presents to us in this lesson.

1. There is always joy in true Christian living.
2. Paul gives us the pattern for a joyful life.
3. Pleasing Jesus makes our own hearts happy.
4. Joy comes from obedience.

THE LESSON COMMENTARY

I. PROGRESS IN CHRISTLIKENESS:
Philippians 2:1-4

A. Fellowship in the Spirit: v. 1

Four things are mentioned here as component parts of a Christian life. The first is "consolation in Christ." The Greek word for "consolation" is *paraclesis*. It comes from the verb *paracaleo*, which means "call alongside (to help)." So the noun means "help, comfort, encouragement." Christ is the one who is always near us to help us.

This fact is highlighted in the Epistle to the Hebrews. There we read that Christ was made like us, in order that He might be "a merciful and faithful high priest"—"merciful" because he knows the frailty of human flesh, "faithful" because He knows how much we need Him every day. "For in that he himself has suffered being tempted, he is able to succour [literally, "come at the cry for help] "those that are tempted" (Hebrews 2:17-18). And again: "For we do not have a high priest who cannot be touched with the feeling of our infirmities, but one who was in all points tempted as we are, apart from sin. Let us therefore come boldly to the throne of grace, in order that we may obtain mercy and find grace to help [when we cry out for help] in time of need" (Hebrews 4:15-16). So there is a lot wrapped up in the brief phrase "consolation in Christ." There is here strength for every need, help for every hour of temptation.

The next thing that is mentioned is "comfort of love." The word for "comfort" is another compound of *para*, "beside." (Paul is fond of using words beginning with the same prefix.) *Parathymion* comes from the verb *parathymeo*, *"encourage, cheer up"*— "especially in connection with death or other tragic events *console*, comfort," and so the noun means *"encouragement, especially as consolation."* So say Arndt and Gingrich, who would translate the phrase here, "if there is any solace afforded by love" (*Lexicon*, p. 626). In the hours of our deepest need, divine love gives us a comfort beyond any human help.

The third item is "fellowship of the Spirit." The word *koinonia*, "fellowship," has become well known in religious circles today. But too often it is used merely for people getting together. As we noted before, this noun means fellowship, communion, partnership, participation, sharing. Here it speaks of that close fellowship that we can have with the Holy Spirit when we are fully submitted to His will to let Him guide us and empower us for each day. We have fellowship with our dearest friends and loved ones. Our closest fellowship, however, unmarred by human differences and limitations, should be with the Holy Spirit.

The fourth thing here is "bowels" and "mercies," which is best translated "tenderness and compassion." The two Greek words mean essentially the same thing. Any religious experience that lacks tenderness and compassion is not Christian experience.

B. Unity of Mind: v. 2

Paul's joy would be full if he knew that the Philippian believers were "like-minded [literally, "thinking the same thing"] having the same love, being of one accord" [this last phrase is a single word meaning "harmonious, united in spirit"] and of one mind

[literally, "thinking the one thing"]." What the apostle is pleading for here, piling up words and phrases to do it, is unity of mind and heart, of purpose and performance. Paul had a passion for the unity of the church of Jesus Christ. He realized that disunity in the church is one of the greatest hindrances to its growth and effectiveness.

C. Lowliness of Mind: v. 3

We are to do nothing out of "selfish ambition or vain conceit" (New International Bible). Rather in "lowliness of mind" we are to consider others better than ourselves. The phrase in quotation marks is one word in Greek, *tapeinophrosyne*. By Greek and Roman philosophers this word was used in a bad sense. But Christianity made it one of the greatest virtues. Human philosophy says, "Know thyself." The Bible tells us to "know God." Exaltation of self is essentially pagan. Humbling ourselves and exalting Christ— this is Christianity.

D. Unselfishness Toward Others: v. 4

Most people believe in looking out for "No. 1." But the true Christian is concerned about the interests and needs of others. The crowning sin of the human heart is selfishness—toward God and man. We are not fully saved from sin until we are saved from self.

II. WORKING OUT OUR SALVATION: Philippians 2:12-18

A. God Working in Us: vv. 12-13

Paul commends the Philippians for the fact that they have "always obeyed." This has been true not only in his "presence" *(parousia)* but also in his "absence" *(apousia)*. The first term literally means "being beside," the second "being away."

Now he urges them to "work out your own salvation with fear and trembling." The verb is in the present tense of continuous action: we are to keep on working out our salvation. But this must be done with a sense of utter dependence on God. It is He who is working in us "both to will and to work in behalf of his good pleasure" (v. 13). This verse could be translated "For it is God who is producing in you both the willingness and the performance in behalf of his good desire."

B. Avoidance of Strife: vv. 14-16

If we are going to maintain the unity that Paul is pleading for in this Epistle, we must "do all things without murmurings and disputings" (v. 14). The New International Bible has it the way we would say it today: "Do everything without complaining or arguing." Arguments are one of the main causes of disunity in homes and churches.

If they avoided these things, they would be "blameless and harmless" (v. 15)—"pure," literally "unmixed"— God's children in the midst of a crooked and perverted "nation" (or, "generation"). They were to shine as lights in a dark world, "holding forth the Word of life" (v. 16). If they did this, Paul would "rejoice in the day of Christ, that I have not run in vain nor labored in vain."

C. Rejoicing Together: vv. 17-18

The word "offered" (v. 17) is *spendo*, found only here and in II Timothy 4:6. It was used literally for a drink offering poured on the animal sacrifice on the altar. So what Paul apparently is saying is this: "I am being poured out like a drink offering on the sacrifice and service of your faith." The apostle always felt that he was expendable; his life could be "poured out" for others. And in this he rejoices with his Philippian friends. In turn he asks them to rejoice with him. "Joy" and "rejoice" (vv. 17 and 18) are *chairo* and *synchairo:* "rejoice" and "rejoice together."

III. WARNING AGAINST JUDA-IZERS:
Philippians 3:1-4a

A. Paul's Concern: v. 1

Again Paul starts out with a note of joyousness: "Finally, my brethren, rejoice [*chairete*] in the Lord." Usually Paul uses the word "finally"—literally, "as for the rest"—to introduce his concluding remarks (e.g., Ephesians 6:10). But here it occurs halfway through the Epistle. Was Paul thinking of closing, but thought of more things to say? We cannot tell. In any case, he felt that for the safeguarding of the Philippians he should warn them against the Judaizers.

B. The Concision Party: v. 2

"Beware of dogs!" That is a familiar sign. But here Paul meant the Judaizers, whom he calls "evil workers." They are of the "concision" (used only here in the New Testament). This word, *paratome*, is in contrast with *peritome* ("circumcision," v. 3). The latter means "a cutting around," which is what circumcision (from the Latin) clearly is. But the former means "a thorough cutting," and so "mutilation." Because the Judaizers were giving such extreme emphasis to circumcision and were practicing this rite in a legalistic way, without any reference to its spiritual meaning, Paul says they are simply mutilating their flesh.

C. The True Circumcision: vv. 3-4a

In contrast to these legalists, the apostle says: "We are the circumcision, who worship God in spirit," that is, spiritually rather than outwardly. The oldest Greek manuscripts have either "worship by the Spirit of God," or simply "worship in spirit." In any case, Paul is calling for a spiritual, rather than legalistic, worship.

Those of the true circumcision— circumcised in heart (Romans 2:29)—"rejoice [or, "boast"] in Christ Jesus and have no confidence in the flesh" (in mere outward religion). Paul reminds his readers that if anybody had a right to put confidence in his heritage of legalistic religion, he was the one (v. 4a).

IV. PAUL'S JEWISH HERITAGE:
Philippians 3:4b-6

If it was a matter of putting confidence in externals, in one's religious heritage and personal practice, Paul had more to present than others. He now proceeds to spell it out.

B. A Hebrew of the Hebrews: v. 5

In accordance with the covenant given to Abraham (Genesis 17:9-14), the baby Saul had been "circumcised the eighth day." This was also enjoined in the law of Moses (Leviticus 12:3). This was the main distinguishing mark of a Jew and was an essential sign that one belonged to the covenant.

Paul was also "of the stock of Israel," that is, belonging to the nation of Israel, God's chosen people. He was "of the tribe of Benjamin," and proud of it. For Benjamin was the only tribe that stayed with Judah in loyalty to the house of David. In fact, he probably received the name "Saul" in memory of Saul, the first king of Israel, who was also from the tribe of Benjamin.

A "Hebrew of the Hebrews" means that his family was of pure Jewish descent. In relation to the law, Saul had been brought up a Pharisee. The Pharisees were more loyal to the entire Old Testament as of divine authority than were the Sadducees. Paul obviously felt that it was a great advantage to be a Pharisee.

C. Zealous for the Faith: v. 6

As a Pharisee, Saul had been zealous in defending the faith. He had gone so far as to persecute the Christians, believing that their calling Jesus "Lord" was blasphemy, and a threat

to the crucial monotheism of Jewish religion. If Jesus was allowed to enter as the Son of God, the basic foundation of Judaism would be destroyed. The one true religion would degenerate into polytheism like the pagan world around it. Young Saul had felt that it was his duty to stamp out this heresy.

Paul also declares that as far as the righteousness of the Mosaic law was concerned, he was "blameless." This is a strong claim. It is apparent that Saul's life as a Pharisee had been marked by strict adherence to all the many rules and regulations of the law. He had obeyed the best he knew how. He testified to the Sanhedrin: "I have lived in all good conscience before God until this day" (Acts 23:1). As far as Judaism was concerned, Saul's record was A[+].

V. DISCOUNTING THE PAST:
Philippians 3:7-11

A. Gain and Loss: v. 7

Paul now makes a startling statement: "But what things were gain to me, those I counted loss for Christ." Chalked up to his account were years of doctrinal loyalty, conscientious observance of the whole law, and zealous service for God. It was a noble record—all gain. But Paul deliberately transferred it from the credit side of his ledger to the debit side. What was gain he counted "loss." This is a strong word meaning "damage, disadvantage, loss, forfeit" (Arndt and Gingrich, p. 338). It was a drastic step on Paul's part, involving a radical change in his concept of true religion. It was not conformity to the law, but to Christ.

B. Christ Worth More than All Else: vv. 8-9

The apostle proceeds to amplify this declaration. With a strong "Yea doubtless," he asserts that he counts "all things" as loss "because of the surpassing greatness of personal acquaintance with Christ Jesus my

Lord." For Paul, knowing Christ was worth more than everything else in all the world. And why not? What would it all be worth without Him? The only answer is, "Nothing." So we sing sincerely, "Take the world, but give me Jesus." Nothing is of real, lasting value except in relation to Him.

Paul had been willing to lose "all things." He had even been willing to count them as "dung." The Greek word means "refuse, rubbish, leavings, dirt, dung." It is found only here in the New Testament. Paul used about the strongest word he could find to show his utter disdain for his own righteousness.

All this was in order that he might "win Christ." The Greek says "gain Christ." Paul had learned that legalism was a liability. Now it was listed properly on the debit side. But Christ was an asset that more than balanced all the liabilities.

Paul wanted to be found in Christ, "not having my own righteousness, which is from the law, but that which is through faith in Christ, the righteousness that is from God, based on faith" (v. 9). Here we have the very heart of the conflict with the Judaizers. They were still advocating a work-righteousness; Paul was contending for a faith-righteousness. The difference between these two is one of the emphases of the Epistles to the Galatians and to the Romans.

C. The Only Thing That Really Counts: vv. 10-11

"That I may know him"—this is all that really mattered for Paul. This does not just mean "know about Him." There are millions who know about Christ who do not actually know Christ. This means personal acquaintance, knowing Him as Savior and Lord in our own lives, and having fellowship with Him as our best Friend.

Paul spelled it out a bit further. He wanted to know not only Christ as a person, but also "the power of His resurrection." The same power that

raised Christ from the dead can operate in our lives as a real life-force (Romans 8:11). But this involves knowing "the fellowship of His sufferings." No crucifixion, no resurrection. Until we have identified ourselves with Christ in His death, we cannot experience the resurrection power of His life. We must be made "conformable to his death" in order to live in His life. This is the price we pay for resurrection power. And only thus will we "attain unto the resurrection of the dead" (v. 11).

VI. PRESSING ON TO THE FUTURE: Philippians 3:12-16

A. Pursuing the Prize: v. 12

There are some things that we cannot experience in this life. One is physical death which comes at the end of life. Another is our bodily resurrection, which obviously can come only after death. The completion of our redemption will come in our glorification, when Christ returns. Paul here says that he had not yet attained to the resurrection (vv. 11-12). And so he was not yet "perfect." This is a verbal form meaning "brought to completion." His redemption would not be completed until his resurrection.

What was he doing in the meantime? He says, "I keep on pursuing, so that I may lay hold of that for which also I am laid hold of by Christ Jesus." He had not yet finished, had not arrived at the goal. But he was pursuing it.

B. Pressing Toward the Mark: vv. 13-14

Again Paul declares that he has not yet achieved the final goal. But one thing he is doing: "Forgetting those things which are behind, and stretching forward to those things that are ahead, I press toward the mark." Success in life depends on our taking the right attitude toward the past, the present and the future. Paul lived an unusually successful life. Fortunately he has told us what his attitudes were in these areas.

What is the first thing? Forgetting the past. The past confronts us with two dangers: discouragement and complacency. We must forget the past with its failures, or we will get discouraged and fail again. But we must also forget the accomplishments of the past, lest we become complacent about our ability to cope with life. Either can be disastrous.

The second thing is: Facing the future. We must have a good goal in life. If we don't we'll drift or go in circles. Paul not only forgot the past, but he was stretching forward toward the future. We only go ahead as we reach ahead.

The third thing is: Improving the present. Paul says: "I keep on pursuing." Life is one long pursuit, and it should not end till death. What was Paul pursuing so earnestly that he kept forgetting the past and stretching toward the future? It was "the mark for the prize of the high calling of God in Christ Jesus." A better translation for "mark" is "goal." The picture here is of a runner in a race. He keeps pushing on toward the goal, where he will receive the "prize." The Greek word for this is connected with the word for "umpire" or "judge," the person who decides who won and then awards the prize. What this prize is Paul tells us clearly in II Timothy 4:7-8. There he says that he has at last come to the end of life's race. He has competed well and has kept the rules. So now he knows that there awaits him "a crown of righteousness, which the Lord, the righteous judge, will give me at that day: and not to me only, but to all those that love His appearing."

One further comment might be made. The "high calling of God in Christ Jesus" (v. 14) is literally "the upward calling." We are always being called upward as long as we live in this life. If we keep moving upward "in Christ" we shall some day arrive in heaven to live forever with Him.

C. Perfection the Goal: vv. 15-16

On the surface, verse 15 seems like a contradiction of verse 12. There Paul said: "Not as though I had already obtained, either were already perfect." Here he writes: "Let us, therefore, as many as be perfect." While it is a verb in verse 12 and an adjective in verse 15, the root is just the same—*telos,* which means "end." But the context is different. In verse 11 Paul says that he wants to attain to the resurrection. Then in verse 12 he writes: "Not as though I had already obtained." It is obvious that in verse 12 he is talking about resurrection perfection which is neither attainable nor obtainable in this life. In verse 15 he is talking about Christian perfection, a purity and maturity that keeps us pressing on toward the final goal. We should keep our mind on this without faltering: "Let us . . . be thus minded."

Verse 16 is very brief in the best Greek text: "Nevertheless, to what we have reached, let us keep on walking by the same thing." That is, let us keep on following the same course which has brought us thus far.

It is interesting to note that three different Greek verbs are translated "attain" in verses 11, 12, and 16. The first means to "arrive" at a certain point. Paul says he had not yet arrived at his resurrection. The verb in verse 12 means "obtain" or "receive." Paul

---

DISCUSSION QUESTIONS

1. How is humility related to unity in the church?
2. How are love and unselfishness related?
3. How is arguing related to unity?
4. What is the true meaning of circumcision?
5. In what way may baptism, confirmation, and church membership be a liability instead of an asset?
6. What part does perfection play in the Christian life?

had not yet obtained resurrection perfection. The third means "reach." Whatever the point we have reached in our Christian progress, we should press on higher with the same zeal and earnestness.

VII. THE CULMINATION OF REDEMPTION:
Philippians 3:17-21

Paul had set a wonderful example in pressing on toward the goal. Now he says, "Be followers together of me" (v. 17). Here he uses *synmimetai*, "fellow-imitators." The Philippians were to join other Christians in following Paul's example. Unfortunately, there were some people setting a very bad example. Paul calls them "the enemies of the cross of Christ" (v. 18). They are sensual, selfish, earthly (v. 19).

This causes the apostle once more to turn the attention of his readers upward. He says, "For our conversation is in heaven" (v. 20). We have already noted the verb *politeuomai* in 1:27, translated "let your conversation be" (KJV). We said that the correct

meaning is "live your life as a citizen." So here "conversation" is the cognate noun *politeuma* (only here in the New Testament). It means "citizenship"— "Our citizenship is in heaven." So we should behave in this world as citizens of heaven. Since Philippi was a Roman colony (Acts 6:12), with the privileges of Roman citizenship, Moffatt translated this passage, "You are a colony of heaven." We should be aware of both the privileges and responsibilities of our heavenly citizenship.

It is from heaven that we await "the Saviour, the Lord Jesus Christ, who will change our vile body, that it may be fashioned like unto his glorious body" (v. 20-21). But the Greek does not say "vile body." It says that Christ will "change the body of our humiliation in conformity to the body of His glory." The human body, in and of itself, is not "vile." God created it and said it was very good (Genesis 1:31). Nevertheless, it is a body belonging to our lowly life on earth. In the resurrection we shall receive a glorified body, fitted for heavenly existence.

CONTEMPORARY APPLICATION

As we write this lesson, *Jonathan Livingston Seagull* is making a big hit as the book of the year, if not the decade, selling over a million copies in 1972. The main thrust of the book is how the seagull reaches out for perfection, striving for it by perfecting his skills. The whole story glorifies self and self-effort in the achievement of perfection.

Very different is Paul's presentation in Philippians. It is only through Christ that any of us can reach perfection. The upward calling is "in Christ Jesus" (3:14), not in self and its efforts. We fear that the author of *Jonathan Seagull* is leading his readers down a blind alley, a dead-end street.

A THREATENED CHURCH

| DEVOTIONAL READING | Matthew 5:13-20 |

ADULTS

Topic: *Prayer for a Threatened Church*

Background Scripture: Colossians 1:1-14; 2:1-7; 4:7-18

Scripture Lesson: Colossians 1:1-14

Memory Verse: *As therefore you received Christ Jesus the Lord, so live in him, rooted and built up in him and established in the faith, just as you were taught, abounding in thanksgiving.* Colossians 2:6-7

YOUTH

Topic: *Take a Good Look at Your Church*

Background Scripture: Colossians 1:1-14, 2:1-7; 4:7-18

Scripture Lesson: Colossians 1:1-14

Memory Verse: *As therefore you received Christ Jesus the Lord, so live in him, rooted and built up in him and established in the faith, just as you were taught, abounding in thanksgiving.* Colossians 2:6-7

CHILDREN

Topic: *A Messenger for Paul*

Background Scripture: Acts 20:4-6; Ephesians 6:21-22; Colossians 4:7-8; II Timothy 4:12; Titus 3:12

Scripture Lesson: Ephesians 6:21-22; Colossians 4:7-8

Memory Verse: *Serve the Lord with gladness! Come into his presence with singing!* Psalm 100:2

DAILY BIBLE READINGS

Mon., July 29: A Prayer for the Church, Colossians 1:1-14.
Tues., July 30: "Established in the Faith," Colossians 2:1-7.
Wed., July 31: Servants of Christ, Colossians 4:7-18.
Thurs., Aug. 1: Salt and Light, Matthew 5:13-20.
Fri., Aug. 2: The Church's Message, I Corinthians 15:1-11.
Sat., Aug. 3: Dangers to Avoid, I Corinthians 3:1-9.
Sun., Aug. 4: Life in the Redeemed Community, Romans 12:3-13.

LESSON AIM

To show the necessity of being firmly rooted in Christ and established in the faith.

LESSON SETTING

Time: The Epistle to the Colossians was written probably in A.D. 60.

Place: It was written in prison at Rome.

411

A Threatened Church

LESSON OUTLINE

SUGGESTED INTRODUCTION FOR ADULTS

Most of Paul's Epistles are hard to outline. As we have noted before, they were occasional letters, written to meet specific needs in the individual churches. In the case of Philippians we have a spontaneous outburst of love and gratitude that defies reduction to a systematic outline. Colossians presents nearly the same problem. There is, however, a clear division between doctrinal explication in the first half and practical application in the second half. This is especially prominent in Ephesians and Colossians. In the former we have three chapters of each and in the latter two chapters of each.

The main topic of the Prison Epistles is Christology. Since Philippians is highly personal, there is only a short discussion there, the so-called Kenosis Passage (2:5-11). This is sandwiched into next week's lesson. Ephesians has a much longer treatment but the main emphasis is on Christ as the Head of the Church. In Colossians we find more of straight Christology, which is the doctrine of the *person* and *work* of Christ. It is this that we shall be noting in our study of this Epistle.

Paul's reason for writing to the Colossians was apparently to warn them against the insidious threat of Gnostic ideas that were creeping into the church there. The answer was a correct view of Christ.

SUGGESTED INTRODUCTION FOR YOUTH

"Take a Good Look at Your Church." What do you see? What you should see first of all is a group of men and women, young people, and boys and girls, with all the human weaknesses that belong to a group of people, but also with a desire to please God. Since all of us have our faults, we should be willing to overlook the faults in others.

But are there any faults in our church as a whole that we could help to correct? If there is a coldness in the services, are we willing to let our own hearts be warmed by the Holy Spirit? If there is a lack of friendliness toward new people, are we willing to be friendly and welcome them? If there is lack of outreach for others, are we willing to take time for visitation evangelism? We are the church, and what we do will influence the whole.

Take a good look at your church and then do something to change it. But don't condemn it; that never helps.

CONCEPTS FOR CHILDREN

1. Tychicus didn't write any of the letters we have in the New Testament but he carried some of them.
2. If we can't do big jobs, we can do important little ones.
3. Boys and girls can sometimes be messengers.
4. God will reward us if we are helpful and faithful.

THE LESSON COMMENTARY

I. SALUTATION:
Colossians 1:1-2

A. Addressor: v. 1

Paul begins this Epistle, as usual, by calling himself "an apostle of Christ Jesus." As in the case of I and II Corinthians, Ephesians, and II Timothy, he adds "through the will of God." He was Christ's special envoy to the Gentile churches, speaking with apostolic authority. And this was not something that he had chosen; he was appointed to it by the will of God.

We note, too, that Paul again shows a beautiful spirit of humility and courtesy by including his younger colleague, Timothy, in the salutation. The apostle also does this in the two Thessalonian Letters, in II Corinthians, and Philippians. It shows the greatness of Paul's spirit.

B. Addressee: v. 2a

The apostle's way of identifying his readers differs with each Epistle. Here it is: "To the saints and faithful brothers in Christ that are at Colosse." We may be sure that this included also the faithful sisters! Colosse was in the Lycus Valley, some sixty miles inland from Ephesus, in the Roman province of Asia. This was the western part of Asia Minor (modern Turkey).

C. Greeting: v. 2b

Once more we find the twofold greeting: "Grace . . . and peace." This was more than a formality with Paul. It was a heartfelt prayer that God would give to these Colossian Christians His grace and peace in abundant measure. It was more than a "Hi" or a "Hello," or even "Greetings."

If you are using a recent translation you may wonder why "and the Lord Jesus Christ" is omitted at the end of verse 2. The reason is that this phrase is not found in our oldest Greek manuscript, Vaticanus of the fourth century, nor in the important fifth-century manuscript, Bezae, as well as other important witnesses to the text.

II. THANKSGIVING TO GOD:
Colossians 1:3-8

A. Faith, Hope, Love: vv. 3-5

After the salutation, all of Paul's letters have a thanksgiving (except Galatians). Here he says: "We give thanks to God the Father ["and" after "God" is omitted in some of the earliest manuscripts] of our Lord Jesus Christ, praying always for you." From the many similar references in his Epistles it is evident that Paul had the habit of praying daily for all the Gentile churches. He felt a special responsibility toward them, and he discharged it by both praying for them and writing to them. His heart was large enough to take them all in.

In I Corinthians 13:13 we find the great Pauline trilogy of the Christian life: "And now abides faith, hope, love, these three; but the greatest of these is love." We also discovered it in I Thessalonians 1:3: "Your work of faith, and labor of love, and patience of hope." Here we have it again, in verses 4 and 5. Paul says that he had heard of the Colossian Christians' faith in Christ Jesus and their love for all the saints. All this was "because of the hope laid up" for them in heaven. They had received this hope from listening to "the word of the truth of the gospel."

Faith brings us into Christ, love unites us in Christ, and hope leads us to Christ at His second coming. These are the three essential factors in the Christian life.

B. Fruitfulness of the Colossians: v. 6

This gospel had reached the Colossians in their inland city, as it had "in all the world"—that is, the Roman Empire, which was the world of that day. And it was bearing fruit everywhere in the conversion of pagans, as it had at Colosse.

C. Good Report from Epaphras: vv. 7-8

Paul speaks of Epaphras as "our dear fellowservant." The word for "dear" is *agapetos*, which occurs sixty-two times in the New Testament. In the King James Version it is translated "beloved" forty-two times and "dear" only three times (here; Ephesians 5:1; I Thessalonians 2:8). While the latter term is more contemporary, the former brings out more fully the force of *agape* as pure, unselfish love.

"Fellow servant" is *syndoulos*—literally, "fellow-slave." Paul uses this compound only in Colossians (1:7; 4:7). It is one of his many terms expressing Christian togetherness. Epaphras was a partner with Paul in the work of the gospel. He was also "a faithful servant of Christ on behalf of us"—better Greek text than "for you." But probably Epaphras acted in both capacities, as Paul's "minister" (*diaconos*, "servant") to the Colossians, and also as their minister to him. He probably carried messages back and forth between Colosse and Rome. In 4:12 he is called "one of you," which shows that he was from Colosse. In Philemon 23 Paul speaks of him as "my fellow prisoner in Christ Jesus." Now he writes that Epaphras had told him about the love the Colossians had "in the Spirit" (v. 8). It is only the Holy Spirit that can fill our hearts with love. This message must have cheered Paul's heart.

III. PRAYER FOR THE CHURCH:
Colossians 1:9-14

A. Knowledge of God's Will: vv. 9-10

Ever since the apostle had heard of their love he had prayed unceasingly for them. It was another church added to his prayer list. His special prayer and petition for them (in the Greek "pray" and "desire" is "praying and asking") was that they "might be filled with the knowledge of his will in all wisdom and spiritual understanding."

This is typical of the language that Paul uses in his Prison Epistles. In his earlier Letters to the Galatians, Corinthians, and Romans there is considerable theological argument and stern reprimand for faulty situations in those churches. But in the Prison Epistles we see the overflow of love pouring out of the apostle's heart in language that borders on hyperbole: "All wisdom and spiritual understanding." We shall never actually have this on earth. But Paul asked for it anyway for these people.

The frequent use of "all" in the Pauline Epistles is but one of the many reflections of his great spirit. There was nothing niggardly about his gracious, loving personality, especially after three or four years in prison.

The purpose of this spiritual knowledge was that they "might walk worthy of the Lord unto all pleasing, being fruitful in every good work, and increasing in the knowledge of God" (v. 10). Walking so as to please God fully—that should be the goal of every Christian.

This verse beautifully combines the practical—"bearing fruit in every good work"—and the intellectual— "increasing in the knowledge of God." When we give attention to only one or the other, we are lopsided. Both of these functions are spiritual. It is just as truly spiritual to live a godly life and win others to Christ as it is to deepen our devotional fellowship with God.

Paul had a strong personality and loved strong terms. This is reflected in the fact that the Greek word for "knowledge" in verses 9 and 10 is the compound *epignosis*, rather than the simple word *gnosis*. Fifteen out of the twenty times *epignosis* occurs in the New Testament, it is used by Paul.

B. Longsuffering with Joyfulness: vv. 11-12

"Strengthened with all might" is literally "empowered with all power" (... *dynamei dynamoumenoi*). This is "according to His glorious might."

When we think of the glorious might that God displayed in creating this universe, we realize that we do not need to be weak and defeated. There is all the power we can possibly need, made available to us through faith.

For what are we to be empowered? For "all patience and longsuffering with joy." We have already seen that the Greek word translated "patience" in the King James Version does not convey the negative notion that the word often suggests—a lack of getting angry or upset—but rather the positive idea of "steadfast endurance." The second term "longsuffering" carries with it more the connotation of not reacting impatiently. So the better translation here would be: "great endurance and patience" (using "all" in the sense of "great").

On Paul's calendar Thanksgiving was never far away. "Giving thanks unto the Father" (v. 12)—the phrase comes naturally and spontaneously from his lips, and his secretary knows very well how to write it. Why is he thankful this time? Because God has "made us meet ["qualified us"] to have a part in the inheritance of the saints in light."

Some versions have "you" instead of "us." This might be the place to remark that these two terms are very often confused in the manuscripts. In the Greek the two words sound so much alike that a scribe could easily mistake one for the other. There are dozens of passages in the New Testament where we cannot be absolutely certain whether the original text read "you" or "us." But fortunately the difference in meaning is minor; either term fits in most cases.

C. Redemption in Christ: vv. 13-14

God has "rescued us from the authority of darkness and transferred into the kingdom of the Son of His love" (v. 13). So reads the Greek. This is a good exchange: from darkness to light—the light of the love of Him who is Love Incarnate, Love Eternal. The

truth here is far beyond our comprehension. But the glorious experience
can be ours in increasing measure
throughout life.

In God's Son we have "the redemption" (v. 14). The added phrase
"through his blood" was not in the
Revised Standard Version when its
New Testament appeared in 1946,
causing a great deal of caustic criticism. One prominent religious editor
wrote: "They have taken the blood
out of many passages in the Bible,
because they don't believe in the
blood atonement." But he could only
cite this *one!* Of course the reason it is
omitted here in all versions today is
that it is not in the Greek text. It is
genuine in Ephesians 1:7, but not
here. A later scribe inserted it here
from that passage, and so it got into
the King James Version.

We have already noted the meaning
of the Greek word for "redemption":
a ransom price paid to free a man from
slavery. This redemption brings "the
forgiveness of sins" because Christ
paid the penalty for them. When we
accept His atonement, the debt of our
sins is canceled; we are set free.

IV. CONCERN FOR THE CHURCH: Colossians 2:1-7

A. Reason for the Concern: v. 1

Paul writes: "I want you to know
what great concern I have for you and
those in Laodicea and as many as have
not seen my face in the flesh." This
alerts us to the fact that the apostle
had never visited Colosse. He had
spent three years in Ephesus, the leading city in the province of Asia (Acts
20:31). The result of his intensive ministry there was that "all those who
lived in Asia heard the word of the
Lord Jesus, both Jews and Greeks"
(Acts 19:10). Paul's policy was to concentrate on the big cities, building a
strong church there and letting others
evangelize the surrounding areas. Probably church growth across the centuries would have been much greater if
this method had been followed. J.

Hudson Taylor had the good sense to
adopt it when he founded the China
Inland Mission—and with notable success. Unfortunately some missionary
societies have sunk their money in out-
of-the-way places, with meager results.

The apostle felt a special concern
for Gentile Christians who had been
saved as a result of his work, but who
had never seen him in person. He realized that they lacked the impact of
personal contact and so needed all the
more his ministry in writing.

B. Doctrinal Concern: vv. 2-5

Paul was concerned that the hearts
of the Colossian Christians "might be
encouraged, being bound together in
love" (v. 2). This is typical Pauline
language and it lies close to the Johannine emphasis on fellowship and love.

But then the apostle goes on to
express a doctrinal concern. It was
that they might have "all riches of the
full assurance of understanding," that
they might have full knowledge "of
the mystery of God—Christ." That is
the reading of the two oldest Greek
manuscripts (Papyrus 46 of the third
century and Vaticanus of the fourth
century). The reading in the King
James Version is found in only a few
late manuscripts (tenth century and
later).

So here Paul puts it very succinctly. What is the mystery of God?
It is Christ! Hidden from eternity,
Christ was finally revealed at Bethlehem and Calvary. He was God's great
Secret, the Savior who would come in
due time to die for the sins of the
whole world, and to offer salvation to
all men, Gentiles as well as Jews.

One of the important Christological statements of the New Testament
is made in verse 3: "In whom are hidden all the treasures of wisdom and
knowledge." Christ is omniscient,
because He is the Son of God. From
all eternity He has been the All-
knowing One.

The word for "knowledge" here is
gnosis. The Gnostics of that day
claimed to have a secret knowledge,

superior to that of all other people. Paul declares that all true knowledge is to be found in Christ. What he is saying is that Christ is the answer to Gnosticism. We shall find this point developed further in a later lesson on this Epistle. But he hints at it here when he tells them: "And this I say, lest any man should beguile you with enticing words" (v. 4). The word translated "beguile" is better rendered "deceive" or "mislead." "Enticing words" is a single term that means "persuasive speech." Perhaps here it means "persuasive argument."

Paul writes to the Colossians that though he is absent in body, he is with them in spirit, rejoicing as he sees how orderly they are and as he views the "steadfastness" of their faith in Christ (v. 5). The Greek word is *stereoma*. It comes from the adjective *stereos*, which means "firm, solid," and which we have taken over in the popular term "stereo." So the best translation here is "firmness." The Colossian church was an orderly congregation composed of solid people. Instead of being torn by divisions, they presented a solid front to the world. No wonder Paul rejoiced at this!

C. Established in the Faith: vv. 6-7

Paul continues: "As therefore you received Christ Jesus the Lord, walk in Him" (v. 6). The verb "walk" is *peripateo*, which literally means "walk around." But in the New Testament it is frequently used in a figurative sense. This is particularly true in the Pauline Epistles, where the metaphorical meaning occurs thirty-two times. The three Johannine Letters have this usage ten times. Thayer says that it means "to regulate one's life, to conduct one's self" (*Lexicon*, p. 504).

So this verse says: "As therefore you received Christ Jesus the Lord, live in Him." This could be interpreted two ways. The first is: "Since you received Christ Jesus the Lord, keep on living in Him" (present imperative of continuous action). The second is:

"In the same way that you received . . . you must keep on living." You received Christ in humility and faith; you must keep on with that same attitude. You did not receive Him when you were saying no, but when you were saying yes to Him. You will keep Him in your heart by continuing to say yes all the way through.

We have noted before that Paul is fond of uniting the metaphors of planting and building (see Ephesians 3:17; I Corinthians 3:9). The Christian is to be rooted in Christ and built upon Him as the foundation. The first verb is a perfect passive participle, while the second one is a present passive participle. So it means, "having been firmly rooted and now being built up in him" (NASB).

And so we become "established," or "made firm," in the faith. And we keep this effectively as we are "abounding in thanksgiving." Praise is always an important factor in growth in grace.

V. CLOSING GREETINGS: Colossians 4:7-18

A. Paul's Two Messengers: vv. 7-9

Tychicus was the one who was carrying this Letter to the Colossians. He is also mentioned in Ephesians 6:21-22 as the bearer of that Epistle. We have previously noted that these two Letters were sent at the same time and by the same messenger from Rome to the province of Asia.

Paul tells the Colossians that Tychicus will inform them of his present state. He is "a beloved brother and faithful minister and fellowservant in the Lord." Once more the affectionate love and feeling of the apostle for "togetherness" show through clearly. We ought to thank God for older saints whose love overflows so constantly and abundantly that it spills on everyone around. This is *holy* love, divine love filling the hearts that are fully surrendered to the Holy Spirit.

Paul and John especially display in their Epistles this abounding love that the world so sorely needs. May their tribe increase!

"Whom I have sent" (v. 8) should be "whom I am sending." This is what is called the epistolary aorist. Though the aorist indicative ordinarily indicates past time, when used in a letter it sometimes signifies present time from the standpoint of the writer, which will be past time when the recipient reads the letter.

Paul is sending Tychicus as his messenger not only so that the Colossians may be brought up to date on how the apostle is getting along in Rome, but also that he may learn of their "estate"—the Greek simply says "the things concerning you"—and might "comfort" (or, "encourage") their hearts. Paul's messages and messengers were intended to bring cheer to the saints everywhere.

Tychicus was going along "with Onesimus" (v. 9). The latter was the runaway slave who had been converted under Paul at Rome (Philemon 10). Now the apostle was sending him back to his legal owner and master. He realized that the young convert might "get cold feet" before he reached Colosse and be tempted to defect again. For the custom at that time was that if a runaway slave was caught by his master he could be beaten to death as a warning to other slaves. Paul was very thoughtful about such contingencies. So he sent Tychicus with Onesimus to be a comforting companion and a watchdog. Now that Onesimus was saved, Paul could tell the Colossian Christians that he was "one of you." The new convert had proved himself so well that the apostle could speak of him as a "faithful and beloved brother." The two messengers would report "all things which are done here" (in Rome).

B. Greetings from Paul's Associates: vv. 10-14

Aristarchus, Paul's fellow prisoner, is named also at the close of the Epistle to Philemon (v. 24), as well as three times in Acts (19:29; 20:4; 27:2). In the Kings James Version, Mark ("Marcus") is called "sister's son to Barnabas," but the correct translation is "cousin." If Mark comes to Colosse, the Christians there are to receive him.

It is interesting to find "Jesus" used here (v. 11) as a name for someone other than Christ. But we must remember that at that time many Jewish boys were given this name, which is simply the Greek form of the Old Testament "Joshua." To distinguish him from others, this Jesus is further identified as the one who is "called Justus."

The three men named in verses 10-11 were Jews—"who are of the circumcision." Apparently they were the only "fellowworkers" Paul had with him at the time, and they were a "comfort" to him.

There was one more, however, Epaphras, who was from Colosse. He had not forgotten the people back home, for Paul says he was "always laboring fervently for you in prayers, that you may stand perfect and complete in all the will of God" (v. 12).

C. Greetings to Colosse and Laodicea: vv. 15-18

Epaphras was concerned not only for the Christians at Colosse, but also

---

DISCUSSION QUESTIONS

1. What was the purpose of Paul's Epistle to the Colossians?
2. What are some doctrinal threats to the church today?
3. What part do faith, hope, and love play in the Christian life?
4. What "knowledge" is most important?
5. Does the local church still have a valid place in modern society?
6. How can your church become more effective?

for those in Laodicea and Hierapolis (v. 13). These were three cities very close together in the Lycus River Valley, forming a sort of triangle. They were at a considerable distance (for those days) from Ephesus, and so the believers there needed fellowship together.

Paul also sends greetings from "Luke, the beloved physician" (v. 14), the author of the third Gospel and Acts, and a frequent companion of the apostle; and from Demas. It is sad to read that Demas finally forsook Paul and went back into the world. But Luke stayed loyally by him to the end (II Timothy 4:10, 11).

Paul instructs the Colossian Christians to "salute the brethren who are in Laodicea" (v. 15), and especially Nymphas and the church that met in his home. There is no evidence from the first century of separate church buildings being erected. The believers apparently met for worship in private homes most of the time until the middle of the second century.

When the Colossian congregation had heard the Epistle read in public service, the Letter was to be sent on to Laodicea to be read there (v. 16). The Colossians were also to read the Letter that Paul sent to Laodicea. We know nothing with certainty about the Epistle referred to here. It would appear that it has been lost. In the second and third chapters of Revelation, Laodicea is the only one of the seven churches about which nothing good is said. Could it be that this church did not even treasure the Epistle that Paul had sent?

Archippus (v. 17) is mentioned also in the second verse of Philemon, where reference is made immediately to the church that met in Philemon's house (at Colosse). Here he is told to take heed to the ministry he had received of the Lord, to "fulfill it"—or, "fill it full." This is the challenge to every minister of the gospel.

Then Paul took the quill pen from the hand of his secretary and signed his own name to the Epistle—"the salutation by the hand of me Paul" (v. 18). We saw in our study of II Thessalonians (2:2; 3:17) that the apostle had to do this because of false letters being sent in his name. It was his "token" in every Epistle.

CONTEMPORARY APPLICATION

The Colossian church was threatened by the heresy of Gnosticism, which denied the deity of Jesus. Today the threat to every church is from the Jehovah's Witnesses, who likewise claim that Jesus Christ is not the eternal Son of God, fully divine. They attack the churches and propagate their erroneous teachings in homes and on the streets. Always the lure is "Bible study," but they distort its truths to fit their teachings.

If Paul were here today he would sound a note of warning against these false teachers, who are winning converts from the churches. The antidote to error is always a careful study of the truth. What we need in all our churches is more sound Bible study.

CHRIST ABOVE ALL

DEVOTIONAL READING	I Corinthians 3:10-15

ADULTS

Topic: *Christ Above All*

Background Scripture: Colossians 1:15-29; Philippians 2:5-11

Scripture Lesson: Colossians 1:15-27

Memory Verse: *In him all the fulness of God was pleased to dwell, and through him to reconcile to himself all things, whether on earth or in heaven, making peace by the blood of his cross.* Colossians 1:19-20

YOUTH

Topic: *Putting Christ First*

Background Scripture: Colossians 1:15-29; Philippians 2:5-11.

Scripture Lesson: Colossians 1:15-27

Memory Verse: *For in him all the fulness of God was pleased to dwell, and through him to reconcile to himself all things, whether on earth or in heaven, making peace by the blood of his cross.* Colossians 1:19-20

CHILDREN

Topic: *A Slave Set Free*

Background Scripture: Colossians 4:9; Philemon 8-21

Scripture Lesson: Colossians 4:9; Philemon 10-18

Memory Verse: *Teach me thy way, O Lord, that I may walk in thy truth.* Psalm 86:11

DAILY BIBLE READINGS

Mon., Aug. 5: The Divine Christ, Colossians 1:15-20.
Tues., Aug. 6 The Incarnate Christ, Philippians 2:5-11.
Wed., Aug. 7: The Spirit-anointed Christ, Matthew 3:1-3, 11-17.
Thurs., Aug. 8: The Authoritative Christ, Mark 1:21-28.
Fri., Aug. 9: The Qualified Christ, Hebrews 1:1-12.
Sat., Aug. 10: The Living Christ, Colossians 1:21-29.
Sun., Aug. 11: The Victorious Christ, Revelation 5:1-10.

LESSON AIM

To seek to grasp the truth that Christ is above all, through all, and in all.

LESSON SETTING

Time: A.D. 60

Place: Prison at Rome

Christ Above All

LESSON OUTLINE

SUGGESTED INTRODUCTION FOR ADULTS

Many people are afraid of magnifying Jesus too much. Paul wasn't worried about this problem! What concerned him was the tendency of some people in the early church to reduce Christ to a mere man—a good man, a great teacher, but not the eternal Son of God and our Savior.

That is one of the main threats to the church today. It is probably safe to say that by the middle of this century the majority of Protestant ministers in the United States were weak on the doctrine of the deity of Jesus. We thank God that the pendulum has swung somewhat the other way in the last twenty years. But there is still too much hesitation in ecclesiastical circles to give Christ His proper place as Lord of all.

There is no question about the picture in the New Testament. From Matthew to Revelation Jesus Christ is portrayed as the Son of God who came to earth to reveal God to man, and then to die on the cross as the divine Sacrifice for our sins. Paul especially presents a very lofty Christology, as we shall find in our lesson today. Christ is above all!

SUGGESTED INTRODUCTION FOR YOUTH

"Putting Christ First." How? First in our *minds*. We must recognize that Christ is the eternal Son of God and the Creator of the universe, that He is the only Savior from sin.

Then we must put Christ first in our *wills*. That means that we submit our will to His will—completely, forever. It means that we let Him be Lord of all in our lives. The surrender of the will is the most crucial point in Christian experience.

Christ must also be first in our *affections*. Love for Him *must* take precedence over all other loves in our life. Until we love Him with all our heart, soul, mind, and strength we are not fully Christian.

Putting Christ first must be a daily discipline if we are going to live our lives at the highest and best level. But it is a joyous experience to do so.

CONCEPTS FOR CHILDREN

1. Belonging to Christ does not free us from our responsibility to others.
2. Onesimus had to go back and make things right with his master.
3. We must ask forgiveness when we have wronged others.

THE LESSON COMMENTARY

I. CHRIST AND CREATION: Colossians 1:15-17

A. Before All Creation: v. 15

There are three passages in the New Testament where the deity of Jesus is asserted in especially strong terms. They are found in the first chapter of John's Gospel (1:1, 18), of the Epistle to the Hebrews (1:3, 8) and of the Epistle to the Colossians (1:15). Of course this concept underlies every Book of the New Testament and shows through clearly at many points.

Jesus is here declared to be the "image of the invisible God." The Greek word for "image" is *eicon*, from which comes "icon." Abbott-Smith says it means a "likeness," such as that of "the head on a coin or the parental likeness in a child" (*Lexicon*, p. 131). Thayer writes that the term is applied to Christ "on account of his divine nature and absolute moral excellence" (*Lexicon*, p. 175).

In the Synoptic Gospels this word is used for the image of the emperor on the denarius, a silver coin (Matthew 22:20; Mark 12:16; Luke 20:24).

Josephus uses it the same way. So it signifies an exact representation. Paul has already spoken of Christ as "the image of God" (II Corinthians 4:4).

Some critics have tried to tone down the thrust of this term. But Lightfoot writes: "Beyond the very obvious notion of *likeness*, the word *eicon* involves two other ideas: (1) *Representation* . . . *eicon* implies an archetype of which it is a *copy* . . . (2) *Manifestation* . . . The Word, whether pre-incarnate or incarnate, is the revelation of the unseen Father" (*Colossians*, p. 145). Ellicott says: "Christian antiquity has ever [always] regarded the expression 'image of God' as denoting the eternal Son's perfect equality with the Father in respect of His substance, nature, and eternity" (*Epistles of St. Paul*, II. 134).

Eadie has a beautiful treatment of this passage. He writes: "The clause dazzles by its brightness, and awes by its mystery. . . . The invisible God—how dark and dreadful the impenetrable veil! Christ His image—how perfect in its resemblance, and overpowering in its brilliance!" (*Colossians* p. 43). He further comments: "In His incarnate state He brought God so near to us as to place Him under the cognizance of our very senses—men saw, and heard, and handled him—a speaking, acting, weeping and suffering God" (pp. 45-46).

In Kittel's *Theological Dictionary of the New Testament* the editor himself declares that in Colossians 1:15 "all the emphasis is on the equality of the *eicon* with the original" (II, 395). Phillips translates this verse: "Now Christ is the visible expression of the invisible God." Jesus Himself said, "He who has seen me has seen the Father" (John 4:9). Paul and John are affirming the same truth.

The last phrase of verse 15 poses a problem. It says that Christ is "the firstborn of every creature"—better, "all creation." Jehovah's Witnesses seize on this, as did the Arians of the early church, to prove that Christ is a created being even though He was the first one to be created.

The Greek for "the firstborn" is *ho prototokos*. This was evidently a Messianic title. Lightfoot, in his outstanding commentary on Colossians, quotes a rabbinical interpretation of the term and then says: "Hence 'the firstborn' *ho prototokos*, used absolutely, became a recognized title of Messiah" (p. 146). He states that the expression conveys two ideas: priority to all creation and sovereignty over all creation. He goes on to say: "In its Messianic reference this secondary idea of sovereignty predominated in the word *prototokos*, so that from this point of view *prototokos pases ktiseos* would mean 'Sovereign Lord over all creation by virtue of primogeniture'" (p. 147). The New English Bible reads: "His is the primacy over all created things."

B. Creator of All Things: v. 16

The great passages on the deity of Jesus referred to above agree in asserting that He created all things. So here we read; "For by him were created all things in heaven and on earth, both visible and invisible, whether thrones or lordships or rulerships or authori-

ties; all things have been created through Him and to Him."

To what do these four created things refer? Lightfoot writes: "Some commentators have referred the terms used here solely to earthly potentates and dignities. There can be little doubt, however, that their chief and primary reference is to the orders of the celestial hierarchy, as conceived by these Gnostic Judaizers." He adds: "The names, too, more especially *thronoi*, are especially connected with the speculations of Jewish angelology" (p. 152). Paul is affirming here that Christ is supreme, far superior to all the celestial powers postulated in the Gnostic schools of thought. As the Revealer of God and the Creator of all things, He stands apart from and far above all His creation. And He is the final good of all creation—all things are "to Him."

C. Sustainer of All Things: v. 17

This verse has tremendous cosmic and scientific implications: "And he is before all things, and by him all things consist." What does the second clause mean? The correct translation makes it very clear: "and in Him all things hold together." As Lightfoot says, "He is the principle of cohesion in the universe. He impresses upon creation that unity and solidarity which makes it a cosmos instead of a chaos" (p. 156). Christ is not only Creator but Coherer. He upholds what He brought into being (cf. Hebrews 1:3).

Some years ago a noted American scientist made this statement: "If the creative force residing in the universe should be withdrawn for a moment, the whole universe would collapse." The Bible tells us that this creative force is Christ.

II. CHRIST THE HEAD OF THE CHURCH: Colossians 1:18

One of the important things said about Christ in the Prison Epistles is that He is the Head of the Church, which is His body. The implications of this are far reaching. If Christ is the Head and we are the body, we should be in complete obedience to Him. Suppose our hands or feet could do as they please, without reference to the head. The result would be utter chaos. The only way our bodies can function properly is for the muscles throughout to be controlled by motor nerves from the brain. In the case of the church as the body of Christ, there is nothing automatic or mechanical. For, unlike hands and feet, the members of the church all have wills of their own. When each one wants his own way, the result is still chaos and confusion. But when all seek and do the will of the Head, there is harmony and efficiency.

Because of His divinely appointed position it is only fitting that in all things Christ should "have the pre-eminence." The Greek literally means "have first place." And that is what He wants in our lives—first place in every-thing. To give Him that is to live life successfully and victoriously. It means that our will is never allowed to inter-fere with His will. It means that when He calls we obey, regardless of per-sonal desires or consequences. To put Christ first is to live at the center of life, not on its periphery.

III. CHRIST THE RECONCILER:
Colossians 1:19-22

A. Reconciling All Things: vv. 19-20

We have already noted that one of the reasons Paul wrote the Epistle to the Colossians was to counteract the insidious influence of Gnostic ideas that were infiltrating the church there. A favorite term with the Gnostics was *pleroma*, here translated "fulness," denoting "the totality of the divine powers and attributes." The truth that the apostle is emphasizing is that Jesus is fully divine. At the same time, as both John and Paul emphasize, He was truly human. But the latter did not in any way detract from the former.

Verses 20-22 deal particularly with Christ's work of redemption. It was through the blood shed on the cross that peace was made between God and man.

It was also through Christ that God was able "to reconcile all things to himself" (v. 20). Does that mean that all things in the universe—"things on earth" and "things in heaven"—are now reconciled or ever will be recon-ciled? The answer is: "Yes and no." Potentially everything has been recon-ciled to God through the atoning sacri-fice of Christ. But actually only those who believe in Christ and accept His death for them will be saved.

The word for "reconciled" is a strong double compound, *apo-cotallasso*, found only here (vv. 20, 21) and in Ephesians 2:16. It means "reconcile completely." Lightfoot comments: "The false teachers aimed at effecting a partial reconciliation between God and man through the interposition of angelic mediators. The Apostle speaks of an absolute and complete reconciliation of universal nature to God, effected through the mediation of the Incarnate Word." He goes on to say: "Their mediators were ineffective, because they were neither human nor divine. The true mediator must be both human and divine" (*Colossians*, p. 159).

The central emphasis of Gnosti-cism was that all spirit is good, all matter is evil. Hence God, who was pure spirit, could have no direct con-tact with a material world. So the Gnostics postulated a long series of aeons, sometimes thought of as angelic beings, between men and God. What Paul is saying is that Christ alone and in Himself is the only Mediator between God and man (cf. I Timothy 2:5).

Christ is the only one who has ever lived that could bridge the gap between Deity and humanity. To span a chasm a bridge must be anchored on both sides. Since Christ was both human and divine, He could do this. He who was the eternal Son of God became the Son of man, and across this Bridge we are reconciled to God.

B. Reconciling the Gentiles: v. 21

Paul is writing to a Gentile church. So he speaks of his readers as having been "alienated." It is the perfect passive participle of the verb that means to be "estranged." We have already noted the same construction in the only other places in the New Testament where this verb occurs (Ephesians 2:12; 4:18).

These Gentiles were also "enemies" in their "minds," or "thoughts." Their former thinking had been in opposition to God, in rebellion against His authority. And this attitude of mind had born fruit in "wicked works."

C. Reconciliation and Perfection: v. 22

When the Gentiles were in this unfortunate relationship of rebellion against God, He loved them enough to reconcile them "in the body of his [Christ's] flesh through death," to present them "holy and unblameable and unreproveable" in His sight. The last adjective is *anengkletos*, which literally means "not to be called to account" or "that cannot be called to account." That is, no charge can be laid against us before God. That is because we are in Christ. All the sins of the past have been forgiven, and we are walking in obedience to His will. We are not perfect in ourselves, but in Christ we stand before God blameless.

IV. CHRIST'S MINISTER: Colossians 1:23-29

A. Minister of the Word: vv. 23-25

A very important condition is attached to this promise of being presented to God unblameable. It is simply this: "If you continue in the faith grounded and settled, and be not moved away from the hope of the gospel" (v. 23). That is a big "if," and a very important one it is! Being a Christian is conditioned on our continued belief and obedience. The Greek word for "continue" has the figurative sense of "persist" or "persevere."

The word for "grounded" means "having a solid foundation," and so "firmly established." The Greek term translated "settled" is found elsewhere in the New Testament only in I Corinthians 7:37 and 15:58. There it is given its correct meaning, "steadfast," which fits well here.

Paul goes on to say that the gospel in which these Colossians have placed their hope "was preached to every creature under heaven." This is a general statement, indicating that by this time the Christian gospel had spread throughout the Roman world. Now it has covered the globe.

Paul declares that he had been made a "minister" or "servant" *(diaconos)* of this gospel. He had certainly performed his service well. Probably it could be said that in the entire history of the church few have equaled him and none has excelled him in this total contribution to the cause of Christ.

Then Paul makes an amazing statement. He says that he rejoices in his sufferings for them and fills up "that which is behind of the afflictions of Christ in my flesh for his body's sake, which is the church" (v. 24). The word translated "fill up" is a double compound meaning "I fill up on my part." The apostle actually carried far more than his fair share of the burden of the gospel ministry.

"That which is behind" is literally "that which is lacking." What does Paul mean by saying that he is supplying what is lacking in the sufferings of Christ for the church? Roman Catholics have taken this passage as a basis for their doctrine of the merit of the saints, and so of the system of indulgences. But we know that Paul is not furnishing any teaching of that nature. What, then, does he mean?

Lightfoot provides a good explanation. He says that the sufferings of Christ may be considered from two different points of view. "From the former point of view the Passion of Christ was the one full, perfect and sufficient sacrifice, oblation, and satisfaction for the sins of the whole world." But, "From the latter point of view it is a simple matter of fact that the afflictions of every saint and martyr do supplement the afflictions of Christ. The Church is built up by repeated acts of self-denial in successive individuals and successive generations." He adds; "But St. Paul would have been the last to say that they bear their part in the atoning sacrifice of Christ" (p. 166).

In a very real sense it is still true today that only a suffering ministry can be a saving ministry. The preacher of the gospel must live redemptively if he is going to be used by the Lord in redeeming men from sin. And to a great extent this also applies to laymen in their personal evangelism.

Again Paul says, "I was made a minister" (v. 25, same as v. 23). He says that this was according to the "dispensation" of God. But the correct translation is "stewardship," as we have noted before. God had given to Paul the stewardship of the gospel, to share it with the Gentiles through fully preaching the Word.

B. Mystery of Christ in You: vv. 26-27

We have seen this word *mystery* several times already this quarter. Jesus used the term once, as reported in all three Synoptic Gospels (Matthew 13:11; Mark 4:11; Luke 8:10). He was speaking of the "secrets" of the kingdom of God. The word is also found four times in the Book of Revelation (1:20; 10:7; 17:5, 7). But elsewhere in the New Testament it occurs only in Paul's Epistles (20 times). Half of these are in Ephesians (6 times) and Colossians (4 times).

In Paul's writings the word *mystery* refers to God's secret plan to save the Gentiles along with the Jews through faith in Jesus Christ. This secret had been "hidden from ages and from generations, but is now made manifest to his saints" (v. 26). To them "God wished to make known what is the riches of the glory of this mystery among the Gentiles, which is Christ in you, the hope of glory" (v. 27). The mystery, then, is that true religion is not a matter of conformity to certain rules and regulations nor performance of ritual acts. Put in briefest form it is simply this: "Christ in you." That is exactly what Christianity is. It is not a creed or a church; it is Christ. The tragedy of the ages is that so few people have grasped this truth.

C. Mighty Working of God: vv. 28-29

Paul was not only preaching doctrine and ethics, though he certainly did not ignore these very important areas. But primarily he was preaching Christ. Without Christ neither doctrine nor ethics can save a soul or make a Christian. "Preach" is literally "proclaim." The great proclamation that many people have not yet heard is that Christ has come to be the Savior of the world.

The apostle says that he is "warning every man." The verb literally means "putting in mind." So the closest English term would be "admonishing."

The aim of Paul's preaching, admonishing, and teaching was to "present every man perfect in Christ." The apostle was concerned not only for the salvation of souls but for their growth in grace. "Perfect in Christ"—

DISCUSSION QUESTIONS

1. What is the real test of Christian doctrine?
2. Why must Christ be supreme?
3. What do we mean by "the cosmic Christ"?
4. What is God's "mystery," according to Paul?
5. What are some heresies today that deny the deity of Jesus?
6. How can we demonstrate that Christ is the Lord of all?

there is no other place where we can be perfect. "In Christ" . . . "Christ in you"—these are the two keynotes of Paul's Prison Epistles, and actually of his whole theology. What the apostle is pleading for is the working out of the implications of this in daily life.

To this end Paul was toiling ("I labor"), "striving [or, "intensely struggling"] according to His work that works in me mightily." This last part is literally: "according to His energy which is being energized in me in power."

V. CHRIST'S HUMILIATION: Philippians 2:5-8

A. In the Form of God: vv. 5-6

Some of Paul's greatest doctrinal passages, particularly in the Prison Epistles, come out of a practical exhortation. This is the case here. The apostle pleads, "Let this mind be in you, which was also in Christ Jesus" (v. 5), and then he gives us the great Kenosis Passage. He presents the eternal Christ who was in the "form" (essential being) of God, but did not consider this a prize to be greedily grasped.

B. Emptied Himself: v. 7

The theological term *kenosis* comes from the verb here translated "made . . . of no reputation"—all one word in Greek, *ekenosen*, which means "emptied." Christ laid aside the outward symbols of His heavenly glory, taking the form of a servant (literally, "slave") and being made in the likeness of men.

C. Obedient to Death: v. 8

Being found in fashion as a man, Christ humbled Himself, "becoming obedient to death, even the death of the cross." This was the depth of His humiliation. Crucifixion was a cruel, disgraceful death, reserved for slaves and dangerous criminals. But that is the way Christ died.

VI. CHRIST'S EXALTATION: Philippians 2:9-11

A. A Name Above Every Name: v. 9

Because Christ, as an obedient Son, was willing to go to the most shameful depths of human suffering, "God also has highly exalted him and graced Him with a name above every name." We are told to humble ourselves under the mighty hand of God, that He may exalt us in due time (I Peter 5:6). Christ set the supreme example of this.

B. Submission of All Creation: v. 10

God has exalted His Son in order that "in the name of Jesus every knee should bow, of things [or, "those"] in heaven, on earth, and under the earth." All heavenly beings, all earthly beings, and even the dead will bow to His will, whether they wish to or not.

C. Universal Confession of His Deity: v. 11

There will come a time when "every tongue will confess that Jesus Christ is Lord, to the glory of God the Father." That hour has not yet arrived; but it will come, as surely as God's Word is true. Those who have denied the deity of Jesus will be compelled to confess it. All rebellion will be put down and Christ will reign supreme.

This is what the world has been waiting for during many weary centuries. We can only pray that the hour will come soon.

CONTEMPORARY APPLICATION

Paul exhorts us to have the mind of Christ. But what is this mind, or attitude? The apostle spells it out very clearly in Philippians 2:8. It is (1) the mind of humility ("He humbled himself"), (2) the mind of obedience ("became obedient unto death"), and (3) the mind of sacrifice ("even the death of the cross").

Humility is not looking pious and saying, "I can't do anything." It is looking up in faith to Jesus and saying, "I can do all things through Christ who strengthens me" (Philippians 4:13). Someone has said that humility is "love's forgetfulness of self." An evangelist once declared: "The humble man is not engaged in promoting the big pronoun I, but the great I AM."

Obedience is the test of love. Jesus said, "If you love me, you will keep my commandments" (John 14:15). The mind of sacrifice is expressed best in Romans 12:1-2. That is where we should live.

FREEDOM IN CHRIST

DEVOTIONAL
READING

Galatians 5:13-26

ADULTS

Topic: *Freedom in Christ*

Background Scripture: Colossians 2:8-23

Scripture Lesson: Colossians 2:13-23

Memory Verse: *For freedom Christ has set us free; stand fast therefore, and do not submit again to a yoke of slavery.* Galatians 5:1

YOUTH

Topic: *How Can I Be Free?*

Background Scripture: Colossians 2:8-23

Scripture Lesson: Colossians 2:13-23

Memory Verse: *For freedom Christ has set us free; stand fast therefore, and do not submit again to a yoke of slavery.* Galatians 5:1

CHILDREN

Topic: *Attitudes for Living*

Background Scripture: Colossians 3:12-17

Scripture Lesson: Colossians 3:12-15, 17

Memory Verse: *Put on then, as God's chosen ones, holy and beloved, compassion, kindness, lowliness, meekness, and patience.* Colossians 3:12

DAILY BIBLE
READINGS

Mon., Aug. 12: Freedom Is Coming Alive, Colossians 2:8-15.
Tues., Aug. 13: Freedom Is Broken Chains, Romans 6:12-23.
Wed., Aug. 14: Freedom Is Equality, I Peter 2:4-5, 9-17.
Thurs., Aug. 15: Freedom Is Responsibility, Colossians 2:16-23.
Fri., Aug. 16: Freedom Is Commitment, Galatians 5:13-18.
Sat., Aug. 17: Freedom Is Life in the Spirit, Galatians 5:19-26.
Sun., Aug. 18: Freedom Is Exciting, Romans 8:18-25.

LESSON AIM

To show that Christ died to set us free, and how we may gain and maintain that freedom.

LESSON SETTING

Time: A.D. 60

Place: Prison in Rome

429

Freedom in Christ

SUGGESTED INTRODUCTION FOR ADULTS

When Paul wrote to the Galatians he was dealing with one main problem: legalistic Judaism. But the situation was more complicated at Colosse. There the church was threatened by two things: incipient Gnosticism and decadent Judaism. One cannot understand this Epistle unless he knows what those two problems were.

We are somewhat familiar with Judaism from the Old Testament, although this term is properly applied primarily to the religion of the Jews after the Babylonian captivity. The four Gospels give us many glimpses of the Judaism of Jesus' day. When we speak of "decadent Judaism" we are speaking of the dead, legalistic form that this religion had largely taken by the first century. As we see from the teachings of Jesus, the religion of the Pharisees was outward, formal, ceremonial, legalistic. It lacked that inward spiritual character that marks true religion.

We have also used the expression "incipient Gnosticism." All scholars agree that Paul is attacking Gnosticism in his Epistle to the Colossians. But many have claimed that Gnosticism did not arise until the second century, and so this Epistle must have been written at that late date and is therefore not genuine. But recent research has demonstrated that Gnostic ideas were circulating freely in the first century in the province of Asia, where Colosse was situated. It is the mixture of this incipient Gnosticism with decadent Judaism that Paul confronts here.

SUGGESTED INTRODUCTION FOR YOUTH

"Freedom" is one of the main catchwords of modern youth. Freedom from all authority—of home, school, church, or government—is what many are demanding.

But the question confronts us all: "How can I be free?" Efforts to free oneself from all restraints have proved futile and frustrating. Too many young people have broken away from "the Establishment," only to find themselves the helpless slaves and victims of drugs. True freedom is found only in Christ, never in ourselves.

<table>
<tr><td rowspan="1">CONCEPTS FOR
CHILDREN</td><td>1. The secret of happy, successful living is taking the right attitude toward God and others.
2. Kindness and love are the main Christian attitudes.
3. We should seek every day to develop right attitudes.</td></tr>
</table>

THE LESSON COMMENTARY

I. FULLNESS IN CHRIST:
Colossians 2:8-12

A. Christ the Fullness of Deity:
vv. 8-9

The apostle warns: "Beware lest any spoil you." We think of spoiled fruit, of a spoiled child. What does the word mean here?

The verb is *sylagogeo*, found only here in the New Testament. It comes from *syle*, "booty," and *ago*, "carry." So it literally means "to carry off as spoil, lead captive" (Abbott-Smith, *Lexicon*, p. 422). Arndt and Gingrich say it is used "figuratively of carrying someone away from the truth into the slavery of error" (*Lexicon*, p. 784). So the basic idea of the verb is "to capture." The King James Version reflects the usage of 1611, of which the *Oxford English Dictionary* gives several examples. It says that when the word "spoil" meant "to strip [persons] of goods or possessions by violence or force; to plunder, rob, despoil" (X, 650). But that is not the way we use the verb today.

The Colossian Christians were to see that they were not robbed of their faith "through philosophy and vain deceit." Our word "philosophy" comes directly from the Greek *philosophia*, which is found only here in the New Testament. Due to the fact that it is used here in a derogatory sense, in connection with "empty deceit," some have wrongly assumed that all philosophy is bad. A Bible school student overseas recently wrote in his paper: "No philosophy can be Christian." This, of course, is not true.

The Greek word means "love of wisdom." Pythagoras was probably expressing his humility when he called himself "a lover of (divine) wisdom." Lightfoot comments: "In such a sense

the term would entirely accord with the spirit and teaching of St. Paul; for it bore testimony to the insufficiency of the human intellect and the need of a revelation" (*Colossians*, p. 179). But by this time it had come to be used for "subtle dialectics and profitless speculation," he continues. Phillips captures the meaning well when he translates it here "intellectualism."

Paul says that this was "according to" (KJV, "after") the tradition of men and the "rudiments" of the world. There has been endless discussion as to what this term means. The Revised Standard Version and the New English Bible both have "elemental spirits," but this is questionable. The New American Standard Bible is probably more accurate in translating it "elementary principles." The Greek word *stoicheia* first meant "the letters of the alphabet" and then "rudimentary instruction." The simplest translation is "elements." Just what Paul meant by this we do not know. The New International Bible translates it "basic principles."

The real trouble was that the empty intellectualism at Colosse was "not according to Christ." Christ is the touchstone of truth. He is the only absolute standard by which all truth can be measured.

Then comes one of the greatest statements in the New Testament on the deity of Jesus: "For in Him dwells all the fullness of the Godhead bodily" (v. 9). What is meant by "Godhead"? The Greek word *theotes* (only here in the New Testament) comes from *theos*, "God." A more correct translation of *theotes* today would be "Godhood." But the simplest rendering is "deity." It means the essence of the divine nature.

The fulness of deity dwells in Jesus. It is difficult to conceive of a stronger statement of His full deity. Any effort to make Jesus less than God is a denial of the inspiration and authority of the New Testament.

B. Christ Our Fullness: v. 10

The King James translation, "And ye are complete in him," loses the connection indicated in the Greek between verses 9 and 10. In the former, "fulness" is *pleroma;* in the latter, "complete" is *pepleromenoi.* So the correct translation here is: "And you are brought to fullness in Him."

This is a tremendous concept. Christ possesses the fullness of deity. When we are in Christ we share in a measure in this fullness—"partakers of [or, "sharers in"] the divine nature" (II Peter 1:4).

Pepleromenoi is the perfect passive participle of *pleroo,* which can be translated both "fill full" and "fulfill." This suggests the very beautiful truth that we as individuals can find fulfillment only in Christ. Every normal person desires a sense of fulfillment in life. Without this we can never know real satisfaction. But we cannot find this fulfillment in ourselves alone, nor in other people. Only when Christ dwells in our hearts in the fullness of the Spirit can we find that wonderful sense of fulfillment that gives purpose to life and makes it really worth living. This is a part of our salvation in Christ. In Him we cease to be *frustrated* persons, as too many people are today, or even *fractured* persons, as many Christians. When we surrender ourselves completely to Christ we become *fulfilled* persons. That is eternal life even here in time.

Christ is the Head of all "principality and power"—rather, "rule and authority." When we are in Him and completely under *His* rule and authority, we are a free people.

C. Circumcision and Baptism: vv. 11-12

In the Christian church baptism takes the place of circumcision in Judaism, just as the Lord's Supper takes the place of the Passover Supper. They are all symbolical acts whose spiritual meaning should be understood and appreciated.

Paul says that those who are in Christ "were circumcised" (past tense in Greek) with a circumcision "not handmade" (one word in Greek). What is this? It consists "in putting off the body of the sins of the flesh by the circumcision of Christ"—that is, the circumcision performed by Christ and which marks His people. This is not a literal cutting of physical flesh, but the cutting off of sin, a spiritual circumcision (cf. Romans 2:28-29).

Baptism is a symbol of this. We are "buried" with Christ in baptism, in order that we might be "raised with him through faith in the working of God, who raised him from the dead" (v 12). This is the real meaning of baptism. Obviously the physical act of baptism must be accompanied by faith if it is to have any spiritual value.

II. FREEDOM FROM THE LAW: Colossians 2:13-17

A. Made Alive in Christ: v. 13

Paul reminds his Gentile readers that they were once "dead in [their] trespasses and the uncircumcision of [their] flesh." They were dead spiritually and had no part in God's covenant with Israel, the sign of which was circumcision. But now God "had made [them] alive together with Him [Christ], having graciously forgiven [them] all trespasses." Salvation means not only the forgiveness of all our sins. That in itself would be glorious! But it is far more than that. It is being made alive with Christ. Christian conversion is not only justification from the sins of the past, but a new life in Christ.

B. Made Free from the Law: vv. 14-15

One of the benefits of Christ's death is described in v. 14: "Blotting out the handwriting of ordinances that was against us, which was contrary to us." Several of these words call for comment.

The first verb has the literal sense of "wiping off" or "wiping out," and so "erasing." But here it is used in a metaphorical sense. Probably the best translation is "having canceled," as we would cancel a note today.

That leads us to the question as to what is meant by the "handwriting." The Greek adjective *cheirographon* (only here in the New Testament) literally means "handwritten." Thayer says that as a substantive it meant "specifically a note of hand, or writing in which one acknowledges that money has either been deposited with him or lent to him by another, to be returned at an appointed time ... metaphorically applied in Col. ii. 14 ... to the Mosaic law, which shows men to be chargeable with offences for which they must pay the penalty" (*Lexicon*, p. 668).

Adolf Deissmann points out the fact that the custom of canceling a promissory note has been abundantly illustrated by the ancient papyri from the sands of Egypt. He says: "We have learnt from the new text that it was generally customary to cancel a bond (or other document) by crossing it out with the Greek cross—letter *chi* (X). In the splendid Florentine papyrus, of the year 85 A.D. ... the governor of Egypt gives this order in the course of a trial: 'Let the handwriting be crossed out'. ... We have moreover recovered the originals of a number of 'crossed-out' I.O.U.'s" (*Light from the Ancient East*, pp. 333-34).

The startling coincidence of the cross is impressive. Just as in Egypt in the first century a document was crossed out by marking the large letter X over the handwriting, so for us who accept Christ by faith the Cross has been stamped on the demands of the Mosaic law, setting us free from its many minute obligations. No longer does the broken law stand against us like an unpaid promissory note. It is all canceled by the cross of Christ.

Probably the best translation for "handwriting" is "bond," and so the phrase would be "having canceled the bond." The New American Standard Bible has: "having canceled out the certificate of debt."

Another significant word here is "ordinances." The Greek term, taken over into English, is *dogma*, which meant a public decree. In Luke 2:1 and Acts 17:7 it is used for the decrees of Roman rulers. Josephus, the Jewish historian, uses *dogma* for the Mosaic law, and that is clearly its meaning here.

"Contrary to" is one word in Greek, found only here and in Hebrews 10:27. It is an adjective that literally means "set over against, opposite," and so "opposed, contrary, hostile" (Arndt and Gingrich, *Lexicon*, p. 846). Moulton and Milligan affirm that this strong sense is illustrated by its use in a second-century papyrus from Oxyrhynchus (*Vocabulary of the Greek Testament in the Light of the Papyri*, p. 651). The Twentieth-Century New Testament has captured the full force of the Greek in its translation: "the bond standing against us, which was in direct hostility to us."

The Mosaic law stood as a bond of decrees against us. But Christ "took it out of the way, nailing it to his cross." In His perfect life on earth He had fulfilled the righteousness requirements of the law—loving God with all one's heart, soul, mind, and strength, and one's neighbor as oneself—and so His atoning death canceled the note against us. Today the cross stands between us and our debt.

"Having spoiled" (v. 15) is a strong double compound in Greek. The verb means "to *strip off* clothes or armor." What follows in this verse suggests that the proper sense here is "having stripped off the armor of rulers and authorities." That is, by His death and resurrection Christ disarmed the rulers and authorities arrayed against Him.

He went further: "He made a shew of them openly." Except for "openly," this is all one word in Greek, the verb *deigmatizo*. A very rare verb, it has now been found in a Tebtunis papyrus of about 14 B.C. Lightfoot says that it means " 'displayed,' as a victor displays his captives or trophies in a triumphal procession" (p. 191).

The last clause of this verse—"triumphing over them by the cross" (New International Bible)—proves that this is the meaning here. The New English Bible spells it out very well: "He made a public spectacle of them and led them as captives in his triumphal procession." It was the familiar picture of a conquerer returning to Rome and leading the captured kings and warriors in chains in his triumphal procession. That is what Christ did on the cross. He vanquished all His opponents and stripped the armor from His enemies. In a very real sense they are now in chains. Over the cross is inscribed: CHRISTUS VICTOR.

C. Maintaining Our Freedom: vv. 16-17

"Let no man therefore judge you in meat, or in drink" (v. 16). Does Paul mean that we should avoid condemnation by abstaining from certain kinds of meat or beverage? Actually he is saying the opposite. The Greek word for "meat" simply means "eating." The literal translation here is: "Do not let anyone judge you in eating and drinking." The last part could be translated "in what you eat or drink," or "in food or drink."

The rest of the verse shows clearly that Paul is referring to the problem of the fault-finding Judaizers. They wanted all the Gentile converts to be subject to the Mosaic regulations concerning clean and unclean foods. Paul is writing to a Gentile church and telling them not to submit to the law; they are free in Christ.

And so he goes on to say: "Or in respect of a holyday, or of the new moon, or of the sabbath days." These three observances are all unmistakably connected with the Jewish religion. In fact, all four mentioned in this verse were religious rites that distinctively

set the Jews off from the Gentiles throughout the Roman Empire. The most observable one was the keeping of the Sabbath (Saturday) in a rigid manner. The Jews also had a special religious celebration at the time of "new moon," which always marked the beginning of the Jewish month. Then there were other holy days or "festivals," such as the Passover season. Also, the strict abstaining from eating pork would soon be noticed.

Paul told the Gentile Christians that they were not to let the Judaizers act as judges in condemning them for failure to keep all those regulations. In Christ they were free from them.

It will be noticed that no moral principles are involved here. We are still obligated to keep the moral law of the Old Testament, but not the ceremonial law. Paul tells us that this is only "a shadow of things to come, but the body is of Christ" (v. 17). Obviously "body" is better rendered "substance." All the types and sacrifices and symbols of the Mosaic law were but an anticipatory shadow cast by the cross. The substance is found in Christ. We ought to rejoice that we are not now living in the time of shadow, but in that of solid reality.

III. FREEDOM FROM FALSE PHILOSOPHY
Colossians 2:18-23

A. False Humility: v. 18

In verse 8 Paul warned against vain philosophy. But then he shifted to talking about the dangers of Judaism in the intervening verses. Now he returns to the threat of Gnosticism. It is apparent that these two together posed a real problem at Colosse, so that we speak of the "Colossian heresies" (in the plural). We now know that in some places the Judaism of the first century had been infected with Gnostic ideas. So there was clearly a pre-Christian Gnosticism.

Here Paul says: "Let no man beguile you of your reward in a voluntary humility and worshiping of angels, intruding into those things which he has not seen, vainly puffed up by his fleshly mind." There are several significant terms here.

"Beguile" is the verb *katabrabeuo* (only here in the New Testament) It comes from *brabeus*, which means "an umpire." So the verb means "to decide as an umpire against one, to declare him unworthy of the prize; to defraud of the prize of victory" (Thayer, *Lexicon*, p. 330.) Lightfoot comments: "The Christian's career is the contest of the stadium ... Christ is the umpire, the dispenser of the awards (2 Timothy iv. 8); life eternal is the bay wreath, the victor's prize (*brabeion*, 1 Cor. ix. 24, Phil. iii. 14). The Colossians were in a fair way to win this prize; they had entered the lists duly; they were running bravely: but the false teachers, thrusting themselves in the way, attempted to trip them up or otherwise impede them in the race, and thus to rob them of their just reward" (p. 195). The verb may be translated either "disqualify" or "rob you of your prize."

What did Paul mean by "voluntary humility"? The word for "voluntary" means "taking a delight in" or "devoting himself to." Lightfoot well observes: "Humility, when it becomes self-conscious, ceases to have any value" (p. 196). The best translation for "humility" here and in verse 23 is "self-abasement." These false teachers made a religion out of asceticism.

"Intruding into those things which he hath not seen." The negative ("not") is omitted in the best Greek text. The best translation here is: "taking his stand on *visions* he has seen" (NASB). The verb *embateuo* is used that way in second-century inscriptions relating to the Mystery Religions, which were prevalent in the area around Colosse. These three things—voluntary self-abasement, worship of angels, and mystical visions—were exactly the kinds of things to cause a person to be "vainly puffed up by his fleshly mind."

B. Christ the Answer: v. 19

What was the answer to all this religious rubbish? It was Christ. The trouble with these false teachers was that they were not holding to the Head of the church. Leaving Him, they wandered into all kinds of ridiculous vagaries.

This verse gives a beautiful description of the church as the body of Christ. He is the one who nourishes the whole and binds it together, so that it "grows as God causes it to grow" (New International Bible).

C. Freedom from the Rudiments: vv. 20-22

"If you have died with Christ, from the elements of the world [same phrase, as in verse 8] why, as though you were living in the world, are you subject to decrees" (dogmas)? These dogmas would probably be both Gnostic and Jewish regulations, though mostly the latter.

Then Paul names three of those dogmas that they are not to be subject to: "Touch not; taste not; handle not" (v. 21). It is unfortunate that the WCTU saw fit to take these words out of their context and use them in exactly the opposite way from which they are used in the Bible.

These are all "to perish with the using, according to the commandments and teachings of men" (v. 22). It is only the spiritual which is eternal.

DISCUSSION QUESTIONS

1. How can we keep free from error?
2. How can we be freed from slavery to self?
3. What place do rules have in the Christian life?
4. Why is legalism such a threat to Christianity?
5. What Gnostic ideas are still alive in our world?
6. What should be our attitude toward asceticism?

D. Falseness of Asceticism: v. 23

One who holds that the body is evil, as the Gnostics did, will go in one of two directions: into immorality or into asceticism. Apparently these Gnostic teachers at Colosse were advocating the latter, treating their bodies with severity.

The thought of this verse is brought out best in the New American Standard Bible: "These are matters which have, to be sure, the appearance of wisdom in self-made religion and self-abasement and severe treatment of the body, but are of no value against fleshly indulgence." The safeguard against sensuality is not asceticism but the power of the Holy Spirit in the life of the Christian.

CONTEMPORARY APPLICATION

There are many false philosophies and religions afloat today. We need to be grounded in Christ in order to be kept safe and "on the track." There is also no substitute for serious Bible study. The living Word and the written Word together can guide us safely.

But we need to be alert to the fact that Bible study is the lure used by the heretics as well as the orthodox. Many are being led astray. One of the safest procedures is to belong to a spiritual evangelical church and seek guidance from the pastor about uncertain doctrines.

PERSONAL RELATIONSHIPS IN CHRIST

DEVOTIONAL READING	Colossians 3:1-11

ADULTS	Topic: *Developing Christian Relationships* Background Scripture: Colossians 3:1—4:6 Scripture Lesson: Colossians 3:12—4:1, 5-6 Memory Verse: *Put on then, as God's chosen ones, holy and beloved, compassion, kindness, lowliness, meekness, and patience, forbearing one another.* Colossians 3:12-13

YOUTH	Topic: *Getting Along with Others* Background Scripture: Colossians 3:1—4:6 Scripture Lesson: Colossians 3:12—4:1, 5-6 Memory Verse: *Put on then, as God's chosen ones, holy and beloved, compassion, kindness, lowliness, meekness, and patience, forbearing one another.* Colossians 3:12-13

CHILDREN	Topic: *Love for Others* Background Scripture: Colossians 4:2-6 Scripture Lesson: Colossians 4:2-6 Memory Verse: *Love one another with brotherly affection.* Romans 12:10

DAILY BIBLE READINGS	Mon., Aug. 19: The Law of Love, I John 2:7-11. Tues., Aug. 20: Raised with Christ, Colossians 3:1-11. Wed., Aug. 21: A New Attitude Toward People, Colossians 3:12-17. Thurs., Aug. 22: Strong Backs and Open Hearts, Galatians 6:1-10. Fri., Aug. 23: The Christian and Everyday Life, Colossians 3:18—4:6. Sat., Aug. 24: God's People and the Poor, Deuteronomy 15:1-11. Sun., Aug. 25: Love Goes Beyond Resolutions, James 2:1-8, 14-18.

LESSON AIM	To show how the life in Christ affects our relationships to others.

LESSON SETTING	Time: A.D. 60 Place: Prison in Rome

Personal Relationships in Christ

LESSON OUTLINE

**SUGGESTED
INTRODUCTION
FOR ADULTS**

Living in Christ makes a difference! We cannot be the same as before. In another place Paul writes: "Therefore if any man is in Christ, he is a new creature: old things have passed away; behold, all things have become new" (II Corinthians 5:17).

That is what this lesson is all about. If we are in Christ, we have a new life. The old life of living for self is gone. We have become a new man in Christ and we must act like new persons. We have a new set of attitudes that will show up in our daily lives. There will be a new atmosphere, both inside and outside. There will be new interpersonal relationships. And we will bear a witness to those outside the church by our new life in Christ.

Being a Christian, then, is more than being baptized and joining a church. It is letting Christ come into our hearts as Savior from sin. And then it is letting Him live in our lives as Lord of all. The Christian life is the "Christed life."

The trouble with too much Christianity today is that it has little of Christ in it. Creed, liturgy, organization—none of these is a substitute for Christ. He is the one who makes a difference in our lives—when we let Him.

SUGGESTED
INTRODUCTION
FOR YOUTH

"Getting Along with Others." How are we making it in that area? This is the real test of the Christian life. We may profess to belong to Christ, but if that doesn't help us to show a better attitude toward those around us, people are going to raise their eyebrows and ask what difference Christianity makes. There is a sense in which we put Christ on the spot every day by the way we live.

Getting along with others starts in the home. That is where it is hardest to live the Christian life. We are so close that we often rub elbows with each other, and this creates friction. We need to ask the Lord to help us to be patient and forgiving every day. Then we need to supplement our prayers by rigid self-discipline, watching our attitudes and words.

The best secret of success in this area is to keep our thinking positive, rather than negative. If we think kind thoughts about others, we will feel kindly toward them. We cannot directly control our feelings, but we can control our thoughts. Starting the day with Bible reading and prayer is the key.

CONCEPTS FOR
CHILDREN

1. The best way to love others is to pray for them.
2. If you feel angry at someone try praying for him.
3. The most important place for us to show the right attitudes is in the home.

THE LESSON COMMENTARY

I. THE NEW LIFE IN CHRIST: Colossians 3:1-7

A. Majoring on the Spiritual: vv. 1-2

Paul tells his readers: "If then you have been raised together with Christ, keep on seeking the things above, where Christ is seated at the right hand of God." After His resurrection Christ ascended to heaven. If we have risen with Him, we also should live in the heavenly realm. We should no longer be merely earthly people, like the unsaved people around us. We are to live a new life in Christ.

He goes on: "Set your affection on things above, not on things on the earth" (v. 2). "Set your affection" is all one word in Greek, *phroneite*. The verb comes from the noun for "mind." So the best translation would be: "set your mind." In other words, we should direct our minds away from earthly things and toward heavenly matters. It is of course true that we have to give considerable attention to things on earth, or we could not keep alive physically. But most of these things can become fairly routine. The real interests and concerns of our minds should relate to the spiritual rather than the material. The man who is engaged in secular employment must spend most of his day thinking about his job responsibilities. But when he is freed from this, his mind should turn to things relating to his own spiritual life and to the kingdom of God.

B. Hidden with Christ in God: vv. 3-4

"For ye are dead" should be translated, "for you died" (aorist tense). It means that there was a time when we died to the old life of sin and selfishness, to be resurrected into a new life in Christ. Now that our lives are hid-

den with Christ in God, we should no
longer live as merely earthly men, for
we are now citizens of heaven as well
as of our nation, and our first loyalty
must be to our heavenly Lord. That
means that He gets first place in our
thoughts. And the most obvious application of this is that we should begin
each day with prayer. For fifty years
we have had the habit of never reading
the newspaper until we have read the
Bible, or never turning on the radio (or
television) until we have tuned in to
heaven. The first thing we need to do
each day is to turn our waking
thoughts toward God and get our sig-
nals clear for Christian living.

If Christ is really "our life" day by
day, then when He appears at His second coming we will also "appear with
Him in glory" (v. 4). The fact that our
minds are set on Him is not only the
necessary condition of being prepared
for that epochal event, it also gives us
assurance that we shall live with Him
there because we have daily lived with
Him here.

C. Mortifying Fleshly Desires: vv. 5-7

Today we speak of being "morti-
fied" when we make some little mistake. All we mean is "embarrassed."
But the term "mortify" comes from
the Latin *mortus* which means
"death." And the Greek verb used
here is based on *nekros*, "dead." So it
very clearly means "put to death."

Paul told the Colossian Christians
to put to death "your members which
are upon the earth." The list that follows suggests that this means "the
things of the flesh," as Paul calls them
elsewhere. He first mentions "fornication," which in Biblical usage includes adultery. After "uncleanness,"
a very broad term, he has "inordinate
affection." In the Greek this long
expression is one short word, *pathos*,
which means "passion." This is followed by "evil concupiscence"—the
Greek simply says "evil desire." "Covetousness," or "greed," is declared to
be "idolatry." That is, it is caring more

for things than for God. Idolatry is a
common sin of human society in all
countries. Paul says that these things
bring down the wrath of God on "the
children of disobedience."

Formerly the Colossian believers
had indulged in all of these, as most of
the pagans of that day did. But now
they were living a new life in Christ
and must be dead to these sins.

II. THE NEW MAN IN CHRIST: Colossians 3:8-11

A. Putting Off the Old Man: vv. 8-9

The more serious sins are to be put
to death. Now Paul lists some less atrocious ones that he says must be "put
off," or "put away."

The first two are closely related.
"Anger" is often translated "wrath"
and describes God's attitude toward
sin and wrong. The word translated
"wrath" suggests a "boiling over"
anger, or "rage" (New International
Bible). "Malice" translates the general
word for "badness," but here it seems
to mean "ill-will."

"Blasphemy" transliterates the
Greek word *blasphemia*, which originally meant "speech injurious to another's good name," and only later
"impious and reproachful speech injurious to the divine majesty" (Thayer,
Lexicon, p. 102). It is used both ways
in the New Testament. But here the
correct translation is "slander."

"Filthy communication" is a
mouthful! In Greek it is one word,
aischrologia (only here in the New
Testament). It means "abusive language" (Abbott-Smith, *Lexicon* p. 14).
Thayer defines it as "foul speaking . . .
low and obscene speech" (p. 17).
Lightfoot combines these in his translation, "foul-mouthed abuse," and
notes that Greek writers use this word
to express both ideas (p. 214).

In both Colossians and Ephesians,
written at the same time and to the
same general area, Paul warns his readers against lying. Here he gives as the
reason: "since you have put off the

old man with its practices." It is not enough to put off the old man in a general way; we must be sure that we have in one crucial act (aorist tense) put away the habits of the old life.

B. Putting on the New Man: v. 10

Again, it is not enough to "put off" the old man with its practices; we must "put on" the new man. These two verbs were used particularly for taking off clothes and putting them on. We must lay aside the old life, as a filthy garment, and put on the clean clothes of a new life in Christ. This new man is "renewed in knowledge according to the one who created him." That is, the new man knows how to live like Christ, the Creator. The new man is the man in Christ. He is the "Christed person."

C. All one in Christ: vv. 11

In this new fellowship in Christ the old barriers of race, religion, and culture are broken down. In Christ there is "neither Greek nor Jew"; there are only Christians. The Gentiles have just as much acceptance as Jews. The Greeks looked down on the Jews as being inferior in culture and learning. The Jews reciprocated by holding the Gentiles in contempt as unclean. But in Christ they are one, all distinctions set aside.

The religious question comes still more to the front in the expression "circumcision nor uncircumcision." The uncircumcised Gentiles were outside the divine covenant. But not since Calvary! Now there is a new covenant, ratified by the blood of Christ.

The term "barbarian" is *barbaros*. Thayer defines this word fully: "1. properly, *one whose speech is rude, rough, harsh,* as if repeating the syllables *barbar* . . . hence 2. *one who speaks a foreign or strange language which is not understood by another.* . . . 3. The Greeks used *barbaros of any foreigner ignorant of the Greek language and the Greek culture* . . . with the added notion, after

the Persian war, of rudeness and brutality" (p. 95).

Who was a "Scythian"? The word refers to "an inhabitant of Scythia, i.e., Russia and Siberia, a synonym with the Greeks for the wildest of barbarians" (Abbott-Smith, p. 410). Lightfoot says, "The savageness of the Scythians was proverbial."

But in Christ all these different groups—including slaves and free men ("bond or free")—are one in Christ, who is "all and in all."

III. THE NEW ATTITUDES IN CHRIST:
Colossians 3:12-14

A. Compassion and Kindness: v. 12

In verse 10 we were told to "put on the new man." Here this is spelled out more in detail. "As God's chosen people, holy and dearly loved," we should clothe ourselves with "a heart of compassion ["bowels of mercies" KJV], kindness, humility of mind, meekness, and longsuffering" (or, patience). The old man was characterized by anger and ill-will. The new man is characterized by compassion and kindness. These are the two most significant manifestations of the divine love that is implanted in our hearts by the Holy Spirit. And as we have noticed before, humility always goes with true holiness.

B. Forbearance and Forgiveness: v. 13

"Forbearing one another, and forgiving one another." The first verb literally means "bearing with." As Christians we have to bear with each other's faults, and we have to keep this up as long as we live on earth. The thing we need to remember is that we also have faults that other people have to bear with. So it is a mutual proposition.

For the same reason we should be forgiving. We want others to forgive us for our faults that hurt their feelings, and so it is only fair that we should forgive them for their faults that bother us. ("Quarrel" should be translated "complaint.")

The criterion, as also the challenge, is "even as Christ forgave you." And this leads us to note the verb that is here translated "forgiving" and "forgive." It comes from *charis*, "grace," and so means to "forgive graciously." The word usually translated "forgive" literally means "leave off." But this is a much stronger term. It carries the deeper sense of wholehearted forgiveness. A better translation would be: "freely forgiving each other . . . as Christ freely forgave you." Weymouth has "readily forgiving," which suggests that our forgiveness of others should be extended gladly, not grudgingly. God forgives freely, fully, and forever. We should do the same—"so also do ye."

C. Perfect Love: v. 14

This phrase is found in I John (4:1). But the idea is also expressed by Paul: "And above all these things put on charity, which is the bond of perfectness."

One of the worst mistakes made by the King James translators was their treatment of *agape*, which means the highest kind of unselfish, holy love. Twenty-seven times the King James Version translates it "charity," which today suggests handouts and cast-off clothes. It should be remembered that the King James Version was a revision of the Bishops' Bible, and the bishops loved their Latin. So "charity" was brought in from the Latin Vulgate *caritas*. The good old Anglo-Saxon word is "love," which is still preferable even though it has been degraded by Hollywood and the Hippies.

The Greek for "bond of perfectness" is difficult to translate, a fact which is evidenced by the great variety of renderings in the different versions. The word for "bond" means "that which binds together." The noun "perfectness" is *teleiotetos*, which means "completeness." Lightfoot comments that what this passage says is that love

is "the power which unites and holds together all those graces and virtues, which together make up perfection" (p. 222). Since Paul is using here the figure of putting on clothes (v. 12), it would seem that love can be thought of as the belt that holds everything in place. This is to be put on "above all these things," to tie them together. Phillips puts it this way: "Love is the golden chain of all the virtues." Lightfoot thinks of it as an outer cloak. He paraphrases the passage this way: "And over all these, robe yourselves in love; for this is the garment which binds together all the graces of perfection." Either figure makes very good sense.

IV. THE NEW ATMOSPHERE IN CHRIST:
Colossians 3:15-19

A. Peace in Our Hearts: v. 15

"Let the peace of God rule in your hearts." The word for "rule" is *brabeuo*, (only here in the New Testament). It comes from *brabeus*, which means "an umpire." So it properly means "act as an umpire," and then "arbitrate, decide" (Abbott-Smith, p. 85). Lightfoot paraphrases this clause: "And let the one supreme umpire in your hearts, the one referee amidst all your difficulties, be the peace of Christ." He comments further: "Wherever there is a conflict of motives or impulses or reasons, the peace of Christ must step in and decide which is to prevail."

Some scholars have objected to imposing the literal meaning of *brabeuo* on this passage. But Moulton and Milligan conclude: "We may endorse accordingly . . . Lightfoot's insistence on the element of *award* or *decision* in a conflict between two impulses, in the remarkable phrase of Col. 3:15; whether the figure of the games is present we need not argue" (*Vocabulary of the Greek Testament in the Light of the Papyri*, p. 116). Stauffer says: "Paul uses the verb of the peace which settles all strife and preserves

the unity of the Christian community"
(Kittel, ed., *Theological Dictionary of
the New Testament*, I, 638). C. B.
Williams translates the passage: "Let
the peace that Christ can give keep on
acting as umpire in your hearts." For
the last clause of the verse he has:
"And practice being thankful."

B. Singing in Our Hearts: v. 16

Paul urges his readers: "Let the
word of Christ dwell in you richly."
Probably "in all wisdom" should go
with what follows: "teaching and
admonishing one another." It takes
divine wisdom to teach the Word of
God and to counsel one's fellow Christians. Only the Holy Spirit can give us
that wisdom, but He will do so as we
seek His help.

The rest of the verse is almost
exactly parallel to Ephesians 5:19.
Both passages suggest that three types
of songs should be used in Christian
services.

The first is "psalms" *(psalmois)*.
Strictly speaking, this would perhaps
refer to chanting parts of the Book of
Psalms as is done in Jewish services
today. There are also some small Protestant groups that will only sing the
Psalms, following the practice of the
old Scottish Covenanters. But perhaps
we could give it a slightly wider connotation for our circles and apply it to
those ancient hymns that are composed almost entirely of words of
Scripture.

The second type is "hymns"
(hymnois). These are songs of worship
and adoration, addressed to Deity or
speaking directly about Him. To refer
to such testimony songs as "I'm Going
Through" as "hymns" is to show the
grossest ignorance. Good examples of
hymns are "Come, Thou Almighty
King" (addressed to Deity) or "Majestic Sweetness Sits Enthroned" (speaking about Deity).

The third classification is "spiritual
songs." This takes in what are generally called "gospel songs," as well as
some of the new "youth music" in the
churches. The Greek word is *odais*,

from which we get "odes." It refers
properly to songs of praise to God.

Not many denominations today
restrict themselves to the use of the
Psalms. But in regard to the other two
types a word might be said. Perhaps
those churches that use only hymns
would be wise to branch out somewhat into gospel songs. On the other
hand, some evangelical churches use
altogether too few hymns. Especially
in the Sunday morning worship service
it would seem that hymns are most
appropriate. During that one hour of
the week, at least, we need to point
our people away from themselves and
their own feelings to the Eternal One.

C. Thanksgiving Always: v. 17

"And whatever you do in word or
deed, do it all in the name of the Lord
Jesus, giving thanks to God the Father
through Him." How many of us really
carry out this admonition fully? It is a
real challenge. To do everything in the
name of Jesus and with thanks to
God—what an ideal! But like everything else, "practice makes perfect." It
is not difficult to form the habit of
seeking God's guidance and blessing in
all we do, and then taking time to
thank Him for answered prayer. Too
many Christians voice hundreds of
petitions without remembering to
thank the Lord for the answers He
gives day by day.

Thankful always! This should be a
daily challenge and reminder. Only
those who have formed the habit of
thanking the Lord constantly know
how much joy and blessing this adds
to daily life.

V. THE NEW INTERPERSONAL RELATIONSHIPS IN CHRIST: Colossians 3:18—4:1

A. Of Wives and Husbands: vv. 18-19

These relationships need to be
studied in pairs, as they are presented
here in Scripture. To tell wives to submit themselves to their husbands,

without also telling the husbands to love their wives, would be grossly unfair and unreasonable. The truth is, as attested by many Christian wives, that when the husband truly loves his wife with *agape* love—which is always unselfish—and with tenderness, she is happy to "be in subjection" to him. The heaviest responsibility, as we noted in connection with Ephesians 5:25, lies with the husband. If he fails to carry out his side of the relationship in holy, selfless love, he has no right to ask his wife to be subject to him.

"As it is fit in the Lord" could be translated "For this is your Christian duty" (C. B. Williams). "Be not bitter against them" recognizes a common fault of husbands. The verb comes from an adjective meaning "sharp, pointed," so perhaps the best translation is "Do not be harsh toward them." T. K. Abbott writes: "The word would seem, then, to correspond more nearly with the colloquial 'cross' than with 'bitter' " ("Ephesians and Colossians," *International Critical Commentary*, p. 293).

B. Of Children and Parents: vv. 20-21

Again there is a twofold relationship. Children are commanded to obey their parents, as in the Ten Commandments. This is a foundation stone of society. But the parents ("fathers") have their responsibility not to "provoke" the children to disobey by being unreasonable. Our two oldest Greek manuscripts have a verb which means "irritate" or "exasperate." Weymouth translates verse 2: "Fathers, do not fret and harass your children, or you may make them sullen and morose." Lightfoot comments: " 'Irritation' is the first consequence of being too exacting with children, and irritation leads to moroseness" (p. 227). The result is that children may "be discouraged." The verb means "to be disheartened, dispirited, broken in spirit" (Thayer, p. 14). That is exactly what happens to some children.

C. Of Slaves and Masters: 3:22—4:1

Slaves are told to obey their masters not with "eyeservice" as "menpleasers." (Since we have already commented on these same two compounds in our study of Ephesians 6:5-6, p. 391 we forbear here.) Rather, they are to serve "in singleness of heart, fearing God."

Verse 23 contains a great admonition: "And whatever you do, work heartily, as for the Lord, and not for men." The adverb translated "heartily" is actually a phrase, "from your heart." This is the way to be happy in our work.

We can be assured that if we do so we will receive "the reward of the inheritance" (v. 24). "Reward" is literally "recompense." We can be certain that we will receive a full recompense for all we do for the Lord. What we, as well as servants, need to remember, is that we are actually serving the Lord Jesus, not just our masters or employers.

The other side of the coin is stated in verse 25: "But he who does wrong will receive"—better, "be paid back"—for the wrong he does. Again we are told that with God there is no partiality ("receiving of face," cf. Ephesians 6:9).

DISCUSSION QUESTIONS

1. What is the most important interpersonal relationship on the human level?
2. What would you list in second and third place?
3. How does our relationship to God affect our relationship to our fellowman?
4. How does our relationship to our fellowman affect our relationship to God?
5. What are some guidelines for happy relations in the home?
6. What responsibilities do parents have in this regard?

The masters have their instructions, too (4:1). They are to grant their slaves what is "just and equal"—or, "what is right and fair." They are also to remember that they have "a Master in heaven," and they should treat their servants as they want to be treated.

V. THE CHRISTIAN AND OUTSIDERS:
Colossians 4:5-6

Paul is concerned not only with the believer's relationship to his fellow Christians but also with his relationship to those outside the church. And so he says: "Walk in wisdom [or "conduct yourselves wisely"] toward those who are without" (v. 5). Weymouth puts it well: "Behave wisely in relation to the outside world."

And then Paul adds: "redeeming the time." This can best be translated "making the most of your time" (RSV) or "making the most of your opportunities" (Phillips). The Greek word here for "time" means "opportune (or, appointed) time." Lightfoot paraphrases this verse: "Walk wisely and discreetly in all your dealings with unbelievers; allow no opportunity to slip through your hands, but buy up every passing moment" (p. 230).

The Christian's speech should always be "with grace, seasoned with salt" (v. 6)—or "seasoned with the salt of grace" (Weymouth). The New English Bible gives an excellent translation: "Let your conversation be always gracious and never insipid [lacking salt]; study how best to talk with each person you meet."

CONTEMPORARY APPLICATION

There never was a time when it was more important to give attention to interpersonal relationships than today. Our vertical relationship to God is the primary thing, but our horizontal relationship to those around us is also of extreme importance. We need all the help we can get from God's Word, from the Holy Spirit, from books on social psychology (by such men as Paul Tournier), and from common sense. And then we shall need to watch and pray every day, seeking to be more Christlike in our attitudes toward others.

SUGGESTED COMMENTARIES

The Gospel According to Paul

ARCHER, Gleason L., Jr. *The Epistle to the Romans.* "Shield Bible Study Series." Grand Rapids: Baker, 1959, 103 pp.

BARCLAY, William. *Letter to the Romans,* 244 pp.; *Letters to the Corinthians,* 298 pp. "Daily Bible Study Series." Philadelphia: Westminster, 1957-1958.

BRUCE, F. F. *Commentary of the Epistle of Paul to the Romans.* "Tyndale Bible Commentaries." Grand Rapids: Eerdmans, 1963, 288 pp.

HOBBS, Herschel H. *The Epistles to the Corinthians.* "Shield Bible Study Series." Grand Rapids: Baker, 1960, 127 pp.

LANGE, J. P. *Commentary on the Holy Scriptures: Romans.* Grand Rapids: Zondervan (reprint), 455 pp.

MORGAN, G. Campbell. *The Corinthian Letters of Paul.* Old Tappan, N. J.: Revell, 1946.

MORRIS, Leon. *Commentary on the First Epistle of Paul to the Corinthians.* "Tyndale Bible Commentaries." Grand Rapids: Eerdmans, 1958, 249 pp.

MOULE, H. C. G. *The Epistle of Paul to the Romans.* "The Expositor's Bible." Grand Rapids: Eerdmans, 1943 (reprint), Vol 5, pages 513-623.

TASKER, Randolph V. *Commentary on the Second Epistle of Paul to the Corinthians.* "Tyndale Bible Commentaries." Grand Rapids: Eerdmans, 1958, 192 pp.

The Gospel of John

BARCLAY, William. *The Gospel of John.* 2 vols. "Daily Study Bible." Philadelphia: Westminster Press, 1955, 600 pp. Sparkling. Human interest. Available in paperback.

BARNES, Albert. *Notes on the New Testament.* "Luke and John." Grand Rapids: Baker Book House, 1949, 220 pp. (reprint). Good brief explanations.

BLANEY, Harvey J. S. "Gospel According to John." *Wesleyan Bible Commentary,* Vol. IV. Grand Rapids: Wm. B. Eerdmans Publishing Co., 1964, 120 pp. Excellent spiritual interpretation of the poetic drama of this Gospel.

ERDMAN, Charles R. *The Gospel of John.* Philadelphia: Westminster, 1916, 178 pp. Excellent brief exposition.

HARRISON, Everett F. *John: The Gospel of Faith.* Chicago: Moody Press, 1962, 128 pp. Very useful paperback, inexpensive commentary.

HENDRIKSEN, William. *New Testament Commentary: John.* Grand Rapids:

Baker, 1953, 1954, 757 pp. Thorough, rich treatment for study in depth, but clearly written.

LAURIN, Roy L. *John: Life Eternal*. Chicago: Moody, 1972, 287 pp. Good devotional commentary.

LENSKI, R. C. H. *The Interpretation of John's Gospel*. Minneapolis: Augsburg, 1943, 1444 pp. A solid conservative commentary, with full treatment of every verse.

LINN, Otto F. *The Gospel of John*. Anderson, Indiana: Gospel Trumpet Co., 1942, 160 pp. Good brief exposition.

MAYFIELD, Joseph H. "John." *Beacon Bible Commentary*, Vol. VII. Kansas City, Mo.: Beacon Hill Press, 1965, 226 pp. Clear exposition, with helpful applications.

MORGAN, G. Campbell. *The Gospel According to John*. New York: Fleming H. Revell, n.d. By "the prince of expositors."

MORRIS, Leon. *The Gospel According to John*. "The New International Commentary on the New Testament." Grand Rapids: Eerdmans, 1971, 936 pp. Thorough doctrinal exposition by a leading evangelical scholar.

TASKER, R. V. G. *The Gospel According to St. John*. "Tyndale New Testament Commentaries." Grand Rapids: Eerdmans, 1960, 237 pp. One of the best brief commentaries.

TURNER, George A. and MANTEY, J. R. *The Gospel According to John* "Evangelical Commentary." Grand Rapids: Eerdmans, n.d., 420 pp. A good combination of exegesis by Dr. Mantey and exposition by Dr. Turner. Up-to-date treatment.

Acts: How the Church Grew

ALEXANDER, J. A. *Commentary on the Acts of the Apostles*. 2 vols. in 1. Grand Rapids: Zondervan Publishing House, 1956 (reprint), 960 pp. One of the best of the older commentaries.

BARCLAY, William. *The Acts of the Apostles*. "Daily Study Bible." Philadelphia: Westminster, 1953, 213 pp. Compact, but meaty.

BARNES, Albert. *Notes on the New Testament:* "Acts of the Apostles." Grand Rapids: Baker, 1949 (reprint), 391 pp. Full, helpful treatment.

BRUCE, F. F. *Commentary on the Book of Acts*. "New International Commentary on the New Testament." Grand Rapids: Eerdmans, 1954, 555 pp. Excellent exposition by a leading British evangelical scholar.

CARTER, Charles W. "The Acts of the Apostles." *Wesleyan Bible Commentary*, Vol. IV. Grand Rapids: Eerdmans, 1964, 275 pp. Excellent exposition.

EARLE, Ralph. "The Acts of the Apostles." *Beacon Bible Commentary*, Vol. VII. Kansas City, Mo.: Beacon Hill Press, 1965, 350 pp.

ERDMAN, Charles R. *The Acts*. Philadelphia: Westminster, 1919, 176 pp. Very satisfying exposition in compact form.

LENSKI, R. C. H. *Interpretation of the Acts of the Apostles*. Minneapolis: Augsburg, 1934, 1134 pp. Thorough study of each verse.

RACKHAM, Richard B. *The Acts of the Apostles*. "Westminster Commentaries." London: Methuen & Co., 1901, 513 pp. One of the standard works on Acts.

Letters to Young Churches

BARCLAY, William. *The Letters to the Galatians and Ephesians*, 219 pp.; *The Letters to the Philippians, Colossians and Thessalonians*, 253 pp. "Daily Bible Lessons." Philadelphia: Westminster Press, 1959.

BARNES, Albert. *Notes on the New Testament: Ephesians to Colossians*, 288 pp.; *Thessalonians to Philemon*, 314 pp. Grand Rapids: Baker, 1949 (reprint).

BRUCE, F. F. *The Epistle to the Ephesians, The Epistle to the Colossians*. "New International Commentary on the New Testament." Grand Rapids: Eerdmans, 1957, 328 pp.

ERDMAN, Charles R. *Ephesians; Philippians; Thessalonians*. Philadelphia: Westminster, 1917-1936.

ERDMAN, Charles R. *Ephesians*, 143 pp.; *Philippians*, 155 pp.; *Thessalonians*, 105 pp. Philadelphia: Westminster, 1917-1936.

HENDRIKSEN, William. *New Testament Commentary: Ephesians*, 290 pp.; *Philippians*, 218 pp; *Colossians-Philemon*, 243 pp; *I-II Thessalonians*, 214 pp. Grand Rapids: Baker, 1955-1967.

LENSKI, R. C. H. *The Interpretation of St. Paul's Epistles to the Galatians, to the Ephesians, and to the Philippians*, 901 pp; *The Interpretation of St. Paul's Epistles to the Colossians, to the Thessalonians, to Timothy, to Titus, and to Philemon*, 974 pp. Minneapolis: Augsburg, 1937-1939.